A MEMOIR OF
CREATIVITY

A MEMOIR OF CREATIVITY

Abstract Painting, Politics & the Media, 1956–2008

PIRI HALASZ

iUniverse, Inc.
New York   Bloomington

A Memoir of Creativity
Abstract Painting, Politics & the Media, 1956–2008

This book is a memoir and for the most part contains real names, but where
indicated, some names and details have been changed to protect identities.

Cover illustration: *Representational, Semiabstract, Abstract.*
For discussion, see Introduction, Pages 3—4

The e-mail address of Piri Halasz is piri@mindspring.com. Her website,
From the Mayor's Doorstep, is at http://piri.home.mindspring.com

iUniverse books may be ordered through booksellers or by contacting:

iUniverse
1663 Liberty Drive
Bloomington, IN 47403
www.iuniverse.com
1-800-Authors (1-800-288-4677)

ISBN: 978-1-4401-2323-8 (pbk)
ISBN: 978-1-4401-2322-1 (cloth)
ISBN: 978-1-4401-2324-5 (ebk)

Printed in the United States of America

Library of Congress Control Number: 2009923105

iUniverse rev. date: 3/23/2009

For the survivors:
my living blood female relatives,
plus Bethie, Mike, and Elsa

WITH LOVE

CONTENTS

ACKNOWLEDGMENTS

MY BIGGEST DEBT, of course, is to the journalists, artists, critics, scholars, and friends whom I know (or have known) personally and have written about in this book.

Secondly, I owe thanks to all the authors of the books and articles whom I quote, but whom I haven't known personally.

Third, I thank my readers, not only all of those whom I hope to reach upon publication of this tome, but even more those who have already read all or part of the manuscript, and given me the benefit of their insights: Kenneth G. Craven, Beatrix Gates, the late Robert E. Doherty and three special individuals who not only read my manuscript in its entirety, and critiqued it, but were willing to go into print for me: Terry Fenton, Katherine B. Crum and Leigh Winser.

It goes without saying that all flaws in this book are nobody's responsibility but mine.

Furthermore, I thank the great libraries I've used: especially the Columbia University system and the New York Public Library, with their many capable reference librarians; also the libraries and/or archives, with their librarians, at the Museum of Modern Art, Metropolitan Museum of Art, Musée Picasso, Musée de Montmartre, Pollock-Krasner House and Study Center, New York University, Parsons School of Design, Archives of American Art, New York Psychoanalytic Institute, American Jewish Committee and Time Inc. I am, of course, also grateful for search engines, and the many reliable Web sites on the Internet that I've consulted, especially those of *Refdesk, Time,* and *The New York Times.*

I'm grateful to the people and institutions who've funded me with actual dollars. I owe especially the Virginia Center for the Creative Arts, including Suny Monk, Sheila and Craig Pleasants, Dorothy and the late Robert Johnson. I also owe Helen A. Harrison, director of the Pollock-Krasner House and Study Center. The Smithsonian's National Museum of American Art (now the Smithsonian American Art Museum) also gave me an early grant.

In addition, I'm grateful to Shawn Levy, for jump-starting this book, when previous rejections had caused me to abandon work on it; to "Editor T," whose positive response to the letter of inquiry I sent galvanized me into revisions so drastic that in the end she would relinquish her claim to it; and to Robin Davis Miller, whose emphasis on boiling my message down to few words, and exposition of "creativity," played a key role in bringing the disparate elements of my narrative into a unified whole. As I shall repeat in my conclusions, I am even grateful to all those other recipients of letters of inquiry, proposals and the finished manuscript whose rejections (however phrased) helped me toughen up my arguments, and ultimately told me where I had to go to publish them.

That place is iUniverse, and I'm grateful to it as an institution (for reasons I shall explain in my Introduction), as well as to all the members of its staff who have seen my project through to completion, from Kim Melichar, Sarah Loury, Eric Kingery, Susan Driscoll and Joy Owens to Krista Hill, Melissa Dalton, Pamela Hawkins, Steve Furr, Natalie Chenoweth, and especially Cherish Denton.

Four people I owe especially because in different ways they helped me make this book what it is: Randy Bloom, Shanshan Ding, Brandon Batista, and John Kois. I'm also grateful for the legal expertise of Michael Gross and Debra Kass Orenstein.

Another debt is to fact-checkers: Caitlin Quinn Bernstein, Lynne Glasner, Leona Li, Angela Palmer, and Chris Thomas. Many thanks are also due to Robert Zolnerzak, for his help with my Index, and to Marjorie Mahle, for zealous proofreading that bordered upon copyediting.

Further thanks are due to Rachel M. Allen, Milagros Alzola, Jan Angilella, Michele Anish, Donna Anstey, Jo-Ellen Asbury, Kathleen Ausman, Andrew Avery, Andrea Bagdy, Jane Bain, Tom Barron, Charles C. Bergman, Sheelagh Bevan, Oliver Botar, Blondine Bouret, Christina Brianik, Susan Todd Brook, Joel Buchwald, Mary Burke, Diane Cardinale, Irene M. Castagliola, Eunyoung Cho, Michael Denneny, Ariane De Pree-Kajfez, Drew Dir, Mark Donnelly, Florence B. Eichin, Michelle Elligott, Sherri Feldman, Daniel Fermon, Lois Fink, Ann M. Fotiades, Elizabeth Franzen, Sylvie Fresnault, Mary Mathews Gedo, Carey Gibbons, Stephanie Gonzalez-Turner, Bette Graber, Amanda Lynn Granek, Nancy Gravatt, Miriam Dressler Griffin and Jasper Griffin, Mary-Bess Halford, Tim Hanson, Neil Harris, Hollee Haswell, Linda Healey, Steve Hipple, Adam Hirschberg, George Hofmann, Kim Hogeland, Bill Hooper, together with Cub Barrett, Evelyn Carranza and Regina Feiler (all of Time Inc.), Alice Hopcraft,, John Hull, Pauline Hyde, Jo Isenberg-O'Loughlin, Elizabeth Joffrion, David Jolliffe, Judith Josephs, Alison Jurado, Namrata Kanchar, Gary Kappel, Amy Kiberd, Lina Kopicaite, Elizabeth Kosakowska, Barbara Kurcz, Irma Kurtz, Mark Landers, Karen Lee, Glenn Loflin, Harriman Logan, Stephen Long, Abraham Lubelski, Robert MacDonald, Marilyn McCully, Chris McNamara, John G. Manning,

Gina Medcalf and Charles Hewlings, Etan Merrick, Diane Meuser, Matt Miskelly, Pam Moir, Carol Morgan, Kenneth Morgan, Robert Morton, Bryon S. Moser, Robert Myers, Kathleen Mylen-Coulombe, David Nielsen, Francis V. O'Connor, Dr. Gerda S. Panofsky, Frank Parente, Constance Roche, Carol Rodman, Rona Roob, Sheik Safdar, Linda Lou Salitros, Christopher Schwabacher, Raymond Shapiro, Robert and Sandra Shapiro, B. Smith, Edrena Smith, Sarah Snook, Robert M. Solomon, Evelyn Stickley, Eumie Imm Stroukoff, Ruth Tellis, Diane Tepfer; Judith Throm, Zoë Timms, John Trause, United Media, Janice Van Horne, Tessa Veazey, Beth Vannelle, Anne Verplank, Watson Wang, Joy Weiner, Nancy Welles, Lloyd Wise, Marisa Young, Lydia Zelaya, and Patricia Zline. I apologize to anybody I've inadvertently omitted, but in fifteen years it's easy to mislay at least a few of one's notes.

The people I never can thank enough are those friends and relations without whose loving support I could never function. The list of friends begins with Elsa and the late Edgar S. Bley; it also includes Alison Bond and Evan Schwartz, Sylvie and H. Stafford Bryant, Jr., Andria Hourwich, Marion Steinmann and Charles Joiner, Anne Stewart FitzRoy (who deserves a whole paragraph to herself); finally the delightful people I play bridge and silly games with in the Special Interest Groups of Mensa.

I'm blessed with an extended family whose company I'm able to enjoy over the web, on the phone and even on those rare occasions when we get together: Suzanne West, Molly Anderson (daughter figure), Tracy Doherty, Rinda West, Jill Anderson, Beth Anderson, Beth Herwood and Michael Herwood. Finally, I owe a debt that can never be repaid to the Ruth West Foundation for the Advancement of the Arts. Under the management of Arthur B. Greene, this exemplary foundation recognizes that, in order to be free of the strictures of the marketplace, truly creative endeavors may have to be subsidized.

Introduction: What This Book Is About
(2008)

THIS BOOK IS a memoir, but not written for the usual reasons. True, my mother may have been a bit difficult, but who can bear a grudge for sixty years? She gave me life (and along with the negatives came many other positives). I've no husband or children, so none of them have suffered from addictions, horrible ordeals, or diseases. Nor have I – except for maybe twenty-five puffs of marijuana back in the Ancient World of 1969 to 1972, all the drugs I've taken were prescription pharmaceuticals, and only in prescribed dosages. True, I've had mental problems, but isn't this rather common? Seems like every time I research mental illness, I read about a new book by somebody with depression or bipolar disorder, and my symptoms have mostly been mild and infrequent by comparison with those tales of woe. I've never been a threat to myself or others (except perhaps for occasional bashful bachelors who panic when I get manic and come on to them strong). No way can I be classed as a celebrity. Maybe I'm not completely unknown within that curious little subcommunity in American society that we call "the art world," but my fifteen minutes of fame in the larger society (national and international) came again in the Ancient World of 1966, when *Time*, the weekly newsmagazine, ran a picture of me up front. I'd written a cover story for it on "Swinging London." The story was controversial then, and has survived surprisingly well, but that's still not why I wrote this book. So – what is?

Those who must have categories might want to call this an "issue memoir." After the London cover, I was assigned in 1967 to write *Time*'s Art page, and after doing this for thirty months, I cared more about art than I did about *Time*. Particularly, I cared about the arcane subject of abstract painting, and an art critic named Clement Greenberg, whose taste in abstract painting of the '60s was more arcane to many than abstract painting itself. I thereupon quit *Time* in 1969 and eventually went back to graduate school, taking my PhD in art history from Columbia University in 1982. One year later, I developed a radical theory that finds meaning and subject matter in abstract painting, and introduced it in an article in *Arts Magazine* in 1983. I wrote this book because I want the theory to become more widely accepted, in hopes of making both abstract painting in general, and Greenberg's kind of abstract

1

painting in particular, more broadly accessible, but I've wound up presenting my ideas very differently from the way I originally expected.

I had envisaged an art-historical tract dealing exclusively with my theory. This instead is a three-part narrative telling how I developed it from varied personal and professional experience, and how I fit it into a broader political and cultural context. Part One, after a chapter on my progressive childhood, deals with my first ten years on *Time*, then a conservative magazine. I show how it was put out, how I started as a researcher, especially in its Business section, and how I graduated to the writing staff, first in two gossip sections, then in foreign news. As one of few women writing for *Time* in the '60s, I see it differently from the many men who've done books about it. As the first woman within living memory to write a cover story for *Time*, at a moment when *Time* was especially unpopular, I became a bit of a media target. How I got to write that cover, and the response it evoked, form the climax of Part One.

Part Two takes me from my initiation into art on through the lengthy experience of leaving *Time*. Leaving was so traumatic that I escaped into a dream world for two years, ending (for three weeks) in a London mental ward before returning to reality. As I knew little about art in 1967, I introduce my readers to the subject as I learned about it (this procedure may help educate readers as innocent as I was). I tell of the people I became friendly with in the art world (especially Greenberg), and of what I learned in grad school. The climax to Part Two is the discovery of my theory in 1983.

Part Three brings me up to the twenty-first century, and tells what I've learned about art, art history, and history itself since 1983. It shows how writing this book made me look back on the times I'd lived through, and rethink them. Part Three wasn't envisaged when I started the book, but creating it forced me to plug gaps in my knowledge of art history and sociopolitical history that led to a broader and (I like to think) deeper understanding of both. The climax to Part Three is a startling insight into the U.S. electorate that came to me in 2001, triggered by the appalling swing to the right of the body politic in the wake of 9/11. While substantiating this insight, I learned that all three climaxes exemplified the creative process of problem solving, as described by Graham Wallas and others, so in addition, the book became a study in creativity.

Now to my theory of abstract painting. Normally, abstract painting is opposed to representational painting. People assume that if a painting is a pure abstraction (what some call a non-objective painting), it doesn't represent or refer to any object in the natural world. My eleventh edition of *Merriam-Webster's Collegiate Dictionary* (2003) defines "abstract (painting)" as "having only intrinsic form with little or no attempt at pictorial representation or narrative content." Grove's 34-volume *The Dictionary of Art*, published in 1996 and updated online, as of June 2008 still defined "abstract art" as "term applied in its strictest sense to forms of 20th-century Western art that reject representation and have no starting- or finishing-point in nature."[1] Still, dictionaries are the work of human hands. At best, they're indices of usage, a means of facilitating communication between people trying to speak the same language. In this case, they need revision. There can be another definition for an abstract painting, even a pure abstraction. Maybe not every one of them, but many, can be seen as a new, richer form of representation (or mimesis, a Greek term primarily meaning "the imitation of life").

In a traditional representational painting, each object on the surface of the canvas refers to a single object in external nature. You see an apple in a Cézanne, and, however many secondary or tertiary meanings a scholar might find in that apple, primarily it corresponds to an apple in external nature: that is to say, the painting is uni-referential.[2] In an abstract painting, the image is ambiguous. It refers to or looks a little bit like a lot of things, but not a lot like any one thing, so one viewer may be reminded of one object in external reality, and another viewer, of another object. The way I say this is that this abstract painting is *multireferential.*

You may protest that my idea makes an abstract painting like a Rorschach inkblot: you can see anything you want in it. But not even with a Rorschach blot can you see anything you want (if you're reasonably sane and normal). The ten blots in the test were chosen because each offers a different set of possibilities.[3] In books for psychologists interpreting these tests are lists of "popular responses" to each blot, objects that people most often see in them, and are therefore to a degree inherent in the image. Abstract art has a similar range of possibilities. Let me show what I mean.

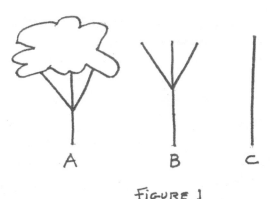

FiGURE 1

3

Figure 1 shows the difference between a traditional representational painting, a semiabstract one and a pure abstraction. A, on the left, shows a tree with trunk, branches and foliage. This is traditional representation, unireferential imagery, a one-on-one image. In B, the foliage is gone, leaving trunk and branches. It could still be a tree, but also a fork, candelabrum or Triton's weapon. This semiabstract image can suggest or refer to more than one thing, but still has enough detail so the number of allusions is limited. Giving a title to such a painting limits the allusions further. If I'd called this picture "a fork," it would have been harder for you to see the tree or candelabrum. With C, I've taken away the branches and left a vertical line. This is a pure abstraction, very multireferential. It could be a tree, but also a knife, person, obelisk, building, phallus, and dozens of other things, but it's never going to suggest a horizon line, or a person lying down (for most people, anyway). You'd need a horizontal line for that, just as you'd need a circle if you wanted to suggest a doughnut. If every abstract painting suggested an infinite number of objects, all would look exactly alike.

I further maintain that the reason viewers are reminded of certain objects by an abstract painting is that the artist herself or himself has seen such objects, or seen objects similar to what the painting's viewers have seen. Nobody can paint a picture of something he or she has never seen, so the abstract painting becomes a synthesis or composite of many things the artist has seen – not everything, but many things that for one or another reason are relevant to that particular artist's personality. In other words, not only the artist's feelings about things seen in the external world, but images of the things themselves are communicated to viewers through the painting. The artist wasn't aware of embedding these images in the painting, and couldn't have done so if she or he had been trying to do it. The abstract painting communicates so many different images to so many different people because the artist (again without being aware of doing so) has synthesized these many images of nature within her or his unconscious, and presented this synthesis as one ambiguous, abstract image on the canvas. (Some people have a problem with the concept of the unconscious. If that's your problem, then substitute the word "memory" for "unconscious" in the following paragraphs. If you have trouble with the concept of "memory," too, then this book may not be for you.)

Every artist (and every human) has a vast storehouse of images in his or her unconscious (or memory), things that she or he has seen. All artists (like all humans) synthesize these images within their unconsciouses. You can identify a tree as a tree, even if you're seeing one you've never seen before, because you've seen so many other trees. All these sightings have caused images of different trees to be stored within your unconscious, and synthesized into a composite picture of what a tree can look like. When you see a new tree, your mind compares it with the many different images of trees that it has previously assimilated, enabling you to identify the sight you have never before seen as a tree (people who through surgery have been enabled to see for the first time after they're grown often can't recognize what they're seeing).

Abstract artists differ from most of us in that they can synthesize many images stored at the back of their minds to a far higher degree; they can even combine disparate, often diametrically opposed images into composite painted images whose components refer back to their origins only in a very simplified, stylized way. I haven't yet figured out how they do it, but the fact that they do at the moment is enough for me.

When I explain this theory in conversation, people outside the art world often get it immediately – so immediately that they are apt to exclaim, "But that's so *obvious!*" Then they look at me suspiciously, and ask, "Are you *sure* nobody else has thought of this before?" Proving a negative is practically impossible. As a Renaissance scholar of my acquaintance remarks, you are always going to be up against the Norwegian *Festschrift*, the obscure article that somebody else will know about, even if you don't. Abstract painting has been with us for nearly a century. Thousands of books and articles have been written about it. I haven't read more than a fraction of them, but I have read some writing from the '60s to the '80s by scholars dealing with subject matter in abstraction. I'll discuss it in more detail further on. Here I'll just say that nothing I've read has offered multireferential imagery as a general principle in abstraction, incorporating objects from the natural world that have been assimilated by the artist's unconscious, and synthesized in that unconscious into an ambiguous, abstract image on the picture plane through which different objects in the natural world are suggested to different viewers. Nor has any of this writing applied its theories to a range of artists, as I've done, publishing my ideas in relation to Picasso, Jackson Pollock, and two lesser-known artists (Friedel Dzubas and Jules Olitski). If anybody else has done what I've done (and before I did), it hasn't made a dent, as those dictionary definitions attest.

Many people like the idea that an abstract painting depicts nothing. As this concept has never had much appeal for me, I find myself at a loss to explain it adequately, but I suspect that in some (if not all) cases, the appeal may be almost mystical: one's ability to admire a painting about nothing becomes proof of one's capacity to accept the reality of all things unseen. For artists, the thrill may lie more in discovery. This view was expressed by a very great abstract artist, Helen Frankenthaler, when I interviewed her for *Time* in 1969. She described how, in the early 1950s, when she was young, she and her then boyfriend, Greenberg, would go to the country, set up easels, and paint the landscapes they saw before them, in a style that inevitably owed much to nineteenth-century French impressionism. Afterwards, they'd return to Manhattan, and Frankenthaler would paint abstracts in her studio. "The landscapes were the discipline, the abstracts were the freedom and the joy," she recalled. "Though I enjoyed the discipline, one was confined within a tradition that was *déjà vu*. For me, just about everything has been said about landscapes, but I don't think everything has been said in terms of colors and shapes."[4]

Frankenthaler's abstractions have had many admirers, but from all I've seen, in the four decades that I've followed art, there are and have always been many more people for whom the apparent lack of subject matter in an abstract painting is a drawback: while they may respect the abstraction, they find it difficult or impossible to love. That fact, more than any other, explains to me the giant reaction against abstract expressionism in the early '60s, after a decade when it had reigned as the avant-garde. This reaction against abstract expressionism (which was really a reaction against abstraction in general) relegated the abstract art made after 1960 (even that of Frankenthaler) to a secondary role within the art world, condemning most of it to near oblivion in America at large, and fundamentally altering our entire society's way of looking at and evaluating not only art but culture in general.

In future chapters, I'll consider that reaction, away from the multireferential and back into the uni-referential, together with its implications. Here I'll merely say that it has led to many forms of uni-referential art that, despite superficial novelty, are to me fundamentally backward-looking. To me, abstract art (or, any rate, the best abstract art) is still the most daring, truly avant-garde art style that we have. But in this, I'm in the minority. To lovers of the status quo, who vastly outnumber me and the people who share my taste, we're the old-fashioned ones. It's a real looking-glass situation.

My theory of abstract painting developed out of my grad school experience, seeing how little time my professors devoted to abstract painting, and how limited was what they could say about it. I hoped to provide a teaching tool to rectify the situation, so I planned a theoretical book for academics to be published by a university press. Seeking funding, I applied during the 1993–94 academic year for a grant from the National Endowment for the Humanities. I didn't get it, but since the NEH is a government agency, I could ask to see readers' reports on my application. Once I saw them, I began to suspect I'd have to rethink my book. The readers were presumably typical of the prevailing esthetic in academia, one in line with the prevailing esthetic in the contemporary art world. They didn't really understand what I was trying to do. To the extent that they did understand it, they didn't want it. I shall analyze these responses more in Part Three; all I need to share here is that they told me no university press was going to buy the book I'd proposed to the NEH. In 1995, I sent a proposal for a similar book to a non-academic art book publisher. It, too, was rejected, and again I got hold of one of the readers' reports. Same ignorance and negativity.

I was already thinking of turning the theoretical tract into a memoir telling how I'd developed the theory out of many past experiences. I hoped this approach might make the theory more accessible to art historians. Equally importantly, I hoped that the material about *Time* might enable me to sell the book to a trade publisher. Shortly after I'd left *Time*, I'd tried to make a nonfiction novel out of my experiences there, and though I hadn't been able to sell it, trade publishers had been willing to read it. I knew that trade publishers weren't interested in art theory, but I thought that a memoir would enable me to prattle on about the art world people I'd known (in addition to all the *Time* types). Weren't books about artists and their bohemian life styles reasonably popular?

By January 2006, I had a completed manuscript (or so I thought, though obviously it's been revised since). I started trying to sell it. Since I thought that my art-in-context approach might be more academically acceptable than an art-as-theory approach, I sent proposals to the three university presses most likely to publish a book like mine. One sent me a form letter of rejection after a week. The second kept my proposal for a month (leading me to hope that they'd sent it out to readers). Then I got another form letter of rejection. The third kept the proposal six weeks, then sent a letter written by a real person telling me that my proposal wasn't "scholarly" enough. This (I suppose) is a valid objection, to the extent that I've long since outgrown some conventions of the academic niche that I occupied in grad school, just as I'd earlier outgrown my niche on *Time*. Today, I see myself as an independent scholar (and art critic), equidistant from journalism and academia, freer to use the tools of each to critique the other, therefore capable of more substantive comments on both. Both disciplines are dedicated to the gathering of information and the dissemination of knowledge. Both have been powerfully affected by changing technology since I was closest to them. My hope is that students of both will be able to take the lessons I learned in the print world, and apply them to a world dominated by cyberspace.

I sent letters of enquiry to seven or eight literary agents. None were interested, the two most honest admitting that they didn't know enough about art to be able to sell my book. (The retired editor for an art-book publisher with whom I had an e-mail correspondence told me that few books he'd worked on were represented by agents, and that most agents don't handle art books because they so rarely earn much money.) I sent six letters of enquiry to editors in trade houses whom I'd selected because they'd worked on books about art. Enclosed were self-addressed, stamped postcards with three boxes to check: 1) Yes, I'd like to see the manuscript; 2) Yes, I'd like to see a proposal, and 3) Thanks but no thanks. Five out of the six sent back the postcard with box 3 checked. One, whom I shall call Editor P, checked box 1.

Editor P kept my manuscript for three months, then returned it with a warm note saying that I'd blended the genres to create an esthetic whole, and gone far toward defying the received wisdom on abstract painting, but it wasn't right for his list. P probably knows more about art than anybody else in trade publishing (he has relatives in the business). When I got his note, I said to myself, if he isn't going to publish my book, nobody else in trade publishing will, either. My fantasy is that he regretfully decided that publishing it didn't make economic sense. I know that trade publishing these days is big business. Virtually all the major houses are owned by big companies who demand that every book make quantities of money. This can only be done by selling many copies. To judge from what art books get published by trade houses, the only ones that might sell enough copies to justify publication are a) about a famous artist, b) by a famous critic, and c) with lots of pretty, almost invariably representational pictures. My book meets none of these criteria.

People in publishing will tell you that smaller "independent" houses are willing to make only a little money by publishing a book with shorter press runs, but having cased displays by small presses and independents at several book fairs, I've found that to the minimal extent that they publish art books at all, they subscribe to the common fallacy that the prevailing art-world esthetic is what's "revolutionary" in art, whereas abstract painting is old hat. Heigh-ho! I've heard stories about books rejected by thirty-six publishers, and then become bestsellers when published by the thirty-seventh, but I didn't want to spend the years needed for that process. The material in my closing chapters was already getting dated, and the longer I waited, the more rewriting I'd have to do. That's why I signed a contract with iUniverse, a publishing house that I pay to put out my book. I'll get royalties from every copy sold, but the odds are overwhelming that I will at best turn a trivial profit. I still have something to say that needs to be said, and I don't know any other way of getting it into print.

In the old days, what I'm doing was known as vanity publishing. Today, it's called self-publishing. The two differ in procedure and content. In vanity publishing, a publisher printed a few hundred or thousand copies, and left the author with few ways of disposing of them beyond selling or giving them to family and friends. Self-publishing is "print on demand." Thanks to improved technology, iUniverse will only print a copy of my book when somebody has placed an order to buy it. This saves money. Thanks to the Web, my book can be bought beyond my immediate circle (assuming I can get word out that it exists, though many publications refuse to review self-published books, and "brick and mortar" bookstores rarely stock them).

Self-published books may also differ from traditional vanity publishing in terms of content. The prevailing attitude toward both is that they're written by untalented amateurs who can't compete in the real world of publishing, and that because a "legit" publisher isn't putting them out, they're not worth reviewing, buying, or reading. Many self-published books are the work of untalented amateurs, but some are limited not by the capacities of their writers but by the capacities of their readers. Only a limited number of readers may have the necessary aptitudes to understand a subject, also the background and interest in it – the sum total of factors that determine the potential audience for a book but reveal nothing of its innate quality (unless you're the most vulgar sort of a populist, whose only definition of quality is sales). Despite all I've done to broaden my appeal, this book is still largely about art, and, although artists like to think that the world is fascinated by everything they do, my experience suggests that most Americans couldn't care less. Admittedly, museums are increasingly crowded, but art books are still only a tiny slice of the publishing industry's output, and my take on art (as already indicated) is very much a minority take, within that slice.

With six years' experience as a writer on *Time*, and more than two hundred articles published in over a dozen periodicals since I left *Time*, I don't see myself as an untalented amateur. Therefore I conclude that the limited numbers of copies that this book can expect to sell are due to the limitations of its audience, not my own (except to the extent that I'm not interested in targeting a mass audience). But I'm not alone. Once upon a time, the publishing world had more room for books with a limited audience, but given increased costs of production, declining numbers of books bought per capita, and consolidation of publishing facilities under profit-hungry overlords, that's less true today. The result, I think, is that many books that once would have been published by trade houses now must be self-published.

There may be increasing recognition of this, at least to judge from iUniverse titles good enough for some of our most distinguished libraries to acquire. I checked the databases of ten such libraries, and found that of the ten, only Harvard was the holdout. The other nine listed the following numbers of iUniverse titles: Princeton, 36; Yale, 36; UCLA, 36; University of Chicago, 40; Berkeley, 44; University of Michigan, 49; Columbia, 51; City College of New York, 67; New York Public Library (research and lending divisions), 164. Some of these were reprints of books originally published elsewhere. Others must have been written by alumni of the schools in question, and of course iUniverse books represent only a tiny fraction of all these libraries' total holdings. Even so, those numbers suggest that, in terms of quality, the line between publishing for profit (however modest) and publishing for what is primarily (though not exclusively) the love of it may not be as firmly drawn as it was.

9

Having signed the contract with iUniverse in February 2007, I began fact-checking the manuscript. The contract stipulated that I turn it in within a year. I figured that would be ample time to fact-check it, since I'd gotten much experience in doing this as a researcher on *Time*. Shortly after I'd begun fact-checking this book, I fell ill with a bad back that required major surgery. When I got out of rehab five months later, I was way behind schedule. Hoping to catch up, I recruited fact-checkers to help me out. By the end of 2007, I'd spent as much on fact-checkers as I could afford, and still had far to go, so I got an extension on the contract and finished the job myself. I don't regret hiring those fact-checkers. All were younger than I was, and some of their responses told me more than they knew about reaching readers of their age.

One prospective fact-checker I interviewed had majored in psychology in college. During our interview, I told her that my theory of abstract painting was based in Freud, and that my understanding of creativity owed a lot to Graham Wallas (whose ideas in turn owe a lot to Freud). After our interview, this young lady sent me a charming e-mail in which she offered to provide me with a reading list of more recent psychology books on the mind and creativity. I began hearing about negative attitudes toward Freud in college psychology departments when I myself was an undergraduate, and I've been getting complaints about my own Freudian methodology ever since I unveiled my theory, so I reconstructed the thinking behind this e-mail as follows.

Oh my God, its author had most probably been thinking. This old woman is way out of touch. Doesn't she know that Freud is totally exploded? Doesn't she know that you can't prove that the unconscious exists? I'll deal with such attitudes at greater length further on, but only after I've told what I learned about psychology during my fifteen years on the couch, and in the thirty-nine years since I left my last Freudian (having become profoundly discontented with him). Anybody who assumes that I just got up off the couch and am hopelessly brainwashed by my shrink is making a mistake.

My theory of multireferential imagery is admittedly derived from what I learned about dream interpretation in analysis, but only because what I learned in analysis has been confirmed by other experiences I've had, and will deal with in this book. Freud believed that the dream image is a composite or synthesis of things people have seen while awake. I many times found this true in analyzing my own dreams. Freud likened these composites to the multiple exposures of Francis Galton, the nineteenth-century British geneticist, who superimposed photographs of the faces of family members to create what he thought was a picture of their common ancestor.[5] In the twenty-first century, Conan O'Brien on late night TV similarly combines photos of celebrity couples to create an image of their possible child.

For Freud, dreams expressed unconscious desires that present themselves to our conscious minds in sleep; ergo, we all have an unconscious mind as well as a conscious one. For me, he was dumb about some things (most notably, art) but right on target about the unconscious. I know I have one, and I've heard much evidence that other people do, too (even when they won't admit it). My expertise is in art, not neurology, but I'm confident that neurologists will locate those portions of the brain which keep people from being continuously conscious of the vast amounts of information stored in their minds; I'm also confident that these neurologists will discover the biological mechanisms that allow specific information to be accessed (if they haven't already, as recent popularly written stories about neurology in *The New York Times* seem to hint).[6] There must be a scientific explanation for the simple fact that if I say, "How much is three and two?" you can answer, "Five," even though two minutes ago, you weren't consciously thinking of the number five.

Another aspect of preparing this book for publication was securing permissions to quote from books and periodicals. That, too, was illuminating, forcing me to look carefully at how I'd quoted such passages, and be sure I wasn't doing so out of context. One article I quote appeared in *Esquire* and concerned *Newsweek* in the '60s. During this crucial decade, *Newsweek* and *Time* were engaged in an epic rivalry that centered around opposed views on Vietnam, but showed in other topics, too. Around 2000, in one of the many revisions this manuscript has gone through, I'd realized that I was biased on behalf of my former employer, and that what I'd written was correspondingly unfair to *Newsweek*. Since I wanted to give the fairest possible coverage of the rivalry, I'd added every good thing that I could find about *Newsweek*, and made sure that my portrait of *Time* included plenty of warts. Still, drafting the e-mail requesting permission to quote the *Esquire* article, I reviewed what it said about *Newsweek*, and how I'd handled what it said. Bit by bit, I had to revise that part of my manuscript still further, forcing me to admit that while my head tells me that *Newsweek* was expressing my own political opinions in the '60s, and *Time* was doing just the opposite, nevertheless my heart belongs to *Time*. This is nothing I can help, so I simply warn the reader of my bias.

Analyzing that bias, I see three reasons for it (none relating to *Time's* politics). The first reason is purely professional: *Time* made me into a writer – not that I couldn't write well when I was first named to the writing staff, but I wasn't writing like a professional until after I'd spent those six years in its great glass writing school. The second reason I'm biased is personal: I liked almost all the people I worked with. When I was contemplating going to work at *Time*, I was told that the people were nice, and they were. Many of the nicest aren't mentioned in this book. Space required that I limit myself to people who were most relevant to my career, or to my life in other ways.

The third reason *Time* means a lot to me is both personal and professional: it allowed me to enter the art world on a level where its members were eager to teach me all they could about art. Representing as I did more than fourteen million readers, I was in particular cultivated by a high-ranking curator who introduced me to the art he most admired. This would enable me to relate to Greenberg when I eventually met him, and that meeting was the beginning of the rest of my life. I'm biased on behalf of Greenberg, too, though again I've tried to present him as fairly as I could, and with understanding of the many people who have trouble relating to him. I think that he was a truly great human being and our greatest art critic. I also believe that the art of the '60s and since with which his name was (and still is) associated is the finest art of these years, despite the neglect and/or hostility that both the man and the art so often (though most certainly not always) continue to encounter.

Another issue that arose during fact-checking was the extent to which any memoir must be fiction – not because the author is lying, but because nobody remembers everything perfectly. There must be some unintentional fiction in this narrative, but also no guarantee that any of my readers who remember situations in which they and I interacted will remember them more accurately than I do. I have a pretty good long-term memory, but I haven't relied upon it any more than I could help. Whenever possible, I've checked my recollections against the written record (published and unpublished), and I've lived closer to that record than many other people. My account of the events in my life described in greatest detail (from March 1965 to April 1966) is based on the nonfiction novel that I wrote in between 1969 and 1971, when I was closer to the action and remembered it more clearly. The account given in second-greatest detail (from February 1969 to October 1969) is based upon another nonfiction novel that I wrote in 1974. In both cases, I'd substantiated or qualified my recollections whenever possible by consulting published sources and my engagement calendars.

Most people you'll read about in this book go by their real names, and are described as I remember them, but in a few cases, names and attributes are disguised (such people are introduced with advisory catchphrases such as "whom I shall call" or "shall we say"). Partly this was done for legal reasons, but partly because I don't want to cause any more pain or embarrassment than necessary in order to present the key elements in my narrative, the essential links in my chain of events. Sometimes I felt I could be franker and even engage in a little levity by referring to former colleagues as "A," "B," or "Z." One psychoanalyst, two psychiatrists, a literary agent and sundry editors are also designated by letters (none of which correspond to their initials). I know (or fantasize) that some of these people are still part of my life.

About creativity. I'm well aware that many latter-day psychologists have dealt with the subject, and I've browsed through a few of their theories, but the one that best corresponds to my own experience is still the oldie but goodie outlined by Graham Wallas, the Fabian political scientist, in *The Art of Thought* (1926). According to Wallas, the creative process has at least four steps. First is "preparation," the definition of a problem and accumulation of information needed to solve it. Another stage is "incubation," when the thinker puts the problem aside, and lets the unconscious select the key information and rearrange it in a new configuration: synthesize it. Next comes "illumination": the story of Archimedes shouting "Eureka!" (having realized that, since his body displaced its volume of his bath water, he could use this to measure the gold in a king's crown).[7] Last is "verification," substantiating or qualifying the insight.

Non-Freudian psychologists prefer explanations that don't rely on the unconscious. Robert J. Sternberg, a cognitive psychologist, described problem-solving in a textbook of the 1990s as 1) identifying a problem, 2) defining it, 3) developing a strategy for solving it, 4) organizing information about it, 5) allocating resources, 6) monitoring the solution, and 7) evaluating the solution. His example is a student writing a term paper, and makes no reference to incubation or illumination (though a recent article on "The Eureka Hunt" in *The New Yorker*, without mentioning Wallas or using the term "incubation," reaffirms its importance).[8]

The climaxes to Parts Two and Three of this book occurred to me on the Eureka model, with realization flooding up out of my unconscious. The climax to Part One was a conscious creation (Sternberg's model). As it occurred on *Time*, it was "collaborative creativity," a type beloved of how-to books offering ten easy steps to greater creativity. This book is only incidentally a how-to book. Still less is it a medical study by a psychologist, psychiatrist, or psychoanalyst. I've learned about creativity in fifty years of observing artists and writers, by trying (unsuccessfully) to write plays and novels, but above all, I learned from thinking about the climaxes of this book, and how they did or didn't progress through Wallas's stages of development in the order he specified. Call me a test case (if you want to be polite), or a guinea pig (if that suits you better).

Psychoanalysis gave me practice in retrieving source material for my dreams. This is done through "free association," letting your mind lead you through links of reminiscence until you can access much in the past. Free association has helped me retrieve many sources for creative insights achieved while I was awake, so in each of my climactic creative insights I'll be describing my sources, an approach that may help readers to take fuller advantage of their own experience.

13

The biggest debate among creativity scholars is how to distinguish between the merely new and the truly creative. A doodle on a scrap of paper may be unlike any other doodle ever made, but does that make it truly creative or merely new – in other words, is it of value to anybody else? Beyond that, the art critic must ask, how much value? A Warhol soup can and an abstract painting by Pollock may both be creative, but does that give them equal esthetic value? I'll revisit these thorny issues, saying at present only that some claim "beauty is in the eye of the beholder," and as a creator I had to consider which beholders mattered (practically, not esthetically: what audience was I trying to reach?). J. K. Rowling wrote Harry Potter books for many beholders of varied ages at the time she wrote. T. S. Eliot wrote poetry for a few literate contemporaries, hoping his following would swell in the future. I write for my circle within the art world, but also for the larger art world, and beyond that for people not unlike my former colleagues on *Time*, intelligent people who may not know much about art but do have an interest in the larger society around them. My hope is that they will be curious to learn how and why developments within the art world helped to shape that larger society, and how in particular publications like *Time*, *Life,* and *Newsweek* interfaced between the two.

As I see it, synthesis is the most important element in creativity, the mysterious process that goes on during "incubation" of integrating previous insights or information into a new ideological configuration. I also see synthesis as the essence of abstract painting, this equally mysterious process of integrating into a new visual configuration the dozens or even thousands of disparate images stored in the artist's unconscious (or memory). To help explain the kinship between these two experiences, I argue that modernist abstraction is descended from a tradition of artistic synthesis going back centuries. The ancient Greek Zeuxis was said to paint grapes so realistically that birds pecked at them. Yet Cicero tells us that when the artist was invited to do a portrait of Helen of Troy for a temple in Crotona, he asked the five loveliest maidens in Crotona to pose. Then he combined the most beautiful parts of each to create his ideal portrait.

Leonardo da Vinci synthesized images of things he'd seen to create a new world of *fantasia*, though he too was famed for his ability to depict the real world. In his *Treatise on Painting*, he told "How one ought to make an imaginary animal seem natural....If, therefore, you would have an imaginary animal appear natural, and assuming, let us say, that it is a dragon, for the head take that of a mastiff or hound, and give him the eyes of a cat, the ears of a porcupine, the nose of a greyhound, the brow of a lion, the temples of an old cock, and the neck of a sea turtle."[9]

Mozart experienced synthesis. In a letter, he described thinking of a theme, related melody, counterpoint, part of each instrument, and so on, until "I have the entire composition finished in my head though it may be long....It does not come to me successively, with its various parts worked out in detail, as they will be later on, but it is in its entirety that my imagination lets me hear it."[10]

Eliot's poem *The Waste Land* incorporates passages by other authors. In an essay, he wrote, "When a poet's mind is perfectly equipped for its work, it is constantly amalgamating disparate experience; the ordinary man's experience is chaotic, irregular, fragmentary. The latter falls in love, or reads Spinoza, and these two experiences have nothing to do with each other, or with the noise of the typewriter or the smell of cooking; in the mind of the poet these experiences are always forming new wholes."[11]

I didn't see the parallel between abstract painting and creativity until the twenty-first century. I might not have seen it at all if I hadn't already experienced my third creative insight, of discovering the "disenfranchised left." Since 1950, the proportion of U.S. voters who (by virtue of their occupations) were more apt to vote Democratic had declined in relation to the proportion of U.S. voters who (by virtue of their occupations) were more apt to vote Republican, forcing the Democrats toward a "centrist" position and enabling the Republicans to move to the far right. The "disenfranchised left" was all the people outside the U.S. who made goods for the U.S. market, but couldn't vote in U.S. elections because they weren't U.S. citizens. These were the economic descendants of working-class Americans who in the '30s, '40s and even '50s had backed liberal fiscal policies that made it harder for the rich to get richer, and the poor to get poorer.

Aided by this insight, I also saw how art and U. S. history since 1945 have been interrelated, so in my conclusions, I bring them together, placing the art of our time in a political context that may differ from the usual art-historical one. I also summarize those aspects of my creativity that may benefit others (though for me creativity is more a life style than ten easy steps).

PART I:
THE MEDIA: "SWINGING LONDON"

1. Preparation
(1935–1956)

A VERY FINE reporter once said, "I firmly believe that any good journalist must essentially be temperamentally an outsider. I don't think [a] full sense of belonging and security is conducive to creativity."[12] Students of creativity talk of "thinking outside the box." I was born (in New York City, in 1935) outside two of the many subcommunities into which American society is divided. My brilliant, beautiful mother, Ruth West, was the daughter of a blind Anglo-Saxon Methodist minister from Michigan. My handsome, literate father, George Halasz, had left his native Budapest and immigrated to New York. My parents split up when I was three, and my father moved to Los Angeles. My mother took back her maiden name, and I was raised by her, seeing mostly her side of the family. I was the only one with a Hungarian name in such family gatherings, which made me feel outside of the Anglo-Saxon box. Since I didn't speak Hungarian, I would learn that I was outside the Hungarian box, too. Two more boxes I was outside of came to me with my first name. Only Hungarians are apt to know it's a girl's name, so over the years I'd get many letters addressed to "Mr. Piri Halasz." These suggested I was a boy, hence outside the girl's box, yet I am a female, so I'm outside the boy's box, too.

My parents had met around 1930, when he was (briefly) a drama critic for the *Brooklyn Daily Eagle,* and she, a (regularly employed) advertising copywriter. The Rev. Julian S. West, my maternal grandfather, died in 1940; I remember him dimly as dour and unforgiving. His wife, Bertha Mae Carter West, didn't die until 1956. When I was little, she made clothes for my dolls and taught me to make fudge. In her youth, she'd kept house for Grandpa West and their three children, looked after the missionary society and church socials, and read books and magazines to her husband. He dictated his sermons to her. She read them back to him until he had them memorized. By Sunday, she'd be so tired that she took a hatpin along with her to church, to jab herself awake when she felt herself nodding off, but she still had a twinkle in her eye, and a fiendishly competitive streak. She taught me croquet in the summer of 1940, when my mother rented a house in Bucks County, and loved to whang my ball far into the rough.

Unlike many Americans, my mother's friends didn't look down on Eastern European immigrants. They thought Hungarians rather glamorous, if crazy, but then she mostly mixed with liberal-minded professionals like herself: in advertising, public relations, magazines, fashion, design, and retailing, plus creative writers and occasional doctors and lawyers. The Gentiles were mostly fleeing the piety of their Middle-American backgrounds. The Jews were pretty assimilated. Not until second grade did I even hear the word "Jewish," but then a classmate at the upper-class Brearley School asked me if I was Jewish. I asked my mother. She replied that my father said he must have some Jewish blood in him, because there was no such thing as a pureblooded anything in Mittel Europa. (In 1995, after he was dead, I'd learn that he'd been all Jewish, but "some Jewish blood" was what I lived with during my formative years.)

*   *   *

In 1942, I was sent to North Country School, on a farm in the Adirondacks near Lake Placid, New York. Created by Walter and Leonora Lacey Clark, NCS was progressive, coeducational, and so wonderful that I've already written a memoir all about it.[13] NCS was a little subcommunity of its own, to which all of us felt we belonged, and it encouraged creativity. We made art in our arts and crafts classes, wrote poetry and fiction in our English classes, made up plays and even a song. Much of our art came right out of our lives: the song was about the school horses going out to pasture in spring, and a poem of mine concerned an early fall snowstorm. My favorite teacher was Edgar S. Bley; he and his wife Elsa would become lifelong friends. Ed taught my English and Social Studies classes, and the ultraliberal outlook that he brought to Social Studies reinforced that of my mother and her friends.

Franklin D. Roosevelt was president, and Democrats controlled Congress. Enthusiasm for how FDR had confronted the Great Depression had handed him a landslide victory when he ran for reelection in 1936 (if Americans had been able to watch the returns on TV, only two of the forty-eight states would have been red). In high school, I'd learn about the benevolent New Deal legislation enacted in the '30s: the Tennessee Valley Authority (TVA) and Rural Electrification Administration (REA) to bring flood control and cheap power to rural America; the Securities and Exchange Commission (SEC) to protect investors; Social Security to protect the elderly and unemployed; and laws to protect the workingman – including a minimum wage, overtime pay, and especially the Wagner Act, with its "bill of rights" for organized labor, and its National Labor Relations Board (NLRB) to adjudicate disputes. As a child, though, all I knew was that FDR was president, and my elders considered him great.

World War II had begun. I'd been sent to NCS because my mother wanted to go to Washington and work for the Office of War Information (OWI). When I graduated from eighth grade at NCS in 1947, the war was over, and FDR had been succeeded by Harry S Truman, his vice president, who then won an election on his own in 1948. The country was still dominated by liberals, and to show us what "liberal" meant Ed drew a semicircle on the blackboard when I was in eighth grade. He explained that the terms "left" and "right" came from seating arrangements like this for many representative assemblies. When you looked at the speaker (who sat facing the delegates), those delegates who identified more with the working class sat to your left, and those who identified more with employers sat to your right. Immediately to the left of the center aisle sat liberals, with radicals farther around the semicircle to the left. Immediately to the right of the aisle sat conservatives, with reactionaries farther around the semicircle to the right. Liberals favored moderate reforms; radicals, extreme ones; conservatives wanted to maintain the status quo; reactionaries, to turn back the clock.

Democrats were more likely to be liberals, and Republicans more likely to be conservatives. Reactionaries were apt to be fascists, and radicals were usually socialists or communists. We had no fascists in our Congress, but clearly remembered the fascism of Nazi Germany and Mussolini's Italy. We had no communists or socialists either, but the Soviet Union was communist, and during World War II it had been our ally. Socialism came to power in Great Britain in 1945, when the Labor Party got elected. Around 1949, I learned that socialists and communists believed that the state should own the means of production, so that all of its citizens might share equally in the profits, but that socialists believed this had to be accomplished through the democratic process, with socialist governments peaceably elected. Communists believed that the end justified the means, i.e., that the overthrow of a government by force and violence was an acceptable way of gaining power (they liked to call themselves "socialists," too).

My bedroom at home had poster paints and an easel in it long before I got to NCS, and I'd been introduced to the Museum of Modern Art and the Metropolitan Museum of Art when I was six or seven. A smaller proportion of the population went to museums in the '40s.[14] Fewer still went to look at modern art, but one was Ed. In the '30s, as a college student in New York, he'd wanted to become an artist, and haunted the galleries on Fifty-Seventh Street, where new European art was shown. During my last two years at NCS, he and Elsa were my house parents; I often saw him sketching and doodling. He made Christmas cards, as we all did, but his were in the style of "curvilinear cubism," which Picasso had developed in the '30s, twenty years after he and Braque had created Analytic Cubism. Around 1910, Analytic

Cubism had been the most abstract painting the world had yet seen, and it revolutionized art.

Besides cubist Madonnas, Ed painted pictures suggesting he also admired other abstract artists of the '30s: Wassily Kandinsky, Joan Miró and that purest of abstractionists, Piet Mondrian.[15] I don't think I saw many of these paintings as a child, but enough of his attitude rubbed off on me so that I wasn't shocked when my mother took me over spring vacation in 1945 to the retrospective exhibition of Mondrian at MoMA. I must have been told that these pure white pictures, with their straight black dividing lines and squares or rectangles of red, blue, or yellow, weren't meant to depict anything, and I didn't love them, but I respected them. Next to me stood a man who said angrily, "My kid could do it." I was pretty good at my arts and crafts classes, very likely better than his kid, and I knew I couldn't have made those paintings.

The seventh grade edited and mimeographed the school magazine. It had been all stories, poetry, and drawings from students throughout the school, but Ed had our class make the front part a newspaper. He taught us to write news stories for it, using the classic formula, with the first sentence telling Who, What, Where, When, Why, and How. He explained that the opinion of the newspaper was supposed to be in the editorials, and news stories were supposed to give just the facts, but he brought New York papers into class, and showed us how even news pages reflected the opinions of the people who put together the paper, and influenced how readers felt about the news. This was done with loaded words, slanted headlines and copy, size of headlines and length of story, choice of photographs, and placement of stories. Tabloids like the *Daily News* used a smaller vocabulary because they were intended for people with less education; *The New York Times*, intended for more educated people, used a larger one.

Time sponsored a student quiz program, and we were given the quizzes at NCS, but they bored me. The magazine was rarely seen on my mother's coffee table, and, among the magazines at NCS, the large-format ones with more pictures interested me more: *Life, Look,* and *The Saturday Evening Post.* My mother subscribed to *The New Yorker.* I loved its cartoons and squibs at the bottoms of its columns, but, although I didn't know it, *Time* and *The New Yorker* had been on a collision course for decades. *Time* preceded *The New Yorker.*[16] Its initial issue, dated March 3, 1923, had a circulation of fewer than 9,000 copies, but by 1940, that was up to nearly a million. The magazine was the brainchild of two recent Yale graduates, Henry Robinson Luce and Briton Hadden. Both could trace ancestors back to America's founding fathers. Hadden grew up in Brooklyn Heights; Luce was the son of Presbyterian missionaries, and spent his early years in China. Both appear to have been creative – Luce especially, who besides co-creating *Time* went on to build an empire upon it. At first, Hadden ran the editorial side of *Time*, and Luce, the business side, but Hadden died in 1929 of a streptococcus infection. Luce took over the editorial direction of *Time* as well as its business side, using managing editors to retain the clever, breezy editorial style Hadden had created.

In 1930, Luce founded *Fortune,* a business magazine, and in 1932, he purchased *Architectural Forum.* In 1933, *Time's* first imitator commenced publication under the name of *News-Week* (it changed its name to *Newsweek* in 1937). By 1934, Time Inc. was considering starting a picture magazine, and Luce met Clare Boothe Brokaw, a divorcee who had been a managing editor at *Vanity Fair* (which was closed down by Condé Nast in 1936, and revived in 1983 in altered form). The *Vanity Fair* of the '30s had elegant photographs of actors and actresses, lively satirical drawings, color reproductions of what polite society considered "modern art," and articles by celebrities as well as journalists. Mrs. Brokaw had written a memorandum for Condé Nast about a picture magazine, so she and Luce discussed picture magazines when they met. Time Inc. introduced *Life* as a picture magazine in 1936, by which time, Luce had divorced his first wife and married Brokaw (the corporate tradition of serial monogamy started early).

Vanity Fair published a satirical two-part article by my father on Hollywood society in 1934. My mother was closer to Time Inc., at least on a personal level. After my father left, she had two lovers who were or would be employed by that company. John Fistere was a divorced man whom I think was already on the publishing side at *Fortune.* During the summer of 1939, when my mother rented a house in the Atlantic Highlands, he came out from the city with her on weekends, and they remained friends after he remarried. His new wife had a daughter named Susan from a previous marriage, and, when Susan grew up, she married a *Time* correspondent, Lee Griggs.

My mother's other Time Inc. lover was not yet associated with *Time* when she knew him best. Robert E. McLaughlin, a red-headed divorcé from Chicago, was writing short stories for *The New Yorker* during the summer of 1940, when my mother had the house in Bucks County where Granny West taught me to play croquet. This house was at the back of a farm. Next to it stood a renovated chicken coop used as a guest cottage, where Bob pecked away at a portable typewriter. He was nice to me, letting me watch him shave in the morning and teaching me a great game called "fixing people's wagons." He, too, remarried but remained friendly with my mother on through the '50s, after he'd become a writer for *Time*.

Bob's fiction experience served him well on *Time*, for the magazine was still famous (or infamous) in the '50s and even the '60s for its writing. Although most of the specific mannerisms that Briton Hadden had introduced were discarded by the time I got there, members of the editorial staff still used them in conversation. I remember "great & good friend," a euphemism for lover or mistress, "the late, great" for well-known dead people, and "the good gray *Times*," an impish catchphrase doubtless dreamed up to needle the magazine's illustrious competitor.

Time itself was not invulnerable to needling. One particularly cute aspect of early *Time*style was the curiously inverted sentence structure that Hadden had somehow or other managed to develop out of the Homer he'd loved in school. This mannerism came under fire in 1936 in *The New Yorker*, when Wolcott Gibbs published a famous Profile of Luce. *The New Yorker* had begun publication in 1925, two years after *Time*, and its editor, Harold Ross, had made it clear in his prospectus that his magazine would be written for metropolitan New Yorkers. *Time* was designed to provide fast, easy information for the less metropolitan (though not less wealthy) Yale grad who got bored plowing through the daily papers on his morning commute.

The formula worked for Manhattan-bound Yalies, and for their opposite numbers in smaller communities across the U.S. James L. Baughman has shown that *Time* in its early years was most read by the more affluent citizens of medium-sized cities where the newspapers emphasized local news.[17] Luce himself said that the magazine was edited for "the Gentleman of Indiana and for Madame the Lady of Indiana."[18] *Time* was satirized in two Broadway comedies of 1939, *The Man Who Came to Dinner* and *The Philadelphia Story* (both later movies). The *New Yorker* Profile was the most lethal, above all the killingly funny phraseology with which Gibbs parodied the reverse word order of early *Time*style.[19] Luce was apparently deeply hurt, but twenty years later, his employees were still quoting those passages from Gibbs.

In our English classes at NCS, Ed had us model our poetry on tough moderns: Gerard Manley Hopkins and e e cummings. He read aloud to us from Homer, Howard Fast, and Swift, and, in eighth grade, assigned us Shakespeare and G. B. Shaw. The modern poetry in particular was highbrow stuff, but then Ed was a highbrow, unlike my mother and her friends, who were merely upper middlebrows. These distinctions I'd learn in 1949 from a delightful chart in *Life* based upon an article in *Harper's Magazine* by Russell Lynes.[20] Upper middlebrows, said *Life*, read *The New Yorker*, drank very dry martinis, bought records of show tunes, and played The Game (a.k.a. charades). All these my mother did. Highbrows read *Partisan Review*, drank a modest but carefully chosen wine, listened to very early or very recent classical music, and made art their worthiest cause. "Art" was symbolized in the *Life* chart by a little drawing of a Picasso, much like one of Ed's doodles. Outside class, I devoured quality children's books and pun-ridden joke books like Bennett Cerf's *Try and Stop Me*, and Ed Zern's *To Hell with Hunting*. A pun has a double level of meaning, and experts say that humor is good training for creativity. Nothing gave me more pleasure than to get off a really awful pun at the dinner table, causing other kids to giggle, and Ed to say sternly, "A pun is the lowest form of humor!"

*   *   *

After NCS, I was sent to the Putney School, in Putney, Vermont, also progressive and coeducational, but not as well-run as North Country. In my sophomore year, a group of the teachers formed a union and went on strike. The director was supposed to be progressive politically as well as educationally, but she crushed the union, convincing me that labels like "progressive" and "conservative" didn't mean much. My grades collapsed, so my mother withdrew me from Putney. In the fall, she took me to Europe for several weeks. I fell for London and the English in a big way.

Back in New York that spring, I did little beyond stare off into space all day, so my mother sent me to Sylvan Keiser, a psychoanalyst who according to her was known for treating adolescents. I remained with him the following fall, when I entered the Dalton School in Manhattan, and until I graduated from Dalton, in 1952. He turned me loose for college, but I still saw him once a month, sitting across from him. In high school, I'd lain on the couch, and analyzed my dreams. Dr. Keiser was a Freudian, though in retrospect I think he used Freud as updated to the '40s. He introduced me to the Freudian unconscious as that part of my mind that I wasn't aware of. I had no trouble with this concept, as I knew there were things that I knew, yet couldn't always remember. It was like the cupboards in our kitchen, whose lowest shelves were above my head: I could see the little cans of mushrooms and Vienna sausages at the front of those shelves, but not the bigger cans in back, though I knew that they were there. Dr. Keiser explained how my unconscious revealed wishes in dreams, and how free association could unravel the riddles of those dreams. I had no trouble with the idea that my unconscious might be more powerful than my conscious, as I knew I did things that I didn't want to do (lose my temper), and couldn't do things I did want to do (flirt with boys).

I had no difficulty with the idea that images in a dream were a composite of things I'd seen during waking hours, and that dream images therefore had more than one meaning. Here were the origins of my theory about abstract painting, though the theory was decades away. The point of bringing traumatic experiences to consciousness through dream interpretation was to "abreact" them, or expose them out of existence, so that I could see the present undistorted by earlier traumas. Psychoanalysis would never give me all I wanted from it, but it has helped me see unpleasant things as they are – a

25

capacity that, according to the books, helps with developing creativity. Dr. Keiser published an article about my case in 1953. I found it while researching this book. At first, it upset me. Then I thought, everybody says they had an unhappy childhood, but who else has an independent witness to testify to it? If you want the grimy details about my difficult mother, go read Dr. Keiser, whose article also said that I had "an unusually high intellectual gift," and added that I had "outstanding" talents in painting, sculpting, and creative writing, "according to teachers' reports."[21]

I was introduced to Marx as a teenager. Around 1950, I read *The Communist Manifesto*, borrowed from my mother's latest lover, William J. Herwood, who lived in the apartment next to ours. In 1951, two actor friends of my mother's, Karen Morley and Lloyd Gough, turned up. The U.S. was engaged in a cold war with the Soviet Union, which had taken over most of Eastern Europe, and installed puppet governments there. China had been conquered by Mao Zedong and his communist army, and the United Nations, led by the United States, was carrying on a hot war with Chinese and North Korean communists in Korea. Even before North Korea had invaded South Korea, the cold war in the United States had led to "witch hunts," when suspected Communists were imprisoned or at best blacklisted. Karen and Lloyd (so I was told) had fled Hollywood because they didn't wish to testify about their possible membership in the Communist Party before the House Committee on Un-American Activities, which was holding hearings on communism in the movie business. My mother put them up in Bill Herwood's apartment. He was away on a business trip. (Both Karen and Lloyd did eventually testify, taking the Fifth Amendment, but this wouldn't happen for another year or two.)[22]

For a month or so, Karen and Lloyd came over to our apartment often for dinner, and the *Daily Worker* joined *The New Yorker* and *Vogue* on our coffee table. We sang folk songs, union songs, and "message songs" to Lloyd's concertina, and my mother gave parties where we played The Game (Karen and Lloyd, being actors, excelled). I admired their willingness to sacrifice their jobs for their beliefs, and shared their sympathies with women, minorities, and the working class, but at a certain moment, I became disenchanted. I was arguing with Lloyd about an article in the *Worker*. He got angry and tried to force me to accept his opinion, but at North Country, children had been listened to with respect, and argued with rationally, so I concluded that he and Karen were basically irrational, hence intransigent fanatics. Since I didn't want fanatics running my government, I rejected communism, but still liked Karen and Lloyd as people. I also liked British socialism, particularly since the socialist Fabian Society had helped found its Labor Party, and Shaw, whom I adored, had been a Fabian.

Rhys Caparn, my sculpture teacher at Dalton, had us sculpt a figure in plasticine as naturalistically as possible (our model was a schoolmate in a leotard). Then the model took another pose, and Caparn had us simplify our sculptures, strengthen the dynamic lines, and eliminate the superficial ones. This gave me an attitude toward abstraction that differs from most people's. They look at the word's Latin root, which means "to drag away," and assume abstraction means taking away the essential – but Caparn showed us *how to take away the non-essential, in order to reveal the essential.* Thanks in part to her, I had no trouble with what I was told were abstract expressionist paintings, when I first saw them in 1956, the autumn after I'd graduated from college, at MoMA's Guest House on East Fifty-second Street.[23] Abstract expressionism was said to be the latest art movement. The paintings I saw were unlike the clear, rectilinear shapes of Mondrian that I'd seen in 1945. Rather, I recall them as having had large, serene areas of color that blended into each other, and again, I wasn't shocked or moved. I liked the pictures better than not, but it was no big deal with me, as by that time I had only a passing interest in the visual arts as a whole.

All the girls in my set at Dalton idolized our English teacher, Dora Mabel Downes. She introduced us to Eliot, and talked about poetry as poetry instead of its relationship to society. Her approach may have resembled the "New Criticism" then in vogue at many universities. New Criticism in literature has been equated to the "formalist" approach to paintings, since formalism emphasizes the forms of a painting, as opposed to its subject matter, and formalism, too, was in vogue in the '50s, given its suitability for discussing abstract expressionism (not that I knew this at the time). Formalism is often equated to "art for art's sake," but I was suspicious of this doctrine. My sympathies lay with the "Epistle Dedicatory" to *Man and Superman* (1903), where Shaw rejected the idea of art for art's sake, arguing that style is the result of having something to say.

In Social Studies at Dalton, we did "research projects." I used mine to explore subjects that had presented problems for me ("problem-solving" on an adolescent level). In junior year, my research project was on labor unions, done to satisfy myself that the Putney union had been treated badly. In senior year, my project was the debates over nuclear disarmament at the United Nations, where the Soviet Union had insisted upon the need to ban the bomb – until it detonated its own bomb in 1949. I suppose I was trying to find out how realistic was the admiration of Karen, Lloyd, and my mother for the Soviet Union.

Rebecca Straus, our twelfth-grade Social Studies teacher, also assigned us *The State of Europe* (1949), by Howard K. Smith. This book was to influence my views on Vietnam in the '60s, and on George W. Bush's right-wing world after 9/11, but I didn't realize this until I reread it for this book. A correspondent for CBS, Smith was described as a liberal by reviewers of this book, yet like many liberals of that time, he verged upon being a socialist in the British sense of word.[24] He disapproved of how the communists had seized power throughout Eastern Europe in the wake of World War II, but *The State of Europe* nonetheless showed how Eastern Europe was doing a better job of recovering from the war than capitalist Western Europe was. Smith called for the United States to encourage Western Europe to elect governments favoring "planned economies operating in obedience to the incentives of the people's welfare and not to the workings of the profit motive or the market."[25] The biggest lessons I got from his book were that

> an important factor in the growth of the predominant tradition of liberal democracy in western Europe has been the existence of surplus wealth as coin for compromise between classes....Another prime social requisite for the functioning of democracy is the existence of a large middle class – people who own something, like the possessing classes, and at the same time live principally by their own efforts, as does labor – to act as a go-between through which compromises can be negotiated. In a Western democracy neither owning-class nor working-class political parties can hope to win an election without support from this broad stratum, and the need to woo it saves party politics from being narrow, antagonizing class politics.[26]

*   *   **

Where to go after Dalton? My mother thought that I was so talented that I should become an artist. She tried to get me to apply to Cooper Union, an art school, but I thought it over and decided I didn't have what it took to become a great artist, and the world had no use for second-rate artists (except for commercial art, which with my highbrow education at North Country I looked down upon). On the other hand, the world had lots of uses for second-rate writers. I might never become a poet, playwright, or novelist, but I could always go into advertising or public relations (to say nothing of journalism, though it wasn't part of my thinking at that time, any more than I knew how many commercially unviable artists were employed by art schools). A writing career required a college education, but I'd had enough of progressive schools, so I chose a traditional college: Barnard, the women's college of Columbia University on Morningside Heights in Manhattan. I graduated in 1956, cum laude, Phi Beta Kappa, and with honors in my major, English literature. In my writing courses, I never got above a B+, but the editors of *Focus,* the college literary magazine, invited me to submit a paper, and the brightest student in my class persuaded me to join the college newspaper, the *Barnard Bulletin.*

Thomas Peardon, who taught European government, admired the English Parliamentary system. This was fine by me, still a passionate Anglophile. The papers I did for his course were more problem-solving, still trying to get Karen and Lloyd in perspective. One was on the Third Republic, France's first working democracy. The other, published in *Focus,* dealt with the anarchist Bakunin. It suggested that nineteenth-century Russia was so autocratic that only violence could change it. No government at all was the only feasible alternative, so Bakunin hadn't been as crazy as he appeared, but had been responding realistically to the society he lived in. The paper also implied that, while Lenin's policy of violent overthrow was needed in Russia, it wasn't in the United States.

I took two great art history courses with Julius S. Held, on the Italian and Northern European Renaissances. Held introduced me to Erwin Panofsky, the art historian who'd elucidated literary and religious symbolism in Renaissance paintings. Dealing with subject matter in paintings, as opposed to their style, is the "iconographic" approach as opposed to the "formal" one. I'd eventually apply iconography to abstract painting, but the best Barnard course I had was Shakespeare, taught by David Allan Robertson (campus heartthrob). He situated Shakespeare in relation to his time and place, giving us the Elizabethan World Picture, as described by E. M. W. Tillyard – the late medieval view of the cosmos, with its "chain of being": angel above human, king above subject, human above beast. This hierarchy would today be dismissed as hopelessly Western European, but to myself, whose upbringing had been so insecure, it offered structure.

Robertson taught us the rhetorical devices that Shakespeare would have studied in school: metaphor, simile, metonymy, synecdoche and others. With many of these devices, one word or phrase can become an equivalent of, or a substitute for, another word or concept. Thus they are related to the lowly pun, and verbal equivalents of the visual symbolism I'd learned about in my art history courses. These nearly simultaneous introductions to double levels of meaning in art and literature would make it easier for me, years later, to perceive analogies between them, but I learned most from my senior thesis, on the Notes to *The Waste Land*, by Eliot. I'd chosen the Notes because I considered them pretentious and phony, and the poem meaningless, but my first draft came back peppered with acid marginal notes by my wise advisor, Eleanor Tilton. "Heavens!" she wrote. "Read the little magazines of the period!"

I did, plus all I could find about *The Waste Land*, and above all, Eliot's essays. In the end, I had to admit that the Notes served a purpose. After generations of scholars had worked with them, one named George Williamson had used them (and much other writing by Eliot) to explain what *The Waste Land* was "about." He showed it had characters, a story line, and meaning in the conventional sense, but I also learned that in the literary circles to which Eliot belonged, these qualities were unnecessary. Eliot had been writing for such readers, a small, discerning group who didn't mind if a poem was difficult; it succeeded with them because it conveyed mood and feelings. In this, it was like abstract art, though there's only an indirect reference to abstract art in the thesis.

In 1995, Anthony Julius published *T. S. Eliot: Anti-Semitism and Literary Form*. The *Times* ran two pieces about the storm this book was kicking up, like it was news that Eliot had been anti-Semitic.[27] I knew it in 1955. It hadn't bothered me because he belonged to my grandmother's generation, and like her, had been raised in the devout Middle West. The only time I'd heard her angry was when she called the Jews "Christ-killers." I felt that Eliot had grown up with this same old-fashioned anti-Semitism in his childhood, and that it stayed with him, despite his evolution into a modern poet, something he shared with many others, not what made him unique or worthy of study.

In my senior year, I was made features editor on the *Bulletin*, and campus correspondent for the *Times*. The *Times* job consisted almost entirely of taking press releases from the Barnard public relations office downtown to the *Times* offices, and transferring their contents to newsprint. It did let me see that huge old newsroom of the *Times*, but I had no interest in journalism as a career, so, after a month or so, I decided that my time would be better spent on my thesis, and quit. My dream was to get an MA and teach college English part-time. It would leave me time for my children, but my mother wouldn't pay for grad school, and my grades weren't good enough for fellowships. I'd have to earn my tuition, and I was ready for a brief break from academia. Then Dr. Keiser told me I should go back into analysis, if I wanted to get married. He said I was still neurotic, since I hadn't had any sexual experience in college, and this was when most women had their first experience.

Today, women taught to dismiss Freud as an outdated male chauvinist might laugh at this advice, but in 1956, I didn't laugh. I wanted to be married more than anything, not because society demanded it or I was looking for a meal ticket, but because marriage seemed to me essential for a normal, happy life. Even the novel I wanted to write was to be about a happy marriage. I figured unhappy marriages had been done to death, but my mother had by this time been divorced twice, and I'd heard that people tended to repeat the neurotic patterns of their parents.

Looking back, I wonder if there weren't some extenuating circumstances for my virginity. The Barnard subcommunity differed from those that I'd grown up in (and that Dr. Keiser moved in: he said he'd sent his sons to Dalton). That world was upper middle class, progressive, sophisticated. Premarital sex was more common with their adolescents in the '50s, but Barnard women, and the men they dated from Columbia's undergraduate college across Broadway, mostly came from more traditional and/or lower-middle-class homes. They might share the politics and culture of people I'd grown up with, but in social behavior, it was another world. Students on Morningside Heights were more conventional, more conscious of their religious backgrounds. More of the women believed in chastity until marriage, including those whom I considered most likely to marry and stay married, thus becoming my choices as friends and role models.

Barnard and Columbia had their bohemians. They must have been more progressive, but I avoided them because I didn't want to marry a neurotic writer, like my father, who stayed home and took care of me (so my mother said) while she had to go out and work. I wanted a non-neurotic man willing and able to support wife and children: doctor, lawyer, teacher, even businessman (with cultured tastes). Yes, I was shy and inhibited, but I still wonder if my romantic difficulties weren't a bit exacerbated by the fact that what we called "nice Jewish boys" wanted to meet and marry nice Jewish girls (Americans married younger in the '50s than they do today). Nice Gentile boys presumably wanted to meet and marry nice Gentile girls. I was a shiksa (as my Jewish roommate told me, since Jews count descent through the mother). Yet my name probably sounded Jewish to most Gentiles (though nobody said so). Here were two more subcommunities I was outside of, without being aware of my isolation.

Among people I'd mixed with through twelfth grade, Jews and Gentiles were fully integrated, but Morningside Heights was more like American society as a whole, where in the '50s, one Jew in about twenty married a Gentile (by the '90s, the ratio was more nearly one in two).[28] I'd had some dates, and gone out a lot with one very secular Jew and one very secular Gentile, but neither was ready for marriage, so there was no point in going "all the way." Also, one nice but very Jewish premed had quietly broken my heart by taking me out once, then dumping me after I told him that my father said he had only some Jewish blood. I'd also encountered a type that I mentally classed as the "neurotic Jewish boy." Neurotic Jewish boys found me sexy, but their sarcasm scared me, so I avoided them. (Reading *Portnoy's Complaint* in 1969, I recognized the type.)

In 1956, I only knew that Dr. Keiser said I was still neurotic, so I decided to follow his advice. I couldn't afford his $25-an-hour rates, so he sent me to an analyst whom I shall call Dr. G, and who, being younger, would take me for $15 an hour. I needed a job to pay him, and asked the Barnard placement office. Their suggestions included *Time*, so I applied there and was offered a job as trainee with a weekly salary of $59.50. After a year, I'd be promoted to research, starting at $75. This was good money for women in 1956, and I knew two people at *Time*. One was Andria Hourwich, a fellow Daltonite who was already a trainee, as secretary to a senior editor. The other was Bob McLaughlin, my mother's friend and onetime lover. Andria liked her work. McLaughlin said, "The magazine's not much, but the people are nice." I took the job.

2. STARTING AT TIME
(1956–1959)

I STARTED WORK in June 1956, in what I would later come to call "the old Time & Life Building" at 9 Rockefeller Plaza. Six magazines were written and edited there: *Time, Life, Fortune,* and *Architectural Forum*, plus *Sports Illustrated* (founded in 1954) and *House & Home* (spun off from *Architectural Forum* in 1952). Luce remained the company's editor-in-chief, but was now fifty-eight and so successful that he could delegate most day-to-day management. Still, his controversial journalistic philosophy and Republican outlook continued to dominate his magazines, especially *Time*.

In the twenty-first century, magazines tend more to be niche publications, targeted toward smaller audiences interested in special subjects. The major print media as a whole appear more peripheral than they once were; indeed, many are struggling to stay alive, given the millions of people who now get news primarily from TV or the Web. Already in 1956, TV was siphoning revenues from mass-circulation magazines like *Life, Look*, and *The Saturday Evening Post,* but there were still more than enough advertising dollars to go around, and the newsmagazines, targeted at a more educated audience, were relatively untouched. Nobody would have confused *Time* with *The New York Times*, in 1956 as in 2008 widely regarded as the finest journalistic enterprise in the country, but *Time* in its heyday, when I worked there, had to be counted among the most influential publications, and unique in the reactions that it provoked.

Time's original argument (echoed by *Newsweek*) was that busy modern people wanted to learn all the week's events within a single sitting, at most an hour's reading. To this end, the magazines divided the news into sections, almost all of which appeared in every issue, and carried stories whose basic size, while I was at *Time*, was seventy lines, or a column in length. A major article, or "takeout," might be two hundred and ten lines or a page, and the cover story occupied an average of seven hundred lines. (In today's changed media environment, *Time* and *Newsweek* have completely different formats, and, from what I hear, are prepared rather differently from the way that they were prepared when I worked there.) In 1956, Time had a worldwide circulation of 2.4 million (including export editions published in Canada,

Latin America, and elsewhere), and a "pass-along" readership several times that size. By 1967, when I began writing the Art section, circulation would have nearly doubled, and the magazine's ads would be claiming a readership of 14.5 million.[29] I would be awed by how many people read what I wrote.

In the '30s, even liberals had viewed *Time* with the indulgence that greets a baby taking its first steps, but in the post-war world, most resented it. Though one reason must have been that the magazine was bigger and richer, the political landscape had also shifted. Luce had never made a secret of his sympathies, but as long as Democrats had been in the White House, there seemed limits on how much damage he could do. Since 1953, a Republican had been President. Dwight D. Eisenhower was a moderate. During most of his term in office, Democrats still controlled Congress, so New Deal domestic reforms were preserved. Nevertheless, the fervor with which *Time* supported Ike and his administration distressed Democrats.

In college, I'd paid little attention to the papers. At work, I soon sensed that *Time* was most appreciated in regions without good local ones. When interviewed for the job, I'd been asked if I read the magazine. I confessed I preferred the *Times*, but my interviewer merely said something about how if one had the *Times*, one didn't need *Time*. In retrospect, I believe those regions without good local papers may also have been the more conservative ones, where *Time*'s Republican bias was most welcome. Important people in Washington read the magazine, too, but I believe less for what it said, and more for how it said it, the assumption being that it reflected the outlook of readers who could alter the course of government with their votes. The magazine was read in other big cities, by people who read many other publications, but the more they read, the more likely they were to disagree with *Time*. The antagonism it inspired had become as much as part of its mystique as the many readers who read it with touching faith in its accuracy and reliability. Successful people who disliked it nonetheless might feel they hadn't really arrived until it had done a story on them.

Before I started at *Time*, I'd seen practically nothing of it except in waiting rooms of dentists and doctors. Then, I'd leafed through it from back to front, amused by its book and movie reviews, and its gossip sections, Milestones and People, but if I had time to work my way up to the political news, I'd get so exasperated at how slanted it was that I'd sling it down in disgust. At *Time*, I was to learn that the cultural sections I liked were called "back of the book," while the political ones I didn't like were "front of the book." *Time* was rarely seen on my mother's coffee table, except perhaps when a friend had been attacked by it. This may have been the case when it reported that "Karen (*Scarface*) Morley" testified before the House Committee on Un-American Activities in 1952.[30] The movie title in parentheses was a mannerism

Time still used in the early '50s to identify actors or writers by their roles or books, but choosing such an ugly title for Karen served the second purpose of suggesting that she was ugly (*Time* routinely used language that conveyed double levels of meaning).

As a trainee, I started on the "clip desk," one of five young women who clipped stories out of newspapers from New York, across the U.S., and Canada, and sent the clips to researchers assigned to the *Time* story on the same subject scheduled that week. We also took new stories pouring out of the wire-service machines (AP and UP), and sent them to sections most likely to schedule their own stories on them. To learn what each *Time* story would concern, we attended "story conferences" held at the beginning of each week by the senior editors overseeing a section or group of sections. Writers and researchers, along with other interested parties, gathered in the editor's office to draw up "story lists" for the upcoming issue. One writer in each section presented a list of suggested stories, while the editor decided what went on the final story list. A head researcher jotted down this list, together with the names of the writer and researcher assigned to each story, and, after these lists had been "dittoed" (duplicated), we on the clip desk used them to address clips and wire-service copy.

Thus I was introduced to how *Time* worked, and to its employees. The senior editors and the writers were all men. The researchers, such as I would become, were all women. Researchers kept quiet at story conferences. Writers presented the lists as entertainingly as possible, and editors responded with as much wit as they could muster. Droll performances resulted, since all had been hired because they could write in lively *Time*style. The men in Foreign News were hard-bitten veterans; the men in National Affairs looked browbeaten from the need to grind out Republican propaganda. Back-of-the-book writers were funniest. The hierarchy of the sexes reflected U. S. society at a time when men expected to spend their adult lives at jobs, but women (at any rate, upper- and middle-class ones) expected to work only until they married or had a child. Our president, at Barnard, had urged us students to combine marriage with a career. This was advanced thinking for the '50s, but it was assumed the career would be interrupted when children were small. My mother's world had working mothers, but in this, as in other respects, it was more advanced than national norms allowed. *Time* was more typical. Most researchers were single, and the married ones often (though not always) left when they became pregnant.

Soon after I started work, I attended a presentation for new employees. We were given facsimiles of the first issue, which ridiculed both *The Waste Land* and *Ulysses*. The prospectus for the magazine by Luce and Hadden was quoted to us. To a remarkable degree, I would learn, it continued to serve as corporate dogma. According to it, *Time* was "not founded to promulgate prejudices, liberal or conservative," but it admitted to a few. Among them were "An admiration of the statesman's 'view of all the world,'" "A general distrust of the present tendency toward increasing interference by government," "Faith in the things which money cannot buy," "A respect for the old, particularly in manners," and "An interest in the new, particularly in ideas."[31]

Time would give both sides of every question, but indicate "which side it believes to have the stronger position." It might verge on the controversial, but "only where it is necessary to point out what the news *means*."[32] While many people thought this made it different from, say, the *Times*, Ed Bley had shown me at North Country how *all* newspapers expressed opinions when presenting news, so I welcomed *Time*'s willingness to be open about it. This feeling would grow as I came to be more knowledgeable about specific topics. Then I could see how other publications were also slanting their coverage of those topics, in a different direction from ours.

Graphs projected on a screen showed that, while *Life*'s circulation was growing in proportion to population increases, that of *Time* was growing faster, in relation to the increase in the college-educated population. This was the first time I heard that the college-educated population was growing faster than the population as a whole. The idea that college-educated people were more likely to read *Time* may have enabled some of us at the presentation to feel smug, but I knew how few of my own college friends read it. A short, but memorable, summary of those graphs was expressed by a professor whom I'd heard about, maybe a Harvard professor: "*Life* is for people who can't read," he was said to have told his classes. "*Time* is for people who can't think."

Nevertheless, I wanted to do a good job, and this meant reading (or browsing) the free copy of the magazine that plopped into my in-box every week. This helped me figure out which section should receive wire-service copy and clips on stories that hadn't yet been scheduled. I read some of the dittoed "files" telexed in from correspondents that also showed up in my in-box. Together with clips and wire-service copy, these files formed the basis for the magazine's stories. Besides being much longer than the stories based on them, they were written more dispassionately. Some dealing with foreign countries gave so much background detail that I began to see a rationale for published stories that would have irked me before I joined the magazine. I was surprised by the number of back-of-the-book stories dealing with English culture, and implying that Luce shared my Anglophilia. I began to feel that *Time* might not be wholly bad.

My fellow clip-deskees were intelligent and friendly. Eleanor Tatum, our boss, sometimes asked one of us to lunch with her. As she swigged away at her second or third martini, she gave us inside dope: for instance, that Luce was or had been involved with Lady Jeanne Campbell, granddaughter of Lord Beaverbrook, the English press tycoon.[33] According to Tatum, Luce and Lady Jeanne used to eat together at a Chinese restaurant on Fourteenth Street, a working-class neighborhood in those days where I suppose they figured they wouldn't run into anybody they knew.

Andria Hourwich and her researcher friend, Marion Pikul, invited me to lunch as well. I did things with one or both of them on Mondays and Tuesdays, since most of the editorial staff worked "the edit week" that ran from Wednesday to Sunday, and enabled the magazine to go on sale at the most advantageous time. Sunday nights, when the magazine was going to press, a buffet was set up, and everybody got free dinner (so they wouldn't dawdle away the evening in restaurants). The clip desk didn't have to work late, but we got free dinner, too, and a chance to attend the informal drinks party held before dinner, often in our bullpen. Everybody was on a first-name basis, from the copy boys on up to Roy Alexander, the managing editor, though to maintain professional detachment in this narrative, I'll use last names or a combination of first and last names, unless it's somebody with whom I socialized outside the office.

The "edit staff" made me feel young again, since everybody else was older. I was a freshman again, no longer a senior, but as I had during my last year in college, I still felt world-weary, especially on November 4, 1956, when the wire-service machines spat out the news that Russian tanks were rolling into Budapest. It was exciting to see tomorrow's headlines today, but I hadn't realized how much I identified with my father's homeland. "It'll all blow over," I said cynically to my fellow clip-deskee, "and the Russians will come out looking better than ever." Next morning, I clipped *The New York Times*. Its banner headlines dealt both with the crushing of the Hungarian rebellion, and the ill-fated invasion of Suez by Great Britain and France. A photograph on Page One showed crowds of Labor Party sympathizers massed in Trafalgar Square to protest the Conservative government's role in the Suez invasion. I remembered that square, with all its pigeons, from my visit to London in 1949. The futility of Suez, and the sun setting on a once-mighty empire, saddened me, but I remained proud of the democratic tradition that ensured the minority's freedom to disagree, and contrasted it with the repression in Hungary. This was my mother's heritage.

In the fall of 1956, I moved into a $70-a-month studio of my own, in a walk-up building on East Ninety-fifth Street. When the building was torn down a year later to make way for a school, the city relocated me to a two-and-a-half-room walk-up for $46 a month, on East Eighty-eighth Street. Such rents were cheap even then, but I needed them, because going to Dr. G forced me to live frugally. For the next thirteen years, I would again be lying on a couch three or four times a week (as was usual in those days). I would be interpreting my dream images as composites of things I'd seen while awake, recently or in the past, prompted to appear by my emotions and fulfilling symbolic roles. I would again be made aware of how things I did and said revealed unconscious attitudes, and that such actions could have a double level of meaning.

Dr. G also increasingly analyzed how people in the news and my coworkers revealed unconscious attitudes and double levels of meaning by things they did or said. In retrospect, he represented a '50s flavor of psychoanalysis, conservative concerning social relationships, but surprisingly advanced about women's professional behavior. True, he felt that my mother, with her many affairs, had over-sexualized personal relationships, and I should try instead to develop relationships that combined sex with "friendly feelings." Unlike Freud, though, Dr. G didn't feel that it was neurotic or masculine for a woman to want to work outside the home. Women as well as men had aggressive drives, he believed, and both should channel or sublimate those drives into their work. I have more than once surprised critics of Freudian analysis by telling them about this attitude of Dr. G. Whatever his flaws, he didn't fit the feminist cliches.

Dr. G gave advice. This seems to have been not uncommon among analysts in the '50s.[34] Following this advice on the job often proved fruitful. I used to think of him as my secret weapon after I became a writer on *Time*. Though some of what he said about how men regarded jobs and women in job situations now sounds condescending or platitudinous, it was true enough then to help me professionally. He was less helpful for social situations, where I could *not* do what he told me *not* to do, but also could not *do* what he thought I should. For example, I could restrain myself from crossing the room at a party to talk with a man I liked (Dr. G considered taking the initiative in this way aggressive, castrating behavior). But I also could not playfully tell a man that I wanted to be taken out to dinner, rather than let him cook for me at home (Dr. G believed that a man and a woman alone together in an apartment at night was a "sexual situation," not to be undertaken until the man had developed those "friendly feelings").

However many edit staffers may have been in analysis, few admitted it to colleagues. In thirteen years, I heard of only two whose alcoholism reached a point where they were in danger of being fired, and so sought help. Nor was I surprised by this paucity in numbers, given the magazine's lukewarm attitude toward Freud. In the later '50s, it ran about as many stories about him as did *Newsweek, The Saturday Review,* and *The New Republic*, according to the *Readers' Guide to Periodical Literature* (which doesn't index all magazines, or always correctly classify the stories it lists, but still affords an overview of how

38

many stories were appearing in the country's major magazines during relative periods of time). *Time*'s stories were polite, but even in the later '50s, at the supposed peak of Freud's influence, almost all got in a dig.

A cover story published in April 1956 (shortly before I started work) quoted "a bright, up-and-coming" British psychologist, Hans Jurgen Eysenck, saying there was no proof that mental cases improved more often under analysis than without it. The story sarcastically suggested that arguing with a Freudian was like arguing with a member of any other religion.[35] In March 1969, *Time* became one of the first general-interest publications to suggest that the "long domination" of Freudian theory and practice which had "ruled the field of psychiatry in the U. S." since World War II was "at an end." As an example of the junior medicos who were increasingly skeptical, the magazine brought back Eysenck, saying that traditional Freudian treatment had "nothing to say to us, and there is nothing we can do for it except ensure a decent burial."[36]

With Freud as with so much else, *Time*'s didacticism in 1956 revealed both the suspicion and the ignorance regarding psychoanalysis in U.S. society outside the major cities and across the U.S. As the cover story indicated, Freudian concepts had become part of the culture: people used them in conversation and cartoonists for jokes. Freudian theory was used by many psychiatrists who weren't themselves analysts, and it had influenced everything from social work to aptitude tests, but even *Time* could point to only 619 "hard-core analysts" in the country, with maybe 15,000 patients in treatment concurrently. The total number of Americans who had ever even tried analysis was only in the low six figures.[37] Not wanting to be classed as lunatic, I'd never mentioned my analysis at Dalton or Barnard. Given attitudes at *Time*, I became even less willing to discuss it, but I had to tell head researchers in order to get vacations in August, when Dr. G was on holiday. I don't know how widely the word of my therapy got around, but one drunken writer, at an office party, asked why I needed "a head-candler" ("candling" being a technique for examining the interior of an egg).

In the spring of 1957, I was promoted to research, starting in the Business section. Like other sections, Business had a bullpen for the researchers and individual offices for the writers. I'd requested back of the book, but most of these sections had only one writer and one researcher. I was told I'd have to begin in one of the larger, front-of-the-book sections, which had four or five writers, five or six researchers, and a head researcher in the bullpen with me, to instruct me. The Business head researcher was Mary Elizabeth Fremd, a young but very competent woman. The senior editor was Joseph Purtell. The weekly routine throughout the magazine began after story conference on Wednesday, with the writer telling the researcher what he wanted to know, from local sources and correspondents in the field. "Queries" were then typed up and telexed to the correspondents, outlining what was needed.

Next, the researcher prepared a folder for each story. Into each went wire copy, news clips, background material from the magazine's morgue (reference library), and "research" the researcher had done: memos typed from morgue material, or on the basis of phone calls to and interviews with outside "sources." The folders were given to the writers, who wrote most of their stories on Friday night or Saturday, after the files came in from correspondents. Then the stories were sent to the copy desk to be properly typed (the entire staff used manual typewriters throughout my stay on *Time,* and very few of us were expert typists).

These "writer's copies" went to the senior editors, who edited them or called in the writer, and told him what he wanted in the "new version" (researchers got copies of the story on regular paper at each stage of the process, while the writers and other interested parties got copies on tissue paper, called "flimsies."). After the story or its new version was edited by the senior editor, it went to the managing editor (or, with some sections, the assistant m. e.). Here, the story was "top-edited." Then it had "checking copy" stamped on it, and was "checked" by the researcher. This meant comparing it with the original material, and placing dots over each word that corresponded to the facts as shown in this material. Inaccurate statements, or statements that couldn't be checked on the basis of the material at hand, had check marks put over them instead of dots, and these "checkpoints" would have to be eliminated one by one, by asking the morgue's reference librarians to dig up further information, telephoning sources, or sending "checking queries" to correspondents.

When everything that could be confirmed had been confirmed, and the only material with check marks left over it was wrong, the researcher had to take the story to the writer, and get him to make "fixes" to ensure accuracy. The story was next read for grammar, spelling, and punctuation by the women at the copy desk, sent to Production, set in galleys, and transmitted to Chicago to be printed. Since so many people worked on each story, and none were signed, how they were put together was known to us (jokingly or angrily) as "group journalism" or "the editorial process." Critics used to complain that it made the magazine sound like it had all been written by one person, but it could also be seen as a pastiche, collage, composite, or synthesis of many different people's input – and, since synthesis is the most important single aspect of creativity, could be called collaborative creativity.

"Group journalism" was the basis for the magazine's authority, and its fatal flaw. I suspect neither Luce nor Hadden had envisioned it originally. The magazine had always used researchers (initially called "secretarial assistants" or "checkers").[38] In its early days, though, it relied solely upon the newspapers for information. The network of correspondents had only grown up over the years, and correspondents had no control over what was done with their files in New York. Even the writers didn't necessarily have that much control, let alone the researchers, though both might have helped gather information. All of it could be used to support only the opinions of the man or men at the top, and, particularly with the larger, hard news sections, this all too often happened, but not usually because the top man or men had given orders.

More often, editors and writers already knew what was expected (a new writer learned through how his copy was edited, and what he was asked for on the new versions, a.k.a. NVs). But senior editors got their evaluations into the magazine, and writers, at least in back of the book, often saw in print almost exactly what they'd written, once they'd developed expertise in their subjects. Writers and senior editors usually tried to use the files as fairly as possible. Many stories were based on huge amounts of information funneled into New York from many places. If we in New York allowed ourselves to be guided by that information, we could distill it into meaningful conclusions that no single individual could have reached, except over far more time.

I didn't know that in 1957. All I knew was that while preparing the folders was interesting, getting fixes made could become a nightmare. Less experienced writers were more sensitive than I'd realized a man could be (beginning my real education concerning men). No matter how heavily their stories had been edited, they identified with them, and having researchers criticize them could be the last straw. Unless the researcher was very tactful, and had perfect fixes to suggest, she might find herself accused of "nitpicking," though all that was usually happening was that the writer was taking out on her the anger he felt toward his editor, but dared not express to him. More experienced writers afforded worse headaches. They knew how to make fixes that altered a story just enough so that technically, it wasn't incorrect, but just as slanted in a conservative, Republican direction, and just as misleading as it had been. This happened especially with "value judgments," often placed in the most telling positions of a story, the "lede" (at the beginning) and the "kicker" (at the end). (It was "lede" instead of "lead," I was told, because such misspellings were a journalistic convention used to alert typesetters that something was a reference to a text, not the text itself. The title of a *Time* story was its "two-hed," not its "two-head," and the abbreviation indicating material due to be inserted later in a story was "TK," for "To Kome.")

Writers would argue that since "value judgments" were only opinion, they couldn't be disproved by facts. Any clear misinformation that the researcher could point to would be qualified by ingenious "hedge words" or "weasels" that would leave her as dissatisfied as ever, but deprived of reasons to say something was literally wrong. During those early days in Business, I remember this happening especially in stories about relations between Washington and the private sector. Raised amidst the heady idealism of the New Deal, I saw big government as a friend, but given *Time*'s stated distrust of "interference by government," its stories might well portray Federal programs as monsters of wasteful spending and unjustified meddling.[39]

How does a weasel work? Let's take the way I described *The New York Times*. Suppose I'd written that it was "the finest journalistic enterprise in the country" (and suppose, for the moment, that "finest" is susceptible to proof, although of course there are so many ways to measure excellence that "finest" itself is rather a value judgement than a fact). Suppose further that my researcher takes exception to "finest." In the '60s, she had most probably studied at some school like MIT, under Noam Chomsky, the antiwar activist who in those days considered the *Times* a tool to manufacture consent for the special interests. In the twenty-first century, she'd more likely be from some place like Oklahoma, have ties to the religious right, and view the *Times* as a ringleader in the liberal conspiracy to dominate the East Coast media.

"How can you say it's 'the finest in the country?'" she asks. "I don't think it's the finest, and I know lots of people back in Cambridge/Tulsa who don't think it is, either." Fine, I say, I'll fix it, and insert the weasel "widely regarded as" at the beginning of the phrase, so that it reads, "widely regarded as the finest...." This shuts up the researcher, since the phrase is now clearly opinion (not fact), and allows for the possibility that some people (including her) might not consider it true. Nevertheless, it still conveys the impression that I originally intended to convey. Most readers, I think, would skate right by that little qualifying phrase, or take it as merely a literary embellishment, and come away convinced that I (who, with all my experience in the media, ought to know) have stated *as fact* that the *Times* is Numero Uno. Unscrupulous though weasels sound, they were fine training for writing precisely. Even today, I find myself weighing my words at the keyboard, searching for means to say exactly what I want to say and no more.

Although writers and editors determined the angle of the stories, the researcher was responsible for their factual accuracy, and shown up in public if she goofed. The chief of research was a tartar. If a reader claimed that *Time* had made a mistake, the researcher had to reexamine the packet of material used in preparing that story (known as a "carbon"). If an error had slipped through, she had to fill out a long, humiliating "errors report." This was attached to all copies of the story in the morgue, and included in a semiannual summary of errors sent to the entire staff. It was like the old-fashioned method of housebreaking a puppy by shoving its nose in its urine, but it had the desired effect of making researchers desperately insistent on accuracy. It also cast them as writers' adversaries, a role that with me would only gradually evolve into cooperation.

As a junior in Business, I was frequently assigned to "Goods & Services," a regular feature consisting of short items on new products and services. This was my first experience of public relations men, and it didn't include the stars of the profession. I got press releases claiming that this, that, or the other was the first, biggest, cheapest, etc. To verify the claim, I'd go to our morgue, where I'd often find other press releases, annual reports, or clippings saying somebody else had already brought out the first, biggest, cheapest, or whatever of its kind.

Dr. G considered a woman calling a man for social reasons aggressive, but saw nothing wrong with her doing so for business (simply healthy sublimation). Still, I was so shy that I dreaded telephoning or interviewing sources. One Wednesday, I started trembling when I came into the office, and I trembled all day. The next, I went to the chief of research, and begged to be transferred to a section that didn't require so much outside research. I was made a "floater" in back of the book, filling in for regulars on vacation (we all got extra weeks off to compensate for working weekends). Almost all the writers on *Time* were Democrats. Every presidential election year, the Science writer polled them, and the Democratic candidate always got more votes (as McLaughlin remarked, "One of Luce's great sorrows must be that so few Republicans can write"). In front of the book, these Democrats often had to slant stories in ways they didn't agree with. This tended to make them bitter. In back of the book, fewer stories involved politics, so the writers were happier in their work, and easier to work with.

After a week or so in Sport, I was sent to Religion. The visiting writer there was John Skow (known as Jack), a tall, droll bachelor in his late twenties. When he asked me out, I was delighted, but after three dates, began to worry. He was a writer, like my father, and my father had left me. Worse, I suspected Jack was a frustrated creative writer, and I thought fiction writers were even more neurotic than nonfiction ones. Jack didn't say he'd written fiction. He'd been on a newspaper before joining *Time*, but he said that when writers applied to *Time* for a job, editors liked to see their fiction, published or not. Aside from what this told me about him, it showed how writing for *Time* was related to writing fiction, and made me see all *Time* writers as fiction writers manqué. What if I wrote successful fiction, I wondered. Could Jack handle that, or would he walk out on me, too? I found myself imagining a host of possible scenarios, each worse than the last, nor was Dr. G any help. I told Jack to stop asking me out.

I didn't think my distress showed, but my next assignment amounted to a rest cure: Hemisphere, where two sections, Latin America and Canada, were prepared for export editions of *Time*. Although abbreviated versions of major Hemisphere stories also ran in the domestic edition, the export editions were only read outside the United States, so the brass wasn't very concerned about them. Editor and writers again felt freer to give the news as they saw it, creating another more relaxed environment. After some weeks in Latin America, I was shifted to Canada. There I learned to suggest fixes that satisfied me and my writers, with the aid of Dr. G and Dorothy Slavin Haystead, the warm-hearted Hemisphere head researcher. The trick was to suggest changes that "built" a story instead of destroying it, cooperating with writers instead of opposing them.

After two years, I was senior Canada researcher, working more with senior writers, especially Robert Parker. He was solid and steady, much more the journalist, much less the fiction writer manqué. He taught me to write queries. Some stories were scheduled from "suggestions" sent by full-time correspondents in the bureaus. Others were scheduled from suggestions by "stringers"(part-time employees), or from wire copy or the papers. If a bureau suggested the story, all the query usually had to say was, "File as suggested," but otherwise, it had to "lead the correspondent by the hand." I'd use this training when I wrote the cover queries for "Swinging London." Almost all Canada stories dealt with events in Canada, so researchers did little telephoning or interviewing, yet sending queries and checking taught me so much about what a *Time* story should be that, after two years, I could look at my copy of the writer's copy and tell whether the senior editor would edit it, or whether he'd kill it or send it back for an NV. I learned enough about Canada, and became so good at suggesting fixes that I could get sweeping changes made, up to whole lead paragraphs. When that much had been done, I began to feel I'd had a hand in a story's creation myself.

Saturday nights, when we were checking, "Dottie" Haystead, the Hemisphere head researcher, would lead a group of us to dine at a chop house, where we'd gossip about recent events on the magazine, and she'd tell us tales of its past. Occasionally, we'd be joined by a writer, but I interacted with the men in other situations, too. In a nearby office sat a Press writer whom I'll call Silas Haynes. He had a lean face, bony body, and saturnine smile. One evening, he came to the Hemisphere researchers' bullpen, when everyone else had gone. I was standing over a counter, reading a book. He came up to me, and toyed with my bracelet, one that I'd been given by a college boyfriend. "That's a very unusual bracelet," Haynes said (as best I recall–with all quotations in this book, please bear in mind that they are only the best that I can recall). "That's what this man'll say to you, on the bus going home tonight. You'll get to talking. His name'll be George Williams, and he'll be a playwright, with his first play optioned, and it'll be produced, and be a big hit, but that'll be after you met him. He'll drive a Lancia or, no, it'll be an Aston-Martin, and he'll take you to dinner at this fine French restaurant in Chappaqua." A delightful tale, and, in retrospect, Haynes's fantasy of what he'd like to be and do, though he was married, and lived (in Chappaqua) with wife and twins.

I was more at ease with Parker, though the only time I spent outside the office with him was in July 1959, when we did a big takeout on the Yukon and Northwest Territories. I wrote a long piece of research for it from morgue sources, and Parker took me with him to interview an Arctic explorer who lived near Mt. Kisco. On the drive back, we stopped for lunch. He introduced me to Manhattans, and told me that his ambition, when he'd saved the money, was to go back to the Middle West, buy a small-town newspaper, and edit it. "*Time*'s a young man's game," he said.

3. THE NEWSMAGAZINE AS VILLAGE
(1957–1959)

DURING THOSE PEACEFUL years in Hemisphere, I began identifying with *Time*, and getting upset by hostility I encountered socially because I worked there. Today, liberals may get nostalgic about Luce. Next to Rupert Murdoch, he looks like a pussycat, but in the '50s, at parties, one of my mother's progressive friends or a young man would nail me against the wall and ask angrily how I could justify Luce's support for the China Lobby. This had little to do with me. I knew Luce had been raised in China, and was close to Chiang Kai-shek, the big cheese in China before the communists took over in 1949. I gathered that *Time* had continued to defend Chiang's right to the mainland after 1949, but by the later '50s, he'd retreated to Taiwan, and the Asian rim was fairly peaceful.

I hadn't worked on the relatively few stories about Chiang we'd done since I'd joined *Time*. I wasn't in Foreign News, where they appeared (I didn't even read it, or National Affairs, more than I could help: they were too aggravating). The attacks made me particularly unhappy when the young men making them were attractive. I didn't care about the little old lady from New Jersey who cooed, "I just adore *Time*, especially the Religion section!" So I developed a shell. In the '60s, *Time* would come under heavier fire for its Vietnam coverage, but by then, the shell was hard enough so my initial reaction was: okay, they don't like what we say about Vietnam, but they've been bitching about our Far East coverage as long as I've been here, so what else is new?

That I didn't incur more hostility than I did in the '50s probably reflected the political apathy characterizing many young people. We were "the silent generation" (a term given currency by *Time*, though not invented by it).[40] My contemporaries didn't organize, march and protest, as young people had in the '30s and would in the '60s. Why should they? By and large, the country was peaceful and prosperous. Jobs were plentiful: we were "Depression babies," born in the '30s, when the birthrate had dipped to an all-time low, so there weren't as many of us to claim those jobs. Perhaps the single biggest reason we seemed silent was that there were so few of us. In 2001, one cultural critic would characterize the period of the cold war as having a "pervasive atmosphere of guilt, secrecy, terror, and dread."[41] That was not my experience. Somewhere, people were building bomb shelters in the '50s, and schools were holding air-raid drills, but none of that was happening to anybody I knew.

Books about the '50s written in the '70s, '80s, or '90s sometimes dramatize deeply rooted problems to explain the unrest that would surface in the '60s. I don't entirely deny their premises, but they may say as much about the decades when they were written, and the people who wrote them, as they do about the period they depict (this book being no exception). Other authors dealing with the '50s may be more typical of the decade than I was, and present aspects of it I was unfamiliar with, but as I recall it, the national media in the later '50s and early '60s offered a comparatively placid view of the domestic scene. Even the struggles of Southern "Negroes" to end segregation in the busses of Montgomery, and schools in Alabama and Arkansas, didn't impinge upon the national consciousness as much as the crusade for civil rights would in the mid-to-later '60s ("Negro" was the term used by Northern progressives and the media throughout the '50s and well into the '60s. "Black" didn't come into general use until the later '60s, and "African American" is yet more recent. Since I'll be quoting articles from the '60s that used "Negro," I shall employ the term until my narrative reaches the period when it went out of use, hoping that African American readers will realize I'm only trying to be historically accurate). In Volumes 20 through 28 of the *Readers' Guide to Periodical Literature*, articles listed under "Negroes," "Negroes in the United States," and various categories under "civil rights," occupied an average of nearly six columns per year from March 1955 to February 1963, but doubled to nearly twelve columns a year from March 1963 to February 1969.

The national media's view of American society will be of consequence during later chapters of this narrative, as I came to feel more a part of it, but even when I did, that society didn't necessarily reflect my own experience. Indeed, I was becoming more and more atypical simply by staying single. In 1960, when I was twenty-five, only one in ten women in the U.S. between the ages of twenty-five and twenty-nine had never been married (as opposed to more than one in three more recently). I was and would remain unaware of this, partly because I was surrounded by single women on *Time*, partly because an increasing proportion of my personal friends would likewise be single working women, and partly because I lived in a metropolitan area in the Northeast, where the proportion of single women to the population as a whole was higher.[42]

That I had a job was also atypical. One adult female out of three in the U. S. was employed outside the home in 1960, as opposed to two out of three in the twenty-first century, and though I never saw myself as serious about my job, I was. This too was atypical, and the edit week dramatized it. Not only did I have to work weekends, but late on weekend evenings. I missed parties given by friends outside *Time*, or arrived after everybody else was on their third or fourth drink, and/or paired off. I missed football games and Sunday brunches. Meeting suitable mates only late at night meant I was more likely to encounter them in what Dr. G. called "sexual situations," while the men about whom I had the best chance to develop those "friendly feelings" he considered so important were my coworkers, single or married.

I don't know how well the married *Time* writers who lived in the suburbs integrated themselves into their communities, but the single ones, and the single researchers, mostly lived in the city, and socialized with their coworkers to an almost incestuous degree, if only because of the edit week. They went skiing with colleagues during the winter, and shared group houses at the seashore with them in summer. At parties, they tended to club together, and talk to nobody else. Everybody gossiped. From my friend Andria, I heard about Jack Skow long after I'd stopped dating him. If I recall correctly, his next relationship was with a Jewish cello player who lived in Greenwich Village, but this was among the more innocuous kinds of information one might hear by attending to that overactive office grapevine.

Besides news of marriages, divorces, deaths, affairs, problems with alcohol or children, analysts, and other personal matters, it thrived on politics, inside and outside the office. I heard of news developments, sometimes minutes after they'd happened, and, in an era before TV could leap within instants to every scene of action, this immediacy made me feel intimately involved. I began to care about the news more, and to learn to analyze it as dispassionately as knowledgeable coworkers were doing. Maybe all they had to contribute was speculation about news events, but even so, it was often very informed speculation. Then there were office politics: which writer was being "put through the mill," whose proposal for a cover story had been rejected and why, what worthy causes an editor or writer might be promoting, and so forth. Even while I was still at *Time*, however, I learned to suspect that grapevine of disseminating fantasies about fellow workers. Since then, I've become yet more aware of its misconceptions, but since I accepted them as true at the time, they affected my outlook and conduct. My colleagues always sounded so sure of what they were saying, and, since they were in the information-gathering business, I preferred to assume they knew what they were talking about.

To me, the inbred situation at *Time* resembled that of journalism in general, and *Time* was only a cell in the larger organism of that profession. Many men on the magazine, like Skow, had previously worked on newspapers, and morning newspapers went to press at night. Their reporters were thus also apt to socialize late at night with fellow reporters, often in bars. From the frequency with which I witnessed alcoholism among older members of the staff, it was an occupational disease (aggravated by the fact that they'd been young during Prohibition, when booze was as much a sign of independence as pot would be in the '60s. I saw similar drinking among some of my mother's friends). I came to feel that writers were shy, that they'd developed skill in writing as children because they'd had trouble communicating in speech. Small talk came hard for these people (as it did for me). If they could start the ball rolling with a job-related discussion, they were more at ease (and so was I).

Another reason *Time* staffers may have clubbed together was that all must have been subject to the same cocktail-party attacks that I got. Somewhere outside Manhattan were millions of Americans who admired our magazine, but in Manhattan's predominantly liberal and Democratic professional circles, I can't have been the only *Time* employee who took shit on Luce's behalf. Maybe one's colleagues weren't ideal companions, but at least they didn't put one on the defensive. This helped to develop a loyalty to the magazine not entirely explained by the lavish salaries, extended vacations, generous expense accounts, profit-sharing, medical insurance, free meals and booze (plus free office supplies). Being close to the news, to history in the making, had to be part of the magazine's allure, as did the fact that the work was never boring, but above all, I think it may have been the camaraderie that came from knowing we were all part of the same high-class leper colony.

A relatively high number of edit staffers dated or had affairs with each other. In my early years at *Time*, I often heard about single writers dating single researchers. These relationships not infrequently led to marriage, and were mostly conducted quite publicly. I also knew there were extramarital affairs, but during the '50s, these were mostly carried on with extreme discretion. Around 1957, my mother had a conversation about me with Bob McLaughlin. "I suppose she'll have an affair with a married writer," he'd said. "That's what all these little researchers do." My mother repeated this to me, and I said to myself, this is one little researcher who's going to be different.

The way I and my fellow employees interacted with each other created what I now look back upon as an unusually cohesive subcommunity, a village with a population of several hundred souls. There were about 140 edit staffers in New York on the magazine's masthead. These came in contact with maybe another fifty in support jobs in New York, as well as about eighty correspondents listed in the out-of-town bureaus, and maybe another hundred stringers. Correspondents came in to the New York office, and writers went out to the bureaus, on permanent assignment or to visit, so the names on the files we got belonged to people we might know, if only casually.

Relations with other Time Inc. magazines weren't as close. Occasionally, a *Time* staffer moved to *Life*, *Sports Illustrated*, or *Fortune*, but rarely did anybody come to us from other Luce magazines. What we learned about such people came from meeting them socially, or through *F.Y.I.*, the company house organ. *F.Y.I.* was known (all around Manhattan) for its classified ads on everything from apartments to rent or share to requests for country-bred kittens. Neither those who placed ads nor those who answered them necessarily worked for Time Inc. All you had to do was know some cooperative body who did.

On the edit staff, we knew little about "the publishing side," meaning the advertising and business staffs. We weren't supposed to know: Luce was fervently committed to "the separation between church and state." This liberated us from pressure by advertisers, and while I valued this while I worked there, I only realized after I left how many journalists don't enjoy such freedom. Mary Liz Fremd, the Business head researcher, told me about the time a Business story panned the new car models from Detroit. General Motors, the biggest advertiser in the country, demanded that the man who wrote it be fired. Time Inc. stood by him, though GM yanked all the advertising for its Buick-Oldsmobile-Pontiac division from *Time* and *Life* (big bucks). GM backed down. I heard that our Medicine writer was respected by doctors for his coverage of the link between cigarettes and cancer, despite pressures to qualify his stories from tobacco advertisers. Once, so the story went, Sherman Billingsley, proprietor of the Stork Club, called up an editor and asked him to kill a story. After the editor hung up, he said, "It isn't a very good story, and I was going to kill it, but now I guess we'll have to run it. We can't have Billingsley thinking he can shove *Time* around."

When I discussed the cocktail-party attacks on *Time* with Dr. G, he asked why I couldn't say I wasn't responsible for the whole magazine. That wouldn't have satisfied my attackers, who acted like I had no right to stay on its payroll. Besides, in a way, I agreed, not because I felt responsible for the whole magazine, but because I felt that if I was taking money from it, it would be hypocritical to disown it. Sometimes, I used Bob McLaughlin's defense: the magazine might not be much, but the people were nice. I was getting fond of those people. The writers were sensitive and intuitive, as writers must be, but I came from a family of writers, and had known more growing up, so I was at home with them as well as made nervous by them. The nervousness faded as I learned, mostly in Canada, that *Time* writers and editors were more responsible than my father had been. Most had families to support, and it was one of the most reassuring revelations of the job that male writers could want to support families.

The office atmosphere was civilized. Voices were rarely raised, and when an editor wanted a story redone, no matter how extensively, he didn't order the writer to do it. He "suggested." Within the profession, Time Inc. was viewed, if less often as a good place to work, nevertheless almost always as a good place to have worked. Former writers and correspondents had become well known: Dwight Macdonald, James Agee, Theodore H. White, John Hersey. I knew of no famous former researchers, but opportunities for women were limited outside as well as inside *Time*. Even the *Times* still carried separate columns of classified ads for "Help Wanted – Female" and "Help Wanted – Male." Few listings for reporters or writers ran in the female columns.

On *Time* men wrote, women researched, and writers made more money than researchers. To the extent that this division of labor was based on sexist assumptions, it was said that men were dreamier and more creative, while women were more down-to-earth and practical, but little was made of this. Essentially, men had the better jobs because that was how it was. When I was being hired, I'd been told that I wouldn't be doing any writing on *Time*, and I didn't want to, since my ambition was creative writing. Women who resented not being able to write at *Time* were, in my opinion, not being realistic: if they wanted to write for a magazine, they should try another employer.

I must have realized quite soon that the masculinity of the men was bound up in their identity as writers, though while I was still a researcher, this didn't matter. At some point, I became aware that the amount of money these men earned was also a prop to their egos, and that without that income, they could become demoralized (or, in Freudian language, feel castrated). The men justified their higher salaries by saying they had families to support. I had an analyst to support, but I let the argument pass, partly because I knew that some men who said this admitted that women could write. Eric Wagner, an NCS graduate whom I dated in 1956–57, had introduced me to the word "WASP," and our masthead had many of them. Most names at the top (where editors and writers were listed) suggested Northern or Western European ancestry. Only a handful implied Southern or Eastern European ancestry, and virtually none represented the rest of the world (except for a few correspondents in appropriate bureaus). Many of my coworkers were graduates of the snobbier Ivy League schools and Seven Sisters, most of the rest having attended the top Middle Western state universities, or elite private colleges in the Midwest or South. I didn't know of any Columbia graduates who worked on *Time*, though, and only two fellow Barnardites.

On Morningside Heights, Jews had been a substantial minority, sometimes seeming a majority, and my mother's world had been a mix of non-religious Gentiles and Jews, but on *Time*, the atmosphere was subtly (sometimes not so subtly) Christian. There was a special cover story for the Christmas issue (on art, religion, or showbiz). There was a special Easter cover, too, for instance on a prominent clergyman or theologian. Luce was the son of missionaries, and some of his employees were related to members of the clergy or priesthood. Roy Alexander, the managing editor, had a Jesuit brother (so I was told). Otto

Fuerbringer, the assistant managing editor, came from a family of Lutheran churchmen. Having a Methodist minister grandfather made me feel like a member of this club, but, given my non-WASP name, I could be reminded I didn't belong, not really. As a child, I'd believed that the Holocaust had shocked this country out of its anti-Semitism, but all through the '50s and even into the '60s I was learning that it hadn't been entirely wiped out.

Maybe while I was still in school, I'd heard about the quota system, which limited the number of Jewish students in some colleges. It was said to be a thing of the past, but it wasn't such a remote past that some of my classmates hadn't worried about it. After I got to *Time*, a man I'd dated in college with a Hungarian name chose to change it in order to get a job in Wall Street. One of my mother's friends made reservations at a hotel, and when he got there, the desk clerk assured him the hotel was restricted. He had an Irish name, but his wife was Jewish, and so was his mother. He told the clerk this, adding that his son was three-quarters Jewish, and canceled his reservation.

Also in the '50s, I witnessed two anti-Semitic outbursts from women my age (not at *Time*, but in social situations). Both came from rich WASP families. This persuaded me that prejudice lingered longest in the top strata of society, but in the '60s, I occasionally dined with an older ex-Catholic of working-class Irish parentage, a family friend. When he got drunk, he'd rave on about how the Jews had gotten Roosevelt into the war, and nothing I could say would stop him. All this is only what social scientists call "anecdotal evidence." It doesn't mean that quotas, restricted hotels, and prejudice in Wall Street were nearly as prevalent in the '50s as they had been in the '20s or '30s, but every part of that evidence was consistent with every other part and nothing I heard contradicted it.

On *Time*, anti-Semitism was much subtler and less virulent, but many otherwise enlightened Gentiles still made an instinctive distinction between themselves and those they considered Jewish, including me. Nobody ever said anything overtly unpleasant, but I used to get awfully tired of how some people gushed about my name (both on the job and elsewhere). "Piri," they'd say. "What a *bee-utiful* name! What an *unus-ual* name!" Then (what they really wanted to know): "What *kind* of a name is that?" This hasn't been a problem since the '60s, and it's one of the biggest reasons I'm grateful for the watershed of that decade. People still tell me what a beautiful name I have, and sometimes ask what kind of a name it is, but praises be, they no longer gush.

The magazine had one Jewish senior editor, Henry Anatole Grunwald, who worked in back of the book, and whose secretary Andria had been. She liked him, and told me over lunch that he was an Austrian refugee who'd worked as a copy boy on *Time* while attending NYU. The story was that he'd edited stories while carrying them from office to office, and also tried psychoanalysis.[43] That Grunwald would admit he'd tried analysis indicated a strong personality, given the office climate on that subject. Andria said he'd married late, to "a nice Jewish woman." She suggested he favored liberal causes – more opportunities for women, I think as early as 1956. His chief distinction was as "a real intellectual." Andria told me how he'd persisted, against opposition, in getting a favorable review of *The Outsider*, by Colin Wilson, into the magazine. I read the book myself, decided it was pretentious mysticism, and remained to be convinced that Grunwald was a real intellectual.

(My failure to be impressed by him was to render me increasingly atypical as he rose from senior editor to assistant managing editor to managing editor. After I left, he would become editor-in-chief of all Time Inc. publications, then serve as ambassador to his native Austria. In 1997, his autobiography got a page-long review in the Sunday *Times*, plus publicity there and elsewhere. When he died, in 2005, the *Times* devoted a half page to his obituary, as the editor who had turned *Time* into "a more centrist magazine."[44] While I was on *Time*, Grunwald was popular most of the time with almost all of my colleagues. In the eyes of a staff that saw itself as predominantly liberal and Democratic, he enjoyed the reputation of a liberal, though his autobiography presented him as more of a centrist. Not long after I left in 1969, he would be getting criticism from feminists for failing to promote more women, but I don't think I'd have been made a writer six years earlier without many people believing that he favored more opportunities for women. Because I continue to think this belief was at least partially justified, I remain grateful, regardless of what else I may say about him. My direct contacts with him were few, and here I shall often be concerned with his public persona, as created by the office grapevine, rather than what he may actually have believed, said, or done.)

Around 1957, I wrote a short story inspired by a college boyfriend named Kevin. It was based on a letter he'd written me in 1955, the summer after we'd dated, telling me about his NROTC training cruise. He'd visited Barcelona, and danced with a young Spanish woman at a nightclub, but in my story, I made him fall in love with her, or rather, convince himself that he was in love, so that he could go to bed with her. My story also had a second source. In the summer of 1954, I'd been a waitress in Manitou Springs, Colorado. The night before I came back to Manhattan, I'd been in a parked car, necking with a man whom I didn't particularly like, even though (or perhaps because) he'd taken me to see a striptease. I'd realized that I could do anything I wanted with him, because I'd never see him again, but all I did was think, This must be one of the great lures of travel, the notion that some purely biological sexual adventure could happen to you.

Dr. G never tried to analyze my creative writing. To him, it was another way of channeling instinctual drives into constructive uses – more sublimation, though he rarely used that term. Instead, he emphasized "feeling," and told me to put my "feelings" into my writing. He thought they weren't used enough in contemporary literature, and, echoing the cliche, criticized "those *New Yorker* short stories that never have any point." I rarely read *New Yorker* short stories, but I wanted to be published there. They rejected my story about Kevin, as did *Esquire* (though Rust Hills, the *Esquire* editor, said he'd like to see more of my work). If I'd sent the story to little magazines, I might have sold it, but as an employee of a national magazine, I was only interested in the major leagues, so I put the story aside and started a play.

I'd always been stage-struck, and had taken a playwriting course at Barnard, so I decided to write a modern-dress *Othello*, with the time frame "next year," and the hero America's first five-star Negro general. *Jubilo* (as I called it) was influenced by what I'd learned in analysis about prejudice. As I understood it, prejudice was a form of fantasizing, a neurotic process in which a person with a repressed desire "projected" that desire onto persons of another race or faith, so a white person who was repressed about sex would tend to think of Negroes as sexy, a Gentile who didn't want to admit that he loved money would think of Jews as avaricious, and so on.

First, I wrote out descriptions of the characters. My general, Tom Jones (named after Henry Fielding's hero) was the only non-neurotic, a steady, hardworking man whose brilliance and dedication had taken him to the top despite the handicap of his birth. My Desdemona was named Peggy after Peggy Seeger, a folk singer whom I'd briefly met through my mother's left-wing friends. In my play, she was a dirndl-skirted, guitar-playing Radcliffe girl who'd gone to a progressive prep school like Putney, and was the daughter of a Southern senator who'd thought he was a liberal until she married Tom Jones. Iago was a racist alcoholic State Department aide, also from the South. Cassio was a *New York Times* reporter who'd been in love with Peggy since college. He was patterned on J. Anthony (Tony) Lukas, a reporter for *The Baltimore Sun* whose father had been briefly married to my mother in 1945, when I was ten and Tony was twelve. We'd spent that summer together as a family, and I'd followed his career from a distance since our parents split up. After Putney, he'd gone to Harvard, where he'd been on *The Harvard Crimson*. While I'd been on the clip desk, I'd clipped some of his stories from the *Sun*.

4. Reporting the Business Scene
(1959–1963)

In August 1959, I vacationed in Los Angeles, seeing my father for the first time since 1939. He owned the Mercury Bookshop in Beverly Hills, while my stepmother Sari worked at UCLA. Learning to know him better may have assuaged some of the insecurity that his departure when I was three had caused in me, because soon after I returned, I found I'd outgrown Canada (or at least the limited view of it that our magazine published) and was ready to move on. Again, I went to the chief of research (a new one, who'd discontinued those awful errors summaries). I asked to be transferred again, anywhere, though I'd prefer back of the book. I was sent back to Business, arriving around Thanksgiving 1959. It was top-edited by Otto Fuerbringer, the assistant managing editor and a conservative Republican, but I was so good at fixes that I felt the stories I checked were fair. Mary Liz Fremd was still head researcher, Joe Purtell still senior editor. Both encouraged researchers to do telephoning and interviewing, and I'd matured enough so that I could. My first week, I got a story on Christmas shopping with John Gregory Dunne, a younger writer who would later become a well-known novelist and screenwriter. "Give me *ideas!*" he said. In a store, I saw a demo typewriter with "Why don't you wait on me?" typed on the paper in it. I put this into my research, and Dunne used it in what I (as a good journalist) had learned to call his "lede," hooking me into *Time* yet more firmly.[45]

Another story I worked on in the first year after I returned to Business concerned how more Americans were now in service occupations than in goods-producing ones. While some service occupations were humble (dry cleaners, diaper services), others were professional (dentists, teachers). Written from the businessman's point of view, *Time* took an upbeat attitude. Spending on services would insulate the economy against depressions, since it continued even when manufacturers were cutting back.[46]

In early 1960, Time Inc. moved to the new Time & Life Building, at 1271 Avenue of the Americas (a.k.a. Sixth Avenue). It was designed on the modular system, which was supposed to be new, but the main building at North Country School had been designed on the modular system around 1938 by Douglas Haskell, brother-in-law to Walter and Leo Clark, directors of NCS, and editor of

Architectural Forum by the time that the new Time & Life Building went up.[47] He was said to be less than happy with the Time & Life Building. Still, every researcher had her own inside cubicle, one module big, no door. Writers got two-modular outside cubicles, with windows and sliding doors; senior editors got multi-modular rooms with hinged doors, and the managing editor and assistant m. e., mammoth expanses on the corners of the building.

The week we moved, Roy Alexander was "kicked upstairs" by top management to a make-work job on the executive floor of the corporation. Fuerbringer was made managing editor of *Time*. Thomas Griffith, a rare liberal who'd made it to the upper echelons, became assistant managing editor. Fuerbringer would change National Affairs and Foreign News to "The Nation" and "The World." He'd make the magazine more responsive to late-breaking news, scheduling "crash covers" on a last-minute basis much more often. He changed the magazine's closing day to Saturday instead of Sunday, and put most back-of-the-book sections on a Monday–Friday week. People in those sections could now socialize with the rest of the world, and even those in sections that went to press Saturday still had Sunday to mingle with non-edit staffers.

As most of my college friends were having babies or moving out of town, they were no longer introducing me to men. Hoping to widen my acquaintance, that summer I moved in with a roommate, in a walk-up on East Eighty-second Street. My half of the rent was $67.50, and my roommate was a charmingly proper Englishwoman my age, Carolyn Mullens, with hatty hats for Sunday churchgoing, and crisp print dresses for the office. Although I met her through *F.Y.I.*, she worked for an encyclopedia. We got along well, and she dealt me in on parties given by herself or the men in her circle. This circle (which she laughingly called "the Small Set") was more like my male coworkers than people I'd known before I started work. Most were WASPS, and had known each other at Harvard, or in the traditional prep schools they'd attended before Harvard. None asked me out, but at least they didn't attack me for working on *Time*.

The Business section would have appealed particularly to their relatives on Wall Street. Its star researcher knew many securities analysts whom she called for stock market comment. She put them on the section's Rolodex, so we could call them, too. Then she became a correspondent. Because of hers and other departures, I was senior researcher in Business by May 1961, when it got a new senior editor, Robert C. Christopher. I assumed Purtell had left because Fuerbringer wanted his own team (most other senior editors had been or would be replaced). Later, we learned that the SEC had found that Purtell had been buying stock in companies that *Time* was going to do stories on, then selling it after the magazine came out, profiting from the price rise occasioned by the stories. *Time* insisted that it had known nothing of this.[48] Still, Christopher altered the section. Stories about the economy became longer and more serious. We ran much more about international business. Newsworthy companies were discussed, but without the rosy earnings estimates that Purtell had demanded, and that boosted stock prices when the magazine was published.

Christopher was a tall, skinny, blond man in his late thirties with glasses and courtly manners. He'd been in World, where researchers did little reportage; in Business, he was quoted as saying, "These researchers really research!" The quotation came from Marcia Gauger, his new head researcher. I was invited to fill in for the Washington bureau's economics correspondent when he went on vacation that August, although I'd just taken a share in a summer group house near Quogue, on the South Shore of Long Island, where I hoped to meet new people (i.e., men). I'd learned about this particular group house through an ad in *F.Y.I.* placed by Marion Steinmann, who worked on *Life*, but nobody else in the house was at Time Inc. Nor were most of the people I was to meet in Quogue, then or in successive summers.

I'd joined the Sand Bar Beach Club there. It was a club for single people, most of whom belonged to other group houses (in those days, still all-women or all-men). Most of the men were Gentile, often WASP, usually in banking, advertising, the stock market or other businesses. *Time* was read at the beach. The women tended to have more interesting jobs, but they were on the whole pretty WASPy, too. I'd meet dates through the Sand Bar, and one permanent friend, but none of the dates led to romance. Looking back, I wonder if one problem was that the kind of men who liked *Time* were also the kind less apt to appreciate a woman who took her job seriously.

Much as I'd been looking forward to Quogue, I jumped at the chance to fill in at the Washington bureau. It was exciting to be in the field, writing files in response to queries, and exciting to be in Washington so near the beginning of the New Frontier. Eisenhower had bored me, but John F. Kennedy didn't, and not only because he was a Democrat, or a liberal. He hadn't been that liberal before he became President, and my mother was always suspicious of what she called "pretty boys," but I'd voted for JFK and liked his inaugural address, which I'd seen on TV. Being a Shavian, I also admired his political skills, and I thought him more intelligent than Adlai Stevenson, who'd run against Eisenhower in 1952 and 1956, and been billed as an intellectual.

"The Washington Report" was a series of confidential items telexed to New York every Tuesday. Known informally as "the memo," it was distributed only to writers and editors, but writers permitted researchers glimpses. I'd seen one titillating item in which Hugh Sidey, our White House correspondent, had interviewed the President in the White House swimming pool, with JFK in the nude.[49] Most of Kennedy's biographers say he was often dissatisfied with *Time*'s coverage of him, but one book by friends of his says he liked Sidey personally, and the warmth of this relationship came through in "the memo," together with an exhilarating sense of intimacy (as I still skipped over The Nation, I didn't know how our magazine treated JFK in print).[50]

Our Washington bureau chief got me in to a presidential press conference. Kennedy didn't say anything much, but he was charming about it. Shortly afterwards, the Berlin Wall began going up. Perhaps that was what he hadn't wanted to discuss. Bureau life made me feel even closer to history in the making, but it was also relaxing. I had only the equivalent of research to do, no checking, and the civil servants I talked to, to get government statistics, were a pleasure to work with. This was *my* government they represented, and they knew it. In New York, I was dealing with a better class of public relations men, representing big corporations. They were suave and informative, but, when push came to shove, cared more about getting their employers a good rap than about helping me.

On this trip, and later visits to bureaus, I saw how correspondents had more self-esteem than writers in New York. This reflected the greater respect shown them by their opposite numbers on rival publications, and the ease with which they moved to those publications. Correspondents were considered real reporters, while the writers in New York were scorned as what on newspapers were called mere "rewrite men." Still, there was a trade-off. When stories based on correspondents' files were slanted in ways that distressed them (or their sources), they could (and did) blame the editors in New York, but by the same token, they had less power within the corporation. A correspondent who truly wanted to influence what the magazine said could do so only if he became a writer in New York.

Barbara Foley Wilson, a Barnard classmate, had given me names of two men to call in Washington. One was a reporter named David Halberstam, whom she'd dated in high school. She told me that he'd gone on to Harvard, where he'd been on the *Crimson* with Tony Lukas, my ex-stepbrother. Now Halberstam was in the Washington bureau of *The New York Times*. I also heard, from a *Time* stringer, that Halberstam had worked for newspapers in the South. When I called him at the *Times*, I was told he'd gone to Africa with Robert F. Kennedy to cover the independence-day ceremonies of the Ivory Coast, and his byline soon began emanating from there. This I would use in my modern-dress *Othello*, which I started writing in the evenings that month, in my Washington hotel room, because I felt so rested and relaxed.

Act One took place in a Georgetown living room, at the home of the senator, Peggy's father. David Cohen, the *New York Times* reporter who was Cassio, was watching a ball game on TV. When the senator learned that his daughter had married Tom Jones, America's first five-star Negro general, he was furious and threatened to get the marriage annulled, but because Jones was being sent to represent the United States at the independence-day ceremonies of the mythical African nation of Ard, he was dissuaded. Cunningly, my Iago, the racist State Department aide, arranged it so that Cassio could go along, to cover the ceremonies for the *Times*.

Even in New York, my bureau experience made me feel more like a reporter, and I made my research look like a correspondent's file. On work nights, I still dined with fellow researchers. Once, we discussed three reporters about our age on the *Times*: Halberstam, Tony Lukas, and Max Frankel. Frankel had been on the *Columbia Daily Spectator*, and had married a *Barnard Bulletin* editor. I'd only known her by sight, and the first time I'd heard his name mentioned was when another *Bulletin* staffer referred to him as "the *Spectator* editor who's going to marry Tobi Brown." According to the dinner conversation with fellow researchers, he'd gone to the *Times* straight from Columbia, and started out as a copyboy, while Halberstam, and by this time, Tony, had joined the *Times* at a higher level because they'd worked on out-of-town papers.[51] We thought they'd been smarter than Frankel. (By 1986, he'd be executive editor of the *Times*, while Halberstam quit in 1967, and Tony in 1972, both going on to write major books.)

Bob Christopher, known as "Chris," was much liked by the Business writers. He edited stories so they didn't seem heavily edited (even when they were). I liked him because I got to file major pieces of research (fifty pages or more) based on phone calls and interviews as well as morgue material. The first big piece I did was for the annual "Year-End Review" of business, at the close of 1961. Christopher devoted it to the impact of computers (the big mainframe ones that were still the only kind in existence). Marcia Gauger told me that after he'd read his copy of my file, he said to her, "I was tempted to edit the research, and not wait for the writer's version." That in itself was a very good reason to imprint this story in my memory.

"Business in 1961" was subtitled, "Automation Speeds Recovery, Boosts Productivity, Pares Jobs," and sizeable passages concerned what automation was doing the U.S. work force and organized labor. Still hymning the joys of capitalism, the magazine described how the increased use of computers was making even low-level jobs more interesting and lucrative: instead of being stuck on blue-collar assembly lines, some employees now wore the white overalls of better-paid technicians, and even clerks had fewer papers to shuffle. Aided by a dazzling array of statistics (many of which I helped assemble), *Time* told how all this automation, coupled with the shift from manufacturing to the service industries, was altering the U.S. work force. Though as a whole it was growing, the number of production-line employees was diminishing, particularly in industries best situated to capitalize on automation: automobiles, steel, and textiles. Employment was rising among white-collar workers: not only were more clerks and technicians needed, but more administrators. The country's manufacturing segment was employing 13 percent more clerks and 65 percent more professional and technical workers than in 1952, but this was bad news for organized labor, because assembly-line workers had formed its backbone since the 1930s, and white-collar and service workers were hard to organize. Union membership had declined from 18.5 million to 18.1 million in the previous five years.[52]

Also in December 1961, my roommate Carolyn went home to England, to marry Timothy Harford, a childhood friend. I found a new, equally nice roommate through *F.Y.I.*: Shirley Carmichael, a cute Baptist from Boston who worked for RCA. In August 1962, I spent my vacation in Quogue, and on weekday mornings worked on the second act of my play. It took place in Ard, a former colony of Switzerland in Africa. After General Tom Jones and his Peggy attended its independence-day ceremonies, communists murdered the prime minister. To keep them from taking over the country, Jones had to stay on as strongman. As months passed, he became more distant and authoritarian, Peggy lonelier and more listless, Cassio increasingly frustrated as his dispatches were relegated to the back pages of the Sunday *Times*, and Iago ever more dangerous as he lapsed into drunken, racist invective. I was still channeling my "feelings" into my writing, as Dr. G recommended. He evidently meant my aggressive feelings, but I'd later realize that libido was also involved.

That fall, I met (through Shirley) a man whom I shall call Fred Freund. He was (let us say) a junior airlines executive from Australia: smart, amusing, and wonderfully sane. He fell in love with me, and plied me with bridge games, theater tickets, candy on Valentine's Day, and roses on my birthday. When the summer came, he'd sign up for a men's group house near Quogue, and join the Sand Bar. From the pleasure he gave me in bed, and the apparent ease with which he did so, I thought he must be one of the world's great lovers (though he sure didn't look it). One night, I asked him his secret for success. He said it had started at the family dinner table, where his father had taught him to notice if somebody wanted the salt, and then to pass it before it was asked for, the principle being "consideration in all things." Eventually, Fred would propose, but though I loved him, I turned him down. I wasn't *in* love with him, and I think that even if I'd married him, I'd have dumped him when I truly fell in love with somebody else, as I eventually did. At first, though, Fred said he didn't ever want to get married, so I enjoyed the moment for what it was worth.

In January 1963, I spent some weeks in back of the book, with a Monday–Friday week. Riding down in the elevator on a Friday night, I ran into people from Business, who told me Bob Christopher was leaving. He'd accepted a job as long-term research director for Corning Glass. I took the elevator back up, and went to his office to say goodbye. Other people were having drinks, so I joined them, and without thinking about it, stayed until he and I were alone. Then he said he wanted to hire a researcher to help him, and had been thinking of me, adding he'd pay me more than I was getting, but didn't expect an immediate response. We got our coats and went out to stand waiting for the late-night elevator. Christopher said softly, "May I?" and, without waiting for an answer, put his arms around me and kissed me. Then the elevator came. Since it had an operator, we stood apart as we rode down. On Sixth Avenue, Christopher flagged a cab, and got into it with me. In silence, we rode up to my apartment, and the cab stopped in front of it. I got out. So did Christopher. "May I come up?" he asked.

He wasn't the first married man on *Time* to hit on me. One Friday evening, I'd run into Silas Haynes, the lean Press writer with the saturnine smile. He said there was a *Life* party in the eighth-floor auditorium, and invited me to go down and see what was going on. We visited the party, and, as we were coming back up (in an unmanned elevator), he leaned across and kissed me on the cheek. "What's that for?" I asked. He smiled, and said, "Oh, just because you're a girl." That was the end of it, but I'd told Dr. G about it, and we'd discussed extramarital affairs. Having said earlier that it was easier for men to split off sex from "friendly feelings," Dr. G argued that in an extramarital romance, the woman was apt to get more emotionally involved than the man, and suffer accordingly. Besides, though I liked Christopher, sex with him would have meant two-timing Fred, and I couldn't have done that. I said to Christopher that my roommate slept in the living room (true, except that Shirley was away skiing that weekend). "I understand," he responded, got back into the cab, and rode away.

To my surprise, Dr. G didn't dismiss Christopher. He encouraged me to see whether "the man" might not be in love with me (he called every man I discussed "the man"). After Christopher had gone on to Corning, he asked me to lunch once or twice. The conversation never got romantic, but he did want to hire me, and I'd wanted for years to leave *Time*. Working there left me no time or energy for my own writing except on vacations, while working late nights and Saturdays continued to limit my chances to meet men. I'd looked into other jobs, but none paid enough to let me continue analysis, particularly since, whenever I got a raise, Dr. G raised his fees. The Corning job would pay more than I was earning, and I'd have a nine-to-five, Monday–Friday week. The work would be so dull I wouldn't want to work overtime, but Dr. G remained unsatisfied.

"What do you really want?" he asked.

"I want to write," I said.

"Why can't you write for *Time*?"

His Socratic question forced me to think. Roy Alexander had said he didn't want women writers, but Fuerbringer had never committed himself, and Henry Grunwald was said to be in favor of "more opportunities for women." Grunwald was still only a senior editor, but looked upon increasingly as a comer. He'd promoted one researcher to the writing staff, Johanna Davis, starting out by letting her write fashion stories for him in the Modern Living section. After months of double duty, researching and writing, she was now a full-time writer there, but married, and due to go on maternity leave. If she could write for *Time*, why couldn't I? For the first time, I thought, Maybe I could, though I know now it was unusual for the media in general. *Newsweek* listed a few women as writers on its masthead, but most of the women on its edit staff were researchers. The *Times* had a few women reporters covering hard news, a few more dealing with cultural topics, and a handful for the page euphemistically called "food fashions family furnishings" (i.e., that journalistic purdah traditionally known as "the women's page").

Betty Friedan would publish *The Feminine Mystique* in April 1963, an indictment of how women had been conditioned to believe they should only be wives, mothers, and housekeepers. Neither *Time* nor *Newsweek* reviewed it. It got a good review in the *New York Herald Tribune,* but Friedan attacked Freudian analysis for deluding many women, so the *Times* gave the book to a dedicated Freudian who'd written a bestseller about her own analysis. Surprise! The review complained.[53] I was dimly aware of this book, and I now know that it became a bestseller, but, as again the *Readers' Guide to Periodical Literature* shows, "women's lib" as a whole wouldn't become a mainstream crusade until the early '70s.[54] Months after I'd quit *Time* in 1969, its researchers would rise, demanding more opportunities as writers and editors. In 1970, *Newsweek*'s researchers would conduct their uprising, and only after this did both magazines (and the *Times*) slowly begin employing more women as writers and editors.

I asked Fred what he thought about my applying for a writing job on *Time*. "There are so many things people don't get because they don't ask for them," he said. I decided to apply, but since I'd never worked with Grunwald, I didn't see how I could go to him. I asked for an appointment with James Keogh, who'd joined Griffith as a second assistant managing editor, and interviewed prospective writers. I gave him my portfolio, as male applicants did. In it were my best pieces of research, since correspondents were brought in to write in New York on the basis of their files. Jack Skow had said the editors liked to see fiction, even if unpublished, so I also put in my short story about Kevin. Looking for the path of least resistance, I said I'd like to start by filling in for Josie Davis in Modern Living, while she was on maternity leave. Keogh, a conservative Republican who did little without Fuerbringer's approval, passed my portfolio to him. Later, Keogh called me in, and said they'd be willing to "work me in gradually," but didn't want to put me in Modern Living, because they didn't want it to get the reputation of being "a women's section." Since it dealt with fashion, fads, food, and travel, it was already the next thing to a women's page, but I couldn't say so.

"Any other ideas?" Keogh asked, or words to that effect.

"How about Books?" I asked. Outside writers, even a few researchers, had done book reviews. They got paid even if the review wasn't published, but had been top-edited and made checking copy. I liked this because I didn't want to play a passive feminine role, as Davis had, and let myself be exploited. I felt it would reinforce whatever prejudices the men had against women writers. Dr. G said one reason women had trouble in business was that men weren't sure what they wanted. Men, he said, worked primarily for money, while women looked on jobs more in terms of emotional satisfaction; men found this hard to understand or accept. "It's only a job," Dr. G liked to say. "Just a job."

Writing in Business would have made more sense than Books, but the senior editor who'd replaced Christopher was Edward L. Jamieson, who would play an important role in my life later on. He'd been a junior writer in Business in 1957, when I'd started my career in research there, and, by the time I returned in 1959, was the senior writer. Then he'd begun "sitting in" for senior editors, though his name hadn't gone onto the masthead as a senior editor until he'd taken over Business. He had a dry sense of humor, and, though married to a handsome platinum blonde former researcher, was usually very prim in his office manner. He was said to be a practicing Catholic, but the incident I remembered best had taken place in the fall of 1960, while I was making checking fixes with him. Clearly I was being too aggressive, for he'd leapt to his feet and roared down at me – a long, loud, wordless animal roar. I was very upset, worked to be extra tactful, and was forgiven – but when, in early 1963, I'd asked him if I could write for him in Business, he'd said no. He didn't approve of women writers, because "women get too emotional." Coming from him, that was rich.

Keogh suggested I ask A. T. Baker for a book to review. "Bobby" Baker had been World's senior editor, but according to the grapevine, had such a problem with alcohol that he couldn't get the section to press on time (World had many late-breaking stories). Now Grunwald was editing World, and Baker had taken over Grunwald's back-of-the-book sections, including

Books. He gave me the journal of General "Chinese" Gordon, written when Gordon was under siege at Khartoum in 1884–85. Rereading it now, I can see that it has some juicy stuff, but then, I lacked the know-how to get it into the magazine (if I'd written it short, say at forty lines, it might have stood a chance, but I wrote it at four times that length, which would have been considered appropriate only for a masterpiece by a major author). Baker didn't edit my review, and, though it was on the next week's story list, didn't edit it then. The third week, I went to him and said if he didn't like what I'd done, would he tell me what he did want, so I could do a new version.

Dr. G said another reason men had difficulty accepting women in business was that they were afraid women couldn't take criticism, and would cry. Having an editor dictate an NV meant accepting his criticism of the first version, but hadn't I taken the criticisms of Drs. Keiser and G on far more delicate and personal matters for years? Baker stalled, but then told me what he wanted, and I wrote a new version. He edited it. Fuerbringer top-edited it, and a researcher checked it, but it was "killed in makeup," meaning it wasn't among the stories the editors selected on Friday to run. For weeks, my review was again put on the list, again sent through, again killed in makeup. I'd told Christopher, and through him sent a portfolio to *Newsweek,* where he knew people. He thought I might write Business there ("I don't know whether or not you can write," he said. "But you sure know business"). I didn't hear from *Newsweek*, and Christopher hired another Business researcher to work for him at Corning Glass.

Finally, on a Saturday in June, Keogh told me I was to start writing Milestones the following Tuesday. George G. Daniels, known as Gus, would be my editor. Two writers gave me cardboard keys to the men's room. One came from Jon Borgzinner, a floater who'd been filling in at Milestones as a vacation replacement. He'd started in Milestones himself, when it was edited by Christopher, so his office had been near mine, and I'd come to know him slightly. At Yale, he'd majored in art history, and I was told that his dream in life was to write about art for *Time*, not least because his mother worked in a gallery that had exhibited a new style in art just becoming famous as pop.

Time had published a big takeout on pop art in its May 3 issue, with color illustrations of Andy Warhol's garishly tinted Marilyn Monroe, a huge stuffed-canvas hamburger by Claes Oldenburg, a comic-strip painting by Roy Lichtenstein, an American flag by Jasper Johns, and a "combine painting" by Robert Rauschenberg. Both Bruce Barton, Jr., the Art writer, and Fuerbringer disliked pop. They only ran the takeout because pop was indubitably "news," but the text sourly suggested that it was only a "passing novelty."[55] People today may find it hard to appreciate how shocking such art appeared in 1963, derived as it was from sources outside the centuries-old tradition of the fine arts, sources that included commercial art like advertisements and package design, comic strips, corporate logos, billboards, and other objects and artifacts designed for or targeted toward mass audiences. Today, such cultural sources for fine art – generally referred to en masse as pop culture or popular culture – are so common that they sometimes almost appear to amount to a requirement, but I suspect I didn't even read *Time*'s angry text on pop art, merely glanced at the brightly colored pictures and thought them amusing.

Borgzinner had read a flimsy of my review of the Gordon book, and thought I had the makings of a *Time* writer. He showed me how to "green" Milestones. This meant adding or deleting words in a green pencil on the galleys, so stories fit properly into the layouts. It was done when the section was going to press, and whoever did it had to stay until Production said the greens fit and the section was "closed."

5. Enter Newsweek and Vietnam (1963–1967)

WHILE WRITING MILESTONES, I'd become aware of Vietnam, and of the competition *Newsweek* was starting to give *Time*, but I didn't read *Newsweek*, and I resisted Vietnam, too. More even than the China Lobby, Vietnam awoke conflicts between my progressive childhood and the employer toward whom I now felt redoubled allegiance because it was letting me write for it. Because I had ascended to a position of relative authority within it, I also had to read more of it regularly, and, while this experience would ultimately become painful, I learned from it. Obviously, I'm not the first to write about either Vietnam or even the rivalry between *Time* and *Newsweek*, but nobody has yet given my particular perspective on either subject. Though I may flatter myself, I feel that what I have to say about both not only advances the discussion of them, but feeds into the larger picture that this book as a whole seeks to present.

Milestones reported births, marriages, divorces, and deaths, in items of ten to fifteen lines, and was used for training new writers. Gus Daniels also edited People, Sport, and what was left of Hemisphere, since the Latin America edition had been discontinued, and Canadian news was now written and edited in Montreal (where my friend Andria was on the staff). All Daniels's sections went to press Saturday night. I had an office with a window in the row of writers edited by him. Our researchers had a row of inside cubicles across a narrow corridor from us. Behind the back walls of the researchers' cubicles lay a wider corridor that ran around the entire floor. My office faced the entryway from this corridor, so I saw – and was seen by – everybody coming in and out, the custom being that writers didn't close their doors unless they were actually writing. This meant that I was constantly exposed to all of my coworkers in those sections.

Though he came from a sophisticated theatrical background, Daniels behaved like the archetypal all-American boy. Fuerbringer had no more loyal lieutenant, though the m. e.'s conservative politics and authoritarian way of running the magazine led to many complaints among writers and researchers (even if writers became elated when he indicated he'd liked a story they'd done). At first, I found Daniels maddening. I'd send each Milestone in to him as I completed it, but he'd let them pile up. Late Friday evening, he'd bring all of them back to my office, sit down in the chair across from me, lean it back against the wall, put his feet up against my desk, and, whistling, completely rewrite each item, after which he'd read it back to me. I'd sit there, silently stewing as my deathless prose was ripped to shreds, but I had to show I could take criticism.

Daniels said that a Milestone should have a rhythm, and I could hear the cadence when he read aloud his finished products (eventually, I'd acquire enough skill so he had little left to do in editing them). Elsewhere, one "late man" did the greens for all the stories under one editor, and the job was rotated from week to week. Daniels made me, the Sport writer, the People writer, and one of the two Hemisphere writers stay until the greens were completed every week, so I didn't get to Quogue until Sunday morning. During the summer of 1963, Fred would pick me up at the train station in his sporty little Triumph, and sympathize as I let loose with my accumulated rage.

On Mondays, I finished the third and last act of *Jubilo* by August. General Tom Jones was stripped of his powers by a communist coup, and found Peggy embracing her Cassio. That was my switch on Shakespeare: Desdemona guilty as charged. My affair with Fred ended that fall, too, when I turned down his proposal. I said I hoped we could still have lunch. Then JFK was assassinated. This event made me realize that some of my coworkers were reading and admiring *Newsweek*, though its circulation was roughly half of ours, and though they denied their interest to outside reporters.[56]

Newsweek's remarkable surge had begun in 1961, when the Washington Post Company, led by Philip Graham, bought it. In the summer of 1963, Graham killed himself, and his widow Katharine became president of the company. Philip Graham had put three very able editors in charge of *Newsweek*: Osborn Elliott was editor, while Gordon Manning and Kermit Lansner were executive editors. In January 1965, Manning left, Lansner became managing editor, and Lester Bernstein became executive editor. The original threesome were known as "the Wallendas," after the circus trapeze artists, and they set the style that would prevail throughout the '60s. "With Kermit, we had a Jewish intellectual from New York, and with Gordon, an Irish Catholic sportswriter from Boston, and in my case, a WASP from the Upper East Side," Elliott once observed in an interview. "It made for a wonderful balance."[57] Looking in the twenty-first century at issues of *Newsweek* between 1961 and 1963, I can already see changes taking place, but I wasn't reading it at the time, and didn't become aware of any change in my colleagues' attitudes toward it until after Philip Graham's death.

Personal History (1997), Mrs. Graham's best-selling autobiography, indicated that she didn't have that much to do with *Newsweek*, but Elliott, in his memoir, wrote that she and Frederick S. Beebe, chairman of the Washington Post Company, "did not hesitate to pour the money in. The editorial budget, which was $3.4 million in 1960, increased to more than $10 million by the time the decade ended." The extra funds "made it possible to pay better salaries, and attract new talent."[58] One new talent was Bob Christopher, who, after less than a year at Corning Glass, joined *Newsweek* that November. As foreign news editor, he would distinguish himself within the profession for his supervision of the magazine's Vietnam coverage.

Philip Graham had been a good friend of Kennedy's, and so was Benjamin Bradlee, *Newsweek's* Washington bureau chief. *Newsweek* covered the assassination exhaustively, using a photograph of JFK on its cover. *Time* used Lyndon Johnson. *Time* usually portrayed the new leader with changes in government (looking forward, not back), but opinion in our office was that we, too, should have gone with JFK. My colleagues also felt that *Newsweek* had written about the assassination better. A Letter From the Publisher, at the front of our magazine, had been offensive (not to say hypocritical), talking about what a high opinion JFK had had of us.[59] Not long thereafter, Griffith, the assistant m.e. responsible, was kicked upstairs.

To me, South Vietnam in 1963 resembled South Korea in 1950. Both were parts of what had been one country, partitioned into northern communist and southern capitalist halves since World War II. Both were developing nations trying to repel communists. Both were run by "presidents" who were more nearly dictators (in South Korea, the president had been Syngman Rhee; in South Vietnam, it was Ngo Dinh Diem). Both had armies so inadequate to deal with the communists that they were relying on U.S. aid, though the U.S. soldiers in Vietnam were as yet only "advisers."

In the wake of Vietnam, I've found, a lot of people have forgotten how the Korean conflict actually began, progressed, and ended (otherwise, I wouldn't feel a need to summarize it here). By June 1950, the North Koreans had crossed the boundary at the 38th Parallel and invaded South Korea, occupying almost the entire country. The U.S. and other U.N. forces, entering to defend South Korea, drove the North Koreans back to the 38th Parallel and crossed it, pushing the North Koreans back to their northern border. When the U.N. forces threatened to go on, into China, the Chinese entered on the side of the North Koreans, and forced the U.N. forces back to the 38th Parallel. The situation stalled, and the two sides started talking. The talks dragged on for two years, while sporadic fighting continued. The U.S. public had initially supported the war, but turned against it as soon as the Chinese entered, and remained at best ambivalent thereafter.[60] Still, the final settlement, arrived at in July 1953, retained pretty much the original boundary between the two countries.

More recently, the tendency has been to emphasize how unpopular the war became in its later stages, and say that it resulted in a stalemate. Still, a stalemate isn't a defeat, and my recollection is that prior to Vietnam, the war was seen in a more positive light. South Korea had retained its independence, after all, and the communist invasion of it had been repulsed. The cold war policy of containment had worked, and though, by the early '60s, South Korea hadn't gotten that much richer, it had achieved a marginally greater measure of representative government, Rhee having been deposed by a student uprising in 1960. When he died in 1965, at the age of ninety, the *Times* ran his obituary on the front page, describing him flatteringly as "the Tiger of Korea." The obit implied that he had only become corrupt after the Korean conflict.[61]

As nearly as I could tell, in 1963 there were two big differences between Korea and Vietnam. The first was that the war wasn't going anywhere, and the second was that the *Times* was playing up how badly it was going, how undemocratic the Diem regime was, and how vehement were Buddhist protests against it. I didn't know whether the *Times* had criticized Rhee while the Korean war was going on, but the notion that he was a despot was one that Karen and Lloyd, my mother's left-wing friends, had gotten me accustomed to. I've since learned that the *Times* had published stories, prior to the North Korean invasion, telling how South Korea's opposition leaders had been detained and its opposition press largely eliminated, while police brutality had become a way of life.[62] But after the invasion, when communist propaganda attacked the Rhee government as incompetent, corrupt, wasteful, stupid, and reactionary, the paper editorialized that such attacks were a technique that "all totalitarians have developed industriously [to] slander a prospective victim," comparable to how Hitler had showered abuse upon the governments of Austria, Poland, and Czechoslovakia before invading them.[63]

In 1963, our magazine was supporting the South Vietnamese government. This surprised nobody familiar with Luce's views on communism and China. Volume Three of the official company history, which discussed Vietnam, maintained that Luce wasn't that interested in Vietnam, or influential upon *Time*'s policy about it.[64] True, his role has been exaggerated by detractors, but I don't think it was as minimal as the company history suggested. Hedley Donovan, a former *Fortune* editor, would take over from Luce as editor-in-chief of all Time Inc. publications in the spring of 1964. I don't think Luce would have picked him if he hadn't seen eye to eye with Luce on communism, especially in Asia. Even in retirement, Luce made public speeches and statements defending U.S. involvement in Vietnam, and attacking the press for failing to report the situation fairly.[65] Excerpts from one such speech were printed in *Fortune* as late as January 1967, the month before he died.[66]

Neither *Time* nor *Life* would alter their positions on Vietnam until after Luce's death. Only in the summer of 1967 would Donovan conclude the war was unwinnable, and *Time*'s position on it begin to change, but Volume Three wasn't published until 1986. By then, the people writing it knew that *Time* had discredited itself with many journalists, and made itself detested by many members of the informed population, for its initial support of the war. Faced with the unenviable task of digging out from under this still-growing mountain of opprobrium, the company historians apparently decided that the best damage control lay in distancing Luce and the people still in charge.

In 1963, I was only marginally aware of *Time*'s coverage of Vietnam. One occasion did arise that August, when World was doing a cover on Mme. Ngo Dinh Nhu, sister-in-law of President Diem. Daniels was on vacation that week, and Michael Demarest, a World writer in training to become a senior editor, was sitting in for him. Demarest only edited one Milestone, describing Stephen Ward, the osteopath who'd been involved in the Profumo scandal, as Britain's "prince of ponces."[67] I had to look up "ponce" in the dictionary, so I was impressed. Midweek, Demarest was called back to edit World. The writer who had been doing that, Edward Hughes, had been called away suddenly. On Saturday, my friend Marion Pikul, who was researching in World at that point, dropped by and told me that Hughes's wife had died. Both Hughes and Demarest will reappear in this narrative.

From the brief reading I gave our Vietnam stories, I felt that the Diem government had a legitimate right to govern South Vietnam, having assumed power in 1954 shortly before the Geneva Conference partitioned the country. As *Time* said in the fall of 1963, elections to unify the country "were supposed to be held in 1956, but Diem repudiated this with the argument that any election in the Communist North would be rigged."[68] I didn't think the communists would have allowed free elections, any more than he did. As far as I knew, no country except San Marino had ever put communists in power through a free election, but I was thinking more of the intransigence I'd witnessed in Karen and Lloyd.

When I reflected upon how much poorer and more desperate the Vietnamese communists must be, I was sure they'd be a lot more intransigent than two well-fed American actors. The primitive economy of Vietnam also mattered to me, because of the economic determinism I'd picked up from Karen and Lloyd, Howard K. Smith, and Shaw. They made me feel that any country which didn't have a solid industrialized economic base and a sizeable middle class had a tough time supporting democracy, so the only choice most developing nations faced was between capitalist dictatorship and communist dictatorship. I felt that the former was more likely than the latter to evolve into democracy, and that was why I favored it, though I was pretty sure that some people I respected and loved, like Ed and Elsa Bley, might not agree.

Still, the dispatches from Vietnam in the *Times* were often bylined David Halberstam. This made me keep an open mind about them, because it was the *Times*, and because he'd been the high-school boyfriend of my Barnard classmate, Barbara Foley Wilson. I read an item about him in the Washington memo (which, now being a writer, I received). As I recall it, the item (most likely by Sidey) described Kennedy asking why he was having to learn all about Vietnam from Halberstam, and berating his own staff for not providing such information. The item probably appeared during the summer or early fall of 1963. In later books, Halberstam wrote that Kennedy was angered by his dispatches and those of other newsmen reporting bad news from Saigon, but he also suggested that the president came to have more confidence in what he read in the papers than in what the military was telling him.[69] Certainly, JFK's administration did nothing to stave off the coup by a junta that overthrew the Diem regime in early November 1963.

Halberstam was the subject of an enthusiastic article in the January 1964 *Esquire*. That spring, he shared the Pulitzer Prize for foreign news reporting with Malcolm Browne of the AP, who was about his age (b. 1931; Halberstam was born in 1934). Together with Neil Sheehan of the UPI (b. 1936), Halberstam and Browne had been providing U.S. newspapers with the lion's share of the stories coming out of Saigon. Their view of the situation was disputed by two well-known older journalists, Marguerite Higgins (b. 1920) and Joseph Alsop (b. 1910). I didn't know that, but in retrospect I suspect the attitudes of Higgins and Alsop, like mine, were colored by the experience of Korea, since both had been combat correspondents there. *Time's* correspondents in Saigon, on the other hand, had also filed copy critical of the Diem regime, and saying the war was being lost.

Rather than airing their point of view, a story in our Press section for September 20, 1963, said to have been all but dictated by Fuerbringer, described the entire Saigon press corps in such insulting language that Charles Mohr, our Southeast Asia bureau chief, resigned in outrage (and was hired by the *Times*; Merton Perry, a *Time* stringer who had worked closely with Mohr, also resigned; by 1965, he would be reporting from Vietnam for *Newsweek*). This incident caused such a commotion that as of 2004, it had been mentioned and often dealt with at length in at least sixteen books, only one of which could be seen as siding with *Time*.[70] (This is what I mean by a mountain of opprobrium.) Clearly, many writers saw it as the symbol of everything they objected to in *Time's* coverage of Vietnam, but such was my need to insulate myself that I managed to pay almost no attention to it when it took place.

I didn't dislike Fuerbringer. He'd given me a chance to write, so I didn't consider him conservative in terms of women. Rather, he seemed to confirm what I'd learned through the teachers' strike at Putney: labels like "conservative" and "progressive" didn't mean much. Also atypically, I was less appreciative of *Newsweek*, if only because my portfolio had been returned, more than two months after I started Milestones, with a kind but unsatisfactory letter from Gordon Manning. He wasn't turning me down, but he sure wasn't hiring me, though he called my reporting "absolutely first class," and my short story, "a tender piece of writing." One question, he said, was "promise vs. performance," but that didn't mollify me, since I knew the path from *Time* to *Newsweek* was well-trodden. More relevant, I suspected, was his comment that "there's no ducking the question, much as I'd like to, that some female writers sometimes are more female than writer." He said he was confident this would not apply to me, but "the question lingers in some minds."[71]

I did have to fight my femininity. I hadn't had a crush on any male colleague since my early one on Jack Skow, but something happened after I became a writer, which I didn't (and don't) fully understand, but which between 1963 and 1966 would leave me vulnerable to crushes. In retrospect, this seems very silly adolescent behavior, but it was serious business at the time (not least because the analyst took these attractions seriously). One reason it happened may have been that I was doing so much the same thing as these men were, and in such similar circumstances. This led to feelings of identification – and sympathy – with them, whereas in research I'd been teamed up with other women, all of us no more than friends, and viewing the men as friendly adversaries. Also, due to my ingrained shyness, I'd always been more at ease in relationships with men that started out on an intellectual level (as had my relationship with Ed Bley).

The first time a crush of sorts happened was with Charles Parmiter, the Sport writer. If Fuerbringer had been amused by a phrase when he edited a story, he wrote an "ah!" in the margin. If he liked the whole story, he wrote a "good" at the end. Parmiter could often be heard in the corridor, chortling over his "ah!s" and "goods." He was gallant, complimenting me on hairdos and dresses, but he was married, and in my opinion neurotic, with a penchant for gambling and a cracked-up Bentley, so I thought that all I had for him was "friendly feelings." He asked me to dinner on a Friday. Since we had to get back to the office afterwards, I didn't see any harm in it, but Dr. G told me I was unconsciously attracted to "the man," and trying to put the relationship on a dating basis by letting him pick up the check. The next time we had dinner, I offered to pay my share. Parmiter laughed, would only let me pay the $7.50 that Time Inc. would repay me – and didn't ask me to dinner again. Still, he'd remain a friend and ally.

My next crush was on Jose M. Ferrer, III, my predecessor in Milestones who was now writing People, and I was conscious of it. I had to read his Milestones (in the scrapbook kept of previous issues) to find out how to write mine, and I liked his writing. Fuerbringer did, too, so I could hear Ferrer chortling about his "goods" and "ah!s." He was handsome and offered suggestions for my section. He was younger than I, but I looked up to him because he was ahead of me in the writing game. I'd been a senior researcher, but as a writer, I was a freshman again. At times, he seemed about to ask me out, but he never did, so Dr. G started analyzing him. "The man" had inhibitions about dating me. To overcome them, I had to make it impossible for him to indulge his liking for me by seeing me on the job. Easier said than done.

While I and Daniels's other writers were waiting on Saturdays to green our galleys, we ate our buffet dinners in Daniels's office and watched TV on his set, the only one in the area. Daniels had organized himself, myself, Parmiter, and Ferrer into an after-dinner hearts game, and I could see no way to escape these games without appearing stand-offish or silly. The hearts continued after I was promoted to People, in early 1964. Ferrer was moved up to Hemisphere, so he remained one of Daniels's writers. Again, I had to model my items on his, and again, he'd drop by with advice. Occasionally, I wondered if he was dating Penelope Oster, my attractive young researcher, but I saw no definite evidence the two of them were going out, so Dr. G started analyzing my attraction to "the man" instead. He told me that since Ferrer hadn't shown any interest in me, he was for me not a "reality man," but only a "fantasy man." This lesson would haunt me. It didn't help at the moment, but in early 1965, Ferrer was transferred to Show Business in a different group of offices. Since I never saw him, I stopped thinking about him.

A People item was a bit longer than a Milestone, twenty to twenty-five lines on individuals who'd made minor news. I heard that the section had the highest readership of any in the magazine. Daniels said its items should be like peanuts: after you read one, you had to go on to the next. Even more than in Milestones, I had to figure out which persons in the papers were suitable for *Time,* so I had to read (or skim) more of the magazine than I had in Milestones. I was entering a new phase of seeing the world *Time* wrote about, learning to define it in terms of its audience. Somehow, the word "heartland" had swum across my consciousness. I was learning the extent to which *Time* was targeted at this heartland audience, and how this made it different from *The New Yorker.*

Around 1943, *Time* seems to have commissioned the Columbia University Bureau of Applied Social Research to interview residents of a town of eleven thousand on the Eastern Seaboard, and find out what it could about the relationship between its readers and members of that community. The findings of the study that resulted were discussed by Robert K. Merton, the Columbia University sociologist, in *Social Theory and Social Structure* (1957). Although Merton didn't say specifically that *Time* had commissioned the study, he called the town "Rovere," and indicated there were in Rovere two kinds of influential people: the "local," to whom their neighbors turned for advice about everyday affairs, and the "cosmopolitan," whom they consulted for news of national politics, culture, and other developments in the world beyond Rovere.

The "cosmopolitan" influentials, it turned out, were apt to read *Time*.[72] The magazine must have been delighted. Apparently it reached tastemakers and opinion-molders in Rovere, but what was "cosmopolitan" there might look pretty provincial to a big-city type, so really what *Time* had to be written for (though this was never said) were readers largely less sophisticated than the people who wrote it, an audience that, by comparison with the hip insiders on the staff, were more apt to be outsiders and squares. To reach them, a writer had to know how much they might not know, explain things to them that big-city types would know about, and share or at least take into account their outlook. Nobody said this meant talking down to them, but this was what it often meant.

In People, I began to be aware of the extent to which I was writing for *Time*'s real, square, heartland audience, if only subliminally. I thought of many of my items as "heartwarmers," upbeat paragraphs about prizes, overcoming odds, or a pleasant event enjoyed by some celeb. I saw myself as Pollyanna, the Glad Girl, because this was the kind of item Fuerbringer would give me an "ah!" or a "good" for. The fact that *Time*'s audience was on balance less sophisticated than my own acquaintance also made it much more numerous and widespread. Most of the people I could do People items on, at least with Fuerbringer in charge, had to have instant name recognition across the country, and only certain people usually had it. Entertainers often did, as did sports and military heroes, royalty, politicians, and rich people, but novelists and scientists were far less likely to, and about the only artist I felt sure would rate a People item was Picasso.

I did do one item on Jackson Pollock, but only because somebody had made a jigsaw puzzle out of one of his perplexing abstract expressionist "drip" paintings.[73] That was funny enough for an item, though I doubt Fuerbringer would have considered him famous enough by himself. I knew practically nothing about Pollock. The only time I'd heard his name before was in late

1956, when a college friend said he'd been killed that summer in an auto accident, and indicated this was a major loss. For the People item, I must have looked at material in Pollock's "bio folder" from the morgue. Those folders had clips from newspapers, Luce magazines, and files clear back to the '40s (occasionally the '30s). The article that *Life* did on Pollock in 1949 would have been in his bio folder, showing how he laid his canvases on the floor and swirled paint upon them from a stick.

Fuerbringer may have been right about what our heartland audience wanted to read, at least in the early '60s. Most of these readers probably still did relate to Luce's priorities, as stated in his prospectus: a faith in the things money couldn't buy, and – despite an interest in the new, particularly in ideas – a respect for the old, particularly in manners. I think many of the magazine's writers found these attitudes congenial, more so than they did Luce's politics, though they didn't think about it any more than I did. Still, as I reread what we published, I can also see how by the mid-'60s, maintaining this outlook was becoming harder. Social change and cultural developments would be equated by us more and more with "manners," while science was seen as "ideas," and, while *Time* remained enthusiastic about breakthroughs in medicine and physics, it could become obtuse or even hostile when confronted by social and cultural developments. Not always, to be sure. Our writers and editors were never all that square, or that committed to presenting the news in a manner that only an outsider audience would find sympathetic, but by comparison with *Newsweek,* they would begin to look so.

In terms of standard demographics (education, category of occupation, income, age), the two magazines were still similar.[74] But, while *Time* evidently saw itself as serving the nation, *Newsweek* appears to have begun targeting a segment of this audience – the more liberal, more sophisticated one. *Newsweek's* writers and editors didn't necessarily see themselves as doing this, but Oz Elliott, in his memoir, suggested that their almost unconscious mindset was oriented in this direction. "In retrospect, we were making a risky bet," he reminisced, "that we could elevate the intellectual level of the magazine and still keep readers buying it. We hardly gave it a second thought. But it paid off."[75]

In 1965, *Newsweek* boasted that its circulation was up by 200,000, the biggest one-year gain in its history.[76] In 1969, an article in *Esquire* by Chris Welles called *Newsweek* "the new hot book" to the advertising world. He reported that in 1968, for the first time (except for a fluke in 1958), *Newsweek* ran more pages of advertisements in its domestic edition than *Time,* 3008 to 2913. He added that *Time's* ad pages had been declining for four years, while *Newsweek's* had been rising sharply (though, since *Time's* audited circulation was still nearly double that of *Newsweek,* and space rates are based on circulation, *Time's* total ad revenues were still far greater).[77]

In 1979, Herbert J. Gans, also from Columbia but of the next academic generation after Merton's, would publish *Deciding What's News: A Study of CBS Evening News, NBC Nightly News, Newsweek, and Time.* It's a landmark opus, celebrating its twenty-fifth anniversary in 2004 with a second edition, but for me it was particularly valuable for how it reflected an attitude that began to develop in the later '60s, a perception that all the mass media were essentially alike and equally wanting. Now that I am no longer a member of the mass media, I can see many similarities and room for improvement, but I also feel that the tendency to emphasize shortcomings and similarities was to some degree a response to larger historical events of the later '60s, rather than (or at any rate, in addition to) what the media themselves were doing. Whatever the reason, educated people even today are more skeptical about journalists than they were when I was growing up (sometimes to the point of paranoia). As an adolescent, my image of a journalist (and I think that of many other people) was the gentler, more romantic one of *The Front Page,* the classic 1928 comedy by Ben Hecht and Charles MacArthur: a seedy outcast with cynical exterior but heart of purest gold.

Gans's equating of *Time* and *Newsweek* can be further explained by the fact that he didn't start his on-site research at *Time* until after Grunwald succeeded Fuerbringer as managing editor of *Time* in May 1968, and Grunwald (as Gans said) was trying to make *Time* more competitive with (hence more like) *Newsweek.*[78] For this book, I trekked up to Columbia, where as an alum I have library privileges, and studied in detail the coverage of not only *Time* and *Newsweek* for the three years of 1965, 1966, and 1967, but also that of *The New York Times* for the same period. My examples of difference between all three publications mostly date from those years, when the gap between *Time* and the other two yawned the widest, but I also think Gans may not have realized the full extent to which his outlook was conditioned by his environment.

He may have thought he was contemplating the amoral world of journalism from the detached, objective, cloistered halls of academe, but Morningside Heights wasn't *that* detached about Vietnam or any of the other major issues of the period. Admittedly, it had its conservatives, and most of its students were apolitical (as were most college and university students throughout the country).[79] But in the spring of 1968, Columbia would become the site of a major student upheaval that resulted in its administration calling in New York City policemen to restore order. A Barnard classmate of mine had a job in a computer lab on the Columbia campus at the time; years later, she recalled that the fact that the police had been called in, plus the way that they'd treated the demonstrators, radicalized a far larger proportion of the student body.

Gans tried to find out what audiences the media thought they were writing for, and discovered differences between the newsmagazine audience and that of the networks. But from how he quoted writers and editors on the newsmagazines about whom they thought they were writing for, it's clear he wasn't trying to establish differences between the audiences of *Time* and *Newsweek*. Most of these writers and editors were jumbled together; the only one I could find identified with one publication was a *Newsweek* senior editor, quoted saying that the attitude of his magazine was that of a "well-educated, decent liberal, in the sense of being an open-minded, fair person, but also one who is bemused and ironic."[80]

James Landers described the rivalry between *Time* and *Newsweek* in *The Weekly War: Newsmagazines and Vietnam* (2004). He did call *Newsweek* liberal, and *Time* conservative, but only dealt at length with their Vietnam coverage. I'd argue that besides being more liberal politically, *Newsweek* also dealt more sympathetically with cultural and lifestyle changes, partly because its editors and writers felt closer than we did to what my colleague, Mike Demarest, called "the nervous trades." He meant those occupations closest to the nerve centers of society: the arts, fashion and design, publishing, entertainment and communications (from newspapers, magazines, radio, and TV on to advertising and public relations). This was the world I'd grown up in, my mother's friends (and some of mine). Most were moderately or well to the left politically.

Geographically, such occupations were clustered more in the Northeast Corridor and on the West Coast, but *Newsweek's* staff also seem to have sensed that many other readers across America had become more hip and progressive than *Time* realized. The magazine could have found statistics to explain why such readers, even in the heartland, were more in sync with the trendsetters in the Northeast Corridor and on the West Coast than they had been back when Luce and Hadden were formulating their ideas, or even the more recent past. In 1956, when I'd started work on *Time*, 71 percent of U. S. households had TV sets; by 1963, that number was up to 91 percent. During that same period, the number of paying passengers on domestic airline flights was up 66 percent, and those on international flights had more than doubled. Even heartland readers were seeing more of the world on their TV sets, and getting out to partake of it more often.

Newsweek may also have been aware of the greater sophistication and sense of social responsibility that characterized many (though far from all) members of the generation entering high school and college in the '60s, the generation to become known as the baby boomers. Both magazines tried to reach students, hoping to hook them in for life. Again, in terms of standard demographics, both were probably succeeding in the '60s to a comparable degree. When I was in college, however, nobody I knew on Morningside Heights read *Time*, and I'd heard of that Harvard professor with his crack about "*Time* is for people who can't think." I don't imagine many of *his* students would have bought it. More recently, a friend who attended Cornell in the '60s told me about a professor there who never missed a chance to lambaste *Time*. True, this is only more anecdotal evidence, but again, all three anecdotes are consistent, and add up to a pattern.

Studies cited in the '90s by David W. Levy showed that when college students as a whole were polled during the '60s, they were apt to uphold the war in Vietnam, but that when polling was limited to students at one hundred fifty or two hundred "elite" schools, it was another story. At these schools, with national student bodies and reputations, pro-war sentiment was always present, but antiwar sentiment was especially vigorous, grew more so as the hostilities continued, and at times in the late '60s and early '70s became all but irresistible.[81] I've seen no statistics on what schools the students who read *Time* or *Newsweek* were more likely to attend, but again my anecdotal evidence suggests that students who read *Newsweek* were more likely to be at elite schools, while those who read *Time* more likely stretched across the full range of institutions.

In the '60s, many minorities and disadvantaged groups carried on an arduous campaign toward equality. It was the decade of the underdog. The '60s themselves saw big change in race relations, and a parallel (though as a rule, indirectly addressed) recognition of Jews. With women and homosexuals, the '60s only witnessed the beginnings of a dialogue, but members of all these groups sympathized with one another, as did progressives who didn't belong to any. I think one reason that *Newsweek* made common cause with such underdogs was that it was itself the underdog, in relation to *Time*. *Newsweek's* writers and editors opted for this role, though not necessarily because they realized it as such. In his memoir, Elliott explained that *Newsweek's* advertising and circulation staffs had been promoting it on the basis of its superiority to *U.S. News & World Report,* third in circulation behind *Time* and *Newsweek*. In this context, *Newsweek* could claim that it was top dog, but that wasn't enough for Elliott and his staff. As he recalled, "We editorial types set out after Harry Luce's *Time*; we figured it was vulnerable because of its set ways, its predictable politics, its snideness...."[82]

Newsweek's shift, from looking down at its competition to looking up at it, made it into the archetypal underdog and positioned it to identify with and express the most dynamic and significant aspects of that era. As the underdog, *Newsweek* wanted change in the world in general and the magazine world in particular. *Time,* as top dog, was far more satisfied with the status quo, and these opposed attitudes would express themselves in many ways. Eventually,

Newsweek would find that change was taking place more drastically than it could keep up with. It could never be radical enough for some of the radicals it wrote about, or even for some of the radicals on its staff, but reviewing the record, it's clear that it was considerably more activist than *Time*.

For his *Esquire* article, Welles interviewed many people in advertising. They didn't perceive *Newsweek* as targeting the audience I've described and only explained their enthusiasm in general terms. "There is a real flair about *Newsweek*," one said. "There is a whole atmosphere of involvement, a sense of riding with what is happening in society. It talks to you in people terms. It's a much more contemporary package." According to another, "When you buy magazines, you look for editorial values, for the contribution of the medium to the ad message. If the book has vitality, if it's with the times, then it reflects that on our advertising." The nearest awareness that *Newsweek* might be aiming for a different sort of reader was suggested by one of its editors. "*Newsweek* is edited for Madison Avenue," he claimed. "We'll do anything if it will make the guys at J. Walter Thompson [the country's largest ad agency] talk about it in the john."[83]

Welles maintained, "Over the past few years, *Newsweek* has often been superior to *Time* in assessing the meaning, significance, and implication of the news," adding that it had also excelled in "recognizing many of the major trends of the 1960s," and citing among his examples "the awakening of black aspirations" and "changes in the mood of the younger generation." Although this was certainly true, his explanation for why *Newsweek* had been able to accomplish this, and *Time* hadn't, reflected his sympathy with *Newsweek*. He argued that *Time*'s "rather conservative ideological stance" had led it to downgrade the importance of what was going on, while *Newsweek*, being "uncommitted to any formal ideological position, was more receptive to deviations from traditional thinking and as a result usually covered these events with more perception and accuracy."[84] It's human nature to think that somebody who comes to the same conclusions that you have is "uncommitted," while somebody who comes to opposite conclusions is "ideological," i.e., biased. *Time* was biased in a conservative direction; *Newsweek* was biased in a liberal one. A liberal bias may well render it easier to appreciate new trends, but that doesn't make it any less a bias.

In many ways, the two magazines had a lot in common. Both dealt with the week's news primarily in unsigned articles, and in sections that matched each other, though titles might differ (our lifestyles section was Modern Living, theirs Life and Leisure). Reflecting its claim to be the newsweekly that separated fact from opinion, *Newsweek* carried signed columns of commentary, but even Welles realized that the claim as a whole was pretty silly and that *Newsweek*'s news stories also expressed opinions. Ultimately, it was those opinions that counted. The magazine appealed to more sophisticated, more hip readers, especially younger ones, because it shared their politics, and their interests in the latest art, books, clothes, and music. It offered a package in which every section played a role, and the cultural sections in back of the book enhanced the news sections up at the front.

By the mid-'60s, the contrast was evident even before you opened the magazines. All you had to do was look at their covers, often side by side on newsstands. *Time* still relied primarily, as it had since its inception, on art for its cover image: paintings, drawings, occasionally sculpture. It was proud of this, and though its regular stable of artists were at best equipped to capture only good likenesses, it employed some with independent reputations (Ben Shahn, Pietro Annigoni, Bernard Buffet, Rufino Tamayo, Marisol, Warhol, and Rauschenberg, among others).[85] The magazine most often used a well-known person as its cover subject, and built its cover story around that person.

Newsweek had almost always used photography on its cover; by 1963, this was usually color photography. Though it often did cover stories on famous people, it was equally if not more likely to deal with a subject of interest. When the cover story was a subject, the cover itself might show a person or persons as a symbol standing for a group of people, unknown persons thrust into the spotlight by the week's events, or even an image with no people. *Time* occasionally did covers on subjects. By the mid-'60s, when Fuerbringer was running more and more crash covers, *Time* was increasingly likely to use a black-and-white cover photo, and/or devote the cover story to a subject, but on the whole, it remained committed to the idea that individuals made history, while *Newsweek* often appeared to favor the idea of impersonal social forces, composed of many individuals. As the '60s advanced, I'd hear more and more gripes among my colleagues about *Time*'s covers, and mutters that *Newsweek*'s covers looked more "contemporary."

I'd also begin to hear how *Newsweek* had beaten us to the punch with cover stories. The first occasion was in 1965, when we'd scheduled a Christmas cover on *Doctor Zhivago*, a likely Oscar contender, only to find that *Newsweek* had done a cover the week before on Julie Christie, the movie's star. After I started writing Art, I'd hear how Jon Borgzinner, who'd taken over the section in late 1963, had wanted to do a cover on Willem de Kooning. Since Pollock's death, de Kooning was regarded as the leading abstract expressionist, but *Newsweek* dashed Borgzinner's hopes by putting de Kooning on its cover in January 1965. Nor would this stop after Grunwald succeeded Fuerbringer, though it became less frequent. I'd hear that our staff wanted to do a cover on Norman Mailer, but we took so long that *Newsweek* did its cover on him in December 1968 (*Time*'s Mailer cover wouldn't appear until 1973).

True, all these subjects were newsworthy enough to have interested any newsmagazine, but some *Time* staffers hinted at espionage. Others thought a *Time* cover in the works had been gossiped about by people in the world of the subject (entertainment, publishing, or art) until word got back to our rival. Fuerbringer, according to our grapevine, said that *Newsweek* was always going off "half-cocked," but that didn't keep most of us from feeling that we'd been scooped.

The covers on Christie, de Kooning, and Mailer were all in back of the book, where *Newsweek* seems to have had unusually good contacts. This area was the special preserve of Lansner, who had taught philosophy at Kenyon College and been an associate editor for *Art News* before joining *Newsweek* in 1954. He was married to an artist, and, though the *Newsweek* masthead in the '50s listed him only as Books editor (later general editor), for quite a while nobody was listed as Art editor; I think it likely that during this period, he wrote art stories, too. In 1963, he hired Jack Kroll to assist him – first as an art critic, later as senior editor overseeing the arts sections. Kroll had been on *Art News*, too, and was another Renaissance man interested in music and theater as well. Under the leadership of this remarkable pair, *Newsweek*'s arts sections were very much in sync with insider taste, and by "insider," I mean not only those creating and disseminating culture, but also consuming it: not only writers, editors, and booksellers, but also book-buyers, not only professional musicians, but also concertgoers and record-buyers, not only artists, art critics, dealers, and curators, but also people who bought art and/or went to galleries and museums.

In January 1966, when Truman Capote published *In Cold Blood*, his "nonfiction novel," *Newsweek* put him on its cover, calling his nonjudgmental posture about the violence in the book "super-contemporary."[86] The book went to the top of the bestseller lists, and Capote reciprocated by throwing an enormous "Black and White Ball," with Katharine Graham as guest of honor. It was the social event of the season, perhaps the century. In October 1967, *Newsweek* did a cover on William Styron. The "peg" (short for "news peg") was his publication of *The Confessions of Nat Turner*. With a novel about a Southern slave who rebels against his masters, after a summer of race riots, Styron again appealed to a "contemporary" audience. His book, too, became a bestseller. *Time* also did covers on authors: John Cheever (March 1964), Phyllis McGinley (June 1965), and Robert Lowell (June 1967). Though gifted in their various ways, they (and their subjects) were WASPs and/or beloved by Middle America. Styron's hero was black, not white, and though Capote's book was set in the heartland, it was at least as sympathetic to the two men who had killed off one of its most respected families as it was to the family itself.

Top dog v. underdog showed up in reviews of two more bestsellers. Saul Bellow's *Herzog* concerned a Jewish antihero, antiheroes being a popular form of outcast in the '60s, and Jews the quintessential underdogs. When the book appeared in 1964, *Newsweek* called it "a literary event of the first importance," with the title character the "perfect protagonist."[87] *Time* felt that individual episodes were "brilliant," but the novel as a whole was "disappointing," and Herzog himself "everybody's doormat."[88] That same year, Louis Auchincloss published *The Rector of Justin*, about the headmaster of a WASPy elite prep school. *Time* gave this Establishment tale a quite favorable write-up.[89] *Newsweek* accused the author of flattering some readers by dropping names into his text, either "to 'place' a pasteboard character, milk a stock emotion, or inject the dry veins of tired sentimentality with a dose of second-hand atmosphere...."[90]

Newsweek appealed to sophisticated readers by assuming they knew something about the subject under discussion. To choose just one of many examples, when Nat King Cole died in 1965, *Time* heavy-handedly recapitulated almost his entire career; *Newsweek* worked his basic biography in around the edges of its narrative, focusing upon the tributes occasioned by his death.[91]

Newsweek was more at home than *Time* was with the esthetics of the avant-garde. When *Bonnie and Clyde* opened in 1967, both magazines panned it, *Newsweek* for its violence, *Time* for its "tasteless aimlessness."[92] Both returned to it, with *Time* doing a cover, and *Newsweek,* a reconsideration by Joseph Morgenstern (by 1967, *Newsweek* had begun to use signed reviews). *Time* employed the movie to show, rather self-consciously, that Hollywood could make European-style "art" films, too.[93] Morgenstern apologized for his earlier review, saying the movie's "dazzling artistry" made it "an ideal laboratory for the study of violence, a subject in which we are all matriculating these days."[94]

Needless to say, the expertise that Lansner and Kroll brought with them from *Art News* showed up particularly in *Newsweek*'s art coverage, but I shall save the details of this situation until the reader has read more about art itself, and progress here to other less specialized areas in which the two magazines competed.

6. Lifestyles, Pop Culture, Civil Rights
(1963–1967)

Both *Time* and *Newsweek* wrote about lifestyles and social change. In July 1965, both did cover stories on vacations, with color photographs of women in bathing suits as cover pictures. *Time* showed a wholesome young married woman striding briskly along a beach at Sea Island, Georgia, in a modest two-piece suit, to accompany a color photography spread on U.S. resorts (in those days, most photographs in both magazines were still in black-and-white. Since the '50s, *Time* in addition had used a page or more of color reproductions of works of art in its Art section, but these went to press weeks before the rest of the magazine. By the '60s, both magazines had also begun to experiment with special inserts in color to accompany stories in other sections of the magazine. These "fast color" inserts went to press on the same week as the rest of the issue, and the spread on U.S. resorts was one of these).[95]

Newsweek's cover showed two sultry babes in what would probably have been considered daring bikinis in 1965, seductively reclining at an Italian resort, for a story on "Europe's Biggest Season." *Time* patriotically emphasized that Americans were following Lyndon Johnson's plea to help the balance of payments by seeing America first. *Newsweek* implied that only squares were staying home, and the record invasion of Americans in Europe would be of "new, more sophisticated" third-trippers who knew what they wanted and "where to go to get it."[96] Pictures and text suggested that the magazine was writing for more sophisticated, fashion-conscious readers, more apt to travel abroad; it also suggested the sensual and pleasure-loving. *Time*'s cover image of the wholesome Sea Island matron appeared, by comparison, a bit dowdy and uptight.

More serious developments similarly evoked contrasting responses. If they could be treated as "ideas," or science, *Time* welcomed them. Besides sympathetic stories on the legalization of abortion and the beginnings of estrogen therapy, *Time*'s Medicine section did a cover on the newest contraceptive, The Pill.[97] But with "manners," or social behavior, *Newsweek* was far less censorious. Both magazines wrote on homosexuality. Both still felt it was psychological in origin, not genetic, but *Time* (in a long, only occasionally sympathetic article) called it "a pathetic little second-rate substitute for reality, a pitiable flight from life, "and "a pernicious sickness."[98] *Newsweek* reviewed Martin Hoffman's book *The Gay World*, quoting his explanation for why the U.S. homosexual subculture was so unhappy: because of "the attitude toward homosexuality on the part of the larger straight world, an attitude which itself is the result of the dread of homosexuality which pervades the culture and which goes hand in hand with repressed homosexual feelings on the part of millions in that culture."[99]

Newsweek was quicker than *Time* to see that, in the wake of pop art's success, popular or mass-audience culture as a whole was beginning to be taken more seriously. The magazine was happier about it, too, with a surer sense of when to treat it as fun, and when to emphasize its significance. Both magazines did stories in 1965 on the fad for comic books. *Newsweek* quoted one fan who saw them as "a document of American times and changes," but mostly the story was gently humorous.[100] *Time* poked heavy-handed fun at the intellectual pretensions of comic-book fanciers ("Why has Donald Duck become a masochist? Does the disappearance of Mickey Mouse's goodness presage a decline of the West?").[101] Using a cover by Roy Lichtenstein, *Newsweek* did a cover story in April 1966 on "pop," surveying the enhanced status of mass-audience culture in fine art, advertising, fashion, movies, theater, TV, and merchandising.[102]

Nowhere did *Newsweek*'s speedier acceptance of mass-audience culture show up more clearly than in its coverage of pop music. When I'd been in college, my boyfriend Kevin was a Mozart freak, and loaned me LPs of Mozart, Schubert, and Bach. The few records I'd bought were mostly classical. Some of my classmates (and professors) liked jazz. Some liked folk songs, but I only heard pop over the jukebox by accident, when I and my North Country schoolmates were taken to a diner on the way to a ski resort, or in bars during the summer I'd waited table in Colorado. Nor would I have been considered a snob by other graduates of elite schools. The first time I heard the name of Elvis Presley was in the later '50s, when *Time* was doing a story about him. Its researcher was my friend Andria, a graduate of Dalton and the University of Minnesota, and her tolerant smile indicated indulgent amusement. Elvis the Pelvis was fine for teenagers, I think we both felt, but too corny for educated adults. By 1964, however, younger writers on *Time* (whom I now looked up to for cultural guidance) were enthusiastic about pop music, starting with the Beatles, whom I'd come to love myself.

Both *Time* and *Newsweek* ran a Music section almost every week. *Time* focused more on classical music (including ballet, opera, avant-garde dance and experimental composers); it also ran occasional stories on popular music. *Newsweek* divided its attention about evenly between classical and popular music.[103] Not surprisingly, *Time* often trailed *Newsweek* in covering the "coolest" pop music and trends with the greatest appeal for the young. The two were neck and neck in their stories on "folk-rock," but *Time* was behind *Newsweek* by six months in discussing the San Francisco sound, by eleven months in its story on innuendoes in pop lyrics, by nearly a year in its discussion of Motown and the Supremes, and by seventeen months with the Rolling Stones, "bad boys" of the British invasion.[104] *Time*'s cover on rock'n'roll preceded a *Newsweek* takeout on the pop record business by five months, but the Beatles were conspicuous by their absence from *Time*'s cover photo montage, and the lag with the Beatles themselves was ludicrous.[105] *Newsweek* did its cover in February 1964, when the group was on its first trip to the United States and appearing on the Ed Sullivan show; *Time*'s didn't appear until September 1967. By then, the group's new album was *Sgt. Pepper's Lonely Hearts Club Band*, middle-period Beatles; the magazine tried to compensate by quoting praise for the group from an orchestra conductor, a musicologist, a classical composer, two psychiatrists, and a clergyman.[106]

Sometimes, though, *Time* could be as with-it as *Newsweek*. In December 1964, it ran a "quotepiece" from "Notes on 'Camp,'" Susan Sontag's article that had just been published in *Partisan Review*, and has since become a classic.[107] Sontag related "camp" to the sidelining of high culture and rejection of moral seriousness, linking it instead with homosexual taste and an interest in mass-audience culture. Given *Time*'s attitude toward homosexuality and comic books, I suspect that whoever scheduled this piece hoped it would cause its readers to reject mass culture because of its associations with homosexuality. Instead, Sontag's definition of camp became part of the language, and herself, according to one biography, "an instant intellectual celebrity."[108]

The biggest domestic hard-news story of the early '60s was civil rights, and the way *Newsweek* handled it did much to augment its reputation. The way *Time* handled it becomes more understandable when you realize the magazine was trying to present it in ways that its conservative, mostly white heartland readership could appreciate. Even today, reviewing their coverage, I'd say that both magazines favored full equality for Negroes, and *Time* had even earned something of a progressive name for itself on the subject of race in the '20s, when Briton Hadden reported lynchings. The fact that *Time* was *Time* made whatever it had to say on behalf of civil rights that much more memorable, but *Newsweek*'s presentation of them was more sympathetic to Negroes, and more acceptable to liberal whites who sympathized most strongly with them. I'm sure even *Newsweek*'s coverage looked like white-man's coverage to Negro readers, but itself being an underdog, it was more likely to emphasize what they were suffering and doing to change things. *Time*, as top dog, identified more with the white community, especially its Republicans, and tended to emphasize what white people were doing.

Time put Everett Dirksen, the white Republican Senate minority leader, on its cover in June 1964, when Senate Republicans teamed up with Northern Democrats to muster the two-thirds vote needed to end the filibuster by Southern Democrats against the Civil Rights Bill, and let it pass. The magazine did a cover in May 1967 on Frank Johnson, a white Republican judge in Alabama whose rulings were helping to break down segregation and enable Negroes to register to vote. In January 1965, the magazine dealt at some length with John Doar, the new white Republican chief of the Justice Department's civil rights division, right after his appointment.

Newsweek ran a cover in June 1963 on Vivian Malone, the Negro woman who, with James Hood, was determined to enter the all-white University of Alabama. That same week, the civil rights leader Medgar Evers was killed in Mississippi, sparking protests all over the U.S. *Newsweek*'s cover story dealt with all of these events, as did its Top of the Week, at the front of the magazine.[109] That September, a black church was bombed in Birmingham, killing four little girls. *Newsweek*'s cover was a stark black-and-white photograph of the mother of one of the girls, weeping in the arms of another woman. The contrast on the newsstands would have been particularly striking that week, as *Time*'s cover was on George Wallace, the racist Alabama governor who'd tried to keep Malone and Hood from integrating the university. The magazine had a story on "The Sunday School Bombing," but the cover story was largely about Wallace and the State of Alabama, trying to explain why they were what they were, and calling him "a smart, capable lawyer who has in many ways been a first-rate Governor."[110]

With its first issue of 1964, *Time* made the Rev. Martin Luther King, Jr., its Man of the Year, but this title wasn't necessarily a compliment, for the magazine conferred it on the person or persons who'd done the most to alter the course of history during the preceding twelve months, for better or worse (Hitler was Man of the Year for 1939). The magazine was happier with moderate Negroes, doing covers on Roy Wilkins of the NAACP (August 1963) and Whitney M. Young, Jr., of the Urban League (August 1967). *Time* liked to emphasize how much progress Negroes were making through the lawful means of the ballot box, so it also did covers on Edward Brooke, the first Negro U.S. senator since the nineteenth century (February 1967), and Carl Stokes, Cleveland's first Negro mayor (November 1967). These were legitimate topics, but two other covers were more problematic. One on "The Negro in Viet Nam" (May 1967) showed how Negroes were being integrated into the military, while the other reported on the marriage of the daughter of Dean Rusk, Johnson's secretary of state, and a Negro (September 1967). Doubtless both were meant to show how Negroes were becoming a respected part of American society, but both also suggest that the magazine was trying to publicize the liberal-mindedness of Lyndon Johnson's administration, to enlist support for his pursuit of the war.

Time reflected the fears of conservative white Americans that integration was coming too fast, but the way that the magazine covered what in those days were considered extremists could make those fears seem justified, for example in its story on the assassination of Malcolm X in 1965. Above the text were police mug shots of the Black Muslim leader, front and profile, wearing a hyper-spiffy hat in the frontal view, and with untidy hair slicked back into a ducktail in the profile. He looked like a hood, and the story began, "Malcolm X had been a pimp, a cocaine addict, and a thief."[111] *Newsweek* used a head shot of Malcolm X, too, but with his hair neatly cut short, and scholarly-looking spectacles. Its story began, "He was born Malcolm Little, an Omaha Negro preacher's son...." The second sentence did mention his criminal record, but added that it dated from his teen-aged years, and implied it was only to be expected from "a Harlem hipster," nicknamed Big Red.[112]

Time looked on the bright side of the racial situation, emphasizing how far the Negro had come. The title of its Man of the Year cover story for King was "'Never Again Where He Was,'" and the story included an eight-page color photography spread on famous and successful Negroes.[113] The first page of its cover story on Wilkins was illustrated with two photos. One was a grisly picture of a lynch victim, taken in 1880, and the other, a photo of James Meredith, in cap and gown, receiving his diploma from the University of Mississippi in 1963.[114] *Newsweek* was more likely to look on the dark side, and point out how far the Negro still had to go. Between July 1963 and August 1967, it commissioned six major polls from the Louis Harris organization examining attitudes about race. Four of these polls accompanied cover stories on race.[115] In November 1967, the magazine devoted a cover and a 23-page special section to "The Negro in America: What Must Be Done." This won it a National Magazine Award, and drew an impressive array of congratulatory letters from distinguished readers.[116]

Newsweek's popularity with liberal insiders showed on other occasions in its letters section. The rule seemed to be that when *Newsweek* did a story you liked about a subject on which you were an authority, you wrote in to congratulate it, but you practically never wrote to *Time* unless a) your economic interest had been served or b) you could point to a mistake. Occasionally *Newsweek* ran letters correcting mistakes, and occasionally a celebrity with no axe to grind wrote a nice letter to *Time*, but commoner were Romain Gary, the French novelist, and James S. Plaut, director of the Boston Institute of Contemporary Art, writing to praise *Newsweek*'s cover story on de Kooning; Willard Van Dyke, director of the film department at the Museum of Modern Art, writing to say how much he liked *Newsweek*'s article on the underground cinema; and Joshua Logan, the Broadway director-producer, writing to salute the *Newsweek* movie critic who'd reversed himself, after panning *Bonnie and Clyde*, as "probably the first brave man of all of them."[117]

Also typical were letters to *Time* from Truman Capote, correcting its account of his Black and White Ball; from Roy Wilkins, to dispute a statement made in the magazine's cover story on "The Negro in Viet Nam"; from Tony Barrow of NEMS Enterprises, Ltd., to discuss a mistake in the obituary of Brian Epstein, the Beatles' manager; from I. M. Pei, the architect, to point out an error in the story on his National Center for Atmospheric Research; and from comedian Jerry Lewis (in a particularly striking contrast with *Newsweek*), angrily condemning *Time* for its review of *Bonnie and Clyde*.[118]

In 1985, when I was applying for a job in Minnesota, the professor interviewing me said firmly that when she'd been in college, *Newsweek* was her magazine. This suggests how much bright students liked it, but I knew nothing of them, and felt sure that Jon Borgzinner of *Time* was a true art-world insider. I didn't read his section carefully, but the fervor of his commitment, in our occasional conversations, convinced me that *Newsweek* couldn't be handling contemporary art any better than he was. By the time I was in People, he'd advised me that pop art had replaced abstract expressionism as the new avant garde. He told me he'd proposed a cover story on Rauschenberg, when that artist had won the grand prize for painting at the Venice Biennale in the summer of 1964, but Fuerbringer had rejected the idea because pop art was "too New York-y." The only cover on a contemporary American artist *Time* did when Borgzinner was writing Art was on Andrew Wyeth, a traditional realist painter beloved by the heartland.

I think Joe Ferrer told me how much he liked the Beatles, adding he thought we should do a cover on them. This also would have been in 1964, and again, according to the grapevine, Fuerbringer couldn't be persuaded.[119] Still, in other ways the office was moving with the times. Men's hair was a tad shaggier. Men's office attire, at least on Saturdays, could be more casual (occasionally even silk turtleneck shirts instead of the usual crisp collared ones that took a jacket and tie when the men went out for lunch). There was now a woman writer (me), and several new young male writers were forthrightly Jewish. Besides Grunwald, there had been a few Jews on the writing staff in the '50s, but they'd seemed to me less comfortable in that WASP environment.

One subject I didn't discuss with my colleagues was Vietnam, not even on the evening when I shared a cab home with John Gregory Dunne, who seemed to remember that we'd worked together in Business. I knew that Dunne was now in the World Section, and was presumably well-informed about Vietnam. Still, all I recall us discussing were how he'd decided to quit, and was getting married. We didn't discuss why he was quitting. Somehow I knew that my willingness to tolerate the war in Vietnam was a minority position, though Fuerbringer was a hawk, and favored pursuing it (the terms "hawk" and "dove" with relation to Vietnam already being in use by 1964). I also imagine that *Time*'s most faithful readers would have been likely to agree with him, and, though the public at large was dissatisfied with how the war was going, polls showed it expressing contradictory opinions on what to do about it.

The polls were not invulnerable to criticism. In the '60s, people often disagreed with what they said, and Michael Wheeler's *Lies, Damn Lies, and Statistics* (1976) described many ways that pollsters did fail to report public opinion accurately. Wheeler said that the Gallup polls had been accused of a Republican bias, while the Louis Harris polls were accused of a Democratic one, but that fellow pollsters liked George Gallup and disliked Harris, and that in some ways, Harris's polling techniques were even less reliable than Gallup's.[120] Harris only commenced publishing the Harris Survey in 1963, but his polls have received more attention in books about Vietnam. One that appeared in March 1964 showed that 35 percent of those queried favored the establishment of a neutral government in South Vietnam, and only 28 percent opposed this step, but 56 percent also favored continuing to resist communism there, and only 18 percent disagreed (in both cases, the remainder were "not sure").[121]

At least one younger historian has wondered why we ever got involved in Vietnam, and implied that public opinion didn't support such an engagement.[122] Such an impression can be supported if one studies only opinion polls that specifically mentioned Vietnam, and were taken during the war itself. Most such polls were divided, and even when a majority supported the war, there were still a sizeable number of negative responses, but, in my opinion, these responses didn't necessarily mean that such people were opposed to the war on principle. As Korea (and more recently, Iraq) have shown, Americans lose interest in wars they don't appear to be winning, and Halberstam wasn't the only newsman reporting bad news about the conflict in Vietnam almost from the moment it hit the headlines in the United States.

If one studies Gallup polls taken prior to the conflict and dealing with communism in general, it's easier to believe that a reservoir of anticommunist sentiment in the United States initially rendered the conflict in Vietnam more palatable than later polls would indicate. Gallup conducted few polls about communism per se in the later '50s and early '60s, but he did several in the later '40s and early '50s that indicated many Americans were concerned about it (even making allowances for his Republican bias). In 1949, the largest number of those interviewed (if not necessarily a majority) a) felt that the House Committee on Un-American Activities should not be done away with; b) approved of the law requiring labor union officers to swear that they were not communists before they could take a case before the NLRB; c) didn't believe that a man could be a good Christian and also a member of the Communist Party, and d) disagreed with the idea that Party members should be allowed to teach in schools and universities. True, America is not and never has been monolithic. Whether or not liberals of the '40s and '50s were opposed to the spread of communism abroad, millions of them felt that American Communist Party members, like every other citizen, had a right to their beliefs. Senator Joseph McCarthy never enjoyed majority status in the Gallup polls. Still, 38 percent of those interviewed as late as 1954 had a favorable opinion of him (46 percent had an unfavorable opinion, 16 percent no opinion at all).[123]

Gallup's polls indicated that the U.S. public as a whole was much less concerned with communism abroad, but that it was still an issue. A majority of those expressing opinions in 1949 felt there was nothing the United States could do to keep China from going communist, but a poll taken the next year still showed that the largest number of those interviewed felt the United States should send military aid to Chiang Kai-shek. Another 1950 poll showed that 71 percent of those interviewed felt the United States should help West Germany build up an army equal to that being created in East Germany, while 72 percent felt the United States should also help the Japanese build up an army in case the communists attacked them.[124] Even in the '60s, the spread of world communism remained one of the "most important" problems facing the United States today, according to a handful of Gallup polls (though it was fourth or fifth on the list). As late as 1969, 54 percent of those interviewed thought communist China should not be admitted to the United Nations.[125]

Given these statistics, it becomes more understandable that the containment of communism enjoyed bipartisan support in Washington through the '50s into the early '60s. Republicans liked to accuse Democrats of being "soft" on communism, but if they could make their charges stick, they might have a campaign issue. Lord knows, *Time* did what it could to scare up support for the cold war, but even Democrats who read only *The New York Times* could still find major stories up until 1963 that showed communism on the offensive. Both the *Times* and *Time* covered the Hungarian rebellion in 1956. While the paper's coverage was more restrained than *Time*'s, it agreed with *Time* in its essentials. When Fidel Castro was still a guerilla up in the hills, the *Times* sent a reporter, Herbert L. Matthews, to interview him, and Matthews was impressed. *Time* sent a writer, Sam Halper, and Halper, too, was impressed. Only after Castro had taken over Cuba in 1959 did both publications learn he was more doctrinaire than he'd said he'd be, and the *Times* wasn't any happier about it than *Time* was. As late as 1961 and 1962, the *Times*'s reportage on the erection of the Berlin Wall and the Cuban missile crisis had been consistent with *Time*'s, and continued to suggest the advisability of resisting communist aggression. When the United States was going into Korea in 1950, the *Times* had editorialized, "Korea is not a faraway and unimportant country. It is every country which is or may be threatened by a Communist attack."[126] Though this sentiment may have been less passionately felt by many Americans in the early '60s, it was still far from extinct.

Not only did many Americans thus perceive a need to fight in Vietnam, but I don't think they seriously considered the possibility that United States wouldn't win. It had won its independence from Great Britain in the Revolution, and defended it in the War of 1812. It had defeated the Mexicans in the Mexican-American War of 1846–48. It had defeated the Spanish in 1898, in the Spanish-American War. It had won big in World War I, bigger in World War II, and although the Korean conflict wasn't a victory, it couldn't reasonably be called a defeat. This was history that people all over the country had learned in school; most had lived through some of it themselves.

My fellow writers were more conscious of the unsatisfactory situation in Vietnam, and even while I was still writing People, I gathered that most of them were already doves, favoring less, not more, involvement. Their hero was Grunwald, who (though editing World in seemingly complete accordance with Fuerbringer) was said to be calling in the corridors for "more enlightened coverage of Vietnam." The Real Intellectual was said to be on the side of the angels in the cultural battles, in favor of proposed covers on the Beatles and Rauschenberg. When you combined these positions with his reputation for favoring opportunities for women, you got a formidable campaigner building a massive power base. His chances to succeed Fuerbringer had been enhanced by the departure of Tom Griffith. Keogh was nominally in line ahead of him, but nobody I talked with expected Keogh to rise any higher than he had.

For one thing, Keogh had no pictorial sense, and even if Fuerbringer didn't like pop art, he understood the visual as a whole. Unlike Milestones, People used photographs, and he'd tear photos from the papers, and send them to Daniels for me to do People items on. I learned he liked pictures of beautiful women looking their best, pictures that were easily readable and well-composed. I think already I'd heard it said that he had "an eye," and learning to see pictures as he did helped me develop my own. It got so that sometimes I could spot a photo he'd ask for before he did.

I'd asked Bob McLaughlin, my mom's old friend, to read *Jubilo*, because he'd had a play of his produced on Broadway. He liked my play, too, but no producers wanted to put it on Broadway (and again, as a major leaguer,

I looked down on off Broadway). In the summer of 1964, I wrote a comedy about a summer group house in Quogue. Its heroine was Harriet (named for the heroine of the Lord Peter Wimsey detective stories, or so I thought at the time). She was a glamorous free-lance writer, as I wanted to be, and came out for a weekend with an IBM salesman whom she was hot to marry. His housemate was a stockbroker whom I patterned on Fred Freund, though I named him Harry after another college boyfriend. Harry and Harriet had been pals when they worked on a business newsletter together, and naturally, they wound up together, but McLaughlin didn't like this play, so I put it away, too, and concentrated on turning out heartwarmers for People with as much wit and wordplay as I could muster.

Puns and double-entendres were so much a part of the '60s. The prudery of the '50s was evolving into the license of the '70s, and the burgeoning desire to say more than what was generally acceptable found expression in many situations. Both *Newsweek* and *Time* had done those stories on the coded messages in pop music. Both wrote about Shirley Polykoff, who, to promote Clairol hair coloring, dreamed up the most famous double-entendre in advertising, "Does she or doesn't she?"[127] I also perceived double levels of meaning in the great English plays that I saw on Broadway, starting in the later '50s. The bitterness of the lower classes was expressed by Jimmy Porter in John Osborne's *Look Back in Anger*, and the emptiness of former imperial glory by Archy Rice in Osborne's *The Entertainer*. With Harold Pinter's *The Caretaker*, it seemed to me that the sick old man, Davies, embodied the weakness of Britannia, while the two younger men, Mick and Aston, were Russia and America.[128]

I loved the great English films whose mood was shifting from grim to lighthearted. *Room at the Top* and *Saturday Night and Sunday Morning* had somber lower-class heroes, played by Lawrence Harvey and Albert Finney, but Finney became cheerful in the rollicking movie version of *Tom Jones*. Also droll was *The Knack*, with Rita Tushingham playing a naive young lady come to the city to learn about sex. Many of these movies I saw with Anne Stewart FitzRoy, who'd replaced Shirley as my roommate in 1963, when Shirley went back to Boston. Like Carolyn Mullens Harford, Fitz was a Briton, but mod not trad, with high boots, "dolly dresses," and British English that enabled her, with a laugh, to classify Finney's accent as "Narth Coontreh" (North Country) and "frightfully pleb." She worked for a company making TV commercials and told me over breakfast how Richard Lester used devices he'd learned doing TV commercials in the United States when he directed *The Knack*.

In People, I learned I might use double levels of meaning without knowing it. This happened with an item about Jane Fonda making a movie directed by

Roger Vadim. I knew the two were lovers, but the item I wrote was obscene. I thought I was using harmless colloquialisms, and Daniels edited the item without noticing its blue overtones, but Fuerbringer spotted them. He called Daniels, who pointed them out to me, amazing me at my unconscious prurience (the double-level verb involved had been "having").[129]

Occasionally, a secondary level of meaning was used for legal purposes. In 1965, James T. Aubrey "resigned" from the presidency of CBS-TV, and our Show Business section scheduled a story. Apparently the brass at CBS, the parent corporation, had wanted for a while to fire Aubrey, but one incident made them dismiss him immediately. According to the story circulating on our office grapevine, Aubrey had gotten rough with a pretty lady at a party – so rough that he'd broken her arm. I don't know whether or not this story was true. All I can say, on the basis of what I heard, was that Fuerbringer believed it and wanted to publish it, but no rock-solid source would confirm it, and our legal staff was warning him that without such confirmation we might be sued for libel. Finally, a senior editor started joking about it and handed Fuerbringer the line he needed. Our article ran, "CBS suddenly discovered it needed Aubrey like it needed a broken arm."[130] This told insiders that we'd heard the story, left outsiders believing we'd merely used a colloquialism, and Aubrey with no grounds for litigation.

Like Milestones, People was a training section. Eventually I'd graduate from it. One evening when Daniels and I were hunting up a cab to share back to our homes, he asked where I'd like to work next. I said, Nation or World. Both sections were large enough so that I might get covers, but I didn't want to say this because I was afraid it would make me sound too single-minded. My long-range ambition was my own back-of-the-book section, where I could establish myself as an authority on a subject, and write covers on it that might lead to a book or a job elsewhere. Covers were the only articles big enough to interest outside editors, but I was pretty sure that as a female without a cover on my record, I'd never get my own section. Instead, I'd be made second writer in a larger back-of-the-book section like Modern Living, and never get any covers.

I couldn't ask to be a floater, because they had to work with many editors; some, like Jamieson, might be opposed to women writers. I couldn't ask for Business, as he was still editor there. I didn't want Hemisphere, because I was afraid that if I only worked for Daniels, people would start saying that we were sleeping together. This was already hinted of Josie Davis and Grunwald, though he was short, bespectacled, and (to use his word) pear-shaped, while she had a very attractive husband.[131] Top management (by this time, Hedley Donovan) was most likely to meddle in Nation, so I suspected it would be considered too sensitive to trust to a woman, but World was edited by

Grunwald, who had such a reputation for helping women that working for him would mean nobody would believe I was competent in my own right. If I said World, it would look like I wanted such preferential treatment, and since I didn't, I had to say, Nation or World. "So you want to play with the big boys, hunh?" said Daniels.

In late February 1965, Fuerbringer invited me to a dinner party that he and his wife were giving on a Sunday. Another writer and his wife gave me a lift to the Fuerbringers' large house in Greenwich, Connecticut. The party was in honor of the Bangkok bureau chief and his wife. The guests were all fellow employees of Time Inc., with wives (if married). As I recall, the house had Ming vases and/or a Tang horse, anyway chinoiserie appropriate for a high-ranking Luceling. The dinner was formal, men alternating with women at the tables. After it, Mrs. Fuerbringer led the ladies upstairs for coffee and dessert in a smaller room. I was the last to use the john there, and emerged to find her alone, picking up coffee cups. She congratulated me on my new job in World. This was how I learned I had it.

After dinner, the Bangkok bureau chief offered me a lift back to town in a limo provided for him, his wife, and Eric Pace, a witty young bachelor from the Hong Kong bureau also visiting New York. When we reached my neighborhood, Yorkville, I asked to get out. Eric got out, too, to take me for beer at a brauhaus. The week I started writing in World, he would ask me out for another nightcap. This one was at the Stork Club, where he told me that Joe Ferrer was going to marry Penny Oster. Since my feeling for Ferrer had faded, I wasn't hurt, but I was afraid I'd acted like a fool. True, I hadn't chased after Ferrer like a dumb young researcher, but my silent suffering must have been evident. I realized there had been signs that the couple were seeing each other, but oblique ones, probably because Oster had wanted to keep the romance private.

Extramarital relationships in the office were being conducted much more openly by the '60s than they'd been in the '50s. Oster and I had discussed one, when we'd gone out for a sandwich. A, a married writer, she said, was carrying on with B, an unmarried researcher. Since A was Jewish, and B was a German woman, the notion of A screwing B struck me as poetic justice, but Oster hadn't felt that way. "You see them coming up together on the elevator, and you know just where they've been," she'd said, as I recall it. I know she used the word "tacky," and I imagine she felt that such situations gave office romance a bad name. All the same, I said to myself in the Stork Club, if I hadn't wanted to believe Ferrer was unattached, I'd have realized what was going on, so let me not delude myself again.

Keogh confirmed I was going to World the Tuesday after Fuerbringer's party. Grunwald had also said so riding up in the elevator that morning. He added he'd been in favor of it. I said I was looking forward to working with him. You won't be, he said: he was leaving World to start a section called Essay. My senior editor would be Ed Hughes, already sitting in for him. Saturday night, I went around to introduce myself to Hughes, whom I found in his big senior editor's office. I remembered that Marion Pikul had told me his wife had died (though I wouldn't be working with Marion in World, as she was going with Grunwald to Essay).

Hughes was a widower, then, and quite presentable: in his early forties, not tall, but trim. From one of the bottles distributed on nights we went to press, he offered me a drink and asked what countries I wanted to write about. I said England, because I was an Anglophile, and South Africa, because I'd dated a man from there. Hughes had been in the Johannesburg bureau and started rhapsodizing about it. Silas Haynes came to the door, probably to ask about picture captions. He'd been made a senior editor, overseeing those special color photography projects. When he saw us talking, he smiled his saturnine smile, and said something like, "Oh, so *that's* what's keeping you." Gossip linking myself with Hughes was obviously starting already.

7. On the Office Battlefront
(March 1965–January 1966)

WHAT COMES NEXT, the Bangkok bureau chief had wondered, in the limo back from Greenwich. "More escalation, I suppose," was what I recall Eric Pace having said. "Escalation" was much used, to describe the U.S. response to the continued inability of the South Vietnamese armed forces to expel communists from their midst. On February 7, Lyndon Johnson had begun bombing North Vietnam. On March 8, my first week in World, the first U.S. combat troops went ashore in South Vietnam. Henceforth, American boys would be getting killed in open, increasingly bloody battles.

World's office layout was the stage on which the next mini-drama of this narrative would unfold. It resembled that of Daniels's sections, but my cubicle was at the end of the narrow inside hall. Next to me was Jason McManus; on his other side sat John Blashill, and Robert F. Jones just beyond. After Jones, the inside hall met another narrow hall which led, on the right, to the central corridor, and, on the left, to the windowed (but door-less) cubicle of Nancy McD. Chase, the World head researcher. Beyond her was Ed Hughes's office, and elsewhere were two more offices used by World writers, among them Bob McLaughlin, but I was rarely aware of their presence.

I was conscious of McManus, Blashill, and Jones. All three were tall, good-looking men about my age, and of Northern European Protestant extraction (to the best of my then knowledge). McManus and Jones had been born in 1934, and Blashill was only a few years older. All three had been raised in the Middle West, and worked as correspondents in various bureaus before coming to New York to write. All were married, with young children. I didn't know Blashill or Jones, but I had known McManus around 1960 in Business, when he'd been a writer there and I was still a researcher. He was a clean-desk type, with crisp white shirts and close-cropped hair, clever and funny but with decency and earnestness underlying surface wit. In Business, he'd told us a funny story about how, as a Rhodes Scholar, he'd eluded the dorm proctors at Oxford, but he'd also loaned me a collection of short stories that included a moving one he'd written about a college student who'd dreamed of becoming a minister. Already in 1960, McManus had friends on "the publishing side." This made me think he must be adept at office politics and ambitious to get ahead. The Shavian in me admired this. McManus would rise through the ranks until, in 1988, he'd become editor-in-chief of all Time Inc. publications, the job which by that time had been held only by Luce, Hedley Donovan, and Henry Grunwald (McManus retired in 1994).

At my first World story conference, I noticed how young and idealistic these three writers appeared, contrasting with the hard-bitten veterans I remembered from when I'd been on the clip desk. The researchers also seemed younger and prettier. True, I was nine years older, and far more inculcated in *Time*, but I think the section had changed somewhat, too, if only in response to the world it wrote about. Since 1956, China had split with the Soviet Union, so instead of attacking everything communist, we now operated on the principle of "divide and rule," occasionally saying nice things about Russia and countries in its orbit, as the lesser of two evils.

The writing was cooler and more direct, without the ham-handed anticommunist propaganda so common in the '50s, but the stories were still built of the same twenty-line paragraphs I'd used in People. Three or four made up the average story, seventy lines – or one column – long. The section combined hard news stories about politics and military actions with features on social or cultural phenomena. My first week, Hughes assigned me two feature stories, both about women.[132] He sent what I wrote through with minimal editing, but only military and political stories normally led to World covers, so features were dead ends, especially features about women.

I had two weeks of vacation coming up, and knew that World writers sometimes visited the countries they wrote about, so I decided to see if I couldn't establish a claim to political stories on some country or countries by visiting them. I didn't think I'd ever be asked to deal with military encounters (nor did I want to), but I thought I could handle politics. Most countries were already divided up among the other writers. McManus and Jones did the Vietnam stories, and McManus also wrote about France and Great Britain. Jones handled communist bloc stories, and some on developing countries. Blashill wrote about Spain and Africa, while McLaughlin did most of the Middle East.

Outside of Europe, the status of women was so low that I'd never be accepted by the locals, but no other writer appeared to handle West Germany, so I asked McManus who did. He said they all did, and they all hated it, because Hughes had been the section expert on it before he'd become editor, and rewrote every story (he'd been in the Bonn bureau after Johannesburg and before he'd come to New York). I didn't like the idea of being rewritten, but the country would have an election in the fall. If Willy Brandt, leader of the opposition Social Democrats, ousted Chancellor Ludwig Erhard, leader of the Christian Democrats, we might do a cover on Brandt.

I'd have time to visit one other city. In London, I knew people whom I could fall back on if the bureau didn't cooperate. Besides, I was still a passionate Anglophile, so I decided to go there. Hughes was startled when I told him my plans, but after he checked with Keogh, told me the company would pay for my plane fare. He alerted the bureaus to book hotels for me and show me around. Before I left, he took me to lunch, and listed the famous people I should be interviewing. I tried to decide if I was attracted to him, decided I wasn't, and was rather relieved (I would also wind up charging all of my trip expenses to the company, except for the day I spent skiing in St. Moritz).

Murray J. Gart, the London bureau chief, didn't suggest any interviews I could conduct by myself, but Honor Balfour, the bureau's Parliamentary correspondent, took me to the House of Commons, and another correspondent took me to a press briefing at one of the ministries. Gart took me to dinner with Barry Farrell, a correspondent from the Paris bureau visiting London to research a cover on Rudolf Nureyev. Gart's wife was still in Chicago, as he'd only recently been transferred from the Chicago bureau to London. Farrell had recently been sent to Paris and had previously been a writer in the New York office. He was in love with Marcia Minns, a researcher in New York. Gart, Farrell, and I went to a gourmet French restaurant, then on to the Ad Lib, which they said was the disco of the moment. Couples were doing the hip-juggling frug on the tiny dance floor, the young women in skirts far shorter than any I'd seen in New York. On my right sat Gart, telling me how his wife could still get into her wedding dress. On my left sat Farrell, saying he wished "old Marcia" were there. This was my first experience of "Swinging London," as sinful and wicked as one of my grandmother's church suppers.

The city looked prettier and more prosperous than when I'd seen it in 1949. Tulips and daffodils bloomed in parks, flower beds, and flower boxes. I noticed many young people, stylishly dressed, strolling in pairs along Oxford Street. At a dinner given by one of Anne FitzRoy's friends, I was told that Prime Minister Harold Wilson was carrying on with his secretary, and about some hot boutiques – where I later bought a Gerald McCann dress and Foale & Tuffin trousers. Over the weekend, I visited my friend Carolyn (Mullens) Harford and her husband at their home in western England.

On to Berlin, where I took a bus tour around East Berlin, and the *Time* stringer drove me around West Berlin. With his wife, a stringer for a Washington paper, we went to dinner with other American reporters. My next stop was Bonn, then capital of West Germany. The bureau chief did little beyond taking me to a cocktail party where a reporter from *The New York Times* glared at me and said he didn't approve of women reporters. Another correspondent in the *Time* bureau had been stationed in Africa, where he'd run across Tony Lukas, my long-lost stepbrother. This Bonn correspondent's wife had gone to high school with my college boyfriend Harry. It seemed that in Bonn I was meeting up with many friends of old friends. Thanks to an introduction from one of my mother's friends, I had an interview with the U.S. ambassador to Bonn. The bureau's economics correspondent and other women in the bureau filled me in on local politics and economics. Back in New York, I wrote a memo to Hughes about what I'd learned from the ambassador, and started getting West Germany political stories. I also got a few political stories about the UK.

In June, Hughes took a week off, and Mike Demarest sat in for him. Demarest was now officially a senior editor, but still filling in for vacationing regulars, without a section of his own. In 1963, I'd been impressed with his use of the word "ponce," but I'd learned more about him when he'd sat in for Daniels in 1964. He'd told a group of us at dinner how his parents had divorced, and his father moved to England. Then the father kidnaped Mike and his brother and put them in English public schools. I thought it must have been tough, growing up without a mother, but he'd gone on to Oxford, and was very much the English gent, with an Establishment accent, polished manners, expensive English tailoring, and an editing style that included plays upon Anglicisms (he was particularly fond of variants of "old hat," such as "*vieux chapeau*").

Also in 1964, he'd told me how, earlier that year, he'd revisited England, and, on the basis of what he'd seen, written an interoffice memo to Fuerbringer, arguing we should do a cover on the Labor Party's Wilson. Demarest had predicted Wilson would unseat the Tories in the next election because a bloodless social revolution had taken place. He'd been right, but Labor's majority had been slim and other major events had occurred that week, so Wilson had been only one of four people on the cover, and the article on him was condensed. I'd always liked the Labor Party's Socialist heritage, but given Luce's dislike of government "interference," plus Hedley Donovan's background on *Fortune*, *Time* never liked speaking kindly of Labor. Other *Time* covers on Wilson had referred to British socialism as "more Methodist than Marxist" and said that Wilson's favorite word was "pragmatic."[133]

I'd had no problems with Demarest in 1964, and he started his week in World by asking me if my Gerald McCann dress was English and complimenting me on it, but he rewrote my stories more than I considered necessary, and, instead of asking me for a new version of one story, took the files for it into his office, and rewrote it himself. I was glad my permanent editor was Hughes, who let me write my own new versions. It wasn't like I had a "feminine" style of writing. This I learned, at a company party, from Roy Alexander, the former managing editor now working on the executive floors. He'd tried to guess which World stories I'd written but had to get up the carbons from the morgue in order to find out. I was also beginning to learn that Josie Davis and I weren't the only women writers *Time* had ever had. Over the years, I'd hear about more and more women who'd done it. While researching this book, I found that a woman, Anna North, had written a cover story for *Time* during World War II, when so many men were in the service. In 1965, nobody remembered her; virtually all my predecessors except Davis had been shoved out of corporate memory or maligned by it.[134]

Over the summer, I'd been doing the stories about the West German election campaign, but when Erhard was reelected, my chance for a cover there ended. In July, a crisis developed in Greece when handsome young King Constantine dismissed Premier George Papandreou, and, despite demonstrations by angry students, tried to form a new government without him. I was writing these Greece stories, so I proposed a cover on Constantine to Hughes. He passed the idea along to Fuerbringer, and a cover was scheduled, but then other crises erupted, and that cover was dropped, too. While working on those Greece stories, though, I developed more insight into Vietnam. I didn't read the stories on the fighting there, sure that a mere female wouldn't be asked to write any. I knew that they supported the U.S. involvement, but neither McManus nor Jones, who wrote them, talked about them much in my hearing.

God knows, these weren't stories in which puns and humor played a role, so they weren't passed around on Saturday evenings, when the section's writers and researchers gathered in Nancy Chase's office to have a drink, unwind, and find out what Fuerbringer had given a "good" or an "ah!" to that week. During the week, I was occasionally conscious of the vehement indignation felt by a beautiful, platinum blonde researcher. She checked a lot of the "Nam" stories, and I remember her exclaiming angrily about the bad taste Fuerbringer had shown by running a shocking photograph. McManus wasn't happy about how we were covering the fighting, either, but he didn't say anything about it to me, beyond once mentioning that he'd been so concerned about how Fuerbringer had edited a Nam story that he'd stayed until after Fuerbringer left on Saturday night, then altered the galleys.

Sometime that spring, I asked McManus what was really going on in Vietnam. As nearly I can recall, he said, "It looks like a war we can't win. With that long, undefended border, there's no way we can stop the North Vietnamese from keeping on trucking in supplies over the Ho Chi Minh Trail...." Maybe if I'd known more military strategy, his words would have been less effective, but as it was, they told me why the situation in Vietnam wasn't like Korea, as I'd been assuming. The Korean conflict had been capable of a more or less successful resolution because Korea is a peninsula.

South Korea's northern boundary, at or near the 38th Parallel, runs across the peninsula: the U.N. forces could extend their battlefront clear along it and fight a conventional war.

South Vietnam occupied only the eastern edge of the Southeast Asian peninsula. Thus, the communists could always send men and materiel from North Vietnam on down the peninsula by the Ho Chi Minh Trail, which ran through Cambodia and Laos. Then they could attack the U.S. and South Vietnamese forces from behind their lines in guerilla operations, and guerillas are harder to combat than the enemy in a conventional war. The only way the United States might have stopped the enemy from using the Trail was by carrying its offensive into the rest of the peninsula, but such an action could have brought China and possibly the Soviet Union into the struggle, with World War III ensuing on a nuclear as well as global scale.

Since the United States didn't choose to risk this, it was condemning itself to a no-win situation, as authors more knowledgeable than I am have maintained more recently.[135] In 1965, it wasn't as clear. *Time* had discussed the Trail in two stories when it was becoming apparent that North Vietnamese troops had joined the South Vietnamese guerilas, the Viet Cong, in the fighting.[136] Since then, however, this topic had given way to others, while the fighting remained just as inconclusive and the number of American soldiers in Vietnam kept mounting. Halberstam's disquieting experiences in Vietnam had been incorporated into his first nonfiction book, *The Making of a Quagmire*, written in 1964 and published in 1965. In it, he'd discarded withdrawal of the U.S. presence and the neutralization of Vietnam as options, thereby suggesting that the least unpalatable course open to the U.S. might be the commitment of ground forces – though he was obviously unenthusiastic about the prospect.[137]

In 1963, his dissatisfaction had been shared by Charles Mohr of *Time* and Neil Sheehan of the UPI. By the time I got to World, Halberstam had been assigned to Warsaw, and Mohr and Sheehan were covering Vietnam for the *Times*, along with A. J. (Jack) Langguth (another Harvard alum who'd been on the *Crimson* with Halberstam and Tony Lukas).[138] In private, Mohr, Sheehan, and Langguth may well have felt as McManus did, but they weren't saying so in the *Times*. The paper also published Hanson W. Baldwin, a stateside military analyst who made the case for more escalation, and its Sunday magazine carried many articles discussing pros and cons of the war. A Sunday magazine article by Langguth, in September 1965, vividly described how awful things were but stopped short of calling for a pullout. In another Sunday magazine article, in October 1966, Sheehan's descriptions were equally devastating, but his equal ambivalence was summed up by the title: "Not a Dove, But No Longer a Hawk."

Jason McManus read the *Times* (as we all did). He told me he also read *Newsweek*, saying that he thought its war coverage "more intelligent." Since *Newsweek*'s way of covering the war resembled that of the *Times*, and differed equally from ours, this wasn't anything he could afford to proclaim, inside or out of the office. Looking at *Newsweek* more recently, I can see why McManus considered it so intelligent. Many *Time* stories can be cited to show that for the larger part of the period from 1965 to 1967, our magazine continued to back up LBJ.[139] *Newsweek* was implying subtle dissatisfaction with the Administration as early as January 1965, by stories with titles like "Vietnam: Where Will It All End?" and "The Deadly and Perplexing War." The magazine may not have claimed that the war might be unwinnable, but it emphasized problems more than did *Time*.

Both magazines ran covers about the bombing of North Vietnam in February 1965, but *Time*'s (top-dog) cover gave the story from the top down, with a cover portrait of General William C. Westmoreland, commander of the Vietnam forces, and a lede describing the National Security Council meeting in Washington, with Johnson arguing his case for bombing.[140] *Newsweek*'s (underdog) cover photograph showed a staff sergeant, one of the U.S. "advisers," on duty with South Vietnamese soldiers in a rice paddy in Vietnam. *Newsweek*'s lede described the arrival in California of the coffins of dead soldiers, and wounded soldiers strapped to their litters.[141] Both magazines used pictures of the flag-draped coffins, but *Time* used a smaller, black-and-white photo in the middle of a text page, while *Newsweek* reproduced its image in color, full-page size.

In August 1965, with the United States fully committed to the ground war, *Newsweek* started a new section, The War in Vietnam, which combined news from Vietnam with stories on related developments in Washington and elsewhere. This section occasionally ran in front of the National Affairs section, and almost always before other foreign news, ensuring maximum readership. Fuerbringer continued to use *Time*'s Nation section to deal with developments relating to Vietnam but taking place in the United States. Stories about the fighting were shunted back and forth between Nation and World, with lesser ones buried in the less prominent World section. Sometimes they ran in the middle or at the end of World, where readers were least likely to see them.

Time gave statistics that showed heavy enemy casualties; whenever it could, it indicated how they vastly outnumbered those of the United States.[142] Whenever it could, it also emphasized U.S. victories or "progress."[143] *Newsweek* reported it when enemy losses outweighed those of the United States, but suggested that these statistics were unreliable, and that the military failed to release them when American casualties were high, or that it under-reported U.S. casualties.[144]

With *Time*, whatever modest measure of representative government that war-torn South Vietnam could achieve was seen as a major accomplishment.[145] *Newsweek* reported it when South Vietnam's government acted democratically, but also dealt with how unrepresentative, ineffective, corrupt, and dictatorial its leaders were.[146] *Time* reported that the Vietcong used terrorism and executed civilians. In May 1965, its Nation section carried a story giving Pentagon statistics on village chiefs and other civilian officials killed or kidnaped. The story was illustrated with the gruesome photograph of a beheaded and mutilated Viet Cong victim that seems to have been the one that the beautiful blonde so much disliked.[147] Other stories would echo the same theme.[148]

Newsweek reported Vietcong terrorism.[149] But it concerned itself more dramatically with the cruelty and destructiveness of the war, running one photograph of a U.S. plane dumping napalm, and another at full-page size of a peasant woman holding her child and wailing in anguish over the burning of her home.[150] After one battle, both *Time* and *Newsweek* said the enemy had executed prisoners, but while *Time* added one had been left hanging head down from a tree, *Newsweek* (in two places) reported that U.S. soldiers had also executed enemy prisoners.[151] (This was an early, still-isolated example of an atrocity committed by U.S. soldiers. Most major stories dealing with them didn't break until the latter part of the war. News of the My Lai massacre, for instance, didn't reach the public until November 1969, although it took place in 1968. Stories about soldiers "fragging" officers by throwing hand grenades at them, and stories about the widespread use of drugs in the military, also mostly date from these later stages of the war, especially after the U.S. began reducing troop levels in Vietnam – a policy that, however necessary, was very hard on morale.)

Neither magazine was lying. Each was merely selecting those facts and ways of presenting them that appeared fairest and most meaningful to its editors. *Time* reflected Fuerbringer's optimistic conviction that the war could be won, and his resulting desire to pursue it (an outlook that Donovan, at this juncture, still shared). *Newsweek* reflected its editors' more pessimistic view of the war. Reporting on U.S. victories strengthened the hand of those arguing that the war was being won, and emphasizing the murders of South Vietnamese civilians by the enemy bolstered the case for keeping on with the war. Contrariwise, reporting on the destructiveness of American troops strengthened the hand of those arguing the United States was doing more harm than good, and emphasizing that Saigon was undemocratic reinforced the idea that its government didn't deserve and couldn't take advantage of U.S. support.

The outcome of the war shows that *Newsweek*'s coverage between 1965 and 1967 was more on target than was *Time*'s, but, since I wasn't reading *Newsweek*, I didn't know this. And, even if I had been paying closer attention to the war, I wouldn't – at that stage – have found newspapers, magazines, TV, or radio commentators agreeing with McManus's assessment. *Time* has been attacked for backing the war, but it wasn't the only publication still doing so at that point, nor was it out of step with the electorate. According to Harris polls taken in mid-1965, 32 percent of those polled thought the United States might not be able to win in Vietnam should it become a big war, but 62 percent continued to endorse LBJ's way of dealing with it, and 79 percent felt that South Vietnam would lose to the enemy if the United States didn't back it up.[152]

I know McManus's opinion about the war sank in with me because I was reading about ancient Greece, and seeing upsetting parallels between it and Vietnam. I'd heard that Plato badmouthed democracy in classical Greece, and since democracy in modern Greece was giving Constantine a hard time, I'd gone to the morgue to look for zingers from Plato to use as epigraphs for my stories. His dislike, I found, was evidently based upon history as originally recorded by Thucydides, the sad story of the later Peloponnesian wars: how Athens, the world's first democracy, tried to conquer distant Syracuse, on the island of Sicily. The decisions that led to and carried on those wars were made by popularly elected leaders of the Athenian city-state, but Sparta, a dictatorship, came to the aid of Syracuse, and Athens not only lost the wars, but her independence. Lyndon Johnson had been elected President in 1964 by a landslide, and by voters who mostly continued to support his Vietnamese policies. (Nor, I've since learned, have the parallels between Thucydides and Vietnam escaped the attention of other observers. Though I was far from alone in this insight, I achieved it on my own.)

The heartland may have been behind LBJ, but in my corner of the country, protest was already looming. An authority on the Students for a Democratic Society, which would play a leading role in the protest, has pointed out that in January 1965, the SDS was already calling for a major antiwar protest in April.[153] Still, the *Times* paid scant attention until after Johnson's bombardment of North Vietnam in February showed how the war was escalating, and the paper didn't begin to deal at length with the protest until March, after U.S. combat troops had gone ashore. This timing reflected the fact that Americans didn't really get emotionally involved in the war until American casualties started to grow. Some young people were already critical of U.S. society, and on March 15 the *Times* front-paged a long, sympathetic article by Fred Powledge about "the Student Left," but the second half of the article merely only mentioned rather vaguely that leftist organizations like the

SDS were planning demonstrations on issues other than civil rights, including "conscription" and "the war in South Vietnam."[154]

The first antiwar protests covered by the *Times* in detail were faculty "teach-ins," reported on March 25 as having begun at the University of Michigan and, in later stories, spreading to many other campuses.[155] On April 11, the paper gave Page One coverage to Dr. Benjamin Spock, the 61-year-old baby doctor, leading three thousand protesters in a rally at the United Nations.[156] A week later, a still bigger demonstration, organized primarily by the SDS, took place before the White House, drawing a crowd estimated by the *Times* at more than fifteen thousand. It made Page One on Easter Sunday.[157]

During the year which followed (up to April, 1966), the *Times* ran dozens more protest stories. Besides marches and rallies on Page One, many smaller stories on inside pages dealt with student activities: with the onset of the ground war, young men on many campuses were becoming increasingly aware that they might be drafted. The paper also reported opposition from clergymen, pacifist organizations, and religious groups; academics and intellectuals; artists, writers, singers, and actors; lawyers and scientists; military men and politicians ranging from candidates in local primary contests on up through the Senate and United Nations to foreign leaders. In December 1965, the Pope's Christmas message was front-paged. It called for "sincere negotiation" on Vietnam.[158] There were "read-ins" by poets and intellectuals, fasts and immolations, reports on study groups and editorials in professional journals, as well as full-page advertisements. The ads were signed by long lists of people, some distinguished, others members of an occupation or organization. They were sometimes accompanied by news stories about them, a practice that the *Times* didn't follow for ads of department stores or automobiles.

In November 1965, *Newsweek* ran a cover story on "The Demonstrators: Who? Why? How Many?" The cover photograph showed young faces, and the Top of the Week referred to "the angry young men who have decided that they do not want to fight for their country – at least not against the Viet Cong."[159] Included was a separate box, offering droll advice on how to avoid the draft, at least partially facetious.[160] The magazine had also run an article on the student left, in the wake of Powledge's article on the same subject, and it published many others related to student discontent, including a takeout on the draft in December 1965, and a cover on the same subject in April 1966.

Still, it conceded that many students supported the war, and that, while the protest cut across all ages, it was still numerically small. The *Times* agreed on the small size of the movement, and was even more likely than *Newsweek* to emphasize that a cross section of American society was protesting. Covering the march in Washington over the Thanksgiving weekend of 1965, Max

Frankel (b. 1930) wrote that it included "more babies than beatniks, more family groups than folk-song quartets," and a sidebar by John Herbers was entitled "Typical Marcher: Middle-Class Adult."[161]

When forced to deal with the protest, *Time* emphasized that dissent was one of the privileges of democracy. It coined "Vietnik" to refer to the youthful demonstrators, an insulting term that didn't stick, and expressed its feelings about them in an Essay in October 1965 called "The Vietniks: Self-Defeating Dissent." Among adult protesters were two people I'd grown up with, Ed and Elsa Bley. In later years, Elsa would mention that she and Ed had demonstrated in Washington, and while researching this book, I found Ed's name among many others in one of those full-page ads in the *Times*.[162] Still, I can't recall either of the Bleys talking about Vietnam with me while I was in World (or for a long while thereafter). The only personal acquaintance whom I recall raising the subject was Alice Mayhew, a woman in book publishing whom I'd met at Quogue. She suggested lunch, then asked angrily over the meal about *Time*'s Vietnam policies.

Over the summer, I'd moved into my first elevator building, on East Seventy-ninth Street. My share of the rent was $107.50, but as a writer I could afford it. My new roommate, Thelma Stevens, was a Southern gentlewoman with a neat sense of humor. During this period I was also (briefly) dating Eric Pace (b. 1936), who'd left *Time* and was reporting in New York for the *Times*. Eric told me that when he'd quit, Bob Jones had taken him to lunch, and tried to talk him into staying. Jones had told Eric about his house in the country, with an apple orchard and a trout stream. "It's like the Garden of Eden in Upper Westchester," I recall Eric as saying. "And the Jewish wife," he went on, referring to Jones's college sweetheart. "Why would anybody like that want to work for *Time*? He's so *normal*." Why would Grunwald want to work for *Time*? was Eric's next question. "Henry's a real intellectual," he added (if memory serves correctly). "The kind of guy who takes Renata Adler to lunch" (mentioning the *New Yorker*'s latest star reporter). My response just popped out. "I don't know," I said, then asked, "The power?" I hadn't known I felt that way until I said it, yet once it was out, I believed it true.

Maybe it was a footnote in our March 12 issue, saying that the Chinese foreign minister had been carrying a copy of *Time* with his portrait on the cover when meeting with the president of Pakistan.[163] Maybe it was the top officials who lunched with the editor and writers of World in the executive dining rooms atop the Time-Life Building, but whatever it was, I'd begun to suspect (oddly enough, for the first time) that *Time* might be influential. Obviously, Grunwald, with his politicking, loved power, but Jones, too, struck me as powerful, if only because of his looks and stamina. Stockier and more muscular than McManus, he'd written a cover on India overnight, sixty lines an hour, napping on the couch in Hughes's office, like a truck driver pulled over to the side of the road.

In October, my standing in World began to deteriorate, though it happened so gradually I didn't realize it at first. Hughes gave me a story on Rhodesia, whose prime minister was threatening to leave the Commonwealth rather than accept integration. This situation had cover potential, but when it escalated, Hughes gave the stories to Blashill. Blashill got the cover. I didn't blame him. I liked him. We were usually alone in the World offices on Thursday evenings, and he'd sit in my office and chat. His wife sounded like a firebrand. He described going to a P.T.A. meeting with her, where he was introduced as her husband. After he left my office, I'd write one story. Going home, I'd pass his door, and see him, staring at the paper in his typewriter with at most one sentence on it, but when his stories did get written, they were complex and funny.

Next, Hughes assigned me a review of a memoir by a Russian spy. Before I'd written it, he took it away, saying Books was going to do it. Then it came back to World, but he gave it to Blashill. Indonesia's president, Sukarno, had stayed in office for years by playing off the military against the communists, but earlier in the fall, a supposedly communist group had attempted to staged a putsch against top generals, and claimed control of the country. Other military leaders had speedily put down this movement.[164] They were now engaged in mass slaughters of communists, making Sukarno's position increasingly tenuous. If he were replaced, the new leader would be worth a cover, but as far as we in New York could see, no one had yet emerged who could be our cover subject. Again, I got to do two stories, but later ones went to Blashill.

In November, Silas Haynes sat in for Hughes for a week. He didn't edit one story he assigned me, and killed the other in makeup, so I was "aced out of the book" for the first time since I'd become a writer. In mid-December, Hughes rewrote a Poland story I'd written, though I'd done a new version. As Christmas approached, he gave me a story about the Ginza in Tokyo, where Japanese businessmen drank in nightclubs with hostesses. Before I could write it, he killed it, then a week later revived it, and assigned it to Blashill. Over New Year's, I went to ski at Stowe with a friend. There was no snow, but the lodge had *The Death of Kings* (1954), a novel by a former *Time* correspondent about a newsmagazine. Its editors made coarse remarks about the anatomy of a researcher, resembling the attitudes toward women shown in the Ginza story, which I also read in Stowe. Blashill and Hughes made it sound like those nightclub hostesses doubled as hookers.[165] Also at the lodge, my friend ran into a friend who asked me if I knew Hughes. Her brother knew him from Yale, she said, adding significantly that Hughes was a widower. She thinks widowers are better marital bets than divorced men, I said to myself, but she doesn't know Hughes. I thought I did.

The previous spring, I'd had a phone call from Susan Griggs, stepdaughter of John Fistere, my mother's boyfriend circa 1939. Susie's husband Lee had replaced Hughes in *Time*'s "Jo-burg" bureau; then they'd divorced, and she was back in New York, working on a non-Luce magazine. I'd asked her to dinner, and she'd told me a story about Hughes's wife, which she'd heard from a reporter who'd covered South Africa for the *Times*. As best I recall it, Susie said that after Hughes and his wife split up, the wife got involved with a man who dumped her, and she'd killed herself. Dr. G called suicide an expression of anger turned inward, a way to get the last word in an argument. It was meant to make survivors feel guilty, but left them angry. Was this so with Hughes? Was he venting his unconscious anger on me, as I was the woman he saw most?

When I returned to work Tuesday after New Year's, McManus told me he'd left his wife and was getting a divorce. At first, I was shocked, but soon realized I really liked him. I'd only allowed myself to experience those "friendly feelings" for him that Dr. G approved of, but by Thursday, I was thinking how much nicer, funnier, and smarter he was than many men I'd gone out with simply because they were single. I'd been drawn to him all along, but repressed the feeling because it was neurotic to get involved with a married man. That evening, Blashill came to my office to chat and dropped an oblique remark implying that McManus might care about somebody else.

The next evening, I heard McManus, in his office next to mine, repeatedly dialing the same four digits that indicated an interoffice phone call. The first digit was a few clicks, followed by two with more clicks, then one with a lot. When the right person answered, he said one quick, laughing French word or phrase, *"Alors!"* or *"Alors donc!"* Whomever he was talking to knew his voice so well that he didn't have to identify himself, and his own voice was so joyful that it was clear he cared about this person very much. I hadn't intended to eavesdrop, but I had to know if there was somebody in his life so I wouldn't make a fool of myself, as I had with Joe Ferrer. By reasoning too convoluted to recapitulate, I deduced that the person McManus had been calling must be the beautiful blonde researcher who'd been so angry about our Vietnam coverage. She was now in Modern Living, but I could see how she and McManus might have come to care for each other through working with each other, just as feelings had developed between Bob Christopher and myself, back in Business. I looked at the staff list. The blonde's extension was 3780 or 3870, anyway something that fit the clicks I'd heard.

Hughes had been particularly infuriating at Tuesday conference, giving me the worst stories on the list. Did I deserve this? I went to the morgue, and got out the carbons of all my World stories, comparing them with those of McManus, Blashill, and Jones. During my first six months in World, my copy had been edited more heavily, so the printed stories carried only 76 percent of my prose, as opposed to an average of 90 percent for the others, but I'd been asked for fewer new versions, on only 38 percent of my stories, compared with 90 percent for the men. I thought my troubles might have begun when Silas Haynes had sat in for Hughes. Had Haynes implied to Hughes that Hughes was favoring me? Was Haynes sour on women in general? (I'd come to suspect that his marriage was not going that well.)

"Why can't you write for other sections?" Dr. G said. Asking for a permanent transfer would be a confession of failure, but Grunwald's new section borrowed writers for individual Essays: if I could do one of those, it might make Hughes think twice. In several third-world countries, a democracy had recently been overthrown by an enlightened military, so I sent a suggestion about this to Grunwald. "Nice suggestion," he said, when he passed me in the corridor, but that was it. "Why can't you write for some other magazine?" Dr. G asked, next. I called Mitchel Levitas, an editor at *The New York Times Magazine* who'd written at *Time*, and, when he was leaving *Time*, had invited me to call him. He asked me to lunch in the *Times*'s dining room, but when I suggested an article on the enlightened military, he said something like, "That sounds like a great idea for Essay. Why don't you suggest it to Henry?" I was so mad I began to cry, though I knew men hated women crying, and dashed for the ladies' room back at my office when I couldn't hold back tears. Next day, I called Bob Christopher, at *Newsweek*, and made a lunch date with him for the following week. I was angry enough to join the enemy.

8. The London Cover
(January–April 1966)

MEANWHILE, HUGHES WENT on a two-week trip through the Latin America bureaus. The first week he was away, Bob Jones sat in for him. Most of what I knew about Jones was that he'd won many "ah!s" and that he lived in the "Garden of Eden in Upper Westchester" with the Jewish college sweetheart wife (given my background, I welcomed the Jewish). Though he wrote many of the Nam stories, I hadn't heard him criticize *Time*'s position on the war. I had heard the beautiful platinum blonde joke about his being a "Ho-lover." Maybe this was when we did a cover on Ho Chi Minh that said Ho was responsible for a land-reform program which had eradicated "perhaps as many as 100,000 peasants," and added, "Still the survivors love him."[166]

Jones liked hunting. In Nancy Chase's office, he'd told us how in the woods, he'd seen a doe drinking from a pond. She'd raised her head to gaze at him, and, he said, "I found myself thinking like a buck – you know, that's one hell of a good-looking doe!" Jones had looked irked while Hughes and I were talking to each other at Thursday "rescheduling conferences," when writers estimated the length of their stories. I'd assumed at the time that he was irritated by my talking angrily to Hughes, but now I thought, Maybe he feels I should be getting better stories.

On Tuesday, he gave me the best story I'd had in months. In Moscow, two writers, Andrei Sinyavsky and Yuli Daniel, were being tried for sedition because they'd published "underground" satires. Jones thought the story important, too. At rescheduling conference, I asked for seventy lines, but he insisted on ninety. When I started to write it, I realized I hadn't prepared enough, letting myself get careless because I'd been so angry. Even before editing, Jones had taught me this. I did what I could, but he called me into his office for a new version, and asked if I'd had any other ideas for a lede. I mentioned one. He listened, then proposed a better one, reading aloud from wire copy quoting Radio Moscow's report on the trial. It sounded like a satire Sinyavsky or Daniel might have written, beginning with a phrase that Sinyavsky had actually used as a book title, and that Jones would use as our two-hed: "The trial begins...."[167]

We worked out the rest of the story, and I got up to leave. At the door, I turned and asked how long the story should be. As best I can remember, he said firmly, "Don't worry about the length. Just put it all in." I got it. *This* was what he'd wanted to say, all along, and why he'd been irked in Thursday conferences. I'd been worrying about the length, meaning what Hughes wanted, instead of what *I* felt needed saying. "Put it all in" meant be more aggressive, use *my* ideas. Back in my office, I started to write, and found that I was learning to write all over again. The story took on a life of its own, pace and climaxes pouring out of the typewriter almost by themselves. Jones liked what I wrote, but it still wasn't long enough for him. He added more, and sent it to Fuerbringer at about a hundred and forty lines. Then he proposed a crash cover for the following week on Sinyavsky, with me to write it. To my relief, Fuerbringer rejected the idea.

All thoughts of looking for a new job had evaporated by the time Christopher and I lunched the following week. He spoke of Ed Jamieson, the senior editor who, besides thinking women were too emotional to be *Time* writers, was reputed to be one of few men on the masthead always faithful to his wife. Christopher said that he'd heard that Jamieson thought he was being railroaded off *Time* because Fuerbringer at New Year's had taken him out of Business, and made him a swing editor. Jamieson sat in for Hughes that week, and scheduled a China story. There was no news to report, but he was lunching with Hedley Donovan, who as Luce's successor might like a story on China. After lunch, Jamieson dictated many ideas about the story to Jones, who as the section expert on China was writing it, but Jamieson still asked for a new version. I was standing in Nancy Chase's cubicle when a copyboy arrived with the flimsies of the edited NV, one for her and one for Jones. He took his, I took hers, and we stood reading them. Jamieson had rewritten the entire story, producing the sort of heavy-handed propaganda World hadn't used since the '50s.

Glancing at Jones, I realized that he was furious. He said nothing, but his arm, with the shirt-sleeve rolled up on it, almost quivered. Then he dropped the flimsy like it had bitten him and walked away. I could have told him Jamieson was feeling insecure, but I didn't say anything, because suddenly, I felt that he and I were a bit too close. The week he was editing had done it, the way he'd turned me around, and because I'd realized that I'd been attracted to McManus when he'd still been married: I could no longer so easily repress any other attraction I might feel for a married man. I was still benefitting from Jones's help, applying the same aggressive approach to the stories Jamieson had assigned me, and though Jamieson had given me one new version, on the whole he'd accepted my copy and sent it through. It would be the same with all my editors after that. I still got edited, but much more lightly, and I still had new versions, but much less often.

I was grateful to Jones, but didn't want to be attracted. The evenness with which he'd treated me told me he respected women and convinced me he must have a good marriage, so there was no future for him and me together. He had two small children and seemed to care about being a father. Still, he might get into an office affair, not because he meant to, but because the pressures of the job promoted it. We worked so hard, and in such proximity, that the people we worked with came to seem more real to us than anybody else, better at understanding us than spouses. Jones must have thought he only wanted to help me with my work, but I suspected this was self-delusion.

When I'd been in Milestones, I'd lunched with a Business researcher whom I'd known when I was in Business. She'd told me how Z, one of the nicest writers in Business, had gotten involved with the researcher who'd replaced me, an ambitious young woman who wanted to become a correspondent. In his innocence, Z, too, had imagined that he only wanted to help her with her work, but before he knew what was going on, they were (said my informant) "doing everything but lying down in the corridors together." It wrecked the man's marriage, but he hadn't stayed with the researcher. I visualized Jones and myself, cooped up in a Manhattan apartment for reasons of finance, both of us plagued by guilt and anger. This wasn't my idea of marriage, so I muttered a few words to him that, I liked to think, warned him off.

Back from Latin America, Hughes assigned me his usual lousy stories. Two Brazilian LPs of bossa nova arrived in my in-box, with a note that read, "A souvenir of *carnaval*." I slammed them down on my windowsill, thinking why in hell couldn't he have given me something I wanted, like a decent story? I wrote the lousy ones so well he sent them through with only light editing. Next week, I got a slightly better story, and did a good job with that. Saturday, I had late duty, greening and writing picture captions, so I went with Hughes to "picture conference," where he and the pictures editor chose photos to be used. Hughes made little jokes, glancing now and then at me.

The following week, I got three decent stories. The first was about a student protest in Cuba, where Castro put the students to cutting sugar cane. How appropriate for a woman, I thought. Aren't women interested in children and young people? I wrote it Thursday night at seventy lines, though Hughes had put it on the list for fifty. Friday morning, he showed me how to cut it, but appeared happy and put in a pun for the two-hed, "Caning the Students." My other stories also made me feel I had something special to contribute because I was female. One dealt with a woman charged with spying in Canada, the other with the wedding of Princess Beatrix in the Netherlands, where more young people called Provos were protesting because she was marrying a

German. Saturday, I came into the office to read my flimsies of the edits. Hughes had sent the stories through almost exactly as I'd written them. At that moment, I discovered (or thought I discovered) that Hughes was in love with me, and I was in love with him.

He'd been so sad when I wrote badly and become so happy when I wrote well. Gradually, I thought, we'd grown closer through the three writers in the offices between us. Eric Wagner, the IBM research mathematician whom I'd dated fresh out of college, had told me that computers were made of interchangeable bits, and I'd often visualized *Time* as a giant computer, with writers and editors interchangeable bits. First, I'd known McManus, then become friendly with Blashill, finally developed a rapport with Jones, and, when Jones sat in for Hughes, all the bits had meshed. I was as charming as I could be to Hughes for the rest of the day. He seemed to keep on getting happier. I played his bossa nova records over the edit weekend. The following Tuesday, in story conference, he gave me what I perceived as a scorching glance and assigned me the story I wanted most: Indonesia, where events were building to a climax. After a six-month campaign to eliminate the communists, the generals were consolidating their power, and one, Suharto, was emerging as the leader. We finally had a cover subject.

For the third time in two weeks, I was dealing with youth. The generals were being supported by crowds of youngsters demonstrating against Sukarno, but the story also involved military activities, and they made me uncomfortable. I was glad when Hughes told me what he wanted in the NV, and particularly admired how he then rewrote the lede, putting it in the imperfect tense: "Ever so politely, yet ever so firmly, Lieut. General Suharto, 45, the new strongman of Indonesia, was stripping President Sukarno of his last vestiges of power...."[168] I read the other flimsies, and admired how Hughes edited them, too, letting McManus go his own way, giving Blashill the push he needed, and reveling in Jones's bold style. Hughes let himself be carried away by the forcefulness of one of Jones's stories, and a draft went through that I knew was longer than it should have been. Fuerbringer asked for a shorter new version.

Saturday night, Hughes and I discussed an Indonesia cover. On Wednesday, he proposed it at the senior editors' weekly "cover conference." It was scheduled for two weeks after that, to give a correspondent time to get into the country, and me, time to read background material (a week's lead time was usual with covers, and writers who'd never done one could get as much as a month). Hughes was still acting happy and being nice to me, but he hadn't asked me out for so much as a drink. I told myself it was because he was my editor, and it wouldn't be fair to the other writers for us to establish a personal relationship. As soon as the Indonesia cover went to press, I would ask for a transfer. I'd wanted back of the book all along, but a transfer took on new urgency because then (I thought) Hughes could date me up.

The next Tuesday, I drafted cover queries. Blashill, McManus, and Jones were guffawing as they concocted an April Fool's Day story together. It was based on an article in an African magazine about the garrison stationed at the private zoo created by Kwame Nkrumah, Ghana's deposed leader. The soldiers were killing and eating the animals in the zoo, and the three writers made up a story about this with dozens of puns on the names of wild animals. Boys will be boys, I thought, but they sent it on to Hughes, who edited it, adding puns of his own. Around six or seven PM, I finished the queries, and left for home. The only other person in the down elevator was Jamieson, who said that I was working late. I said I'd been writing the Indonesia cover queries. He said something like, "That's interesting. You know, I may be editing that cover." "I didn't know," I said. Jamieson told me Hughes was going on a six-week trip around the world, and, though I acted like this made no difference, I knew it did. Hughes had told me Fuerbringer wasn't wild about the cover. The m. e. was going along with it because he himself was pushing it. I suspected that if he wasn't around, the cover would be postponed, then killed. I didn't think Fuerbringer would trust Jamieson to edit it. Normally, if a cover was written by a writer who'd never done a cover, the section's regular editor worked with him. Visiting editors were teamed with experienced cover writers, but a neophyte writer and a visiting editor? Not likely.

I'd come to World to write covers, but been disappointed with West Germany, Greece, and Southern Rhodesia. If I didn't get Indonesia, I might never get any, but it would be an admission of feminine weakness to go to Hughes. If he'd ever asked me out, I might still have gone, but as it was, I had to conclude that, to use Dr. G's phrase, he was (in terms of a personal relationship) only a "fantasy man," so I wrote an interoffice memo to Fuerbringer that night. It was him I wanted to hear from, anyway, whether he was serious about letting me do covers the way other writers did. I said I'd learned from Jamieson about Hughes's trip, but still wanted to do the Indonesia cover. Since Jamieson wasn't the regular editor, my ideas might be more important than they would have been if Hughes had been editing. I outlined three ideas: first, the strategic significance of Indonesia; second, its natural beauty, making it a possible future tourist destination; third, how children and teenagers were helping to force Sukarno out, just as young people had been making history in other stories I'd worked on: Greece, Cuba, and the Netherlands. Knowing how Fuerbringer felt about American youth protesting the war, I doubt that I mentioned them, but I'm sure they were at the back of my mind – as well as his.

Wednesday morning, I put the memo into the interoffice mail. Late Thursday afternoon, Hughes called me to his office, and said something like, "You're going to write a cover, but not Indonesia. I want you to imagine yourself picked up and flown halfway around the world, to London." A travel cover on London had been scheduled in Modern Living, but Fuerbringer had decided to run it in World, and thought I might like to write it. I was grateful, and knew that even Jamieson could edit a travel cover. I was also afraid that I'd made Hughes look bad with Fuerbringer, but I'd had no alternative, and Fuerbringer wasn't making it easy. The cover was scheduled for the following week. We had nine days to get it researched and written.

Instead of the usual lengthy cover suggestion, all I had to start with were memos dashed off by members of the London bureau in January, when a senior editor had been visiting from New York. A group had lunched together, and the idea dreamed up in what a creativity consultant might call a "brainstorming" session, but the memos were mostly short, thin and vague: pretty girls, short skirts, not much else. I had ideas based on English plays and movies I'd seen, my two English roommates, my two trips to London, and the literature and political commentary I'd read over the years. That evening, I bought LPs of British rock groups, took them home and played them. Next day, I wrote the cover query to the London bureau, leading it by the hand, as Bob Parker had taught me.

Pretty girls and short skirts were fine for Modern Living, I thought, but a World cover should get below the surface to show why this was history. Though I tried to dress stylishly, writing about fashion bored me, so whatever I might say about it and the tourist appeal of London, my story would also deal with politics and society. For the cover design, a British artist, Geoffrey Dickinson, had been commissioned to assemble a mixture of London sights, and my cover query asked the bureau to supply vignettes showing how life in London was being lived. I requested statistics and scholarly interpretation, documenting (or contradicting) what I saw as the major trends behind the phenomenon. The beauty of group journalism was that I could use the bureau to test my theories.

Remembering the young people I'd seen in London, I believed this was yet another situation where a new generation was playing a key role. I knew the birthrate in the United States had skyrocketed after World War II; I thought it likely the same had happened in England. I believe I'd first learned about U.S. birthrates in Business, where after successfully suggesting a story on the Mattel toy company, I hadn't been able to get one on a church pew manufacturer off the ground.[169] Mattel had been riding the crest of the baby boom, while in the '60s, the pew maker was still only benefitting from smaller increases in the population as a whole.

The idea that the younger generation was playing a key role in London may appear obvious today, but it was much less so then (especially within *Time*). Our culture has developed a picture of the '60s as synonymous with youth and revolution. We often see it as the decade when a generation gap opened between the baby boomers and their elders, when youth overthrew the Establishment in art, music, lifestyles and above all, politics, forcing the United States to withdraw from Vietnam. There are elements of truth in this appealing image, but like all popular images, it has only coalesced with the passage of decades, the blurring of distinctions, the telescoping of time sequences, and the elimination of experience that doesn't coincide with the observer's preferences. To the extent that this image is true, it's truest of the end of the decade, when Theodore Roszak and Charles Reich were writing their books about it, but in April 1966, the varied aspects of the youth culture hadn't yet come together. The London cover would help to meld them and create the image (though many other writers contributed to it, too).

As I said earlier, for this book I've gone back to *Time* and the *Times* for these years, to see how I might have been influenced by them (I've also read *Newsweek*, to see what I couldn't have been influenced by). All three publications were interested in young people and aware of their growing numbers, but (in retrospect) the ways that they dealt with them were piecemeal and sometimes contradictory. On the *Times*, education reporters viewed with approval the idealism of the current generation of students, and the large numbers expected in colleges and universities, but business reporters wondered if the job market would be able to absorb all the high school students when they graduated.[170] Business and fashion reporters gloated that the purchasing power of the young was boosting sales of everything from cosmetics to greeting cards, but a correspondent covering Hollywood for the *Times* was so fed up with the plethora of movies for teenagers that he was delighted to be able to report on an "anti-teenager" movie.[171]

As I've also said, the *Times* had tended to present the antiwar protest as an expression of all age groups, but its serious style allowed it to convey the outlook of younger demonstrators more convincingly than when it handled stories about the more frivolous aspects of youth. Long hair on boys, short skirts on girls, and rock 'n'roll were already well-known symbols of youthful rebellion, but the *Times* still treated them with amused condescension. It headlined the prevalence of girls among the Beatles' shrieking fans when the group visited New York, and its Sunday magazine carried arch articles by women decrying the "little girl" styles that no adult female could wear.[172]

Nowadays, the paper deals calmly enough with oral sex and vaginal dryness, but in the '60s, it was still abiding by its slogan "All the News That's Fit to Print" (to say nothing of our catchphrase, "the good gray *Times*"). The slogan had been adopted in 1897, to distinguish the paper from the yellow journalism that dominated newsstands at the time.[173] But, by the 1960s, the news coming out of police stations and discos could have redeeming social value, and rated treatment that the paper wasn't yet prepared to give it. Hair styles and dress fashions were confined by the *Times* to its glorified women's page. Pop music would acquire more importance than the *Times* could adequately address, and younger people who had been treated as not yet capable of mature judgment would have to be accorded more respect.

As I also said earlier, *Newsweek* had focused to a greater degree upon the younger antiwar demonstrators than the *Times* had. It was less condescending on topics of special interest to younger people, and employed a lighthearted approach in stories about the lifestyles of the young, for example on how long was too long for a boy to wear his hair.[174] The magazine ran one cover story on "The College Generation Looks at Itself and the World Around It," in March 1965, and a second on "The Teen-Agers," in March 1966. Both included extended Harris polls of their subjects, but both still focused on a wholesome, all-American type of youngster, not the terrifically hip or politically involved. Both cover photographs showed a blonde, natural-looking young female dressed in very conventional clothes. The college student was even making a fashion statement out of the '50s: she was wearing a sweater with a white Peter Pan collar, just like the "dickeys" we used to wear at Barnard, to create the illusion that we were nice girls who wore blouses beneath their sweaters. The teenager was a little more the image of a nice girl gone excitingly bad: she was riding a motorcycle.

Time also thought it had a stake in the young, especially the college-educated. Its ads in the *Times* boasted about how many of its readers were college-educated, and touted its College Student Edition.[175] The magazine was competitive with *Newsweek* in lighthearted stories about youth: it, too, did one on how long a boy's hair should be.[176] *Time* ran a cover in January 1965 about a California high school class that seemed as carefree and wholesome as the girls on the cover of *Newsweek*. When confronted with adolescent discontent, however, particularly antiwar protest, *Time* took positions that its editors doubtless thought mature and adult, but that, especially in retrospect, sound patronizing and unsympathetic. One Essay in December 1965 was titled, "On Not Losing One's Cool About the Young."

By April Fool's Day of 1966, when I was writing my cover query to our London bureau, neither *Time*, *Newsweek*, nor the *Times* had really integrated the different angles of the youth story, combining the significance of population statistics with the pop culture that young people espoused, and the social revolution they represented. The *Times* was furthest away, because it categorized stories – as either education or business news, for instance

– and because of its primness. The newsmagazines were more attuned to synthesis, at any rate in cover stories, and *Newsweek* had come closest in its covers on teenagers and college students. Even *Time* had shown a bit of awareness in a few of its Essays, but *Time* was impeded by its conservatism, and *Newsweek* inhibited by its conscientiousness. It's tantalizing to see how its cover on teenagers, published weeks before my London cover, deals with its subject in the same detail that I tried for, yet never organizes its details into a comprehensive whole that would enable it to draw conclusions with real impact.

The media were beginning to discuss generational conflict in the U.S., but from what I could tell, nobody yet used the term "generation gap," and, though "baby boom" had been in use since the '40s, neither *Time*, *Newsweek*, nor the *Times* yet spoke of "baby boomers." The closest anybody on these three publications had apparently come to suggesting the social and political implications of the rising tide of youth were Russell Baker, in two of his humorous columns for the *Times*, and James Michener, the novelist, in an article about rock'n'roll in the *Times* Sunday magazine.[177] In the first of Baker's columns, he'd reported that, since over half the population was now under the age of twenty-six, a "new minority," i.e., grownups, had been disenfranchised in radio, publishing, fashion, movies, and TV. In the second, he discussed the man with a "middle-aged teenager" for a son who wanted to keep his hair short, preferred the foxtrot to the frug, and insisted his father's generation had done things right.

When writing my query, I must have been at least subliminally aware of what the *Times* and *Time* had written, and of the need not only to incorporate their insights, but go beyond them. After asking for statistics on the youth in London, I went on to the second and third aspects of the situation as I saw it: I believed the new leaders in London society were more apt to be from working-class backgrounds, and from parts of Britain once deemed unfashionable – the industrial Midlands, what my British friend, Anne FitzRoy, called the "Narth Coontreh." These ideas were suggested by rock stars like the Beatles, actors like Michael Caine, Peter O'Toole, and Albert Finney, and the recent social evolution of England, as Mike Demarest had laid it out in that interoffice memo proposing a cover on Harold Wilson in 1964. The week I was writing my cover queries, Wilson was winning his second election, and by a much wider margin than he'd had in his first. Conveniently forgetting that Socialism wasn't *Time*'s favorite brand of politics, I borrowed Demarest's memo from him. Besides its emphasis on youth, the cover would also deal with politics and pop culture.

I claim only partial credit for the inclusion of pop culture, since much of it developed out of the original intention to make this a travel cover, with advice for tourists on where to go and what to buy. The bureau supplied this without my asking for it (Fuerbringer may have added a request for it to my query). One contribution of mine was the presentation of "Swinging London" as a single, unified phenomenon. It was an early example of my tendency to synthesize different, even opposed aspects of a situation, but this tendency was enhanced by my experience of a newsmagazine, with the cover story also including the input of the London bureau, Jamieson, and even Fuerbringer. It was a collage, pastiche, composite, or synthesis of words and ideas contributed by many people. This made it group journalism at its finest, a.k.a. collaborative creativity, but my own input would include memories of personal experiences as well as professional ones. I'd done a bit of this before, but I'd never felt as passionately about it, and, as my CPA once told me, the line between personal and professional activities isn't always firmly drawn with creative people.

The best idea in those memos from the bureau came from Peter Forbath, a cool, sharp, younger correspondent. He'd said that every decade had its city, and London was the city of the '60s. My query to London asked him to expand on this idea, and I sent shorter queries to bureaus in the United States and on the Continent asking whether their sources agreed with it. I took the queries to Hughes, who carried them to Fuerbringer. Later, Fuerbringer stuck his head into Hughes's office, where I was sitting, talking. "Looks like you've got the cover written already," he said, or something like that.

Back in my office, I thought about how the whole huge organization was being galvanized into action. Correspondents were gathering information, photographers shooting a color spread. Millions of people would read this cover, but I thought I was writing it for one – Hughes. Since the magazine would go to every correspondent he'd be visiting, I figured he'd have to read it, and I wanted to use it to cheer him up. His dead ex-wife had been English, and I visualized her as a Deborah Kerr type, old-style English, but I wanted to show him that there were newer, less neurotic Englishwomen around. I felt that everybody in the section knew how he'd let me down, and was sympathizing with me. Blashill told me how much he liked the Beatles, and how much Jones liked them, too. He asked if I'd heard their latest song, and sang a few bars of "Nowhere Man." I felt he was saying that Hughes was the real nowhere man.

On Tuesday, Jamieson said everything would be all right – I'd have my picture in the Pub Letter, and get lots of marriage proposals. Files from outside London were coming in, agreeing London was the new "In" spot for U.S. teenagers and European media. As the London files hadn't arrived, and it was my birthday, I was going to the theater with my mother and Bill Herwood, her longtime lover and latest husband. Toward the end of the day, Bob Jones stuck his head inside the door of my office, and said something like, "Come on, I'll buy you a drink, and tell you how to write a cover. Fifteen minutes." We went to Eddy's, a restaurant on West Forty-Eighth Street that stank of beer and cigarette smoke, but was favored by many of the writers, I suppose as a no-nonsense drinking place (the menu didn't go much past burgers). Jones and I sat across from each other at a table, and he said the most important thing to have was a lede. I said I had one, Forbath's idea about London as the city of the '60s.

Jones said before I'd come to World, England had been one of his countries. It wasn't a fussy, Victorian sort of place, he told me, but real he-man country, as it had been back in Elizabethan times, with lusty country lads and lassies tumbling in the hay. I noticed he had a bandage on one finger, and asked how he'd done that. He said he'd been clearing land for a new co-op kindergarten for his son; the co-op president, Eric Wagner, had said he knew me. "Sure," I said, "I used to date him." Jones said, as nearly as I can recall: "I can't see the two of you at all. He's middle-aged, and you're young." How nice! Truly, the years had rolled back for me since I'd started on *Time*. I'd been so world-weary as a senior in college, but starting afresh as a writer, and moving from section to section, had kept me open, and staying open was staying young.

Wednesday, the files from London started to come in. Murray Gart had a short introductory overview, written in hip slang. Forbath had done the vignettes, and reported on the fashions, including the shops for boys in Carnaby Street, and the appropriate length for what Londoners were now calling "miniskirts" (three to six inches above the knee, though most true London minis were shorter than that). The term "miniskirt" was new to me. Honor Balfour filed on traditional London society, and Marshall Clark provided statistics and scholarly interpretations that confirmed my hypotheses about youth, the invasion from the North, and the working-class meritocracy. He listed casinos, restaurants, discos, and pubs. Horace Judson filed on the strip joints and porno bookstores in Soho, as well as theater and movies. He quoted a Tory journalist who considered "Swinging London" as decadent as John Ruskin had said sixteenth- and seventeenth-century Venice were. Jamieson stuck his head inside my door, and told me to be sure and get that good stuff about decadence into the story.

Pausing in my writing, I went downstairs to Production, to see the photographs chosen for the color spread. Silas Haynes's researcher, whom I shall call Claire Bellini, showed the transparencies to me on the light box. A tall, good-looking young woman with long black hair, she sometimes wore see-through blouses and brief, tight skirts. Prior to this assignment, she'd been in Education, where she'd very publicly gone around with the Education writer. The pictures ran the gamut. There was a City of London businessman with brolly and bowler, a park, a discotheque, a boutique, an art gallery, a mod miss in a pants suit, and a young man celebrating Wilson's most recent electoral victory by clambering into a fountain in Trafalgar Square. The hemlines of seven young women were well above the knee, shorter than I'd seen in London the year before, far shorter than street wear in New York. These women were so innocent-looking that they didn't seem indecent to me, but a photograph of a striptease was more suggestive, and, as we stood there, Bellini began to sniff.

I asked her what was wrong. She burst out, "Sex, sex, sex! That's all anybody thinks about around here!" Claire, I thought, you don't exactly take their minds off the subject, but I sympathized, too. Haynes had flown to London for the color spread. Whether he'd been touching or merely looking didn't matter. Given what I imagined his marital situation to be, he'd have been full of cutting little jokes and remarks upon his return. Going back upstairs, I mused upon Bellini's outburst, and suspected I'd have to deal in my cover story, too, with the fantasy that I'd first become aware of in Colorado in 1954, when I'd realized that the idea of faraway, free-and-easy sex was such a part of the lure of travel. I thought, the guys here will exaggerate whatever sexuality they can find in London, reflecting their own (and appealing to their readers') fantasies.

Turning into the main hall, I saw Blashill up ahead, entering the inner corridor of the section. He had the week off, but maybe he'd come in to deal with tax problems. He'd been groaning about those. I followed him into the section, and, as I walked past his office, saw him on the phone, looking happy. I'd seen him looking happy on the phone before in the past few weeks, and suddenly thought, there's only one reason a man would come into the office on his week off, just to make a phone call. Blashill had a girl. I felt as if a bomb had gone off, several floors below, but I had to ignore it, and get down to work. Fred Freund called. He'd moved to the Midwest, but we still had lunch when he visited New York. He wanted me to do a bit of research for him, but I told him that I was busy, and that, if he read the magazine next week, he'd understand.

It was eerie, barricaded in with all those files, writing the most ambitious story I'd done for publication. I remembered something Bob Christopher had said, about a feeling he'd gotten when writing covers in World: sitting on top of the world, able to see over the edge. That was how I felt, sensing how the power centers had shifted from London to New York, so that we now bore the burden of responsibility, and London had been liberated to share pleasure with its workers and its youth. For my lede, I used Forbath's idea of every decade in the twentieth century having been epitomized by a different city. Quoting from the files, I added that in the '60s, it was London, "so green with parks

and squares that, as the saying goes, you can walk across it on the grass."[178]
Next, I put in the vignettes (pausing to call my friend Fitz because I wanted
to say that they looked like the film techniques of Richard Lester which she'd
told me about, and I needed a few more details from her). In the vignettes,
Mick Jagger strolled through Chelsea; Leslie Caron, the movie star, gave a
party in her Kensington town house; and Lady Jane Ormsby Gore, whose
father had been UK ambassador to JFK's Camelot, went to a party at the art
gallery, then on to a disco with her boyfriend.

I quoted the Ruskin, but a bigger point, to me, was that losing the empire
and devaluing the pound had enabled England to regain the free and easy
spirit crushed out of it by the weight of commanding the globe. This was
my idea, not from the files. Reflecting what Jones had said, I suggested that
London in 1966 was not unlike the London of Shakespeare's day, and I quoted
the joyous song from *As You Like It* that refers to "a lover and his lass, that
o'er the green cornfield did pass." Then, echoing Demarest's memo but also
embroidering upon it, I went on to show why "Swinging London" was social
and political history: I described how the dark days of the Tory-instigated
Suez crisis of 1956 had by stages given way to a new and more democratic
leadership community in which many young and relatively young people,
from pop singers and actors to intellectuals and photographers, had come
from Britain's lower classes, yet still won national and even international
renown.

Putting together all this history was exhausting, though, and took time.
By early Saturday, I was so tired that I could only summarize the material in
the files on the theater, Carnaby Street, nightclubs, restaurants and gambling.
I did get in a key statistic that the bureau had provided: nearly a third of
London's population was in the teenage-young adult age bracket, a far larger
proportion than the national average.[179]

I dealt with the new affluence and sexual freedom, though I believed that
there was more fantasizing about what was going on than what was actually
going on. I also felt that however much easy sex there was in London, there
was more of it in America (a month earlier, *Time* had done a story about the
"free-sex movement" on U.S. campuses).[180] England wasn't as affluent as we
were, and had been so straitlaced for so long that any sexuality would seem
like a lot to it. The word "swinging" could mean promiscuous, but it could also
mean lively, fun-loving, up to the minute – and in my lede, I said that London
was swinging in both senses of the word. I quoted Jagger saying that "the girls
have become as emancipated as the boys," but I also cited a 1965 survey by the
Nuffield Foundation showing that only 20 per cent of British boys between
fifteen and nineteen had had sexual intercourse, and only 12 percent of the
girls.[181] In addition, I mentioned the naivete of *The Knack*, one of my favorite

movies. Working from the files, I described how London, with its unique combination of parkland and buildings, was more "accessible" socially than American cities. My story ended with Ormsby Gore rejoicing that the barriers between the different streams in London society were down.

The sun was rising Saturday when I gave the story to the copy desk. After a few hours' sleep at home, I returned and asked Jamieson if I could do anything to help him edit it. He said something like, "At first, I thought I was going to have to throw the whole thing out and write it myself. Now, I wish you'd take these and shrink them." He gave me the vignettes. I cut them down, gave them back to him, and got my hair done, so that I could pose for the Pub Letter. No matter what Jamieson did to the cover, Fuerbringer was going to make it look like I was solely responsible. Jamieson finished in the early evening. About 40 percent of the cover was still mine, though condensed and reordered, with phrases and sentences of his slivered in, and sizeable additions. Most of these were material from the files that I should have included, but hadn't been that interested in: the newest clothing fashions, boutiques, pubs, discos, and so on.

Jamieson deleted the Nuffield Foundation and *The Knack*. The idea that "swinging" had two meanings was deleted, too. The Jagger quote stayed, twice as salacious in isolation, and a kinky reference was added to a strip joint where an exotic dancer performed with a cheetah. This was sleaze, but the color spread had that picture of the stripper, so the story had to mention it. I could see how it and the rest of the tourist stuff were needed for a travel cover. Our readers in Rovere would want to take the story along when they went to London that summer. Jamieson changed the cover's tone. Where I'd been innocent and idealistic, he was sophisticated, worldly. Since *Time* was supposed to know the score, I felt (consciously) that I liked the whole story. In his conclusion, Jamieson wrote that London had "shed much of its smugness, much of the arrogance that often went with the stamp of privilege, much of its false pride...."[182] Fuerbringer made only two changes. He deleted a reference to "Chelsea pot parties," probably fearing it would make a negative impression on *Time*'s readers, and put in a new two-hed, "You Can Walk Across It On the Grass." Then he came to the door of my office, smiling. "Take a trip to London," he said. "You earned it."

Mary McConachie, the researcher on the story, had to finish checking it. I was worried about Ormsby Gore. We had a quote implying she was sleeping with her boyfriend, and didn't care who knew it, but I wasn't sure she felt that way. She could have said it without realizing how it would look in print. She might be a Claire Bellini, who had been seen with her man friend around the office, or she might be a Penny Oster, who'd kept her romance private, but the bureau insisted the quote was okay to use. At four AM, Jamieson and I went home in one of the company limos. As I dropped him off, I recall him as saying, "I've changed my mind. A woman can be a writer for *Time*." His generous concession should have capped my triumph, but next day, I flew to Washington for an art show by a friend of a friend. Years later, I would see this flight from Manhattan as a wish to get as far away from *Time* as I could.

9. The Response: Amateur, Ruthless Girl Agent, Harlot (1966–2006)

So many papers excerpted and/or commented on the London cover, especially in England, that *Time*'s promotion office made a scrapbook of clippings, which they presented to Fuerbringer, who presented it to Jamieson, who presented it to me.[183] I was interviewed on a local New York radio station, and letters poured in to *Time*'s Letters department, where (as usual) they were summarized in the weekly interoffice Letters Report. I expressed pleasure over how many letters my cover was getting to McManus. "Well, it's about sex," I recall his saying. "Everybody's always interested in sex." (At the time, I thought sourly that he was jealous; in retrospect, I'll admit he had a point.) Readers divided on whether or not they approved of "Swinging London." At the beginning of May, the Letters Report would say that the cover story had so far elicited 172 letters, and that 60 to 56, they'd "scoffed" at it.[184]

Heartening personal congratulatory notes came to me from two senior editors; four researchers; the publisher of *Time*; a correspondent in Los Angeles who'd been a Business writer; a woman on the publishing side whom I'd met socially; an executive at the *Saturday Evening Post* who was a friend of my mother's; Tony Egan, an adman who was the son of two of my mother's other friends; a student who wanted me to sign a copy of the issue because she was collecting signatures of people who'd been involved in writing *Time* covers; three public relations men I'd socialized with; and Fred.

Best of all was a call from Ellis Amburn, an editor at Coward McCann, asking if I'd like to write a guidebook to "Swinging London." I leapt at the chance. I couldn't leave New York for long, but I could ask one of the London bureau correspondents to round up listings of hotels, restaurants, shops, and so on, in exchange for coauthorship and half the advance and royalties. I could also say what I felt about London, which wasn't what *Time* had said – and I soon learned that other people had problems with the cover story, too. Jane Ormsby Gore wasn't a Claire Bellini. She was definitely a Penny Oster, and she was just as hurt as I'd feared she'd be. "Swinging London" sympathized. On the elevator, I heard somebody say that *Life* had wanted to give a big party at the estate of John Paul Getty, the oil billionaire, for all of those cool people, but they were so mad at *Time*, because of how it had treated Ormsby Gore, that nobody came. The Rolling Stones had a hit ballad not long after called *Lady Jane*, and I never could hear it without thinking it'd been written in defense of a lady we'd abused.

John Blashill was almost in tears, the Tuesday after the cover. He was indeed in love, with his children's au pair girl, but I couldn't deal with my colleagues' problems anymore, so I zeroed in on my guidebook. After Hughes got back from his tour, I told him I'd like to be transferred to back of the book. I still fantasized that he might ask me out, once I'd left his section, but as it seemed he hadn't even read my London cover, it was a pretty faint hope. I'd always wanted back of the book anyway, and assumed that, since I'd now done a cover, Fuerbringer would give me a section of my own.

I took the trip to London that he'd said I earned between May 28 and June 6, to research my guidebook. I got to a lot of places, saw a lot of people, and had a great time, but nobody from the bureau would help me. Forbath, whom I'd called before going to London, had agreed but got transferred to another bureau for the summer, and had to cancel. Judson turned me down after I got to London. Clark said he'd do it, but had to back out, too, after Richard M. Clurman, chief of correspondents, told him he'd be endangering his career if he worked with me. Since Clurman was presumably also responsible for reassigning Forbath, I dimly suspected that somehow, I'd gotten on his shit list, but didn't know why. Fortunately, my roommate Thelma, who worked for Time-Life Books, had an opposite number in London who agreed to do some research for me. When she got sick, she passed the job along to a freelance whom I shall call Marianne Foster. My youngest cousin, then studying at a Midlands university on a Fulbright, also did some research for me, but she wasn't (and wouldn't have wanted to be) a swinger in any sense of the word, and Foster seemed to know the with-it places.

To be sure, the two hundred dollars' worth of restaurant bills that she submitted as "expenses" was a bit much, considering the base payment I'd promised her was only five hundred, but she did appear to move with an in-crowd, and contributed some lively copy. She mentioned having gone to an art gallery with Demarest (who had since become senior editor of Nation). Amburn wanted the book in a hurry, so I wrote it over my August vacation. What I felt made it good was my discussions of hip London society, and my advice on how visiting Americans could integrate themselves into it, but Amburn wanted more listings, especially of menswear shops. I cribbed some from *Esquire*, which had begun a special issue on London before our cover appeared, but not published it until July.

In the fall, I was transferred to Books for a month. Then I was made junior writer in Modern Living, and told this was to be my permanent slot.

The senior writer there had less seniority than I did. He'd never done a cover, but since he was the senior writer, he'd get any covers scheduled in Modern Living. I complained about this to Fuerbringer. The moment he chose to give me an audience meant I missed the wedding of McManus to his beautiful blonde, but I got to the reception. My senior editor in Modern Living was Cranston Jones, a dapper gent. He also edited Art, and had written Art stories back in the '50s. His visual aptitudes were considerable, but since practically nobody else on the edit staff possessed comparable ones, his weren't appreciated, and since his writing was not that good, he was despised as a sycophant who didn't deserve his job. He was nice to me in "Mod Liv," giving me a takeout on Hawaii hotels with a color spread that required I go out to Hawaii over Thanksgiving. Alas, that gave me too much time to walk along sandy beaches and miss Hughes.

At Christmas, Fuerbringer demoted Hughes to Essay writer, and gave World to Jamieson to edit. I knew Hughes had resisted the way Fuerbringer wanted to cover West Germany, but still wondered if his demotion and Jamieson's new job might not also be a response to the different ways the two had treated me. At some point, Blashill would divorce his wife and marry the au pair. Bob Jones wrote the Man of the Year cover, on the "Twenty-five and Under" generation, at the end of 1966 for Demarest in Nation, and stayed on in Nation. He said he'd gone "stale" on World. This put McManus in line to become an editor in World, but I no longer cared about World, or paid much attention to front-page news. The grapevine would tell me if a major event occurred, and *A Swinger's Guide to London* was due for publication in the spring.

It seemed to me that other magazines were following in our footsteps. I noticed one article on London in *McCall's,* a mass-audience "women's service" magazine, and two in *Look, Life's* big rival.[185] All three took at least an open-minded view of the scene, but I'd also begun to suspect it was provoking controversy in the news media. Over the summer, I'd been asked to write an Essay about the worldwide spread of American pop culture. I didn't enjoy doing it, and did a poor job with it – I think because, on a subliminal level, it made me feel somebody had been complaining to Grunwald or Donovan that "Swinging London" was American pop culture stuffed down English throats in a display of Yankee imperialism, and that *Time's* cover on it was only more of the same. Around Labor Day, a second Essay appeared: "How the Tea Break Could Ruin England." It dwelt upon the country's economic problems, and suggested that "Swinging London" was at best superficial, at worst a sign of decay.[186] Since Essay was the closest thing to an editorial section that *Time* had, it looked like official policy was now to disown my cover.

I was haunted by a feeling that the words "swinger" and "swinging" were being used differently since our cover. They'd been popular before it, but mostly in the innocent sense. The London cover (as edited) had a bit too much sleaze for me, and I came to feel that, without meaning to, we'd cheapened and vulgarized not only London itself, but the words we'd used to describe it. For this book, I've reexamined the record. Among other things, I found that three small liberal magazines – the *Saturday Review, The New Republic* and *Commonweal* – had all endorsed "Swinging London."[187] *Business Week* condemned it, and that was fine with me, too.[188] I wouldn't have expected (or wanted) a businessmen's magazine to applaud a story about the rise of the working class. But the sadder progression of "swinger" and "swinging" I could trace in the tabloid New York *Daily News*.

A society column in the *News*, the month before my cover, was headlined, "Society: PB Swings as the Young Hold Sway."[189] The younger set at Palm Beach was staging nothing more decadent than a beer party. The paper also used "swinger" and "swinging" playfully in stories about golf swings and a boxer swinging.[190] But after our cover came out, I found more cases of the words having hard-core associations. Later in 1966, the *News* would use "swinging" (or "swingin'" or "swinger") to describe an actress known for erotic dances; a murdered woman who'd worked in a disco; and a group arrested in a Greenwich Village apartment allegedly containing heroin and barbiturates.[191] By 1969, when I was leaving the magazine, "swingers" had become synonymous with married couples who exchanged partners for sex.

Another possible sign of *Time*'s influence was the entrance of the word "miniskirt" into the American vocabulary, the adoption of the style, and the tendency to see it, too, as a sign of the "sexual revolution." Considering what a commonplace the miniskirt is now, it may be hard to appreciate the sensation it created when introduced to the U.S., but the slowness with which the top U.S. female fashion magazines picked up the term and the style itself was even exceeded by the reluctance of most American women to buy miniskirts and wear them (a reluctance that the *Times* dealt with in more than one story).[192] Studying *Vogue, Mademoiselle,* and *Seventeen* in the months immediately before and after the London cover, it looks like *Time* forced them into showing a truly short skirt, and calling it a miniskirt, just as we seem to have forced U.S. manufacturers into making it.

Admittedly, skirts had been getting shorter in America before the London cover, and much had been written about that, but, as the editors of all the fashion magazines were evidently aware, most American women were reluctant to hike their hems as high as women wore them in Europe. A month before our cover appeared, *Seventeen* had featured dresses for teenagers that Mary Quant, the top young English designer, had created for an American manufacturer, but the photographs showed their hems lowered to the same length that appeared in stories and ads about American fashions.[193] The word "miniskirt" wasn't used by *The New York Times, Newsweek, Time* (or the *Daily News*) before our cover. The first use of "mini" with regard to clothes I found in the *Times* was in a Bonwit Teller ad a month after the cover, but only for "Mini-lingerie."[194] The first ad that I found in the *Times* to use "mini-skirt" didn't appear until early June.[195]

The first appearance of "mini-skirt" that I saw in the paper's editorial columns was at the end of July. The story quoted a French designer sneering at it.[196] *Vogue* had used the word "mini-skirt" once in January 1966, but for a beach outfit, not street wear.[197] I didn't find the word again in any of the fashion magazines until the late summer of 1966 and early fall. Then it suddenly appeared in all of them (the time lag probably due partly to the fact that these monthly magazines prepared their issues further in advance than a weekly newsmagazine, and partly to the fact that the manufacturers advertising in them had to make the clothes, and get them to retail outlets).

Mademoiselle, which was written and edited for "smart young women," especially college students, used the word "miniskirt" in its August "college" issue, and several layouts featured it.[198] *Seventeen* used the term "mini-skirt" for a layout in its August issue entitled "Carnaby Street: USA." It featured the mildly masculine, vaguely kinky clothes that U.S. manufacturers associated with the London mini. "Dig the new London beat of Carnaby Street," it wrote. "How does one tell the girls from the boys?"[199]

Vogue, the haute couture magazine, didn't get with-it until its August 1 issue. Then the magazine excerpted *Quant by Quant*, a forthcoming book by the designer, and illustrated it with a photo of Patti Boyd, bride of Beatle George Harrison, in a London-length mini. Quant explained that the miniskirt appealed to younger women because they alone could wear it. "Never before have the young set the pace as they do now," she proclaimed, discussing their outlook. "They don't worry about accents or class," she wrote. "They are superbly international....there may be a chance that you can't swing a war on a generation which does not think in terms of 'us' against the foreigners...."[200]

With a few exceptions (like Paraphernalia), American manufacturers and stores still hesitated to offer the shortest lengths. Manufacturers' ads in the December 1966 issues of the fashion magazines almost all showed hemlines much where they'd been the previous January, one to three inches above the knee. Department-store ads in the *Times* in August had shown a true mini of at least four inches above the knee, but only in "college shops," and mostly in "junior" sizes (for adolescents and petite women).[201] By December 1967, the miniskirt would have caught on widely enough across the U.S. so that *Time* would do a cover story on it (chauvinistically using an American designer as its cover subject, and relegating Quant to a ten-line reference).[202] Initially, though, miniskirts were for radicals, youth, and Anglophiles in the fashion magazines and the *Times*, all of which were written primarily for the more educated and/or affluent reader.

To the less affluent and educated readers of the *News*, miniskirts suggested the depraved upper class. How immoral it had become was presented in two long articles in the *News* in April 1966, about the "Campus Sexplosion"; they discussed orgies, free sex, illegitimacy, and the decline in virginity among college students (who were still often regarded as children of the privileged classes).[203] The sexual revolution may have been further advanced than I'd been prepared to admit while I was writing my London cover story, but even Tom Wolfe, hardly a Puritan, has pinpointed the shift from propriety to promiscuity as not having taken place until the 1970s.[204] He was speaking of U.S. society broadly, and his conclusion was shared by the pollster Daniel Yankelovich.[205]

The class distinction that still existed between the abandoned upper classes and the more prudish lower middle classes shows in how the *News* presented skirt lengths in the spring and summer of 1966. It ran occasional photographs in its editorial columns of women in skirts four inches above the knee, but the women were mostly actors or models, from whom amoral behavior was expected.[206] The ads in August give a better idea of what *News* readers might buy. Expensive stores like Saks Fifth Avenue and B. Altman didn't advertise there, so there were no notices for "college shops," and Gimbel's, a medium-priced store that had promoted miniskirts in the *Times*, limited itself to more conventional skirt lengths in the *News*. The only store that I could find mentioning miniskirts there did it in an ad for the children's department.[207]

The equation between miniskirts and sex was underlined in a *News* article in August, which ended with a quotation from "a fuzzy-faced youth," saying, "You wanna know why I dig these chicks in those miniskirts? I'll tell you why. They're more makeable, that's why, man, they're more makeable."[208] Nor was this perception limited to the uneducated, or to those writing at the time. One latter-day historian of the "cultural revolution" of the '60s would cite a study on the upsurge in rape during this period, implying that miniskirts were in some sense responsible.[209] Dr. G said a man could get an erection from looking at a woman in one. Not wishing to distract my male colleagues from my professional accomplishments, I kept my daytime skirt lengths as demure as fashion allowed, but Dr. G was having trouble with other aspects of the sexual revolution, too – for instance, the increasing use of explicit language.

He associated the word "fuck" with "uck" and "muck," arguing it was healthy for a woman to be shocked by it, and a denial of her femininity if she wasn't. Likewise public nudity: healthy for a woman to be shocked, in denial if she wasn't. He'd never approved of the Kinsey Report, feeling that sex was a private thing, and that people who talked about it to pollsters were by definition exhibitionists. He disapproved of the studies in sexual behavior by William Masters and Virginia E. Johnson, whose *Human Sexual Response* was a big story in 1966, saying there was a name for people who got paid for sex. He must have felt that all society was heading in the neurotic direction he'd deplored in my upbringing, where (as he saw it) my mother's overemphasis on sex had disrupted its connections with love and affection. Though I tried to appear shocked by nudity and bad language (when I was out on dates), I was at that point less disturbed than he was, especially by short skirts and extramarital affairs, if only because so many of my favorite colleagues wore one and/or engaged in the other.

Most dismaying was the response to the London cover of the U.S. news media, both in my magazine and more liberal publications. Some of it I must have read at the time, because my guide book took into account those criticisms that struck me as valid. Some of it I didn't know about, for example *Newsweek*'s attack that July in a story on Britain's economic problems. To reinforce its argument that these problems stemmed from the failure of Britain's traditional leadership community to adopt modern management techniques, it observed that "In a curious way, 'swinging London' typifies not the modern professional spirit of the age to come but the engaging eccentricities of Britain's amateur past."[210] My first thought, when I read this, was: the Beatles, the Stones, Finney, Vanessa Redgrave, Peter O'Toole, Caine, Pinter, Julie Christie and Vidal Sassoon – all of whom our cover mentioned – *amateurs*???? My second was to wonder whether this might not be a dig at the person whose photograph had been featured in the Pub Letter, a woman writer doing a cover for the first time in living memory. Did it imply she didn't know how to write, and had just lucked out? A third thought – and it hurt – was that this passage had been written or approved by my old friend Christopher. Had he been referring to those brief kisses we'd once exchanged as my "amateur past," and suggesting that I was now a "modern professional"? Were the media so dominated by men that a woman writing a *Time* cover could be explained only by assuming that it wasn't her writing talents which had won her the job?

The first attack from the good gray *Times* was delivered in early June by Anthony Lewis, its London bureau chief. In a story headlined "Frivolity in Britain," he disapprovingly described Britons ignoring their economic problems in favor of discussions of hemlines, and mobs of Yankee tourists arriving in search of "Swinging London." "One of the things they may find is a lot of puzzled talk about what it is that is supposed to be swinging about London," Lewis continued. "Sex is probably most of it – short skirts and plays about lesbians and movies about a comic-strip character like Modesty

Blaise, ruthless girl agent in funny boots."²¹¹ The cover hadn't mentioned lesbians (though in London that summer, I saw *The Killing of Sister George*, the play Lewis meant, and liked it). Nor had the cover mentioned *Modesty Blaise*, a lousy movie that hadn't opened in the United States or the UK when I wrote the cover. Was I (again, on a conscious or unconscious level) a lesbian or ruthless girl agent? Lewis couldn't refer to the good plays and movies our cover had mentioned. It might have detracted from his case for London as economically and morally sick. This idea was continued the following Sunday by an article in *The New York Times Magazine* that suggested England was "willing to sink giggling into the sea."²¹² This article was by Henry Fairlie, a much-discussed British writer working at the *Times* that summer.

As Lewis's article indicated, part of the standard attack on the idea of "Swinging London" was that it was news to the English, and this idea was perpetuated over the summer in *The New York Times* in articles on the Beatles and Michelangelo Antonioni.²¹³ The paper debunked the "myth" again in August, when Herbert L. Matthews, by that time a member of the paper's editorial board, told how he'd visited England. Having been mostly outside of London, he reported that "There are some swingers, especially in London – young people, mainly, long-haired and short-skirted, but they are such a tiny minority...."²¹⁴

Then there were the humorists. Art Buchwald, the syndicated columnist whose flagship paper was *The Washington Post*, reported in July that when he'd visited London, the only place he'd found "Swinging London" was in our bureau, where he saw "reporters doing the Watusi with several comely researchers," and a champagne bucket on every desk.²¹⁵ Again, I wonder if this description of *Time*'s men and women drinking and dancing together wasn't influenced by the fact that a woman writer had been featured in the Pub Letter. Its writer found Buchwald's column so funny that he quoted from it extensively in one of our midsummer Pub Letters, ostensibly to show that *Time* could take a joke.²¹⁶ Satirist Russell Baker was so impressed that in November, his column in the *Times* told how he'd hunted all over in London for "Swinging London," only to be told by a Scotland Yard inspector it was merely "a handful of boys who won't cut their hair and girls who don't have the decency to cover their legs."²¹⁷

By February 1967, Baker was reporting that the outrage surrounding pop icons like Andy Warhol and Batman had died down. "'Swinging London' is a dying joke," he wrote. "We seem to have assimilated the pop-culture outburst of the early sixties, so that suddenly it all seems a little old and stale...."²¹⁸ Fortunately for his career as a humorist, that week *Newsweek* introduced the picturesque phenomenon of the San Francisco hippies to a national public (to be followed in March by *Time*).²¹⁹ But the *Times* carried one last big attack on my cover story. A British travel writer implied that *Time* had been the first American magazine to write about "Swinging London," but resented its emphasis on models, popular musicians, and showbiz types, calling them outside the moral order, obnoxious, and about as "accessible" as an "expensive harlot...."[220]

Look, the cover story wasn't perfect. Among other flaws, we'd implied "Swinging London" enveloped the whole city, enabling critics to claim that the phenomenon was composed of only a few people. True, not all London was swinging. The action was mostly concentrated in a few neighborhoods (Chelsea, Kensington, South Kensington and the West End), or at least made itself most visible there. Still, "Swinging London" was more widespread than merely its star performers. Every successful movement has followers as well as leaders, and "Swinging London" had tens or hundreds of thousands of followers within London, and millions beyond it: all the young people who bought the mod clothes, cut their hair like the Beatles or in knock-offs of Sassoon, went to the movies and less exclusive discos, bought the records, and attended the concerts.

Our treatment of youth in the cover story presented it as too squeaky-clean (not for the first time in *Time*). Fuerbringer's deletion of the phrase about pot parties pulled a discreet curtain over what seems to have been a not-uncommon practice (though again, probably no more common than it was in the U.S., where many younger people were using marijuana, as we'd also said in March 1965).[221] The whole cover was unrelentingly upbeat, reflecting my need to escape the depressive elements in my own environment at that moment. This made a pleasant change from the usual way our magazine dealt with the UK, especially under a Labor government, but the cover could have mentioned the country's (and the city's) economic problems (though I should point out that by boosting the onslaught of Yankee visitors to London, our cover probably did more for Britain's balance of payments than any sour editorials in *The New York Times*).

The reaction against the cover exaggerated its shortcomings, and was influenced by factors that had nothing to do with the cover itself. That the leaders of "Swinging London" were only a minority didn't make them any less significant. Usually, a majority begins as a minority, and advance guards exist in culture as well as politics. The *Times* and *Newsweek* had devoted considerable space to the New Left in the U.S. and student protests against Vietnam, even when both publications knew (and wrote) that the percentage of students involved was minuscule.

In both the UK and the United States, much outrage came from older, more conservative people who liked traditional English culture: tweeds and crumpets. These people were most likely to find "Swinging London" immoral and decadent – not only the miniskirts, which invited sexual congress and recalled orgies of ancient Rome, but even more the unisex fashions: boots and pantsuits on young women seemed mannish, while long hair and ruffled shirts on boys appeared effeminate. With Yanks, such complaints also reflected the American tendency to favor the old in Europe – just as Europeans went for the new (and preferably crude) in America. Compare the French fascination with Jerry Lewis, reported in *The New York Times Magazine* in February 1966, with a letter to the *Times* from Victor G. Fourman, praising the traditional English things he'd seen during a recent visit and dismissing the swingers as not worth bothering with.[222]

Other letters to the *Times* were more sympathetic. Both an American reader, M. Pezas, and an English one, Richard Blomfield, wrote in to say how happy they were that the swinging society meant a more democratic Britain.[223] To find prominent Britons expressing his own views, Fairlie had to quote Conservative party leaders Edward Heath and Reginald Maudling. How odd: conservative *Time* cheering on Labor (on the rare occasion of my cover), while the more liberal *Times* voiced Tory sentiments!

Until *Time* did its cover, *Newsweek* and the *Times* agreed that "Swinging London" existed, and for the better. The *Times* had said so in an article about Jean Shrimpton, the model, in May 1965; in an article on Julie Christie in November 1965; and by quoting Kenneth Tynan, the theater critic, in an article on him in January 1966.[224] *Newsweek* had said so in its cover story on Shrimpton in May 1965, its article on "Britain's With-It Society" in December 1965, and its cover on Christie, two weeks later. In its travel cover in 1965, it had devoted about a column to the new London. A photo of the Buckingham Palace Guards was captioned "Out," and one of "Carnaby Street threads" captioned "In." The story quoted Diana Vreeland, editor of *Vogue*, saying that "London is the most swinging city in the world at this moment."[225] Apparently something was true if Vreeland and *Newsweek* said so, but if *Time* said the same thing, it had to be a figment of its imagination.

To the extent that my cover incorporated social commentary often found in *Newsweek*, and its familiarity with the hip and In, you might say I'd written a *Newsweek* cover that by a twist of fate had wandered into *Time*. To the extent that my cover decried "decadence" and had tips for tourists, it was still for *Time*'s square heartland readers. To the extent that it was a *Newsweek* cover, it antagonized *Time*'s usual readers, and to the extent that it was a *Time* cover, offended those who preferred *Newsweek*. *Time* didn't create "Swinging London."[226] We only popularized it, but our coverage showed that the situation was no longer exclusive to insiders, and the hip often don't like sharing their space with squares. In the wake of our cover, invading tourists overwhelmed the phenomenon we'd described. When I was there in the summer of 1966, the city was still unspoilt, but when I returned in the summer of 1967, the bloom was gone.

Finally, there was how *Time* was dealing with Vietnam. For me, this explains better than anything else the long-lived anger that the London cover provoked. The contrast between *Time* and *Newsweek* on Vietnam was at its height during of the week of my cover, when the South Vietnamese government was threatened by a Buddhist uprising. To *Time*, the government was putting up a heroic defense against an "ambitious, extremist" Buddhist monk, Thich Tri Quang.[227] Sensing a silver lining in the cloud, *Newsweek* hinted at the possibility that if Tri Quang got his way, "a neutralist government might take over and ask the U.S. to get out."[228] The cover of *Newsweek* that ran opposite the London cover showed Buddhist-inspired rioters, but I suspect *Time*'s cheery escapism outsold it on the newsstands. This could have angered *Newsweek* and its supporters.

Vietnam was the defining issue among thinking people in the '60s. Even more so than civil rights, Vietnam colored how people saw nearly everything else. To many of them, *Time* was so wrong on Vietnam, and was causing so much death and destruction by being wrong, that it couldn't be right about anything else, least of all the revolutionary social and cultural arenas in which *Newsweek* had enjoyed such supremacy. The fury *Time* provoked could be seen in the *Times* the month before my cover, reporting a "read-in" at Reed College in Oregon. The poet Robert Bly was quoted saying that *Time* had made General Westmoreland its 1966 Man of the Year, and that "Time Magazine would make Pontius Pilate the Man of the Year."[229]

Two personal letters are even more illustrative. One was from Tony Egan, child of my mother's friends, congratulating me when my cover came out. "I never thought I would be writing a fan letter to Time Magazine," it began, "but just this once...."[230] The second was from David Merrick, the Broadway producer, who'd been asked (through yet another one of my mother's friends) to give Coward McCann a blurb for my book. Generously, he did so, but first, he sounded off. Admittedly, he hadn't liked the cover story we'd done on him, but his remarks went beyond that. Comparing my book to *Time*, he suggested that everything that *Time* had ever printed was a lie, and that my book must in all probability therefore be more of the same.[231]

Most newsmagazine cover stories are like yesterday's newspapers, but *Time*'s cover on "Swinging London," a product of the mass media, has become part of the pop-cultural phenomenon it described. I've found twelve histories of London or books about British culture published between 1969 and 2001 that discussed "Swinging London" as a phenomenon, in U.S. libraries and bookstores alone.[232] Most were written by Britons; most mentioned the *Time* cover (though rarely with approval).[233] A thirteenth called the story "famous," "influential" and "the initial catalyst" in terms of media response.[234] A Tate Gallery exhibition catalogue in 2004 mentioned it, and a BBC program coinciding with that exhibition showed the cover design and map of "The Scene" that had illustrated our story.[235] In the '90s, when London was said to be swinging again, magazines on both sides of the Atlantic had cited the 1966 cover.[236]

In 2002, Shawn Levy would publish *Ready, Steady, Go: The Smashing Rise and Giddy Fall of Swinging London* in U.S. and UK editions. He'd interview me and quote me at length in his book. In 2005, Max Décharné would publish in the UK *King's Road: The Rise and Fall of the Hippest Street in the World*; Décharné, too, would interview me (via e-mail) and discuss the *Time* cover at the beginning of his introduction.[237] In 2006, Dominic Sandbrook would in the UK publish *White Heat*, an 878-page "history of Britain in the Swinging Sixties." It would use a full-page color reproduction of the cover to lead off a section of color photographs of period celebs, and quote and discuss the cover, myself, and even some letters to the editor prompted by the cover.[238] I might add that even somewhat used copies of *A Swinger's Guide to London* (1967 price: $3.95), as of 2008 commanded quite a respectable premium at Amazon, and that a fresh copy of it was featured in *Summer of Love: Art of the Psychedelic Era*, an exhibition commemorating 1967 that was originally organized by Tate Liverpool and played the Whitney Museum of American Art in New York in the summer of 2007.

As Christmas 1966 approached, I heard Cran Jones wondering aloud in the corridor whom he could get to write Art over New Year's, as Borgzinner was going skiing. I volunteered, was given the assignment, and Fuerbringer liked what I wrote. A week or so later, I heard that Borgzinner was going to *Life*, and a week or so after that, I learned I was to be his permanent replacement. I could leave Modern Living, and at last have a back-of-the-book section all my own.

PART II
THE ART WORLD:
"MULTIREFERENTIAL IMAGERY"

10. ENTERING THE ART WORLD
(JANUARY 1967–DECEMBER 1968)

THE BIGGEST THING going for me in Art was having made art from kindergarten through twelfth grade. This had introduced me to how it was made, but more importantly, taught me that making it wasn't easy and that people who could make it were to be respected. My progressive upbringing had taught me to admire the avant-garde, which I understood in a cultural sense as well as an esthetic one. I knew that the term "avant-garde" originated in the military before it acquired an artistic meaning, that it meant troops who went on ahead of the main army, to reconnoiter the territory, explorers. I believed that the avant-garde in art led the way in society as well as art, that artists were more sensitive to the world around them and responded to change more quickly than other people. I believed what many people in the '60s believed, that abstract expressionism had been the reigning avant-garde all through the '50s and more or less monopolized the scene. I believed that by the '60s, it had become The Establishment, and had to be overthrown by a revolutionary new avant-garde. Again, like many other people, I believed that art progressed by revolution, not evolution, so that avant-garde art was always shocking when it was new. This meant that I should remain open to all new art even if it was shocking, because in time, it would become accepted.

In January 1967, I saw pop art as the new avant-garde, since that was what Jon Borgzinner had told me. I knew about op, because he'd done a takeout on it in 1964, and kinetic art because he'd done a takeout on that in January 1966. All three takeouts had been accompanied by several pages of color reproductions, as part of *Time*'s ongoing commitment to bring the best of art to its readers in color (the plates were corrected by hand, a laborious process that made possible a high degree of faithfulness to the originals which impressed even our art-world readers). In weeks when no such big takeout was scheduled, one story in Art in each issue was illustrated by one or two pages of color reproductions. As I hadn't read the section in such weeks, I'd missed the single color page that had accompanied the story on *Primary Structures* at the Jewish Museum in June 1966. This show had marked the beginning of widespread gallery exposure of an extreme form of abstraction known as minimalism, but neither minimalism nor op nor kinetic art had supplanted pop. Rather, they complemented it, elevating the pop artists to Old Masters within the art world, while themselves remaining secondary in the larger society that responded only to cataclysmic change.

To this larger world, the shift from abstract expressionism to pop had been cataclysmic, turning art (for most of those people who liked to consider themselves with-it) from seriousness into humor, making fine art out of soup-can design, and comic books into collectors' items. *Newsweek's* 1966 cover story on pop as a cultural phenomenon that I mentioned in Chapter Six had suggested many spheres of endeavor that pop art had influenced, directly or indirectly, from TV to fashion. The cover had quoted Lawrence Alloway, the British art critic associated with the coinage of the term "pop." For *Newsweek*, he defined it as "an affectionate way of referring to mass culture, the whole man-made environment."[239] Pop was part of the London scene: the *Newsweek* cover mentioned Carnaby Street's unisex look – so, as the poster child for "Swinging London," I also entered the art world as something of a poster child for pop.

I didn't know the people who constituted that art world. I didn't realize they formed a subcommunity, just as the people on *Time* did, or students on Morningside Heights. I'd seen only a handful of museum exhibitions during and since college, and had been inside only two or three galleries (for openings of relatives or friends of friends). On Borgzinner's last day at *Time*, he took me out for a drink, bringing along a copy of the *Gallery Guide*, a pocket-sized monthly listing galleries and museums in Manhattan. He leafed through it with me, grading the galleries he felt most worth visiting. Not surprisingly, Leo Castelli, the dealer who represented Rauschenberg, Johns, and most of the other big pop artists, got an A. Borgzinner also gave A's to Marlborough-Gerson, a big gallery that focused on older and foreign artists; Richard Feigen, which showed op and kinetic art; André Emmerich, known for American abstract painters; and Dwan, which was new but making a name for itself in minimal art. "Look," Borgzinner said. "And look – and look." I still can't give anybody better advice.

Because Art's color pages were printed in advance, the section couldn't get killed in Friday makeup conferences: it ran in every issue. It had a Monday-Friday week, so in summer, I got to my beach house in Quogue on weekends. Otherwise, I spent Saturdays at the galleries (in the '60s, they were mostly on Fifty-seventh Street or the Upper East Side). I flew to other cities to look at art that we were reproducing in color, and looked at pictures in the art magazines, but avoided their texts (*Time* frowned upon technical "jargon," and I didn't want any art jargon creeping into my prose). Museum PRs were more reliable than the corporate ones I'd dealt with when I was in Business. Being nonprofit organizations, museums may have attracted more idealistic practitioners. They didn't yet introduce new exhibitions with "media previews," as they do today, but I got invites to evening openings, especially from the Museum of Modern Art and the Whitney Museum of American Art. There I'd mix with all sorts of people, getting free drinks and useful leads. Two dealers asked me to parties, and I'd meet Rauschenberg in 1968 at a promotional party given by Marion Javits, wife of the U.S. senator, and introducing a big Rauschenberg poster.[240] Rauschenberg told me that he'd been required to make so many new versions of his cover design for *Time* on *Bonnie and Clyde* that he was thinking of having a show of *Time* rejects.

Starting out, I would have been lost without group journalism. I knew more about art than most Americans, but far less than most people involved with art professionally. Upon the basis of the one Mondrian show I'd seen in 1945, and the one "abstract expressionist" show I'd seen in 1956, I thought I understood abstract painting. Fortunately, I had two fine researchers, Leah Shanks Gordon and Susan Howard (later Biederman). Gordon was especially helpful, and Cranston Jones, even more so. He'd done books on architecture, and scheduled our stories about it.[241] Initially, he also scheduled most "art news" stories (fakes, record prices, museum appointments, etc.), and most stories on older artists (abstract and representational). He showed me how we had to balance off recent and earlier art, using the color pages for recent art one week, and earlier art the next, doing a story with only a black-and-white illustration on earlier art when the color spread was on recent art, and vice versa. This was my first hint that not all my readers were as gung-ho about the avant-garde as I was – not that I didn't enjoy looking at earlier art, but when I wrote about it, I had to rely on books or exhibition catalogues. Because we interviewed contemporary artists, I fantasized that centuries hence, scholars might come back to read our stories about them as original source material.

At first, I was irked by Cran Jones, because he liked abstract expressionism and was lukewarm about pop. To me, this made him the Old Guard, The Establishment, though John Canaday, senior critic on *The New York Times*, could occasionally disparage even earlier twentieth-century art (its junior critic, Hilton Kramer, was somewhat more open, and Grace Glueck, an art reporter for the paper, did news stories about pop, kinetic art, etc.). Our Old Guard on *Time* also had Fuerbringer and the ghost of Luce. Luce died a month after I started in Art, but his spirit lingered on. Leah Gordon told me she'd sat next to him at a company party in 1966, and he'd asked whether she thought abstract expressionism was for real. This resembled how Alexander Eliot had dealt with abstract expressionism when he was writing *Time*'s Art page in the '40s and '50s. Eliot had attacked Jackson Pollock, calling him "Jack the Dripper."[242]

Still, Luce had liked, maybe even loved, older art, and in his later years been a trustee at the Metropolitan Museum of Art. While I was still on *Time*, I'd hear that in the '40s he'd been a trustee at MoMA, and that Mrs. Luce had been on *Vanity Fair* while she was still Clare Brokaw. Having been told that *Vanity Fair* pioneered with color reproductions of modern art, I'd come to think of *Life*, the picture magazine, as the child she and Luce had together. I knew the marriage had settled into convention, but I romanticized it, I suppose because of Richard Sherman, a sweet, shy writer whom my mother had known in the '50s and early '60s. At her parties, he'd stand in a corner, talking to nobody and drinking too much; he'd died at the age of only fifty-six in 1962. My father had known him in the '30s, when Dick was publishing short stories in *Vanity Fair*. His first novel, *To Mary, With Love*, became a bestseller in 1936, and then a movie.[243] My father said it was really about Dick's unrequited passion for Clare.

Though Fuerbringer didn't like pop, my experience in Art confirmed what I'd learned in People: that he had an eye. When he came to approve our color photography layouts, he'd sometimes shift around the transparencies; the layout always looked better. At Harvard, one of his friends had been Charles Cunningham, who by 1967 was director of the Art Institute of Chicago; another was Perry Rathbone, by 1967 director of the Museum of Fine Arts, Boston. In April 1968, *Newsweek* would do a cover on Thomas Hoving, the Met's new director. The story said that the Met would be reattributing some of its Rembrandts.[244] Rathbone told Fuerbringer that other museums had been doing this for years, so Fuerbringer had me do a big story on all the other museums reattributing Rembrandts. Even experts didn't always agree upon whether a painting was a true Rembrandt, or one done by assistants in his workshop, disciples, or eighteenth- or nineteenth-century copyists.[245]

Borgzinner had done stories with color pages on Rauschenberg and Johns. He hadn't done full-length stories on Warhol or Lichtenstein. By 1967, Warhol was making movies, so stories about him were done in Cinema, but I'd write about Lichtenstein, Oldenburg, James Rosenquist, and Tom Wesselman. Jones left these stories much as I wrote them, nor did he do much to stories about younger and/or lesser-known artists whom I discovered in the galleries. Looking back, I admire his forbearance: to put it mildly, most of my early discoveries were undistinguished.

Jones edited stories about abstract expressionism heavily, especially in my early months, adding much I didn't know to them but also to my resentment of his Establishment bias. MoMA had a big Pollock exhibition in April 1967, and Jones insisted we do a story on it, though I protested that Pollock was old-fashioned. Hilton Kramer, in the *Times*, called him "an interesting artist of, say, the third class," and I used that quote as the kicker for the shortest story I thought I could get away with. Jones added paragraphs describing how younger artists like Johns had admired the show. His kicker was a well-known quote from de Kooning, Pollock's best-known rival, saying that "Pollock broke the ice."[246]

During my first week in Art, Jones suggested a story on Tony Smith, an older minimalist. Smith was exhibiting big black sculptures in Bryant Park, and showed them to me. Built of geometric forms, many were more complex than the work of younger minimalists, but even when they were simple, Smith told me what they reminded him of. This laid the foundations for my theory regarding subject matter in abstract painting, though of course I hadn't a clue at that point to the theory itself. Smith and I played the game of free association that I'd used to interpret dreams on the couch, but I didn't think that his associations meant that he'd intended to portray such subjects. Some sculptures reminded him of more than one idea (the germ of what in 1983 I'd call "multireferential imagery"). His most famous piece, a cube, was called *Die*, and it suggested a matrix, or mold, the imperative of the verb "to die," and one half of a pair of dice.[247]

Marianne Foster, the English freelance who'd done research for my guidebook, turned up in New York. She was a short young woman, with short, curly black hair, a short red minisuit and high red boots. I introduced to her to a friend of mine whom I shall call Suzie Brown; Suzie later told me that one reason Foster had come to New York was that she was in love with Mike Demarest, and wanted him to get a divorce and marry her, but he refused. From this, I (rightly or wrongly) concluded a) that Demarest had been unfaithful to his wife while he was over in England, and b) that Foster was a swinger in both senses of the word. *A Swinger's Guide to London*, published that spring, got three positive reviews, two positive brief references, two negative reviews, one noncommital one, some good publicity, and a few nice fan letters, but never took off.[248] Still, I was glad that I'd written it.

On the July Fourth weekend, Silas Haynes (of the saturnine smile) gave an outdoor party at his home in Chappaqua for many edit staffers and their mates. My date and I got a lift to the party from Penny and Joe Ferrer, my onetime colleagues from People. On the way home, Penny was telling her husband what terrible taste Haynes had shown by inviting his researcher to the party. Evidently she thought the two were lovers. I'd thought they were only coworkers, but when I said so to Gordon, next day in the office, she was surprised by my ignorance. Later that summer, during my vacation, I revisited the scene of *A Swinger's Guide*. "Swinging London" had become a tourist gimmick, with tacky souvenirs and bad, vulgar guidebooks hawked in Piccadilly Circus.

143

That fall, the editors held a conference in East Hampton. Grunwald was now an assistant managing editor, directly in line for Fuerbringer's job. I heard he'd again argued for more enlightened culture and politics, so I sent Fuerbringer a cover suggestion on Tony Smith. Fuerbringer scheduled it, then made Cran Jones and me rewrite it for the benefit of all those good people in Rovere who still couldn't relate to the avant-garde. In spite of the NV, most of our regular readers were irked or bored anyway, to judge from the few letters that the cover elicited, but thereafter I felt more at home in Art.[249]

In November, Jones decided we should do a color page on de Kooning, who was having his first exhibition of new work in five years. He lived at the far end of Long Island, so the Time Inc. travel service borrowed a small plane from the Rockefeller Brothers, and Leah Gordon, a photographer, and I flew out to interview him. He must have been drunk when we got there, because all he wanted to do was paw Gordon and myself. The only quotable thing he would say was, "I am ambitious, ambitious to be a fantastic artist."[250] Finally, he curled up on the sill of a picture window, and went to sleep. I was so mad that I found it hard to write about him, but I decided this chutzpah was part of what made him great, so I wrote my anger into the story.

The next week, I did a color page on the brilliantly hued, minimalist paintings that Frank Stella had designed with a compass and protractor and was going to show at Castelli's.[251] When I'd visited him at his studio to prepare a shooting script for our photographers, his attitude had been defiant, even hostile. This exasperated me, as did abstract art in general. Though I respected it as art, I couldn't see what it had to do with life, and I could understand why it bored so many of my readers. Didn't *Time* measure its success by the size of its circulation? Didn't our Art stories allude to the size of the crowds a show was attracting, and the record prices that works of art had sold for (higher prices reflecting bigger demand)? Wasn't the greatest art that which appealed to the greatest number, then, and wasn't such art usually representational, not abstract?

Near Christmas, I ran into Ed Hughes in the corridor. He said he was going to the Beirut bureau. How appropriate, I thought, the Middle East, with all those Arabs who believe that women have no souls (or so I'd been told in my childhood).

Early in 1968, I got a press release from MoMA announcing a spring exhibition, *Dada, Surrealism, and Their Heritage*. It was being organized by William Rubin, MoMA's new curator of painting and sculpture. He was replacing the celebrated Alfred H. Barr, Jr., who'd been with MoMA since its inception, but had retired in 1967. Since dada and surrealism were both new to me, I thought the show might be good for a color page or two, so I called Elizabeth Shaw, MoMA's PR director, and asked her to set up a lunch for herself, Rubin, and me.

Rubin had gone to Columbia, which made me, a Barnard graduate, feel at home. He was forty, about the right age for me, but I assumed he was married. He'd taught at Sarah Lawrence and Hunter colleges, and carried a pedagogical manner into our conversation over lunch in the museum's members' restaurant, but that was all to the good, as this show was to be my first in-depth exposure to twentieth century art prior to abstract expressionism. I knew practically nothing about the cubism that had preceded dada, nor did Rubin go into it, but I easily understood the idea that dada was a protest against World War I, given the protests against Vietnam at the back of my consciousness.

Rubin defined dada for me as based in chance or accident, a universe devoid of logic. Its creators called it "anti-art." The show would display "Readymades" that Marcel Duchamp had constructed out of household objects. One was *Bicycle Wheel* (1913), a bicycle wheel mounted on a stool, and a work of art primarily because Duchamp had taken it out of a domestic context and placed it in an esthetic one. The Readymades had introduced the idea, now widespread, that anything can be art if the artist says it is. Some people found this shocking, but to me, it was only avant-garde. I could see parallels between the Readymades and the household artifacts of pop featured in the "heritage" section of Rubin's show. Indeed, Rauschenberg and Johns had been known as "neo-dadaists" in the '50s, before the soup cans and comic strips of true pop came along.

What Rubin said about surrealism provided another link in the chain of experiences leading up to my theory about abstract painting as based in the artist's unconscious synthesis. Rubin explained that the surrealists in the 1920s had tried to utilize the unconscious in the creation of art. They replaced dada's celebration of chance, accident, and the illogical with the seemingly illogical logic of the Freudian unconscious and dreams. I'd lived with the logic of the Freudian unconscious most of my life. Rubin divided the surrealists into two groups. The academic or illusionist branch, led by Salvador Dalí, depicted dreamlike or bizarre images using perspective, modeling, and shading: traditional techniques taught in art schools. The automatists experimented in their picture-making, utilizing chance, accident, and the unconscious.

Rubin told me how Joan Miró painted *The Birth of the World* (1925), one of his greatest pictures, by daubing paint freely onto a canvas, then emphasizing images that he felt his unconscious had suggested.[252] I began to see how surrealism in general and automatism in particular had evolved into abstract expressionism (and this was my first concrete exposure to the concept of modern art as evolution, not revolution, though this implication didn't register with me at the time). With Miró, vestiges of representation remained, but the mature works of artists like Pollock and Mark Rothko were pure abstractions. Rubin's "heritage" section also had semi-representational transitional paintings made by those two and other abstract expressionists when they were younger.

Rubin suggested which pictures we should use in our color layout, but I had to call him to double-check them. His secretary mentioned she'd been buying him shoes. Husbands had wives to buy shoes for them, so Rubin must be single. Then he came on the line, and said something like, "You must come to my place and have lunch. I have quite a little collection of my own." My heart skipped a beat. Nobody I'd met in Art had yet extended such a personal invitation. We made a date for Saturday, but he called again, to say he was having a house guest that weekend, a young lady from Boston, and did I still want to come? If I said no, I'd be saying I only wanted to see him if I could be alone with him, implying a personal relationship, but lunch wasn't like a real evening date, so he wasn't committing himself. Suppose, if I did, he then asked me to dinner? I didn't consider it ethical to get involved with somebody I had to write about. It would be hard to do so with the detachment needed in good journalism (and even if I could, the rest of the world wouldn't believe that I was being detached), so if we were going to get involved, I'd have to ask for a transfer to another section. As I really didn't want to leave Art just then, I had to say, no, I'd still like to come to lunch that Saturday.

Before lunch at Rubin's loft on Lower Broadway, we sat around a coffee table in the living-room area. He served me Harvey's Bristol Cream sherry, which Fred Freund had introduced me to. To my right sat the young lady from Boston, legs crossed and exceedingly visible up her very short skirts. To my left sat Rubin, talking away, and in front of me hung a large, totally abstract "drip" painting by Pollock: rich, predominantly red swirling webs or skeins of paint. I couldn't help noticing it. Even when my head was turned, I saw it out of the corner of my eye, and subtly it began to get to me. Rubin started to show me the rest of his collection. In the bedroom hung a Stella over the conspicuously unmade double bed. The kitchen was semi-enclosed. I asked Rubin if he'd designed this layout. He said no, he'd asked the architect to make it like that because his wife (now his ex-wife) had wanted it. So, he was divorced.

We sat around the dining table, eating hamburgers made by somebody in the kitchen. On one wall hung a large Rothko, with its radiant rectangles of color. Beneath it stood a large abstract sculpture made out of wiry black steel and resembling a mighty insect. This was *Australia* (1951), the masterpiece of

David Smith, a contemporary of Pollock's, and today, I'd say, the U.S.'s greatest sculptor. In 1968, I'd never even heard his name. On another wall hung a tall, narrow abstract painting that Rubin said was by Helen Frankenthaler. I'd never heard of her, either, but he said she'd been about to throw it out and he'd rescued it from the trash. In addition to paintings by Lichtenstein and minimalists I knew about, there was work by Jules Olitski, another unfamiliar name. To judge from my subsequent behavior, I must also have seen paintings by Larry Poons and Kenneth Noland, two more abstract painters whose names, if I'd heard them before, had never struck me as important.

After lunch, Rubin's limo took the three of us to Fifty-seventh Street and Madison Avenue, and we went to Marlborough-Gerson, where a show of paintings by Lee Krasner, Pollock's widow, was just opening. Krasner greeted us. Rubin said hello, then back in the elevator growled that he hated being "hovered over" by the artist. We walked west. Knoedler's had shiny, busy little abstract sculptures by Bernard Rosenthal. Rubin growled here, too, saying a trustee wanted the museum to acquire one of these, but he was going to have to vote against it. Nor did he like the next show, of gilded canvases by a younger minimalist. He'd bought an earlier painting by this artist, but said this show wasn't up to his last. So one didn't have to stay open to all the new art one saw!

Our last stop was Dwan, where Robert Smithson had a minimalist sculpture that resembled a staircase.[253] Rubin said it was interesting, how the artist played with the idea of Renaissance perspective. I realized that my idea of the avant-garde as revolution, not evolution, needed revision. We passed a chestnut vendor. I said I liked chestnuts. Rubin said he'd had bagels as a child, when he, his father, and his brothers walked across the Brooklyn Bridge. This was so New York that again it reminded me of my college world. We came to Sixth Avenue. It began to rain. I said I was going to my office. Rubin reached out an arm, and gave a little swipe in the air, almost like he wanted to caress me. He asked if I'd like a lift, but I said, no, I'd run between the raindrops, and darted off. From then on, I cared about him, and it wasn't fun.

The week that the dada and surrealism show opened, Cran Jones was on vacation, and Bob Jones sat in for him (Fuerbringer was grooming Bob Jones to become a senior editor). I liked the way Bob Jones edited my story, though he made me do a new version, and wrote in stuff about Yippies demonstrating outside MoMA (Yippies being hippies with political involvement).[254] Most of the time, the antiwar protest was like noises heard from a distance for me, so deeply had I buried myself in art, but I paid more attention to the political scene, because I had to know who to vote for.

In late 1967, Senator Eugene McCarthy from Minnesota had announced that he'd run against Johnson in the 1968 Democratic primaries on a peace platform. On March 12, 1968, he'd gotten many more votes in the New Hampshire primary than anybody had expected, and three days later, Robert F. Kennedy, junior senator from New York, had announced that he, too, would run against Johnson. On March 31, the Sunday evening after the dada and surrealism story went to press, I was ironing in the living room of our apartment. Margot Forbes, the roommate who'd replaced Thelma when Thelma moved to Washington, was watching LBJ make a speech on TV in her adjoining bedroom. I heard him say that he wouldn't run for re-election that fall. The way now seemed open for Bobby Kennedy to get the Democratic nomination, and end the war.

The next week we did the Rembrandt story. Then I had a week off, and went back to North Country School, which I'd attended in the '40s. I wanted to move from *Time* to *The New Yorker*, and fancied I might swing it if I could first sell them a series about the school. John McPhee had done something like this with an article about Bill Bradley. The man at *The New Yorker* whose name McPhee had given me wasn't encouraging, but Leo and Walter Clark, the school's directors, were delighted to help. I spent the week interviewing and observing them and others at the school. Martin Luther King, Jr. had been assassinated, and the students were watching his funeral on TV. His assassination and the ensuing riots were more distant noises for me, one big reason being that Fuerbringer didn't put him on the cover. *Newsweek* did, but Fuerbringer again favored the living over the dead, giving the cover to LBJ and his decision not to run.

One child at North Country was Lauren Olitski. As I'd seen work by her father in Rubin's loft, I wanted to do a color page on him, but to justify this notion on more rational grounds, I found that he'd been featured in *Artforum*, and had exhibitions scheduled. These were enough to rate him a story in *Time*, according to the more informed picture I was developing of my readers. As I said earlier, *Time* had claimed 14.5 million of them in 1967. This included "pass-along" readership, but to compare *Time* with its competition in the art scene, I'll use the smaller paid circulation statistics. Even by those, *Time* reached 40 percent more people worldwide than *Newsweek*, and more than three times as many as the Sunday *New York Times*. *Time* had nearly seven times the circulation of the Saturday *Times*, where the week's gallery reviews were published, 113 times the circulation of *Art in America*, 121 times that of *Art News*, 160 times that of *Arts Magazine*, and 390 times that of *Artforum*.[255] When we wrote about art or an artist for the first time, we were exposing them to millions of people who'd never known about them before.

A Chicago pop (and op) art collector had pointed to one painting in his house when I visited him, and said he'd ordered it by telephone after it was reproduced with one of Borgzinner's stories. In 1969, somebody would say to me, "Have you any *idea* what happened to Stella's prices after you did that story on him?" I didn't, but in 1984, *The New Yorker* would do a Profile on Stella, and – without mentioning our story on his Protractor Series – report that they'd tripled in price very quickly.[256] In January 1968, I'd done a big story, with four pages of color, on *Romantic Art in Britain*, an exhibition of art from 1760 to 1860 that I saw at the Detroit Institute of Arts. Later, I'd gotten a letter from the Institute's PR man, telling me that the show had broken attendance records.

As I analyzed it, the Tony Smith cover had failed because most *Time* readers were more conservative about art than I'd realized, and less involved in it. The vast majority apparently didn't read the section unless it had the cover or a major takeout. Among those who did read it more regularly, the largest group read only stories on representational art. A smaller group read those stories, plus any on modern art from the first forty years of the twentieth century (up to Picasso, say, or Mondrian). Next came a still-smaller group who liked all this, and also the abstract expressionism of the '40s and '50s, but couldn't stand pop (any more than either of the first two groups could, though depending on whom they could stand, they'd attack Picasso or Pollock instead of Warhol). Finally came the smallest group: people who read everything I wrote, especially stories about new art. Such people were a very small portion of our readership, but the most likely to be my sources. They belonged to that subcommunity I was learning to call "the art world."

I admired everybody in that world, especially artists who'd made it without the umbrella of a big corporation. I was glad this world had many women critics (though few women artists or curators). Still, I wasn't part of it, no matter how many openings and parties I attended. Rubin was the only member of that world who'd extended a personal invitation to me, and it hadn't been that personal. Lunch was included, but not dinner. Such treatment, repeated in other subtle ways, made me feel more a spectator on this scene than a participant, an outsider not an insider. No doubt the feeling was augmented by my personality, but representing *Time* had something to do with it, too.

The Washington Post Company owned *Newsweek*, which in turn owned *Art News* (a magazine much more about esthetics and less about art news than it is now). *Newsweek* had those two *Art News* graduates I mentioned in Chapter Five: Kermit Lansner, the managing editor, and Jack Kroll, the senior editor who edited some Art stories, and wrote others. Both were admired in the art world. Whenever *Newsweek* did a story on a subject *Time* hadn't covered, somebody always asked if I'd seen it. I started to pause at the newsstand in the lobby of our building on my way in to work, and thumb furtively through *Newsweek*'s latest issue to see what its Art section said. I didn't think that their section was better than ours, making me feel still more strongly that I and *Time* were outsiders. Much as I would have liked to be an insider, though, I say today that by seeing the art world from the outside, it was easier to see it whole.

I saw myself as a bridge, taking artists who'd achieved recognition within the art world, and introducing them to "the larger community." In the '60s, I had no statistics on the size of the art world or this larger community. In 1984, I assembled some for an article in *Arts Magazine*. The main thing it indicated was that even this "larger community" was smaller than I'd thought it was while I was at *Time*. True, the audience for art was increasing faster than the population as a whole, but even as late as 1984, the number of Americans who cared enough about art to go to an art museum on a regular basis was still only around four million out of a population of more than two hundred million. The number of people who went to MoMA was only a quarter of those who went to the Met, and even those who patronized MoMA were still far more numerous than those who cared enough about contemporary art to go to galleries, and see it fresh from artists' lofts.[257]

Members of the art world then (as now) tended to ignore how many millions of Americans didn't care what they were doing, but I was always somewhat aware, if only because I'd been one of those millions for so long. Most of my coworkers still belonged among them. During the thirty months I was writing Art, only one or two of them mentioned having seen an exhibition (aside from Art editors and researchers). Only one other colleague (Demarest) did I actually see at a museum – yet all were intelligent, educated people whom I'm sure considered themselves reasonably cultivated, and up-to-date on all the latest. As I said earlier, this book is written at least partially for such an audience. I can't deal with the people who think art has been going downhill ever since the Renaissance, but I hope there are some progressively minded adults out there who don't realize how the way they look at so many other things has been influenced by art-world developments.

In my capacity as bridge, I felt obligated to cover the whole scene, whether I liked an artist or not. And I developed a mental metaphor for what I was doing, no doubt influenced by the outsized manufactured objects that Oldenburg drew as "monuments" set into landscapes. I visualized *Time*, in its skyscraper on Sixth Avenue, as a huge vacuum cleaner, sucking in stories from the ground of Manhattan, siphoning them up above the skyline, then spewing them forth, all across the country, and around the world.

In this context, I decided Olitski was well enough known in the art world so I could legitimately introduce him to the larger society through a color page. More ambitiously, I wanted to do a cover on Miró. To judge from how Rubin talked about him, Miró was relevant enough to contemporary art so insiders would appreciate a cover on him, but he was old enough, and his style well enough accepted, so that less sophisticated people who only read my section when it had a cover or a major takeout would like him, too. The revisions Fuerbringer had asked for on the Smith cover led me to hope my reasoning was in line with his, but the day I sent in my cover suggestion, he was kicked upstairs, and Grunwald named managing editor. One of Grunwald's first acts was to return my suggestion, with "Nice try, but too old" scrawled on it. He'd been promoted in hopes he'd bring a younger, more "contemporary" quality to *Time*, making it more competitive with *Newsweek*, so Miró could be only a major takeout, with four pages of color.

Not long after Grunwald's accession, I had lunch again with Rubin, who'd invited me when I called him to get a quote for my Miró suggestion. The lunch was again at the MoMA members' restaurant. When I got there, Rubin was reading *Newsweek*. After I sat down, he asked why *Time* wanted a "swinger" for its managing editor (the *Times* had reported Grunwald's appointment). I said, "What do you mean?" Rubin said he'd seen Grunwald having lunch with a woman not his wife. "How do you know?" I asked. Rubin reiterated that the woman was not his wife. I asked whether Grunwald had called him. When the color spread for the dada and surrealism show had to be approved, Fuerbringer had been away and Grunwald had taken his place. While approving our layout, he'd asked for Rubin's phone number, but Rubin said that Grunwald had merely offered a surrealist painting he owned for inclusion in the exhibition. Fortunately, the picture had been done after the period covered by the show, so Rubin could gracefully decline.

I wrote the Olitski story in early June. To prepare the shooting script, I'd visited the artist in his studio. He was pleasantly beefy, but his canvases were nearly monochromatic, with stained or sprayed-on paint in radiant clouds of pink, mauve, pale green, or yellow. I asked about the drawings of female nudes I saw on the wall. Olitski said that he, "Clem" Greenberg, and other friends liked to sketch from a model. I told Cran Jones about this. After we'd made up the color page, Jones said the pinks and yellows might strike our readers as "airy-fairy" (that being how even progressive people talked in those days). He wanted them to know that Olitski was "a real mensch," so for our black-and-white illustration, we should photograph him with a drawing behind him, and put the sketch group in our lede. I did so, though Greenberg's name meant nothing to me.[258]

This may surprise current art-world denizens who believe that "Greenbergian formalism" ruled the art world in the '60s, but the fact was that, of the many galleries I visited, most featured pop, op, kinetic art, minimalism, "funk art" from California, Karl Wirsum and the Hairy Who from Chicago, representational painting by artists like Philip Pearlstein and Jack Beal, and other varieties of non-Greenbergian art. Sure, I'd gone to some abstract shows, but out of duty rather than pleasure, and, even rereading the reviews in *The New York Times* of that period, I find that most of those abstract shows were of artists who may have wished they were Greenberg's intimates, but weren't. My only direct exposure to him had been an article by him in the June 1967 *Vogue* that I'd read under the hair dryer in the beauty salon, but by 1968 I'd blotted out its memory because it irked me. Greenberg had argued that what I liked to think of as the new avant-garde was too easy and familiar to be true avant-garde, that it was only "novelty art."[259]

I was planning a story on conceptual art, a style beginning to reach the galleries. In conceptual art, the idea was more important than the finished object, so it used words instead of pictures, or photographs instead of real objects. My story had begun with a group show of such art at Dwan, but I decided to include Christo, an artist with an exhibition at MoMA who used sketches and photographs to show how famous buildings might look if wrapped and tied with rope. I called Rubin, to get a quote to use with this story; again he invited me to lunch. We ate at a French place, and argued about abstraction. I said that it couldn't be universal, because it didn't appeal to most ordinary art-lovers. Rubin asked me what would happen if ordinary art-lovers were let into a gallery with genuine and workshop Rembrandts. How many could tell the difference? I had to concede the answer would be, Not many. Rubin said that only a few of his undergraduates could respond to great art. He added that in a hundred years, abstract art would be the established mode, so enthusiastically that I cried out, "But what's abstract art *about?*"

With great intensity, he replied, "What *all* great art's about – *feeling.*"

My life was never the same after that. Obviously, my feelings about Rubin made anything he said more meaningful (I don't know who it was that first said that we learn about art through love, but in my case, it's been true). What Rubin had said about surrealist automatism and its relation to the unconscious laid the basis for my accepting emotion as a subject for art, but the word "feeling" tied abstract painting into two more experiences of mine. The first was the conclusions I'd come to about "feeling" as the basis for modern poetry in my college thesis on *The Waste Land*. I hadn't thought about that in years, but Rubin's words activated the memory, and what he said about greatness in art not being determined by the breadth of its appeal activated my recollection that Eliot's poetry had been addressed to a small, discerning audience.

Secondly, Rubin's emphasis on "feeling" gave new value to Dr. G's advice to channel my feelings into my creative writing, and suggested that the feelings which (I already knew) an artist like myself put into her or his work could be transmitted to the viewer or reader. After that lunch, I'd find it easier to respond to abstract painting. Thinking of feeling as its subject matter freed me from the need to perceive images, and permitted me to look at it for its own sake, let its shapes and colors sink in, and evoke emotions of my own.

The only compliment I ever got from Grunwald was on my Miró takeout in July, but *Newsweek* for the same week (by a funny coincidence) had a big takeout with four pages of color on "The New Art." It was mostly about younger artists, and, according to the magazine's Top of the Week section, had been planned as a cover, but downgraded when the Soviet crackdown in Czechoslovakia necessitated a cover on that instead.[260] Even the takeout dramatized the difference plaguing *Time* and boosting *Newsweek*'s ad sales: one chronicling age, the other, youth. I thought I'd been falling down on the job because I liked Rubin; that would have to end. He seemed to want it to: I got a letter from him, saying he'd been misquoted in the Miró piece. Even if *Time* hadn't done the first story on the latest art, I decided, it could at least do the definitive one, and I might get a cover out of it, so over my vacation in August, I saw far-out art at the Venice Biennale and Documenta, an equally big German show.

Alas, this was no holiday, and Grunwald's campaign to make *Time* more competitive with *Newsweek* was wearing. Our covers were more often the same as *Newsweek*'s, and the greater immediacy with which we handled such news sensitized me to it more than I wanted. By June, when Bobby Kennedy was assassinated, Grunwald had taken over, and both magazines had run RFK on their covers. The race to beat *Newsweek* to the newsstands was accelerating, and with it, pressure to get our sections closed earlier, but Grunwald took longer to top-edit stories, so it became harder to get to press. In retrospect, I think he was trying, especially with Vietnam, to help our heartland readers better understand what was going on. This was necessary, ergo desirable, but I hadn't read the front of the magazine since I left World, so I didn't know about that. Every Monday, when I stopped by our lobby newsstand, I looked anxiously to see whether *Time* was on sale yet, and whether *Newsweek* was there, too.

The *Newsweek* takeout on "the new art" had dealt with a range of it. I decided the real news was conceptualism, and two more recent, related developments – earthworks and process art. The former meant piles of dirt on a gallery floor and vast outdoor projects on empty or previously unspoiled tracts of land. The latter meant sculptures made of materials (like rolls of felt) lacking permanent shape. I planned a big color spread with work by many younger artists, but none was famous enough to use as a cover subject, so I proposed Oldenburg for that role. The soft fabric sculptures he'd made of everything from hamburgers to toilets could be seen as forerunners to process art, and he'd arranged to have dug a very conceptual hole in Central Park, proclaiming it an "underground sculpture."[261]

Preparing the color spread was exhausting. The first page showed Oldenburg with his sculptures. Next came a two-page photo of seven mostly younger process artists, each with his work, plus three more pages of art. I knew Grunwald would only approve a cover if he loved the color spread, and I thought that as a real intellectual, he'd be interested in the avant-garde, but he disliked the transparencies intensely. All I got was another takeout, to run in late November. Writing it was even more exhausting, and the only reaction I got from anybody at *Time* came from a man in space sales I saw in the elevator. *Newsweek*'s opposing issue (by another coincidence) had a cover story in Life and Leisure on "Male Plumage '68," with four pages of color photographs showing male celebrities and models in high-style, expensive fashions. Quite a contrast with our big photo of the process artists, since they were wearing what young artists normally wore: jeans, ordinary sport shirts, and the like. The space salesman was furious with me because the *Newsweek* piece had so much more appeal for menswear advertisers.

I was so tired I got the flu, and was out for three weeks. I dragged myself back for the Christmas issue, but Grunwald had postponed the carefully nonsectarian color spread on children in art that I'd prepared, and scheduled instead *Yellow Submarine*, the Beatles' animated movie. It was cute, but its art styles were years out of date, so the story really belonged in Cinema. I got so tired trying to write it that I had to go home for another week, and missed Bob Jones's going-away party. He was moving to *Sports Illustrated*. When I saw him in the corridor, he said Grunwald had told him that he wasn't going to make him a senior editor, that he needed "more seasoning." It must have been a heavy blow for Jones, but after he got to *Sports Illustrated*, he'd begin to publish a whole series of highly literate adventure novels, far more distinguished than anything he'd written for Time Inc.

Two more of my allies on *Time* were also suffering under Grunwald. Cran Jones was told that he had to go to the Washington bureau; instead, he left Time Inc. at the end of 1968 for a New York job with another company. Charlie Parmiter had been taken out of Sport and put in Modern Living. He told me Grunwald made him write the same Modern Living story over five times in five weeks. "It's hard to get it up five weeks in a row," he said, adding, "Pardon my French" (this being a phrase that gentlemen in 1968 still employed to apologize for using off-color language in front of a lady). Parmiter added that he'd heard that Grunwald had been seen entering a midtown hotel with a platinum blonde black woman. I was sore enough to place the worst possible construction on that remark.

11. I Meet Clement Greenberg
(January–May 1969)

WHILE RECUPERATING FROM the flu in January, I wrote the memoir of North Country School that I'd publish in 1990. In 1969, I saw no hope of getting it into print, but wanted badly to get something published outside *Time*. I called the editor of the *Columbia Journalism Review*, and asked if he'd like a piece on art criticism. He said he might, so I started work on that. Meanwhile, Bill Rubin's brother Lawrence (Larry) opened a gallery on Fifty-seventh Street. He was going to do a show of Kenneth Noland, whose paintings I'd seen in Bill Rubin's loft, along with those of Larry Poons. I'd done a story on Poons in the autumn of 1968, so I decided to do a color page on Noland. We met at the warehouse where his paintings were stored, to pick out paintings to photograph. Lean and keen, he asked, "Haven't I met you at Clem's?" I didn't know what he meant.

Helen Frankenthaler had a retrospective opening February 20 at the Whitney. I'd seen a painting by her in Bill Rubin's loft, too, and she was married to Robert Motherwell, the abstract expressionist. Readers bored by abstract painting might respond to such human interest, I thought. I saw the show, and loved its big, bold paintings, with their luscious colors and flaring shapes. Maybe I could do a cover on Frankenthaler. The show was getting good reviews. To find out how it was going over with the public, I called Stephen Weil, administrator at the Whitney. When I asked about Frankenthaler, he said something like, "Just imagine! She was Clement Greenberg's mistress!"

"Who's Clement Greenberg?" I asked. Weil sputtered, then said he was a very influential critic, the one who'd discovered Pollock. I got Greenberg's bio folder from the morgue. It told me he was important. I suggested a cover on Frankenthaler to Bobby Baker, who'd taken over Art after Cran Jones left. Baker had dealt with his drinking problem, and was a very cultivated gent. He agreed to let me write a cover proposal. While we waited for it to be discussed, we prepared a four-page color layout of her paintings. If I didn't get a cover, I'd do yet another takeout, but neither of my regular researchers was in Art that week. I'd have to report this story as well as write it.

My first interview took place on Monday, March 10, at the artist's studio. It was a block from where I'd lived on Eighty-second Street, which made me

155

feel at home. Slender and stylishly dressed, she told me that she'd started at Brearley, and transferred to Dalton. I'd attended both schools, in the same order. She mentioned having been in analysis as a young woman. It was such a relief to hear analysis referred to openly, after thirteen years in that WASPy *Time* environment where nobody admitted they needed help. I asked her to call Greenberg for me. She did, putting me on the line after she'd talked to him. He invited me over for a drink that Wednesday.

Tuesday, I met her at her townhouse in the East Nineties. She introduced me to Motherwell, and later on, told me how she'd met him at a party around 1957. He'd been sitting talking to other people, and she couldn't get him to pay attention to her until she grabbed a toy pistol she had in her purse (a humorous gift from her sister). She slung the pistol in his lap, after which he paid attention, but I tell this incident because of how she described the way she slung the pistol. "It was such a surreal gesture," she said, and repeated it: "So surreal." At least, that is what I recall her saying, and this use of the word "surreal" was to affect me profoundly. I've since learned that it was common slang in hip circles in the '60s. What luck I didn't know that then! Because of my blessed ignorance, I was able to relate the word to what I'd learned about surrealism as an art form that tried to express the unconscious. Frankenthaler was using it in the context of everyday behavior, linking it up to what I'd learned about the unconscious in analysis, how it was expressed through accidental gestures and slips of the tongue with double levels of meaning.

My interview with Greenberg took place in his apartment on Central Park West, on March 12. When he opened the door, I saw an ordinary-looking man. He was sixty, and with his balding pate, keen eyes, and somewhat fleshy nose and cheeks, resembled many elderly Jewish gentlemen I'd seen on Manhattan streets. His most distinctive facial feature was broad but exquisitely delineated lips. The spacious living room was hung with beautiful paintings by Noland, Olitski, Frankenthaler, and so on.

I took out pad and pencil. He made me put them away, saying that he wasn't going to say anything for publication, just as he'd never write about a "girl" he'd gone to bed with ("girl" being what all kinds of people still called women of all ages). He did say, "She's a real painter," adding that in the '50s, she'd been grouped with Joan Mitchell and Grace Hartigan, but that she alone had developed. He was modest about his contribution to her work, saying that it was like the way Krasner had interacted with Pollock, as a "sounding board." He understood the difficulties Frankenthaler encountered as a woman, saying that Frank Stella went to parties uptown in paint-stained clothes, but "a woman has to be soignée." I took trouble with my appearance, and had been complimented on it, but Greenberg's comment went beyond compliment, showing he realized how much effort being "soignée" required.

He recalled that as a young woman, Frankenthaler had been "aggressive." To Dr. G, aggressiveness was undesirable in a woman, but Greenberg made it seem an aspect of youth that Frankenthaler had grown out of, but that might have been important for her development, and all but inevitable in a talented young artist. My identification with her stepped up a notch, and with it came a sense of feeling more at ease with him, not that I wasn't in awe of him, but this was becoming a more personal encounter. He was defining her talents and accomplishments in human terms.

I asked him when he and Frankenthaler broke up, and he said 1955. I said Frankenthaler had said they'd split up in 1954. He countered fiercely, "It was '55. I keep diaries. I know my dates." I could see that arguing with him would be tough. I said that after Frankenthaler split up with him, and before she married Motherwell, her painting hadn't been very good. "There were some good ones," he said. "There was *Eden*." The sympathetic way he spoke of her reminded me of how Fred took me out when he was in Manhattan, and kept hoping I'd reconsider my rejection of him. I must be ambitious in the same way that she had been, I thought guiltily. I'd taken advantage of Fred's feeling for me so I could learn about love, and become able to write about it, and, while Frankenthaler must have loved Greenberg, I thought that part of his appeal for her had been what he could teach her about art.

The fact that he could still speak so warmly of her made me feel me that he absolved her for having exploited him, and, in so doing, also absolved me. Since I knew Fred still loved me, I assumed that Greenberg must still love Frankenthaler, and I would put this into the manuscript of the nonfiction novel I wrote in 1974. When I gave it to Greenberg to critique, he'd deny that he'd still been in love with her, and continue to deny it the rest of his life. The more he protested, the surer I became that feeling for her still lurked, though I now believe I exaggerated its extent when we met. It was my first experience of Greenberg's remarkable intuition: as I'd just met him, I couldn't understand how he knew the guilt that I was feeling, so I concluded it was because of a mutuality of experience. I could tell that he was highly intelligent, and I sensed that his aesthetic standards were rigorous. "Read Kant," he said. "Read Croce. Read Susanne Langer." This was a really real intellectual speaking.

We were joined by a friend of his from California. She had a drink, and played with Sarah, his little girl, who entered shortly after. Noland came in. I felt like a little play was being staged for my benefit. Greenberg, Frankenthaler, Olitski, and Noland were all friends, part of this sub-subcommunity of the art world whose existence I'd never suspected, but which had clearly been flourishing right along, a village within a village. I told Greenberg I'd gone to the school Lauren Olitski was attending. He said that Margaret Marshall, the

Nation editor who'd starting him writing art criticism, had sent her daughter there. "It's a good place," he added. Circles in my past were linking up.

Noland left. Word came up from the lobby that Bill Rubin had come to take Greenberg out to dinner. Rubin belonged to this village, as I should have realized sooner, given the paintings in his loft. Greenberg told me to come downstairs with him and the California woman; Rubin could give me a lift downtown. He was waiting out front, in a Jaguar. Greenberg and the Californian got into the back seat, and I got in next to Rubin, Greenberg introducing me as "a girl from *Time*." Rubin stared at me. His surprise was almost comic, but he quickly recovered, and invited me to join them for dinner. At last, I thought, I can have a purely social evening with him, without feeling we had to get back to our respective offices afterwards.

In the backseat, Greenberg said (as best I recall), "I like this girl – she has character." I realized it was a quality he admired, and got a boost from his words. We went to an American-type restaurant in midtown, and the men had hamburgers (again). I flirted with Rubin, casting my eyes down when he said "fuck," and forcing him, with a laugh, to cut it out. He and Greenberg talked about the current de Kooning retrospective at MoMA. Since we'd done that other story on de Kooning so recently, I'd covered this show with a color reproduction of *Excavation* (1950) above a block of text. I'd titled it, "De Kooning's Masterwork," because Rubin had said this picture was the artist's masterpiece, but Greenberg insisted sharply that some of the earlier portraits of men in the show were better. Rubin muttered something about *Excavation* that made me think his opinion was related to something Greenberg had said earlier.

The Solomon R. Guggenheim Museum had scheduled a David Smith retrospective for February. Having seen *Australia* in Rubin's loft, I'd wanted to do a story on Smith, but the retrospective had been postponed.[262] I now learned why. As an executor of the Smith estate, Greenberg had threatened not to lend the pieces owned by the estate unless the whole museum was given to the show, and that couldn't be done right away. In a note on my 1974 manuscript, he'd explain that the museum had promised to let the show use the whole museum, and was trying to welsh on this promise, but this didn't explain why he hadn't acted until the week before the show was to open.[263] At this first dinner, I asked why he'd waited, and he said, "It was my unconscious." I was amused by his chutzpah; besides, it was nice to hear him admit he *had* an unconscious, more evidence I was back in a Freud-compatible world.

After dinner, Rubin dropped the Californian at her hotel, and Greenberg gave me a lift, on his way home uptown. In the taxi, he told me that Rubin was engaged to a woman named Beryl Barr, who was getting a divorce in order to marry him. This made me feel terrible, but the fact that Greenberg was volunteering the information, together with the gentle way he did so, convinced me that he realized how I felt about Rubin. In later years, Greenberg would insist he'd been unaware of my feelings, but I'm sure he must have sensed them, if only on an unconscious or subliminal level, because again my whole experience was that he was so intuitive.

He reactivated an emotion I'd tried to kill off. To Dr. G, it might be only a neurotic attraction to "a fantasy man," but Greenberg's attitude convinced me that it had been real and true. This was one reason I concluded, on the basis of that one evening, that Greenberg would be remembered long after nearly everybody else I'd known. I'd met artists whom I believed would be remembered as great artists, but I felt that Greenberg would be remembered for his greatness as a person (I still feel this way). From that day forward, I wanted his good opinion more than I wanted anything else, but I suspected nothing I could ever write for *Time* would earn it. Simply meeting him made *Time* seem less important.

The next day, I interviewed Motherwell, who spoke of Greenberg's "moral earnestness," and said that Frankenthaler had "internalized" his "eye." Writing the article on her was painful but mind-expanding. I saw a parallel between her relationship with Greenberg, and mine with my editors as well as with Fred. They'd been my critics, I thought, as Greenberg had been hers. After she'd "internalized his eye," she'd been able to go on by herself, and I'd have to leave *Time* because only by writing on my own, and editing myself, could I achieve artistic maturity. I felt I was seeing light at the end of a tunnel (an expression then used about Vietnam, but I felt it in this context as a physical sensation). *Time* was an underground experience, but I'd found someplace else I could go – Greenberg's sub-subcommunity. Rubin used a French word, *milieu*. I felt that this village had come into being because Greenberg wanted to build a milieu for artists he admired. He'd said Pollock had sold only a few pictures from his greatest show in 1950, and I knew Pollock had gone back to the bottle at around the same time, getting killed six years later by driving his car into a tree while drunk.

I felt (and continue to feel) that Greenberg's milieu-building was intended to prevent similar situations, but in 1969, I saw it as designed primarily for Frankenthaler. Today, I'd say he was more aware of wanting to help other artists. I knew he'd been criticized for supporting artists he admired informally, instead of writing about them, but these were difficult painters. They needed particularly sophisticated supporters, and I thought I knew who some of them were. Curators like Bill Rubin. Dealers like André Emmerich, who represented Frankenthaler and other artists Greenberg believed in. Collectors like Eugene and Barbara Schwartz, whom I'd become friendly with. Gene had mentioned Greenberg's article, "Avant-Garde and Kitsch."

My cover proposal had been turned down, and Baker took so long to edit the takeout that I wondered if he was showing it to Greenberg. Neither had said they knew each other, but Frankenthaler had told me that Greenberg had read an article about him written for *Life*, and that it never appeared. This suggested he had influence, as I'd been told as a researcher how important it was never to show stories to sources. (Greenberg didn't deny that he'd read the *Life* story, when I mentioned it in my 1974 manuscript. He merely wrote a question mark in the margin, and a note saying "*Life* itself hadn't been too eager to print it."[264]) Finally, Baker asked for a new version. He wanted "less about Greenberg. This story is about Frankenthaler. You can do another story on Greenberg." I said I didn't think he'd permit it, but the NV I wrote was pretty much what appeared in print. Grunwald made us revise the first paragraph, to emphasize the museum setting in which Frankenthaler's pictures were displayed. This dramatized the role men played in stage-managing her work. Baker also took out the passage in which I'd said that, although Frankenthaler painted confused and unhappy pictures right after she split up with Greenberg, she was painting well again by the time she met Motherwell. This created the impression that she didn't paint well again until after she'd married Motherwell, and was incapable of accomplishing anything without a man around, but it was so typical of the male chauvinism on *Time* that I let it pass.

*   *   *

The next two months led up to a moment when I would begin moving in and out of a fantasy world for more than two years – although, until the very end of this period, I seem to have appeared to be more or less in my right mind to observers, judging from how they treated me. Even Dr. G didn't behave like he thought I'd lost touch with reality, but I'd already had a mildly paranoid thought when I supposed at Greenberg's apartment that a play was being staged for my benefit. I don't think this timing was coincidence. I believe my meeting him had much to do with the development of my curious mental state, though I don't blame him, or underestimate other factors, including my genetic makeup and childhood conditioning. There is even the possibility that the analysis itself was taking its toll on my sanity.[265] Yet, looking back, I can't help feeling that the stresses I was undergoing were the key precipitating factors.

Some ordeals, such as the loss of a beloved or being in a war, have been accepted for centuries as affecting mental health, though the systematic study of the relation between stressful "life events" and mental sickness only began within the past century or so.[266] Since then, however, much research indicates that stress can affect the body's chemistry, including that of the brain.[267] Whole books have been written on how to measure and evaluate different sorts of stress, discussing job-related stress, and arguing the importance of environmental factors affecting mental health as opposed to simplistic assumptions that mental illness is exclusively due to genetics, and/or that medication is the solution to every problem.[268]

Short-term stress, such as that felt by a cat at the bark of a dog, can prepare the body for "fight or flight," and thus be seen as adaptive. Long-term stress may exhaust the body or kill it, but the editors of one recent compendium of stress research have emphasized the positive, arguing that "Certainly, chronic stress can produce maladaptive consequences, but invariably, learning, growth, and evolution are also the by-products of stress."[269] God knows, I don't want to repeat my state of mind between March 1969 and July 1971, nor would I wish it on anybody else, but my progressive-school upbringing has taught me to learn from any situation, and my fantasies did serve several purposes, including weaning me from *Time*, and partially cleansing my system of the effects of having been too immersed in it. Maybe the short way to say this is that *Time* was such a great job, I'd have had to be crazy to leave it – so I went crazy.

In some ways, to be sure, working on *Time* had always been stressful, with its constant emphasis on accuracy, deadlines, and hierarchical setup, nor did it help that I'd been working a forty- to sixty-hour week since I'd come to Art, but in the spring of 1969, to all this was added the increasingly upsetting news in the papers, as the antiwar protest swirled to new heights. The fact that *Time* and *Newsweek* gave the protest increasingly sensational coverage also played on my nerve ends (which since childhood had been far too sensitive anyway). The increasing pressure on all of us at *Time* to compete ever more aggressively with *Newsweek* accentuated this situation. Another source of stress must have been the fact that Grunwald didn't like my work as well as Fuerbringer had. At the time, I'd believed he and I liked each other, but looking back, I can see danger signs: he'd rejected three cover suggestions of mine, reacted violently against my transparencies of conceptual art, and postponed my Christmas color spread. Writers and editors at *Time* were rarely fired; much more commonly, they were harassed into quitting (and I was well aware of this practice). Grunwald had already engineered the departure of Bob Jones and Cran Jones, and he was making life as tough as he could for Charlie Parmiter – three men who (like me) had been particularly appreciated by Fuerbringer.

Most important, however, was the inner conflict between my desire to stay on *Time*, with all its perks, and my growing wish to strike out for myself, even if I'd have to give up the entire way of life I'd so painstakingly built up over thirteen years: roommate, beach house, hairdos at Saks Fifth Avenue, and lavish Time Inc. expense account, but especially the analyst and my long-standing ambition to marry a nice "normal" man and have babies. Greenberg threw this whole carefully constructed edifice into question. His esthetic standards, I sensed immediately, were far too rigorous to admit much admiration for my career up to that moment. This abruptly prompted me to raise my own standards, and made me even more determined to concentrate on creative writing.

Finally, beyond my wish to make him respect my intellectual accomplishments lay a deepening hunger for life more fully lived, not insulated from direct experience as I'd so far made mine with the aid of Dr. G's well-meant but ultimately stifling "advice." Looking back over the progress of my relationship with Greenberg, I now believe that from our first meeting, I was attracted to him not only as a critic of creative endeavor, but also as a man – more powerfully than I'd been drawn to any other man, but, because he was married, and seemingly devoted to his wife, unwilling to admit it to myself (more than a year would pass before I could allow myself to think that my attraction to him was physical as well as mental). If I left *Time* (and Dr. G) for Greenberg and all he stood for, I'd have to begin a new life, and this prospect was so daunting that I couldn't bring myself to face its full consequences. I had to do it by stages, taking refuge from the implications of my decision by cloaking it in fantasy.

A certain body of evidence suggests that the incidence of mental illness may be higher among artistically creative people than it is, say, among insurance salesmen or stockbrokers, but nobody has yet shown that one *must* be mental in order to become a great writer, artist, or musician.[270] Almost all the artists I know today are more than ordinarily resilient – neurotic about their love lives sometimes, and often strapped for money, but still very much in touch with the workaday world. I dwell at some length upon the fantasies I had between 1969 and 1971 partly because I see this period as the most unconventional in my life, a period when commonplace words and incidents seemed strange and wonderful, even magical, and partly because some of what I learned during this period would help me understand the art scene better. Most of all, it's because my most persistent symptom, reading secondary meanings into things I heard and saw, had developed largely (though far from entirely) out of prior, perfectly rational experience, and would play a key role in helping me to develop my theory of multireferential imagery in 1983. Granted, some of my fantasies between 1969 and 1971 were pretty wild, but I've heard it said that a fantasy is like a pearl: the pearl forms around a grain of sand, and similarly at the center of every fantasy lies a seed of truth, though what that truth may be is almost always unknown at the time.

*　　　　　*　　　　　*

The Monday that my story on Frankenthaler appeared, she called me to say how much she liked it. I saw Greenberg that Friday at the preview for the David Smith show. He said, "That was some piece about Helen!" Then he walked on. I was very aware of the feelings for Bill Rubin that Greenberg had reactivated in me; that was why I'd invited a man whom I'll call Dustin Maine to escort me to the preview. Dustin, a PR man for (shall we say) NBC, was a decent guy who'd taken me out a bit, but the prime reason I wanted to seduce him was so I could drive the engaged Rubin out of my head.

After I'd written about Smith, I did the story on Noland for which I'd chosen paintings earlier: blazingly serene horizontal stripes in many colors. I'd gone with my researcher to interview him at his loft, and he'd flirted with us. "You're involved with someone as long as something is developing, changing or insightful," he'd said. "Painting is the same way."[271] Then I went to his show. Neither of the paintings we'd chosen were in it. Those on view were similar, but galleries normally featured our selections. I thought Larry Rubin was trying to show he didn't care about *Time*, so I gave him hell.

Then Greenberg called, and invited me for a drink the next evening. I was surprised and honored. While we were having our drinks at his apartment, he pointed out that *Time* hadn't mentioned the good paintings that Frankenthaler had done after she'd split up with him, but before she married Motherwell. Unlike my editors, he conceded that a woman could accomplish things without a man in her life. Larry Rubin had told Greenberg how I'd chewed him out. Greenberg said he couldn't understand why I'd gotten so upset, adding that I must be paranoid for thinking the choice of paintings in the show had anything to do with *Time*.

I remembered the word "paranoid" particularly because Frankenthaler had also used it, though as a joke (saying something like, X is just as paranoid as Y is, but then all my other friends are paranoid, too). Today, I'd suspect that she was using it as it was then used by a certain group of Neo-Sullivanian psychoanalysts, to denote a merely neurotic personality type. These Neo-Sullivanians were much patronized by the sub-subcommunity to which she and Greenberg belonged, but I didn't know this, so I took Greenberg's use of the word "paranoid" in its dictionary sense, as having psychotic delusions of persecution and/or grandeur.

He and I discussed Robert Morris, a minimalist and conceptualist who'd evolved into process art and earthworks. I'd written about him eagerly, but Greenberg quashed my enthusiasm by saying something like this: "Morris is a nice guy, but his work is too tasteful." Suddenly, I visualized Morris's art: all in tasteful shades of gray or brown, too sterile to withstand the test of time or beget artistic descendants. This made it taste as opposed to art. I must have picked up that opposition in my avant-garde youth, but Greenberg reactivated it just as Bill Rubin had reactivated my memories of Eliot. Rubin had taught me it was okay to criticize individual artists and exhibitions, but Greenberg was inviting me to criticize the whole "new avant-garde." It was an invitation that I would find it increasingly hard to refuse.

After our drinks, he took me to a loft party downtown, given by young artists I didn't know, with spaghetti, cheap wine, and dancing. Olitski was there with a young woman not his wife, and a stick of grass was passed around (Greenberg courteously saying that he didn't feel like it that evening). Greenberg and I frugged: it was a sight to see this sixty-year-old man, twitching and shaking like an adolescent. As he was driving me back to my apartment in his modest Chevy, he asked if I'd ever been married. I said, No, I was in analysis. "A lot of the girls I like best aren't married," he said, and added that he'd been in analysis until recently but quit.

I can't remember what prompted his next remark, but it may have been something to do with Olitski's young woman. "My Jenny would never act like one of those young girls," Greenberg said, with such pride and respect for his wife in his voice that I was sure this was a great marriage. She went around with her friends, and he went around with his, but she was an actress, so her friends must be theater people, just as his must be art-world people. That she had a social life of her own seemed to me further evidence of how enlightened was Greenberg's attitude toward women.

I did see her with Greenberg the next night at a party Frankenthaler had gotten me invited to, given by Alexander Liberman of *Vogue*. Michael Steiner, a young sculptor I was talking to, said he always felt uncomfortable at big parties like this one. I said everybody did. An elderly man in glasses lunged across the room, threw an arm around me, and said, "Will you marry me?" I said to Steiner, "See what I mean?" The elderly man lunged off, and I asked Steiner who he was. "Rothko," he replied.

Later that week, I asked Dustin Maine to escort me to a dinner at the Chase-Manhattan Bank, which collected art. I shook hands with David Rockefeller, president of Chase-Manhattan, but was put at the table of a mere vice president, while Kermit Lansner of *Newsweek* rated Rockefeller's table. In retrospect, I should point out that Lansner was a managing editor, whereas I was only a writer, but then, all I thought sourly was that here was yet more evidence of how much more popular *Newsweek* was in the art world than *Time*. It wasn't only because *Newsweek* employed two *Art News* alumni, Lansner and Jack Kroll, but also its liberal politics, especially on Vietnam. *Newsweek*'s smaller circulation must also militate in its favor, as this made it the underdog, while *Time* was the journalistic Establishment. Neither it nor I seemed to be getting the credit we deserved, and this was forcing me to work yet harder. The strain of doing so made me impatient to make it with Dustin Maine. If I could marry him, I could leave *Time* and do creative writing that might earn me the respect of Greenberg. I spent that Saturday night with Dustin, but it didn't convince me I loved him.

Pop and neo-dada cast abstract expressionism as The Establishment, and themselves as revolutionaries against it. This was becoming disturbing for me. I'd been amused by the Yippies who'd picketed MoMA in 1968, but by the spring of 1969, such demonstrations were merging into national turmoil. Bobby Kennedy's assassination in June 1968 had left the Democrats with no clear choice for the Presidential nomination. They'd nominated Hubert Humphrey, Johnson's vice president, at their convention in August 1968 in Chicago. Party regulars thought he had the best chance of getting elected, but his nomination had angered antiwar activists, who wanted McCarthy or George McGovern of South Dakota. The convention was marred by a violent battle between activists and the Chicago police, with many arrests, and much rage.

In November 1968, Humphrey had lost to Richard Nixon. During the campaign, Nixon hadn't offered any concrete ideas about the war, but there was little doubt in my mind (and, I believed, those of many others) that he'd won because he was less closely tied to it than Humphrey was, and more likely to get us out. During his first months in office, the press had been easy on him. It seemed willing to wait and see how he'd extricate us, but nothing was happening, beyond a continuance of the peace talks in Paris that Johnson had started, so the situation was getting desperate. The usual remedy of democracy, a peaceful change of the party in power, didn't seem to be working, so maybe the only recourse was a forcible overthrow of the government itself.

By May, campus upheavals were so widespread that the *Times* was running almost daily stories about them on Page One. Harvard was thoroughly disrupted. An even scarier situation developed at Cornell, where militant black students carrying guns seized a building ("black" was coming into use more, being considered less condescending than "Negro"). Columbia was under siege again, as were the three major campuses of the City University of New York (in Manhattan, Brooklyn, and Queens).[272] The tension was heightening in our office, too, as Grunwald got the magazine more in sync with the news – and more competitive with *Newsweek* – by using the same people on the cover, and by dealing at cover length with the same kinds of situations. One *Time* cover that spring was on the Harvard disruptions. *Newsweek* did its cover on Cornell. I was becoming frightened by how things seemed to be getting out of hand. When I went to Production to look at color transparencies for Art, I was where the cover images were being designed, and the gossip I'd hear there was even more up-to-date and upsetting than what I heard in the less pressurized corridors outside my office.

Saturday, May 3, I spent preparing dinner for Dustin, as he was taking me to the theater that evening. Sunday, I learned that Bates Lowry, director of MoMA, had been fired after less than a year in office. Saturday's *Times* had run the story.[273] I should have read that paper, I thought guiltily, but it also meant that the announcement must have been made on Friday, while I was at the office. Why hadn't I been informed? Monday, I learned that *Newsweek* had done a story on Lowry. If we couldn't be the first newsmagazine with the story, I thought, at least we could do the definitive version, but when I started investigating, the situation got stranger and stranger. The official line was that Lowry hadn't been sufficiently interested in fund-raising, but that didn't explain the suddenness or secrecy surrounding his "resignation." I was visited by Simone Swan, an art-world PR representing a trustee who'd liked Lowry. Swan set up a not-for-attribution interview for me with Lowry, but what he said made matters more confusing. He'd begun re-installing the art in one of the galleries, but hadn't been allowed to finish.

When I called Bill Rubin to ask him about this incident, he only asked how I knew about it. "A little bird told me," I retorted, thinking of Swan. Fred called. He'd planned to visit New York, and I'd arranged to take him to meet Greenberg, but since his plans were postponed, I had to call Greenberg about the postponement. I asked about Lowry. Greenberg said that a junior patron of the museum had said Lowry hadn't been interested in fund-raising. Greenberg added he'd liked the looks of Lowry, growing his hair the way the kids did. Putting that together with progressive policies Lowry had instituted, I saw him as representing the younger generation, and became afraid that his dismissal meant a reactionary turn at the museum. I felt a feverish need to give his point of view. Otherwise, I thought, the museum would become a mausoleum, and cancel a show of abstract expressionist work that Rubin was planning for June.

On Friday evening, I came to Baker's door, found it closed, and through it heard him on the phone with Liz Shaw. It sounded like she was trying to talk him out of running the story. He sent it through, but I overheard him asking one of my researchers to get up from the morgue a story we'd killed the week before, on a show of black art in Brooklyn. It looked like he was planning to substitute that for the MoMA story. I sat in my office, crying, too upset to go to the ladies' room. Baker said that the MoMA story would run, but I came in to the office on Saturday and found that he'd persuaded Ed Jamieson, who'd become assistant managing editor and was sitting in for Grunwald, to run black art instead. I marched into Jamieson's office and told him about Baker's conversation with Shaw, asking if he wanted a source to dictate policy. Jamieson said that he'd talk with Baker. Then he called me, telling me to relax, that they'd run the story. I couldn't relax. That whole weekend, I was on edge.

Monday, I got to the office and looked at the new issue. My story was in it, with a cryptic conclusion that "perhaps some petty incident triggered the downfall, some minor outrage in a sculpture gallery or hall."[274] Suddenly, I thought that the unconscious reason I'd wanted that story to appear was the opposite of what consciously, I'd intended. I'd thought I was trying to save Rubin, but now I believed that unconsciously, I'd wanted to destroy him. Dr. G had talked about hate as the flip side to love, and it seemed that this had happened with me. I became fearful that it was Rubin who'd witnessed the scene in the gallery, and that my reporting it would mean the loss of his job. Frantic to try and reverse the chain of events I thought I'd set in motion, I took a cab home, and started telephoning around. This led me to Liz Shaw, who assured me that the story was all right, adding that Lowry hadn't even had a checklist when he started rearranging the gallery. The image this summoned up – of him singlehandedly moving around precious artworks, with no plan for where he'd put them – convinced me that he hadn't known what he was doing. I thought that he, like me, had become so depressed by his job that he, too, had become destructive, and, without being aware of it, was trying to wreck the museum. Obviously, they'd had to let him go. Equally obviously, they couldn't say why.[275] Baker, I thought (confusedly), must have been trying to save me from my own destructiveness when he tried to kill the MoMA story. I called him and said he'd been right, the story shouldn't have appeared, but I wasn't feeling well. Would he mind if I took the day off? He said, not at all, so I drifted off to sleep.

Early in the morning of Tuesday, May 13, I half-awoke and lay, half-asleep. My memory drifted back to the apartment where my parents lived, when I was a baby. There I visualized my father and Bob McLaughlin playing chess. Although McLaughlin had been my mother's lover, he'd also known my parents before they split, and had played chess with my father in reality. I'd seen little of him around the office, but Baker and Christopher had told me that he'd told them that he'd known me when I was a child. I fantasized that McLaughlin had always looked out for me, and that his sense of responsibility for me had been transferred to *Time*.

My next fantasy was that Lowry's dismissal and the concealment of its reason had been staged by *Time*'s editors to bring me back to my duty as a journalist, away from Dustin, a mere PR. I believed that my new art-world friends had collaborated with *Time* in this charade, telephoning each other behind my back. I realized that this fantasy was paranoid (a delusion of grandeur), yet even so, I remained convinced that it was true. I felt that I hadn't always been so angry, that I'd turned against Rubin only after he rejected my Miró article, with his letter saying I'd misquoted him. Because of this, I'd become destructive, and, with my takeout on conceptual art, begun promoting anti-art, and its ambition to destroy the traditional values of art.

That Tuesday, I went to work thinking that I must control these destructive instincts of mine, and determined to defer to Baker in every way. In retrospect, I think it likely that this deference was a way of concealing my paranoia: if he told me what to do, I wouldn't make any false moves. I did break off with Dustin that afternoon. Wednesday morning, I said to Dr. G that I'd discovered there was good in the world, because so many people had cooperated in helping me. "People are basically good," he said, as though I'd happened on an ultimate truth.

That evening, Frankenthaler had gotten me invited to a cocktail party at the home of a well-known art historian. Both Emmerich and Bill Rubin treated me like a distinguished guest, but the big event was meeting the fabled Alfred Barr. He said he didn't read *Time*, but subscribed to *Newsweek* (of course). He asked if I played tennis. I said I did. "In tennis, you have to pat the ball, not slam it," he said. For the first time, I had a thought that would become the hallmark of my obsession, the thought that somebody was conveying an idea to me in "surreal" language. Frankenthaler had described slinging that toy pistol in Motherwell's lap as a "surreal gesture." I believed she'd been suggesting that besides being a playful gesture, her act had also been a come-on. Likewise, I felt that Barr was saying that I shouldn't have knocked myself out with my story on Lowry, that to deal with it gently would have been enough.

The word "surreal" suggests a second level of reality, on top of (in French, *sur*) the real. I felt that Barr's words similarly conveyed a second, hidden level of meaning on top of the obvious one about tennis, and from his courteous treatment of me, I felt that he thought the Lowry story was a good one. The way everybody else was behaving made me think that they admired it, too. I've since read about what psychologists call "delusions of reference." This is a thought disorder some mental patients suffer from: they overhear a conversation on the street, and think that it's really about them, or they believe that people on TV are sending them coded messages. My experience with Barr could be described as the start of this delusion, but only to the extent that I believed his discussion of tennis was a deliberately disguised message to me.

After all, for thirteen years, I'd been hearing from Dr. G about the unconscious or symbolic significance of remarks or behavior. He'd told me about hidden meanings of my own words and gestures dozens of times, and done the same with public figures and my colleagues. I'd spent fifteen years interpreting my dreams with Dr. G and with Dr. Keiser before him. Time and again, I'd seen how images in these dreams were symbols, to be deciphered by free association, nor was my experience of double levels of meaning in words, sentences, or incidents confined to what I'd learned on the couch. I'd been exposed to the concept many other ways, from the puns I'd read as a child to the metonymy and synecdoche I'd studied in college; from the symbolism in modern English plays to double-entendres in ads and coded messages in songs.

I'd used double levels of meaning while writing for *Time*, sometimes without knowing it. My colleagues used them as wit or to avoid a libel suit. Frankenthaler's use of the word "surreal" had linked art and life together for me intellectually, but not until Barr talked to me about tennis did art and life fuse. Yes, it may have been somewhat deranged of me to believe that this was happening. I know that sometimes I did have genuine "delusions of reference," but even today, I'd argue that on many occasions, the "surreal" messages that I received (and sent) made an eerie kind of sense.

When I read that secondary – or surreal – level of meaning into Barr's remark about patting the tennis ball, I was doing so upon the basis of my knowledge of art, language, dream and gesture, but also (without thinking about it) because of other things I knew. Many art-world people didn't admit they read *Time*, but that didn't mean that they didn't read it, and if Barr hadn't read my story, somebody might have told him what was in it. Considering his long association with MoMA, he might have been interested in knowing what 14.5 million readers were being told about a major upheaval in its management. He could also have been told that I'd run myself ragged in researching the story, since it was known to more than one person at that party. Barr's words about tennis, as I interpreted them, made me feel important, understood and soothed. Who is to say that this wasn't what he intended to accomplish (on some level or other)?

12. QUIDNUNC
(MAY–AUGUST 1969)

THE STORY ACCOMPANYING our color page the week after the Lowry story dealt with a London church, bombed out in World War II, being rebuilt in Missouri.[276] As I wrote, it acquired meaning on a secondary or surreal level: I was the church, and the story was telling all my art-world friends that I'd been blasted, but was re-created, and rededicated to a worthier cause. The "cause" was the restoration of true art – as opposed to anti-art, or what Greenberg might have called "novelty art."

Earlier in the spring, researching my piece for the *Columbia Journalism Review*, I'd lunched with Hilton Kramer of the *Times*. He'd said that in the '50s, a rivalry between Greenberg and Harold Rosenberg had divided the Manhattan art world. Rosenberg had written for *Art News*, where he and its editor, Thomas B. Hess, had promoted de Kooning as the greatest abstract expressionist, while Greenberg stood by Pollock. Kramer intimated that Hess had been "too close" to Elaine de Kooning, Willem's wife.[277]

Following that up, I'd read an article that Rosenberg had published in *Art News* in 1952 on "The American action painters." In it, he'd applied what was initially taken to be an existentialist interpretation to abstract expressionism. "At a certain moment," he wrote, "the canvas began to appear to one American painter after another as an arena in which to act – rather than as a space in which to reproduce, re-design, analyze, or 'express' an object, actual or imagined. What was to go on the canvas was not a picture but an event."[278] By saying that the *act* mattered more than the result, Rosenberg in effect linked up abstract expressionism with the dada of Duchamp, since Duchamp had argued that his household objects became art by his *act* of placing them in an artistic context. My realization of this must have owed something to an article by Barbara Rose in the May 1969 *Artforum* on "The Politics of Art," which I read the week I was writing about that bombed-out church. Rose saw Rosenberg's article as "the main channel through which Dada ideology and esthetics" entered abstract expressionism.[279]

She dismayed me by suggesting that the media were corrupting the art scene in the very act of reporting it. "The minute Pollock ceased to be 'Jack the Dripper' for the Luce publications," she wrote, "the radicality of extremism

170

was doomed."[280] I'd tried so hard to get *Time* away from rear-guard phrases like "Jack the Dripper," but now I felt as if I'd been rendering greatness and sophistication merely shallow and commonplace by writing about them in my mass-media magazine. Guiltily, I remembered how London had been cheapened by our cover, the sleazy souvenirs and vulgar guidebooks, how even the word "swinging" had become a synonym for wife-swapping and promiscuity.

Friday night, I took Fred, my old boyfriend, to see Greenberg. I gave Greenberg a copy of *A Swinger's Guide;* he gave each of us one of the drawings he'd made during his sketching sessions with Olitski and other friends. He made us choose the ones we wanted, and after I'd made my choice, he said, "You picked a good one." Evidently he thought I had an eye. The three of us went out for dinner. I was so engrossed with Greenberg that I ignored Fred. After dinner, we went to a pub for a drink. I sat with my elbows on the table, propping up my chin. Greenberg gently disengaged one wrist, and waggled it slowly, from side to side. "You may be a good art writer for *Time*," he said. "You may be the best art writer that *Time* ever had, but you're never going to amount to anything, as long as you stay on *Time*. It's just a job." Dr. G had been saying that *Time* was "just a job" for years, but only when Greenberg said it, did it sink in.

Saturday, he'd gotten me invited to a party that Larry Poons was giving at his multistory loft downtown. I asked Fred to escort me, then again forgot him, climbing by myself to the top floor, where Greenberg asked me to dance. It was a slow number, and he cradled me in his arms as a father cradles a baby. I thought of him as the father I'd never had. "See? No sex," he said, carefully disengaging himself when the music stopped, and going to dance with Stephanie Noland, while I sat with her husband. He'd liked the article I'd done on him; she hadn't. That marriage was in trouble. Greenberg had come to the party with a woman who worked at (shall we say) the Marlborough-Gerson Gallery. They drove Fred and me back to my apartment, me talking all the way to Greenberg from the backseat. (The next time I heard from Fred was in September, when he called to tell me he was engaged.)

Time's cover the following week was on Vladimir Nabokov. Its conclusion said, "Perhaps he knew, even then, that the best way for an artist to triumph over time was to vanish like the Cheshire cat, leaving only a smile behind."[281] My taste had grown too sophisticated for *Time*, I thought, so Grunwald was suggesting that the best way for me to triumph over it was to vanish. Clearly, this was a delusion of reference, since even if Grunwald had written that sentence, it was unlikely that he'd directed it to just me, but in retrospect the idea that he wanted me to vanish seems quite possible. This delusion of reference could have been my unconscious telling me – in surreal or symbolic language – what my conscious mind couldn't yet accept.

That summer, I heard that Ed Hughes, my onetime editor in World, had left the Beirut bureau and the company, but Baker, my present editor, took me to two fine lunches with corporate bigwigs.[282] This nourished my delusion that, by insisting *Time* run my story on Lowry, I'd become a model of heroic journalism, an oracle for the company. I fantasized that Greenberg had called Dr. G; this was why Dr. G spoke so respectfully of him. "Why can't you leave it to this Clem Greenberg to run the art world?" he asked. Was he jealous? It was the first time in thirteen years that he'd referred to a man I knew by name.

Further research showed me how Rosenberg used the reputation he'd developed within the art world as an apologist for "action painting" to legitimize pop and neo-dada for the wider community that read *The New Yorker*. In the fall of 1962, the Sidney Janis Gallery staged *The New Realists*, a big exhibition of pop. *The New Yorker*'s regular critic, Robert M. Coates, had lived in Paris in the '20s. There he'd evidently seen lots of dada and surrealism; to him, pop was just more of the same.[283] This apparently meant he had to be replaced, for *The New Yorker*'s first art column of the 1962–63 season was by Rosenberg, who wrote, "Today it is felt that a new art mode is long overdue, if for no other reason than that the present avant-garde has been with us for fifteen years."[284] One month later, the Janis show had come along, enabling Rosenberg to report that this overdue new mode had "hit the New York art world with the force of an earthquake," and adding that "Within a week, tremors had spread to art centers throughout the country."[285] Pop didn't really become a household word until *Time* did its big color spread on it the following spring, but as I saw it, Janis and Rosenberg had forced *Time* to follow suit.

In her article, Rose suggested that Greenberg had abandoned socialism for "a reactionary political attitude."[286] This made sense to me, because clips from *Time* and *Newsweek* in his bio folder had told me about a letter he'd written in 1951 to *The Nation*, criticizing its foreign affairs editor for following a pro-Soviet line.[287] Admirers of pop and related dada-descended art welcomed this apparent correlation between Greenberg's preference for more traditional painting and sculpture and his supposed political conservatism. The art world was (and is) predominantly leftist in its politics, so calling Greenberg a political reactionary afforded added grounds for his opponents to reject his esthetic preferences. In my innocence, I accepted this correlation. *Art News* was owned by *Newsweek,* and to me, *Newsweek* had been celebrating anti-art in its aborted cover on "The New Art." This, I figured, made Greenberg into my ally as a *Time* employee (weird as that alignment sounds to me in retrospect – in later years, when I knew him better, he'd always say that he preferred *Newsweek* to *Time*).

To a dadaist (as I then understood it), there was no order, logic, or reason in the world, and no sense or meaning in high art or the bourgeois society that produced it: a political conviction as well as an esthetic one. It made me think of art in the tradition of dada as dangerously political. Barbara Rose's article reinforced this impression. Antiwar protesters were finding fault with capitalism, and, as she saw it, a parallel feeling had developed among artists making process art, conceptualism, or earthworks. "The artist," she wrote, "does not cooperate with the art market. Such non-cooperation can be seen as reflective of certain political attitudes. It is the esthetic equivalent of the wholesale refusal of the young to participate in compromised situations (e.g., the Vietnam war)."[288] Such political allusions helped me to feel that a community of interest – political as well as esthetic – bound together neo-dada, pop, and related styles like conceptualism with *Art News*, *The New Yorker*, and above all, *Newsweek*. Weren't the precedents that *Newsweek* set for *Time* only making bad things worse? From the sadistic violence of *In Cold Blood* to Cornell's gun-toting militants, *Newsweek* seemed to me (in my nervous state of mind) to be publicizing and thus accentuating nearly every negative trend in American society.

Somebody called to say demonstrations would be taking place at Yale, and would I like to send somebody to cover them? I said I didn't think it was an Art story. Somebody else called to say a new Oldenburg sculpture, a giant lipstick, was to be set up, also at Yale. I felt we'd done enough on Oldenburg. Yale was the most conservative, stuffiest school in the Ivy League. In 1969, it was still the only one of the top four Ivy League schools that had so far escaped serious disruption.[289] To me (at that moment), this made it the last bastion of civilization. If even Yale went up in flames, everything else would go.

Then I heard that *Time* was going to do a Show Business cover on "Sex in the Arts." It would outdo in prurience even *Newsweek*'s 1967 cover on "The Permissive Society." *Time*'s peg was *Oh, Calcutta!*, a musical with an all-nude cast, but it would also deal with explicit sex in other plays, movies, and books. This was the antithesis of what Dr. G considered sane, healthy attitudes toward sex: he'd so often said that people who engaged in public displays of it were neurotic exhibitionists. The cover story was to be written by Mike Demarest and edited by Silas Haynes, both of whom I liked but believed had been unfaithful to their wives. Grunwald would top-edit it; and Bill Rubin and Parmiter had suggested that he had outside interests, too. Dr. G said that adultery was easier for men, because they had less difficulty splitting sex off from love. How could one expect three adulterers to deal with sex in the only way that mattered: in relation to love? The cover seemed the clearest example yet of *Newsweek*'s cheesy practices forcing *Time* to outdo it in gutter journalism. It upset me so much that I decided to write an interoffice memo to Grunwald, arguing we shouldn't do it. Looking back, this strikes me like telling the tide not to rise. As Jason McManus had said, everybody's interested in sex, but Dr. G was all for my writing the memo, and even suggested I should send copies to other people on the staff, because "the man" might not be "responsive" to what I said. (When even your shrink is promoting lunatic behavior, what do you do?)

After months of campus unrest, the *Times* on Monday, June 9, headlined Nixon's first major troop withdrawals, but the number of soldiers involved (only twenty-five thousand, out of a total of more than half a million) seemed to almost all of his many critics far too small.[290] What I overheard, in galleries and museums, made me think of the art world as still dangerously inflamed. I talked about it with Baker, who was related to a Harvard student, and sympathized with this student. "It's this war that's really responsible" he said, with passion. "Nixon's doing what he can," I replied, arguing with equal fervor that if the withdrawals were any larger or faster, they'd be taken as weakness. I scheduled a story to calm things down by showing that Nixon patronized art, even by minorities. The story was to include a "paint-in" on a wall hiding construction in Lafayette Park, across from the White House. The wall was decorated by largely black area high school students, and Tricia Nixon, the President's daughter, joined in for a few ceremonial dabs.[291]

Production needed a photograph to illustrate this story. I remembered from my first year at *Time* that the clip desk got the Washington papers, and went to where they were shelved. *The Washington Post* had a photograph of the paint-in. I took it to Production, suggesting they request it (*Time* and the *Post* belonged to the Associated Press, and AP members shared photographs). Obviously, I knew the Washington Post Company owned *Newsweek*, but I wasn't thinking of that. After greening my section, I took a Friday-night train to Quogue, where I still had a share in a group house. Saturday, I called Production, to be sure my greens had worked, and the man said yes, they'd worked. "Everything worked," he added, with what seemed unusual satisfaction.

Sunday night, June 15, I came back from Quogue to attend the disco party that MoMA was staging for the opening of Bill Rubin's abstract expressionist show. At the entrance, I met Greenberg, leaving. He kissed my hand. Fred had kissed my hand, too, but when Greenberg did it, it became his signature gesture. Inside, Liz Shaw said, "They're burning New Haven." Yale, I thought, dimly, Luce's alma mater, but I was dazed, and didn't ask what she meant. She introduced me to the man she was with, saying that he was with Time Inc.'s radio division. "I work for the same corporation," I said, making a joke of it.

"You *are* the corporation," he said (doubtless making a joke in turn, though naturally I took it as another tribute to my status as oracle).

The Monday papers said nothing about a fire in New Haven, and *Newsweek* wasn't yet on sale at our lobby newsstand. I checked every time I went in and out of the building, but the magazine didn't arrive until late Tuesday afternoon. Its cover was a collage built around a student's mortarboard, images of campus strife and the militant's clenched-fist salute. The headline read "Class of '69: The Violent Years," but the text was only a rehash of earlier confrontations, with the most guarded reference possible to Yale ("Yale's Kingman Brewster is credited with staying 'one step ahead of trouble' by seeking out students and anticipating their needs").[292] Nevertheless, there had been a fire at Yale in the early hours of Saturday, June 14. It caused damage estimated at between five hundred thousand and two million dollars to the art and architecture building designed by the modernist architect Paul Rudolph, and much criticized for its "brutalist" design.

The blaze had begun with violent explosions. Their cause was still unknown even by the time I read about it, in the August 11 *New York*. The article was by Peter Blake of *Architectural Forum* (now owned by a nonprofit organization). Blake wrote that, though the fire had made Page One in Denver, San Francisco, and Washington, the *Times* didn't report it for almost two weeks, and then only after it "had been repeatedly needled about this business by fascinated parties, including reporters from the *Architectural Forum*." The paper sent a reporter to New Haven only after it was "stung into action by suggestions that Yale President Kingman Brewster had actually kept the story out of the *Times*."[293] (Was this my paranoia or somebody else's?)

I felt sure that this fire must be linked to antiwar protests. yet both the *Times* and *Newsweek* seemed to be suppressing news of it. I thought of the man in Production saying, in that odd tone of voice, "Everything worked," and put together a scenario which seems fantastic now, but was real enough to me then. I reasoned that if even *Time* had been told of the demos scheduled for Yale, and Oldenburg's monster lipstick, then surely *Newsweek* had. *Newsweek*, as I saw it, would have decided to feature this concerted protest in New Haven at cover length, with artists and students united. The protesters would have hoped to trigger demos on other campuses, as news of their efforts was spread by the media, and, given the vehemence of the moment, who knows how far the protest could have gone? Then I'd done my story on the paint-in, and made *Time* ask the *Post* for the photo. Maybe the *Post* told its sister publication this picture had been requested, and people there wondered why. They could have found out, I thought, remembering people on *Time* who knew people on *Newsweek*, plus all those curious coincidences between *Newsweek*'s coverage and ours.

In retrospect, I think it possible that *Newsweek*'s cover on the "Class of '69" didn't mention the Yale fire on Saturday night because it had gone to press on Friday, with the rest of back of the book, but in 1969, my overactive imagination put together a livelier scenario. I imagined that when *Newsweek* had learned *Time* would portray the Nixons as art lovers, directly at variance with their cover, they'd decided to play down the situation in New Haven. It would have taken time to create a new story that didn't mention the fire. Time to design and print a whole new cover – yet, judging from how late the magazine had arrived on our newsstand, that time had elapsed. Even in 1969, I found my theory hard to believe, but I didn't know how else to explain the facts, so I concluded that I'd become an oracle for *Newsweek* and the *Times*, as well as *Time*.

Given all this, I was sure my memo would force Grunwald to abandon "Sex in the Arts." I can't remember exactly what it said, but I know it was rambling and fearfully indiscreet. I argued that *Time* was being trapped into destructive, sensationalist journalism through its efforts to compete with *Newsweek*, that *Newsweek* was driven by pernicious art criticism, and by an aggressive woman, Katharine Graham, its owner. I also argued that her two principal instruments were Kroll and Lansner, gifted paranoids who'd risen from the dada-inspired misdirections of *Art News* to drive Greenberg into exile, and promote chaos throughout America in the cynical interests of building advertising and circulation.

I maintained that *Time* had been trapped into imitating *Newsweek*, described how destructive a cover on "Sex in the Arts" would be, and closed by saying that Moses may have decided to tell his people that the Ten Commandments came from God, because although he himself might sin against them, he didn't want them discredited on that account. This passage was meant to be a way of telling Grunwald on a secondary or surreal level of language that I thought he might himself have violated the Seventh Commandment, but could still promote wholesome values as managing editor. I made copies, just as Dr. G recommended, for Demarest, Baker, and Jamieson.

On Monday, June 16, I put all four copies of my memo into the interoffice mail. Wednesday, I went to MoMA, to look at the abstract expressionist show. Minutes after I got there, Rubin hurried in, to show me around. I hadn't told him I was coming, but somebody must have spotted me, and alerted him. More benign supervision, I fantasized. Rubin's seeming desire to be with me kept me thinking he must like me, though Liz Shaw had told me that he was leaving that Friday to summer in France with Beryl Barr. Shaw said that Barr's divorce hadn't come through, and the couple were postponing their marriage until the fall, though I hadn't asked her about that, either.

By the following week, I'd begun to see surreal or double levels of meaning in *Peanuts*, in the *New York Post*. I couldn't imagine how Charles Schulz had become familiar with my situation, but he seemed to know all about it. Charlie Brown was on vacation, just as Bill Rubin was, and Charlie was writing a postcard home to Snoopy.[294] I fantasized this meant that Rubin was going to send me a postcard, and sure enough, a card from France in fact arrived, saying that he'd liked my story on the abstract expressionists. "Sex in the Arts" was proceeding with the enthusiastic support of every male on the staff. When I went to Production, to look at Art transparencies, I found the guys there poring over photographs of *Oh, Calcutta!* "Women just don't understand pornography," somebody remarked, but I let it pass.

My sense of being a corporate oracle was evaporating. Suddenly, I felt no need to do any more than was required, and even started farming out one Art story a week (this was asking to be fired, but naturally I didn't see it that way). These stories were written by Marguerite Johnson, a researcher who would become a writer after I left *Time*, but the artworks chosen to illustrate her stories seemed suggestive to me. Since nobody on the outside would know that I hadn't written them, I felt *Time* was conspiring to make me look like a whore. Today, I'd say this delusion of persecution might be seen as a symbolic expression of real experiences I was having, such as the writer who stuck his head into my office about then, and said (apropos of nothing), "You know, *Time* could get along without you."

I had vacation in July, and wanted to rewrite one of my plays, but the editor of the *Columbia Journalism Review* wanted revisions on my article, so I'd have to do that in July, and only get to the play in August. Dr. G was taking two months off. I wouldn't see him again until after Labor Day, when I planned to resign from *Time* – as I told him on June 27, our last session before he left. If I resigned in the fall, giving a month's notice, I'd have a month to look for a part-time job to cover basic expenses (including Dr. G) but let me do my own writing. Everybody said that getting a new job was easier when you still had the old one, but the art world scattered to the Hamptons and Europe in summer. Nobody who might offer me employment would be back before Labor Day.

*   *   *

I was on vacation when "Sex in the Arts" came out, so I had to buy *Time* to read it. One vicious paragraph began, "The plastic arts have also turned anew to 'genital commotion'...."[295] This paragraph tried to create the impression that porn dominated the art scene, with four almost totally specious examples of explicit art that somebody had dug up without consulting me. As it did create the impression that *Time*'s regular Art writer was very badly informed and/or a hopeless prude, its effect was to shove me violently away from the magazine. When I started revising my article for the *Columbia Journalism Review*, I saw things very differently. I had argued that *Time* had done the best job covering contemporary art. My villain had been *Newsweek*, whose emphasis on art as news had cheapened it, but now *Newsweek* seemed nicer and more idealistic, while *Time* looked arrogant and venal. My conclusion was that all mass-media coverage of art served to debase it, but the revised article was far too long to publish. I didn't mind. It had served a purpose: educating me.

For several summers, I'd had a share in a Quogue group house called the Farmhouse. It was owned by William H. Swan, an eccentric divorced man of indeterminate years who also owned other houses in Quogue. He rented many of them to summer "groupers," which didn't endear him to older, stuffier local residents. Bill Swan didn't like to spend money on upkeep or repairs, but his houses had charm, and he himself was not without elvish appeal. He liked to drift by the Farmhouse at the cocktail hour, and make chitchat while avoiding promises to fix whatever happened to be wrong.

The Farmhouse was part of Swan's family estate, Pen Craig, though reached by a different road from the main Pen Craig house. The main Pen Craig house had been rented to men associated with International House, a Columbia University dorm housing many foreign students. Persons from African or Asian backgrounds in lily-white, Republican Quogue were even less appreciated by older residents than the average grouper, but the "I-House" group was another reason I liked Swan, for all his shifty ways. The other big building at Pen Craig was a renovated barn called the Coach House; I'd dined there in 1961 with Donald B. Douglas, a neurologist I'd met at the Sand Bar Beach Club.

Donald B. had since dropped out of the Sand Bar, and moved into a house of his own. He was still single, but other men I'd met at the Sand Bar had married Sand Bar women and bought Quogue homes. These graduate groupers weren't that different in background or outlook from the people who'd resisted their advent as groupers, and few had much use for Hungarian names, but the town itself was gracious, in an old-fashioned way. The group in the Farmhouse during the summer of 1969 had been organized largely by Alison Bond, a cheerful, skinny, red-haired Englishwoman. All the other members of the group were women except for one married couple (unlike the trendier group houses on Fire Island, Quogue's were still mostly single-sex).

Only one woman in the Farmhouse belonged to the Sand Bar. Sometimes, I'd go to the club with her, but neither Alison nor the others in the Farmhouse were members. When I went to the beach with them, we used Hot Dog One or Hot Dog Two, public beaches a quarter-mile or so west of the Sand Bar.

The I-House crowd also used the Hot Dogs. I liked to stroll along the edge of the water, passing the Sand Bar if I wasn't spending the day there, then arriving at Tiana, a public beach to the east of the Sand Bar. Tiana drew a noisier crowd, in flashier bathing suits. They liked to stand around talking and drinking beer.

On August 4, I returned to work. Baker was on vacation; Gus Daniels was editing Art. For some months, I'd been being encouraged to use "duotone" instead of full-color photography. As the name suggests, duotone was printed in only two colors. It was cheaper, and went to press at the same time as the rest of the issue, giving Grunwald the option of killing my section. I'd resisted duotone, but, as part of my new desire to be less aggressive, I offered to use it for a story about some recently excavated early Christian frescoes. After I'd written it, Daniels said bluntly that he didn't think it was very good, and killed the section. When Fuerbringer had been managing editor, Daniels had cared for me like a father, but with Grunwald in charge, he was not only killing my section but being rude to me about it. What a weathervane! Sad to say, he wasn't alone. I'd run into McManus in the corridor and greeted him with a bright hello, but he'd only muttered a scared little "Hi" under his breath, and scuttled along away from me as fast as he could go.

In the mornings, before going to the office, I was redoing the comedy I'd written in 1964 about a summer group house in a town like Quogue. It gave me insights into the creative process that even people who have written fiction might not know. I thought I was writing fiction, with characters and dialogue completely made up, but time and again, after I'd written something down, I'd realize that I'd really been alluding to something I'd actually seen or heard. In effect, I was psychoanalyzing the play, using free association to unearth the sources of the imagery in it just as I'd so often unearthed the sources of images in my dreams. The experience would turn out to be very helpful in 1983, when I was formulating my theory about abstract painting, because it would show me that images could make the transition from a creator's unconscious to the work of art without the creator's conscious mind being aware that this was happening.

Sometimes, I'd become aware by myself that fictional characters or situations were based upon memories of real people or events. Sometimes, I fantasized that friends had gone into my apartment and read what I'd written, after I left for the office, then made remarks or staged incidents to make me see that I'd actually been writing about this or that factual circumstance. The idea that friends were helping me was, of course, crazy, but the remarks and incidents did trigger awareness of what real circumstances I'd been referring to. For starters, there was the title of the new version: *Quidnunc*.[296] It was the name of the fictional town where the play took place. I thought I'd picked it out of the air simply because it, like Quogue, began with a Q, but at some point I looked it up in the dictionary, and saw that it meant "busybody." I realized I must have known this, on an unconscious level, because it fit the central character in the play – even though, when I'd chosen it, I hadn't been conscious of what it meant, or that he would become the principal character.

I knew it was to be a surreal play, with characters externally based on Quogue people, but internally informed by my art-world experience. I didn't anticipate that, with its hidden allusions, it would turn out to be written on more than two levels, and say as much about *Time* as it did about art, or Quogue. As its plot, throughout August, developed in ways I hadn't anticipated, it made me recognize some hard truths about myself, in this respect also resembling analysis. Looking back, I'd say that maybe this was the purpose of writing the play: to help me understand why I was where I was at that moment.

My basic plot was to be the same as it had been in 1964. The heroine was a glamorous writer who came out to Quidnunc for a weekend with a square Republican named Tom. They arrived on Friday night at a men's group house (where dates slept in a women's dorm). There they met Tom's more interesting housemate, whom the heroine had known when they were working together on a business newsletter (consciously meant to resemble the Business section of *Time*). Needless to say, this heroine was a stand-in for me, and was meant to end up with the interesting housemate. To make this possible, I decided to add a third character, a deus ex machina who would bring the two together. He was to be a Quidnunc landowner with mysterious powers and perspicacity whom I named Simon Murgatroyd. In the context of Quogue, he was to be based upon Bill Swan, but on the surreal level he was informed by Greenberg, the busybody who'd meddled in my life.

In my original draft, the interesting housemate had been modeled on Fred Freund; in this new version, he was to be informed by the spirit of Bill Rubin. In both drafts, he was called Harry. With my conscious mind, I'd named him after my college beau, but during the summer of 1969 I remembered that Harry had also been Luce's nickname, and realized this must have been another reason for my naming my character Harry. In the version of 1969, Harry had a fiancee named Lady Isabel Mountebank, daughter of an English press lord. The only relative of an English press lord whom I knew about was Lady Jeanne Campbell, the granddaughter of Lord Beaverbrook who'd been involved with Luce when I was new on *Time*. This was a second hint that I was writing about *Time* as much as I was writing about the art world, but it was a hint I still didn't want to take.

Late Saturday afternoon in my play, Lady Isabel played croquet with my heroine, and whanged her ball into the rough. When I wrote that, I'd thought I was remembering the summer of 1961, when I played croquet in Quogue with a bond broker I'd met at the Sand Bar, but the weekend after I'd written it, Alison asked me where I'd learned to play croquet, and I recalled that I'd originally learned it in the summer of 1940, from my granny West. I'd been five, and my mother had rented the cottage on the farm in Bucks County. Bob McLaughlin had been staying in the renovated chicken coop next to the cottage, writing short stories for *The New Yorker*. Earlier in 1969, I'd fantasized that he'd stood in loco parentis for me on *Time*, but by August, I was thinking (with more justification) that he'd been awfully tame and domesticated, that summer in Bucks County, in effect castrated by my mother's generosity, the fact that she'd let him live there for free.

Granny West had excelled at croquet, but I also remembered how she'd slaved in caring for my blind grandfather, helping him memorize sermons, raising their children in threadbare parsonages, doing household chores, and fulfilling the church duties expected of her. I realized that, in trying to become a bride of *Time*, I'd turned myself into my saintly granny. Luce had been the son of missionaries. Hadn't I noticed how many of his writers and editors had clerics in their families? It was only natural that I should see myself as a minister's wife, leading a life of obvious chastity, rarely losing my temper, putting up with subtle indignities. With Dr. G telling me again and again how neurotic it was to be aggressive like my mother, I'd fallen back to the previous generation.

My 1964 play had had a single set, an all-men group house. In 1969, there were two group houses. The all-men one was named the Stable, and based on the Coach House on Bill Swan's estate. The all-women one was supposed to be based on the Farmhouse, and had several members who served as a sort of Greek chorus. I named it the Henhouse, meaning it as a joke, but sometime that August, I realized that the renovated chicken coop that McLaughlin had occupied in 1940 must be the unconscious reference I'd intended. Analyzing this in turn, I realized that unconsciously I considered him, the obedient *Time* writer, so tame and domesticated that I'd turned him into a woman.

My fictional equivalent for the Sand Bar I called the Mid-Victorian Club, believing I was satirizing the decorous courting rituals in Quogue. I had the club president hoping for an attendance of two hundred people at the Saturday-night party there, and another character saying, "That'd break Prince Charlie's record." I thought I was referring to a former Sand Bar president named Charlie, but then Charlie Parmiter dropped by my office at work, and I realized that I'd really been referring to him. When I'd been in

People, he'd complimented me on my clothes and hair; more recently he'd said, "Pardon my French." What a gentleman! Men on *Time* observed the conventions in public, whatever they did in private. Again, I realized that in writing about Quogue, I was also writing about *Time*.

Escorted by Tom, my heroine came to the club party, and saw a shy older guy standing in a corner by himself. This character was based, so I thought, upon a shy older member of the Sand Bar, but my heroine said that if this were the sort of party she normally attended, he'd be a distinguished writer, and added that she once knew a writer like that. Asked what he'd written about, she replied, "Himself and the girl he was in love with. A lady editor. He drank himself to death." I'd thought I was making this up, too, but the second these words were on the page, I realized I'd been referring to Dick Sherman, my parents' shy friend who'd worked on *Vanity Fair* with the future Mrs. Luce, written a highly successful novella about his infatuation with her, and stood off in a corner at my mother's parties. When he'd died in 1962, the circumstances suggested acute alcoholism. Yet here he was, surfacing in a way that showed me how even my mother's world, which I thought so different from Quogue, was swimming into its orbit, and how her world and that of *Time*, which I'd always considered opposites, were tied together through Dick.

The most complex associations revolved around my heroine. In the 1964 play, I'd called her Harriet, but in 1969, I decided that Harriet was too much like Harry (and as such, yet another reference to Luce). I renamed her Mary Ann, after a college friend. My Harriet had been a glamorous freelance writer, but Mary Ann had become a travel writer for a hip magazine called *Hot Shot*. Harry confided to Lady Isabel that he couldn't understand how Mary Ann had become so successful, adding, "This girl was nothing when I knew her. I taught her the business. She never did know how to write." Lady Isabel asked how she could have done it. "Some of those places are sinks," Harry said darkly. "Girls like Mary Ann use their editors." I was trying to explain why Rubin hadn't accepted me. Art-world people slept about, and as they hated *Time*, would assume its employees did, too, for more cynical reasons. Why shouldn't they make such assumptions, when *Time* published "Sex in the Arts"? Greenberg could have been suspicious. Somebody had suggested I apply for a Guggenheim fellowship, to finish my play, and I'd called him to ask if he'd be a reference. "I haven't published much under my own name," I'd said, remembering that my writing for *Time* was unsigned. "But I'm a professional," I added. "Oh yes," he'd said. "You're a real professional." Was there a bite in his voice?

The sort of travel article Mary Ann wrote was first suggested in the beach scene on Saturday morning, when the club president led her from the club over to Titty Beach (meaning Tiana). I'd peopled it with (imaginary) busty babes in bikinis, and it resounded to electric guitars. Broken gin bottles littered the sand, but Mary Ann loved it. "Look at those couples, writhing in a frenzy of passion," she said. "That's the kind of performance that makes magazine copy." Then she was led off in the opposite direction to see Cop-Out Beach (meaning Hot Dog One). This was the one Harry went to, with beautiful (though equally invisible) Scandinavian models and handsome black men.

Quidnunc's main street, with one streetlamp shining, was the setting for a scene that took place after the croquet and before the club party. Mary Ann entered to admire an imaginary house. Simon, the mysterious landlord whom she'd met earlier, came up behind her, and said, "You picked a good one," as Greenberg had said of the choice I'd made among his drawings. Mary Ann told Simon that Harry had said there was an article for *Hot Shot* in Quidnunc, but she didn't know where to look for it. Simon told her a witch had been burned there in 1780; she'd really been a reformed prostitute, protesting the town whorehouse. Mary Ann was more interested in the whorehouse, and asked whether Quidnunc had any contemporary equivalents. "Only, of course, taking money for it is kind of square," she added. "What I need is a place where the girls put out for free."

Here she was defining herself as the kind of travel writer who'd created "Swinging London," a woman who knew what sort of travel article paid. Besides being another reference to my job, it referred to my time in World. "Swinging London" had also been implied by Mary Ann's response to Titty Beach, but her language here was cruder. Instead of answering her, Simon took out a map of Quidnunc, and pointed out locations of several houses. She said she couldn't get to all of them in one visit. "Perhaps you'll come back sometime," he said, kissing her hand, as Greenberg had kissed mine, and exiting to leave her gazing after him, as hypnotized by him as Greenberg had hypnotized me.

Harry entered, and was jealous of the map. Mary Ann was convinced that the houses Simon had indicated on it were sites of sinful, illicit activities. "Quidnunc's the cleanest little town this side of God," Harry said. She reminded him he'd told her there was a story in it for her, but he said what he'd meant was the houses in the town. They'd been put up around the turn of the century as private indulgences by famous architects, but were too big to sell or even rent. The summer tenant in the house Harry lived in during the winter had just moved out. She asked why, and Harry said bitterly, "No action. The town wasn't live. He's gotta have action. Just like you." She had nothing to say, and he brusquely announced they had to get back to the Stable, because his fiancee was waiting. "I'm sure she is," Mary Ann said, gently, as the sad end to a scene summing up my relationship with Rubin – how he loved his fiancee, but played up to me for the sake of publicizing his art.

At the real-life Farmhouse, Alison had invited my friend, Suzie Brown, for the weekend. Suzie asked, "Whatever became of Marianne?" I heard "Mary Ann" instead of "Marianne," and for an instant thought she meant Mary Ann in my play. Then I realized she meant Marianne Foster, the Englishwoman who'd done research for my guidebook, and later known Suzie in New York. It hit me with horror that the people coming in to read my play must think I identified with Marianne, the red-hot swinger. This led to the still more unpleasant thought that, in relation to *Time*, I had been not unlike one. The last time I'd gotten a raise, the secretary telling me about it had said I was "the most highly paid woman in New York." Greenberg had called me "a real professional." I'd offered myself to Fuerbringer as a woman who could write, when he needed a woman writer. I'd never sold my writing in the open market, and until I did, the world would look on me as Marianne, the professional woman.

Baker returned from vacation, and said the story on the Christian frescoes was all right. Then he killed it over the weekend, leaving me aced out of the book for the second time in the thirty months I'd written Art.

By this time my play had reached its late-Saturday-night scene. The club party had ended. Outside the Stable, Tom was starting the barbecue for dinner, but Mary Ann was trying to lure him into bed much as I'd lured Dustin Maine, hoping to get him to marry her. Simon interrupted them, and sent Tom off on a pretext. Mary Ann said to Simon, "I have this feeling, of being trapped in a maze. Or toyed with like a mouse. By a very high IQ old cat." These were my feelings about Greenberg, but Simon only exclaimed, "What an imagination!" and asked, "Do you write fiction, young lady?"

She confessed she was unhappy with describing foreign places so they sounded sick and sinful. "It's that combination of horrified innocence and world-weary greed that gets them every time," she said, and with those words, I was back writing "Swinging London." I'd never been to Art. In the ensuing action, Simon and Harry broke up Mary Ann's relationship with Tom, but Harry didn't claim her for his own, and she wandered off. All or most of this I must have written on the Thursday before the Labor Day weekend. The next day, I was going to send my resignation to Grunwald, giving him a month's notice.

Friday morning, I wrote a scene in which Mary Ann wandered at dawn into the Henhouse, to raid the refrigerator. One of the house members came out, and asked about the article she was going to write about Quidnunc. "They'd never believe Quidnunc in *Hot Shot*, or any other magazine," Mary Ann said. "They'd say it was all a figment of my disordered imagination."

Why not write a novel? "My God, if I write a novel, I'd have to admit it was all in my mind," she said. "No self-respecting journalist can afford to do that. Besides, who's to say my novel would be the only one anybody could write? With journalism, you can have the illusion you're telling the only story that can be told."

I planned a third act in which Simon brought Mary Ann and Harry together, but I didn't know how he could do it. My play had arrived where I was in reality, with my having dumped Dustin, but Rubin still engaged to Barr. Offstage, in my play, birds started to twitter. "Gee whiz," Mary Ann said. "You have fantastic birds out here. Do they ever wake you up?" On the far side of the stage, Simon entered, and she asked, "What the hell is he doing here?" Swan never appeared in early morning. "Who?" the Henhouse regular asked. "Simon? Looking for a cup of coffee, I suppose. He loves to make the rounds at dawn. Offhand, I don't know of a bird in town that's more likely to wake you up." This is the last line in the manuscript. Rereading it, decades later, I saw for the first time that it was the perfect ending, as Greenberg – the real hero of the play – had in fact by Labor Day 1969 already rousted me out of the cosy nest that my job had so long afforded me, and put an end to that phase of my life. What came next would be a whole new play.

After I'd finished this scene and gone to the office, I looked at *Peanuts*. Snoopy was sitting on top of his doghouse, typing a novel. Clearly, this alluded to my work. Lucy offered to do a cover illustration. "How about a bunch of pirates and foreign legionnaires," Snoopy thought, "fighting some cowboys with some lions and tigers and elephants leaping through the air at this girl who is tied to a submarine?"[297] I was that girl, tied to the submarine of *Time* – an engine of war, submerged in that its articles were unsigned. Nobody in the enlightened world admitted they read it because it attacked from behind this shield of anonymity, a power of darkness. Pirates, legionnaires, lions, and tigers were people fighting over me. I could only escape by cutting loose from the submarine, so I typed my letter of resignation to Grunwald, put it in my out-box and left to go home.

13. "Swinging London": The Fantasy
(August 1969–August 1971)

THAT EVENING, ANNE FitzRoy gave me a lift to Quogue for the weekend. She said her boss was trying to harass a woman into quitting. The woman thought he was having an affair, and had called his wife. I remembered how I'd suggested to Grunwald that I knew about his supposed infidelity. Bill Rubin and Charlie Parmiter had told me about it, but now I fantasized, what if neither had been telling the truth? What if Grunwald had planted at least one of these reports? He had (in fact) asked me for Rubin's phone number. Rubin had told me Grunwald merely wanted to offer him a painting, but (I wondered now) what if Grunwald had really been asking him to tell me he'd seen Grunwald at lunch with a woman not his wife? What if Parmiter had told me about that platinum blonde black woman as a joke? Considering these improbabilities led me to a much more probable idea that I hadn't been prepared to accept before that moment: the idea that Grunwald might not like me that much.

Sure, I thought, he believed he did, since I was proof of claims he'd made for years, that women could write for *Time*, but when I started in Milestones, I'd deprived him of this issue, and he'd been using it to make Fuerbringer look bad, and advance his own career. I'd deprived him of another issue in 1967, after the editors' conference in East Hampton where he'd argued for a more intellectual stance to the magazine. By proposing my cover on Tony Smith, I'd given Fuerbringer the chance to show he could be as intellectual as Grunwald, so there was no need to replace him yet. Since Grunwald had taken over, I'd shown him up as less of an intellectual than he liked to think he was by proposing the color spread on conceptual art that shocked him. All at once the lack of compliments on my stories, the rejections of my cover proposals, and killing of my section made sense. Grunwald had never liked me, and my memo on "Sex in the Arts" had come as the crowning insult – whatever his conscious mind might think. "What if your boss conned this woman into thinking he was having an affair, simply to have an excuse to get her out?" I asked Fitz. Instead of answering me, she told me to look at a Rolls Royce that the police had called over to the side of the road. She said that it must have been driving with its lights out, but that the cops always loved cracking down on a Rolls. Years before, I'd seen Jean-Luc Godard's movie, *Weekend*, and thought he was using cars as metaphors for people. I didn't think of that movie with Fitz, but I suddenly felt quite sure that she had answered me in surreal language. I'd been told I was like a Rolls, a classy automobile too good to be driving with my lights out. Contributing unsigned articles to a magazine was like driving in darkness, so everybody who valued me had cooperated to wrench me out of my niche.

The whole weekend was like that – an ongoing fantasy that, as I look back on it, becomes almost novelistic in the way it unfolded. Having ceased to accept its paychecks, I saw *Time* from a new viewpoint (though in retrospect, I'd say I exaggerated its evils, to provide myself with more reason for having left). Saturday morning, another one of my housemates found a bit of paper with writing on it, and read aloud something like this: "Eduardo swears he has no soul. I have a soul, but refuse to put it in the collection plate. (IV: 9)." I fantasized this must be a message in surreal language sent to me from my editor in World, "Eduardo" Hughes, who (like me) had left *Time*. Before then, he'd been in the Beirut bureau, where Arabs believed women had no souls (or so I'd been told). Here, I imagined, he was saying that he had no soul, but thought that I had one, and refused to put it in "the collection plate." He must mean (I thought) that by the time I'd arrived in World, he'd placed his soul in Grunwald's collection plate. Grunwald had (in fact) chosen Hughes to succeed him in World, so (I thought now) whatever Grunwald thought of me, Hughes had to go along with.

Here in Quogue, he seemed to be saying that he regretted it, and respected me, no matter what my independence of mind cost him. I thought of other men I'd cared about, from Joe Ferrer to Bill Rubin. All had been ambitious, and at least subliminally aware that getting involved with me might harm their careers, so that I might not have imagined the affection they'd had for me. Perhaps they'd simply repressed it (as so many people, women as well as men, repress feelings that, for one reason or another, cause what a Freudian might call "unpleasure." I may have been indulging in wishful thinking here, but at least it was wishful thinking on a psychoanalytic base).

After breakfast, a group of us went to a Hot Dog beach. Fitz and I walked along the shoreline, passing two houses high on the dunes. They were owned by Donald B. Douglas, the neurologist, and he was standing next to them, beckoning to us. We climbed the dunes to see the two houses. The first was small but charming. Donald B. lived in it himself. This house was like my new world, I thought. Then he led us to the other one, which was bigger and more pretentious. It seemed to me like my old world, *Time*. This house had been rented to a group of burly, surly men who were standing on its sundeck, swilling beer. There was only one woman, and one man was hefting her in his arms, while others picked with undue familiarity at her faded, shrunken bikini. She was giggling, but not happily. "That's Marianne," said another man. "She's got a big, tough brother who's a Marine." He mimicked a hulking ape. "When the brother's around, the guys let her alone, but now he's gone away." Since the woman's name was Marianne, I thought she must be a symbol for me, and the big brother must stand for Fuerbringer. I fantasized that this was a little play being staged for my benefit. Its point was to show that when Fuerbringer had been managing editor, I'd been treated well by colleagues, but as his protege, I'd shared in his unpopularity. Doing my job well had perpetuated his reign, so when he left, everybody who'd disliked him had tried to get rid of me.

As Fitz and I started back, Donald B. warned us about visiting Tiana Beach. "The animals there get kind of rough," he said. "They were tossing a girl in a blanket." This was my second reference to animals in two days. First, I thought of the lions and tigers attacking the girl in *Peanuts*. Then I thought of the funny-animals story that my three fellow-writers in World had written for April Fool's Day in 1966. At that time, I'd been thinking that I was going to write a cover story on Indonesia because Hughes was in love with me. Those three writers had made puns out of the names of wild beasts in the zoo of Kwame Nkrumah, Ghana's deposed leader. As a tiny child, I'd been afraid that lions and tigers lurked under my bed at night. Dr. G had said they were projections of my own unconscious rage, so I applied his interpretation to those three men in World.

My success, I thought, must have brought out the beast in them, and they'd used the funny-animals story as a way of expressing their anger. How polite and civilized everybody at *Time* always seemed. Everybody repressed their anger, but these three, I felt, must have resented a woman writing for the same magazine they did: doing the one thing they could use as an outlet for their own aggressions, earning the same money they'd always prided themselves on as a male prerogative, and exercising the same degree of influence on public opinion, yet another thing they identified (or confused) with their own masculinity. They don't *type* with their penises, I'd often said to myself, but I now suspected they felt like they did.

They hadn't known how much my ability made them feel castrated, my thoughts ran on, because the damage had been done unconsciously. With their conscious minds, they'd probably thought they liked me, but they'd also believed in Grunwald, and been distressed with how Fuerbringer made *Time* play the hawk on Vietnam. They wanted Grunwald to succeed Fuerbringer, since he was promising more enlightened coverage of the war. Their sexual rivalry had gotten confused with politics, and yet how could I blame them, good liberals who, in terms of Vietnam, wanted the same thing I did? I was the Circe who'd turned them into swine, and then only in print, through the funny-animals story with which they'd expressed their rage.

Rage – and jubilation, I thought: those three must have sensed that Hughes had figured out how to demoralize me by dealing me out of that Indonesia cover, thus hastening the day when Grunwald would take over. I thought that Hughes had expressed this belief, again unconsciously, with how he'd edited my earlier story on Indonesia, where he'd used the past continuing tense: "Ever so politely, yet ever so firmly, Lieut. General Suharto, 45, the new strongman of Indonesia, was stripping President Sukarno of his last vestiges of power...." Suharto must have stood for Grunwald, I thought, and Sukarno for Fuerbringer, still the magazine's figurehead, but with his opponents scenting victory in their struggle to get him out.

It was exhilarating to look back, to perceive surreal or double levels of meaning in earlier *Time* stories, and to believe that these stories expressed unconscious feelings of the men who'd written them. But I wasn't conscious of any anger at my former colleagues. They couldn't help what they'd felt, I knew, any more than I could have helped what I'd done. We'd all been living in a situation that evolved without any of us knowing where or why or how it started, and powerless to change the outcome. Subsequent conversations and incidents over the weekend persuaded me that I shouldn't try to finish my play, but write a novel instead – and, that to do so, I should go to London. I was at last convinced that Bill Rubin was really married, but that I'd been kept in ignorance of this all summer so that he could lure me into his world. I'd never have left *Time* without that other world to move to, but Rubin had served his purpose, so I had to put him out of my mind – and that would be easier in London.

As I'd given Grunwald a month's notice, I went to the office on the Tuesday after Labor Day, and attended story conference as usual. Around noon, I went back to Baker's office. He'd gone to lunch, but on his desk was an interoffice memo from Grunwald, one evidently sent to senior editors on a weekly basis, pinpointing highlights of the previous issue. It cited the obituary of Ludwig Mies van der Rohe, the architect, which had run in Art but been written by Marguerite Johnson. The memo called it "the first truly distinguished piece of writing that has appeared in Art in months," or words to that effect. I said to myself, If that's how Henry feels about my writing, he never needs to read another word of it, and typed out a good-bye note to Baker, whom I'd already told I was going to resign. Then I went home – to stay. (*Time* would muddle along for months without a regular Art writer. Eventually, it would hire Robert Hughes, who would turn out to be the answer to Grunwald's prayers, and remain until the millennium.)

As a result of a bridge game that evening, I stopped thinking that people were trying to direct me, and started thinking God was doing it. (I still believe in God, but figure he's got better things to do than supervise me.) I stopped believing in Dr. G. On my first appointment with him after Labor Day, I realized that he'd been repeating himself to me for at least three years, and always from the perspective of the *Time* world I'd left, so I stopped seeing him.

I wrote to friends and acquaintances, telling them I was going to London, hoping we could get together for a farewell drink, and asking if they had friends in London whom I could look up. This led to many social occasions. Barbara and Gene Schwartz, the collectors, had me to lunch at their apartment. I gave them a bowdlerized but still critical picture of *Time* to describe why I'd left it. Then I mentioned my apartment on East Eighty-second Street, my first group house at Quogue, and other things I'd learned about through *F.Y.I.*, the Time Inc. house organ. Barbara said, "You're just like a woman getting a divorce. First, you talk about all the awful things your husband did to you, and then you start nostalgically talking about his organ."

Greenberg called in response to the farewell note I'd sent him, and said he thought I'd done the right thing in leaving *Time.* I invited him to dinner. He brought along a pamphlet reprinting a speech he'd given in Australia. It was inscribed, "For Piri, from her admirer, Clem," and at this point, I shall start referring to him by that name, as our relationship had passed from the more professional to the more personal. I gave him a drink before dinner and we talked, his words so engrossing me that the shish kebab I had in the oven got hopelessly charred.

I told him I'd stopped seeing my analyst. He said the analytic process kept on working for some time after one ceased therapy (as it had over the summer, with my analyzing my play). He said the trouble with most analysts was that they were concerned with getting a person to conform and adjust. How pathetically true this had been with Dr. G, trying to shoehorn me into my wretched marriage with *Time*! Once it had been what I wanted, but I'd outgrown it. People did outgrow relationships. Clem told me of two Neo-Sullivanian analysts who accepted this, Jane Pearce and Saul Newton. He'd been treated by Pearce, and recommended a book she and Newton had written, *The Conditions of Human Growth.* Clem said these doctors believed people got into marriages that reflected their neuroses, so in outgrowing the neurosis, they might have to break up their marriages. I asked my bookstore-owning father to send me a copy.

Clem gave me the addresses of four of his friends in London: Anthony Caro, the sculptor; Leslie Waddington and John Kasmin, art dealers; and Vera Russell, the ex-wife of John Russell, the English critic. After dinner, he and I went for a drink. He spoke of physical need, how distasteful it was to wake up in bed next to a woman whom you'd wanted but then discovered you didn't really like. "It must be even more distasteful for a woman," he said. I realized this was an experience I'd never gotten myself into, and perhaps should. Clem said he wanted to read my novel. I was writing it for him, the story of a thirteen-year sojourn in the land of ordinary people, well-intentioned but lacking vision. I still wanted his good opinion, more than anything else, and I needed what Eliot had demanded for his poetry, an enlightened reader.

I had lunch with Ken Noland. In the cab on the way to the restaurant, he cheerfully put an arm around my shoulders and fondled the back of my neck, a schoolboy gesture and doubly appealing as such. "Look," he said, pointing to the car up ahead of us, "a Princess. A very special kind of Rolls. They only make a few of them." I took this as surreal compliment, and told Ken in return that his looks reminded me of Peter Fonda, star of *Easy Rider*. "I'm a Rough Rider," he laughed. "I carry a big stick." If that wasn't a surreal come-on, I'd be very surprised.

Clem invited me to drinks on the Saturday before I left for London. At his apartment, I found a group gathering to go on for dinner in honor of Poons, whose new show was opening at Larry Rubin's gallery. There would be a loft party afterwards. Clem had invited me along, but before we left, the two of us chatted in his little study. He sat at his desk, and, with the light from the window behind him, his face was in shadow, making him appear to me remote and guru-like. "You have so much to learn," he said. And, "If you can love one person, you can love a lot of people." Finally, "There's no such thing as unrequited love." I thought back through the men I'd known at work, and once again believed (or fantasized) that whatever I'd felt for them had been returned, though they'd repressed their feelings for me.

Only in retrospect were my own feelings beginning to surface. In the background I was dimly aware of *Time* writers and editors. In the foreground stood shadows of art-world people: Bill Rubin, Ken Noland, even Jules Olitski, at that moment having drinks in Clem's living room with another young woman not his wife. After Clem and I joined them, Olitski told me he might be visiting England, and would look me up when he got there. Fine, I thought. I'll sleep with any one of these wandering art-world denizens who calls. If the fondness I'd felt for those men on *Time* had been love, how heartless I'd been not to express it. Who was I to make distinctions between single and married?

*   *   *

I arrived in London on October 8, and found a furnished apartment with a garden where I would live from November 1 until I left London in

August 1971. The apartment was at 139A Blythe Road in West Kensington, a not-at-all-swinging but reasonably priced neighborhood. I could handle the rent of $140, having some savings and getting $16,000 from Time Inc.'s profit-sharing plan. My nice landlords operated and lived behind a nearby luxury grocery shop. When I wasn't working on my novel, I went with friends to theater, dinners, parks, stately homes, tennis, and parties. I also had a few "adventures," ranging from your basic one-night stand to prolonged formal platonic encounters, but almost all this socializing was done with people I hadn't met through Clem. Kasmin, though, put me on the mailing list of his gallery. I went to his openings, and one fine party he gave. Leslie Waddington took me to one chilly lunch, Vera Russell had me to dinner several times, and I remember especially my lunch with Tony Caro. After he'd shown me his sculpture, he said, "Isn't Clem the most lovable person you ever met?" I felt the two of us were on a wavelength when I heard that.

During September in New York, newspaper headlines and magazine covers had upset me with their surreal messages. Clem said I'd be better off if I didn't pay so much attention to the news, and in London, I followed his advice. It helped. I bought only the Sunday papers, and read only their cultural news, nor did I get a TV set. My portable radio was tuned to a music station. Five days a week, nine to five, I worked on my "novel." It was fiction only in using made-up names, altering physical descriptions of people, and saying they came from Wisconsin instead of Missouri, or had gone to Harvard instead of Yale. I looked up back issues of *Time* in a London library, copied out passages, and incorporated them into my text. I'd also brought along my appointment books for 1965 and 1966. All this unearthed many memories for me, but also showed me that some of what I thought I'd remembered wasn't true.

As I wrote, ideas that I thought of as insights came to mind, causing my manuscript to exist on two levels. The first was the purely factual (and completely self-absorbed) account of my life on *Time* that I was actually typing. The second or surreal level was the insights that I was storing up in my mind, intending to add them at a later stage. A third, saner level came into being thirty years later, while I was still trying to write down the second level for this book. I realized then that although the second level differed radically from the first, the reality probably lay somewhere between.

Still, the first two levels would be more important to the development of my theory about abstract painting, because they marked such a prolonged immersion in "divergent thinking" (or what in a sane person might be called divergent thinking). Many books on creativity consider divergent thinking very important. Convergent thinking is the kind most people use, logical reasoning that leads to a single answer. Divergent thinking holds back on any conclusion that doesn't fulfill all the contradictory conditions of a problem. It's the capacity to explore two or more ideas or theories in one's mind at the same time, without committing oneself until they finally resolve or synthesize themselves into a new configuration that admits all possibilities.

Children tend to get divergent thinking drummed out of them in traditional schools. There they are trained to think there is only one "right" answer to every question (which may be true with arithmetic but is much less often true with art, politics, or daily life). I was lucky in having gone to progressive schools, which encouraged more creative thinking. I also benefitted from fifteen years of dream interpretation, because the basic principle of free association, as the psychoanalyst Alfred Margulies has emphasized, is that the patient should suspend judgment about what in the dream is or isn't important, and just say whatever comes to mind.[298] In practice, this leads to finding in every dream image more than one reference. Many people think in terms of "either/or." Freudians accept the principle of "both/and."

I began writing shortly after I moved into 139A Blythe Road, with a flashback to my adolescence. Soon, I began to feel that already I'd been a victim of circumstance. Some of this feeling was undoubtedly a reaction against thirteen years of being expected by Dr. G to find myself responsible for anything bad in human relations that happened to me, but another boost to my battered ego was provided by Clem's continued interest. He and I corresponded while I was in London, every six weeks or so. His letters and postcards (for he loved to write postcards) were wise, kind, and completely personal. His attitude toward marriage must have helped me feel I was more successful than I'd thought I was, since he didn't consider it evidence of maturity.

Nor did *The Conditions of Human Growth*. Though I've since heard the Neo-Sullivanians referred to as "those witch doctors on the West Side," and believe their subcommunity is now pretty well defunct, I found this book helpful at that moment. Rereading it, I see I picked up only on those aspects that appeared relevant to me at the time, but then I wasn't in therapy with Pearce or Newton. My interest in them was a byproduct of my relationship with Clem, which was anything but clinical. Drs. Keiser and G had assumed that the only relationships which really affected me were with my parents, lovers, and themselves. Pearce and Newton argued that anybody with whom an individual interacted constructively enabled that individual to grow and mature, including teachers, friends, even acquaintances.[299] This interaction occurred through "validation," meaning when one's own experience was recognized and confirmed by somebody else.[300] Once this validation had taken place, prior experience which an individual had relegated (or repressed) into his or her integral personality (meaning, roughly, the unconscious) could be admitted to the "self-system" (or again roughly, the conscious), and the individual became more capable of responding to life.

I'd already experienced such validation when Clem had recognized and sympathized with my feeling for Bill Rubin, thus rescuing it from the oblivion to which I'd tried to consign it. But Clem hadn't been the first person with whom I'd been able to establish a constructive interpersonal relationship. My parents hadn't given me the validation I needed, but many other people had since filled the gap. The first had been Ed and Elsa Bley, my teachers from North Country – and at Dalton and Barnard, I'd had good friendships with female classmates. Pearce and Newton considered same-sex "chumships" an indispensable stage on the way to maturity.

When I was about to graduate from college, Dr. Keiser had said I was still neurotic and should go back into analysis because I hadn't had any sexual experience in college, but I hadn't realized that his conclusion might have been based on an imperfect knowledge of the facts. It was in London that I began to feel maybe he'd misjudged me, not knowing how the more traditional and/ or lower-middle-class Barnard subcommunity I was inhabiting differed from his own sophisticated, upper-middle-class one. In college, I hadn't yet learned how different the many villages of society could be, having been exposed only to the closely related ones of home and progressive school. Since then, I'd also become aware of the subcommunity of *Time*, what Carolyn Mullens had called "the Small Set," the three beach communities at Quogue (Sand Bar, Hot Dogs, and Tiana), that wider world west of the Hudson known as the heartland, and finally, the Manhattan art world, which (I'd begun to realize) wasn't even monolithic.

Yes, I decided (in my head, not on the typed page), Dr. Keiser had misjudged me. He hadn't realized how sane and normal he'd helped me to become. Though I hadn't had sex with my two college boyfriends, I'd had constructive interpersonal relationships with both, starting out getting a lot from interacting with them, then outgrowing each in turn. But how could Dr. Keiser have known this, when I hadn't known enough to tell him? As for my other college relationships, or rather, the lack of them, it was also in London that I began to feel they hadn't been due to my neuroses so much as my lack of neurosis. I'd been a Jew to the Gentiles and a Gentile to the Jews, rendering me off-limits to the non-neurotic members of each subcommunity.

During my first years out of college, the problem had continued. I'd been slender and quite nice to look at. Some men even considered me beautiful, but I'd dated and then been dropped by three nice Jewish men – at least two of whom had since married Jewish women. I'd also been shabbily treated by a nice Gentile man who, within the year, had married the daughter of one of his mother's friends. Still, in London I didn't feel angry at him or any of the others, any more than I'd felt angry at the men in World. Again, it was simply circumstances beyond anybody's control.

When I started to write about my first day on *Time* in June 1956, I found that I could recall the weather, the day of the week, and the people I'd talked to. Sights, sounds, smells of the old Time & Life Building rose to memory: the layout of offices and bullpens, how the staff list looked, the browns and greens of furniture, the odors of the catered dinners on Sunday nights. I can't say all these recollections were accurate, but the fact that I thought I could remember so much made me realize that I'd cared about the place more than I'd thought I did, only months before.

When I'd quit, I'd thought I'd only seen myself as the bride of Luce since I'd become a writer in 1963, but in London, I read a story that had appeared in *Time* four years earlier, in March 1959. I'd been only a researcher in the Canada section at that point, and recalled the story as an apology for an earlier story so nasty that it had caused riots in Bolivia. In London, I felt that the second story was if anything nastier than the first.[301] I realized that by 1959, I was already seeing the world from the vantage point of *Time*. The contrast between how nice *Time* writers and editors were in person and how mean they could be in print had become so familiar that I took it for granted.

By May 1970, I'd arrived at May 1961 in my "novel," when Bob Christopher took over in Business. It was spring in London, I was looking forward to writing about Christopher, and most importantly, I'd received a postcard from Clem, telling me that he was going to be in London in late June, on his way to Africa. He said he expected to see me, and would be staying with the Waddingtons.[302] I was delighted, but still because I thought a revered elder statesman would be in town, and I wrote him a respectful letter back. Then a friend mentioned that she'd been sewing, and hurt herself when she'd pricked her finger. It suddenly occurred to me that this expression of pain over a pricked finger had carried a message from Clem on a secondary or surreal level, saying that he was hurt because I was being so distant.

I also realized that he was no longer a remote, mysterious father figure to me, but a man whom I loved with a totally mortal love. I forgot that he was married. The idea that my emotions might be inappropriate because he was a public figure never entered my mind (he wasn't a public figure to me, after all). It was the most complete and overwhelming emotion I'd ever known, and made me very happy. I wrote him a second letter, laying myself out for him. As soon as he was due to arrive, I called the Waddingtons, and was invited over for a drink, only to find that he was traveling with his lady friend from the Marlborough-Gerson Gallery. Boy, was I mad!

Neither the postcard in which he'd said he was coming, nor a subsequent letter from him, had even hinted that he wouldn't be traveling alone.[303] I wrote him a furious letter saying so, and he called me from the London airport, as he was leaving. *Never*, he said angrily, write another letter like that to *anyone*, but as we talked, he simmered down, and promised to write me a letter back, from Africa. He did, too, a nice, kind, long one, but the lodge in Kenya didn't mail it for months. When it arrived, I'd forgotten the incident, and wasn't even thinking about him much.

At least, I didn't think that I was thinking about him, but when I recall the "insights" I had while writing the next part of my manuscript, I conclude that our relationship, such as it was, continued to influence me. On some level or other, I would have to accommodate myself to the fact that if I wanted him, I'd have to share him. This became an incentive to reinterpret my relationships with other men I'd had to share, married men on *Time*, and to find, in those relationships, parallels that would let me develop the relationship I had with Clem.

When I'd started writing about Christopher, I'd felt I could recall his appearance and mannerisms with a vividness equaled only by how well I'd remembered the furniture and smells of the *Time* offices. I felt that without intending to do so, he'd communicated with me through his editing of stories, and that I'd communicated with him through my research. We'd known we were conveying information to each other, but I felt that in addition, we'd conveyed mutual attraction, resulting in yet another one of these interpersonal relationships that had enabled me to grow. I wouldn't have wanted to admit this mutual attraction, partly because getting involved with my editor would have complicated my career, but even more because Dr. G thought getting involved in extramarital affairs was neurotic for most women. Therefore what I'd done, I concluded in London, was channel or sublimate my feelings for Christopher into a feeling for the next suitably single man I met: Fred Freund.

I hadn't known this at the time, of course. I'd thought I liked Fred because he was very smart, very nice, and very eager to make me happy. Nor did these qualities seem any less admirable in London, but there I decided that I'd also responded to him because he was what Dr. G called "a reality man." Since that time, Clem had validated my feelings for Bill Rubin, though Dr. G would have considered him a "fantasy man." Therefore, on Blythe Road, I concluded that the feeling I'd had for Christopher must have been just as real as my feeling for Rubin, though my relationship with Christopher had also been purely professional until the very end of it.

"If you can love one person, you can love a lot of people," Clem had said. Pearce and Newton believed that maturity meant being able to relate to other people besides one's primary partner.[304] Nor had my feeling for Christopher been unreciprocated, if I could believe Clem, who'd said, "There's no such thing as unrequited love." Pearce and Newton said that, too.[305] Considering that Christopher did eventually make a pass at me, I don't think even in retrospect that I'd imagined our mutual attraction, but I also think I exaggerated these emotions in 1970 because Christopher, like Clem, was married, and I was unconsciously looking for precedents and justifications to proceed with my relationship to Clem. In reality, I probably cared at least as much about Fred, but in London I had Clem at the back of my mind, so I was more concerned with Christopher and less with Fred.

It was much the same when describing the situation where I'd been a writer in Milestones in 1963, and People in 1964. After I'd split with Fred, I'd become aware of my attraction to Ferrer, the bachelor writer, but thought I wasn't attracted to Parmiter, the married one. In London, I found myself going on and on about Parmiter, and decided that again, I'd channeled my attraction to Parmiter into a more socially acceptable crush on Ferrer. And again, as I write from a more recent vantage point, I'd say that in 1970, I must have been maximizing whatever I felt for Parmiter and minimizing whatever I felt for Ferrer. What capacities I have for deluding myself!

*   *   *

I went back to New York for Christmas of 1970, called up Clem, and was invited over for a drink. He was alone. At first, the occasion was everything I could have wished. He embraced me tenderly, kissed me, and asked when I'd discovered I loved him. Then he wanted to have sex, and that, too, was flattering and pleasing, but, for reasons I don't choose to discuss, he got me very angry at him (though I concealed the fact that I was angry from myself). When we got into bed, he couldn't consummate the relationship. Years later, when I knew him better, I thought over this incident, and decided that he hadn't been able to make it because I'd been so angry at him that I was radiating waves of rage. I told him this. He listened, then said, "My prick doesn't lie." In 1970, though, he only said philosophically that this sometimes happened with age, and dropped off to sleep, while I (in my paranoia) decided he'd deliberately denied himself to me because I hadn't finished my "novel."

Returning to London, I fell with renewed vigor into the writing of it, and met a man who relegated Clem to the back of my mind (Clem himself was not writing to me during this period, because he was occupied with a series of seminars at Bennington College). I'll call this new man in my life Claude Weiss. He was in his forties, divorced, and (shall we say) a professor of French literature at Swarthmore, in London on a sabbatical, doing research on the British response to Proust. Claude had been given my number by a mutual friend in the art world, and he took me out for the first time on Valentine's

Day, 1971. On our second date, we went to bed, and for the next three and a half months, he took me out regularly, Saturday night into Sunday. To be fair, I made no real attempt to get to know him well, but he didn't make much of an attempt to plumb my personality, either. One weekday evening, I saw him at a poetry reading with another woman. One weekend I went to visit friends in the country, and after I returned, he told me that he'd looked up yet a third woman and gone to bed with her.

I put up with this crap because I thought of Claude as a convenience, sent by the powers supervising me to provide physical gratification, enabling me to get on with my novel. It never occurred to me that Claude might consider me a holiday convenience in turn, though I'd known there was a holiday syndrome since 1954, and that parked car in Manitou Springs, Colorado. It never occurred to me that going to bed with Claude regularly would cause me to fall in love with him. Sure, Dr. G had warned me that men found it easier than women to split off love from sex, but I took that as just another one of his hypotheses which I'd never proved out for myself. As a result, by spring I'd be very attached to Claude, while he wasn't at all attached to me.

Starting in January 1971, I'd been writing about my career in World, which had begun in March 1965. In the library, I'd copied out passages from stories by Jason McManus, John Blashill, and Bob Jones. I'd become accustomed to feeling that colleagues were describing themselves, on a surreal level, through their writing or editing, but it reached a new intensity in World. Our four offices were lined up together physically, and we were in the same section, writing the same kinds of stories, using files from the same correspondents, and sending our copy through to the same editor.

I hadn't thought I was attracted to them at first, since all three were married, and to outward appearances, happily. Getting involved with any of them would have made me feel I was behaving neurotically (and again, been professional suicide as well). Looking back from Blythe Road, it seemed to me that once more, I'd repressed the attraction I'd felt for them, and channeled it once more in the direction of Eric Pace, the unmarried *New York Times* reporter I'd briefly dated (today, I'd say that I probably liked Eric as much as I liked most of those married men, but that in 1971, my need had been to minimize my feeling for him, and maximize my feelings for them).

By January 1966, Hughes was giving me worse and worse stories, and editing them so unpredictably that my self-confidence was increasingly undermined. Then, in February, he'd gone on his Latin American trip, and I was told that Jones would take his place for a week. I'd reviewed what I knew about Jones, and thought it wasn't much, but reviewing it again on Blythe Road, I realized I could remember quite a lot.

I'd begun to write about the story he'd assigned me on the trial in Moscow of those two underground writers. Its title was "The Trial Begins." When I'd reread that title in the London library, it had seemed to refer, on a surreal level, to the ordeal Jones and I would have to undergo: the two Russian writers were surrogates for us. After Jones and I had discussed what I should write in the new version of that story, I'd asked him how long it should be. He'd said, "Don't worry about the length. Just put it all in." This directive had been incredibly liberating. I'd found that I, too, could write in a bold and aggressive, masculine style, though in 1966, I hadn't thought of it as masculine. When Hughes returned from his trip, I'd dazzled him with the strength of my new style. Writing about it in London, I first thought that it was like I'd been inoculated, with Jones's words pumping into me the strength and resistance I had to have, as a needle pumps vaccine into an arm. Then I began to think that the pump hadn't been a needle, but something else, a purely emotional metaphor, of course, but potent nevertheless.

Jones had said, "Don't worry about the length. Just put it all in," and as I typed these words, I realized that they could be read as a humongous double entendre. Consciously, he'd been speaking about writing, but unconsciously, I felt, it had a secondary or symbolic level of meaning. I thought of an old-time father speaking to a son on the eve of his wedding, but it also led me to believe that Jones must have been attracted to me, and was unconsciously expressing this attraction in this way. Knowing he did love his wife, I explained this attraction by how enmeshed he was in the job and its people, but, at the back of my mind in London, I began to visualize ugly fantasies.

In my mind's eye, I saw a scene behind a barn, two boys performing surgery on a horse, but a mare, not a stallion, and not gelding it but grafting testicles onto it – two boys, Jones and Hughes. It was a repugnant picture, but it explained the new power of my writing style in World, In 1966, I'd believed that the good relationship between Hughes and Jones had helped Hughes discover that he was attracted to me, but writing about this in 1971, I felt that I'd been deceived in this belief, and that I'd only persuaded myself that he was attracted. I'd done this in order to channel or sublimate my attraction for Jones into the socially acceptable direction of an unmarried man, and because if I'd admitted to myself how angry I was with Hughes, I couldn't have stayed on in World.

When Hughes had told me that I'd be allowed to write a cover about Suharto, Indonesia's new leader, I'd been overjoyed. Then I'd run into Ed Jamieson, that devout Catholic senior editor, on the elevator, and he'd told me about the trip Hughes was taking around the world. Writing about that incident in the elevator, I became convinced that running into Jamieson couldn't have been an accident. I thought it was part of a divine plan to test me, and, as I sat typing my description of the two of us talking together, I began to hallucinate. I thought I could smell smoke, and feel the warmth of fire. I thought, this elevator hadn't been just going down to the ground floor of the building, but straight on down into hell. I began to fantasize in religious terms (though my fantasies were based more upon my college course in seventeenth-century English poetry than on religious instruction, as I'd gotten little of that).

These fantasies (until I went completely around the bend) helped me understand why the story on "Swinging London" left me with such a feverish desire to get away from *Time*, a desire that had first expressed itself the morning after the cover by my flying to Washington. They also persuaded me that I'd cared about Bob Jones more than I'd realized, and that I'd written the cover more for him than for Hughes. I felt that only Jamieson's willingness to confide in me had kept that elevator from going straight on down to hell. This bond of trust between a man and a woman had set me running, like a rat through a maze, to arrive at correct decisions, for the sake of salvation – not only mine, but that of the rest of the world, all of which was somehow hanging in the balance.

In my memo to Fuerbringer, I'd stressed three things I wanted to write about in the Indonesia cover: youth, Indonesia as a tourist attraction, and its strategic importance. As I saw it on Blythe Road, this memo challenged the old relationship between men and women, the idea that only men could experience God directly, and that women had to go through men ("He for God only, she for God in him" was the phrase from *Paradise Lost* that I'd learned at Barnard). By bypassing Hughes, a man, to appeal to Fuerbringer over his head, I was declaring my equality with Hughes before God, and bringing Christianity into the twentieth century.

This, of course, necessitated believing that Fuerbringer – or somebody in the organization – was God, so my mind obediently explained to me that when Fuerbringer got my memo, he'd bucked the decision on what to do about it clear up to Luce, who must therefore be the risen Christ (how many mental cases would have cast Luce for the leading role in the Second Coming?). Then Hughes had called me into his office, and said something like, "I want you to imagine yourself picked up and flown halfway around the world, to London." As I wrote about his saying this, again a tiny hallucination appeared in my mind's eye. I seemed to see a furry, fiery glint in his eyes, and I thought, he's become possessed by Satan, come to carry away the world, except that I'd prevented him from doing so, by offering up myself to ride on his back in its place. My offer had been made, in surreal language, by my memo outlining those three reasons, and on Blythe Road I equated them with offering up my body, mind, and soul. The offer had been accepted, and, to save the world, I'd let myself be turned into the Whore of Babylon, prostitute of the ages: Marianne, the swinging travel writer.

Then I began describing the drink Jones had taken me out for, the week I wrote the London cover. What that gesture must have meant for me, I can only guess in retrospect by how much I thought I could remember from our conversation. Even on Blythe Road, I knew he must have taken me to Eddy's, that grungy writers' hangout, but, as I tried to reconstruct the scene, I kept visualizing red-checked tablecloths and softer lighting, like the Steak de Paris, a more romantic French place down the block.

The Steak only had banquettes, though, and Jones and I had been sitting across from each other, the way the tables were at Eddy's, so I knew it must have been Eddy's, but my illusion of the Steak led me to believe that the feeling in this encounter was no longer lust, but love. When Hughes had been Satan, I fantasized, Jones had been Beelzebub, Satan's chief lieutenant (more *Paradise Lost*). As Beelzebub, he'd lusted after me, but he'd been metamorphosed into Adam, the first man, by my appeal clear up to Christ. I'd been metamorphosed into Eve, the first woman, and it was as Adam and Eve that Jones and I were having our drink in Eddy's.

By the time I was writing this chapter, I'd reread the "Swinging London" cover, and found its double levels of meaning so disturbing that the pages swam before my eyes. I looked at our cover illustration, and saw that it incorporated many small images. Then, seeing the photograph of myself in the Pub Letter, I remembered the student who'd written asking me to autograph her copy of the magazine. Rereading her letter in the '90s, I saw that she'd been collecting autographs of people involved in preparing *Time* covers, but in the London library, I fantasized that she'd thought I was the real cover subject, not for myself alone, but for what I symbolized, London as a woman. People referred to cities as "she," and I'd become that "she" to the magazine's readers, but even more to the men who'd helped to put the cover together.

I looked at the headline to the color spread Silas Haynes had prepared: "Oh, To Be In London." If London was a woman, I thought, this was obscene. The picture below showed young people on a London street. Its caption referred to A. A. Milne: "Like Christopher Robin, they're walking in all of the squares."[306] On the opposite page, in the story itself, was another way of saying how easily London's squares were traversed, a passage about how the city was "so green with parks and squares that, as the saying goes, you can walk across it on the grass." I thought of the modules in the Time-Life Building, and fantasized that these were the squares referred to in surreal language, implying that every man in the organization had passed through *my* square. I was most upset by the title that Fuerbringer had chosen, "You Can Walk Across It On the Grass." It made me think he equated my having submitted myself to having my story rewritten by Jamieson with an accommodating woman spreading herself on the ground for a man, with the grass being a surreal or symbolic reference to pubic hair.[307]

Only two passages in the cover still seemed friendly. The first came from what Jones had said to me in Eddy's, about London today being like Elizabethan times, with lads and lassies tumbling in the hay. This I'd turned into the song from *As You Like It*, "It was a lover and his lass, that o'er the green cornfield did pass," and the word "lover" seemed to shine like a beacon through a murk of smut. The other thing I liked was the conclusion that Jamieson had written in, saying that London had shed "much of the arrogance that often went with the stamp of privilege, much of its false pride...." It tallied with his saying he'd changed his mind, and now believed that a woman could be a writer for *Time* – but he was an exception. The rule was Haynes, Fuerbringer, and the bureau who had put together that portrait of London, and thus myself, as swinging in the rudest possible sense.

The men in the bureau, who'd provided the passage about parks and squares, had been angry because they were being forced to work for Fuerbringer's woman. Haynes had been angry at women in general. Fuerbringer was maddest of all, because I'd forced him to give me the cover. That he'd ever wanted to give me a cover was debatable, but he'd definitely have preferred to choose his own moment. Even in my wildest moments, though, I didn't think my assailants had known what they were doing, since they'd done it unconsciously, with only subliminally intended double entendres. Their conscious minds had thought they were merely trying to do their journalistic best. As I wrote about this in my "novel," I believed all those unconscious attacks must have registered with me subliminally, and combined to create this horrible self-image I had, of myself as Marianne, the office swinger, a professional woman in the wrong way.

Today, I'd still say that my baroque, exaggerated interpretation in London of the London cover may have contained a seed of truth. Certainly, it would help to explain why outside journalists saw SEX in "Swinging London," and why the word "swinging" itself became debased. Still, in 1971 I must also have been expressing the way I saw myself: as the accommodating woman servicing Claude Weiss. Freud believed that dreams have one foot in the past and one in the present. *Quidnunc* had also drawn from both past and present, so I believe it was really the combination of past and present miseries that led to my nightmare vision of "Swinging London" revisited.

None of my insights into the London cover were in my typed manuscript, which merely described Jamieson and myself, taking a company limo home after the cover had gone to press. Then I had no more urge to write. Claude was going back to the States. He said nothing about wanting to see me again.

I decided he was still married in spirit, even if technically divorced, and all I could do was laugh when I went out with him on June 4, our last date. The next morning he left. The one after that, I completely lost touch with reality. I seemed to hear a voice telling me to write the prophetic books of a new religion, so I did – for six weeks, seven days a week, eighteen hours a day.

After six weeks of gibberish, the prophetic books came to an end. On Sunday, July 18, I was collecting plants in my garden for a witches' brew that I was concocting on my stove, and talking to spirits in the air (imitating mad Ophelia and the weird sisters in *Macbeth*, though again I wasn't conscious of my sources). I still don't know exactly why I went off the deep end. The sorry conclusion I'd arrived at in my "novel" must have been one reason, but psychologists also say the loss of a loved one is the severest stress a psyche can be subjected to. The loss of Claude must have been doubly painful because he'd come to me through the art-world village I'd moved into, and I'd left *Time* full of hope for this village. Given the treatment I'd had from Claude and Clem, I must have felt that all I'd really done was step out of the frying pan into the fire.

I suspect my neighbors heard me over the back fence, talking to my spirits, and notified my kind landlords, because they rang my doorbell, and invited me over to eat Chinese takeout. After dinner, they suggested I might like what in Victorian novels would have been called "a sleeping draught." I accepted this suggestion with alacrity. They drove me to Hammersmith Hospital, where a shot in the backside knocked me out until morning, but when I woke, I was still talking to spirits, so I was transferred to St. Mary Abbot's in Kensington, a hospital with a mental ward. There I spent nearly three weeks, pumped full of tranquilizers whose names I never knew. They were my first experience of psychiatric medication, and they worked. No more spirits danced in the air, and I stopped receiving surreal messages. When I'd started receiving these messages, in the spring of 1969, they'd seemed a strange, wonderful, and even soothing means of communication, but by the summer of 1971, they'd taken over my life. When the tranquilizers freed me from them, I was grateful, and determined not to let myself get into such a state again.

14. Grad School
(Summer 1971–Summer 1975)

When I came out of that mental ward in August 1971, I no longer had the delusions I'd suffered from for two and a half years, but I had no illusions, either, so I was depressed. My "novel" was far too long to publish; the prophetic books, I dumped in the trash. Somehow, I took myself back to New York. There, I found a studio apartment, four flights up, on East Eighty-eighth Street, two doors down from Gracie Mansion, the mayor's residence. By April 1972, I felt better, and, condensing the first five-sixths of the novel into one chapter, created a 360-page manuscript chronicling my first year in World, and ending with the writing of "Swinging London."

I called Clem, and he invited me over for another drink. Jenny had moved out. He and I spent the night together, and it was great. I let him read the new version of my novel, but he only said that I should get more of my anger at these men into it (at least, he later insisted he'd said "anger," though I remembered him as having said "hate"). Over the summer, he'd call me occasionally, and invite me over for a drink, after which he'd cook me dinner, and we'd go to bed. In the morning, he'd make me breakfast, and I'd be on my way. At first, I liked this, but began to like it less and less. He never took me out to dinner, and was no gourmet chef. Worse still, he was losing sight of me as a person. One evening he didn't call until after dinner. The instant I walked into his apartment, he started tearing my clothes off me, and insisting we go straight to bed.

On the morning of September 8, I told him I loved him, though he'd never said anything about love to me. He glanced wildly around the bedroom, and his eye lit on a group of framed prints and watercolors lined up against the wall, the gift of Jack Bush, a Canadian painter he esteemed. He grabbed one of the prints, thrust it into my arms, and said, as nearly as I can remember, "Here, don't sell it for less than two hundred dollars." I glanced, just as wildly, at the rest of the pictures, and gesturing vaguely at a smaller (and what looked to me like a less expensive) one, said, "That's nice." Clem looked at it, and said, "That's a watercolor. I'm not giving it away." Some women might have considered the print a handsome gift, and I wasn't aware of feeling insulted. Only afterwards did I realize that I felt like he'd been putting a price on my favors, saying that sure, he liked me, too – two hundred dollars' worth, not a penny less, but (since watercolors are more expensive than prints) not a penny more.

I went home, clutching the print, and started trying to revise my novel in line with Clem's criticisms, but the more I got into it, the more I thought, I didn't hate these men, I loved them. I got angry at Clem, for wanting me to write like I'd hated them, and started writing around the clock, but, fearing I'd go off the deep end again, flung the manuscript aside. I had a part-time job by then, on the New Jersey edition of *The New York Times* (thanks to my fine longtime contact, Mitchel Levitas). I was reviewing art shows in New Jersey, and remember sitting on a train in the tunnel under the Hudson River going to a museum, visualizing in the blackness beyond the window a wicked little Satanic Clem, dancing angrily up and down and haranguing me. Getting home, I called the real Clem up and told him I didn't want to see him anymore.

That ended the hallucinations, but also made me feel like I had no reason to go on living, so I went to a hospital and was sent to a psychiatrist – not a psychoanalyst, but a psychiatrist. He told me that the best way to prevent a further recurrence of my symptoms was to go back on tranquilizers. Since this meant I had to keep on having them prescribed to me, I also had to keep on seeing him – or rather (after a brief period), his replacement at the hospital, whom I shall call Dr. I and whom I'd stay with for decades. I saw Dr. I mostly once a month, sitting on a chair, and telling him only what I felt he had to know. He was younger than Dr. G, and more up-to-date in his outlook on society. This made him much more tolerant of my behavior. He also taught me some cognitive therapy, which, I believe, was relatively new in the '70s, and which is the antithesis of Freud. Its premise is that depression is caused by flawed thinking in the present, and treatment is analyzing for oneself what's flawed with that thinking – in the present, again, without going back to one's childhood. I found it helpful.

Meanwhile, my mother (who'd split up with Bill Herwood) was asked to "assist" a diet doctor, Robert Atkins, with a book about his new diet. She'd already published a diet book under her own name, said to have sold at least a million copies, but *Dr. Atkins' Diet Revolution* would become an even bigger success after it was published in 1972. Knowing she was going to be rich, my mother asked me what I really wanted to do. I said, go to graduate school. I still wanted to write about the "color-field" painters whom Clem and I admired (Frankenthaler, Noland, Olitski, and Morris Louis being the big four I knew about at that point), but mass-circulation magazines wouldn't buy articles about such art, since few of their readers wanted to read about it, and the art magazines only paid peanuts. I had to have an additional source of income. Why not teach?

If I stayed in the art world, I could stay in touch with Clem. I was no longer in love with him. I'd fallen out of love when he shoved the Bush into my arms, and put a price tag on it, but I still wanted him in my life. Dr. G had said it was all right for a woman to call a man for business reasons, and, if I stayed within the art world, I'd have business reasons to call Clem. On some level or other, I also wanted to learn more about how abstract art said whatever it had to say. Bill Rubin's idea that it was about "feeling" had enabled me to respond to it, but my big story on Helen Frankenthaler, though it stressed the importance of feeling in her paintings, had been greeted with a spate of angry letters from readers.[308] Another form of presentation would have to be developed, if I were going to overcome such objections.

While I was still at *Time*, I'd already had some ideas about Jackson Pollock. I'd looked closely at his most abstract, dripped or poured paintings (often also called his "allover" paintings). I'd asked myself what associations I had with those skeins of paint. I'd decided that what I was reminded of was semen, exuberant loops and swirls of it, but I knew that I'd never dare say that in *Time*. Its square heartland readers would have been stunned, outraged, or laughed their heads off. To me, Pollock's swirls imparted a subtly sensuous mood and feeling, but I knew that some words triggered emotional rather than rational responses, and couldn't therefore be expected to convey the same idea that a writer wanted to convey. "Semen" was definitely one of those words.

Having put this idea to one side, I'd wondered if color might not communicate something. During my last summer at *Time*, I'd read Lionello Venturi's *History of Art Criticism* (first published in English in 1936, though the revised version I read was dated 1964). From it, I'd learned that the two essential building blocks in painting were color and form, or color and line (sometimes called "drawing"), and that color (in the eyes of many painters and critics of earlier centuries) corresponded to emotion, while the use of line, or draftsmanship for drawing images, corresponded to reason or logic. From all this, I'd concluded that artists were equally likely to put color first, but that writers (including those on *Time*) were more apt to favor line or form. I thought Clem must be exceptional in that he understood color as well as line. I hoped that if I could understand color myself, I might discover how abstract painting communicated.

Before I entered graduate school, I had to take three undergraduate art history courses. For one, an introductory survey taught by Mirella Levi D'Ancona at Hunter College, I wrote a term paper on Titian's *Venus and the Lute Player* (ca.1565–70). Frankenthaler (or Helen, as I hope I may now call her) admired this great Venetian Renaissance artist. He was said to be especially brilliant in his use of color, but I couldn't find any books about that, so instead I used Erwin Panofsky's writing on Titian's subject matter. Though I didn't know it, Panofsky (1892–1968) was a German art historian who came to the United States in the 1930s, having already become known for his "iconographic" school of interpretation or methodology. Iconography deals with the subject matter in a painting and what it symbolizes, especially in relation to its cultural and religious milieu.

Panofsky had developed his approach in the 1920s; it was often seen as a reaction against the previous reigning form of interpretation, formal analysis, especially as practiced by Heinrich Wölfflin (1864–1945), a native of Switzerland who taught in Germany, and was most influential from about 1890 to 1930. I shall say more about formal analysis shortly. Here I note only that it's a type of interpretation based exclusively on how a painting looks, in terms of its forms and colors, with no attention to its subject matter. Wölfflin is supposed to have said that you should be able to describe a painting of a horse without saying that it is a horse.

I had fond memories of Panofsky from Barnard, where Julius Held had discussed his ideas on "disguised symbolism" in lecturing on the Northern European Renaissance. In 1973, I loved what Panofsky said about the allegorical significance of paintings like the Titian I was writing about, and their relation to the Neoplatonism of Marsilio Ficino in Quattrocento Italy.[309] Ficino's devotees, though Christians, had celebrated a pagan goddess, Venus, as an emblem of divine beauty and love. This Neoplatonic way of conflating Christian ideals with pagan imagery paralleled the way that dreams and gestures, according to Freud, conflated more than one meaning into single images. It also equated with the double levels of meaning that I'd lived with for two years in London (though I didn't think of either parallel while doing my paper for D'Ancona. They would contribute to my insight into abstract painting in 1983).

Throughout the '70s, I'd pay little attention to politics. Though I voted for George McGovern in 1972, I wasn't surprised when Nixon beat him. McGovern's reputation was based on his antiwar position, but Nixon deprived him of this as a campaign issue by having already withdrawn many U.S. troops from Vietnam. With fewer body bags coming home, the public was losing interest. The euphemism for troop withdrawal was "Vietnamization." This meant the war effort was being turned over to the South Vietnamese military, but since they hadn't been able to withstand the communists by themselves before the United States came in, I had no confidence in their ability to do so after the United States got out. In 1973, the last U.S. soldiers left South Vietnam. In 1975, Saigon fell, and South Vietnam ceased to exist as a separate country. Having anticipated this outcome for ten years, I didn't feel strongly about it. I merely watched it happen.

It was the same with Watergate and the ensuing presidency of Jimmy Carter. I wasn't surprised to learn of Nixon's deceit, and I was pleased when Carter won, but I mainly noticed economic policies during Carter's administration, partly because of my experience as a Business researcher, and partly because of the economic determinism learned in my left-wing childhood. Those policies included the deregulation of airlines and trucking. I was reminded of my first years on *Time*, when I'd checked stories condemning big government for all its "unnecessary" supervision of free enterprise. This had been Republican dogma and Democratic anathema in the '50s, but now, it seemed, even Democrats thought government was "too big."

I was removed from contemporary art, though I occasionally went down to SoHo, which had become known as a neighborhood for galleries within a year or so after I left *Time*. I still didn't read about contemporary art in art magazines, and picked up general magazines only in waiting rooms, but I gathered that "performance art" and video were attracting critical attention, these being ways that visual artists could venture into suitably existentialist forms of acting and movie production. Almost everything else I saw in the galleries in the '70s seemed a continuation of the late '60s, especially the conceptual art. A very literal style of painting, based on photographs and known variously as hyperrealism, superrealism, or photorealism, was selling well, but many critics sneered at it. Since buyers and critics couldn't agree, there didn't seem to be any hot new trend in the art world. Instead, the buzzword was "pluralism."

People no longer spoke of the "new avant-garde," since even its admirers had to admit that pop, minimalism, and their related movements had become too widely accepted to qualify as "avant-garde." Some critics argued that the age of the avant-garde itself was ended. One thing pluralism meant was that I would have been able to see quite a number of shows by color-field painters (though I didn't, since I wasn't familiar with the names of the lesser-known ones). Helen kept me on her mailing list and I went to her openings. We even had lunch a couple of times, and I was irked by the way she was treated in H. W. Janson's *History of Art*, the text for my Hunter College course. Janson implied that the stain technique which she'd pioneered was the invention of one of her imitators, and gave him a full-page color reproduction without even mentioning her.[310] It looked like male chauvinist piggery to me, but my Hunter classmates would probably believe Janson's version of events, if only because they knew so much less about it.

My mother gave me all the money I needed, but I didn't want to be any more dependent on her than I could help. Besides my job on the *Times*, I was selling articles on non-Greenbergian subjects in Manhattan to *Smithsonian* and *ARTnews* (now the preferred spelling for *Art News*, since it was under new management). I didn't therefore want to leave town to go to graduate school, so I applied to NYU's Institute of Fine Arts and to Columbia. The Institute turned me down, even though I asked Bill Rubin (together with Henry Grunwald) to furnish me with references to it, and Rubin taught there. I figured if he'd really gone to bat for me, I'd have made it, and I wondered if his estrangement from Clem was relevant. The rift had begun developing while I was in England, and by the time I returned to New York, it was complete. Clem never explained the split, beyond saying that Jenny said Rubin "smelled bad," but the contemporary art that MoMA was exhibiting and acquiring during this period paid only minor attention to art Clem admired, and was heavily stacked in favor what that he'd have considered lesser if not outright "novelty art."[311]

Under Rubin's leadership, MoMA acquired much earlier art that Clem considered great, and would stage great shows of earlier art, but Clem was never content to sit around being congratulated for having spotted the greats of the last generation. He wanted to advance the greats of the next ones, too, and in this, Rubin wasn't willing or perhaps even able to help. For Columbia, I asked D'Ancona and another professor with whom I'd taken an undergraduate course to be my references. They obliged, and I got in, entering in the fall of 1974. I'd complete the requirements for my MA in that first academic year, and complete course work for the PhD and pass my oral examinations two years later, depositing my dissertation in 1982.

*　　　　　*　　　　　*

Columbia's graduate art history program in the '70s was one of the top half-dozen, maybe even one of the top three or four in the country. It may not have been the most "advanced," as measured either by its taste or by its methodologies, but it was far from being the most "conservative"(however "conservative" the education it gave me may appear to twenty-first-century scholars). Columbia defined "modern" as meaning European painting and sculpture beginning in 1785, with the neoclassicism of Jacques-Louis David, and centering in Paris until after World War II, when "the mainstream" crossed the Atlantic with the triumph of American abstract expressionism. For my second area of major concentration, I eventually settled on American painting and sculpture of the nineteenth and early twentieth centuries (up to 1945).

Over six semesters, I'd learn about modern and American art and architecture from eight professors: Meyer Schapiro, Theodore Reff, Allen Staley, Kirk Varnedoe, Barbara Novak, Rosemarie Bletter, Gerald Silk, and Milton W. Brown. During my first year in grad school, the first four would have most effect on me; during my second and third years, the last five. Schapiro was such a celebrity that *ARTnews* had already asked me to do an article about him in 1973.[312] He was famous as a medievalist and as a modernist, but by 1974 he was semiretired. The only course I could take with him was on the theory and methods of investigation in art history, so I took it. Much of his material was new to me, so I don't entirely trust my notes (which I still have, along with those I took for most of my other courses). Reviewing my notes from Schapiro's course, I conclude that if I didn't understand what he was saying, one reason may have been that we were going in opposite directions.

Schapiro listed eminent art historians on the blackboard; one was Wölfflin. Clem had mentioned Wölfflin in the pamphlet he'd given me, so I decided to do my term paper on him. Formal analysis came to me as a surprise, and even after doing that paper, I'd still be fuzzy about it. Later in grad school, I'd learn to know it better, but only since I've left the academic environment have I come to appreciate what a vital tool it is. How in the world, I ask myself today, could I have spent two and a half years writing about art for a national magazine without knowing about it? The answer, I suspect, is that most of my readers didn't know what it was, either, so when I didn't talk about it, they never missed it. As for my editors, if I could get by without referring to it, that was so much less "jargon" to be translated into universal English.

The average art lover, I believe, thinks as I'd been thinking up to that point, primarily in terms of subject matter (though she or he is more apt to call it "content" or "meaning"). Most people aren't aware of how different arrangements of shapes and colors can affect their overall impression of any picture, nor do they stop to analyze this effect on them. Artists do so, of course, especially abstract artists, and to the extent that I'd come to know a few abstract artists, I'd learned a bit about their kind of formal analysis, but without being aware that this was what it was. In my article for *Time* on Helen, I'd quoted her talking about how some paintings "worked," and some didn't, and how the way to learn the difference was by developing one's "eye."[313] If anybody had told me this was related to formal analysis, I'd have been as surprised as Molière's Would-Be-Gentleman, who was amazed to learn that all his life, he'd been talking prose. Even more surprising is the fact that, until I entered grad school, I didn't know that Clem was often called a "formalist," and that the art with which his name was associated was often called "formalism," because he used formal terminology when discussing paintings, and because so much of the work he discussed was abstract (formal analysis seemed the best way to discuss abstract art).

These code names were already in use in the art world while I was on *Time*, but if I heard them, I didn't know what they meant. Nor did I learn with my paper for Schapiro, for Wölfflin's books concerned the Renaissance and baroque eras of the sixteenth and seventeenth centuries, calling the Renaissance ideal "linear," and the baroque, "painterly." Many people equated this to line v. color, but Wölfflin meant not only opposite ways of organizing a picture, but also opposed ways of rendering it. He described how two sketches, one "linear" and one "painterly," would compare. The linear one would be drawn with a pen or silver-point pencil, creating a neat, tight, hard line, while the painterly would achieve a softer, looser effect by using charcoal, red chalk, or a broad watercolor brush. Every object in the linear sketch would have sharp, unbroken outlines, while the painterly sketch would utilize broad, vague masses. Wölfflin specifically denied that "painterly" was the same as "colorful," citing Rembrandt as an artist who was painterly but preferred the medium of etching, which works only with variations of light and dark. [314]

Reff (BA, Columbia College, 1952, PhD, Harvard, 1958) taught a sequence of four lecture courses on modern painting that I would take over the full six semesters of my course work. The first two, on nineteenth-century painting, began with Courbet and realism in the 1840s and '50s, progressing through the impressionism of Manet and Degas in the '60s and '70s to the post-impressionism of Cézanne and other avant-garde painters of the '80s and '90s. The next two, on twentieth-century painting, began with the fauvism of Matisse, the cubism of Picasso and Braque, and the dada of Duchamp, continuing through the neo-plasticism of Mondrian and the surrealism of Miró and Magritte in the '20s and '30s, and winding up with the abstract expressionism of Pollock and de Kooning in the '40s and '50s. I took the whole sequence, as well as a seminar Reff gave on the late paintings of Cézanne.

Reff was known for his writing on Cézanne, Degas, Manet, and Picasso, and was doing research on all of them while I was taking courses with him. This research energized his lectures. The first three-quarters of his sequence were a revelation to me, since I'd known almost nothing about his subjects before taking the courses. He was at his best with iconographic analyses, these being what his books primarily concerned, and with representational paintings to which iconography could be applied. Such paintings he might explicate in relation to the literature, politics, and/or social customs of the era in a way that enriched both, but he could also handle formal analysis.

In fact, one of his strongest suits was showing how formal means could be used for iconographic ends. At our first lecture, he showed us Courbet's *After-Dinner at Ornans* (1849). This was a scene of everyday life, and in the nineteenth century such scenes were normally handled in "genre" paintings. "Genre" paintings were usually small, and considered of secondary importance, but Courbet used a large canvas for this one, a formal characteristic that, as Reff pointed out, elevated its humble subject and forced viewers to confront it. Reff would teach me much about art, how it looked, and what to say about it. He would enable me to respond fervently to Cézanne, and I would have him to thank for a dissertation topic that would eventually lead to my theory about abstract painting, but somehow I never really warmed up to him.

One reason may have been his taste, as first manifested in the nineteenth-century segments of his sequence. I loved it when he lectured about the great avant-garde artists: Courbet, Manet, Degas, Cézanne. But he interspersed his discussion of them with work by other painters who didn't impress me as favorably. The vibrant *After-Dinner at Ornans*, for example, was compared and contrasted with Thomas Couture's *Romans of the Decadence*, a stale-looking painting exhibited at the Salon of 1847.[315] With his oversized "genre" painting, Courbet had scandalized the Parisian public that came to these Salons, but Couture was a "history" painter whose idealized classical scenes reflected the values of the French Academy that controlled the Salons, and he was greatly admired by that same public. Reff spoke with equal gravity of both.

This was known as "revisionist" art history, and it was big in the 1970s, but to prepare myself for grad school, I'd read *The History of Impressionism* by John Rewald (originally published in 1946, though I read the revised edition of 1973). This was the nineteenth-century art history that I'd learned as a child, more by osmosis than by reading anything, and to me, it set the stage for the abstraction of the twentieth century. As Rewald told it, the paintings at these nineteenth-century Salons mostly reflected the ideas of Jean-Auguste-Dominique Ingres, who'd succeeded David as leader of the neoclassic school, and whose outlook dominated the French Academy. Ingres proclaimed the superiority of line over color, and reason over emotion. His rival had been Eugène Delacroix, the Romantic, distinguished for his use of color. Delacroix wasn't elected to the Academy until late in life, and was considered a rebel against it.

The followers of Ingres lacked his talent, and used his style for pictures that appealed to a nouveau riche public which, as Rewald put it, "lacked any art education and were satisfied with whatever flattered their eyes and hearts: pretty nudes, sentimental stories, religious subjects, heroic deeds, flowers which one could almost 'smell,' patriotic scenes, and touching tales."[316] Most critics shared this taste, and so, though the young impressionists got some of their gravely beautiful and triumphantly honest paintings shown in the Salons, they attracted little positive attention. Eventually, the group decided to hold exhibitions of its own.

The first, in 1874, was attacked by a number of art critics and ignored by most of the public; its sales barely covered its costs. With scathing indignation, Rewald condemned the reviewers' "blatant injustices or perfidious insinuations, their cruel sarcasms or vulgar mockeries...."[317] Yet it was precisely the taste of such critics that we were now being invited to keep a more open mind about, by examining the Salon paintings they preferred. With Reff and other revisionist teachers, I'd also be invited to admire the equally academic and popular late-Victorian painters who exhibited at the Royal Academy in London, and nineteenth-century Germanic painters formerly classed as lesser lights, like Adolph Menzel and Hans von Marées.

Throughout grad school, I'd keep an open (if not wildly enthusiastic) mind about these painters. As I saw it, I was at Columbia to learn, not teach – on the receiving end of information, for a change, not the giving end. I'd go to local shows of nineteenth-century French and English academic art, and do term papers on Victorian painters and Menzel. Only much later would I be able to put together all the things I was witnessing in graduate school with the outlook that dominated (and continues to dominate) the contemporary art scene, but already in the '70s, I noted vaguely that revisionism had developed in the wake of pop art, and wondered if the two weren't related. Didn't the Salon painters have a lot in common with the pop artists, I thought, in being so concerned with subject matter and storytelling, rather than art for its own sake?

Even Ingres, according to Rewald, had described the Salons as "a picture shop," where "business rules instead of art."[318] And weren't the pop artists also distinguished more for the popular and commercial success they'd enjoyed than for the approval of genuinely highbrow critics like Clem? Wasn't publicizing the Salon painters therefore a way of trying to legitimize pop by establishing a pedigree in earlier art for it, and showing that art which finds favor with a broad contemporary public might not be so bad? Neither my professors nor my fellow students gave any signs to me of being aware that their concern with academic historical art might be influenced by, and reflect prevailing tastes in contemporary art. Why couldn't any of them see it? Why could I?

At the time, I assumed that neither professors nor grad students were up on contemporary art. I thought that I was more aware of its relationships with art history because I'd been keeping tabs on contemporary art (especially in the '60s). In retrospect, I see other reasons, too, such as the fact that I'd spent eighteen years outside academia since graduating from college, so when I came back to grad school, I was more fully formed than I'd been just out of Barnard. I respected, even admired my grad school professors, but I wasn't awed by them, as I'd been in college, and as most of my fellow students, especially the younger ones, still appeared to be.

Moreover, most of those eighteen years had been spent in a subcommunity very different from Morningside Heights. I tried to fit in with the academic community, at Columbia and for years thereafter, but when I was on *Time*, I'd been such an outsider in relation to the subcommunity of the art world that it was hard to start thinking of myself as a member of its academic extension. It wasn't just that *Time* was the media, as opposed to academia. It was also *Time*'s orientation toward less sophisticated, more conservative readers, and its support for the war in Vietnam, which lingered in many left-wing memories for decades after that stance had evolved into a more critical one.

Even today, I get hostile stares from many of my contemporaries when I say I worked for *Time* in the '60s, and Columbia had been very much on the other side of the barricades in those days. Morningside Heights was quiet in the '70s, but souvenirs of its activist past remained – for instance, in one stall in a ladies' room in Butler Library. There, every time I squatted on the toilet, I saw a graffito straight ahead of me which read, "LBJ pull out like your father should have," and it stayed there until the library was completely renovated in the new millennium. If I'd worked on *Newsweek* or in book publishing, I'd have been more welcome in grad school, and felt more at home there.

Maybe the biggest reason I remained a bit detached from Columbia, though, was my friendship with Clem. Other intellectuals of his generation had found niches in higher education, but he remained independent (giving talks and participating in panels on campuses, but turning down offers of full-time jobs). He shared the academic tendency to look down on me as a journalist, saying that my journalistic experience made my prose too "sprightly," but he looked down on most art historians, too. Some few he respected, but the phrase I recall him using about my teachers at Columbia, even when I was being most enthusiastic about them, was "mediocre minds." Academia mostly responded in kind. Both Clem's writing, and books by critics and art historians who shared his outlook, would appear in bibliographies my professors gave me, but always labeled "Greenbergian" and/or "controversial." One incident during my first semester demonstrated the animosity with which many art-world people viewed him. Rosalind Krauss, an art critic and Hunter College professor, published an article in the September–October 1974 *Art in America* that suggested the David Smith estate was being mishandled by its executors. Since Clem was the executor who had been and was caring for all the sculptures unsold when Smith died in 1965, this was really an attack on Clem.

Using photographs taken at Smith's former home in Bolton Landing in upstate New York, *Art in America* presented what looked like evidence that Clem was ignoring the wishes of Smith by having some sculptures stripped of the paint Smith had applied to them, or by allowing the paint on them to deteriorate by leaving the sculpture outdoors.[319] Many people knew that Clem had often felt that Smith's work looked better unpainted. Quite a number of them assumed that Clem was taking advantage of the fact that Smith was dead to alter the artist's esthetic decisions. He was widely attacked, including by lots of people whom he'd thought were friends, while others who'd quietly resented him for years now found it respectable to vent their venom in public. Thus, in retrospect, this article marked a turning point in his reputation.

Hilton Kramer in the *Times*, Robert Hughes in *Time*, and *Newsweek* in an unsigned article all picked up the Krauss attack.[320] Hughes was the most censorious, and *Newsweek*, most knowledgeable and sympathetic. All three publications interviewed Clem, as he took full responsibility for the situation, but he maintained that the paint which had been stripped was only the preliminary undercoat, known as primer, not the finished overcoat. "David said that these works were unfinished," he was quoted by *Newsweek* as saying. "I know damn well what he wanted." Smith had always left many of his sculptures outdoors. Clem further indicated that he wasn't concerned with other people's opinions, only with doing what he thought was right.

It was a long time before I could discuss this incident with him, among other reasons because relations between us were still somewhat strained. The previous spring, I'd written a new version of my "novel" about *Time* that brought events up to 1972, when I'd told Clem I didn't want to go to bed with him anymore. I thought I was presenting it with detachment, but I must have been trying to justify my own conduct toward him by making him look as bad as possible. I sent it to him at his house near Norwich, in upstate New York. Jenny had chosen this house, so I understood, because it was near a theater group she'd been involved with, but Clem now spent a lot of time up there alone. I believe he felt under less pressure there than when he was in the city. In any event, he read my manuscript there, marking its margins with comments from informative to sarcastic. To his credit, he tried to read it as literature, and wrote me an intelligent, remarkably objective letter about it, telling me what was wrong with it esthetically, and how I might improve upon it when I redid it. As always, his esthetic ideals ran parallel to his human values, so the critique was personal, too, but phrased with such insight into his own behavior that it became acceptable (he understood himself better in writing than in person, but so do I).

He was so upset by the attacks on him over the Krauss article that it would be months before I could get him to talk about it. When he did, he still maintained the paint was only primer, and said that only a small number of sculptures had been involved, no more than eight. Actually, it was only five, out of a total of more than four hundred sculptures that had been in the estate originally.[321] Since Krauss's article didn't say how many sculptures had been supposedly vandalized or mention the total number of sculptures in the estate, she conveyed the impression that far more than 1.25 percent of the total were at issue – nor did Kramer, Hughes, or *Newsweek* seriously attempt to correct this impression.[322]

As an executor, Clem's duty was to maximize profits for the estate's beneficiaries, Smith's two underage daughters. The executors of the Rothko estate had been sued for failing to do this, and their trial was reported at length in the *Times* for the better part of 1974. Even in the extremely unlikely case that the paint on all five of those Smith sculptures wasn't primer, I'm sure Clem believed it was, and, given his pathological honesty, would have told any potential client that it was. This would have greatly diminished the market value of the sculpture.

As the '70s progressed, and I was in contact with Clem more, I'd call him in Norwich repeatedly, but the phone would ring unanswered. When I finally got him, I'd ask where he'd been, and he'd say, "Smith estate business." I believed that he was smart about pricing, and I thought he was pricing the Smiths as high as he could, to maximize profits for the daughters, but low enough so the best works went to collectors and museums who'd do the most to ensure Smith's place in history. Nothing I've seen in the Clement Greenberg papers at the Archives of American Art dispels this notion.[323] In fact, the documents there help to explain why, in spite of the Krauss attack and occasional disputes with Smith's ex-wife, Clem was kept on as the executor with primary responsibility for the care and pricing of the sculpture until the girls reached the age of twenty-five. With the younger one, this was not until 1980. Clem later told me he'd made both daughters millionairesses, but the older one had developed into "an artist's widow." "What's that?" I asked. "Just a type," he said, and didn't elaborate.

Shortly after the Krauss article came out, Clem appeared in a panel discussion at the CUNY Graduate Center. In the question period, I saw Kirk Varnedoe, a new, young professor at Columbia from whom I was taking a "proseminar" course, ask him a very loaded, angry question about the Krauss article. I knew why Varnedoe was concerned. He'd done his dissertation on Rodin, and he and Albert Elsen, the top Rodin scholar in the country, were distressed at that moment over sculptors' posthumous reputations, because posthumous castings had been made of sculptures by Rodin and other artists that weren't up to the standard of those made earlier.[324] I could see Varnedoe's position, at least in relation to Rodin, but knowing Clem as I did, I couldn't believe he'd do anything wrong, so I sensed, rather than knew, there must be factors involved I wasn't familiar with, and watched helplessly as Clem got furious at Varnedoe. With all the blistering intensity that could make his words really sting, he shot back that Varnedoe had no business asking that question, and he wasn't going to answer it.

I've asked myself whether I knew, during those early years, of the cleavage between Clem and my professors. The answer seems to be that I only sensed it, and ignored it whenever possible. After all, the painters whom Reff had

216

focused on in my first course with him had been avant-gardists (Courbet, Manet, Degas, and Cézanne), and his use of the Salon paintings could be seen as an attempt to illuminate the avant-garde ones. Still, why hadn't he lectured on Monet and Renoir? To me, they were more important than Degas or Courbet. And why hadn't he had anything good to say about Delacroix, the great apostle of color? Though the impressionists' emphasis on nature differed radically from the "history" painting that Delacroix had practiced, younger avant-gardists still admired him, from Manet and Monet through to Cézanne.[325] Yet Reff had used slides of Delacroix only to show how much more radical Courbet was, and talked only of how Degas had admired Ingres, the upholder of line.

I felt that Monet and Renoir were the colorists among the impressionists, while Degas and Cézanne were more oriented toward line, and concluded that I was once again up against a writer who, like my *Time* colleagues, was more linear than coloristic. During my second semester at Columbia, I'd have to write a research paper in order to fulfill the requirements for my master's degree, so I decided to write it on Monet and his use of color. That way, I'd be able to educate myself about Monet, and also to explore the possibility that color might be some sort of language or form of communication – in which case it might prove as applicable to abstract art as it did to representational.

Kirk Varnedoe shared the teaching of the proseminar with Allen Staley. This course was designed to prepare students for taking seminars, as opposed to lecture courses. Our group had only eleven students, and we sat around a table, with lots of discussion. This made it easy for me to relate immediately to both professors, and I liked them both, finding them scholarly in the best sense of the word, seemingly detached and objective, demanding but considerate of their students. The chatty nature of proseminar helped fill in chinks between my more formal courses. I was taught to take the art magazines more seriously: some of their art-historical articles were assigned to us. We were also referred to Robert Rosenblum's book on Ingres (1967).[326] Evidently, Rosenblum was somebody we ought to know about, a younger scholar who taught at the Institute of Fine Arts. Another book soon mentioned was E. H. Gombrich's *Art and Illusion* (based on lectures given in 1956, but first published as a book in 1960).[327] I'd find his name and theories discussed in more advanced courses, too.

Staley (BA, Princeton, 1957, PhD, Yale, 1965) was tall and thin, with a dry sense of humor, and little spectacles as stylish as they were severe. His specialty was nineteenth-century English painting, and being an Anglophile myself, this prejudiced me on his behalf. He'd done his dissertation on the landscapes of the Pre-Raphaelites, a group of English artists who in the early

Victorian period had painted beautiful little pictures outdoors, directly from nature, before the French impressionists had become known for doing this. In the spring of 1975, I'd take a seminar with him on the Romantic landscape from 1750 to 1850, a lecture course in summer school on French painting from 1774 to 1830, and in the fall of 1975, a seminar on later Victorian painting.

Staley made me feel that iconography was worth pursuing by the intensity with which he spoke about it. His recommended reading list for the summer school course included Rosenblum's *Transformations in Late Eighteenth Century Art* (1967), Hugh Honour's *Neo-classicism* (1968), and Walter Friedlaender's *David to Delacroix* (1930; English translation, 1952). Although Staley called the Friedlaender a basic undergraduate text, he associated it with the "narrow stylistic view," while my notes on the Rosenblum read "revolutionary," with "great emphasis" on iconography, and "relation to history and society."[328] For my presentation (and paper) in the late Victorian painting seminar, I selected "Five O'clock Tea Antiquity" from the list Staley gave us. This meant scenes of domestic life by academic painters like Lawrence Alma-Tadema which, although set in ancient Rome, were more characteristic of middle-class life in Victorian England (ladies playing "he loves me, he loves me not" with daisies, going to the doctor, etc.). During or right after a consultation with Staley at the beginning of the semester, I jotted down ideas to develop in this paper in one of my notebooks. The list ends with, "why? what did it mean? not just narrow stylistic progression."[329]

When Staley wasn't pushing those sappy late Victorians, he had a fine eye, but this wasn't Greenbergian formalism. Rather, it was "connoisseurship," the appreciation of works of art in and of themselves. The slides he showed us in the Romantic landscape seminar captured the exact colors and brushwork of exquisite pictures by lesser-known English painters like Thomas Girtin, as well as famous ones like J. M. W. Turner. Staley's course in French painting was timed to coincide with *French Painting 1774–1830: The Age of Revolution*, a revisionist exhibition at the Metropolitan Museum. This show combined splendid paintings with second-rate ones, but the course emphasized the great and famous. Staley worked value judgments into his discussions. In his seminar on the Romantic landscape, he compared two slides of Mt. Vesuvius erupting by Joseph Wright of Derby and Pierre-Jacques Volaire. "Wright has tremendous sense of calm," my notes read. "v. subtle + extremely sophisticated – much more successful than theatrical extravaganza in the Volaire." [330]

Varnedoe (BA, Williams, 1967, PhD, Stanford, 1972) was boyish-looking, on the short side, on the go, and eager to get ahead. He wouldn't stay long at Columbia before moving to the Institute of Fine Arts. In 1989, he'd succeed Bill Rubin at MoMA, only to die of cancer in 2003 at the age of fifty-seven.

In the fall of 1974, he was starting out in the Big Apple. I asked him to be my advisor for that master's research paper on color in Monet, and he obliged. Though he confided to me halfway through the term that he suffered from color blindness, he read my paper carefully and conscientiously. His real strength was sculpture, where color is less of an issue.

During my first semester in grad school, I also did some reading in two revered art historians. Their attitudes toward abstract art dismayed me. In an essay first published in 1940, Panofsky argued that every man-made object could be seen as a work of art, since each had an idea behind it and a form or shape. The idea might be functional, as with a tool or apparatus, or else involve a wish to communicate something, as in a painting or play, in which case the idea was conveyed by the subject matter. "Content" differed from subject matter, being "the basic attitude of a nation, a period, a class, a religious or philosophical persuasion – all this unconsciously qualified by one personality, and condensed into one work."[331] But content would be obscured to the extent that "either one of the two elements, idea or form, is voluntarily emphasized or suppressed. A spinning machine is perhaps the most impressive manifestation of a functional idea, and an 'abstract' painting is perhaps the most expressive manifestation of pure form, but both have a minimum of content."[332]

Gombrich claimed that *Art and Illusion* wasn't intended as a plea for the return of an art based in illusion, but he joked at the expense of one of abstraction's defenders.[333] To me, the book was essentially an apologia for representational painting, showing the many ways it had served to portray reality and as an independent creation. Gombrich set up an opposition between "conceptual" and "perceptual" art, between "making" and "matching." Matching (perceptual) was the attempt to make a painting look like the external world, while making (conceptual) meant the painting conveyed only basic information about its subject, in a simplified or schematic manner, thereby throwing the viewer's attention back on the painting as an object in itself. He argued a viewer's eye was torn between seeing a painting as an illusion of something else, and seeing it for itself (brushwork, composition, etc.). It was impossible to see both at the same time, and in that sense, every painting was ambiguous. He reproduced an optical illusion from an old Viennese humor magazine that, if you looked at it one way, looked like the head of a duck, and, if you looked at it another way, looked like the head of a rabbit. According to him, the image was either a rabbit or a duck, but could never be both at the same time.[334]

Cubism, according to Gombrich, was "the last desperate revolt against illusion....the most radical attempt to stamp out ambiguity...." He equated Picasso's collages to James Thurber's wobbly cartoons (meanwhile protesting he meant twentieth-century art "no disrespect"). He suggested that Picasso resembled Thurber in the skill with which he utilized accidents. I recognized that idea of abstract art as accidental gesture from my last year at *Time*. It was Rosenberg's dadaist interpretation, and Gombrich cited Rosenberg in his notes. His reproduction of a Pollock was really ugly, and the artist himself was identified only as the "action painter." Gombrich's associations with Pollock's imagery were negative: "the intricate and ugly shapes with which industrial civilization surrounds us," "twisted wires or complex machinery," and "the deserts of city and factory...turned into tanglewoods."

15. Reconciling Duchamp with Pollock
(Fall 1975–Fall 1976)

Varnedoe gave me an A for my research paper on Monet and color, but I hadn't been able to come to any conclusions about Monet's use of color as a means of communication. In the paintings I'd studied, he'd laid dozens of colors around and upon each other; this didn't help me find meanings of specific colors that could tell me how abstract art said whatever it had to say. Nor did I have much luck that spring with more conventional iconography in my presentation for the course on Romantic landscape. From Staley's list this time, I'd chosen pictures by Turner associated with the poetry of Byron, but the pictures mostly ran parallel to the poetry, instead of alluding to it directly.

Trying to discover meaning in Alma-Tadema's domestic scenes in ancient Rome was equally frustrating. Staley said he'd read the phrase "Five O'clock Tea Antiquity" somewhere. I couldn't find it, and concluded that it must have been coined in the twentieth century, because it wasn't even the kind of thing said by the nineteenth-century art critics who'd reviewed these pictures originally at Royal Academy exhibitions. These critics devoted the largest proportion of their discussions to what the twentieth century might have called the formal qualities of the pictures – the accuracy of the drawing, skill with which materials such as metals or marble were rendered, brilliance or opacity of the colors, and anatomical correctness of the figures.

I said so in my paper, which at least let me see how art history might be reconciled with art criticism, and formalism with iconography. The art critic, as I saw it, used formal analysis to explain why he (or she) felt whether or not a work of art was worth preserving for posterity, while the art historian used iconography to find out what the work had meant when it was created in the past. Staley gave me an A for it (just as he'd given me an A for the Turner–Byron paper), but I was no closer to being able to write the kind of iconographic analysis that he'd asked for originally, and the books he'd enthused about in his French painting course emphasized subject matter that demanded such analysis. Rosenblum and Honour used similarities between the subject matter of the Romantic and neoclassic painters to minimize stylistic differences between them, and/or imply that the neoclassicists were better – as was line over color, reason over emotion, and (to use Wölfflin's terminology) linear over painterly (neoclassicists favoring hard clear outlines in their paintings, while Delacroix was notable for his loose, rough brushwork).

The show at the Met similarly devoted most space to the neoclassic period, and I complained about this in a letter to Clem. "The good painters, David and Ingres and Gérard," I wrote, "are certainly very good, but the Delacroix... comes like a welcome breath of painterliness only at the very end."[335] This letter is dated September 2, 1975, and is preserved, like many of my letters to Clem, in the Greenberg papers at the Archives of American Art. To judge from his letters to me, this was the first I'd written him since the beginning of the year, and suggests I hadn't seen or talked with him on the phone in the interim. He could be supportive in letters, telling me I had "the head to swim through art history at any graduate school."[336] But speaking with him was harder. I'd call him up to ask some question about art, and, if I kept him talking, the conversation would become increasingly vulgar, until finally he'd say, "You must come up to Norwich and get fucked." Can you imagine a less gracious invitation? Eventually, I'd realize this was the only invitation I'd get, and even come to believe that its phraseology was due to his insecurity. I'd feel it was because I'd rejected him earlier, and he didn't want to take a chance on being rejected again, once he'd gotten me up to the country. I'd learn to swallow my irritation, get out my calendar and make a date to go see him in Norwich, but while I was still doing course work, it seemed to me he was saying, Sex is the price of admission to my eminent presence, since you're only a lowly graduate student.

The result of my irritation, during those early years, would be that instead of making a date to get fucked, I'd say sure, sometime, and change the subject. In fact, I seem to have been so turned off by these invitations that I let him know I didn't like them, for in a letter of his dated January 10, 1975, he protested that he didn't recall having laid down any conditions.[337] The rest of that letter I seem to have found off-putting myself, and so, though he'd followed it up with a conciliatory postcard, I don't appear to have written back until the following September, and our relationship seems to have been conducted primarily by mail for at least another year and a half.

The presentation I prepared for the other seminar I took in the fall of 1975 was a third exercise in frustration. The seminar was on German Expressionism, taught by Rosemarie Haag Bletter (PhD, Columbia University, 1973). My presentation concerned the paintings of Kandinsky and his use of color (Kandinsky was Russian, but living in Munich in southern Germany when he evolved into abstraction). Again, I was trying to discover whether color could communicate meaning, and Kandinsky had written about color at length, especially in a short memoir, "Reminiscences," (1913), and his theoretical tract, *Concerning the Spiritual in Art* (1912). He was the first abstract painter I'd been able to study since I'd come to grad school.

Bletter told us about a dissertation deposited at Yale in 1968 by Rose-Carol Washton (later Washton Long).[338] It argued that the supposedly abstract paintings that Kandinsky executed prior to World War I were really full of veiled imagery derived from theosophy (among other things). Washton Long wouldn't publish her findings in book form until 1980.[339] The Columbia library, however, had a typescript of the dissertation, and I read it eagerly. It was very encouraging to find another scholar challenging the traditional definition of abstract painting as meaning nothing, but I wasn't happy with the way she did it. She detected saints, apocalyptic figures on horseback, people in boats, and other images in Kandinsky's paintings. I could certainly see such images, but they struck me as cute and cartoonlike, and the whole concept as tending to diminish the artist rather than elevate him. From being an innovative, excellent abstract painter, he became merely a second-rate representational one – so second-rate at representation that he needed an art historian to tell what he'd depicted.

Sad to say, my attempt to establish color as a language in which Kandinsky communicated feelings met with even less success. Different colors evoked different emotions in him, and he associated them with different musical instruments, but the equivalencies that he set up didn't correspond to the way other writers, artists, and even the composer Scriabin had correlated colors to emotions or sounds. I seemed to have come to a dead end in my search for color as vehicle to convey meaning.

Except for Emil Nolde (whom I'd written about while on *Time*), I was unimpressed by the northern branch of German Expressionism: Ernst Kirchner and Erich Heckel weren't nearly as radical (or as good) as Matisse and Picasso. In retrospect, I'd say the growing interest in them in the '70s derived from their being more obviously representational than the French greats, and less approved by genuine highbrows like Clem. Both qualities again reflected the taste for pop's figurative nature in the present, and its popularity as opposed to quality: subject matter again, at the expense of style. My notes suggest that Bletter emphasized the interest of German Expressionism in mysticism, and its contrast between spirit and matter.[340] This was right in line with Rosenblum's new book, *Modern Painting and the Northern Romantic Tradition: Friedrich to Rothko* (1975), listed in a bibliography she gave us.[341]

Modern Painting and the Northern Romantic Tradition was the first book I'd encountered in grad school that dealt at least partially with artists whom I knew a bit about, the abstract expressionists. It irked me even in 1975 (though I was barely conscious of being irked). Rosenblum argued that abstract expressionism was really descended from Northern European painting, rather than the vastly superior painting of Paris, covering up the fact that he couldn't establish any credible line of stylistic descent or influence with a lot of high-minded talk about ideological kinships, describing a mystical search for secular equivalents to outworn religious imagery that began as landscape and wound up as abstract expressionism. The idea that abstract expressionism was really landscape had been around since the 1950s. It had survived into the '60s and beyond because it enabled proponents of pop art to argue that pop alone was all about Society, whereas abstract expressionism, being nothing but landscape, was somehow escapist (and color-field painting even more so, to the extent of being "hedonistic").[342] In addition, as Rosenblum's title suggested, he set up Rothko as the archetypal abstract expressionist, and relegated my hero, Pollock, to a subordinate role.

The third course I took that semester was Barbara Novak's lecture course in American painting, 1760–1900, for which the text was her own influential *American Painting of the Nineteenth Century* (1969). Novak (BA, Barnard, 1950; PhD, Radcliffe, 1957) had curly golden hair and always looked glamorous. I liked all of the nineteenth-century paintings she showed us, but especially the "luminists" she'd helped to rediscover, Fitz Hugh Lane and Martin Johnson Heade. With their clean, clearly outlined landscapes, these little paintings were rarely great, but almost always well-made and appealing. Alas, the epilogue of Novak's book, on the twentieth century, again downplayed Pollock and elevated Rothko, adding a coda on the '60s that all but ignored color-field painting and reproduced neo-dada, pop, and minimalist art. She was married to Brian O'Doherty, who wrote about contemporary art, and (under the name of Patrick Ireland) also exhibited conceptualist varieties of it.

Within the nineteenth century, most of Novak's favorite painters were conceptual rather than perceptual (to use Gombrich's terminology), and linear rather than painterly (in Wölfflinian terms). In her book, only two clearly painterly painters (Albert Pinkham Ryder and Washington Allston) rated chapters of their own. All the rest (including Gilbert Stuart, John Singer Sargent, Mary Cassatt, and James A. McNeill Whistler) were crammed into one chapter on "the painterly mode in America" (in my notes, I find "Q: is it un-American to be painterly?").[343] Again, I wanted to fill the gap left by a teacher by doing a term paper on a painterly American artist, but I worried about doing so, given Novak's preference for the linear. She herself showed me the way out of this dilemma. One topic on our list of suggestions for papers was "great teachers," including John La Farge. In her chapter on the painterly mode, she'd indicated that although La Farge was a painter of modest merit, he was more interesting as an intellect and a writer. By dealing with his writing, I could avoid this whole touchy question of his painterly style.

This approach also let me avoid the larger, even more delicate issue of whether I was going to employ the "narrow" stylistic approach that my professors seemed to frown upon, or try to deal with "content" as revealed through iconography, which they liked, but which I didn't seem to have any aptitude for. Eventually, I'd find that writing about writing would let me deal with abstract painting in a way I never could have if I'd been firmly committed to either formal analysis or the usual iconography. I'd be able to see that the issue with abstraction was not the paintings themselves, but rather how they were thought about (not that I envisaged this possibility at the time). When I took Novak's seminar in American painting, the following semester, I chose a second topic from her list of suggestions that would let me write about art writing: changes in the concept of "sentiment" from 1850 to 1900. This paper wouldn't be completed until fall, and two courses I took that spring would feed into my thinking before then.

One course was Bletter's illuminating Modern Architecture. I learned a lot about Art Nouveau and the giants of the International Style like Le Corbusier and Mies van der Rohe, but again I was vaguely annoyed by tinges of revisionism. Bletter showed us New York buildings like Bonwit Teller and the Waldorf Astoria that were sweet but flaccid. She showed us Paul Rudolph's school of art and architecture at Yale, site of that mysterious fire which *The New York Times* hadn't reported for weeks during the bizarre summer of 1969, my last at *Time*. She set up the "brutalism" of such buildings as a modernist bogeyman that justified the reaction against modernism by younger architects like Robert Venturi: my notes on the Rudolph building read, "RB thinks claustrophobic and too rough."[344] Her lecture on Venturi gave his views more warmly. My notes run, "attacks puritanical mod[ern] arch[itecture]/ likes...'messy vitality' over 'obvious unity.'"[345] I wasn't impressed by this, or by the slides she showed us in relation to the book that Venturi was known for, *Learning from Las Vegas* (1972). To me, Las Vegas architecture was an eyesore – walk-in pop art.

It was in this course that I first heard the term "postmodern" (and/or "postmodernist" and/or "postmodernism"). As nearly as I can recall, Bletter used one or more of these terms in her last class, on April 22. She was discussing Louis Kahn, who is sometimes said to have anticipated the postmodern in architecture, and Venturi, who personifies it for me. Some people think the terms were first used in architecture, and passed from architecture into the art world around 1980. It's true that before then, they weren't as widely used in the art world as they would be in the '80s, but they were already in use there during the late '60s and early '70s.[346]

Leo Steinberg had shown his sensitivity to the *Zeitgeist* of that moment when he applied "post-Modernist" to art in *Other Criteria*, a collection of articles he published in 1972.[347] Besides writing about contemporary art, Steinberg had been teaching art history at Hunter. Though his interests were catholic, he was there perhaps best known as a Renaissance scholar, and he was also – according to a fellow student of mine at Columbia – *the* contemporary critic who mattered in the '70s. I don't know when I bought his book, or how carefully I read it, but rereading it, I see that some of its ideas must have contributed to my thinking, even though in terms of '50s and '60s art, the book focuses on Johns and Rauschenberg, while distancing itself from Clem.

Steinberg used "post-Modernist" to refer to the "flatbed picture plane." This was his term for what he saw as a profound shift in esthetic thinking that began around 1950 with Rauschenberg and (to a lesser degree) other artists of his generation. Steinberg defined it as the shift to a painted surface that "is no longer the analogue of a visual experience of nature but of operational processes."[348] He saw it as "expressive of the most radical shift in the subject matter of art, the shift from nature to culture."[349] He also argued that with this shift, painting was conceived on the horizontal, even when it was positioned vertically for viewing. This last idea never really took with me, but I, too, would come to define postmodernism as having begun with Rauschenberg around 1950, and to appreciate the importance of "process" to it. Steinberg's emphasis on the shift from nature to culture (reinforcing as it did Rosenblum's notion that abstract expressionism was all about landscape) would similarly stay at the back of my mind until 1983, when it would enter into the formulation of my theory.

A second course I took in the spring of 1975 was Varnedoe's Modern Sculpture I. These were exciting lectures, too. Varnedoe gave us the important French sculptors of the nineteenth century, and a wide range of sculpture done across Europe in the first two decades of the twentieth, but his most crucial contribution for me was how he presented Picasso and Duchamp, both for what he did say and for what he didn't (and couldn't). I was seeing Picasso's work in a classroom for the first time, and enough of it so I could begin to appreciate it, but reviewing my notes, I find that Varnedoe didn't give us a complete or altogether coherent picture of its evolution. Partly this was because he was teaching a sculpture course, and only using Picasso's paintings to illuminate the sculpture; but partly, I say in retrospect, it was because neither he nor many other people really understood what Picasso had been up to in the most critical phase of his development – the evolution of cubism into Analytic Cubism from 1907 to 1912.

Even his contemporaries hadn't understood – most notably Duchamp. Today, I'd argue that Duchamp's bafflement at Analytic Cubism led to the creation of his Readymades, and that the admiration for those Readymades, on the part of Varnedoe and many others, stems in large measure from sharing this mystification, but in 1976, I was merely copying down what my teacher said, secure in the knowledge that he was giving me state-of-the-art scholarship (and even in retrospect I'm sure he was). When it came to Duchamp, the daddy of dada and the grandpa of pop, the calmer climate of academia let me view his work with more equanimity than had been possible during my last summer at *Time*. In taking him more dispassionately, I could also take him more seriously. I still do, if only because his work and outlook have answered the needs of so many others.

Since I took Varnedoe's course, I've become more familiar with Picasso and his development. I know how his early, representational Blue, Rose, and Iberian Periods led up to *Les Demoiselles d'Avignon* (1907), the large, startling painting generally considered the first cubist (or proto-cubist) picture. Its five ferocious-looking nudes are still perfectly recognizable as women, and set off very definitely from their background, but some faces and body parts are angular and jagged instead of curved. Working closely with Braque, Picasso continued on into increasingly complex compositions that broke the shapes within them into little "cubes."

Around 1910, these cubes began to flatten out into pointy areas of pattern or design that some call facets: they integrated the central subject of the canvas with its background. *"Ma Jolie"* (1911–12) marks the culmination of this three- or four-year phase known as Analytic Cubism. It's about as abstract as Picasso ever got. When I knew it first, it was subtitled *Woman with a Zither or Guitar*. Today, we can dimly see the figure of a woman holding a musical instrument of some sort amid the panoply of angular shapes, but many observers around 1912 couldn't perceive any subject matter at all in it, or in any of the other Analytic Cubist paintings Picasso and Braque had recently been making.

I've since concluded that this caused a profound disruption which has never really left the Western art world, or the overwhelming part of the globe which has been influenced by Western art. Paintings in the Western tradition had depicted external reality since the cavemen, though the conventions used to do so had varied from century to century, and culture to culture (Chinese, Indian, native American, and African artists, to one degree or another, had also engaged in mimesis, in the sense of imitation of the external world). The issue of what constitutes beauty in art was challenged a little earlier, with the fauvist innovations of Matisse. That's another issue that's never been satisfactorily resolved, but in terms of the meaning of art, it's this moment in Paris between 1910 and 1912 that marks the great divide between art that large numbers of people can relate to, and art that too many people have trouble with – abstract art, that is – and I don't mean just ordinary people. I mean a great many art-world people, too, though in grad school, I still believed that all the people who thought they understood abstraction really did.

Varnedoe tried to use Picasso's paintings to illuminate his sculpture. He began by comparing examples from Picasso's Blue Period, when the subjects of both paintings and sculpture were clearly recognizable. Then he gave us an early cubist painting of Fernande Olivier, the artist's mistress, compared with a bronze sculpture of her head (both 1909). The modeling and casting techniques Picasso used with this sculpture were centuries old, but he divided its face and hair into rigid peaks with sharp edges that resembled the painting.

Then, after only a brief discussion of Analytic Cubism, Varnedoe passed to the collages and constructions that Picasso (and Braque) began to make around 1912 (none of Braque's constructions have survived). The techniques used to make both collages and constructions were unprecedented in Western European fine art, but both again incorporated more recognizable images, or were recognizable as images in themselves. Since this was a sculpture course, Varnedoe paid more attention to the constructions, whose radicalism lay in their being neither modeled nor carved, but built out of separate pieces. The first example that he gave us was Picasso's first and most important construction, *Guitar* (1912), a completely recognizable musical instrument, made out of sheet metal and wire.

Next, Duchamp, who was already known as a cubist painter, had come up with his Readymades, starting with the *Bicycle Wheel* (1913). As Varnedoe presented the Readymades, they went Picasso one better because many of them weren't even constructed by the artist, but simply objects that became art primarily through the artist's act of placing them in an esthetic context. Duchamp had said that he wanted to get away from purely "retinal" painting, and place painting once again "at the service of the mind." This was his way of saying that painting had gotten too abstract, and needed to return to recognizable subject matter, but he didn't want to appear to be taking a step backward, so instead of returning to traditional representational painting, he ultimately developed the Readymades. They were presentational rather than representational, but still figurative in the sense that they had subject matter that could easily be defined in words.

I may have read about "the service of the mind" in 1968, as the phrase appeared in Bill Rubin's catalogue for the dada and surrealism show at MoMA of that year.[350] Still, if I'd read it, it didn't sink in, because I'd been ignorant of its context. Rubin's catalogue had said that dada was a reaction against cubism, and "the autonomy of pure painting," but had also emphasized its role as a political reaction against World War I, and this had carried greater weight with me, as a journalist in the midst of Vietnam. Neither "the autonomy of pure painting" nor "retinal painting" would have meant anything to me in 1968. The first was a formalist code reference to abstract art, and the second was a dadaist code reference to it, but even if I'd known this in 1968, I still didn't know how abstract Analytic Cubism had become, or that anybody had ever viewed it as non-objective, or of the uproar that such a view had caused.

Even when I took Varnedoe's modern sculpture class, I was only beginning to learn this, and though he did his best to teach us what he could, I feel, after reviewing my class notes, that he himself could be seen as a victim of the dismay and lack of understanding that arose in response to Analytic Cubism. In his lectures, he was giving us a fine synopsis of what he'd read, but even that reflected the anger and frustration which many other critics and art historians who also considered themselves sympathetic to cubism had experienced in trying to understand it. Varnedoe spoke of more than one sculpture as "frustrating." Picasso's *Guitar*, he said, looked like you could play it, but you couldn't. Duchamp's *With Hidden Noise* (1916), a hollow ball of twine compressed between two sheets of brass, had inscriptions engraved on the brass that were frustrating because Duchamp omitted letters within each word, rendering the whole susceptible to more than one interpretation.[351]

Part of the frustration that Picasso and Braque inspired (and that Duchamp would incorporate into his work) developed out of the fact that neither of these first two cubists explained what they were doing. Picasso had uttered cryptic remarks over the years, for instance one made in 1935, "There is no abstract art. You must always start with something."[352] This enabled people to say, well, he wasn't really abstract anyway. (Of course he was. His paintings were semiabstract, as opposed to pure abstractions, but even semiabstract's a form of abstraction.) With my grounding in "feeling" as the subject matter of abstraction, I liked an equally cryptic quote from Braque. "Nature is a mere pretext for a decorative composition, plus sentiment," he'd said in 1908 or 1909. "It suggests emotion, and I translate that emotion into art."[353] But most later commentators, it seemed, had preferred other spokesmen or explanations.

Picasso and Braque had lived near each other in Montmartre when they were creating Analytic Cubism. The Italian futurists and other foreign artists came to see what they were doing, but a secondary group of French cubists were associated with two towns near Paris, Puteaux and Courbevoie. These artists, who at one time or another included Léger, Delaunay, and Roger de La Fresnaye, were known as "the Puteaux Cubists." Picasso and Braque appeared to favor nineteenth-century subject matter in their paintings: figure studies, portraits, landscapes, and still lifes. These subjects were so familiar that people thought Picasso and Braque were merely using them as pretexts for "pure painting," or art for art's sake. The Puteaux Cubists and the Italian futurists were more likely to use topics they considered "modern": the city, its industrial suburbs, trains, bicycles, and so on, and the futurists in particular had a whole ideology about the beauty of the truly modern.

Two minor Puteaux Cubists, Albert Gleizes and Jean Metzinger, published a pamphlet, *Cubism* (1912). Among other things, it suggested that the bewildering way that cubists juxtaposed shapes on their canvases could be understood as presenting objects seen from more than one vantage point. This essentially formalist manner of interpretation had become the basis of virtually all later discussions of Analytic Cubism. For writers who could respond intuitively to these pictures, and enjoy them despite their lack of apparent subject matter, formal discussions helped to explain why cubism was so rewarding. They weren't upset by the abandonment of perspective, a technique in use since the Renaissance, but others found it disturbing.

The fact that foregrounds merged with backgrounds in these paintings created spatial ambiguity, which upset many viewers. They couldn't be sure what was in front of what, and some commentators who claimed to be defending cubism found themselves doing so on grounds that it was supposed to be disturbing, and that its ambiguity reflected the ugly, chaotic modern society that had produced it. Among my notes for Varnedoe's course, I find this passage: "Cubist pntg catches on all over Europe, corresponds to 20th cent love of ambiguity, need to admit situations of uncertainty. Instead of an affirmation of reality, a challenge to it."[354] This idea would prove useful to me later on, but only after I'd been able to turn it inside out, and see that ambiguity could be a way of affirming reality.

Other language that Varnedoe used in discussing Picasso was also more of a turnoff than a turnon. *Les Demoiselles* was presented only in relation to Brancusi, to show how differently the two sculptors responded to African and other "primitive" sculpture. The Brancusi was about "reduction" and "simplicity," while the *Demoiselles* was about "disruption, upset, violence." The way Varnedoe described an example of Analytic Cubism led my notes to say, "form has been dissolved in way more drastic than Impressionism. More radical. In breaking up form + interlocking it w. space does without single light source...no atmosphere or space left around an object."[355] Does this make it sound beautiful or claustrophobic?

Lacking explanations from Picasso for why he'd taken up constructions, Varnedoe led up to *Guitar* by showing us paintings and sculptures made by Italian futurists and Puteaux cubists around 1912 and 1913. He implied that the futurists had contributed to Picasso's constructions through their more modern subject matter, but he also qualified this claim. "Cubism deals w. cerebration, contemplation, hermetic art form – subjects deal with studio life," say my notes. "Futurism – city, impulses and energy....Futurism a complete break w. past/typical subjects: activity, motion, politics, aggression." Varnedoe told us about the Technical Manifesto of Futurist Sculpture (1912). My notes call it a "valuable mine of ideas," though I've also written that it's "arguable how influential Futurist sculptures themselves were – ideas were in the air."[356]

Looking at Varnedoe's comparison between the subject matter of cubism and that of the futurists, I realize that many years later, I would derive some of my ideas about the subject matter of Analytic Cubism that lies beyond the titular subjects of its paintings from what he said about the subject matter of the futurists and Puteaux Cubists. But in those days neither he nor I could see beyond those titular subjects, and they indicated that Analytical Cubism was really only about picture-making, while the futurists and Puteaux Cubists were the first to deal in their paintings with the modern world. This attitude has continued to inform the standard distinctions made between cubism and futurism into the twenty-first century. "'Cubism' stood for a revolutionary style in art; 'Futurism' proclaimed a revolutionary style of life," announced the catalogue for an exhibition in 2004 built around *Materia*, Boccioni's futurist painting of his mother.[357]

Varnedoe's presentation was ideological, not strictly chronological, but the effect was to lessen the still more powerful impression Picasso could have made had his work been presented in one sequence. Varnedoe pretty much failed to explain how or why Picasso's constructed sculptures and collages evolved out of his own paintings, and the extended presentation of Duchamp that occupied most of the last class implied that Duchamp was the climax up to which everything else had been building. Rubin's 1968 exhibition had included thirteen works by Duchamp, but Varnedoe showed some that I hadn't seen, including *Fountain* (1917), the famous Readymade consisting of a urinal. He pointed out that the Readymades placed the emphasis more on the artist than on the object, and emphasized the mental or intellectual aspects of art, implying it also de-emphasized art's material and sensual properties. My notes on *Fountain* read: "seems effectively a sculpture of the mind, of the intellect. A maximum amount of conceptual difficulty w. minimum amount of making."[358]

For all its imperfections, this course stimulated thought in me. Over the years, I've put together what I learned from it. Most important was Duchamp's statement that art should be placed "at the service of the mind," and how the Readymades express this view. "The service of the mind" refers to emphasizing art's rational, logical properties – the antithesis of feeling or emotion. Although some dadaists liked to emphasize the movement's elevation of accident and its admiration for chaos, the fact is that we think and reason through words, though our capacities to feel precede words (a baby can cry before it can speak). Only figurative art can easily be described in words: whether it is representational or presentational, it has subject matter. Abstract art has too long appeared to have no subject matter, merely style, and style – like emotion – is nearly impossible to describe adequately in words.

Duchamp, in the teens, and the pop artists, in the '60s, rejected abstraction and reinstated subject matter. A Readymade, being machine-made, bears no trace of personal style, which Duchamp called the artist's *patte*, or paw, and denounced. A Readymade must therefore be discussed primarily from an iconographic point of view, not a formal one. Its concept is what counts: it has no perceptual component, since it hasn't been made to depict something else. It usually has clean, clear, or "linear" outlines, as opposed to painterly brush techniques.

Sharing Duchamp's priorities, my professors at Columbia in the '70s were playing up subject matter or "meaning" (and playing down style).

They were playing up iconography (and playing down formal values).

They were emphasizing line and reason (in opposition to color and emotion: Degas and Manet at the expense of Monet and Renoir, neoclassicism at the expense of Romanticism; Theodore Reff admired Cézanne, who was both a great colorist and a great draftsman, but he'd done his dissertation on Cézanne's drawings, hence, he was closest to Cézanne's linear skills).

Finally, they were emphasizing the linear (the clean, hard outlines of the American luminists, at the expense of the painterly mode).

In short, my generation of future teachers, curators, and critics specializing in modern or American art at Columbia (and I would imagine elsewhere) was already, by the '70s, being sent out into the world conditioned to see art from the vantage point of Duchamp. I don't think my professors were necessarily aware of their own affinities with or possible influence by dada, any more than I was aware while I was taking their courses. Only after decades of hindsight have I been able to put pieces together.

During the summer of 1976, I wrote my paper on "sentiment." I thought (among other reasons, because of the quote from Braque) that sentiment must be related to "feeling" in art, but I had to start by looking it up in the multi-volume *Oxford English Dictionary*. The O.E.D. said that "sentiment" could mean "A thought or reflection coloured by or proceeding from emotion,... *esp.* An emotional thought expressed in literature or art...." The first (1762) example of this definition that it gave came from *Elements of Criticism* by Henry Home, Lord Kames: "Every thought prompted by passion is termed a *sentiment*." I had to find out more about Kames.

Columbia had a biography of him by Arthur E. McGuinness (1970). It related this Scottish esthetician and philosopher to larger issues in his period, specifically a type of ethics called "moral sentiments." These fitted in with nineteenth-century American painting, since landscape then was often seen as displaying God's handiwork. "Moral sentiments" reminded me of Clem. He said he believed only in "art for art's sake," but Motherwell, when I'd interviewed him in 1969, had mentioned Clem's "moral earnestness," and I'd seen for myself how intense he could be about art. If people couldn't see good art, and praised the bad, he could be so dismissive that he reminded many people of the pope excommunicating a heretic. When I came to know him better, my belief that he revered art as a moral good would evolve into a less exalted conviction that he felt great art could reflect, express, and convey admirable human qualities, but in 1976, I was still too much in awe of him to see him clearly.

On the other hand, I must also have known by then of the dichotomies between him and my academic environment. Varnedoe had clashed with him over the Krauss article, then presented Duchamp as the climax of his sculpture course; I knew Clem didn't think much of Duchamp. Bletter had enthused about Venturi; I suspected Clem would like his work no more than I did. Staley had told us to get away from stylistic progressions, and emphasize "meaning." Clem valued style and formal values above all else. In Reff's lecture course that spring, he'd been giving us the bibliography on Renoir, and said something like this: "And then there's Kermit Champa's book, but he's a formalist, and there are certain problems...." His voice had trailed off, and I for one thought, Well, that's one book I don't have to bother with for orals. Finally, there was Novak, whose favorite contemporary art was what Clem would have considered "novelty art," and she would be reading – and grading – my paper on sentiment.

McGuinness said that Kames had come up with "a quite modern-sounding theory" about "felt thought."[359] "Felt thought" alluded to T. S. Eliot's ideas about why Metaphysical poets like Donne were better than Victorians like Tennyson – because the Metaphysicals fused thoughts and feelings, while the Victorians merely ruminated on their ideas.[360] I'd read these passages by Eliot at Barnard, but forgotten about them through the years when I'd fixated on feeling in art by itself. Nor was I fully conscious of the significance of fusing thought with feeling when I wrote the paper (for which Novak would also give me an A). I knew that the word *sentiment* had been so overworked that it had passed out of the critical vocabulary, so I concluded with a plea for its revival, because it applied to both Pollock and Duchamp (and adumbrates how I'd apply Duchamp's demand for verbally describable subject matter to abstract painting like Pollock's, though I was years away from doing so at that point).

"An artist in the act of creation," I wrote, "is rarely laughing or crying, seducing or attacking; he must be detached and concentrating all his faculties, both conscious and unconscious, in the business of making. This is true whether he is a Pollock, painting pictures that appear purely emotional, or a Duchamp, assembling objects that claim to be the epitome of cerebration. In short, whether we call it by that name or not, a successful work of art is still imbued with sentiment as Kames defined it – "thought prompted by feeling or emotion." It might help us to reconcile some of the seemingly irreconcilable polarities in the present, if we could again think in such terms."[361]

16. CG & Me: Just Friends
(Fall 1976–Summer 1981)

In the fall of 1976, I was invited by Gerald D. Silk (PhD, University of Virginia, 1976) to be his reader for two undergraduate courses, twentieth-century American art in the fall semester, modern art in the spring. Silk was new at Columbia, a kind young man who'd only just deposited his dissertation on the image of the automobile in modern art. As his reader, I audited his classes and helped him grade term papers and exams. Once, he told me that a certain dealer in SoHo "knew Clem Greenberg and all those people," or something like that (many people in the art world referred to Clem as "Clem," even when they'd never met him, and/or couldn't stand him). On November 12, I wrote Clem that his article on "Avant-garde and Kitsch" was required reading in Silk's course, and I thought also the one on "American-type" painting, yet "the other day, I heard [Silk] describing your style as 'pompous & arrogant' to a student."[362]

"Young Prof. Silk, now," I wrote, two days later. "I think he does respect you....But he's determined not to be overawed. And besides, I think maybe he finds some of your positions a little hard to accept," since his dissertation surely featured Warhol "& a lot of other artists whom I'd guess you'd find less than world-shakingly significant." Silk did "quite a decent job in his lecture on Pollock. He relied rather heavily on Namuth photographs & talk about 'the ritual of painting' [i.e., Hans Namuth's photographs of Pollock painting, and Rosenberg on 'the action painters'] but he also discussed ideas that owe a lot to you – elimination of the Cubist grid, all-overness (though he didn't use the term), the degree of control & mastery Pollock had over his medium, and so on."[363]

Clem replied, "I loved both yr. missives. And relished hearing what was said about me, not at all irked. Prof. Silk on my prose wasn't so wrong, or at least he shared a common reaction to it."[364] Clem was unimpressed by Silk himself, though, and even I, reviewing my notes from that course, can see that the two had little in common. Virtually all of Silk's lectures on the '60s concerned pop, neo-dada, and their friends and relations. Four color-field painters (Frankenthaler, Louis, Noland, and Olitski) got one slide apiece, each on view for no more than a few instants during the last lecture in the American art course, jumbled in with minimal art, preceded by fifteen Oldenburgs, and succeeded by earthworks, conceptualism, a form of performance art known as "body art," and hyperrealism as the grand climax.[365] Students didn't have to go to grad school to be inculcated with the Duchampian tradition: they got it as undergraduates, too.

I was taking a seminar on problems in nineteenth-century art with Varnedoe, who quoted (or rather misquoted) Clem, to support his own contention that in the '70s, sculpture was more interesting than it had been (Clem had been writing about sculpture in the '50s, with the constructivist tradition and David Smith).[366] This mention, together with how Silk talked about Clem, made me realize that he was eminent, at least within the art world. I'd fantasized that he was omnipotent when I'd met him, but by grad school, I was discounting all my thoughts from those years as fantasies. Thus the fact that he was truly well known came as a bit of a surprise, and not an altogether pleasant one.

> So: you are required reading, & famous, & as far as I'm concerned, it's a nuisance [I wrote, in my letter of November 12]. Of course, I'm glad for you, & for the sake of the recent artists we both admire, but it clutters up your time & it also means I feel embarrassed to talk about you. You're not only famous, but controversial – some of my fellow students would be dazzled to know I knew you, but more – the Salon lovers, especially – would be exasperated, and tend to kiss me off as a slavish Greenbergian formalist – which I'm not, of course, nor do I think any of your admirers are, but in art, as in politics, distinctions tend to get blurred in discussions of The Enemy Camp (in my seminar discussion of the politics of T. J. Clark, some of my classmates were astonished to learn that I made a distinction between 'conservative' and 'reactionary' (apropos of Delacroix). If I'd been talking to a bunch of Reaganites, they'd have been equally amazed to hear I make a distinction between 'liberal' & 'radical').[367]

T. J. Clark (b. 1943) was an English scholar practicing a style of art history called Neo-Marxism. Though I wasn't up to making the connection in 1976, in fact the art-historical Neo-Marxism of the '70s owed much to the broader radical politics of the '60s, as practiced by some members of the antiwar protest in the United States and parallel uprisings in France and elsewhere in Europe. When I was in Varnedoe's seminar, Neo-Marxist art history was just becoming popular on U.S. campuses, so Varnedoe told us to read and to discuss Clark's first two books, *Image of the People: Gustave*

Courbet and the 1848 Revolution (1973) and *The Absolute Bourgeois: Artists and Politics in France, 1848–1851* (1973). Since both books concerned nineteenth-century art, they didn't seem to have much to do with "Soviet Realism," the official art of the Soviet Union in the 1970s. Still, Courbet had been known as a "realist," and Soviet Realism was an academic, propagandized version of nineteenth-century realism, featuring happy workers, heroic portraits of Stalin, etc. The old-line Stalinism I'd been raised with said that modern and especially abstract art was bourgeois decadence, but in Czarist Russia, before and during World War I, artists had created non-objective art as radical as anything in Western Europe – and, in the first years after Lenin and the Bolsheviks seized power in 1917, these artists had worked with the government. Lenin had never liked them, but Soviet Realism didn't take over until after Lenin had been succeeded by Stalin, and Stalin had exiled his own rival, Leon Trotsky.

Trotsky's combination of Marxism with a conviction that art must be judged by its own laws had won the respect of Western literati like T. S. Eliot and Edmund Wilson.[368] Trotsky was murdered by a Soviet operative in Mexico in 1940, but some of his writing appeared in *Partisan Review*, the little magazine that had been started by a band of New York intellectuals in the '30s, and that Clem had been associated with then and since. Being Trotskyist, *Partisan Review* was committed to a Marxism at odds with the Stalinist type; Clem had cited Marx approvingly in "Avant-Garde and Kitsch," published in *Partisan Review* in 1939.[369] The article contrasted avant-garde art like that of Picasso with "kitsch" from Russia and the United States, Soviet Realism being equated to mass-audience American culture like Norman Rockwell's *Saturday Evening Post* covers.

By the '60s, when mass-audience culture was beginning to achieve intellectual status, many art-world people liked to think that Clem's politics had moved to the far right. I'd thought so, too, when I was on *Time,* because I knew that in 1951 he'd written to *The Nation*, protesting its pro-Soviet foreign affairs editor. In the 1974 version of my "novel," I'd said that the Clem-character was an old Socialist who had "decisively broken with hard-line Communism in the early '50s, abandoning one little magazine he'd been writing for because of a pro-Soviet columnist it carried." Next to this, Clem wrote "!? I was never a Comm[unist]," and added, "I'm still a Socialist."[370] He repeated this in the letter he wrote me about the manuscript: "I was never a 'hard-line Communist.' I was a sort of Trotskyist sympathizer until 1942 or '43. I'm still a socialist."[371]

I've never been sure exactly what he meant by "socialist." At a dinner party in the late '80s or early '90s, he said that his family had been "socialist atheist Jews," and that this had been true of many Jews when he was growing up. I believe that he considered himself a socialist just as he considered himself Jewish and atheistic: it was part of his identity. Another time, he told me how the socialist Labor Party had enabled poor English children to get enough milk so that a whole generation grew up taller and more beautiful than the working-class English he'd seen on his first, pre-war visit to Great Britain. Clem being an Anglophile, I suspect his socialism was also to some extent flavored with the English Labor Party variety. In 1974, I didn't know what a Trotskyist was, but today I'd say Clem's attack on *The Nation* wasn't a capitalist attacking a communist, but a battle of Trotskyist v. Stalinist. Nor did I ever see Clem upset by so many younger scholars taking up Neo-Marxism. In a letter he wrote me in 1981, he described a conference on modernism in Vancouver where the talks by the academics made him squirm and left him exhausted

> & yet I had a good time, maybe because I was the main event: everybody attacked me more or less. Also, I liked most of the people, even the one egregious girl art-historian. We were worked hard by the Frenchman in charge – & there were many French there, some from Quebec & others from France. And almost everybody, including the Americans & one Englishman, Marxized. The exceptions, both female, were feminized, & even then w. a Marxist overlay.[372]

He told me once that he enjoyed arguing with "Tim" Clark, so my reaction to Clark's *Image of the People* had nothing to do with Clem, and everything to do with Neo-Marxism in a grad-school context. The Neo-Marxists were said to be terrifically hipped on history – social and political history, that is, as opposed to art history. They even had a saying, so I'd been told: "Style is the bourgeois substitute for history." I'd revolved this in my mind, and come up with my own riposte: "History is the blind man's substitute for style." Given the wonders of Braille, I reasoned, even a blind man could write a history book, but you needed eyes to be able to see style. Nevertheless, I, too, am interested in history, as opposed to art history, and I got so involved in the political history contained in *Image of the People* that I remember nothing of the rest of the book.

In it, Clark argued that the spirit which animated two of Courbet's most famous paintings, *The Stone Breakers* (1849) and *A Burial at Ornans* (1849-50), had to be understood in a political context – as did the controversy they elicited in Paris. These paintings depicted petty bourgeois and laborers of Courbet's hometown, Ornans, and Ornans (though itself politically conservative) was near rural parts of France that had horrified conservatives by voting in surprisingly large numbers for left-wing candidates in the May 1849 elections to the Legislative Assembly. It was the year after the Second Republic had come into being in the wake of the Revolution of 1848. This revolution had overthrown the second of two monarchies that had ruled France since Napoleon Bonaparte, the first emperor, had lost the Battle of Waterloo in 1815 and been exiled to St. Helena. After decades when only the upper classes had been allowed to vote, the revolutionaries of 1848 had instituted universal male suffrage.

Everybody had known that the Left was strong in the cities, but the idea that a "red France" also existed in the provinces and especially the countryside struck terror into many right-wing hearts, not least because France was still primarily agricultural, with industry far less developed than in Great Britain. The Right had little to fear, as the Left had won only a third of the votes cast, but the right-wing majority ended even that minority threat by enacting residence requirements for voters that eliminated millions of likely left-wing voters from the rolls, especially in the cities. In December 1851, France swung still further to the right when a coup d'état was staged by Louis Napoleon, nephew of Bonaparte. He'd already been elected president of the Second Republic in December 1848, and, though his coup provoked some peasant uprisings, they were easily put down. A plebiscite held shortly after the coup, again with universal male suffrage, resoundingly endorsed him, and he'd reign until 1870 as Napoleon III in the Second Empire.

Marx had written two books about all this, *The Class Struggles in France, 1848–1850* (1850) and *The Eighteenth Brumaire of Louis Bonaparte* (1852). Since Clark was said to be a Neo-Marxist, I assumed that he was following Marx, and as I read *Image of the People*, began to feel that it didn't jibe with my dim recollections of the reading I'd done for my paper on the Third French Republic in college. I went to the graduate history department at Columbia, and asked a professor there to recommend some history books on the Second Republic. He gave me the names of two or three that I found in Butler Library. They seemed to present a different version of events from Clark's, so different that Clark even appeared to be falsifying election statistics to support his claims. I got all steamed up and presented my findings in Varnedoe's class, trying to be dispassionate about it but not succeeding. He got steamed up in turn, and shouted at me something about how he didn't want the politics of *Time* in his classroom. This was the first time I'd had *Time* overtly held against me at Columbia, and it didn't entirely deserve the rap. True, my years there had augmented my skepticism about Marxism, but I'd been bothered about it since my Stalinist adolescence, and my knowledge of French history had been acquired in college. Still, I was cowed by the intensity of Varnedoe's response, and shrank back in my seat.

When writing this book, I tried to find what incensed me. I could locate only two books in Butler that I might have read in 1976, but one was surely *The Second French Republic: A Social History* (1972) by Roger Price (b. 1944); another was probably *Revolution and Reaction: 1848 and the Second French Republic* (1975), a collection of essays edited by Price and with an introduction by him. Initially, I reread them and compared them with Clark. I couldn't find any falsified election returns, but I did find one passage in Clark, dealing with the primary target of the legislation limiting the electorate, that radically differed from Price. I quoted this contrast, suggesting that Clark had relied too much on Marx and that Price had criticized Marx. Still, when it came to fact-checking this book, I decided to go back and read those two books by Marx as well as rereading Price and Clark. Imagine my surprise when I discovered that I'd been closer to Marx than Clark was! Even Price was closer to Marx than Clark. (Not that I'd read those two books by Marx as an undergraduate, but I suspect some historians publishing books in the liberal '40s and '50s were, like Howard K. Smith, influenced by Marx.)

The big issue was the peasantry. My recollection was that the peasants had been conservative, more conservative than workers in the cities. Clark's colorful narrative emphasized the radical nature of the peasants, and suggested that the city-dwellers had lost interest in taking action. By lavishing detail on "red France," he created the impression that it was far more representative of the rural population than it actually seems to have been. Here and there, his narrative admitted that this wasn't the whole story, but his qualifications reminded me of the "weasels" that *Time* used to put into its political stories, back in the bad old days when the magazine was slanting its coverage in a Republican direction. Clark was slanting his story in a radical direction, dramatizing how important were the left-wing activities of the peasants.[373]

Marx hadn't been that enthusiastic about the peasantry. His heroes were the urban proletariat who'd fought on the barricades in 1848. He didn't ignore the radical peasants, but he said that they were only "a section" of the peasantry.[374] They were even a "considerable" section, but as a class the peasants were "capable of absolutely no revolutionary initiative."[375] As a class, he said, they remembered Bonaparte, and were grateful for how he'd consolidated the gains of the 1789 revolution in terms of land reform. This was a big reason that they'd voted for his nephew, Louis Napoleon, as president in 1848.[376] Marx also wrote that a majority of the peasants endorsed Louis Napoleon in the 1851 plebiscite.[377] As for those French peasants who'd been "revolutionized" at the time of the May 1849 elections, Marx suggested that they had been revolutionized only "superficially."[378]

Price wrote respectfully of Marx, and even quoted him, but he said that Marx had over-generalized, and that neither the peasantry nor the proletariat constituted a single bloc. Price's painstaking analysis of the 1849 election returns showed how "red France" existed in some parts of the countryside and not others, depending on how prosperous that particular region of the country was, how isolated from the rest of it, how strong was the local Church, how large the typical land-holding, etc. He also reported that the percentage of left-wing ballots in some working-class districts of Paris and Lyon got up to 50 and even 80 percent, far higher than the national average, and, although the percentage of left-wing ballots in some rural areas did get as high as 40 percent, other rural parts of the country voted conservative.[379] To Price, "red France" was only part of a larger, more complex story. Such balanced, thoughtful history I find more persuasive than Clark's, and none of this political history really explains for me why Courbet's paintings were so controversial. Rather, the controversy had to do with the dignity and luscious painting with which the artist immortalized his humble subjects, so radically different from the gluey sentimentality and patronizingly small scale which normally characterized such genre scenes at the Paris Salons, and so different from the tired academicism of the latter-day neoclassicists in their larger scale "history paintings." Political history for me is no substitute for esthetics, though under certain circumstances it may help to explain why the right esthetic questions are or aren't being asked.

In the fall of 1976, I was also writing to Clem about Theodore Reff with enthusiasm, since his courses on modern painting had now reached the lectures on Analytic Cubism. There was just so much Reff could do with its subject matter, which seemed so traditional that it was impersonal. He was really happier with Picasso's Blue Period, Rose Period, collages, and other more clearly representational work. Because Analytic Cubism was so abstract, in teaching it Reff had to rely heavily on formal analysis, though he did a fine job with that. Using excellent slides, he showed how Picasso and Braque used *passages*, a technique they'd developed from the late work of Cézanne (the French word *passages* conveys the idea far better than its English equivalent).[380] The two artists had blended subtle grays, blues, and browns by the use of these *passages*: subtly modulated, small pats of paint that enabled them to eliminate distinctions between the parts of a painting which usually contrast with each other, the foreground or "figure" and the "ground" or background. This helped me see why the paintings themselves were so beautiful.

Similarly, I'd fascinated in the spring semester, when Reff showed how Mondrian had painted the surface of one of his most abstract pictures from 1935, a picture made with only red, white, black, and light gray. Reff had another excellent slide, and when he commented on Mondrian's brushwork, I could again see exactly what he was talking about – the thin, almost transparent layers of paint, and the strokes upon the surface, these square little pats. "In originals, quality of execution," my notes read. "Refinement in way in which pigment applied to surface/execution v. rich, no means a flat monotonous surface – layering of paint/builds up surface/one also sees how long he worked on these pix/black did not need repainting, white often did."[381] Yet again, Reff devoted much time to the representational paintings that Mondrian had made as a young man in the Netherlands, before he came to Paris and began to paint abstractly.

Reff gave us Duchamp, but without enthusiasm. My notes show that I heard again about Duchamp's wish to place art "at the service of the mind." To Reff this meant that he wanted to make art "more spiritually evocative and less materialistic, more intellectual." Reff's indications of the negative emotional content of Duchamp's works paralleled those I'd heard in Varnedoe's class of the previous spring. My notes allude to the "pessimism" of the artist's large painting on two pieces of glass, *The Bride Stripped Bare by Her Bachelors, Even (The Large Glass)* (1915–1923). As for the Readymades, my notes describe the *Bottle Rack* (1914) as "a strikingly bristling + aggressive form – menacing, repels one....repressed aggressiveness comes through." The coat rack (1917) was "nailed to floor, so people would trip over it – more playful aggression."[382]

During Spring 1977, I also audited Varnedoe's Modern Sculpture II. Here I got Duchamp for the third time (one time more than I'd gotten either Matisse or Picasso). In Modern Sculpture II, the theme of frustration was even more eloquently emphasized. The bicycle wheel, Varnedoe pointed out, was unusable, because it was upside down, and the stool beneath it couldn't be sat on because the wheel occupied it. He, too, mentioned how *Trap*, the coat rack, was nailed to the floor. The *Large Glass* was "basically a work about sexual separation and frustration," because the abstract shape representing the "bride" was in the top half of the painting, and the "bachelors" are in the bottom half, where they couldn't get to her.[383]

Varnedoe did well by David Smith and Tony Caro, but with minimalism, I felt that I knew more than he did (at that stage, anyway). After all, I'd followed it from galleries into museums, books, and now a classroom. He suffered from a basic misconception (as did and do many others): he thought that minimalism equated to modernism or formalism, apparently unaware that Clem had called minimalism "that latest and most sophisticated form"of "Novelty art."[384] When Varnedoe showed us minimalist sculpture by Donald Judd, my notes include a quote: "Greenberg would approve of Judd." Next comes my comment: "ho ho."[385] Varnedoe showed us Tony Smith's *Die* (1962), the black cube I'd first written about in 1967. I knew that Smith associated it with many things, but my notes for Varnedoe's class read "pure self-enclosure – does not refer to anything," together with my comment: "(?-PH)." I wasn't yet able to argue logically with his position, but on a gut level it seems that I was already dissatisfied with it.

With Novak's aid, I took a seminar in the fall of 1976 at the CUNY Graduate Center that taught me more about abstraction. This seminar, on American painting from 1908 to 1935, was given by Milton Brown, author of a pioneering history of that period first published in 1955. My presentation was on abstract American painters in Paris, including Morgan Russell and Stanton Macdonald-Wright, who in 1913 had unveiled "Synchromism," a form of color abstraction based in cubism and Robert Delaunay's "Orphism." Brown's book said these two Americans had gone "all out for pure art unencumbered by recognizable objects."[386] But in 1965, William C. Agee had written that the June 1913 Synchromist exhibition in Munich consisted "entirely of figurative scenes, interiors or still lifes often adopted from Michelangelo, Rubens, or Rodin." Agee called Russell's slightly later *Synchromie en bleu-violacé* and the oil sketch for it "the first abstract Synchromies," but he also said the painting was "based on the accents of form and movement of Michelangelo's *Slave....*" (in the Louvre).[387]

I borrowed a slide of that painting from Gail Levin, a younger scholar organizing a museum show of Synchromism and related paintings. Her catalogue would expand upon the *Synchromie en bleu-violacé* and its relation to *Slave*.[388] In my presentation, I showed her slide and quoted what Agee had said about its resemblance to *Slave* rather dubiously. Brown walked up to the screen where the slide was projected, and pointed out these resemblances to us exactly. With Wright, the resemblances to figures and so on were even more obvious, once you'd been told to look for them, but I felt that by focusing on them, the paintings themselves became much less valuable. It was like Washton Long finding those cute cartoons in Kandinsky: the representational imagery exposed was so routine and/or silly that it detracted from the power of the paintings, and I believed that a good interpretation should enhance that power. I expressed my distress about these treatments to Clem:

> Iconography has its uses, I think, when applied with imagination – but I haven't read anyone yet who's really imaginative about iconography – at least in relation to 20th century art. The trend today in art history is to pick out the latent images buried in paintings by artists like Kandinsky & Morgan Russell....But I don't think that's going to work when the art historians get to

more recent artists. There's got to be some loosening up in the basic definitions – there must have been some writing on it but I haven't hit any yet that turns me on.[389]

I passed my orals in the spring of 1977. Not having found a dissertation topic, I spent the next academic year adjunct teaching at the C. W. Post Campus of Long Island University (thanks to a wonderful woman, Joyce Rosa, chairman of the art department). As nearly as I can recall, it was during this period that I began accepting those invitations to "come up to Norwich and get fucked" (I've kept many of my engagement calendars, but not those from 1977 through 1979). Thereafter, Clem and I resumed what could technically be called our affair, since I went to bed with him in Norwich (and New York), but this happened so rarely that I'm not sure the term "affair" would be appropriate. I'd have known him for twenty-five years by the time he died, and I estimate I spent a maximum of twenty-five nights in bed with him (a statistic I cite primarily because I fear that if I don't, our detractors may assume it was much more).

In the later '80s, I told a lawyer friend of mine that Clem and I had gotten together on an average of once a year. Her disappointed response: "But that's just *friends*!" Still, our friendship was more than merely the time we spent in bed together. We talked on the phone, exchanged postcards and letters, and got together without sex. While I was still doing my course work, I'd been asked over to Clem's New York apartment for nothing more than a drink, and such purely social intercourse would become almost exclusively the case after I took my PhD.

The first reference to Norwich in my 1980 engagement calendar shows I was "chez Clem" from June 16 to June 18. The next visit was from November 28 to 30, 1980, and the one after that from August 10 to 13, 1981. I didn't visit Norwich after 1981, and the spacing of the 1980–81 visits, five to nine months apart, was most likely typical of the '70s, too. To get to Clem's house, I took a commuter airline to Norwich or Binghamton, in upstate New York. Clem would pick me up at the airport in one of his two cars (a Subaru and a Pontiac, if I remember correctly). Then we'd go to his house, a rambling, unpretentiously modern one in the woods. We'd get drinks and sit at a little table in the dining area of the living room. We'd talk until evening, get ourselves dinner, talk some more and go to bed, usually around 9:30. Next morning, we'd get up, eat breakfast, sit and talk till noon; eat lunch, talk all afternoon, eat dinner and talk until bedtime.

I can't remember what we talked about in detail, though in later years remarks of his would rise to my mind in relation to one subject or another, particularly art – art, that is, not esthetics, looking at pictures and what made some better than others, who was good and who wasn't, what was good about A, not good about B, characteristic of C or D: not elevated theory. I've always been pragmatic, I suppose, so I never brought up art theory. Neither, for whatever reasons, did Clem, but what he said about art in concrete, specific terms never ceased to surprise me. Whatever I expected him to say, he always said something different (an experience, I've since discovered, not unique to me).

I was beginning to learn of his omnivorous appetite for art. He went to all sorts of shows, including many I don't think he expected to like. I believe he always hoped that he might find something to admire, and felt that he couldn't criticize anything he hadn't seen. His reputation was based upon the abstract expressionists he'd discovered, and many who opposed him set him up as a critic who could see nothing but abstraction, but he also thought that a few representational painters, including Andrew Wyeth and Richard Estes, the hyperrealist, had "something" out of the ordinary. He also tended to feel that although the best new paintings he saw were abstract, so were the worst, and that the average quality of conventional representational painting might be better.

We talked about literature, since we'd both majored in English at college. We both admired Eliot. Clem didn't share my passion for Sayers, but then I felt no desire to explore Céline, on the basis of what Clem said about him. Céline sounded like a nasty piece of work, but Clem apparently devoured his books. He loved Jane Austen, and used her as bedtime reading, along with the Bible (King James Version, I'm sure, since he would have been reading it as literature, not for moral instruction). Céline and Austen, what a pair! Particularly since, when Clem got drunk (and we were alone together), he'd use sex talk that would have scandalized Austen (I tolerated it since I couldn't have shut him up anyway). We talked psychology, since we'd both been in therapy, but we probably talked more about people than anything else – people we both knew, ones he knew, even (though much less often) people I knew and he didn't. Clem's understanding of people lent depth to his understanding of art, psychology, and literature. This may surprise some of those who had difficult or unhappy experiences with him, but I mostly saw his kinder side, and was far from alone in this.

He could focus on an individual so wholeheartedly and with such perspicacity that unless his judgment was completely negative, that person could be willing to tolerate any lesser criticisms he might make. What he said about people, I suppose, taught me much of what I learned about art from him, because (as I indicated earlier) I felt the two were closely linked in his mind. I don't mean he thought people had to be the subject matter of paintings, or that a person had to be nice to be a great artist, but he did feel that great art reflected and expressed great human values: courage, ambition, character. I don't recall hearing him say this, but as I look back at what he did say to me or others, and what I learned from him, almost by osmosis, I can see parallels between such human values and their pictorial equivalents.

When he'd dined with me in 1969, I'd had a row of pictures by Oldenburg in my living room, small reproductions of lithographs that Leo Castelli had distributed free as a sales device. Clem examined them carefully. Then he said, "Oldenburg works best at a small scale." This was a formal judgment, but I feel it reflected his feeling that Oldenburg's subject matter, and his treatment of it, were so unambitious that when he made small pictures, he was truer to the level of his ambition. In an interview in the early '90s, he described the paintings Lee Krasner had been making around 1960 as "hollow."[390] In 1990, he was quoted saying Frank Stella's color at that moment was "an authentic scandal."[391] I might have said that Krasner was trying to do more than she had the emotional depth for, and called Stella's color vulgar and ostentatious, but Clem didn't object to size or experimentation if the result was good. He may have felt that Stella's colors reflected a wish to create shocking art. Clem discussed how postmodernist art as a whole institutionalized shock in the seminars that he gave at Bennington in 1971, and that Jenny published after his death as *Homemade Esthetics* (1999).[392]

Clem equated human and esthetic values when he spoke of risk-taking, the willingness to experiment. The first year I met him, I'd realized I had to leave *Time*, and make mistakes if I were going to rediscover myself. This was the same idea. Clem discussed risk-taking in *Homemade Esthetics*. He talked about "a sense of the courage and a sense of the ambition necessary to try for" work on the level of major, as opposed to minor, art. In the same book, he translated another human characteristic into an esthetic value when he related "character" to "inspiration."[393]

One subject off-limits was myself. Once, he said, "Women always want to talk about themselves" in such a disconsolate voice that I tried to avoid the topic. Another time, I shared one of my pet fantasies with him: that when I died and went to Heaven, I could have the body I'd had at twenty-seven, but the mind of my more mature years. "How original," he said, ironically. I don't remember his complaining about his own troubles, though he'd talk about how neurotic he'd been when he was younger, and how he'd outgrown the need to go to bed with "girls" he didn't like as people. He described punching an art critic named Manny Farber in the nose when Farber called him a plagiarist, probably back in the '40s. Such remarks made me think I'd have found him abrasive when he was younger, and glad that I'd come to know him as an older, mellower man (though his earlier writing was more effective than that of his later years).

Despite all his psychoanalysis, I think he was still depressed. This would explain his dependencies on alcohol and cigarettes. In Norwich, he started drinking around eleven in the morning or maybe noon, nursing Scotch or vodka while I drank diet ginger ale. He smoked Camels, a pack a day. Once or twice, in the evening before dinner, we had drinks with neighbors, Al and Doris Vellake. They were working-class people whom Clem enjoyed because they didn't pretend to know high art, and they liked him as a kind, seemingly relaxed old man. He told me that there were people around Norwich who considered themselves cultured, and tried to socialize with him, but he discouraged them. I think he would have considered this sort of person middlebrow, and like many highbrows, he had small use for middlebrows. The Vellakes were cheerfully and unapologetically lowbrows, and this was just fine with him.

One evening, Clem and I drove into the town of Norwich, and dined at a Howard Johnson's, but he'd drunk so much that we had to drive home at a crawl (a city dweller, I'd never learned to drive). He still didn't like spending money on me. Like many insecure rich men, he wanted to feel loved for himself alone, so he only once paid my plane fare up to Norwich, and the sole gift he offered me during this period was a broken little string of speckled beads that his daughter Sarah had picked up at a yard sale. She couldn't have paid more than twenty-five cents for it. In New York, however, we now went out to dinner, if only to Chinese restaurants (abstemious in his eating habits, he adored Chinese food, as well as halvah and expensive chocolate). Once when I was visiting him in Norwich, four of his artist friends from Syracuse came by, with a huge picnic meal.

Clem told me he was divorced from Jenny (and a biography published in 1997 would say that the divorce took place in 1977).[394] Still, I was leery of letting the world at large know about our relationship for many reasons. One was that I was only one of the women with whom he had been (or was) intimate. He would allude to this "girl" or that one, never by name, but often enough so that I believed that there were many of them. Once, he read an excerpt from one of his journals to me, omitting names but making it appear that he'd slept with three to five women within the previous week or ten days (interspersed with references to his sexual partners were considerably more solicitous comments on the health of his cars; the Pontiac was referred to affectionately as "Ponty"). Not all women found him irresistible, but enough evidently did so that I was afraid anyone who knew his habits might class me as a groupie. I still don't think the relationship he offered me suggested that I had any special claims on his affection, though I've been grateful many times for his willingness to spend as much time with me as he did.

It was wonderful to spend entire days simply talking to a man who was assertively male and desired me. None of my previous admirers had ever spent so much time talking with me – not even Fred Freund, who had always been entertaining me with theater or bridge or whatever. Clem liked to say that he was passive, and gave this excuse for rarely calling me, but I knew he called other people, and in conversation he was very assertive. Matching wits with him took enterprise: he was too emphatic for me to disagree with him to his face, thought I did once give him backtalk in a letter.[395] My only precedent for these long talks in Norwich were those I'd had with Ed Bley, when I'd visited him and Elsa at their home in New Hampshire, but Ed was a father figure, very married to Elsa. Clem, though older than Ed, abrogated any claims he might have had to being a father figure by his stated intention of having sex with me, so after these days of monumental conversation, we'd go to bed. Nearing seventy, he was no longer quite the stud he'd been, nor did the booze he consumed help. He knew it impaired his performance, but said he had to have the lift it gave him. Still, spending the night in bed with him was its own reward. In the morning, I'd get to see his backside, as he rolled out of his side of the bed, and stumbled off to take a leak and shave. I've always liked the sight of a man's nude backside: so innocent and defenseless.

Even in Norwich, the disagreements between him and my professors lingered in the background. When Reff called somebody "a formalist," it wasn't a compliment, and Clem referred with equal venom to Reff as "an iconographer." He said that one of his friends had taken a course with Reff, and found it boring. He was sure that Reff had put Varnedoe up to reviewing Charles Millard's book on the sculpture of Degas for *Arts Magazine* (Millard was a friend of Clem's and chief curator at the Hirshhorn Museum and Sculpture Garden in Washington). Reading Varnedoe's businesslike hatchet job (in preparation for this book), I found that its snide remarks about Millard's resemblances to Clem, and its obsequious references to Reff, don't dispel Clem's conviction.[396]

I was still unaware of the numbers of such attacks on Clem, or the animosity that had been and would be expressed, among academics and even more by artists and art critics, but personalities and writing styles weren't the real issues. The bottom line was whether Clem liked the art that you liked or made, and his disapproval hurt as much as it did because his opinion mattered so much more. Nobody I know about got upset if Rosenberg or Steinberg found their work wanting. The bitterness that Clem provoked reflected the respect he enjoyed (perhaps also the fear that he might be right).

Having gone through a convoluted evolution myself, I like to think I can appreciate both the positive and negative responses he evoked. When I'd first met him, in 1969, I'd seen him as a remote, supremely wonderful guru, but by the autumn of 1972, I was visualizing him as Satan. My experience of him in the later '70s and early '80s started the process of demystifying him for me. Eventually, I'd come to realize that he was simply a man who, as the saying goes, put on his pants one leg at a time, and, from what I've seen, this degree of detachment is somewhat uncommon (though far from unique). The fact that Clem placed sexual conditions on my visiting him made me feel that I had to pay for the privilege of his company, but also that I was paying. That I had to pay must have grated, but that I was paying gave me an independence from him that I might otherwise have missed. If he'd been bestowing his valuable company on me gratis, and getting nothing that he considered of equal value in return, I might have felt so obligated to him that I'd have followed obediently in his footsteps, but as it was, I would feel freer (in the fullness of time) to take my own intellectual path.

Moreover, if Clem's only interest in me was sex, and my only interest in him was intellectual companionship, I was definitely getting the better end of the bargain, in terms of the relative amount of time devoted to each activity. He claimed not to know what being "in love" meant, and I was no longer "in love" with him, but the feeling I had for him was still love, not a neutral or negative emotion. He said he wasn't in love with anybody, but this was self-delusion. He was in love with Jenny, and while he gave any love he had to spare to the rest of us, Jenny was always his favorite. He made it clear that she had asked him for the divorce; he'd only agreed because she wanted it. He boasted about how clever she was with money, and described her business activities with relish. When he loaned a painting to an exhibition, the label read "Collection of Mr. and Mrs. Clement Greenberg," and when I asked who would take care of him when he got too old to take care of himself, he said that Jenny and Sarah would, just as he assured me that all those dreadfully incriminating journals and diaries would go to them.

His promiscuity had begun years before I met him. Consciously, he didn't accept the idea that fidelity was necessary in marriage. In one way, there was something very grand in this stubborn denial, this belief that he could love large numbers of women, and every one could love him in return. One might say he was so insecure that he needed the reassurance that only many lovers might give, but I didn't think about it that way at the time. I simply felt that he was a law unto himself, and that I was getting so much out of the relationship that I was willing to put up with its inconveniences.

Whatever else it was, I'm inclined to feel that Clem's insatiable need for lovers was also a neurotic way of punishing Jenny, just as he punished all the rest of us by continuing to proclaim his preference for her. Also, he tended to be attracted to Gentile women, and could be unpleasant about Jewish ones. This was the Portnoy complex I'd first encountered at Barnard, the neurotic

Jewish boys who wanted to screw shiksas because they were angry with their mothers, instead of dating nice Jewish girls whom they respected, and would make their mothers happy. I used to laugh at myself, how I'd tried so hard to avoid those neurotic Jewish boys in college, only to wind up with the champion neurotic Jewish boy as an adult.

Clem was the textbook example of the neurotic married man's split between sex and affection that Dr. G had cautioned me against, the male who looked for sexual satisfaction outside the marriage, but could only feel affection for his spouse (which Jenny remained in Clem's mind, however legally divorced they were). He knew that he suffered from this split, but therapy hadn't been able to help him with it. "Freud was a better philosopher than therapist," he once remarked, sadly. Maybe my unconscious need was to play the role of lover, and maybe I simply found Clem very interesting. Looking back upon the men I dated when I was younger, I suspect that I wasn't that interested in most of them, though I hadn't realized it. This lack of interest may have showed without my knowing it, and explained why they didn't continue to call. Clem never bored me (not even in his last years, when he repeated himself a lot).

My willingness to accept being only one of many lovers may have been conditioned by having been raised so completely by my mother, and, as a child, feeling the need to compete with her lovers for her affection. I'd gotten into my ill-fated marriage with *Time* because it took a whole organization to counterbalance her possessiveness, and in grad school, I was financially dependent on her as well – necessitating the even more powerful counterweight of Clem to keep from being swept entirely into her orbit. She meant well, and gave me money without my asking, but she also smothered me with attentions I didn't dare reject: movies, theater, bridge, and visits to Mexico and Key West. *Dr. Atkins' Diet Revolution* paid for this luxury. When my mother died, in 1989, *Publishers Weekly* had already listed it one of the all-time mass-market top sellers.[397] Still, her pursuit of me made me uncomfortable, especially when she treated me as her escort, her little man. This made me grateful for Clem's insistence on my role as sex object. However blunt this approach, at least it told me that I was a woman.

So I put up with the limitations of my relationship with Clem, hardly realizing that they were limitations. When one really cares about a person, his neurosis becomes a fact about him like any other, to be accepted as part of himself, and however profound, even desperate was Clem's need to be loved by as many people as possible, it led to a seemingly boundless capacity to endear himself, by demonstrating how interested he was in those people, and how sympathetic to their needs. I didn't know the full extent of his interest in his artist friends as people, but I was beginning to learn that he knew the names of all of their lovers, spouses, and children, as well as exactly how to pronounce their own names, even names that nearly everybody else found unpronounceable. Most of all, he realized that the foremost need of creative people is to have somebody respond to their creations. He answered to this need with many people, though it was not until the '80s, and even more the '90s, that I'd acquire specific ideas about the way he was able to offer so much encouragement and reassurance on his studio visits.

Then, bit by bit, I'd learn that he'd looked at and critiqued work not only by all the well-known artists with whom his name was associated, but by dozens of younger and lesser-known ones, too. Even in the '70s, I knew that he read all the many versions of my "novel" (including some not mentioned here). Although he usually gave them back to me with little or no comment, nobody else had any use for them either, so he can be excused for reticence. I did wonder whether my being a woman might have promoted his indifference. He tried to be as objective about women artists and writers as he was about men, and I think to a large extent he succeeded, but given his age and neuroses, he couldn't be completely detached. "Girls have to prove themselves" was how he justified his failure to include any women in the list of artists worth looking at that I heard him read off at a lecture that he gave in 1985. This was true and not true – true in the sense that many women painters who were his contemporaries had quit painting when they got married or started having babies, not true to the extent that by the '80s and '90s, women were much more committed to staying with their careers.

Clem's cracks about women critics, especially "Jewish girls with typewriters," were so well known that detractors called him a male chauvinist. He could be nasty about women in general, too, yet he had many good women friends, not all of whom he'd slept with, and this was a side of his personality that I wouldn't learn about until much later. Nor did I learn for years that he'd visited the studios of many women artists, and critiqued their work, whether or not he considered them desirable as women, and even when he did and they'd rejected his advances. Some remained bitter about the relationships they'd had with him, but then an aging drunk isn't exactly the ideal lover.

The convoluted nature of his relationships with women tell me that his feelings about his mother must have been powerfully conflicted, though he knew this, though he believed that to some extent he'd been psychoanalyzed out of it, and though doubtless to some extent he had. He said that his mother hadn't been a good mother to him, though he'd cried when she died (he'd been sixteen). He told me how once he'd come in from school, and found his mother with one of her friends. The mother had introduced this friend, and Clem had put out his hand to shake the woman's hand, but his mother had rebuked him, saying that he was supposed to wait until the lady put out her hand. Clem told this story like it showed how his mother had tried to undermine his self-esteem, but to me it also suggested how much he had in common with her, because as an adult he was fanatic about etiquette (in theory if not always in practice). All his friends knew of this obsession, and were irked or amused by it, depending upon their mood of the moment.

He showed me how one friend had put her name in the upper left-hand corner of an envelope as part of the return address, and said the polite thing was simply to put your address. He explained that when you had personal stationery made up, you should put only your address on it, not your name, as houseguests might want to use it. More than once, I heard him complain about being seated between women he knew at formal dinners; etiquette dictated that he be seated between women he didn't know. He corrected word usage, criticizing me for saying "hopefully" (which he said was based upon the German *hoffentlich,* and had no place in proper English). He corrected my pronunciation of "Walter Benjamin" and "Giuliani." If this was irritating, it was also a bit endearing, as it showed he was interested in what I was doing, and wanted to see I was doing it right. I think his mother corrected his manners for this reason. Even if it angered him, he knew her intentions were good, because his relationship with her must have been better than that with his father, of whom I rarely heard him speak.

Clem told me that his mother was "deep," that she read Theodore Dreiser, and that she employed African American women as domestics because she thought they were cleaner than white people. He himself could be horrible about *shvartzes,* or so I was told by a mutual friend. He called gay men "queers" (the term has since become respectable in some contexts, but was considered bigoted and/or old-fashioned when he was using it). He had a few art-world friends of African descent, and a few more who were gay. Whether they were nice, and more importantly, what they could accomplish was all that mattered. He may well have made racist remarks to his African friends, and homophobic ones to his gay friends, since to me he could be so objectionable about women, but I found such behavior commonest when he'd had a lot to drink, and/or felt under pressure, nor did it surprise me, since he'd been born in 1909, and raised when such attitudes were far commoner (and far more broadly tolerated) than they are today.

When he was sober and serious, he was as free of prejudice as most people half his age. His best friend in college had been gay, and Clem corresponded with him for years after they graduated.[398] Once I told him a joke I'd read in *Esquire,* in a column on racist jokes. I thought the joke wasn't necessarily racist, but his response was a curt "*Not* funny." A Canadian friend of his told me how surprised he'd been when Clem praised the excessively graceful sculptures of boys by Carl Milles, but that, too, was part of an inner sweetness which also helps to explain why he loved the Beatles and insisted, "You can't not like Dickens." Once, the subject of the '60s came up. During this decade, the art Clem admired had begun going into eclipse, so I expected him to be negative, but he said heartily that "the '60s were the best thing that ever happened to this country." Then, I thought sourly that his enthusiasm had a lot to do with the sexual revolution, which made so many more "girls" available to him; now, I think it also had to do with his dislike of the stuffiness, prejudice, and formality of the '50s.

From Clem's need to correct and criticize etiquette and pronunciation, it was only a short leap to his need (and desire) to correct and criticize works of art (even if or perhaps because he couldn't make great art himself; he boasted that he'd been a child prodigy when he took drawing classes at the Art Students League, but as an adult, his paintings and drawings showed only a modest talent). One of many things that made his studio "crits" so valuable was his honesty. If he liked something, he said so, and if he didn't, he said that, too. This was fine if in a general way he approved of an artist, but over the years, he'd seen and commented on much art that hadn't lived up to his standards: its creators accordingly badmouthed him every chance they got.

I admired him for saying what he thought, but while it meant I could believe him when he praised me, it also meant he could be painfully rude. Once he told me I was "a mediocrity." Tears started to my eyes, and I said, "That's a hell of a thing to say," but instead of apologizing, he reiterated it more emphatically, saying, "Well, you *are* a mediocrity. What have you done with your life so far?" I could absorb such attacks partly because somewhere I felt that when I'd developed more, I'd no longer deserve them. Clem had given me this reason to hope in the letter he'd sent me in 1974, after he'd read the angriest version of my "novel." You must realize, he'd said, that "nothing you've done or has happened to you defines you, characterizes you: you remain free to make anything of yourself that's rationally possible. I.e., you don't have to fear."[399] In other words, if he could be cruel, he could also be wise and kind.

Visiting him in Norwich, I began to realize how many people looked to him for advice and encouragement. Somewhere in the background, along with all his enemies, were those armies of friends, though I rarely saw them. Most of the time, I didn't know who they were: he'd refer to this anonymous "friend" or that one in conversation. I did witness phone calls. One came from Helen, waking him up (grumbling) in the morning, while we were still in bed; another came from Tony Caro, calling across the Atlantic around midday. During my last summer on *Time*, my paranoia had convinced me that Clem and all his friends had been talking about me, but in Norwich, I realized my paranoia had some basis in reality, to the extent that he and his vast acquaintance formed a huge network of gossips who did talk a lot to each other on the phone.

17. Advancing Wave of the '40s
(Summer 1978–Fall 1982)

I WANTED A dissertation topic on New York art in the 1940s, when the abstract expressionists were forming their mature styles, but, for various reasons, I couldn't choose any of the top abstract expressionists. In the summer of 1978, Reff called me to his office to meet Esther Gentle Rattner, widow of a painter named Abraham Rattner. He'd died in February, and she'd called Reff hoping a graduate student would do a dissertation on him. I'd never heard of him, but said I'd investigate. When I looked at reproductions of his paintings from the '40s, I was disappointed. True, he'd lived and exhibited in New York then, but his paintings had been representational, at best semiabstract: still lifes, landscapes, and especially figure studies, including Crucifixions. I saw long-lashed female eyes, a Picasso mannerism. The heavy black outlines surrounding jewel-like areas of color reminded me of paintings by Georges Rouault, a representational French contemporary of Picasso's. Rattner resembled Rouault in religious subject matter, too, and he'd used multiple human figures, piled atop each other, like the Italian futurists. In short, the work looked "derivative": Rattner hadn't developed a style of his own, but Reff had suggested him, and I thought this meant that if I chose him, I'd have Reff for my senior dissertation advisor.

I consulted the two major art-historical books about the '40s in New York that had been published by 1978, Irving Sandler's *The Triumph of American Painting: A History of Abstract Expressionism* (1970), and Dore Ashton's *The New York School: A Cultural Reckoning* (1972). Neither mentioned Rattner, but elsewhere I found that in the '40s, he'd exhibited at a prestigious gallery, and his shows had been well reviewed in newspapers and magazines. Several books written in the '40s had mentioned him, and he'd participated in big annual group exhibitions in New York, Philadelphia, and Pittsburgh. Museums and collectors had bought his work.

Throughout grad school, I'd been getting revisionist art history of the nineteenth century, with teachers trying to rehabilitate academic artists who'd been popular in those days, but since forgotten. To judge from Sandler, Ashton, Silk's undergraduate course, and Reff's graduate course, all that had been going on in the '40s in New York was abstract expressionism, but the wider context of that decade must have differed from how posterity saw it, if Rattner could have been so important. Why not go in for a little revisionist art history of my own, and rehabilitate Rattner by reconstructing this context? Clem didn't think much of Rattner's work. All the time I was writing my dissertation, he'd ask, "Are you still working on that mediocre painter?" For me, this was an advantage: nobody could say I was under his thumb.

I submitted a proposal to Reff. He read it and said he was too busy to be my advisor, but James H. Beck was willing to take his place. Although Beck was a Renaissance scholar, he was interested in twentieth-century art and had tenure (required for a senior dissertation advisor). Gerry Silk (who didn't have tenure) was willing to be my junior advisor, so I started my research. Born in Poughkeepsie, New York in 1893, Rattner had lived between the wars in Paris with his first wife (she'd died in 1947, and he'd married Esther two years later). During the '30s, he'd painted in a surrealist vein, and enjoyed critical success in Paris and New York City. He'd moved back to New York City to live in 1939, when France and Germany officially went to war.

At the home of Esther Rattner, I found a surrealistic drawing that he'd made to illustrate *Scenario (a film with sound)*. This was a book by Henry Miller, published in Paris in 1937. Beck thought the drawing would make a great article, so I called up Richard Martin, editor of *Arts Magazine*, to which I'd already contributed two reviews. I'd been introduced to Martin by a dealer representing a conceptualist, but *Arts* also carried scholarly articles, plus writing by Clem and his friends. My piece about *Scenario* appeared in the March 1980 issue. Reff told me he'd read it, and decided he could be my advisor after all.

As a "preceptor," a job reserved for grad students working on their dissertations, I was teaching "art hum," an introductory art humanities course for Columbia, when Silk suggested I apply to the Smithsonian Institution for a pre-doctoral fellowship. I'd have to move to Washington for a year, and work out of the National Collection of Fine Arts, a Smithsonian museum, but much of my research had to be done at the Archives of American Art in Washington, so I had a legitimate reason for applying. Silk said I'd need a sponsor from the NCFA, and suggested Harry Rand (BA, City College of New York, 1969, PhD, Harvard, 1974). Rand had done his dissertation on Arshile Gorky, the abstract expressionist; he was now a curator at the NCFA, and coming to Columbia to lecture on Gorky. One of those rare scholars trying to find meaning in abstraction, he showed us how Gorky's paintings were more representational than anybody supposed, and delightfully witty, findings that would not be published in book form until 1981.[400] I'd eventually want to go beyond a one-on-one approach to abstraction, but I'd still say that Rand made the strongest case for the one-on-one approach that I've seen. He would also prove a wise and supportive advisor, when I was awarded the fellowship in the spring of 1980 and since.

Before I moved to Washington, the Museum of Modern Art turned over its whole building (as it then existed) to a huge retrospective of Picasso (organized by Bill Rubin). I saw it, and was so impressed that I wanted to write about it. Richard Martin said he'd be interested in a review, so I went back to the show many times. With so many paintings on display, I could see precisely how the artist had evolved from one to the next, especially with his views of women. From the haunting harridans of his Blue Period, he'd progressed into the nubile maidens of the Rose Period, which in turn developed into the formidable earth goddesses of his Iberian period. These paved the way for the nightmare prostitutes of *Les Demoiselles d'Avignon*.

I'd presented the *Demoiselles* to my "art-hum" students at Columbia, and some of them had been shocked. Why did it have to be the one Picasso on which so many art historians fixated? Why couldn't more attention be paid to the far more beautiful and radical paintings of the Analytic Cubism that followed, and also culminated in an image of a woman, *"Ma Jolie"*? To me, the most significant *and* the most deeply satisfying galleries of the exhibition were devoted to Analytic Cubism, yet they were almost deserted, while the galleries with earlier, more conventional work, and what for me was mostly inferior later work, were crowded. Picasso was such an icon that crowds came to see his work without really knowing what was truly great about it. Martin didn't print my review, but what I learned from writing it stayed with me.

Washington was close enough to New York so I could get back to do research in museums and interview survivors from the '40s, but far enough away so I could view the city's art scene with more detachment. It got my mother out of my hair (though I did help out three times when she became sick). I boarded with a very nice college math teacher, and my fellow Fellows were nice, too. We were all capably supervised by Lois M. Fink, and I had a pleasant social life, especially with four people to whom Clem had given me introductions. One was Charles Millard, at the Hirshhorn Museum. Another was Jacob Kainen, the abstract painter known as "the dean of the Washington color-field school"; Clem was especially fond of Kainen's wife, Ruth. A third was Anne Truitt, a sculptor and the only minimalist whose work Clem admired and had written about.[401] In later life, Truitt would publish three journals that made her at least as well known in the literary world as she was in art.[402]

Having an office, and a Monday-to-Friday, nine-to-five routine, was soothing. We Fellows had bullpens on the top floor of the NCFA, which was renamed the National Museum of American Art soon after I arrived (and has more recently been renamed again, the Smithsonian American Art Museum).

Besides books, its library had clippings and exhibition announcements of individual artists, and bound volumes of art magazines, both back to the '40s. For anything I couldn't find here, I had stack privileges to the Library of Congress, the largest library in the world. Here were microfilms of the New York dailies that reviewed art regularly in the '40s, and bound volumes or microfilms of all the other magazines that had dealt with art regularly then.

I could find what Clem had written for *The Nation* and *Partisan Review*, and the amount surprised me. Most of it wouldn't be collected and reprinted in book form until 1986, four years after I'd deposited my dissertation. Aside from occasional recent pieces in *Arts Magazine*, all I'd known of Clem's writing before I started the dissertation was *Art and Culture*, the small group of essays, mostly from the '40s and '50s, that he'd revised and reprinted in 1961. Nor had I heard much from him about the '40s in conversation. I've since learned that he'd talk about that period in interviews or conversations with other friends, but with me, he wanted to live in the present.

Sometime in the later '80s, I went back to the Library of Congress to do more research. In its subterranean corridors, I smelled the peculiar, sweetish scent there, and it took me back, just as the taste of the madeleine brought back memories for Proust. I remembered how hopeful I'd felt while I was working on my dissertation, how confident that once I'd completed it, I'd get a teaching job and could support myself again. I'd been warned before grad school that getting a job wouldn't be easy, but I assumed that, with my publications, I'd have a leg up on the competition. I didn't realize how different I was from my fellow Fellows, most of whom have fitted into the professional art scene more successfully than I (at any rate, in the pecuniary sense). I didn't realize how hard it would be for me to follow this path because I hadn't found my mature esthetic personality. I was trying to be just like every other graduate student, taking refuge in Rattner, a suitably academic subject, noncontroversial if dull.

I devoted months to *The New York Times*'s art coverage. In the '40s, it was far more thorough than it has since become. There were only about ninety galleries in Manhattan, and the *Times* ran about fifteen reviews every Sunday, so it got around to most of the shows on view in the course of a month. Even the abstract expressionists got write-ups, but usually only by junior reviewers or in small paragraphs at the end of the senior critic's long column. Most space was devoted to reviews of artists who had since been forgotten, or were remembered only for earlier, better work. If an artist was old and famous, he rated prolonged, respectful treatment, regardless of how weak his late work might be, but the abstract expressionists were merely promising youngsters. With some few exceptions, it was the same with *Time, Life, Newsweek,* and *The New Yorker,* as well as *Art News* and *The Art Digest* (precursor of *Arts Magazine*).

258

Even within the artistic subcommunity, the abstract expressionists hadn't emerged as leaders of the avant-garde until around 1950 – but the moment of their emergence could be charted with fair accuracy: with the Whitney Annual of 1949, opening on December 16 and discussed by both *Art News* and *The Art Digest* with their inaugural issues of January 1950. At this moment, both magazines emphasized and/or dramatized how much abstract painting there was in the annual.[403] All the twelve top abstract expressionists except for Barnett Newman had already been having solo exhibitions for between two and eight years.[404] Although only eight had yet displayed work in their mature styles, virtually all had been reviewed and discussed individually.[405] Yet museums and private collectors, to the extent that they had acquired any of this work, had gone for only minor examples of it in most cases. The paintings which had been most exhibited, won the biggest prizes, and sold best in the '40s were only rarely abstract expressionist. Far commoner was work almost completely forgotten by the '80s.

Clem was the only critic writing regularly throughout the '40s who'd accorded prominent space and sympathetic treatment not only to Pollock but also de Kooning, Hans Hofmann, William Baziotes, Motherwell, Adolph Gottlieb, and Gorky. Rosenberg, who would emerge as Clem's great rival in the '50s, was already known in what was still the underground of the abstract expressionist art world. He was publishing in the little artists-run periodicals, and even co-creator of one of them, but another scholar, Ann Eden Gibson, was doing her dissertation on these periodicals, so I didn't concern myself with them. In any event, most of Rosenberg's writing in these periodicals was literary or philosophical; only rarely and briefly did he write about the abstract expressionists during the '40s.[406] The only first-generation abstract expressionists who had solo shows in the '40s, and to whom Clem didn't devote meaningful space during that period, were Theodoros Stamos, Ad Reinhardt, Clyfford Still, and Rothko. Clem later said he regretted not having recognized Stamos's talent in the '40s, but he never seems to have thought very highly of Reinhardt. He didn't review Rothko because Rothko asked him not to, and he didn't review Still because he couldn't yet relate to his work. He did discuss both Rothko and Still, however, very favorably when writing about the abstract expressionists as a group, in "'American-Type' Painting" (1955). (He also praised Franz Kline, but as Kline didn't have a solo exhibition until the '50s, I didn't deal with him in my dissertation.)

In a broad way, too, Clem was also riding a wave, for the kind of painting he liked was gradually coming into favor in New York over the decade. I could chart this trend by the relative degree of importance accorded by all reviewers to specific artists and groups of artists, together with the frequency and success of their exhibitions. In subject matter, the trend meant successive moves in the direction of more inwardly turning paintings, with subjective, fanciful, or religious subject matter, and away from the more outwardly directed ones, which had emphasized political or social themes. Stylistically, I could also see a tendency away from what Wölfflin might have called linear compositions, toward more loosely brushed, painterly ones, also away from more representational depictions and toward more abstracted ones.

The terms "expressionist" and "expressionism" were widely used in the '40s, meaning not German Expressionism but any painting that might have been called painterly as opposed to linear. Such work was called "expressionist" because looser brushwork was equated with freer *expression* of emotion. Rattner was an expressionist in this sense, and most painters using expressionistic brushwork in the '40s had been, like him, representational not abstract (Jack Levine, Hyman Bloom, etc.). Robert Coates, the *New Yorker* art critic, knew this when he applied "abstract expressionism" to the new abstract American painting. He did so in a review of Hofmann in 1946, intending to distinguish this work both from figurative expressionism, and from the clearly outlined, linear abstractions of pre-war European leaders like Jean Arp, Miró, and Mondrian, as well as their American followers.[407]

I argued that the recognition accorded the semiabstract figurative expressionism of artists like Rattner paved the way for acceptance of the pure abstractions of abstract expressionism. At the beginning of the decade, his style was controversial. By the mid-'40s, he was being recognized as a leader (though he would be relegated to the sidelines in the '50s, as increasingly abstract styles came to the fore). In subject matter, his Crucifixions of the early '40s referred to the anguish of Europe under Nazi rule. Rattner was Jewish, but by using a Christian theme, he universalized the experience of the Holocaust, employing a Jew (Christ) to symbolize suffering humanity as a whole. By July 1981, I'd written five chapters on him, but when dealing with his career in the '40s, and mentioning critics, galleries, and museum exhibitions, I kept wanting to cross-reference to the context part of the dissertation, which I'd not yet written.

Silk was eager to have me do the context, but he would be going to the American Academy in Rome that year, and couldn't serve at my defense. Reff was going on sabbatical, and told me to ask his replacement at Columbia, Donald E. Gordon, to be my senior advisor. Gordon (BA, Harvard, 1952, PhD, Harvard, 1960) was visiting from the University of Pittsburgh, and working on a book tracing expressionism from Germany in the early twentieth century up to the "neo-expressionism" which, by the early '80s, was already hot on the contemporary scene.[408] When I came up to New York in September, I introduced myself to him, and he agreed to be my senior advisor. Silk's replacement at Columbia, Kenneth E. Silver, agreed to be my junior advisor.

He was interested because his dissertation for Yale had dealt with the avant-garde in Paris during and after World War I, and Rattner had been in Paris for part of that time.[409]

Gordon was interested in the context part of my dissertation, and suggested I put it at the front, before Rattner. I did, and it all hung together much better. Since the first draft of the dissertation was about seven hundred pages, and the context part was about 60 percent of that, it may seem odd that the first draft of that part was written almost entirely between September and December 1981. Nevertheless, as nearly as I can recall, that happened. The context part had a long discussion of Clem's writing in the '40s, yet seems to have been written after we'd come, subtly, to a change in our relationship. My calendar says the last time I visited Norwich was from August 10 to 13, 1981. What must have happened then explains why I never went back.

I believe this was when Clem's preference for Jenny finally got to the point where I could no longer tolerate it on a biological level. In other ways, it seemed that he and I were growing somewhat closer. I'd called him often from Washington to discuss my research, and some of his postcards to me contain affectionate salutations, but written words aren't the same as spoken ones, and Clem never used affectionate language with me in conversation. I could deal with the fact that when I complimented him on the tea in his kitchen cupboard, he said Jenny had bought it. I could handle the photos of his seventieth birthday party that she'd thrown for him, and to which I hadn't been invited, any more than I was allowed to see Sarah (though I heard intimate details of her growing up), but the incident that my unconscious finally drew the line at, I conclude in retrospect, occurred in Norwich in August 1981.

Clem and I went to bed one night, and had unusually good sex. He dropped off to sleep, while I was lying awake, and then he started talking in his sleep. "Dear," he said. Gee, I thought, this is something like. I snuggled a little closer, so I could hear his next word, which was "Darling!" That really made me feel great, but then he uttered a deep sigh, and added, "Oh, Jenny!" His voice expressed enormous loss, and he rolled impatiently over to the far side of the bed, away from me. This made me feel terrible, but the worst of it was that he hadn't been trying to be cruel. He'd been completely unaware of what he was saying, but either it meant that he really loved Jenny, and would always do so, no matter what I did, or else it meant he really loved me, and that was why he was talking to Jenny, to punish me for loving him.

Maybe if I could have dished it as well as taken it, we could have become closer, but I've never been much at riposte. I'd known I'd never marry him, because I couldn't have satisfied him sexually, or tolerated the resulting infidelity. I knew that if we were married, nobody would take my writing seriously. They'd assume I was merely his mouthpiece, and this was the only reason I gave him for not wanting to marry him (not that he'd asked, and he gallantly replied that he admired my ambition). Still, after that night when he talked to Jenny in his sleep, something in me seems to have decided that I didn't want to go to bed with him any longer, for, without intending to, I started to get fatter. By the summer of 1982, I was so overweight that Clem no longer desired me (he'd once given me to understand that he couldn't get it up for a fat woman).

Part of my research for the "context" involved looking up what had been written about the '40s since the '40s. This meant whatever I could find about collectors, museum officials, critics, and so on. Most of the critics had been forgotten. A few had had successful careers stretching on into the '50s, '60s and more recently, but only Clem had had anything written about him, and it was quite a lot. According to these commentators, in the '40s he'd been a hard, cold purist who hated surrealism, tried to force abstract expressionism into a cubist mold, and downplayed the importance of feeling and content in abstract painting. None of this was substantiated by what he'd written, and was in fact contradicted by it, but the condemnation of him for lack of feeling was particularly silly. In my dissertation, I quoted more than a dozen references in his writing of the '40s to "feeling," "emotion," "passion," or being "moved" by art.

Much had been written on Pollock, in the '40s and since. Clem had praised him in the '40s as the greatest painter of his generation, and Clem's writings of that period were already being read by other writers, including some on *The New York Times* and *Life*. Many people in the '80s thought that Pollock's fame originated with the article *Life* did on him in 1949, but when it came out, he was already relatively well known within the art world: *Life*'s subtitle, "Is He the Greatest Living Painter in the United States?" referred to the fact that Clem said he was.

To Clem, the allover paintings of Pollock's "classic" period had no subject matter, but less enlightened critics still likened them to many things. I quoted some of these analogies in the dissertation, often to show how critics using them didn't like Pollock's work. Howard Devree, of the *Times*, was most likely the one who wrote that the paintings in Pollock's January 1948 show made him think of "webs of very white ash with tar judiciously dribbled for accents in what may or may not be meaningful patterns."[410] Emily Genauer of the *New York World-Telegram* (and later the *New York Herald Tribune*) would learn to love abstract expressionism in the '50s (after it became the reigning avant-garde), but in 1949, she was still saying that Pollock's paintings "resemble nothing so much as a mop of tangled hair I have an irresistible urge to comb out."[411]

Alex Eliot of *Time*, Pollock's foremost detractor, likened his abstractions to subjects that ranged from "a battlefield seen from 40,000 feet" to "a culture of bacteria seen through a microscope...."[412] A similar but more flattering analogy occurred to Henry McBride of *The New York Sun*, a more progressive critic. Of the picture that Pollock exhibited in the Whitney Museum's 1949 annual exhibition of contemporary painting, McBride wrote poetically that it suggested "a flat, war-shattered city, possibly Hiroshima, as seen from a great height in moonlight."[413] Sam Hunter, a younger critic on the *Times* in the later '40s who went on to become an art historian of note, described Pollock's most abstract painting as "a pure calligraphic metaphor for a ravaging, aggressive virility."[414] This made me wonder if he hadn't had the same association with Pollock's paintings that I'd had while I was still on *Time*.

In those days, I'd concluded that their liquid, passionate swirls of paint reminded me of semen, but in Washington, I'd also started associating them with the nuclear holocaust. The fact that I couldn't relinquish the semen association kept me from trying to write about the nuclear one, while the nuclear one kept me from trying to write about the semen. I was still committed to a conventional either/or frame of reference, but also engaging in divergent thinking, the creative person's way of holding two opposed possibilities in mind without committing one's self wholly to either. I'd done something of the same thing while I'd been writing my "novel" in London, and that experience may have made it easier for me to use divergent thinking in Washington, but in Washington, I was sane. I quoted Hunter's analogy only in a footnote of the dissertation, and McBride's not at all, but both stayed in my memory, as did many of the others.

Since the '40s, other writers had discussed the associations Pollock's work had for them, but because they'd become able to see the beauty of it, these associations were more positive. Ellen Johnson in 1973 had dealt in *Studio International* with "Jackson Pollock and Nature." Chad Mandeles had written in *Arts Magazine* in 1981 on "Jackson Pollock and Jazz: Structural Parallels." I read B. H. Friedman's biography, *Jackson Pollock: Energy Made Visible* (1972). From it, I learned more about Pollock's life, the countryside in The Springs, on Long Island (where he was living when he arrived at his poured paintings), his fondness for cooking, and so forth, but I was still seeing his classic abstract poured paintings as devoid of subject matter.

During the fall of 1981, I finished writing the first draft of the context part of the dissertation. I'd assembled masses of photocopied research, and wrote my rough draft on pads of yellow paper, sometimes ten pages a day, before typing it up. (My fellow Fellows said that when I left, they wanted my pencils, because the pencils wrote ten pages a day all by themselves.) Besides describing the backgrounds and exhibitions during the '40s of more than a hundred American artists, and discussing critics on all the newspapers and magazines I've mentioned, I dealt with the exhibition and acquisition policies of four major Manhattan museums, listed the leading galleries, outlined the activities of top collectors, analyzed the price structure of the art market, and provided a narrative outlining the overall direction of the decade.

As Christmas approached, I brought the first draft of my manuscript to New York for my advisors to read. Gordon told me how to present my table of contents, and asked me to put the section dealing with the later assessments of Clem into an appendix, shrink the manuscript by a third, rewrite the conclusions at the end of the first (context) part so that they set up the second (Rattner) part better, and rewrite the conclusions ending the Rattner part so that his significance for later art was made clearer. I did as I was told, and, after moving back to my New York apartment at New Year's, I spent the first months of 1982 cutting and retyping the manuscript.

I never said anything to anybody at Columbia about my relationship with Clem, though I thought about the ethics of writing about a lover. I was afraid that my treatment of him in the dissertation might be too partial, yet as I said to myself, he wasn't its main subject, and there was nothing in it about him that wasn't public record. The quotations from his writings could be verified by anybody in libraries across the country. Many women had written about their mates, including Simone de Beauvoir, Lauren Bacall, Ingrid Bergman, and two of Picasso's mistresses, but there hadn't been any secret about these relationships. I wouldn't have denied my relationship with Clem, if anybody had asked me about it, but nobody even asked if I knew him, and I couldn't figure out how to bring up the topic without behaving rather oddly myself. It would have looked awfully strange if I'd sashayed into Gordon's office and announced, apropos of nothing, "By the way, I've slept with Clement Greenberg. Is that an issue?"

In the end, I told myself that having slept with somebody didn't necessarily predispose one in his favor, or else we'd all still be married to the first person we went to bed with. I also thought that having slept with somebody enabled one to know him better, so my dissertation might even have benefitted from the relationship. I didn't take Clem's side on the one occasion when he'd reviewed Rattner's work, in 1944. I quoted his few favorable and many unfavorable comments, but I said that in 1944 he was still only "a very obscure minor critic," pointed out that the *Times* had also criticized the show, and indicated that neither of these reviews affected the show's success, for it was extended an extra week, and sold quite well. I didn't see how I could exclude Clem from the dissertation without giving a seriously flawed portrait of the decade.

I considered my defense committee a preliminary board or panel of review, and felt that if what I said about Clem passed muster with them, it was objective enough to be published. Rereading what I wrote, I see that I was trying to present Clem's writing from his point of view. When the first two volumes of his collected essays and criticism were published in 1986, other reviewers would take the same material, and by selecting other passages from it, use it to draw different (sometimes hostile) conclusions. Yet such was my innocence when I wrote the dissertation that I thought I was merely correcting misconceptions about Clem. I believed that the writers whose oversights I was pointing out had erred out of ignorance, because they'd based their evaluations solely on *Art and Culture* and his more recent writing. I was even naive enough to think that if their mistakes were pointed out to them, they'd be glad to correct them!

Allen Staley assembled my defense committee. Besides Gordon, Silver, and himself, he recruited Arthur C. Danto, a Columbia philosophy professor interested in contemporary art (but not yet reviewing it for *The Nation*), and Greta Berman, a Columbia PhD whose dissertation, deposited in 1975, was on Depression-era WPA mural painting in New York City. The defense was peaceful; the committee asked only for minor changes. Shortly before my defense, Gordon suggested we lunch together. At the lunch, he said that although he was willing to let me defend the dissertation in its current state, it needed more work before it could be published. I'd done nothing more than "skillful reporting," and I should get beneath the surface more. "What about existentialism?" he asked. I told Clem that Gordon had asked about existentialism. Clem said this was the sort of thing that art historians fussed over, but the artists hadn't been concerned with.

After I'd deposited the dissertation, I sent him a copy. He read it and liked it. Modestly protesting that there was "too much" about him, he also said I'd brought back a lot of memories. He remained unimpressed with Rattner, but thought I should try and get the context part published as a book, with the conclusions appropriately revised. This began a new phase in our relationship, where he respected me as a writer and art historian, but no longer insisted on having sex with me, and respect from him was all I'd really wanted in the beginning anyway: his good opinion.

18. Breakthrough
(Fall 1982–Summer 1983)

I WAS READY for a full-time teaching job, but all I got during the 1982–83 academic year was an adjunct course at Hunter. I didn't think I could get my dissertation published. However much Clem liked it, an academic publisher would want the same "digging below the surface" that Gordon had, and I wasn't interested in existentialism. Conventional wisdom said that if one couldn't publish a dissertation, the next best thing was to get articles out of it, and, since I was again starting to notice contemporary art, I conceived a series of articles combining the dissertation with the current scene. The first would present newspaper critics of the '40s, and compare them with those of the '80s; the second would deal with the magazines, then and now. The third would be about Clem, what he wrote in the '40s and what had been written about him since. I outlined my idea to Richard Martin on October 10, and he liked it, especially the article on Clem.

The three installments of "Art Criticism (and Art History) in New York: The 1940s vs. the 1980s" appeared in *Arts Magazine* in February, March, and April of 1983. The first two showed that critics in the major media and the art press in the '80s were still attacking painters whom Clem admired, and that critics of the '40s had celebrated many artists since forgotten, or remembered only for work done earlier. This suggested that the fame of artists popular in the '80s might prove to be just as ephemeral, and the true avant-garde that would be remembered was still the artists associated with Clem.

Needless to say, the articles delighted Clem's friends, but as I also presented the artists of the wider context of the '40s in a nonjudgmental manner, more conventional artists and art historians liked the them, too. I got letters from two all-but-forgotten artists from the '40s whom I'd mentioned, and the widow of a third sent me books about her late husband. An art historian teaching at Yale would tell me she'd put photocopies of my articles on reserve for her students, and Motherwell would say that I'd captured exactly his feelings upon being twitted by the senior critic of the *Times*, back in 1946. I was asked to do a synopsis of the article on Clem by RILA, an international index of art publications that had shown no interest in my publications before.

Clem himself called to thank me, saying it was the first time anybody had attempted his "defense." That was a thrill. Earlier, he'd told me that many people had asked him if he knew me, because they'd been so impressed by my first two articles. Helen Frankenthaler and Charlie Millard sent me notes saying how much they liked them. Another artist was so taken with the piece on Clem that he asked if I'd write the text of a book about his work. He had a publisher all lined up, but I asked Clem about it, and he told me that I didn't need to be anybody's apologist. "Stick to your own work," he said. This boosted my ego further, since it implied that my work was important enough to stick to.

In February, I met Kenworth W. Moffett, one of Clem's friends and curator of modern and contemporary art at the Museum of Fine Arts, Boston, at a symposium in New York. Moffett invited me to Boston, to see a show from the Graham Gund collection at his museum. In April, I flew up for the day, and lunched with him and his fiancee, Lucy Baker, a painter. After the museum show, I was driven by Baker to nearby Framingham, to see a show Moffett had organized of younger artists in New England whose work had grown out of the color-field painting of the '60s. Then Baker took me to her studio, and those of a few other younger artists. All knew my articles and were impressed by them. Moffett also sent photocopies of them to Olitski and other older artists whom he thought would be interested. André Emmerich wrote me a cordial letter saying that he'd been sending photocopies of them to his clients. In June, he invited me to a luxurious lunch at his gallery, and invited me to write about some of his artists. He was so charming that he boosted my ego more than anybody else (except, of course, Clem).

Averaging 9,600 words apiece (plus notes), these three articles were the first in which I'd publicly committed my support to Clem and color-field painting. Looking back, though, one reason these articles were greeted with such enthusiasm by Clem and his acquaintance was that conceptually they were not that radical. For some time, he'd been saying that the best painting always took place away from the center of public attention, so all that my articles really did was reinforce his argument. They didn't explain why color-field painting should be having such a tough time in the '80s, or challenge any received wisdom to the extent that I later would.

It was the heyday of neo-expressionism. Julian Schnabel, David Salle, Eric Fischl, Sandro Chia, Enzo Cucchi, Francesco Clemente, Anselm Kiefer, and Georg Baselitz were the new culture heroes. Neo-expressionism was at last a style that critics, collectors, and a wider public could agree on, for the first time since the advent of pop in the early '60s. Because it was predominantly figurative, it appealed to museum-goers who'd never been able to relate to abstraction, and because it was predominantly paintings to hang on the wall, it was much more salable to collectors than conceptual artworks or artists' videos. Neo-expressionist painters had individual styles (or anyway, individual mannerisms), so critics could find more to say about them than they'd found with the photographic imagery of hyperrealism. Neo-expressionism's clearly delineated subject matter could also be discussed art-historically in iconographic terms.

The consensus of collectors, critics, museum-goers, even art historians meant that the loud colors and crude imagery of neo-expressionism were selling like there was no tomorrow, particularly since so many nouveau-riche collectors were now competing for the same art with collectors who'd been around since the '60s. Prices in the art market were zooming, but then the stock market was also going up, greed was good, and ostentatious vulgarity in clothes and lifestyles was the order of the day. Ronald Reagan was president. His "trickle-down" economics seemed to me a justification for letting the rich get richer, while leaving the poor ever further behind in their wake. I also resented the way he ballooned the budget with military expenditures to fight the Soviet Union, while buying votes by offering to cut taxes. But Reaganomics seemed to have made the country at least superficially prosperous.

Critics and art historians talked about "the return to figuration." This was above all why "modernism" (a.k.a. abstraction, especially as admired by Clem) was being supplanted by "postmodernism." The term "postmodernism" had finally come into its own, with its prefix "post-" implying that modernism was dead. Dealers were dropping younger and/or lesser-known modernist abstract artists whom Clem liked in favor of younger and/or lesser-known neo-expressionists ("My taste has changed," they'd say). Exhibitions of even the better-known color-field painters were being shunted by their dealers into late spring or early fall, in order to leave calendars open for newsier art during those months when more buyers were in town. No amount of writing about abstract art, I must have suspected, could stand up to this onslaught, not at least the way abstract art had been written about in the past.

It was in this context that I discovered my theory of multireferential imagery in abstract painting, the subject that inspired this book. I was writing my article about Clem in the fall of 1982, and trying to explain why he'd been able to appreciate Pollock and the rest of the abstract expressionists so long before anybody else. One reason, I felt, was his conviction that "feeling" lay behind all great art. The other was his belief that an abstract painting could have content without subject matter (he'd distinguished between the two in 1940, writing that "every work of art must have content, but...subject matter is something the artist does or does not have in mind when he is actually at work").[415]

When Bill Rubin had first suggested to me that the content of abstract art was "feeling," it enabled me to respond to it, but later I remembered that according to Freud, nobody "feels" in a vacuum. One "feels" in relation both to one's inner makeup *and* external situations or physical stimuli. Defending Clem's point of view, I was writing that "I think it was the recognition that a picture could have content, whether or not it possessed readily identifiable subject matter, that enabled Greenberg, among other things, to respond initially to the Abstract Expressionists."[416] Then I started to rebut the notion that Pollock had been trying to paint any of the subject matter imputed to him by commentators who'd likened his poured paintings to one thing or another (I'd mentioned several of these analogies in the first two articles in the series).

Suddenly, I realized how Pollock's abstract paintings, over which I'd puzzled for fifteen years, *could* have subject matter: by depicting simplified versions of many subjects simultaneously. The critics who'd been reminded of this or that by his paintings were only wrong to the extent that they believed they'd seen the only possible thing to see. Pollock hadn't intended to paint any of the things they compared his pictures to, but precisely because he hadn't, his unconscious had synthesized various visual experiences he'd had into a single image, just as the images in dreams are composites of different things seen in waking life. I knew this theory came right out of Freudian dream interpretation, but an article about Clem was obviously no place to explore it, so I merely inserted a parenthetical remark that I italicize here: "I have not yet seen any evidence that Pollock was deliberately or consciously trying to paint jazz, nature, or any other subject in his poured paintings of 1947–1950 *(though I would not exclude the possibility that unconscious associations enabled him to allude to these subjects in his canvases, together with a myriad of others)*".[417]

I read a bit of Freud.[418] I discussed my theory with Dr. I, my psychiatrist. "That's just like the Rorschach blots!" he exclaimed, or words to that effect. "You can see anything you want in them, too." "Are you sure?" I asked. "Aren't there some images that more people see in a specific Rorschach blot than others?" Dr. I conceded that there were, and said that in books on interpreting the blots, I'd find these images listed as the commonest or popular responses. Columbia's psychology library had such books, for instance Robert M. Allen's *Student's Rorschach Manual: An Introduction to Administering, Scoring and Interpreting Rorschach's Psychodiagnostic Inkblot Test* (revised edition, 1978). I, however, was otherwise occupied for the rest of the winter, and shoved the subject to the back of my mind.

In May, I went to Europe for three weeks, and attended the opening in London of a show of beautiful Frankenthalers from the '60s at the Knoedler Kasmin gallery. Helen was there, and she introduced me to a Spanish diplomat who collected color-field paintings. She'd trucked my articles clear across the Atlantic so that he could read them, and he and I sat in a back room of the gallery and talked. He said that modernism was being driven back to Boston and Syracuse (the first being where Moffett and his younger artists were; the second, home to other younger artists, most notably Darryl Hughto and Susan Roth). Even Helen's reputation depended on her having followers, the diplomat continued, and this was why it was so vital for younger painters to succeed. He told me about a terrible argument that the junior partner of a New York gallery that I respected had had with its senior partner, because the younger color-field artists who were the junior partner's particular responsibility weren't selling.

In Paris, I taped an interview with Stanley William Hayter, an eighty-one-year-old English painter and printmaker who'd run a workshop for printmakers in New York during World War II, and whom I'd learned about through my dissertation (the interview would be incorporated into an article on Hayter that I'd publish in 1984). Hayter had known Pollock during the war, and told me that Pollock had experimented at his workshop with swirling paint onto a canvas from a can with a hole in its bottom and a string attached so it could be swung back and forth.[419] This antecedent to Pollock's mature technique was a surrealist "automatist" device meant to bring the unconscious into the picture-making process.[420] Rubin had introduced me to automatism, and Pollock had known about the role of the unconscious in creation.

"Most modern painters," he'd said in a radio interview around 1950, "work from within." He'd added that "the unconscious is a very important side of modern art...."[421] In a later interview, he'd indicated that although he himself was a Jungian, "We're all of us influenced by Freud, I guess."[422] Hayter said that even with abstract art, "The sources are exterior, and it starts by looking, doesn't it? An artist is somebody who looks a bit more than somebody else. How are you going to explain to the public that somebody they look on as a naive source of genius – like Pollock – this was a man who *saw*, who *looked* at things. Much harder, and with greater intensity, with greater insight, if you like...and the result of this was that something came out of him, having been completely assimilated, and so on...."[423]

After I returned to New York, I called Charlie Millard, at the Hirshhorn Museum. I was feeling more self-confident than I'd felt in a long time, but also apprehensive about what the diplomat had said. I asked about the retrospective of Friedel Dzubas, a lesser-known color-field painter, that Millard had organized for the Hirshhorn, and that had opened there on June 16. While I'd been living in Washington, Millard had been organizing this show. He'd told me how no other museum had been willing to take it on a traveling basis, though he'd written to many. On the phone, he asked me to come down and look at it, saying it was beautiful, but nobody was coming to see it. I thought I detected a note of desperation. To put years into organizing such a big show, then find that nobody wanted to come and look at it, must have been truly depressing.

I read a one-page review in the May issue of *Arts Magazine* of a Dzubas show in a Manhattan gallery in January–February. The reviewer saw nothing in these paintings beyond abstract expressionism, so classed them as out-of-date. Evidently, he knew nothing about color-field painting, and feeling a need to educate him, I called Martin, and said I'd like to do a one-page review of the Dzubas show at the Hirshhorn. He said he'd be glad to have it, and would be willing to hold the September issue open for it. This would have been around Thursday, July 7 or Friday, July 8. On Monday, the eleventh, I flew to Washington, saw the show and loved it. On Tuesday, the twelfth, I started to write, and began to feel that there was more to be said than I'd previously intended to say. I called Martin and asked for more time and space. He said that the article could be as long as I wanted, and that if I could get it to him by Monday, the eighteenth, he would still be able to use it for the September issue.

The next day, Wednesday, I was working on the piece when Clem called and invited me over for a drink. This elated me further. He had another guest, a photographer and longtime friend named Cora Kelley Ward. They were eating Chinese takeout in the kitchen, and Clem invited me to join them. He'd just returned from a trip to China with Sarah, and he'd sent me a postcard from there, with the Chinese ideogram for "love" on it. Now he gave me one of the small carved wooden combs that he'd brought back for gifts. We started talking about Dzubas. "He's great," Clem said, "but nobody knows it." Then he smiled across the table at me. "You're great!" he said.

If there was one thing for which I'd been striving since I'd met Clem, it was praise like this. I can't begin to describe how terrific it made me feel, because he wasn't using the word in a slang sense, but with its full importance. I felt like I'd arrived at the top of Mt. Everest, after a long, tortuous uphill journey, like Jove himself were congratulating me. I went home, and kept on writing my review. The neglect of this beautiful exhibition (nearly deserted when I saw it) was symptomatic of everything wrong with the art scene, the way third-rate neo-expressionist art was fawned over in the magazines and selling like crazy, essentially because it was figurative, while the marvelous abstract paintings that I so much loved were being rejected, even knowledge of them driven back to Boston and Syracuse.

Images formed at the back of my mind – of all the lectures I'd attended at Columbia. With only rare exceptions, neither Reff nor Silk had found much beyond formal analysis to use in discussing abstraction, so the minutes spent on it had dwindled into insignificance by comparison with the hours devoted to figurative art, since that could be handled with both formal and iconographic analyses. Such lectures must have left generations of students feeling that their teachers considered representational art superior to abstraction. I thought of the special issue that *Art in America* had done on Picasso in 1980, pegged on the MoMA retrospective. Only a relatively brief passage, by Clem, focused on the Analytic Cubism in the show, while the rest of the magazine concerned itself with windy generalities, side issues and less attractive but more representational work. *Picasso in Retrospect* (1973), a collection of essays, dealt with practically every phase of Picasso's career except Analytic Cubism. I visualized twentieth-century art history as a black wall of ignorance and hostility, favoring lesser art, and only a few tiny windows of light allowed to shine through: Analytic Cubism, Mondrian, and abstract expressionism.

What was the reason for this skewing of art history in favor of the second-rate and at the expense of the first-rate, figuration preferred to abstraction at all costs? It must have been the definition of abstraction as depicting nothing, of having no subject matter. This view of abstraction went back to the early years of the century, and was shared by its supporters and detractors. Yet, although many critics, collectors, museums, and art-lovers had admired abstract art, far more people had been turned off by its seeming unrelatedness to the external world. The result was a constant tendency to revert to figuration (representational and presentational), however ugly it might be.

If all these people could only see that in fact abstraction was a new, richer form of representation, they might learn to love it as I did, and the course of art history might be changed. Nor was it necessary to claim for abstraction anything it didn't have. All my knowledge of Freudian psychology, which I'd stuffed down beneath consciousness the previous autumn, came erupting back up – the whole idea that a dream was a composite of images the dreamer had seen during his or her waking hours, since he or she couldn't visualize anything except in terms of what she or he had already seen. The idea that what had gone into the dream had been conveyed to the dreamer by her or his unconscious, and that therefore ideas or images of any kind could be transmitted from an artist to a viewer, without the artist being aware that he or she was doing so.

Other recollections stretched back into childhood. Ed Bley had taught us about abstraction or generalization in language. If you said Willy, you meant one dog of that name. If you said Labrador retriever, you meant not only Willy but all other dogs of that breed. If you said dog, it meant not only all Labs, but all dogs of other breeds, and if you said animal, that meant not only dogs, but also horses, cats, cows, and so on. Simplifying or abstracting a pictorial image from many observations of nature was the visual equivalent to this. I remembered my Barnard senior thesis. *The Waste Land* hadn't seemed to be "about" anything at first. It was praised by the avant-garde because it evoked a mood or feelings. Decades later, George Williamson had figured out the poem's plot, what it was "about." I was doing the same with abstract painting.

I remembered things artists had said to me over the years. Tony Smith had told me how *Die*, his black box, could mean a matrix, or mold, the imperative of the verb *to die*, and one half of a pair of dice. Helen, Anne Truitt, and Hayter had all mentioned ambiguity to me. Agee, Washton Long, Levin, and Rand had perceived images in abstraction, even if their writings didn't substantiate my argument completely. In the catalogue for an Adolph Gottlieb exhibition that I'd attended while I was living in Washington, Lawrence Alloway had listed five dualities that might have been in Gottlieb's mind when he painted his "Burst" series, with a round, hard (and often red) ball at the top and a scratchy patch (often black) at the bottom: sun and earth, male and female, night and day, life and death, Mediterranean and Northern.[424]

Looking back, I see other experiences that contributed to my insight, especially verbal ones, since double and even triple levels of meaning can occur in language as well as art. I was helped by puns I'd laughed at as a child, rhetorical devices learned in college, language as used on *Time*, above all by my two years, from 1969 to 1971, in my world of intermittent fantasy. During those years, I'd perceived so many double levels of meaning in things I'd said, heard, read, and seen that I'd learned to live with ambiguity, to feel at ease with it. Some of these "surreal messages" had been delusions of reference (when I saw them in movies and newspapers), but some I'd been sending myself (when symbolizing myself as a London church). And sometimes I think I'd received them (Alfred Barr's tennis analogy, Ken Noland talking about his big stick).

Maybe because I'd lived with all this verbal ambiguity, I could accept the idea that ambiguity might also be a principle in visual art. Freud knew that babies recognize things before they learn the words to designate them (this may be why his dream interpretations concerned themselves with images first, words second). Still, a double level of meaning seems to be easier for most people to accept when it's verbal. I suspect that visual ambiguity disturbs many of us. We depend so much on our eyes to keep us in touch with the world that we don't like to think of an image having more than one meaning. If we can't say for sure that this is a tree, and be confident that everybody else will agree with us, we are left with the nagging sensation that we may not know what else we're seeing, and doubt about whether we can believe anything we see.

Despite its concurrent fantasies, the play I'd written about Quogue in the summer of 1969 had taught me how something from my unconscious could be conveyed to the outside world without my conscious mind being aware that this was happening, just as I believe happened with Pollock, Picasso, et al. I'd intended my play to have a second, surreal level of meaning, about the art scene in New York, but while I was writing it, I'd become aware of half a dozen other, unconscious allusions that had passed onto the typed page without my realizing they were allusions until after I'd written them down. Among these had been "Harry," the putative hero, as an allusion to Harry Luce, "The Henhouse" as an allusion to the renovated chicken coop of my childhood, and the very title, *Quidnunc*, as a description of Clem's role in my life at that moment.

My article for *Arts* had begun as a review of the Dzubas exhibition, but almost before I was fully aware of what I was doing, I was shoehorning my theory about multireferential imagery into the middle of it, and intertwining the two themes. While I was writing about the theory, I wasn't thinking about my two years in dreamland, or the many experiences I'd had with words having double levels of meaning – though I did realize that what I was writing tapped into other art experiences, from Tony Smith's *Die* on through Alloway's Gottlieb catalogue to my interview with Hayter, and I cited them all as part of my argument in a perfectly logical, understandable way.

> An artist must be able to see [I wrote] in order to paint (or sculpt), and thus he inevitably sees the world around him from the moment of birth....Whatever he paints (or sculpts) must in some way be influenced by what he's previously seen. I cannot see any way around this. The shapes and forms he creates...must in some way be related to the vast storehouse of images from nature he has previously assimilated.

> But there is a difference between the way in which a representational artist's work is related to these previously received images and the way in which an abstract artist's is related to them. The human mind does not just record images and transmit them (like a camera). It can and does think about what the eyes see: it conceptualizes and generalizes.....

> The representational painter can conceptualize and generalize to a certain extent (for example, in creating an "ideal" landscape, or a mythological or allegorical composition). But the abstract painter conceptualizes and generalizes to a far higher degree. As a result,

the representational painter creates images on the canvas that are essentially uni-referential; that is, each image on the canvas refers to a single image that can be observed in nature (or could be, if it existed, such as an angel). But the abstract artist creates an image that is multireferential, ambiguous; that is, the image on the canvas refers to two or more objects to be found in external nature. He does this by abstracting, or generalizing his image, often to the point where it bears no apparent similarity to any single object in nature.[425]

The article segued into a Freudian discussion of how the abstract artist might not be aware of his multireferential imagery and yet create it. I took up and disposed of the Rorschach blots, since I expected other people would respond to my theory the same way that Dr. I had. I mentioned artists I'd talked with who'd been interested in ambiguity, but I also used paintings to illustrate my theory. The first was *"Ma Jolie."* Since this picture of Picasso's beloved "Eva" was subtitled *Woman with a Zither or Guitar* in Rubin's 1980 exhibition catalogue, I argued that the artist had unconsciously symbolized his famously ambivalent attitudes toward women by combining two musical instruments into a single image. It wasn't *either* a zither *or* a guitar; it was *both* a zither *and* a guitar. The guitar, national instrument of Picasso's native Spain, represented memories of his mother, and puritanical Spanish society, while the zither symbolized gypsies and artist's bohemian night life in Paris. The synthesis of the two was a way of saying that with Eva, the artist had achieved balance and reconciliation.[426]

The problem was that I didn't know what zithers or guitars Picasso would have seen, and where he could have seen them, so I couldn't establish a direct link between the artist's visual experience and the image in his painting. To deal with this, I used Dzubas as a test case, studying the transparency of his painting, *Trough* (1972), loaned to me by the Hirshhorn. First, I felt that it suggested four cyclones hurtling down the right side, and a series of flat, stacked green fields on the left. Second, I felt that the vertical shapes on the right also looked like test tubes, and the horizontal ones on the left resembled a stack of heavy books, perhaps scientific.

I called up Dzubas, whom I'd never met, and asked him about his experiences with chemistry and with flat lands and cyclones. He'd studied chemistry in the *gymnasium* he'd attended in Germany as an adolescent, and thought the lab experiments that went with the course "exciting." He'd also lived in Chicago in the early '40s, and seen how flat the land around there was. He'd seen photographs of cyclones, too, and, having always been "attracted to large winds," considered cyclones "an enormous, wonderful, dramatic spectacle."[427] In other words, he had seen things which corresponded to what I'd seen in the painting, so it could be said that he'd communicated them to me through *Trough*.

The most extended example I used was Pollock. It was by far the best documented, both the many associations that different viewers had made with his poured paintings, and what he could have seen and incorporated into his unconscious storehouse of visual impressions (either the objects themselves or photographs and drawings of them). I began by mentioning the analogies to jazz made by Chad Mandeles, and to the dunes, grass, sea, and sky around the Pollock home in The Springs on Long Island, as discussed by Ellen Johnson, but I amplified on her article by saying that she hadn't compared "the delicate webbed linear tracery of Pollock's paintings and the rich clusters of twigs and branches on the trees near the Pollocks' home" (the scenery suggested to me by B. H. Friedman).[428] I passed on to Henry McBride's comparison of one of Pollock's paintings to "a flat, war-shattered city, possibly Hiroshima, as seen from a great height in moonlight," adding that Pollock could have seen many images of wartime devastation in newspapers and magazines, and that, even though the Pollocks hadn't been very involved in politics, "World War II was a cataclysmic event, a giant emblem and symbol of destruction, aggression, and eventual salvation."[429]

Life had compared Pollock's paintings to macaroni. I argued that spaghetti was the pasta unconsciously intended, and that it would have had "powerful associations for Pollock with home, family, nurturing, domesticity, and hospitality." Citing Friedman as my source again, I added that the artist "was very proud of his skills as a cook and had his own recipe for spaghetti sauce. The Pollocks liked to serve spaghetti, with the sauce, to friends."[430] I commented on Genauer's comparison of Pollock's paintings to "a mop of tangled hair" by saying that the hair on people's heads had many "intimate, domestic associations," and remarking that "Lee Krasner's hair must have looked pretty appealing, spread out on a pillow (I hope she will pardon me this familiarity, in the interests of helping to establish an art-historical theory)." I even cited Alex Eliot's crack about "a culture of bacteria, seen through a microscope," finding a possible source for this association in D'Arcy Thompson's *On Growth and Form*, described by Friedman as being one of Pollock's favorite books, with its discussions of the amoeba and many plates of cells, shells, skulls, scales, and snowflakes.[431]

Since 1983, I've done more research, qualifying a few of these analogies and adding many others that demonstrate how Pollock's personal experience would have corresponded to what people were reminded of by his paintings, but I think I've said enough here to show the process. After I'd given all these examples of other writers' associations in 1983, I introduced my own, of semen and urine. I did it carefully, because I knew these were explosive subjects, but I thought that surely artists and art historians, being so much more sophisticated than *Time*'s readers, would be able to accept them in the spirit in which they were presented (what a dreamer I still was). The urine seemed to me to express Pollock's childish desire to shock, but the semen spoke of the relatively sane and stable marriage that the Pollocks had at that time, the facts that Krasner was herself a gifted painter, and that, although the couple had no children, they had interacted with each other particularly well in the creative sphere.

> So I would suggest [I wrote] that the associations with semen I might have shared with Pollock are three in number. First, an association with an act of harmless aggression ("Make Love, Not War," as the bumperstickers used to have it in the '60s). Second, an association with both physical pleasure and the conveyance of the tenderest and warmest feelings a man can have toward a fellow human. Finally, semen can be interpreted as a symbol of generation and reproduction, the perpetuation of the species, and from this it can also be seen as a metaphor for the extension of human personality after an individual's lifetime, in the form of the creation of art for later eras to enjoy.[432]

Here I was thinking of Renaissance humanism. In that era, people began to wonder whether Heaven existed, but artists and writers believed they could achieve immortality on earth through their creations. Shakespeare expressed this, most notably in his sonnet XVIII, where, addressing his beloved, he wrote of his own poetry, "So long as men can breathe, or eyes can see,/So long lives this, and this gives life to thee."

During that Thursday and Friday, July fourteenth and fifteenth, I'd been writing late into the night and getting up early to get on with it. My mother dragged me off for the weekend to a luxury hotel in exurban Amenia, New York, but I brought along pads and pencils, and kept writing. Spewing out ideas that in some cases had been percolating in my mind for decades, on top of the praise I'd received in the weeks leading up to the article, was getting me awfully keyed up, but that didn't stop me. I must have typed up the piece on Sunday night and Monday morning, after I got back from Amenia, though it runs to about 9,800 words (plus notes). I titled it "Abstract Painting in General; Friedel Dzubas in Particular," and delivered it to Martin by midday.

He took me to a memorable lunch. The next day, I called him, and asked what he thought of the article. "It's wonderful," he said.

This original formulation of my theory was, as I see it, a creative act, resembling "problem solving" as outlined by Graham Wallas, and even as emended by Robert Sternberg. Although I certainly wouldn't set myself up as Pollock's equal, I believe that this creative act of mine more or less parallels the way that he worked (with due allowance made for the fact that we were working in different art forms). As Sternberg said, I first had to identify and define my problem. It was how to deal with the shocking lack of admiration for the best art of its time. With Pollock, the problem (probably existing on a much less conscious level) was finding how he could best and most truly express himself and his era. My "preparation" was information I'd assembled over decades, almost entirely without knowing that it would eventually be put to this use. With Pollock, it was his vast accumulation of visual impressions, going back to his childhood and derived from every aspect of his life. "Incubation" for me took place while I was, without thinking about it, putting my solution oh so gradually together, and the same in another sense was true of Pollock, experimenting with different ways to paint. Finally, and most importantly, came "illumination" or synthesis, in my case bringing together my mostly verbal experiences, and in his, bringing together visual ones.

Pollock may have felt the same flash of insight that I did (possibly when he saw how effective looping paint from a stick could be). He didn't mean to synthesize visual experience or create ambiguous images. On a conscious level he was creating paintings that depicted nothing. For this purpose, his association with Clem was particularly helpful, because Clem expressed his own intuitive response to paintings most meaningfully in terms of form; whether or not the paintings depicted anything was for him irrelevant to its quality as art. This attitude must have helped Pollock to repress all imagery back into his unconscious, and to focus entirely on creating a painting that "worked" in formal terms – thereby creating work most likely to last.[433] I didn't linger over this issue of longevity. Rather, I emphasized that viewers should also look at the style and composition of a painting, because that was what best expressed "the inner character of the man and the way he relates to his times."[434]

Every artist intends every picture she or he paints to be a masterpiece, but the viewer has to decide when the result is one. Since Pollock's breakthrough in 1947, his allover poured paintings have come to be accepted as pure, beautiful abstractions, and since 1983 (on a much humbler level), my theory has made sense to a limited number of people, either in its original form or as it has further evolved. It's still in the process of becoming, but the original insight was the decisive synthesis, and to me, synthesis is the stage of creativity that isn't emphasized as much as it should be – because if you don't have that, you have nothing. It's the synthesis of spaghetti, semen, the ravages of aerial warfare, the loveliness of nature, and dozens of other things into single images that makes Pollock's poured paintings into a paradigm or model for the whole creative process. If you can understand one, you may be able to understand the other.

PART III
U.S. POLITICS:
"THE DISENFRANCHISED LEFT"

19. Reactionary Wave of the '80s
(Fall 1983–Fall 1989)

The article on multireferential imagery marked my deepest immersion into art as art. Gradually, this would evolve into an analysis of U.S. politics in the wake of 2001, which in turn would enable me to situate the art of the past half-century in the context of U.S. politics. The process began with my next article – also based upon my dissertation, but intended to compare the contemporary art that the four biggest Manhattan museums had exhibited and acquired during the '40s with what they'd acquired and were exhibiting in the '80s. To write this article, I had to look at (and take notes on) contemporary art as I hadn't done since I'd left *Time*. I found myself aware of the people with me in the museums, and I tried to figure out why they liked the art that was so popular, as well as why they had such trouble with the art that I admired. This was the beginning of my understanding of contemporary art's context.

The Met, the Guggenheim, MoMA, and the Whitney were crowded that August. The crowds gave an added jolt to my heightened mood, caused by writing such a daring, 9,800-word article in six days. I was sure my new theory marked a shift in thinking as radical as Copernicus's, and would change the course of art history, but all that these convictions did was to persuade Dr. I that my foray into dreamland between 1969 and 1971 had been the manic phase of a bipolar disorder, and that this must be a recurrence, so I should take lithium. Horrible stuff! True, my state of mind, after turning in my article on multireferential imagery, had some classic symptoms of mania, but the lithium didn't help. All it did was make my head feel like it was strung up on a wire. I had to have my blood tested regularly, because an overdose could kill me. My mother was terrified. I persuaded Dr. I to let me go off it, and rely on the tranquillizers to bring me back down to earth – which they did by Thanksgiving, with the aid of visits to a spa in Baja California and to relatives on the West Coast. I realized what a pressurized environment I'd been living in as a resident of the Big Apple.

My symptoms in 1983 were never as serious as those I'd suffered from when leaving *Time*. Besides my soon-quashed delusions of grandeur, they included only a few delusions of reference, plus weeks of waking early; being more outgoing socially; looking, thinking, and achieving insights at a fast and highly sensitized rate, plus "hypergraphia," which is the opposite of writer's block. All this led to a manuscript of 150 pages (about 52,000 words) on Manhattan museums. I began to research it right after July 18, when I'd given Martin my article on multireferential imagery. I sent him the new article (or rather, a Xerox of it) before I flew to Baja California on October 8. Soon after I got there, I became dissatisfied with it, called up Martin and told him to kill it. I can't remember why I was dissatisfied. Rereading it, I can see several possible reasons, but in any event, he'd never have had the space to run it uncut.

I was still clinging to aspects of the nonjudgmental stance that I'd cultivated in grad school, but also evolving out of it into a more critical mode, further outgrowing the academic niche that, without realizing it, I'd already started to abandon with my article on multireferential imagery. In that article, I'd tried to show how my theory correlated with the findings of fellow scholars. In this new one, I began to undermine authorities I'd read during my self-imposed apprenticeship, though their formulations did help me to develop new formulations of my own.

The article has big holes in research, and only the beginnings of thinking I've done since. I could see – and did say – that the leading neo-expressionists were borrowing stylistic tricks and an esthetic outlook from pop artists like Warhol and Lichtenstein, who'd first become famous in the '60s, and from Rauschenberg and Johns, who'd already attracted attention as "neo-dadaists" within the art world during the '50s. In other words, the neo-expressionists were really the second generation of what today I'd call "postmodernism," but in 1983, I didn't say that. I didn't refer to abstract expressionism and color-field painting as "modernism" (as I do today). Clem and his friends were saying that all the big names in neo-expressionism "had a little something" (most were at least painters, not makers of objects). With what remained of my nonjudgmental stance, in the article I referred to the artists of pop, neo-dada, and neo-expressionism as "good" artists, contrasting them with the "great" artists of abstract expressionism and color-field.

The problem that I was trying to report was the massive public preference for the second-rate art of the '60s and '80s, and the rejection of the first-rate art of the same period, but I still didn't see the emergence of this body of second-rate art as a trend. Today, I'd say that trend had begun as a trickle in the '50s (with Rauschenberg, Johns and, to a lesser extent, Larry Rivers). It had become a torrent by the '60s, with Warhol, Lichtenstein, and many others (including Oldenburg, George Segal, James Rosenquist, Tom Wesselman, and Jim Dine, among the figurative artists, and Frank Stella and Ellsworth Kelly among the "hard-edged" or "post-painterly" abstractionists). By 1983, postmodernism was a flood: the art world was drowning in neo-expressionism, but I still didn't see it a stage in a progression, and described it only as a static phenomenon.

As I said, I intended to compare the four museums' exhibitions and acquisition policies in the '40s with those of the '80s. Making the rounds of the museums, however, I dimly realized that this original plan had been predicated upon the same assumption upon which I'd based my earlier series about art criticism: the assumption that the '80s were like the '40s, that *plus ça change, plus c'est la même chose.* I also dimly realized that this assumption was wrong. The '80s weren't like the '40s. If they had been, only the good-but-not-great popular art of the '80s would have been on view, while the good-but-not-great popular art of the '50s and '60s would have joined the good-but-not-great popular art of the '40s in museum basements. This was not happening.

Work from the '50s and '60s by all the gods of what I'd now call postmodernism was proudly displayed, while their modernist contemporaries had been driven into storage. Among dozens of paintings on view in those museums in 1983, I saw only one by Frankenthaler, one by Noland, and two by Morris Louis. There were none by Olitski, Dzubas, Poons, or Jack Bush, the other leading modernists of that generation with whom I was familiar, and even when I knew that the museums owned paintings by them. I saw nothing by any younger modernist whom I knew.

One reason that Rauschenberg and Co. were receiving such preferential treatment was obviously that so many younger popular painters looked up to them as father figures. Another, even bigger reason had to be that they themselves were still so popular, still offering the public what they weren't getting from greater work. What could it be? Sometime that fall, I heard a remark that helped me answer that question. I can't remember where I heard it, but it was very simple: "Clem's like the pope."

This is not to say that for Clem or any of his friends, art was a religion. Clem himself always denied this, saying that art merely made life "more interesting." But whoever compared him with the pope instantly told me one big way that the '80s differed from the '40s. My dissertation had shown that all through the '40s, successive waves of more and more abstract art had brought the New York scene closer and closer to pure abstraction. That had been an innocent time, when most art lovers didn't know much about European art or modernism, and were accordingly willing to be instructed. Like pagans before the coming of Christianity, their naivete made possible conversion. New York in the '80s was a more jaded, cynical place, peopled by art-lovers who'd tried to appreciate abstract expressionism, but couldn't. With neo-dada and pop, they'd rejected multireferential imagery, and lapsed back into the uni-referential, so they were like religious recidivists, bitter and angry about the light that had failed and resistant to giving it a second chance. Even in the limited varieties of abstraction that they permitted themselves, negativity prevailed.

I was also writing the catalogue essay for a December exhibition in the Hillwood Art Gallery at C. W. Post. This show had been scheduled in late 1982, and was to deal with Rattner and his fellow figurative expressionists from the '40s. I wanted to do my best for them, but writing about truly great art over the summer had expanded my horizons. By August, I couldn't help but see how pathetically familiar and derivative almost all of the figurative '40s expressionists were. It was just a step to seeing much the same traits in the museums, with the neo-expressionists – and with the big names of the '60s. Sensitized by my mania, I could gaze at a painting from afar and almost intuitively sense its stylistic influences. I could see through these influences and subject matter to the attitudes behind them, what the artists had been saying with them (whether or not they'd known they were saying it). I could see how derivative most of these painters were, and how negative the attitudes they revealed.

At the Met, I'd seen *Man of Faith* (1983), by Georg Baselitz, a German neo-expressionist. Baselitz's image was of a man upside down. This reminded me of a 1947 painting with an upside-down figure in it by Philip Guston that I'd reproduced in my dissertation (in the '50s, Guston would become one of many second-generation abstract expressionists, but in the '40s he was still making representational work). I knew that upside-down figures had appeared in several paintings of the late '30s and early '40s by Max Beckmann, the German painter who'd come to fame before World War II and was sometimes classed as one of the original German Expressionists. This made the Baselitz image doubly familiar, though it could also be seen as disturbing, conveying uncertainty and a reversal of traditional values. I wrote, "The idea's not exactly new, but it's full of those fascinating literary, existential implications."[435]

Here was the first way I was challenging the authorities, by finding existentialism in the neo-expressionism of the '80s instead of the abstract expressionism of the '40s and '50s. I knew that existentialism was said to have been big in the art world during the heyday of abstract expressionism. Besides Donald Gordon's suggesting that I should have concerned myself with it in my dissertation, Sandler and Ashton had discussed it in their books on abstract expressionism.[436] The idea was apparently common in academia, to judge from talks I'd attended at College Art Association conventions, where speakers threw an abstract Pollock on the screen, and referred to "existential nothingness." This was Rosenberg's interpretation of Pollock, the idea that his canvas had only mattered as the site of an action – uniting the notion of existential *geste* or gesture with the art-as-act philosophy of dada. I knew that existentialism had been popular in intellectual circles in the '50s, outside the art world. Some of the brightest bohemians at Barnard had been wild about Sartre, but Pollock's paintings to me were far too richly steeped in the real world to qualify him for those two key existentialist attributes, "alienation" and "estrangement."

Nor did I see alienation and estrangement in most of the other abstract expressionists. I did perceive (and report) a bit of it in de Kooning and Barnett Newman, but the rest (and all the color-field painters) were to me characterized by a robust and heartfelt engagement with the world around them, shown not only through their warm, beautiful colors and visually pleasing shapes, but by the fact that their multireferential imagery fused or synthesized natural and cultural allusions. This insight had come to me after I'd given my first article to Martin. Initially, I'd been so excited to find that Dzubas had communicated images of objects to me through *Trough* that I hadn't stopped to think about the significance of those objects, but since then I'd realized that the science books and test tubes I'd been reminded of were cultural allusions, while the flat lands and cyclones pertained to the natural world.

This combination undermined or subverted Rosenblum's argument in *Modern Painting and the Northern Romantic Tradition* that abstract expressionism was descended from landscape, with its implied corollary that the movement was only about landscape. My idea undermined or subverted Steinberg, who in *Other Criteria* had suggested that the "flatbed picture plane" expressed a shift from nature to culture, with its implied corollary that pop, neo-dada, and their allied varieties of hard-edged abstraction (with its machine-made appearance) had preempted culture and relevance to society.[437] Both positions, with their implications that color-field painting was nothing more than "hedonism," had subliminally irked me for years.

My conviction (though I didn't say so) was that commentators (past and present) who'd found existential alienation and estrangement in abstract artists like Pollock were projecting upon these artists their own feelings of alienation and estrangement, caused by their own (unadmitted) inability to respond to Pollock and abstraction in general. For me, the painters who really qualified as alienated and estranged were those twentieth-century painters who, like Baselitz, still employed uni-referential imagery – in the '40s as well as the '80s. In 1949, when MoMA could have been tanking up on abstract expressionism at bargain prices, it had purchased Andrew Wyeth's adamantly realistic *Christina's World* (1948). This painting had become one of the museum's most popular. "Personally, it depresses me," I wrote in my 1983 article, "with its dreary, grayed-out colors, the colors of autumn and nature dying, and its mood of emptiness and alienation. Christina Olson was a cripple, and she's shown seated, reaching out toward a house on the horizon forever beyond her grasp. Is this the image that millions of Middle Americans identify with? What a sad commentary on the national quality of life and self-esteem. Still, in terms of style, the picture is nice and easy to understand, with its simple, old-fashioned uni-referential imagery – something to give the most naive museum-goer the satisfaction of feeling he or she can relate to art."[438]

With Wyeth (and Edward Hopper, whose equally uni-referential painting, *Gas* (1940), similarly depicted a lonely person in an isolated situation) the real reason for their existential angst to me was that they were out of step with the modern world simply by painting representational pictures. The neo-expressionist paintings of the '80s similarly capitalized on the public preference for the uni-referential. "There's nothing multireferential about the image," I wrote of the Baselitz. "It's the simpler, older type of imagery, uni-referential, the kind we've had around for the last four hundred years." Moreover, "the character has a sort of cartoony quality, something which has belonged to merely good art for a long time, and in this case probably comes right out of pop. Derivative, but for that very reason so easy to look at, and to relate to (much easier than less derivative art). And such fun."[439]

I also referred to Baselitz's color as "garish." This garishness (which he shared with some other neo-expressionists) was straight out of pop, which in turn had borrowed it from art designed to appeal to mass audiences. I did say, in discussing paintings by Lichtenstein at the Met and MoMA, that Lichtenstein's cartoon style was derived from the style of Milton Caniff, the cartoonist who created the comic strips of "Terry and the Pirates" and "Steve Canyon" (which I remembered from my youth, though I'd never particularly liked them). Thus, by imitating Lichtenstein's basic idea of using a comic-strip idiom, Baselitz (along with some other neo-expressionists) was being doubly derivative. Finally, Baselitz (again in common with other neo-expressionists) was using the sloppy, messy brushwork that I associated with de Kooning in the '50s, and his legions of "gestural" followers among the second-generation abstract expressionists – though as I also noted, many European painters in the '40s and '50s had likewise gone in for "the overloaded surface....All this messy brushwork is such an awful lot of fun," I continued. "So wonderfully amateurish that we can feel comfortably superior to it. I mean, this is *really* the kind of thing a kid could do....and then the pleasure of thinking existential thoughts flatters our egos on a second level. No wonder Baselitz is so popular (but popular ain't great)."[440]

To me, existentialism was negative, suggesting that all we can do is try to make the best of a bad situation, but the '80s (and the '60s) had other ways to convey this outlook besides disturbing uni-referential images. One way to reveal inner depression was by making more or less deliberately ugly art, and/or employing worn and/or perishable materials. An example at MoMA was Rauschenberg's combine painting, *First Landing Jump* (1961). I wrote that it was "especially grungy,...with a tacky brown khaki shirt and a tire and some kitchen enamelware and a live blue light bulb, all looking very disheveled and used, except the light bulb, which looks cute....All of these combines are just so flimsy, and made of perishable materials (I bet that little light bulb burns out regularly, even if it is turned off at night)....These objects were built for the moment, not for the ages – built upon the basically despairing (if perhaps unconscious) assumption that there would be no ages, so let's enjoy the moment while we can. Let's cheer ourselves up by making jokes about art and life, let's take the funny idea that flotsam and jetsam, the effluvia of the modern world, can be used to create art."[441]

Indeed, humor was perhaps the most important clue to inner depression – and anger. Besides the Rauschenberg, another example of it at MoMA was Johns's big *Map* (1961). "Oh, the colors are very pretty," I conceded, "kind of candy-box colors. And the brushwork is fine and the whole picture very well done. Johns is one of the best of the neo-dadaists, but he's still a neo-dada, with a ha-ha, let's-make-fun-of-modern-art sensibility. In *Map*, this attitude is there not only in those too-darling colors, but in the slick surface, and above all in the design of the U.S.A., and the names of all the states stenciled in, deliberately machine-made (echoes of Readymades). I find nothing multireferential about this image at all; on the contrary, it's very obvious, uni-referential, and all on the surface. No depth to it."[442]

Another example of humor was *The Marriage of Reason and Squalor* (1959), one of Stella's "pinstripe" paintings. It was "all depressing black, two sets of concentric rectangles on a large rectangular canvas, with those irritating little white lines separating the concentric rectangles." I called it "very black humor." Admittedly, it was multireferential, "but the associations I get are not the pleasantest, primarily because black is not such a happy color. Also, because the surface of the picture is so dead, and the lines so straight and mechanical."[443]

Previously, I'd discussed the differences in surface between good and great art, as seen in paintings at the Met. Merely good art went to extremes – messy brushwork like that of Baselitz, or the hard-edged, impersonal, mechanical surfaces of abstractions by Lichtenstein and Kelly. "Both extremes," I'd written, "leave me feeling totally uninvolved with the content. The type of paint application that does challenge me and involve me (and seems to put some other people off) is the one in the middle range, where the human hand has obviously been at work, but with a great deal of care and deliberation and thought. That's what really bugs a lot of people, and of course it's the kind of paint application that we find in all the greats in the modern tradition from Manet and the impressionists on through Pollock to Morris Louis." Louis's *Crest of Pillar* (1961) had been the only color-field painting on view at the Met, and its brightly colored, blazingly beautiful vertical stripes reminded me of a hand tensely open and scraped down a foggy windowpane, a cat's claw ripping into somebody's arm, all sorts of stalk-and-flower allusions, fluted Ionic columns, the pillar of smoke rising from either the atom bomb or the burning bush in the Bible, and the life-giving rain of heaven coming down. "These stripes are brilliantly cruel and lovely, at one and the same time," I'd concluded. "A simple statement, but enormously rich."[444]

The pinstripe Stella reminded me of nests of Chinese boxes, mazes, cell blocks in jails, and fortresses enclosed with walls and moats, "anything to keep a man from the outdoors and from freedom, and not an iota of landscape imagery in there anywhere, unless it's caves." This off-putting image was "deliberately (if no doubt unconsciously) designed to shock and offend the viewer, and then force him or her into approving it, because he or she has been conditioned into thinking all great art seems shocking at first. The joke's on the observer, because at first he or she doesn't think it's art. But the artist insists that it's art, and various authorities (such as MoMA) have conditioned the public into believing it's great art. Well, of course it's art. Anything is art, if the artist says it is. But the artist can't judge if it's great or merely good. That decision has to be made by the critic, the observer, and my opinion differs from MoMA's. To me, it's merely interesting, lesser art, and I say that because it's not beautiful, and not startling in the way that great art is – without the intention of startling.[445]

"It's also not as original as all that, because Duchamp was there long before Stella, making not pictures that looked like this, but creating art on the same principle – designed to shock and offend. *Fountain* is the most famous example, the urinal." Here I was challenging Kirk Varnedoe, my professor, who'd seen *Fountain* merely as the epitome of cerebration (though I'd also quote him on the frustrations inherent in the Readymades). I agreed that *Fountain* was "not unattractive as an object, very pretty clean white porcelain (tasteful). But so's a water pitcher, and so's a washstand. Why did Duchamp have to choose the urinal, if not for its excretory associations? This selection was consciously or unconsciously designed to shock the living bejesus out of everybody, and enable Duchamp to have the last laugh."[446]

Next, I introduced Freud's famous book, *Jokes and their Relation to the Unconscious* (1905).[447] I knew (and said) that there were newer discussions of humor, but that I found Freud most appropriate (as of 2008, I still do). He'd distinguished between two kinds of jokes, innocent and tendentious. Innocent jokes were funny in themselves. Tendentious jokes expressed repressed emotions, including sexual ones (obscene jokes), and aggression (both simple hostility and the skepticism and cynicism that underlay critical or blasphemous jokes, especially at the expense of authority figures and institutions). Tendentious jokes had a target. If you were the target (or sympathized with it), you weren't amused. Feminists might not laugh at sex jokes (obscene humor); Polish jokes didn't amuse Polish people (hostile humor); and jokes about Reagan didn't make true-blue Republicans laugh (critical or blasphemous humor).

Duchamp's humor, I said in 1983, was tendentious, and I quoted Varnedoe on the frustrations inherent in the Readymades as evidence of their hostility. More importantly, I concluded that the real target of Duchamp's humor had been the abstract art of his day, Analytic Cubism. It had mystified him so much that he'd felt he had to debunk it by satirizing all fine art (after *Fountain*, which had been sent to an art exhibition, his next most famous work was arguably the small reproduction of the *Mona Lisa* to which he'd added a beard and a mustache). The target of the neo-dadaists and pop artists had been abstract expressionism (most conspicuously when Rauschenberg erased a drawing by de Kooning, and Lichtenstein painted comic-strip versions of the abstract expressionist brush stroke). Abstract expressionism had mystified these artists, so they too had used humor to debunk it, but the art thus produced could only be good, not great, "because you can't be funny about art, and still do it greatly. You can't laugh at art, and still utilize it to the fullest. You've got to be serious, and laugh within an artistic context, if you're going to laugh."[448]

Given my sympathy with Analytic Cubism and abstract expressionism, I wasn't amused by dada and neo-dada, but most of my fellow museum-goers, I thought, must be mystified by abstraction, or they wouldn't be so enthusiastic about all this humor at its expense. While I'd been at the Guggenheim, taking notes on the cutesy sprig of mistletoe affixed to a painting by Anselm Kiefer (the most widely acclaimed German neo-expressionist), a younger art historian of my acquaintance had come up beside me. She'd started taking photographs of the Kiefer, evidently to show her classes. "I like this," she'd said. "My kids like it, too. It's such a relief after the high seriousness of abstract expressionism."[449] I didn't consider abstract expressionism "high seriousness." For me, it expressed normal seriousness, but if your norm was Kiefer, then by comparison, abstract expressionism must appear high.

I knew that there was a serious side to pop (and pop's related movements). Besides the respect accorded to them in magazines of contemporary art, many scholarly tracts had been devoted to explicating their deeper significance. But this seriousness reminded me of T. S. Eliot's essay on "Shakespeare and the Stoicism of Seneca" (1927). Stoicism was a philosophy popular in the ancient world when people had lost faith in the old gods, but hadn't yet accepted the new god of Christianity (Seneca was a Roman dramatist whose plays reflected this philosophy, and Shakespeare had probably read some of them in school). Eliot thought that stoicism was popular in Shakespeare's day because people were subliminally losing faith in Christianity, and feeling so alone and lost in the universe that they needed to cheer themselves up. Eliot called Nietzsche a prime example of "cheering oneself up."[450]

From the vantage point of 1983 and art history, I nominated Duchamp and his legions of artistic descendants as prime examples of cheering oneself up. I could also see how the art of cheering-up must strike a responsive chord in the museum-going audience, with the world situation as bad as it was, and the tensions and pressures of life in Manhattan. At the Whitney, I noted that "Robert Morris's suggestive mounds of dark gray felt strips writhe around on the floor, like a nest of pythons. I freaked out over those, back when I first saw them in 1968 (perhaps because I unconsciously realized I was working with a nest of pythons, at the office)."[451] I'd escaped my pythons, but how many people alongside of me in the museum could say the same?

At MoMA, I'd commented upon Elizabeth Murray's *Painter's Progress* (1981). "The colors are obvious," I'd written, "blatant nylon pinks and very commercial greens, sort of like a billiard table perhaps or an indoor swimming pool with a lot of chlorine. This is a painting with an urban sensibility, and no access to nature at all in its spectrum. Too many unfortunate people do have such limited horizons in our modern, urbanized society."[452] Great art was great because it offered viewers something beyond of their immediate environment, but that was also what made it difficult to relate to. Great abstraction offered no easy hooks like uni-referential imagery or familiar stylistic tricks and color schemes that corresponded to most museum-goers' daily lives. Great art was also more challenging than merely good art because of its greater capacity to reach the viewer on a gut level. Though it's not in the 1983 article, I'd never forgotten what Helen had said, when I'd written about her for *Time*. She'd compared looking at a painting and going to a concert. The difference was that no matter how moving the concert might be, it would end and you could leave, but a painting existed outside of time, so it might be able to move viewers on a deeper level than they wanted.[453]

The painters building on the great tradition of abstract expressionism, I wrote, "aren't funny-funny. Their work is serious – beautiful, sensually rewarding and emotionally satisfying – but not har-de-har-har. I don't know what the religious beliefs of most of them are, but their attitude toward life seems to be sufficiently affirmative so that they don't need to make jokes about art in their art. All of this, unfortunately, means that they're not big box office. You can't pack in the crowds with a Poons or a Dzubas exhibition, not in New York anyway. A few sensible, quiet art-lovers come, and of course a lot of younger artists. But mob scenes, no. This seems to make such shows undesirable with the Manhattan museums, all of which now charge admissions and need to hear the cash registers jingle."[454]

I described various ways that these museums were offering shows with popular rather than esthetic appeal, and implied that such policies were motivated by commercial considerations, but at the back of my mind, I was haunted by another point that Eliot had made in his essay on Shakespeare and Seneca. It's nowhere mentioned in my article, but Eliot compared Shakespeare, whose poetry had reflected the skepticism of the sixteenth century, with Dante, whose poetry had reflected the still firm and solid Christianity of the thirteenth century. He'd argued that if Shakespeare had been a better philosopher, he would have been a worse poet, because a poet's job was to express whatever philosophy dominated his own era, regardless of whether or not the philosophy itself was good. Did this mean that Rauschenberg and Co., because they better expressed the skepticism of the '80s, were better artists than Frankenthaler and Co., with their mellower outlook? It would take me years to resolve that issue.

It may have been that in 1983, I exaggerated the positivity of the painting I admired, out of my need to counteract the depressive elements in my situation, just as I had looked overmuch on the bright side of "Swinging London," back in 1966. Today I don't hit the affirmative angle so hard. I merely say that modernist abstraction (synthesizing nature with culture) expresses the modern era better than any other form of art in its difficulty, its complexity, and its incorporation of the vast storehouse of images that inhabit the modern mind – a far vaster storehouse than in previous centuries, because it includes not only sights seen directly, but also billions of images assimilated from books, magazines, newspapers, movies, television, and most recently, the Web. Some of these billions of images have positive associations. Some have negative ones, but truly great abstraction incorporates the entire range, adding up to a portrait of the artist's world in all its goodness and badness that is ultimately profoundly philosophic rather than either shallowly optimistic or shallowly pessimistic.

The 1983 article also describes the multireferential references I perceived in Mondrian, all the major abstract expressionists, and three more color-field painters, but I was only partially able to link up the images I perceived in these paintings with objects that the artists themselves could have seen. With Mondrian and the first-generation abstract expressionists, I had only published sources to rely on, and they weren't enough. With more recent painting, I'd tried to ask the artists themselves (or their widows) about their sources, but I wasn't getting many answers. None of these people wanted to help me. The prevailing attitude was that since my theory wasn't concerned with "quality" and didn't enhance "the esthetic experience," it was worthless (at best). If I couldn't discuss art in formal language, I'd be better off not discussing it at all. I'd asked Emmerich what he thought of my theory. He kissed it off with a remark to the effect of "Oh yes, let's get people seeing things in abstraction again." The word "again" made it clear that he'd missed the point of the article, and thought I was telling people to go back and look at abstraction the way they had in the '40s and '50s (when they'd approached it as resembling one thing or another thing, not many things at once).

Clem was furious with my article. When I called him in Norwich, he barked over the phone that I was "all fucked-up" and "a popularizer, like Barbara Rose." The bitingly angry voice in which he uttered these words instantly deflated my adulation of him to a much more matter-of-fact attitude; for the first time, I could identify with the anger of other people whom he must have snarled at. Still, he simmered down quickly, his most vocal complaint being that Pollock couldn't have made spaghetti sauce because he'd never had it at the Pollock house, and he'd been there to dinner many times. Friedman, my source for the sauce, had gotten it from an interview in *Art in America* with Lee Krasner, Pollock's wife. Short of having been in the kitchen myself, I couldn't imagine a more reliable source, so Clem and I continued to bat this around in correspondence for months.[455]

More seriously, he objected to my theory because it couldn't explain everything that a painting conveyed. I told him I was trying to convey the artists' "world picture" (from the "Elizabethan World Picture" of my college Shakespeare course).

> So what kind of philosophy did Titian or Goya or Manet or Phidias bounce off of? [he'd write, in a postcard of December 1984]. Of course they had a "world picture," but it wasn't to be labeled academically, which is what you want too much – if only in order to generate the correct kind of copy. What about *my* "philosophy"? Lay off the labeling. Those Abst Expists: so much rolled around in their heads, as in yours & mine. And how wd you label your "world picture"? Tell that before you try to tell any one else's.
>
> You can write, handle the language, yes indeed. Don't go off on wild goose chases.
>
> Love, Clem[456]

In my 1983 article, I argued my case with Clem and his friends. The aggravation I felt was compounded by the fact that I was making even less of an impression on the academics I'd hoped to reach. I'd sent copies of *Arts* with my article in it to scholars whom I'd thought might be sympathetic, but their responses were unsympathetic, nonexistent, or at best, exceedingly cautious. As I said in a letter to Anne Truitt, the sculptor (accompanying the copy of *Arts* that I sent her), it reminded me of my experience at Barnard. Just as the Jews there had considered me a Gentile, while the Gentiles considered me a Jew, so, too, the iconographers of academia disapproved of my formalist taste in art, while the formalists of the art world disapproved of my iconographic approach.

When I returned from the West, I was heartened to receive a long, beautiful letter from Truitt. She thought I was correct about multireferential imagery, and said she'd talked about it and written about it in *Daybook*, the only one of her three journals published by 1983.[457] At the same time, she tamped down my enthusiasm by explaining why I was getting such negative responses from artists, and warning me of the tremendous difficulties I would have in exploring the subject further. Emphasizing how difficult and mysterious the process of making art was, she underlined how anxious any probing into it must make the artists concerned, and urged me to treat the subject with the greatest possible tact and insight, lest I lose their sympathy altogether.[458]

Truitt visited New York that Thanksgiving, and in conversation told me how she'd assigned my article to students of hers at the University of Maryland. She also said something about how when she looked at one of her sculptures, she could see seventy or eighty things it reminded her of, dramatizing for me how many allusions there must be in every abstract work, and how unwise it was of me to limit them to just a few. I did a shorter article on Olitski the following spring, based upon a visit made to his summer home in New Hampshire over the Labor Day weekend (before he'd read the article on multireferential imagery). I tried to discuss his work with the reverence that Truitt recommended, and suggest that his paintings might contain as many allusions as Truitt saw in her sculpture. Both Jules and Clem liked the piece, but since that time, I'm often (though not always) cautious about employing multireferential imagery in discussing work by living artists, since the artists whose work appeals to me most tend to prefer formal language, and after all, their formal excellence is what really determines whether or not their work will survive.

Regardless of what Emmerich thought of my theory, he'd put me on his mailing list, and I was attending openings at his Fifty-seventh Street gallery for many artists I admired, or would come to know and admire: Helen, Ken, Jules, Larry Poons, Michael Steiner, Stanley Boxer, and James Wolfe. In 1984, I was invited to a show at Clayworks, a gallery in Greenwich Village run by James and Ann Walsh. The show was paintings by Jill Nathanson, a younger artist based in Boston. At the opening, I met her and Francine Tint, another younger painter. The Walshes were painters, in their early thirties, and among Clem's closest friends. Randy Bloom, another younger painter I met around then, invited me to her studio to look at her work. So did Tint, and so would Pat Lipsky, a modernist painter whom I met at an Emmerich opening in 1985.

At long last, I'd become a member in good standing of Clem's village, that cosy sub-subcommunity I'd glimpsed so enviously from afar in 1969. My writing had won me entree, beginning with my series on art criticism, and even my theory didn't disturb my friendship with Clem, perhaps because I still shared his taste. I met two more writers who also did, and contributed articles written from a formalist point of view to *Arts Magazine*: Darby Bannard, also a painter, and Valentin Tatransky, a tall, thin younger critic (Clem's word for him was "weedy"). I rarely saw Clem at openings, but he knew everybody I was meeting. If I wanted an address or phone number, I'd call him, and he'd give me the information within instants.

In the fall of 1984, I went to a symposium at the Whitney where he was one of the speakers. Afterwards, he invited me to join him and a group of his friends for lunch. There I renewed my acquaintance with Mike Steiner and met Gina Medcalf, an English painter. Both would invite me to their lofts. After lunch, Clem and I and one or two other people walked to Hunter College, where another younger English painter had a show. Clem circled the gallery, pointing at paintings he liked with little jabbing gestures. At Knoedler, Darby Bannard had a show. Clem wondered aloud how the biggest painting would look if hung upside down. It was comical to see how fast two gallery attendants rushed to reposition it. Finally, we had a drink at the New Westbury. "Try your hand at negative criticism," Clem said to me. "I'm working on it," I retorted, having already decided to turn my 150-page article into a series of shorter articles.

The introductory "overview" to this series appeared in *Arts Magazine* for January 1985, and an article on the Met in March. The piece on the Met was a revised segment of the longer manuscript, but the "overview" was all new. In it, I examined the increase in the population that went regularly to contemporary art museums, and the relation of academia to contemporary art. As I indicated in Chapter Ten of this book, I calculated that even as late as 1984, only about a million Americans attended museums of contemporary art regularly. The average museum-goer was apt to be more rather than less educated, and either a student or a white-collar worker (i.e., executive, professional, technical, salesperson, or clerical worker).[459] Besides documenting the rise in the college-educated population, I wrote, "In 1940, 31 percent of the U.S. work force, or

16,082,000 people, were engaged in white-collar occupations. In 1982, the comparable figure was 53 percent, or 53,470,000 people."[460]

In retrospect, I can understand the lack of academic response to my theory. I'd conceived it as a teaching tool, to help teachers find as much to say about abstraction as they did about representational art, but this was the first time I'd presented it, and the presentation wasn't perfect. Also, the theory is creative, and though art historians deal with creative artists, that doesn't necessarily mean they welcome creative art history. My biggest problem was that my theory undercut the whole rationale for postmodernism. The argument that abstraction depicts something (in fact, many things) deprives postmodernists of their justification for reacting back into uni-referential imagery, either traditional representation or Duchampian presentation. Similarly, the claim that abstraction depicts nothing makes minimalism like Tony Smith's black box into the ultimate abstraction, but if abstraction depicts something, then the ultimate in abstraction becomes modernism like that of Dzubas.

I hadn't worked all of this out in my mind by 1985, but in my "overview" I told how courses in contemporary art were commoner in colleges and universities than they'd been in 1940, how critics and curators were more likely to have advanced degrees, and how people attending contemporary art museums might have studied contemporary art in college. But, I added, "In discussing the contemporary scene, academics tend to follow the leads of the most sympathetic critics, the most successful museums, and the best-known artists. Thus, in effect, what we are dealing with is a never-ending circle of participants, the academics being only one more link in the growing chain."[461]

This conclusion came most directly out of two years of hunting (fruitlessly) for a full-time teaching job. I'd gone to conventions of the College Art Association, where besides attending talks, I was interviewed. Yes, I was older than most applicants. Yes, there were many more applicants than openings. Still, in the interviews, I found that colleges wanted teachers who'd boost enrollment: one way to do so was by teaching popular contemporary art such as neo-expressionism. In some of the talks (as well as one job interview), speakers tried to discredit Clem. To me, they were looking for ways to excuse the fact that they couldn't relate to abstractionists like Noland and Olitski.

The next article in my series would have been on MoMA, but before I could write it, Alvin Demick, publisher of *Arts*, died. He was the one who'd wanted Clem and Clem's friends in his magazine, though I'd always operated through Martin (with my *Time* upbringing on the separation between church and state). Now I couldn't even get Martin on the phone. He stopped asking Clem for manuscripts, and stopped publishing Valentin and most of Clem's other friends. I tried to sell shorter articles on contemporary modernists to other art magazines. No luck. Then, in the spring of 1986, my mother moved to what she always referred to as an "old ladies' home" in suburban Rye, New York. The atmosphere was stultifyingly provincial, and I could see she needed me, so I stopped applying for jobs outside New York City, though getting a full-time teaching job in or near it was next to impossible. Every modernist art historian wanted to be in the art capital of the world; the few advertised openings got hundreds of applications. I still went to openings, mingled with Clem's friends, and once ate Chinese takeout with him, Sarah, and her boyfriend of the moment. By 1985, Clem had fallen for Elizabeth Higdon, an art historian. It looked like they might get married, but by the following January, the romance was winding down, and Clem and I talked away the evening of his seventy-seventh birthday in the study of his Manhattan apartment.

In 1987, I was manic again because I couldn't get a job or published. At least, I thought, I could throw a whale of a party and I did, using the temporarily vacant studio apartment next door as well as my own. About fifty people came, including Clem and a lot of artists. In January 1989, he turned eighty. Jenny and Sarah threw a big birthday party for him, and I was invited. It was held in the Chelsea loft of a painter named Elyssa Rundle and her husband, Wright. Elyssa and I became friendly. Clem critiqued her work; for him she cooked pot roast and potato latkes, as well as singing songs he knew from his childhood. The Rundles had me to dinner occasionally with him, and Elyssa and I talked about him. I've always felt that everybody is somebody different with everybody they know, and Elyssa knew a different side of Clem from the one I knew.

In July 1989, my mother died at eighty-four. That same summer, Clem remarried Jenny; she continued to make me feel welcome at their apartment. My mother's death meant I could again look for out-of-town jobs, and by Christmas, I'd landed one at Bethany College in Bethany, West Virginia. Bethany was a private liberal arts college, so small that I would be its only art historian. It prided itself upon being "a teaching institution," meaning it didn't require even a minimum of publications for tenure. I would never need to publish another line if I didn't want to, and since it looked as though I never could, I was delighted to have landed this job.

20. Working Critic in the '90s
(Fall 1990–Spring 2000)

BETHANY OFFERED ONE course in art history, a one-semester survey from cave painting to soup cans, given in fall and spring semesters. My three other courses were ceramics (also offered twice a year), three-dimensional design, and sculpture. All three were "studio courses," where students made art instead of looking at slides of it. I taught myself to teach these courses, but halfway through my third year was told that my contract would only be renewed for one more. This was depressing, but I'd kept my apartment in Manhattan, subletting it during the school year, so I moved back to it in the summer of 1994. By autumn, I was asking myself, why did I ever leave?

My stay at Bethany had been pleasant. I'd played some hilarious bridge, and realized four longstanding ambitions: to teach full-time, learn to drive, live in a small town, and keep a cat (my New York apartments were never big enough for me and a cat). I liked talking with scholars in other disciplines, and a local psychiatrist introduced me to bupropion, a great drug that kept me from mania except in serious crises. Still, I'd compare the town of Bethany to Rovere, the town sociologists studied in the '40s for *Time*. Although Bethany's academics rendered its year-round population of under a thousand more intelligent and educated than most towns of that size, geographically and socially it was closer to the heartland than anywhere else I'd lived. Bethanians thought New York might be a great place to visit, but they wouldn't want to live there, and with the nearest museum forty miles away, interest in the visual arts was minimal.

Bethany felt far from world events. The Gulf War of 1990–91 came and went exclusively on TV, occasioning little if any comment from my colleagues that I can recall. George H. W. Bush was evidently determined not to let public opinion hamper him, and skillfully mobilized it behind him. Since Saddam Hussein had invaded Kuwait, we were defending a helpless ally, but victory didn't preclude the election of a Democratic President, Bill Clinton, the following November. I didn't follow that campaign or the next closely, knowing that I'd vote for Clinton. I was vaguely aware that he wanted to end welfare "as we know it," and that he would get the government on a sound financial basis, but I didn't think about the significance of these positions.

Once told I'd have to leave Bethany, I started the book that I assumed I'd have to start if I wanted a teaching job anywhere else. It was to be a scholarly presentation of my theory of multireferential imagery, applying it to Analytic Cubism, Mondrian, Pollock, and other abstract artists. I began working my way through the twenty-four volumes of *The Standard Edition of the Complete Psychological Works of Sigmund Freud* (getting to Volume Six, enough to see that it resembled the Bible in that not only I but anybody else could find support in it for pretty much anything they wanted to say). I hadn't taken any psychology courses at Barnard, having heard that its department frowned upon Freud and favored behaviorism, which involved helping people to alter habits by rewarding them when they did the right thing, and punishing them when they did the wrong one, as B. F. Skinner trained rats and pigeons. By 1993, I'd long since learned that Freud didn't have all the answers, and wanted to know more about other psychologies.

The chairman of the Bethany psych department was still a behaviorist, but another teacher in the department was a humanist, and the third (the one who told me this) was a social psychologist. After giving me two introductory textbooks sent to her by publishers (in hopes she'd assign them for courses), she said something about how she couldn't accept the idea of the unconscious, so in some ways, I thought, academia hadn't changed. I was more surprised that January. When serving as a committee member from outside the psych department examining a psych major taking his orals, I heard him questioned about defense mechanisms, those unconscious processes (denial, displacement, rationalization, and justification, etc.) that people undergo to ward off anxiety or psychic "unpleasure" caused either by internal conflicts or external circumstances. The student defined the term correctly. I thought that defense mechanisms had something to do with Freud, and, after the student had left, asked the chairman if this wasn't so. He said something like, "Well, after we've given them the obligatory trashing of Freud, we do tell them about defense mechanisms."

To finance my book, I applied for grants. I received none, but the National Endowment for the Humanities lets applicants get copies of the reports made by the readers who'd screened their proposals (with the readers' names deleted). From these reports, I learned that none of my readers had really understood my theory. One suggested that all I was doing was appropriating other people's ideas. A second complained that my Freudian "agenda" would further confuse my already "problematic" methodology. The third argued that even applying psychoanalytic principles wouldn't enable me to *know* that the images I perceived were embedded in the artist's unconscious. The fourth asked a lot of questions that could have been answered by the whole book, but not in the limited space allowed for the proposal. The fifth snottily complained that abstract art was already so well established that it didn't need more defenders. Indeed, the snotty tone was not far from any of these five reports.

What that first reader seemed to have been thinking of was the work of Harry Rand, William Agee, Gail Levin, and Rose-Carol Washton Long. As I knew from grad school, all had dealt with imagery in abstract painters, but none had discussed more than one or two artists, and all had found only uni-referential imagery, not multireferential. Another writer whom the reader might have meant was Anna Chave, who'd published *Mark Rothko: Subjects*, an exhibition catalogue, in October 1983, and *Mark Rothko: Subjects in Abstraction*, a book, in 1989. Chave argued that Rothko's paintings, which show horizontal rectangles of color on a vertical canvas, combined or conflated the conventional (horizontal) shape of a landscape with the conventional (vertical) shape of a portrait. The vertical, she said, also implied a Madonna-and-Child image, while the horizontal implied the dead Christ laid out on the lap of Mary in a Pietà or Entombment scene. This did nothing to challenge the conventional wisdom that abstract painting was all about art for art's sake, nor did Chave attribute any major role to the unconscious, or apply her ideas to any other artist.

Other writers in the '70s and '80s also dealt with "subject matter" in abstraction. This subject had been of interest to a generation of younger art historians eager to go beyond Clem and Rosenberg, younger art historians who perhaps had been subjected to the same injunctions in grad school to focus on "meaning" that I'd encountered, but no other scholar whom I've read (either then or since) came near to the comprehensiveness and radicality of my approach. Even in those extremely rare cases when they perceived more than one reference to external nature, they still behaved as though their observations applied to only one artist or small group of artists, the implication being that this artist or these artists weren't really abstract, and the definition of "true" pure abstraction being still that it made no reference to external nature.[462]

Then there was the NEH reader who disliked my Freudian "agenda" ("agenda" is always a hostile word, implying bias as opposed to scholarly detachment). I'd come up against this attitude before. In early 1994, at the CAA convention, I'd run into Francis V. O'Connor, the Pollock scholar. He told me about a long, controversial article attacking Freud that Frederick Crews had published in *The New York Review of Books* the previous November, and sent me a Xerox of it. It would take me a while to absorb, but already from what O'Connor told me, I realized that Freud was a no-no in some intellectual circles. The reader who complained that Freud wouldn't enable me to *know* that images were embedded in the artist's unconscious chose to ignore how much other art history is unproven speculation. Suppose a scholar wants to prove that Painter C was influenced by Painter D, when C has never admitted it. Even if the paintings of the two look alike, they may have been influenced by a common ancestor, so the scholar looks for places where C could have seen paintings by D, usually exhibitions by D in cities where C lived, and preferably at galleries or museums that C was known to frequent. Even if the scholar can find such shows, they still won't *prove* that C actually saw them, but (as long as the scholar isn't propounding anything controversial), such speculation is usually considered quite an acceptable substitute for proof.

Admittedly, I wasn't presenting my theory as clearly in those early proposals as I can today. But the fact that I hadn't been understood bothered me less than the nastiness in these reports: it suggested that even if I'd made my ideas clear, they'd still have been rejected. Perhaps this attitude was best explained by how I'd set up Rauschenberg, the archetypal postmodernist, as an artist whom my theory challenged. He'd famously said that "Painting relates to both art and life....(I try to act in that gap between the two)."463 This, I felt, was based upon the assumption that there was a gap between abstract painting and the real world that could only be closed by reverting to figuration, as he'd done, but my theory closed the gap without resorting to dada, rendering postmodernism superfluous. Nowhere in my proposals had I mentioned Clem or color-field painting, but those readers seem to have sensed that my theory might enhance the standing of this group of painters – or so I surmised, seeing how similar their nastiness was to how Clem's ideas had so often (though not always) been greeted.

I could see that this nastiness would create problems in getting my book published. If I sent a proposal to a university press, they'd send it out for "peer review" to more readers who were virtually guaranteed to be equally postmodernist and unsympathetic. Even if their rejections were as illogical as were the complaints of those NEH readers, the press's editors would still consider them indications of what kind of sales potential the book might have. University presses don't have to make big bucks with every book they publish, but they must have an audience of some sort, and neither the postmodernists who dominated academia nor fellow modernists who shared Clem's antipathy to my theory would buy a scholarly book all about it.

I'd kept in touch with Clem and Elyssa Rundle over vacations and by phone while I was teaching at Bethany. I had drinks with Clem when I was in town, and the Rundles continued to invite him and me to dinner, or we all went out to eat together. Twice, the party included Valentin; once, Jim and Annie Walsh. Elyssa invited me for studio visits. From those, and my other studio visits, I learned more about how Clem behaved on his studio visits, and the paintings he liked best (always the most far-out). Abstract paintings can be hung with any one of four sides up. By turning them around, you figure out which way "works" best. Most paintings I was looking at had been painted on unstretched canvases, laid on the floor, so when each painting was tacked up on the wall (with a stapling gun) you could also see whether it would benefit from being cropped along this, that, or the other side, and how wide the crop should be.

Clem had a sure eye for the best way to hang an abstract canvas, and he knew just when and how much to crop, but he often had other comments and suggestions to offer (again, always the unexpected). Larry Poons had told me how in 1971, Clem had been in his studio, and admired the way some paint had splashed off the canvas onto an adjoining space. Poons began to set his canvases upright, pouring the paint so that it coursed down the entire canvas and radically revised his work.[464] In a 1978 interview, Clem himself told how in 1957 he'd liked the watercolors Jack Bush was making in his Toronto studio better than he'd liked his oils, and suggested that Bush apply his oils more thinly; again, it revolutionized the artist's style.[465] In 1985, I'd been in an apartment on Third Avenue with Clem, some other people, and a small constructed sculpture by the young artist who lived there. With a gesture of his arm, Clem asked what that extra piece on the right side of the sculpture was for. The young sculptor immediately seized a saw and eagerly sawed the piece off.

A voluptuary, Clem got sensuous pleasure from beautiful art that was somehow related to his appetite for beautiful women. I realized this when I saw a show of nudes by Horacio Torres, a representational painter whom he'd admired. I'd never really understood this artist's appeal for Clem, and wasn't bowled over by this show with its heavy, placid, cow-like females, but their skin was rendered with such a delicate, silvery, satiny texture that I could see how its physical appeal shaded off into the purely esthetic, and told me how passionately Clem loved beauty in all its forms.

He wasn't well. His longtime habit of a pack of Camels a day was catching up with him, and he suffered coughing fits so severe that he had to be taken to the hospital. He said it was asthma, and was given steroids, which is a treatment for asthma, but when he died, his obituary in the *Times* would give the cause of death as emphysema. Whichever it was, the coughing subsided when he couldn't smoke in the hospital. When he got out, he'd stay off the cigarettes for a while, but then go back to them, so he'd be back in the hospital again. In the summer of 1993, he was in the hospital, recovering from an attack, and fell and broke his pelvis. They strung him up in traction, but his lungs filled up in that stationary position and he developed pneumonia. He was very sick, and I and other friends came in to see where Jenny and Sarah were looking after him. Jenny let me feed him dinner one night, while she and Sarah slipped out for a while. He looked so frail in that big hospital bed. It was like a momma bird feeding a baby bird. He'd open his mouth, in an unguarded moment, and I'd pop a teeny piece of hamburger into it.

After I'd gone back to Bethany for the school year, Jenny brought him home, but his hip hadn't healed properly, and he could only get around on a walker. Most of the time, I gathered, he didn't leave his bedroom. I saw him once when I was in New York at Christmas, and twice when I came to New York for the CAA convention in February. In one of my February visits, he was sitting in the living room, being interviewed by a young lady from USC doing a dissertation on the philosophy of Rothko, or some such weighty topic. Clem was maintaining that Rothko's conversation was "banal," and that he himself didn't remember any discussions about philosophy (much as he had in 1983, when I'd asked him about existentialism).

In May, Elyssa called me and told me he was dying. A little later, Jenny called. Then she called again, to say he was dead, and invite me to join her and Sarah for a gathering at the apartment that Wednesday. Clem's body was to be cremated, and the following year, there would also be a big formal memorial for him at the Century Club, but on Wednesday, it was a smallish group, with photograph albums laid out, showing lots of photos of him. Jenny said that people had been coming up to her and saying, "He changed my life." He certainly changed mine, and I'd spend the last part of 1994 and the beginning of 1995 exorcizing my grief by writing out a memoir of him.

I didn't think that anybody would hire a 59-year-old assistant professor, but anyway, I wanted to focus on my book about multireferential imagery, and the modest income I received from my mother's estate meant that I didn't have to work in order to eat. In early 1995, I visited the Pollock–Krasner House and Study Center in The Springs on Long Island, where Pollock and Krasner had lived, and photographed its surroundings. Helen A. Harrison, the center's director, invited me to give a talk on Pollock and multireferential imagery there in the summer of 1995. This required updating myself on Pollock scholarship.

Not all the books I found rejected a psychoanalytic methodology, but that didn't mean they arrived at the same conclusions that I did. Donald Kuspit, whose outlook on Freud was influenced by D. W. Winnicott and the "object relations" school of psychoanalysis, wrote that Pollock "tended more to the psychotic than the neurotic."[466] He added that in his opinion, Pollock's "sense of meaninglessness becomes dominant and overt in the allover paintings, which is what makes them truly untranslatable and uninterpretable."[467] Michael Leja, something of a social historian, attacked the very concept of the unconscious, calling it "a conceptual construction socially determined," and citing the sociologist Peter Berger as a source for this approach.[468] If I could collaborate with a neurologist, I thought, I bet we'd be able to establish a scientific basis for enough of the unconscious to substantiate my theory, but I didn't know any neurologists, and suspected that even if I did, Leja and his fellow postmodernist art historians would find some other pretext to dismiss my ideas.

In the spring of 1995, I'd also gone to Paris and taken photographs in Montmartre, where Picasso and Braque together had created Analytic Cubism between 1907 and 1912. I'd last visited Paris in 1993, and both times stayed with my stepsister, Beth Herwood, whose apartment was in Montmartre, near where the two artists had lived. Montmartre is a hill. Its crooked little streets run up and down, and the irregularly shaped little buildings facing them are set at odd angles with each other. In 1993, it had hit me that these were the visual sources for the straight lines and boxy or angular shapes that had come to dominate the canvases of Picasso and Braque during this period, and led to their style being dubbed "cubism." Likewise, the grays, blacks, and browns of the streets and buildings of Montmartre were to me the source for the "hermetic" color schemes of Analytic Cubism. Braque and Picasso had unconsciously synthesized this urban landscape into paintings consciously intended to depict nothing more than traditional figure studies, still lifes, and landscapes. By so doing, they'd integrated the twentieth-century urban world into their canvases both before, and more completely than, futurists like Boccioni and Puteaux Cubists like Léger and Delaunay.

At least seven experiences had themselves been synthesized by my unconscious to arrive at this insight. Besides clambering around Montmartre myself, there was what I'd learned from Varnedoe and Reff in grad school; a passage Clem had written in 1942 about cubism; *Pablo Picasso: A Retrospective* (1980) and *Picasso and Braque: Pioneering Cubism* (1989), two great shows (organized by Bill Rubin) at MoMA; and a passage in Michel Seuphor's monograph on Mondrian published in New York in the '50s. My conclusion again ran counter to the conventional wisdom, so it brought me no closer to a university press, but as I was no longer thinking in terms of tenure-track jobs, my ideas about my book were becoming more fluid. An art-book publisher might feel freer of academic constraints, I thought, and in the fall of 1995, through a friend, I sent a proposal to one. It was rejected, but the friend got me a copy of the report made by one of its in-house readers. This reader spoke of my "disarming naivete" in thinking that my theory was new or original, but as my supposed antecedents, she made only vague references to Rothko and Kandinsky. This told me that she, too, was confusing my ideas with those of Chave and Washton Long.

Around the same time, I'd also sent a copy of my Pollock talk to Editor Q, a friend of a friend who worked for a trade publisher. Since trade houses publish books for the general reader, I don't know what I expected from him, but I got a kind letter back. Although he'd found my talk very interesting, he wouldn't want to do a book about it because the market for books about art was so small. All the same, he'd been more sympathetic than the NEH readers or the art-book publisher's reader, making me think my best shot would be to broaden out my book so that it would appeal to the general reader, thereby making it a paying proposition for a trade publisher. What about a narrative, I thought, telling how I'd developed my theory – a memoir, in other words? I knew that some ideas behind my theory went back to my years on *Time*, and (from trying to sell my "novel" about *Time* in the '70s) that publishers would at least read manuscripts about *Time*, so in early 1996, I started the book you're reading now.

At first, I felt very alone. I tried to confirm or correct my memories of my childhood and adolescence with library research, but the material I dug up made me remember what an outsider I'd been then, neither WASP nor Hungarian, neither Gentile nor Jew. My feeling of isolation was exacerbated by the art scene. Right after Clem died, even well-known artists he'd admired couldn't get New York shows, and/or saw sales drop to nothing. As for younger and lesser-known ones – forget it. During the 1995–96 season, I saw only one show I liked, by Randy Bloom, at the Gershwin Gallery in March. The gallery was in a budget hotel with ersatz pop art in its lobby and dormitories for wannabe showbiz types. Shortly afterward, I met an editor on *lingo*, a new arts magazine, and got him interested in a story on Bloom, but he was more interested in the hotel. Back and forth went the manuscript, he demanding more and more about the hotel and less and less about Bloom. I hadn't done this much rewriting as a junior writer on *Time*, but I hadn't published anything about contemporary art since 1985, so I hung in there, and assuaged my rage by keeping Bloom posted. Finally, the editor was satisfied, but the article wouldn't be published for more than a year.

Obviously, I thought, my upbringing must have been terribly unusual, if I was nearly the only surviving modernist. Most of U.S. society must have been raised very differently, if so many went for postmodernist art. I dealt with this situation in a talk I gave that October at the National Museum of American Art on "An Atypically Modernist Childhood: How Does It Play Today?" For it, I dug out the *Life* article from 1949 picturing the differences between highbrows, upper middlebrows, lower middlebrows and lowbrows. I read the article by Russell Lynes in *Harper's Magazine* that the *Life* article had been based on. My mother had been an upper middlebrow. North Country had been highbrow. But highbrows and upper middlebrows were only a segment of the population. What about the lower middlebrows and especially the lowbrows?

Further research indicated that millions of Americans my age and slightly older had most likely been served Campbell's soup out of a can by their mothers when they were children, sitting in the family kitchen, just as Andy Warhol had.[469] Millions of children my age and slightly older must have read comic strips or comic books, as Roy Lichtenstein almost certainly did.[470] Both practices were commonest among lowbrows and lower middlebrows. When such people grew up, soup cans and the comics would still have been familiar icons from their childhoods, so they must have augmented the upper-middlebrow market for pop art in the '60s. I had no idea how lowbrow and lower-middlebrow children could have become upper-middlebrow adults, but at North Country soup had been served in our International Style dining room out of handsome ceramic crocks (even if out in the kitchen it had come originally in cans, I never saw the cans). The only time I got to read comic books was during the train trips to and from school. Not Superman but Ed Bley's Picassoid doodles had been my icons.

In my talk at the NMAA, I showed slides comparing my cultural experience with that of the all-American average, using family and school photographs to portray my background and the average represented by Norman Rockwells. *Freedom from Want*, his World War II propaganda poster, showed a bespectacled, motherly woman putting a turkey on the table, with fluffy, lower-middlebrow white window curtains behind her that reminded me of my aunt Emily's home in suburban New Jersey. They contrasted vividly with the elegant, upper-middlebrow, floor-to-ceiling yellow chiffon curtains in my mother's Manhattan apartment. A Rockwell image of little girls showed them wearing skirts, as did most little girls did in those days. It contrasted equally vividly with the blue jeans that girls as well as boys had worn at North Country (we were decades ahead of the times).

Back in Manhattan, I learned that Bloom had pondered my problems with *lingo*, and invited me to write an art column for the online edition of *a gathering of the tribes*, a little magazine for which she was the online editor. The first issue of *From the Mayor's Doorstep* was dated November 1, 1996. I chose the name partly because I lived two doors down from Gracie Mansion, official residence of New York mayors, and partly to suggest I was carrying on with what the mayor of Clem's village (i.e., Clem) would have wished. Bloom put my column online, but I didn't feel comfortable reviewing her shows when she was my "editor." She never altered a word, but people might think she was doing so, or that I was on the take from her. In the summer of 1997, I found John Kois in the yellow pages, a great guy who provided computer services for small businesses, and hired him to put me online instead. I also instituted a "print edition," and two fledgling magazines, *NYArts* and *Night*, published excerpts from the column.

From the Mayor's Doorstep took a lot of time. The column came out seven times a year, at six-week intervals during the art season. This meant devoting three to four out of every six weeks going to galleries and museums, then writing the column and sending out the print edition. It slowed up the book, but I enjoyed praising the few good shows and lampooning the many poor ones in Chelsea, which by the mid-'90s had taken over from SoHo as the center of hot younger art. At least, all the other critics who dealt with such art on an ongoing basis thought it was hot. To me, it was lukewarm, third-generation neo-dada, overblown but weak imitations of work I'd seen back when I was on *Time*. Neo-expressionism was gone with the wind, as were two short-lived fads of the later '80s called "neo-geo" and "appropriations." Both had been essentially old wine in new bottles. The former, best exemplified by the oft-forgotten paintings of Peter Halley, was a variant upon minimalism. The latter, whose stars were (and are) Jeff Koons and Jenny Holzer, might be described as "neo-pop": bigger, shinier versions of pop and conceptual art's practices of copying older art, images and/or lettering from the mass media and advertising.

In 1986, I'd read an article in *Arts Magazine* by Roni Feinstein on the "white paintings" that Rauschenberg had made in 1951 and exhibited at the Stable Gallery in 1953.[471] This article told me exactly where and when the postmodernist reaction against modernism began. Rauschenberg's all-white paintings, made with rollers and completely bare of any human incident, seem to have been a response to the nearly monochromatic paintings that Barnett Newman, the last of the great first-generation abstract expressionists to enter the public arena, had exhibited in his second solo exhibition in 1951. Newman's paintings, with a single or occasional vertical bands of color down their centers, had gone Pollock one better in the matter of abstraction, but they were still paintings with surfaces and incident clearly made by a human hand. Rauschenberg was out to go Newman one better, to carry the premise of abstract expressionism to a logical but ridiculous extreme, to expose it in other words, and this same reductio ad absurdum mentality underlay almost all minimal art, endowing it to me with the same sarcasm and hostility as other forms of postmodernism.

By the late '90s and early twenty-first century, object art and "installations" were in vogue. Object art resembled '60s assemblages (of assorted elements), while installations (roomfuls of objects, photographs, etc.) looked to me like updated versions of what we used to call "environments" in the '60s. Postmodernist abstract painting was also around, but the buzzword for it was "irony," and visual irony was feeble stuff. Photography was popular, as were videos and conceptualist art made out of writing. All three of these modes were just as uni-referential as object art and environments. Not one of the five expanded viewers' horizons into the multireferential. All of this art (except for its pathetic abstractions) could be described in words, which is to say they appealed to viewers' rational or thinking minds. None (again, except perhaps for the abstractions) really attempted to move them on a deeper, emotional level All of it was so fundamentally stale and familiar that it didn't surprise me to find three eminent critics giving their latest books titles suggesting that art history had come to an end (though actually none of the three meant precisely what I did, for I thought in terms of stylistic development and they all had different themes in mind).[472]

Taking the dismal postmodernist scene to pieces got me known in the art world, if not loved, like Clem (though on a far more modest scale). Often with him, always with me, other critics referred to us in code. With Clem, it had been "formalism," "The Establishment," "fashionable art," and "influential critics" (implying that influence was being wielded upon behalf of unworthy art). With me, the references were to "old-fashioned," "historical" or "obsolete" art, "grandmothers," and being "on the margin," but hey, I didn't know any other art critics who stood out enough to rate even negative attention – and I didn't (and don't) consider myself old-fashioned. To me (as I said in my Introduction) modernist abstraction was (and is) still the most radical art we have. Postmodernism's reaction against it, back into uni-referential imagery, was (and is) what's really backward-looking. My detractors may say that I haven't evolved with the times; I say that I have evolved – and developed – but in a different direction from theirs.

By the later '90s, the great artists from the '60s (Frankenthaler, Noland, Olitski, Louis, Caro) were getting more exposure, but I also wrote about those younger and/or lesser-known modernists, reviewing their shows or visiting their studios if they hadn't had a show. Because of them, I didn't feel so alone, and, since their backgrounds varied, I saw that it wasn't necessary to have had an upbringing like mine in order to make or respond to the best contemporary art. Among the younger and lesser-known artists I met or came to know better during this period were Stephen Achimore, Lucy Baker, Thomas Barron, Willard Boepple, Frank Bowling, Peter Bradley, Robert Christie, Paula DeLuccia, Joseph Drapell, David Evison, Terry Fenton, Jonathan Forrest, John Adams Griefen, Charles Hewlings, Peter Hide, George Hofmann, Darryl Hughto, Terrence Keller, John King, Roy Lerner, Anne Low, Sheila Luck, Gina Medcalf, Marjorie Minkin, Jill Nathanson, Irene Neal, Lauren Olitski, Susan Roth, Mitchel Smith, Arthur Yanoff, and more.

I continued to revise my theory of multireferential imagery (Graham Wallas might have called this process "verification"). While at Bethany, I'd heard discussions of deconstruction, a method of literary interpretation that had been chic among art historians in the '70s and '80s, but otherwise, I'd been remote from art-historical action, undergoing a period of what Wallas might have called "incubation." This had let less essential ideas drop from memory, while more essential ones automatically reshuffled themselves below my level of consciousness. In 2005, I presented the latest version of my theory in another talk at the Pollock-Krasner House and Study Center. It began with Figure 1, the diagram I showed and discussed in my Introduction. Next, I continued with Figure 2:

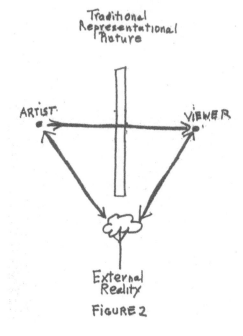

Here you see what happens with traditional representation. We are at right angles to the canvas, and on the canvas is a tree. The painter has seen the tree. That is why she or he can paint it. The viewer has also seen a tree. That is why he or she can recognize it. The canvas is like a window, through which the artist communicates with the viewer by way of his image, since it refers to an object that both have seen.

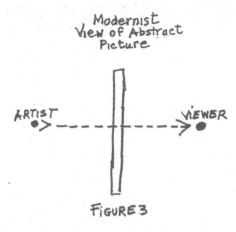

In Figures 3 and 4, I contrast the responses to a pure abstraction by modernists and postmodernists. Figure 3 shows the modernist response. Neither artist nor viewer believe the single vertical line on the canvas depicts anything, but both believe that something created by the artist is evoking a response in the observer, even if neither can define what is being evoked in words. The window is still a window.

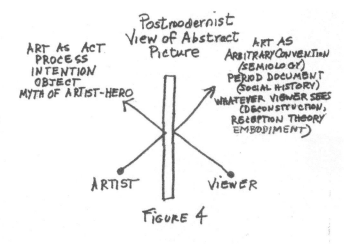

Figure 4 (slightly updated for this book) shows the postmodernist response to abstraction, by people who cannot send or receive any sort of communication through it. Both artist and viewer think the vertical line depicts nothing, and therefore means nothing. It has no intrinsic content, meaning or value for them, but, since it must be accepted as art, all definitions

311

of art must be adjusted to accommodate the assumption that a meaningless, valueless, content-less object can be art. The window of the painting has been changed into two back-to-back mirrors, with the artist forced to fall back upon rationales other than communication for making art, and viewers forced to find other rationales for looking at or writing about it.

On the left are ways that postmodernist artists from Duchamp onward have accommodated themselves to the idea that art in itself means nothing. First, there is the idea of art as act: taking a urinal from a men's room or the image of a soup can out of an advertisement, then sending either to an art show and by this act, defining them as art. Since the emphasis is upon the act of moving the object from its original context to the art gallery or museum, it relegates the work itself to minimal importance and puts into play the fourth dimension: time. This opens the way to various forms of moving art, from kinetic sculpture to videos.

Second, we have art as process, in which the work is permanently in the process of being made, like the loose felt that Robert Morris began exhibiting in the late '60s, or the piles of objects (such as rocks or candies) that other artists have exhibited since.

Third, we have art as intention, where the artist describes what the work of art is supposed to represent, instead of representing it: conceptual art that incorporates writing instead of imagery, and hence (since the eyes must move from word to word) again introducing the temporal or linear element.

Fourth, art as object, in which even an abstract painting is executed so mechanically that it loses all human characteristics and becomes a purely decorative, soulless object.

Finally, the myth of the artist-hero: Pollock in the act of painting (Rosenberg's idea of what was really important about his art), or the performance artists who stage demonstrations of various sorts in which any visual byproducts are purely secondary. In fact, with all variations on the idea of art as act, the art itself is only rarely esthetically pleasing – but then it isn't supposed to be; it doesn't have to be. If it's ugly enough to shock, all the better.

On the right are some of many bewildering post- or anti-Freudian methodologies that postmodernist art historians have employed since I was in grad school. I don't pretend to have studied them in depth, but it seems to me that they mostly boil down to ways to discuss art that is believed to communicate nothing: semiology, social history (incorporating Neo-Marxism), deconstruction, reception theory, and the phenomenology of Maurice Merleau-Ponty, with its concept of "embodiment."

Modern semiology was developed more in relation to written or spoken language than to imagery, and language is arbitrary convention. There's no reason for you and me to say "cat" except that we both speak English, and English-speaking peoples have agreed that those three letters designate the animal that French-speaking people have similarly agreed to call "chat," and German-speaking people call "Katze." Semiologists, seeing no relationship between pure abstraction and any source in nature, tend to look upon it – and all visual art – similarly as arbitrary convention (at any rate, if their orientation is toward the more prestigious European linguistics of Ferdinand de Saussure, not the less prestigious American semiotics of Charles Sanders Peirce).

Social historians see art primarily as historical document and/or commodity. They tend to downplay formal values and may reject psychological interpretations, as these attribute meaning to the work of art, speak to the distinctive qualities of the individual artist, and deflect attention from her or his role as cog in the machinery of the art market, or political pawn, or spokesperson in the hierarchy of gender, race, and/or class.

Deconstruction, reception theory, and embodiment emphasize the impossibility of knowing what the artist is really up to, elevating the viewer to prime importance and relegating the artist to a secondary role. All these schools, from semiology to embodiment, emphasize "context," suggesting that art can only be understood in relation to the time and place where it was made, and by implication if not outright fiat, where, when, and by whom it is to be viewed.

There's some truth to all of this, just as Duchampian art isn't always ugly, but to the extent that such artists and scholars deny any references to the natural world, claim that nothing can be communicated by the artist to the viewer, and insist that art can't be appreciated if you don't know the context in which it was created, they come up short.[473]

In Figure 5 , you see how multireferential imagery works, though

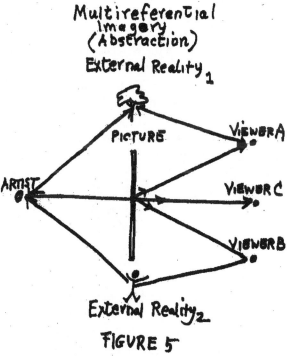

FIGURE 5

I oversimplify it. At the top, viewer A looks at the vertical line on the canvas and thinks it resembles a tree. The artist has seen many trees, and that is why the essence of tree is incorporated into the abstraction, and by it, communicated to Viewer A. Viewer B, at the bottom, thinks the vertical line looks like a standing person, and the artist has seen many people as well, so in this case the experience of standing humans is communicated. C, in the middle, sees the painting as the painter wanted it seen: as a single vertical line.

For some viewers, the insight of C comes easily, without recourse to my theory. Others, I hope, may be enabled to graduate to it because they no longer feel under pressure to do so. Instead of being treated like simpletons if they don't accept the idea that the painting depicts nothing, they are allowed to know that the painting may resemble something they've seen in the external world; paradoxically, knowing this might make it easier for them to cease to rely upon the knowledge. I only hope that such viewers can also accept the idea that what they're reminded of is not the only association that the line may have, and that somebody else may with equal justice be reminded of something different (this may be difficult, given the common resistance to ambiguity).

When I gave this talk in 2005, Helen Harrison pointed out that people can see many different things in clouds, too. I agree that there are some situations when a supposed window is in fact a mirror, and the images that a viewer sees in it relate only to that viewer's experience. This would be true with clouds, or the stain on the wall that Leonardo da Vinci talked about, or with any other marks made by nonhuman means. But, by the same token, when you do have a work made by a person, you must admit that your perception of it is at least in part influenced by that person's input.

Sometimes an observer has a hostile association to an abstract painting. These, too, are valid, but commoner when people dislike the painting (Gombrich, associating Pollock's paintings with "the intricate and ugly shapes with which industrial civilization surrounds us"). When people like an abstract painting, they're more apt to associate it with pleasant things (Ellen Johnson, seeing "nature" in Pollock). Somebody who associates a Mondrian with computer innards is clearly wide of the mark, since Mondrian never saw a computer. The association can only be with something similar he could have seen – the insides of an old radio or the wiring on the back of an illuminated street sign, for example.

In other words, the subject matter of a multireferential painting is time- and space-bound, but this is true of uni-referential painting, too. People today looking at a fifteenth-century Netherlandish Annunciation won't know that its garden enclosed and vase of lilies allude to the virginity and purity of Mary unless they've taken a course in the subject, or listened to a museum docent, but upper-class fifteenth-century Netherlanders might well have recognized these allusions without course or docent. That's why the responses of those benighted New York critics in the '40s to Pollock's paintings are so valuable: because they saw the same external world that he did. Pollock's twentieth-century world has begun to pass, as Flanders did, yet we still enjoy looking at both kinds of paintings because their capacity to transcend space and time doesn't ultimately depend upon their subject matter, but rather upon their style, the way they look. I haven't so far been able to find multireferential imagery in every abstract painting I've liked, but that doesn't bother me, any more than does the fact that I have found multireferential imagery in postmodernist paintings that I disliked, because what really determines the excellence of a work of art is its formal values, not what it depicts, but how. There have been many great paintings of Satan, and many awfully wooden ones of God. In other words, multireferential imagery is value-neutral, as all subject matter is value-neutral, in uni-referential paintings as well.

Why do I bother with multireferential imagery, if it's time- and space-bound, and doesn't tell me whether a painting is good or bad? Because any good interpretation of a work of art can heighten our enjoyment of it. True, some people can appreciate a painting without understanding it on an intellectual level. Clem could, and his friends could (and can), as well as some people beyond his immediate circle. I've more than once heard about the handyman or cleaning lady who comes to an abstract painter's studio and praises the paintings he or she sees there, but I'm afraid that this aptitude is only possessed by a small percentage of the total number of people sufficiently interested in art to go to exhibitions and/or buy it. Otherwise, postmodernism wouldn't enjoy the overwhelming support that it does.

Many, maybe most people can't respond at all to an abstract painting because they don't know intellectually what it's "about." They may respect it, but that doesn't mean they're able to love it. When they do know intellectually that it does have subject matter, they may be able to relax and respond more warmly and intuitively to its style. I can't promise that this will happen with everybody, but something like it happened with me right after I discovered my theory. The experience also made it easier for me to distinguish between better and worse abstraction, another outcome that I'd hope even more keenly may be shared by people who now think they can respond emotionally to abstraction, but still favor second- and even third-rate varieties of it. I dream that my theory may be able to elevate the level of public taste.

In January 2000 I'd already used my online review of the Modern*Starts* exhibition at MoMA to sketch a relation between Analytic Cubism and Montmartre cityscape. Modern*Starts* had a gallery on the "Unreal City," but no Analytic Cubism in it, and, as I wrote, "the whole gallery should have been built around Picasso's and Braque's Analytic Cubism, because that's where the whole idea of cubism as an expression of the urban environment begins."[474] *"Ma Jolie,"* the masterpiece of Analytic Cubism I'd cited in my 1983 article, was included in April 2000 in another MoMA show, *Seeing Double* (organized by Peter Galassi). In my review, I discussed this painting. As late as 1989, MoMA had subtitled it *Woman with a Zither or Guitar.*[475] Now it had no subtitle. A letter by Picasso that MoMA published in 1992 showed that Picasso consciously meant the instrument to be a zither, yet in 1996, John Richardson's biography of him captioned the painting *Woman With Guitar ("Ma Jolie").*[476] It must carry both associations, though Picasso hadn't consciously meant it to. How could I substantiate my belief that for him, a guitar symbolized Spain and his mother, while a zither symbolized gypsies or the sexy cabaret performers of Paris? I used internal evidence.

> At *Seeing Double* [I wrote] I took a hard look at this picture (as I never had before), and now feel that the conflation of zither and guitar is not due to vagueness....Instead, it is due to the juxtaposition of the two instruments: the straight-sided, roughly trapezoidal zither is at the bottom of the picture, on the woman's lap, while the neck of the guitar is primarily in the middle, two parallel diagonal lines running up the front of the woman's torso....Since...the artist consciously intended the instrument to be a zither, the two diagonal lines may have been consciously intended to suggest the woman's neck or the front of her dress....the placement of the two musical instruments supports my theory that on an unconscious level, Picasso associated zithers with sexuality (the zither sits above the woman's genital region) and guitars with maternity (the neck of the guitar sits over the woman's breasts, as a nursing baby might).[477]

21. Youth, Vietnam Protest & the Media (Winter 1996–Summer 1999)

By the latter part of the '90s, I was researching the '60s, but the manuscript I wrote then was unlike the book you're reading now. In particular, that Ur-manuscript had a chapter after the one on the response to my London cover which tried to show how my cover also influenced *Time*'s coverage of the youthful aspects of the antiwar movement in three major stories that the Nation section ran in 1967. As I reviewed the research I'd done at Columbia on *Time, Newsweek,* and *The New York Times* between 1965 and 1967, I was drawn increasingly to the different ways that these publications had handled the relationship between youth and the antiwar protest. *Newsweek* had taken the lead in 1965, but those three major stories in *Time* in 1967 were surprisingly sympathetic, considering the magazine's earlier hostility to the protest, and the *Times* seemed to have interacted with one of them.

Obviously, these three *Time* stories were based on many factors, primarily the events under consideration, but psychologists of perception will tell you that people see what they expect to see, and to overlook what they don't expect (this is one reason that proofreaders are necessary, to spot missing words in manuscripts that the average eye automatically fills in). So, to the extent that my cover story had linked youth, revolution, and even pop culture in a favorable context, I suspected that it had might have fed – just a little bit – into the Nation section's coverage of youth and the protest.

To prepare for this additional chapter, I'd also consulted books about the '60s written in the '70s, '80s, and '90s. Both the news media of the '60s and later books about that era discussed major events that I'd noticed, if at all, only in passing when they occurred. Placing the media in this wider historical context of more recent books plugged gaps in my knowledge and required adjusting some of my recollections in order to develop a coherent narrative – but the process has also (I like to think) enabled me to plug a few gaps in the books upon the basis of my experience.

The first of these three big Nation stories in *Time* was the Man of the Year cover on the "Twenty-five and Under" generation in the issue of January 6. I'd been dimly aware of it when it appeared, but only because it was written by Bob Jones, my friend from World. Mike Demarest edited the Man of the

Year cover, and Otto Fuerbringer not only top-edited it but had probably thought of it. All three men had been, in one way or another, involved with my London cover, and (I believed) respected my writing more than most people (certainly more than the journalists who'd attacked or ridiculed the cover from afar). The Pub Letter for the Man of the Year said that my cover was one of the things that "the editors" had read, preparing for their own, but obviously, what they made out of it and their other sources was uniquely theirs.[478]

True, the overly clean-cut young people in the Man of the Year cover picture reflected *Time*'s myth of American youth rather than reality, and the ebullience of the text rang somewhat jarringly in retrospect. Yet for *Time* the story marked a new sophistication in dealing with the "minisociety" of the young.[479] Celebrated were their clothes, their songs, and their permissive attitudes toward sex and drugs, but particularly notable was the box that accompanied the story. Entitled "Youth Questions the War," it reprinted excerpts from a dignified letter to Johnson by student leaders from a hundred American colleges and universities, questioning "the conduct, rationale and very aims of the war" in Vietnam.[480] Quite a change from the censorious Essay that only fifteen months earlier had stigmatized the "Vietniks" as "self-defeating dissent."

The new attitude toward youthful protest made its next major appearance in April. The previous spring, *Time* had ignored tens of thousands who'd assembled in New York and elsewhere for an "international day of protest." Instead, it had done a story on a demo of only eleven protesters in Boston that had been attacked and overwhelmed by 150 pro-war high school students – thereby suggesting that youth supported the war (an idea not altogether wrong; actually, throughout the war, younger Americans were more apt to be hawkish than older ones).[481] Covering the Spring Mobilization of 1967, *Time* minimized the significance of pro-war demonstrations. Instead, the lede in Nation emphasized antiwar protests across the United States, focusing on 125,000 demonstrators in and around New York's Central Park. Admittedly, the text sourly insisted that all that was really happening was Americans having fun in the springtime, and that the demos would be welcomed by Ho Chi Minh. The tone of the story (I say in retrospect) was so tolerantly indulgent toward the foibles of the young that it must have made the activists themselves writhe, but at least both pictures and text emphasized the youthful aspects of the demo in ways that made it sound relatively harmless, not menacing ("kooky costumes," "painted faces," and "daffodils and roses that the marchers carried in gaudy abundance...").[482]

Neither the *Times* nor *Newsweek* ignored the youth in these demonstrations, but they continued to emphasize that antiwar feeling cut across age brackets.

Page One of the *Times* showed Martin Luther King, Jr., addressing the crowd, and the story described him, Dr. Benjamin Spock, and Harry Belafonte (three adults) leading the parade. No mention was made of younger demonstrators burning draft cards until Page Two, which also pictured pro-war youths in a sideline demonstration.[483] *Newsweek* ran its story in the midst of its National Affairs section. It had two and a half columns rather than the nearly six and a half *Time* gave it, and though *Newsweek* said that most demonstrators were young, it added "there was also a liberal sprinkling of middle-class marchers in business suits and housewives with children in baby buggies."[484]

By the fall of 1967, more publications had begun to call for an end to the war, including *The Washington Post*, *The Saturday Evening Post*, and *The Wall Street Journal*.[485] Johnson lost the support of Tip O'Neill, a prominent moderate House Democrat who had been one of his staunchest backers on Vietnam.[486] By October, polls were showing a decided advantage for a Republican ticket considered likely to oppose Johnson in 1968: Nelson Rockefeller, governor of New York, for president and Ronald Reagan, governor of California, for vice president.[487] Yet more galling for LBJ must have been the fact that only 28 percent of the public continued to approve of his handling of the war, although those who disapproved were split between those who favored increased use of military power (37 percent) and those who wanted the fighting scaled down (48 percent).[488]

Hedley Donovan lost confidence in the administration's capacity to win the war, and *Time* and *Life* began to express the sort of reservations I'd heard Jason McManus voice two years before.[489] Outside observers didn't notice real change until the cover for *Time's* October 6 issue showed a Marine cowering in a fetal position in a bunker with a cover slash that read, "Rising Doubt About the War," and *Life's* October 20 issue ran an editorial advocating a pause in the bombing of North Vietnam.[490]

Robert F. Kennedy, William J. Fulbright, Eugene McCarthy, and other liberal Democratic Senators had long criticized the war. Antiwar politicians were urging Kennedy and McCarthy to challenge Johnson for the Democratic nomination, but neither had agreed to run. Some journalists thought that if a Republican could beat LBJ, the United States would begin troop withdrawals, but Congressional Republicans on the whole were more inclined to back LBJ on the war than were members of his own party. Rockefeller was as liberal as Republicans got, but his recent messy divorce and remarriage had already proved a political liability (the remarriage and birth of a child had kept him from getting the Republican nomination in 1964). Reagan's transition from movie star to politico had begun by attacking communists in the Screen Actors Guild in the '40s; this made it unlikely he'd back away from confronting what he'd later call the "evil empire."

In this dead-end context, *The New York Times Magazine* published "Why the Generation Gap Begins at 30" in its July 2 issue. The title seems to refer to the "Twenty-five and Under" generation of the Man of the Year cover: it's like a correction, because it substitutes "30" for "Twenty-five," and because *Time* in its story had quoted David Riesman, the sociologist, using a phrase then still quite new to journalism and saying, "The generational gap is wider than I've ever seen it in my lifetime."[491] The *Times* article was by C. D. B. Bryan, a gifted younger writer (b. 1936), whose first novel, *P.S. Wilkinson*, had won the $10,000 Harper Prize for 1965. Speaking on behalf of a generation just beyond the thirty-year mark, he was ceding leadership of the protest to a younger one:

> I wish 10 years ago I had had the intelligence and courage that I see in so many of the 20-year-olds today [Bryan wrote]. Most of the over-30's I have spoken with have enormous respect for the young people who are involved, who do place themselves in personal jeopardy....A great number of over-30's marched recently in San Francisco and New York to protest the war in Vietnam....For many of us, it was the first time we so deliberately and premeditatedly rid ourselves of our cool. And we are grateful to the under-30's who made us aware how senseless and selfish being cool is.[492]

The autumn demonstrations, climaxed by the march on the Pentagon on Saturday, October 21, were the most dramatic yet. In *Johnson, Nixon and the Doves* (1988), Melvin Small quoted Ramsey Clark, Johnson's attorney general, calling it "the moment that the fever broke in the whole antiwar movement." According to Small, Clark didn't mean this was necessarily a turning point for the Johnson administration or the movement itself, but that it was "a catalytic event" for the rest of the nation. Small also said that from Clark's perspective, the march "energized antiwar forces and spelled the beginning of the end for American involvement in the war...."[493] Other historians of the movement have demonstrated by the amount of space that they devoted to the event how important and even climactic they considered it.[494] Composed of a peaceful demonstration in front of the Lincoln Memorial, and the more violent assault upon the Pentagon, the event showed the wide range of participants in the antiwar movement, ranging from older, more traditional liberals to younger, more militant radicals – and may even have been the moment when the younger militants wrested leadership of the movement as a whole from the older traditionalists.

Time did a crash cover on these demonstrations, switching from the cover previously scheduled only hours before press time. Again the editor was

Mike Demarest and the writer Bob Jones.[495] The cover picture was a black-and-white photograph showing marchers in front of the Lincoln Memorial. Inside was a two-page layout of more black-and-white photographs showing demonstrations at three California locations and one in Wisconsin. The headline for this layout was, "Youth Battles Against the War," and while two of the demonstrations appeared to have been violent, the other two seemed peaceful: one even showed students carrying candles in Claremont, California.[496]

The story itself described the tens of thousands of demonstrators who had charged that imposing edifice, the Pentagon. Besides telling how members of the military had rebuffed the protesters and arrested hundreds, the story discussed demos across the country. Cold-war rhetoric labeled the more radical protest groups in Washington with various flavors of Marxism, but *Time* conceded that the crowd included "all the elements of American dissent in 1967: hard-eyed revolutionaries and skylarking hippies; ersatz motorcycle gangs and all-too-real college professors, housewives, ministers and authors...."[497] A half-column was devoted to describing the antics planned by hippies, and one photo showed a hippie putting a flower down a gun barrel.

Such combinations of rhetoric with innocent details told me this story was yet another product of group journalism, a collage, pastiche, or synthesis incorporating compromises among different people struggling to get different messages across in the same five pages of text: collaborative creativity. One paragraph ended with a homily about the demo being "a reminder to the world of America's cherished right of dissent," together with a scary reference to the possibility that the demonstrations might get out of hand, but buried in the middle was a passage that would have been of more interest to McCarthy, Nixon, and other politicians contemplating a run for the presidency and searching for the issue that might put them out in front. "To the vast majority, the banners of Communism fluttering in Washington, the fist-flailing clashes and the violent verbiage were unsettling, almost unreal," this passage ran, "Yet the disquiet that suffused the spectacle was certainly shared to a degree by most Americans...."[498]

The *Times* also emphasized youth in its coverage of the march, but not in the Page One portion of its main story on Sunday, October 22. Rather, these introductory passages cited the names only of adult leaders of the day's events. Still, the continuation of the story, on page 58, made frequent reference to the youth of the demonstrators. Page 58 also carried a sidebar by John Herbers reporting that only a sprinkling of the demonstrators had been over thirty, and contrasting it with the previous year's demonstration, when middle-aged people had far outnumbered the young. A second, unsigned, sidebar described youngsters camped out at an all-night sit-in at the Pentagon, but aside from a passing reference in this sidebar to the reek of marijuana, and an almost equally brief reference by Herbers to a group of "Flower People," there was no attempt to classify anybody as a hippie or refer to pop culture.[499]

In 1995, LBJ's defense secretary Robert McNamara would recall how "Young women rubbed their breasts against soldiers standing at attention with rifles at their sides and even unzipped their flies...."[500] The soldiers didn't budge, but this sort of thing was more than the good gray *Times* could take. On Monday, it ran a "news analysis" entitled "Everyone Is a Loser" by the much-respected James Reston. "It is difficult to report publicly the ugly and vulgar provocation of many of the militants," Reston wrote. "Many of the signs carried by a small number of the militants, and many of the lines in the theatrical performances put on by the hippies, are too obscene to print...."[501]

Newsweek ran nearly two full pages on the march at the front of its National Affairs section, but the cover was in Life and Leisure, on "Trouble in Hippieland" among apolitical flower children. The story on the march gave no hint that a majority of the marchers were young, though it mentioned students as among the demonstrators and made passing reference to activist hippies.[502] Equal space, plus color photographs of Rockefeller and Reagan, was devoted to a jaunt aboard the SS *Independence* with more than forty state governors, but *Time*'s cover might have been read with more interest by McCarthy, as his daughter Mary had been among the demonstrators.[503] When even that arch-hawk *Time* felt that the protest merited a crash cover, it had to be taken seriously – and even by the magazine's core readership in cities and towns like Rovere who were mystified by or actively resented the activists.

Whatever politicians may say, they're pretty tough-minded about whether the coverage of an event is negative or positive: ultimately, it matters less to them than the amount of space devoted to that event, and its placement – on the front page, if it's a newspaper, or on the cover of a magazine. The activists may not have appreciated it, but that crash cover, even in its Establishmentarian way, was paying them the biggest compliment that the editors of *Time* knew how to pay. It was saying that to *them*, the march was the most important news of the week (a judgment vindicated by history).

Nobody, as far as I know, has ever said this cover story had any effect on them, but denials concerning the influence of its subject matter, the protesters, were equally persistent, widespread, and to me unlikely. Johnson told his biographer Doris Kearns that "the peaceniks" weren't his enemy; they were too young to understand, they just didn't know what was going on.[504] Hedley Donovan said he concluded that American opinion about the war had changed through talking with "relatively conservative businessmen and politicians," and his "mainly Republican neighbors" in Sands Point, Long Island.[505] Many opinion polls have shown that the public disliked how the protesters went about their business, but that's not the same as saying the protests weren't effective. You may want to shoot the messengers, but you listen to the news they bring.[506]

I don't believe Johnson could have looked at the masses of marchers on *Time*'s cover and not realized, however dimly, that he wouldn't be getting their votes in 1968. Even more disastrous would have been the magazine's decision to publicize them at cover length. All accounts agreed he was extremely angry and bitter at Time Inc.'s shift in its Vietnam position, that he felt Donovan had "'betrayed'" him, and that it was "the worst kind of serpent's bite."[507] When Donovan visited him in March 1968, he told Donovan that he'd only been doing "'what you fellows wanted me to do all along.'" Now, according to Donovan, LBJ felt that "the change in *Time*'s position had made it impossible to conduct the war."[508] To other people, the president said that the defection of Donovan (first evidenced in 1967) ranked with that of Walter Cronkite of CBS (in 1968) in forcing him to back off from the war.[509]

McCarthy was as coy about how much the media influenced him as Donovan and Johnson were on how much they'd been influenced by the protest, but in *The Year of the People*, the senator's 1969 account of his 1968 presidential campaign, he revealed an extraordinary familiarity with well-nigh everything the media had said about him.[510] Just as Johnson might have looked at *Time*'s cover picture of all those marchers and realized they weren't going to vote for him, McCarthy by the same token might have suspected they could become votes for him. Although he'd been approached by politicians encouraging him to run well before the march, he didn't formally announce his candidacy until November 30, making it possible that *Time*'s coverage of the October 21 march on the Pentagon was a factor influencing his decision.[511] One book about McCarthy said that the final reason he decided to run was because he was afraid of the more extreme militants, and anxious to show that reform could be achieved within the system.[512] If so, the presence of so many militants on our cover would have furnished him with yet more incentive to throw his hat into the ring. In this way, the magazine might have been ticking history along – not shoving it in a major way, but contributing a little something to the course of events.

The day before McCarthy announced his candidacy, news broke that McNamara was leaving his post as secretary of defense. Next, beginning on January 30–31, 1968, the Vietnamese communists mounted their massive "Tet" offensive. Some writers (most notably Peter Braestrup) have argued that the communists had actually been repulsed, and that the U.S. media mistakenly conveyed the idea that the offensive had been successful.[513] Still, the fact that the enemy had managed – however briefly – to penetrate the inner circles of the allies' defenses gave it a powerful psychological if not military victory. Cronkite visited Vietnam. Upon his return, he announced over national television on February 27 that "we are mired in stalemate...."[514]

On March 12, McCarthy amazed the country by winning 42 per cent of the vote in the New Hampshire primary. Johnson got 49 per cent, but he'd been expected to do far better, so this constituted a defeat. An NBC poll indicated that five out of ten New Hampshire Democrats didn't know that McCarthy was a dove, and six out of ten of those who'd voted for him thought LBJ should use more force in Vietnam, not less.[515] Bobby Kennedy, however, took McCarthy's triumph possibly as evidence of the depth of antiwar feeling, certainly as a sign of Johnson's vulnerability, and announced on March 16 that he would run. Now Johnson had real trouble. McCarthy still wasn't nationally known, but Kennedy was, and had been since he'd served as his brother's attorney general in the early '60s. According to one poll, Johnson's approval ratings on how he was handling the war dropped to an all-time low of 26 percent during Tet.[516] By the end of March, another poll reported that the number of those with confidence in U.S. military policies in South Vietnam was down from 74 to 54 percent, and the number of those who thought of the war as a stalemate was up from 39 to 42 percent.[517] Nor was this because the media were saying the situation in Vietnam was worse than it was. Johnson's advisors were saying much the same thing.

Among them was Clark Clifford, McNamara's replacement as secretary of defense, but the decisive opinion came from a meeting of the senior advisory group on Vietnam, also known as "the Wise Men" and consisting of fourteen distinguished advisors from outside the government, including Dean Acheson, Truman's secretary of state, and McGeorge Bundy, who'd been LBJ's assistant for national security affairs until 1966.[518] After receiving briefings from diplomatic and military officials, the Wise Men reported their findings to LBJ on March 26. A minority favored holding the line militarily and even escalating if necessary, but the majority favored immediate steps toward de-escalation. Acting as spokesman, Bundy said, "Dean Acheson summed up the majority feeling when he said that we can no longer do the job we set out to do in the time we have left and we must begin to take steps to disengage."[519] Five days later, LBJ announced he wouldn't run for reelection.

This was the beginning of the long, slow process that finally got the United States out of Nam. It didn't matter who got elected in November, because no other candidate was as committed to the war as LBJ had been. During the campaign, as I recalled it, Nixon, the Republican, didn't set himself up as a peace candidate, but he didn't say anything that might make voters think he was opposed to peace, either. As I interpreted the election, enough Democratic voters had thought Nixon would get us out of Nam so they crossed party lines and put him into office. If LBJ had run for reelection, he might very well have won. As the incumbent, his position would have been stronger than any other candidate could have been, and his domestic accomplishments were impressive, including the Civil Rights Act of 1964, the Voting Rights Act of 1965, Medicare, Medicaid, Head Start, loans to college students, food stamps, the Corporation for Public Broadcasting, the National Endowments for the Arts and Humanities, environmental legislation, and other aspects of his "Great Society" program. Many Americans cared more about domestic than foreign policy, but if Johnson had been re-elected, he might have seen it as a mandate to carry on the war.

To the extent that the antiwar protest had encouraged McCarthy to run, that his showing in New Hampshire had persuaded Bobby Kennedy to run, and that Kennedy's announcement in turn contributed to LBJ's decision to withdraw, I felt that the system had worked, and that when Nixon was elected, the political process had brought about a change in policy by throwing out the Ins, and electing the Outs. Accordingly, I believed that in the war to end the war, the antiwar forces had triumphed, and that a victory for democracy had been snatched from the jaws of military defeat, but some of the books up at Columbia raised issues I couldn't ignore.

I'd browsed dozens of books on youth, Vietnam and/or the protest in the '60s. There were hundreds more, but many repeated each other, and I couldn't get to all of them, so I persuaded myself that I'd achieved a representative sampling. Most disturbing were three on how the media had covered the protest. All three attacked the media, suggesting or implying that (with very occasional exceptions) every major news outlet had misrepresented the protest. The parent volume was Todd Gitlin's *The Whole World Is Watching: Mass Media in the Making and Unmaking of the New Left* (1980), but Daniel C. Hallin had also written *The "Uncensored" War: The Media and Vietnam* (1986), and Melvin Small was responsible for *Covering Dissent: The Media and the Anti-Vietnam War Movement* (1994). Gitlin had been president of the SDS; Small had been a petition-signer and a demonstration-attendee; the book by Hallin began as a dissertation for which Gitlin was an advisor.[520]

Only *Covering Dissent* dealt in detail with *Time*'s reportage on the movement. God, was this book hard to take! I felt like my lover was being attacked, but hey, scholars are supposed to be detached and objective, so I'll try to be fair. I could recognize the *Time* that Small portrayed, but it was a very unflattering portrait. The story on the Spring Mobilization was labeled "derisive"; the photograph of the candlelight procession was dismissed as "uncharacteristically peaceful." Small did concede that the cover photograph of the march showed a banner placing the antiwar movement in a favorable light, but discussed the banner purely in terms of what it said about the movement, as opposed to giving any credit to *Time* for having promulgated it.[521] Gitlin, Hallin, and Small all suggested, directly or by implication, that the media had opposed the movement. All three implied that the media functioned as an apologist for the government, even as a branch or organ of it. There was some admission that after public opinion as a whole began to turn against the war in 1968, the media became more sympathetic to the protest, but even this was seen as mere disagreement by the media with individuals in the government, not a critique of "the system."[522]

I'd agree that the Fourth Estate is integral to America's political system, but point out that these three authors appear to have been enmeshed to one degree or another in their own ideologies. I don't know enough about these ideologies to describe them in their entirety, but the attitude toward the media in these three books was just as hostile as the books accused the media itself of being toward the antiwar movement. The value of a critique lies in being able to see ourselves as others see us, but this applies to the movement as much as to the media. I may not have liked what Small said about *Time*, but I concede that I could at least recognize his unflattering portrait of it. Would he (at this late date) be willing to concede that *Time*'s portrait of the protest, even if unflattering, wasn't altogether unrecognizable to him? A journalist's first responsibility is to her or his readers. Whether his or her subjects like what is said about them must be at best a secondary consideration. As an art critic, I know what it's like to have artists I write about sore at me, but it's more important to me that my readers trust me to say what I think.

Gitlin, Hallin, and Small tended to imply that all members of the media were (with occasional exceptions) more or less alike, so "the system" (again) must be at fault. This attitude also appeared in *Manufacturing Consent: The Political Economy of the Mass Media* (1988), by Edward S. Herman and Noam Chomsky, and (to a much lesser degree) in the book by Herbert J. Gans that I discussed in Chapter Five, *Deciding What's News: A Study of CBS Evening News, NBC Nightly News, Newsweek and Time* (1979). Neither of these last two were as passionately written as the books by Gitlin, Hallin, and Small, nor were they as clearly characterized by a deeply felt and widespread bitterness and anger that – even as I read further – I still found hard to explain, given that eventually the antiwar protest had prevailed.

Books by doves were much more numerous and (I must say) much better written than the few books by hawks that I'd found at Columbia, using "Vietnam" together with "media" as keywords in CLIO, the library database, and consulting footnotes of dovish authors for lists of their adversaries. Part of me was inclined to attribute this lopsided situation to antiwar bias in academia, not least because Gitlin, Hallin, and Small had all become college professors. Two more dispassionate scholars, William Hammond and Clarence Wyatt, had written books about media coverage of the fighting in Vietnam. These were known as "owl" books, purporting to stand back from the debates of the '60s, and both books were refreshingly free of dogma. Both concluded that the media hadn't affected the outcome of the conflict, thereby rebutting the doves' argument that the media prolonged the war by accepting the government's claims of victory uncritically, and the hawks' argument that negative press coverage undermined the war effort and forced the United States to withdraw prematurely. Still, neither Wyatt nor Hammond suggested that the war could have been won. In that respect, they had more in common with doves than hawks.

I couldn't explain all the bitterness by saying that academia had as a whole been antiwar in the first place. I remembered an experience I'd had at the Virginia Center for the Creative Arts in 1997. The VCCA, a great artists' colony near Sweet Briar College, had given me a residency to work on my book, and I'd gone to the Sweet Briar library to do research on my Hungarian roots (for a segment since omitted from this book). The Sweet Briar library was much smaller than Columbia's, but I found several decent books about Hungary that I didn't think Columbia had. This raised the possibility that a scholar researching Vietnam in other colleges might find more good hawkish books and fewer good dovish ones.

Besides, it wasn't only scholars' books that were dovish at Columbia. David Halberstam, the journalist who practically invented dovishness, was represented in CLIO by many copies of his books about Nam, as was his friend and colleague, Neil Sheehan, with his book on the debacle. Quite a lot of the dovish books were on reserve, suggesting that they were or had recently been required reading for students. I got so irked by Columbia's bias that I concocted an acid footnote, giving numbers of the books in CLIO that I was familiar with by hawks, owls, and doves. The score was six copies of books by hawks, six by owls – and 107 by doves.[523]

Four books that I'd seen commented on the bitterness and disillusionment which had developed in youth and/or the protest movement in the later '60s. One was by Thomas Powers, *The War at Home; Vietnam and the American People, 1964–1968* (1973).[524] Another was by Landon Y. Jones, *Great Expectations: America and the Baby Boom Generation* (1980).[525] A third was by David Chalmers, *And the Crooked Places Made Straight: The Struggle for Social Change in the 1960s* (1991).[526] The fourth was by Edward P. Morgan, *The 60s Experience: Hard Lessons About Modern America* (1991).[527] Wyatt suggested that the disenchantment with government and the media affected not only the radical left, but public opinion as a whole.[528] Jules Witcover's book about 1968 was titled *The Year the Dream Died* (1997).

Searching for contemporary signs of general disillusionment or disenchantment with the media, the earliest I found was a piece in *Newsweek* in September 1968. "Is The Press Biased?" told how newspapers across the United States were the center of a growing debate over their coverage of the racial struggle and the war. Historically, the magazine conceded, "reporters have run with the hounds rather than held with the hares," and besides, the media thrived on the new and the novel. Such preoccupations might distort coverage. "Anti-war protesters have argued – rightly – that news cameras tend to focus only on the bearded demonstrators and to pass over the ranks of ordinary-looking schoolteachers." In this way, standard journalistic procedures had become exaggerated in the increasingly contentious political climate.[529]

Paradoxically, *Newsweek*'s article was prompted by how some journalists had sympathized with the hundreds of antiwar demonstrators whom the Chicago police had clubbed, beaten, Maced, and arrested during the Democratic National Convention. Still, as *Newsweek* said, the demonstrators were skeptical of the journalists' motives, and for these demonstrators, the outcome of the convention must have been even more embittering. In the wake of Bobby Kennedy's assassination, party pols had nominated Hubert Humphrey, LBJ's vice president, though he hadn't won a single primary. I knew he had a distinguished earlier record in the Senate, but trying to explain the anger in those books, I could see that the people who'd supported McCarthy or George McGovern, both of whom had campaigned in the primaries on peace platforms, must have felt that the system had betrayed them. Humphrey's nomination could have persuaded many of them that the radical element of the antiwar movement, which wasn't even satisfied with McCarthy, must be right, and the system itself at fault.

Such feelings must have been magnified by Nixon, since he wouldn't start announcing specific troop withdrawals until the following June, and then only after many campus upheavals. None of the books I read dealt at length with those upheavals, but I remembered them vividly, as part of my last, manic summer on *Time*. Reexamining the *Times* showed I hadn't imagined them. Four more years would pass before the last U.S. troops pulled out, and disengagement wasn't steady. I'd been in London, but I knew vaguely that Nixon had alternated between peaceable and warlike stances. This would have contributed to malaise, as did the steadily more disturbing news from the battlefront, where troops became increasingly demoralized as their numbers shrank. Another contributing factor must have been the awareness that both the FBI and CIA, under both Johnson and Nixon, had been investigating and even infiltrating the antiwar movement.[530] From beginning to end, the way in which both Johnson and Nixon had lied to the public about the progress of the war also had to be deeply disillusioning.

Nevertheless, as I see it, more distressing than any of this was the sheer fact that the war was being lost, and had from a purely military standpoint been unwinnable since its inception. It must have been the need to deal with the painful, prolonged trauma caused by this basic truth that forced the most agonizing mental revisions among both hawks and doves. I'm not a psychologist, but my Freudian background leads me to think of these revisions as collective defense mechanisms of various types. With the hawks, denial and displacement would appear to have been the mechanisms employed. They had to *deny* that the enemy was stronger than we were. Since they couldn't admit this, or concede that our own military was at fault, they *displaced* responsibility for losing the war onto the media and the media's supposed ally, the protesters.

With the doves, the need to withdraw from the war led especially to collective *rationalization* and *justification*. As I said earlier, America is not and never has been monolithic. Some of the antiwar activists seem to have been "red-diaper babies," raised in far-left homes where they imbibed hostility toward "the system" with their mothers' milk. Still, I think that most of the future protesters and journalists who'd be dealing with Vietnam had been raised by more typically American parents who'd taught them to respect their country's leaders, and to believe that America was both strong and good. When the country was gradually led into the war in Vietnam, most journalists and even (in the very earliest phases of the conflict) most of the people who'd later become protesters would have accepted this decision, if only because they believed that their leaders knew what was best for the country. When, however, it became obvious that there was no way of winning the war, these same Americans were forced to jettison earlier ideals, and develop rationalizations and justifications for withdrawing instead. As I see it, such rationalizations and justifications began (often very early) with the future activists, then spread to larger and larger numbers of journalists and concerned citizens. By the '90s, a great many Americans had long since convinced themselves that it had been immoral to get involved in Vietnam at all because it was purely a civil war, and no wider issues had been involved, least of all the containment of communism. This belief enabled opponents of the war to feel they were doing the right thing in protesting, but being forced to abandon one's reasons for going into war, and adopt reasons for pulling out instead, had to be a deeply embittering experience.

If you don't like Freud, consider "dissonance reduction." "Cognitive dissonance" is a still-controversial theory about human attitudes and behavior developed in the 1950s by Leon Festinger, a social psychologist (not a Freudian). Festinger argued that people need consistency. When they find themselves in an inconsistent situation (with regard to other people), they become upset and uncomfortable and must adjust attitudes and/or behavior to reestablish consistency and equilibrium. A recent history by Joel Cooper of cognitive dissonance over the past fifty years takes as an initial example the case of how an avid American baseball fan, convinced that the best baseball in the world is played in the United States, deals with a world tournament in which the U.S. team is eliminated and the Japanese team wins.

He is upset not only because his team didn't win, but even more because he'd been so certain beforehand that it would: the inconsistency is between his expectations and the outcome of the tournament. He is therefore in a state of "cognitive dissonance," and must deal with this by "dissonance reduction." He therefore persuades himself that the tournament doesn't really reflect the true state of American baseball. Many of the best U.S. major-league players weren't in the tournament. Others were playing for the countries where they'd been born, even if they were now on American teams, and even the players on the U.S. tournament team hadn't been giving it their best, as they were also involved in spring training for the U.S. season and not taking the tournament seriously.[531] At the risk of appearing frivolous, I see Vietnam as comparable to this situation: positive expectations in the early phases of the war, progressively growing disappointment as the negative outcome became increasingly apparent, ever more need for a new rationale to restore equilibrium.

There's another defense mechanism that I think of in relation to the antiwar movement. This will undoubtedly enrage some of my readers even more than what I've already written, but the movement's fascination with Marxism reminds me of the defense mechanism called "identifying with the aggressor."[532] I don't know any non-Freudian psychological term that parallels this, but I do think it has analogies in the folk wisdom of two old sayings: "Nobody loves a loser," and "If you can't beat 'em, join 'em."

On a second visit to the Virginia Center for the Creative Arts, in 1998, I thought about how many journalists I'd written about were – like myself – Depression-era babies. David Halberstam, Malcolm Browne, Neil Sheehan, Max Frankel, C. D. B. Bryan, Eric Pace, Robert F. Jones, and Jason McManus had all been born in the '30s.[533] A number of them had become concerned about Vietnam before students started demonstrating against the draft. It occurred to me these contemporaries of mine had had more influence in the media than most people suspected, and the media as a result had wound up using the younger generation to help force a withdrawal. I could see how the tectonic shift in the debate – from a simple struggle between pro-war and antiwar forces to a battle between generations – might have made it easier for adult moderates to side with the protest. They might have thought, if that's what the young people want, maybe we should go along with them; after all, they've got to fight the war, and live with its consequences longer than we do. I doubt most of my contemporaries consciously followed this Machiavellian line of thinking, or used the younger generation intentionally, but the younger people might still have sensed they were being used, and become bitter and angry as a result.

"We were the officers (without necessarily knowing it)," I wrote. "They were the cannon fodder (though persuaded they were leading the charge). We were the ones who first realized how bad the situation was in Vietnam, and how essential it was to extricate ourselves from it. We (and those a few years older than ourselves) were the ones who realized (on some level or other) that we couldn't do it by ourselves, that we had to enlist a younger, less inhibited and more numerous generation, and we were the ones who told the rest of the world how this younger generation was doing it, with all the gaudy trappings of pop culture which would make its endeavors colorful and more sympathetic to the rest of society, including our own elders....[534]

"It wasn't that the leaders of this younger generation didn't already have their own ideas and distinctive, highly skeptical way of evaluating society, but such ideas could be compared to a heap of dry straw: without the torch of Vietnam to set it ablaze, the resulting conflagration might never have reached the height that it did, or been visible from so far away. Without the imperative need to force a military withdrawal, the entire youth explosion might never have captured the spotlight as it did – and if it hadn't, the values and attitudes it espoused would never have been so widely adopted.

"Throughout history, youth has rebelled against age, but only in special circumstances has the rebellion become a revolution. Commoner are situations in which the older generation has perceived the younger one as going through a stage of development, and the younger generation, as it matured, has adopted the values and attitudes of the older one. In the '60s, the process was reversed, with members of older generations adopting (or trying to adopt) the values and attitudes of the younger ones."

I wasn't satisfied with this, but it did explain for me how the idea of the young having led the protest was to some extent a myth the media had helped create.

By 1999, I had a manuscript that took my life up to 1983, but though it was twelve hundred pages, it had only a fraction of what's in this book. I wouldn't mention it, except that this book is itself an example of creativity, and I want to suggest how it achieved its final form – with the aid of feedback (or further "verification"). My friend Kenneth Craven had read all of it. I'd made many changes in response to his input, but Rosanne Bricker, his wife, was only interested in the part about *Time*. I was grateful for his assistance, but he'd been a Freudian therapist, while she worked with computers, so I thought the general-interest reader would be more like her than him.

If I could get the first part of the book published, I thought, the rest might follow, so I sent a letter of inquiry, offering it as a memoir about *Time*, to Editor R, who'd been associated with the memoir of a famous woman journalist. R responded that she thought there were better ways to write about important subjects than memoirs (the famous journalist, she said, had been an exception to the rule). I wrote to Agent S, said to specialize in art books. S asked for two chapters and an outline, so I sent her an introduction and first chapter. The introduction was as yet far from having gelled, and the first chapter brought me only up to the age of three, so S didn't think any publisher would want it. This response tallied with the tepid one I'd gotten when I'd read passages from that first chapter at the VCCA, so in time I'd condense my first twenty-one years into one chapter, but in 1999, I couldn't yet see the need for this. Instead, I put the entire project on hold.

22. The Shift of Mindsets in the '60s
(Summer 2000–Spring 2001)

FOR MONTHS, I worked on other projects. Then early in 2000, I got an e-mail from Shawn Levy, film critic for the Portland *Oregonian*. He was working on a book about Swinging London, had read my guidebook, liked it, and wanted to interview me. I was touched and excited at having something I'd written more than three decades earlier so warmly remembered, but I was just moving to a new and larger studio apartment, so the interview itself (by telephone) took place in April. Since I despaired of publishing any of my new book, I gave Levy an earful, but some of his questions suggested there was so much he didn't know about the '60s that I couldn't begin to explain it to him on the phone. "There was a war on. Remember?" I recall saying, sarcastically.

Mulling over our exchange, I eventually thought, I must know more about the '60s than many younger people like Levy. They might be interested in reading the first part of my book as history, not memoir. If I pitched it as a first-person narrative by an eyewitness to history, I might have better luck placing it. I sent a letter of inquiry, offering the book on those terms, to Editor T, who'd worked on books about the media and books about Vietnam. Back came a note saying yes, she'd like to read it. Galvanized, I took out my manuscript, but when I started rereading it, I realized it would need revisions before I could send it to her. There was too much about my ancestry, childhood, and private life as opposed to the history I was claiming to have witnessed. I'd been very unfair to *Newsweek* (if you think this book has too much on my private life and is biased on behalf of *Time*, you should have seen that earlier draft). What little I'd said about political and social developments in the '30s, '40s, and '50s presupposed knowledge on the part of my readers that younger readers might not have. I was, after all, sixty-five. Eighty-eight percent of the U.S. population was younger than I was.

One tip-off that in some ways I'd been sleeping as soundly as Rip Van Winkle was a conversation I'd recently had with a Barnard alum who'd graduated a few years after me. Recently she'd revisited the campus, and burbled, "It's all different now – we didn't have any minorities when we were there." "Jewish isn't a minority?" I asked, in astonishment. Evidently, *no más*, though Jews were still the same minuscule proportion of the U.S.

population that they'd always been (and the woman I was speaking to was Jewish). In the new millennium, I realized, the only minorities who really counted as minorities to "enlightened" people were the four who still weren't completely integrated: African Americans, Latinos, Asian Americans, and Native Americans. The minorities of the '30s – Poles, Italians, Greeks and Hungarians like my father – were so integrated that they'd begotten mayors, governors, a vice-president (Agnew), and a candidate for the presidency (Dukakis). I must at least hint to my readers that for my WASP mother to marry a Jewish Hungarian was about as unconventional in 1930 as marrying an African American would be today – not unheard-of, but not something everybody did.

Then there were the politics. I had only one passing reference to Franklin D. Roosevelt in my manuscript, and it would have meant something only to somebody who already knew a lot about him, yet even the baby boomers hadn't been around while he was in office. The post-war baby boom had started in 1946, the year after FDR died. Obviously, I'd have to put in a little more about him, and, since I couldn't remember offhand the most important New Deal legislation of the '30s, I'd have to go up to Columbia and do a bit more research. What I found there on FDR alone showed me that I'd have to do a lot more research. In fact, the more I thought about it, the more I realized that the manuscript was going to need so much surgery that I might as well think big. Maybe I wouldn't get another shot at publishing a book, so why not try to boil the whole twelve hundred pages down to one book? I sent Editor T a note, saying I was having to revise the manuscript, and it might not turn out to be what I'd offered her, but I'd send her another letter of inquiry when it was done, and see if it was anything she was still interested in. Back came a note saying that she'd be glad to look at my manuscript whenever it was ready. This really bucked me up.

Until the following August, I'd be burrowing into yet more books, and Xeroxing yet more pages from them and magazines (especially *Newsweek*). With the dual support of T and the artists who liked my column, reexamining my outsider childhood became a much more positive experience. Ethnic and religious groups, I now thought, were different subcommunities, adjoining villages in the larger society. Never having fully belonged to any, I could look at all with more detachment, just as I could see academia from the vantage point of journalism, and journalism from the vantage point of academia. I was truly an independent scholar. Nor was I alone in feeling that being an outsider had advantages. In 1982, I'd run into Tony Lukas, my onetime stepbrother. He was finishing a book about the bussing crisis in Boston that he'd been working on for years. It would be published in 1985 as *Common Ground: A Turbulent Decade in the Lives of Three American Families*, and win many prizes.

Tony and I had had lunch in 1991. He'd described the new book he was working on, about a 1905 murder in Idaho for which a labor leader was tried. "Why did you choose that subject?" I asked. He said it was about "class," and made me feel that he considered class to be *the* problem in America now as well as then. The book would be published in the fall of 1997 as *Big Trouble: A Murder in a Small Western Town Sets Off a Struggle for the Soul of America*, but Tony didn't live to see it. In the spring, he'd strangled himself (after decades of suffering bouts of depression). One of his obituaries used the quotation that begins my Chapter One: "I firmly believe that any good journalist must essentially be temperamentally an outsider. I don't think [a] full sense of belonging and security is conducive to creativity." Neil Sheehan saw another gifted journalist as an outsider. He wrote that David Halberstam felt himself isolated by the fact that he was Jewish.[535] In 2004, the obituary of John Gregory Dunne, whom I'd worked briefly with on *Time* (and whose death would be commemorated by his widow, Joan Didion, in *The Year of Magical Thinking*), quoted Dunne as having described every writer as a perennial outsider.[536]

The election of 2000 made my heritage look even better. On TV, states that had gone for George W. Bush were red, and states that had gone for Al Gore were blue. In fifth grade, Ed Bley had taught us where the different immigrant groups had settled, and the *Statistical Abstract of the United States: 2001* would confirm the fact that these locations tallied with blue and red state divisions. The largest number of descendants of those earlier waves of migrants from what is now the United Kingdom lived in the West and South, where Bush was strongest, while the largest number of descendants of the later waves from Italy, Greece, and Eastern Europe lived in the Northeast and Middle West, where Gore was strongest.[537] With a Protestant Anglo-Saxon mother, I had a red-state heritage, and with a Jewish-Hungarian father, a blue-state heritage, too.

As a journalist, I might also be better prepared to compare and contrast red v. blue. *Time*'s defining audience in the '60s had been "the heartland." This equated largely to the red states, and because I'd been on *Time*, I might know that audience better than many New Yorkers. The audience *Newsweek* appealed to in the '60s was rooted in the blue states (the Northeast Corridor and the West Coast), and that audience had so much in common with the liberal subcommunity in which I'd been raised that I felt I knew it even better than I knew the red states (I also knew that even in blue states, many voters had a red-state outlook, and many voters with a blue-state outlook lived in red states; ultimately, it wasn't a question of geography but attitudes).

The anger that the disputed election provoked further salved my sense of apartness. Most of my friends were talking about politics often and angrily.

The fury with which they attacked Bush and the Republicans for stealing the election made me feel that as a Democrat and even a liberal, I was far from alone.[538] It was a fine feeling of at long last belonging, and I decided to use it as a climax and ending, a way of coming back to the politics in the first part of my narrative. Carrying the book up to 2000 would also let me incorporate the later thinking I'd done about art, but the politics in it meant that I had to pay attention to current events. The election of 2000 stayed in the news after New Year's, so I kept on reading the *Times* carefully – as I hadn't in decades.

Oddly enough, these years of ignoring politics helped me, because I was confronted so starkly with the contrasts between my early life and the year 2000. People who followed the news regularly witnessed change so gradually that they adjusted themselves to each stage of the progression and never thought about profound or structural change, but as I inserted brief reports on political developments into my chapters dealing with the '70s and '80s, I saw a pattern emerging. It showed steady increases in benefits and power for the wealthier members of the community, and steady erosion of benefits and power for the poorer ones. This longtime drift to the right had taken place under Democratic administrations as well as Republican ones, from the deregulation of business in the '70s under Carter, to the tax cuts of Reagan in the '80s and Bill Clinton's campaign to "end welfare as we know it."

What Republicans and Democrats had stood for in the '40s and '50s had become partially if not entirely obscured with the passage of decades (plus the fact that the Republicans under George W. Bush were becoming as adept as the Democrats at promising welfare-state-type benefits, while the Democrats under Clinton had shown themselves more concerned than the Republicans with fiscal responsibility). If my book were to make sense to younger readers, I needed to say whom the parties had represented in my childhood, as explained to me by Ed in eighth grade, with his semicircle of political opinion: liberals and Democrats to the left of center, representing workers, conservatives and Republicans to the right of center, representing bosses, radicals (socialists and communists) to the left of the Democrats, reactionaries and fascists to the right of the Republicans. With fascism officially destroyed in 1945, communism receding into history since 1989, and the socialist parties of Europe no longer known for advocating the nationalization of basic industries, younger readers might be vague about what these political terms had once stood for.

Conservatives wanted to maintain the status quo; reactionaries, to turn back the clock. Republicans in 2000 liked to claim that some legislation they favored was radical or progressive, but in reality it was reactionary. Liberals of the '40s had wanted change toward greater egalitarianism, political and economic, but now the gap between the wealthier and poorer members of the community was widening toward what it had been in the 1920s and before.

The big government of the New Deal, even its later forms of the '50s and '60s, had meant that taxes levied progressively more on the higher income brackets subsidized government benefits for the lower income brackets, but Bush during the campaign had already called for across-the-board tax cuts, which would in practice benefit the more affluent, and, during the first half of 2001, cuts would be enacted that would indeed mean more money for the upper income brackets.

This was a whole new climate. Because of it, I thought, younger readers of my book might not know just why Roosevelt had been so beloved by ordinary Americans, why his New Deal had been so necessary, and what it had accomplished. They might not appreciate how awful the Great Depression of the '30s had been – with one out of every four workers in the United States unemployed – or how poorly Great Britain, France, Germany, Italy, Spain and the Soviet Union had coped with the crisis. Such ignorance was even being perpetuated by books, as I discovered when I went up to refresh my memory about Roosevelt and the specific accomplishments of his New Deal.

I thought that all I needed was a summary of FDR's accomplishments, since my reference would be brief, so I went to the Barnard library, a branch of the Columbia system with a trendier selection of books than most other branches. Wanting to take advantage of the newest scholarship, I looked up Roosevelt in the nice-looking new *Encyclopedia of the American Presidency* (1994). The essay was by John Braeman, but it wasn't a Roosevelt I recognized. Grudgingly, it conceded that FDR had felt "a genuine sympathy with the depression's victims," but suggested he'd often acted with "deviousness, if not dishonesty." He was "late in throwing his support behind" the Wagner Act, organized labor's Bill of Rights, because he preferred "government paternalism to independent worker action." The section on Social Security, submitted to Congress in 1935, began by saying what the initial legislation didn't do, not what it did (it didn't have universal health insurance, but Truman, Johnson and the Clintons had been unable to get universal health insurance enacted in the last sixty years as well, so why lead off the discussion of FDR's Social Security with this complaint?).

Though there was much other information in the article, I couldn't find any mention of the National Labor Relations Board, the Securities and Exchange Commission, or any other key New Deal legislation that helped enforce the rights of labor and police the business community. The picture of FDR which thus emerged was that of an aristocrat concerned solely with perpetuating the reign of his class. On top of that, Braeman suggested that the president had been a racist and an anti-Semite, saying that FDR "refused to act against the discrimination against blacks practiced by the armed services," and "must be counted an accessory to Hitler's murder of six million European

Jews" because of "his failure to open U.S. doors to larger numbers of Jewish refugees."[539] Where is this guy coming from, I asked myself.

Didn't he know what things were like in the '30s and '40s? Segregation had been the law of the land throughout the South during World War II, and millions of white drafted men in the armed services had been born and raised in that South. I didn't think it likely that they or their relatives back home would have taken kindly to forced integration, and building support for the commander-in-chief was vital in wartime. Washington had racist Congressmen and Senators, as Braeman admitted, but he didn't appear aware that they represented white racist voters (or that African Americans in the South were still effectively disenfranchised through poll taxes, biased eligibility tests, and so forth). Anti-Semitism among Americans had still been a problem even in New York when I was a young woman in the '50s. How much worse it must have been in the '40s I could guess from the novel of *Gentleman's Agreement* (1947), subtly anti-Semitic cartoons in *The New Yorker* of the early '30s, and most of all memories of that elderly ex-Catholic friend of my mother's who, when drunk, raved on about how the Jews had gotten Roosevelt into World War II.

As I remembered it, FDR had been more open-minded than many, maybe most Americans. I knew that when the Daughters of the American Revolution refused in 1939 to rent a concert hall to Marian Anderson, the African American contralto, Mrs. Roosevelt resigned from that organization and FDR's secretary of the interior offered Anderson the use of the Lincoln Memorial as a backdrop for her concert. I remembered the photograph *Life* had used when FDR died, showing an African American serviceman playing a funeral dirge on an accordion with tears streaming down his face. I recalled that FDR had been known for the Jews who were members of or advisors to his administration: Henry Morgenthau, Jr., as secretary of the treasury, Bernard Baruch as a financial advisor, Felix Frankfurter as a member of Roosevelt's "Brain Trust" whom he later appointed to the Supreme Court (the New Deal's enemies even referred to it as "The Jew Deal"). I didn't think my mother's friend had dreamed up this idea about the Jews getting Roosevelt into war. More likely the Nazis had used the claim in the propaganda they beamed over the radio to U.S. soldiers. If FDR had allowed every Jew into the United States who was seeking refuge, it might have lent substance to the claim, and undermined very possibly bigoted U.S. soldiers' eagerness to fight.

Still looking for information on the SEC and NLRB, I consulted *The New Encyclopaedia Britannica* in Columbia's more sedate Butler Library. Its article on FDR was by Frank Freidel (the edition that I consulted in 2000 was copyrighted 1997, but the article must have been written earlier, as Freidel died in 1993). This article mentioned the NLRB and the SEC. It agreed

FDR had been late in getting behind the Wagner Act, but didn't talk about paternalism, and cited additional New Deal legislation to protect stock market investors. Nothing suggested that FDR had been a racist or a bigot, and "trickiness" and "dictatorial ambitions" were mentioned as qualities ascribed to him by his opponents. Freidel concluded by quoting FDR saying that the presidency was "pre-eminently a place of moral leadership." [540]

Thus, we had one article slanted for and one against FDR. It was like they'd been written by people from different worlds, and in a way, this was true, I found when I researched their authors.[541] Freidel had been born in 1916, so he'd been a teenager when Roosevelt became president, and nearly thirty when he died. Braeman was born in 1932, shortly after FDR was elected president, so he'd have been only twelve at his death. By the '60s, Freidel was a full professor at Stanford, making it less likely that he'd been deeply involved in the antiwar protests there, but Braeman had been only an assistant and associate professor at Brooklyn College, also the site of student upheavals. Given his youth, it seemed likely he'd been more directly affected by them.

It looked to me like "before" and "after" examples illustrating the giant shift in mindsets that took place in the '60s, between generations and among them, since baby boomers shared the "after" mindset with many members of my own silent generation who'd committed themselves to the causes of the '60s. I could see Braeman as more sympathetic to the New Left of the '60s, rather than the Old Left of the '30s and '40s, less concerned with the working class as a class, more only with those members of it who belonged to minorities. I could understand the New Left's lack of interest in the working class. Although organized labor became divided on Vietnam as the war progressed, initially it projected a pro-war image, with the AFL-CIO, its umbrella organization, issuing nine statements endorsing Johnson's policies between August 1964 and February 1968.[542] Some craft unions for skilled workers were racist, and some industrial unions for semiskilled and unskilled workers had many members rendered more conservative through prosperity and middle-aged spread.

A Braeman sympathizer might argue that his article showed only "cultural relativism," but to me, his attitude toward FDR also reflected the anger and bitterness that so many people his age and younger felt toward Johnson because of the war. These emotions had become a mental filter through which all previous presidents had to be seen. Braeman didn't consider the idea that Roosevelt's lack of action on behalf of African Americans and Jews reflected a need to accommodate the far larger number of racist and bigoted white Gentile voters who had elected him. This failure to accept the realities of the democratic political process again reminded me of attitudes of those radicals in the antiwar protest who'd surged to the fore in the later '60s, when the democratic process didn't appear to be bringing about withdrawal from Vietnam.

I don't say that the older scholar was perfect, that the younger one was all wet, or that every scholar in each age group shared their characteristics, but I was disturbed to find Braeman's article in an encyclopedia, where it might be the first thing an impressionable college freshman would read and set her or his mind into a rut that could be hard to get out of. By the time something gets into an encyclopedia, it's already been dealt with in more specialized books, so I looked for them, especially by younger scholars. On FDR's treatment of African Americans, I found helpful *The Presidency and the Politics of Racial Inequality: Nation-Keeping from 1831 to 1965* (1999) by Russell L. Riley (b. 1958).

Riley shared many of the post-'60s attitudes that characterized Braeman, with every good thing that could be said about Roosevelt's race relations countered by a wealth of persuasive observations tending to undercut it. He did convince me that most of Roosevelt's achievements in that field had either been forced upon him or were symbolic, but at least he gave FDR credit for being considerably more enlightened than his predecessors, and to that extent reflected the realities of the '30s and '40s as I understood them.[543] I found no evidence that Braeman's condemnation of FDR for his attitude toward African Americans dated back to the '60s, but it sure wasn't a factor in either of two major books published about Roosevelt in the later '50s.[544]

I did find a parent volume dramatizing the Roosevelt administration's neglect of Jewish refugees during World War II. *While Six Million Died: A Chronicle of American Apathy* had been published by Arthur D. Morse in 1968, that climactic year. This book contrasted strikingly with Robert A. Divine's *American Immigration Policy, 1924–1952* (1957). Devine said that although Congress opposed letting more emigrants into the country during the 1930s, "the Roosevelt administration displayed a keen desire to help the refugees in every way possible under law, and as a result administrative policy toward refugees enabled the United States to absorb more refugees than any other nation."[545]

Morse was not alone. In 1982, Leonard Dinnerstein listed five more books published in 1968 or later on how British and American officials had done little to stop the annihilation of the Jews.[546] He himself was less accusatory than Morse, although in *America and the Survivors of the Holocaust*, he told how Congress continued to resist the admission of "displaced persons" after the war, and how this attitude reflected the widespread anti-Semitism that still characterized the U.S. public. Other books documented anti-Semitism in the United States going into World War II more widespread and virulent than I'd known, and at least one suggested that Roosevelt had done as much as he could to respond to pleas by American Jews to admit more refugees.

"Were these Jewish intercessors wrong, then, in their conviction that Roosevelt, for all his dissembling and equivocation, was the Jews' last, best hope? They were not wrong," wrote Howard M. Sacher, in *A History of the Jews in America* (1992). "Almost any other occupant of the White House would have been worse for their people" when anti-Semitism was so rife that even Jewish-owned newspapers like *The New York Times* and *The Washington Post* dealt sketchily with the Holocaust because they "feared boring their readers."[547] My mother's friend could easily have heard that the Jews got Roosevelt into the war from Nazi radio broadcasts, for he'd been in the armed services in Europe, and such diatribes linking FDR with the Jews were documented in books about Nazi propaganda.[548] A book about anti-Semitism quoted an American official, involved in discussions about saving European Jews in 1943, writing in his diary that "one had to be careful not to give credence to Hitler's accusations."[549]

In *The New Dealers' War* (2001), Thomas Fleming would specifically compare Roosevelt to Lyndon Johnson, and the period before U.S. entry into World War II with the situation in the '60s, suggesting the two presidents had been equally duplicitous.[550] Here again FDR was seen through the filter of LBJ, but with older, working-class voters in the '60s, the situation had been reversed. They saw LBJ through the filter of FDR, whose administration had done so much for labor in the '30s. Unless the afterglow of this support were taken into consideration, younger people might not understand why so many voters continued to back LBJ, or why the debate over the war was so divisive. Left-wing scholars trying to discredit FDR were still fighting the battles of the '60s, but their dismissal of the New Deal left them ill-prepared to defend its legacy against the right-wing attacks on it that by 2001 had been going on for more than twenty years.[551] Left-wing radicals, however, may actually prefer reactionaries to liberals, for reactionaries offer targets that enable the radicals to rally forces to their own side. Liberals offer a viable alternative to radicalism. This renders them more of a threat to the radicals than do the reactionaries, and explains why Al Qaeda would have preferred to see John McCain elected to the U.S. presidency in 2008.[552]

*   *   *

The charges of anti-Semitism in Eliot that I'd first encountered in 1996, with the Anthony Julius book, could also be traced back to the '60s. In *T. S. Eliot's Bleistein Poems* (2000), Patricia Sloane summed up the issue and dismissed it as biographical rather than literary in nature, saying, "To date, from John Harrison to Anthony Julius, we have endured thirty years of impassioned 'deploring,' 'denouncing,' indicting,' 'condemning,' 'convicting,' the kind of posturing that by its very nature produces more heat than light."[553] Harrison's book, *The Reactionaries*, had been published in the United States in 1967 (1966 in the UK). Subtitled (in America) *A Study of the Anti-Democratic Intelligentsia*, it charged Eliot, Yeats, Wyndham Lewis, Pound and D. H. Lawrence with supporting or at least condoning fascism, and charged Eliot in addition with anti-Semitism and elitism. Harrison wasn't the first to criticize Eliot's anti-Semitism, but he was evidently the first to make a big impression with it, for in the decades that followed, the subject would become what one scholar has called an "academic industry."[554]

The argument had to do with esthetics as well as politics. It reflected the growing feeling among artists and writers in the '60s (both in the United States and abroad) that art couldn't be divorced from politics – that if it didn't commit itself to radical politics, it must be reactionary. But this was also a postmodernist position, reflecting the desire to dethrone modernism, and modernism's less censorious stance. Anti-Semitism and fascism must have seemed like related weapons to attack a modernist poet in a literary atmosphere that was doubtless equally inflamed with anti-modernist and antiwar sentiment. As I've already said, Eliot's anti-Semitism had never bothered me, and I saw *The Waste Land* as philosophic, rising above politics in the same way that great abstract painting does. Political writing says, This is what's wrong (or what's right) with the world; sometimes also, This is how it can be fixed. Philosophical writing (and art) simply says, This is the way the world *is*, creating more profound insights that outlast politics. Would we care as much about Elizabethan and fifteenth-century Florentine politics if Shakespeare and the art of the Quattrocento hadn't been as great as they were? Nor was I alone in seeking to explain Eliot's anti-Semitism, as opposed to capitalizing on it.[555]

*   *   *

By this time, I'd read the article by Frederick Crews in the *New York Review of Books*. It attacked Freud as a charlatan who'd invented only a "pseudoscience."[556] Crews said Freud's claims couldn't be substantiated empirically, suggesting that psychoanalytic therapy was at best little more than a placebo. I'd always known Freud was controversial, but in my youth, his antagonists had mostly been conservatives, screaming about his emphasis on S-X. Progressives like Walter and Leo Clark had admired him and applied his principles at North Country (to good effect – Leo was brilliant at applying child psychology). Since *The Feminine Mystique*, though, feminists had condemned Freud as a male chauvinist, and Crews gave more evidence that far larger segments of the "avant-garde" were now hostile to him, less because of what he said than because the *New York Review* was so prestigious.

Hoping to learn more about other flavors of psychology, in 1996 I'd audited an introductory psych course at Barnard. The instructor was a social psychologist, and I found that social psychology offered a corrective to Freud: Freudians were apt to find the person's neuroses responsible for all of her or his problems, while a social psychologist might suggest they arose from social situations over which the person had no control (I'd sort of done this in London in 1969, when figuring out why my dating experience at Barnard hadn't been better). Our instructor told us about the Stanford Prison Experiment, where in 1971 an experiment on the psychology of prison life supposed to last two weeks had to be canceled after only six days because the students assigned to play the role of guards were becoming sadistic, and the students assigned to play the role of prisoners were becoming depressed and showing evidence of serious stress.[557] This experiment furnished a welcome corrective not only to Freudian ideas about childhood traumas but also to biological determinism (the handy notion that anything which is wrong with you is all a matter of genes).

I picked up many other useful nuggets, too, but the instructor's attitude toward Freud was (to put it mildly) ambivalent. In one lecture, she recommended reading him, commenting upon his "compassion and flexibility," and adding that it was only his disciples who'd turned his ideas into "rigid doctrine," but in another, she described the unconscious as merely "a concept that was useful for the culture." She gave us a worksheet on defense mechanisms, but credited them exclusively to Anna Freud (who did codify them for the first time, in *The Ego and the Mechanisms of Defense* (1936), but in a context established by her father). This instructor's description of penis envy dripped scorn. "With girls, they see little boy's penis + develops penis envy," run the notes in my class notebook. "Says 'oh my God, I'm so inadequate + I can never win love of my mother.'" In the margin is underlined "*heavy sarcasm here.*"[558]

Stephen Mitchell and Margaret Black offered substantial evidence that not all of Freud's disciples had turned his ideas into "rigid doctrine" in *Freud and Beyond: A History of Modern Psychoanalytic Thought* (1995). Admittedly, they agreed that the classical Freudian image of the impersonal doctor taking notes as a patient lies on a couch and free-associates about his dreams had pretty much gone out of style, surviving mostly in the form of cartoons and movies. They suggested that the growing power of insurance companies and the government to dictate payments might be one factor, as well as the interest in briefer, targeted techniques for treating problems (to which I'd add the growing interest in neurology as explanation and medication as solution). Nevertheless, Mitchell and Black maintained that recent years had seen a dramatic increase in the extension of post-Freudian psychoanalytic concepts outside psychoanalysis itself, with object relations theories and self psychology influencing both social work and nearly every other form of psychotherapy currently in use. Mitchell and Black also pointed out that the philosophy of Freud and followers of his like Harry Stack Sullivan, Melanie Klein, and Heinz Kohut had made contributions to many areas of culture beyond psychology.[559]

Confirming this observation, a computerized study published in the *Journal of the American Psychoanalytic Association* in the spring of 2008 found 1,175 entries referencing psychoanalysis and related topics among the course listings of 150 top public and private universities and colleges, with 86.4 percent of these entries outside psychology departments, principally in the humanities and social sciences.[560] But a review of 23 studies involving 1,053 cases, published in *The Journal of the American Medical Association* in 2008, also concluded that long-term psychodynamic psychotherapy, the classic "talking cure" of Freud, was more effective in treating complex mental disorders than short-term psychodynamic psychotherapy.[561]

All of this didn't alter the fact that in art history (and probably every other discipline in the humanities and social sciences), psychoanalytically oriented scholars (if they valued survival) often had to find some means of accommodating themselves to the socially oriented ones. Crews suggested that the revolt against Freud began in the '70s (a period of consolidation for the '60s). "Since the 1970s," he wrote, "a rapidly growing number of independent scholars...have been showing us a different Freud," the "revisionist" Freud.[562] Some desire to revise Freud doubtless sprang from the larger number of women and minorities in academia in general and the psychological professions in particular: such scholars were apt to find him representative only of his time and place, but, at the risk of sounding megalomaniac, I think the revolt also reflected the shift in the mindset due to Vietnam. "Young people now are not interested in man's struggle against himself, but in man's struggle against society," Anna Freud had said in 1968. "They see that what psychoanalysis may lead to is adaptation to society. That's the last thing they have in mind."[563] Marx was the symbol of "man's struggle against society," and his star rose in the '60s as Freud's declined.

Within art, I saw a relation between the downgrading of Freud and the ascendance of postmodernist art through the polarities of feeling and reason that they represented. By reacting back from multireferential imagery into the uni-referential imagery of his Readymades, Duchamp made art that could again be described in words, words being what the reasoning mind uses.

Abstract art is hard to describe in words. What helped me respond to it in 1968 was Bill Rubin saying it was about "feeling." This had worked for me because the idea of feeling as a source for art plugged into my psychoanalysis and trying to make art in my modern-dress *Othello*.

Freud's career had been devoted to understanding feelings and relieving his patients of the need to be driven by unacceptable ones. Marxists believed that when the classless society arrived, people would behave in the best interests of all because of their innate reasonableness. The hostility toward Freud – and inability to respond with true sympathy to modernist abstraction – among post-'60s scholars influenced by Marx reminded me of the *Daily Worker* in 1951. I may not have read all of it when Karen and Lloyd, my mother's left-wing friends, were living next door to us, but I had read it in the mid-'90s, when revisiting my childhood for the book, and saw that the party line from Moscow viewed both psychoanalysis and abstract art as tools used by capitalists to delude the unwary into accepting their system instead of fighting it.[564]

*   *   *

Though I still planned to end my book with the 2000 elections, reading the papers forced upon me more recent developments. One of Bush's most aggravating campaign promises had been "faith-based" initiatives: funneling government welfare through churches. Religion is a sensitive subject for many people, but it struck a particularly tender nerve in me. Since the '60s, people had been more open-minded, but now it seemed we were regressing to the religious discrimination of the '50s, too.

Three days after his inauguration, Bush announced his education program, including vouchers for children in poor public schools to attend "private" schools (though he carefully avoided using the word, "vouchers").[565] In 1968, Walter Clark had explained to me that relatively few boys and girls attended private schools which were, like North Country, truly independent. Most "private-school" students went to church-affiliated schools, and most church-affiliated schools were Catholic.[566] Catholicism opposed both abortion and all birth control except the rhythm method. The idea that my tax dollars should go to subsidize such teachings infuriated me. Besides, it violated the First Amendment, which among other things was designed to keep members of one church from being taxed by another.[567] I got so upset that I abandoned work on my book to research and write an article on school vouchers for the Op-Ed page of the *Times*. Needless to say, it wasn't published (though the *Times* did air the views of some people who felt that same way that I did, it also published people supporting Bush).

I got more upset when Senator Joe Lieberman, the Orthodox Jewish Democratic nominee for vice president in 2000, came out in support of "faith-based initiatives." I'd expected Bush to fulfill his campaign promises, but I'd voted for Lieberman and Gore expecting they'd oppose him. Lieberman's double cross brought back painful memories of the "nice" Jewish males who, I suspected, had rejected me when I was younger because I wasn't Jewish enough. How would Lieberman feel about letting a son of his go out with me, I wondered bitterly. What chance had I ever stood with "Christians"? I wrote a Lieberman a furious letter. I wrote my senators and congresswoman, all of whom I'd already written about school vouchers. Carolyn Maloney, the congresswoman, replied that she opposed school vouchers, but supported "faith-based" initiatives in principle, adding only that she was concerned because many of Bush's proposals failed to include constitutional safeguards.[568] From the research for my Op-Ed piece, I knew that "constitutional safeguards" were a sham. I sent letters to other newspapers, another article to the *Times*. No response. All my representatives in Washington were Democrats, but none would go on record opposing faith-based initiatives per se. A Democrat had started doling out money to churches for social welfare: Bill Clinton, under the Welfare Reform Act of 1996.

Later, the ACLU and the NAACP publicly opposed Bush's "faith-based" bill.[569] The bill would have allowed church organizations receiving government funding to discriminate in hiring by favoring members of their own religion, and a survey indicated that while three-quarters of the public favored government funding for faith-based organizations, more than three-quarters said they would be opposed if the religious groups that received government money were allowed to hire only people of the same faith.[570] Maloney voted against the bill, but it passed the Republican-controlled House.[571] What disturbed me more was that too many Democratic politicians found fault only with that one provision in the bill. Too many more voters supported "faith-based" initiatives in principle, and too few like me opposed it. This was my first chilling realization that liberals like myself were no longer numerous enough so that politicians had to listen to us, not even Democratic politicians, and not even in this heavily Democratic state, where only months before, Al Gore had gotten 60 percent of the vote.

23. The Reception of Abstract Expressionism in the '50s (Spring–Summer 2001)

The more I focused on the wider shift in the mindset during the '60s, the more I wanted to see how the mindset shifted in art. I knew (or thought I knew) how in the '40s, the Manhattan art world had evolved toward an acceptance of abstract expressionism around 1950. I'd witnessed the reaction against modernist abstraction becoming progressively more vehement since 1967, but I hadn't studied the moment of the turnaround or the period leading up to it – the '50s, in other words, the supposed heyday of abstract expressionism, and the early '60s, when pop sprang into view. In the spring and early summer of 2001, I researched this turnaround, as evidenced in art magazines, mass-media magazines, academia, museums, and the marketplace. I couldn't have told you why I felt this material was important. All I could have said was that somehow it would fit into the picture of the past that I was trying to draw. When I'd drawn it, I'd find that it was at variance with the prevailing art-historical way of looking at that past – just as my picture of the '40s had offered a few surprises in the '80s.

When I first heard about abstract expressionism, fresh out of college, I got the impression that it was the reigning style of the '50s. I'd heard nothing to the contrary by the time I got to grad school, but rather come to believe that its reign had begun in the later '40s. Nor was this impression materially contradicted by Irving Sandler and Dore Ashton, authors of the two major books on abstract expressionism that had been published when I started work on my dissertation in the late '70s. Through the dissertation, I'd learned that in the '40s, much other art had received greater contemporary attention – though I could also see that by 1950, abstract expressionism had been surging to the fore. How far it had surged was what I needed to document in 2001. From the sources I've consulted, then and since, I've concluded that even in the '50s, at the height of its influence, abstract expressionism never took over the entire scene – not even within the art world and certainly not with the larger community who might have read about it only in the mass media, from *Life* and *Look* to *Vogue* and *Harper's Bazaar,* and as opposed to art magazines or little magazines.

Throughout the '50s, abstract expressionism had many passionate supporters within the art world, as nearly as I can tell without having been part of that world myself. Many younger painters wanted to try their hand at it, too, but in retrospect their level of performance indicates that even among adherents, abstraction was poorly understood. As for the world outside the art world, my findings are somewhat at odds with scholars who are sometimes apt to convey the impression that the popular press, en masse, eagerly assimilated and effectively promulgated abstract expressionism.[572] My library research, upbringing in the "nervous trades," and knowledge of the media acquired on the job, all suggest that only by very selective citation can this argument be substantiated. Art historians also tend to behave as though the mass media spoke for society in this supposedly wholesale acceptance of abstract expressionism, when at best they were only attempting to educate it.

In the '30s and '40s, most American art lovers had still been reluctant to accept even the modernist abstraction of cubism, just as most American painters steered clear of it (often falling into oblivion as a result). Such reluctance left many artists (to say nothing of their audiences) ill-prepared to cope with abstract expressionism in the '50s. When pop art arrived, in the early '60s, its supporters talked of an abstract expressionist "Establishment" that had to be overthrown in order to usher in a "return to figuration." This was true only to the extent that 1) the representational painting of the '50s lacked the cachet of being "avant-garde"; 2) abstract expressionism enjoyed this cachet; 3) the pop art of the early '60s had enough in newness or novelty, and created enough controversy, to be able to claim that it was "the new avant-garde"; and finally, 4) its popularity swept most of the secondary abstract expressionists from public view. Still, if we are to understand fully why pop itself should have become so widely and so rapidly popular, I think we need to underline the fact that figuration had never completely gone out of style, and that right through the '50s, many painters created and more art lovers admired even the traditional varieties of representational painting that coexisted with abstract expressionism in generous measure. Not all these people would be enthusiastic about pop. But for many, maybe most of them, anything that meant the end of abstraction as an "superior" form of expression was more appreciated than abstraction itself had ever been. During the '50s, they'd felt the need to respect abstract expressionism, but respect isn't the same as love.

*   *   *

My revisionist portrait of the past began in 1939, when the Museum of Modern Art staged a big Picasso retrospective. Picasso was far more radical than most of the "modern" art that MoMA showed in those days. Sandler and

Ashton reported that in 1936, MoMA staged *Cubism and Abstract Art*, and they suggested that the young abstract expressionists found it an inspiring show.[573] Not mentioned was the fact that this show was radical even for MoMA. Since the museum had been founded in 1929 by Abby Aldrich Rockefeller (Mrs. John D. Rockefeller, Jr.) and two other ladies, most of its solo exhibitions had been much less adventurous. These shows were devoted to late nineteenth-century or early twentieth-century Europeans and American representational painters, from Van Gogh and Cézanne to Edward Hopper.[574] American magazines, on the whole, were no more daring. *The Art Digest* (forerunner of *Arts*) was edited by a man who'd done a book on all the folksy, aggressively representational paintings that *Life* featured in the '30s. *Vanity Fair* was known for its color reproductions of "modern" art. It was more sophisticated than the good people who enthused about "American Scene" painting and Social Realism, those twin bastions of representational painting that dominated the art scene in the '30s, the former reflecting a reactionary political outlook and the latter a radical one. Yet even sophisticated *Vanity Fair* published nothing more abstract than early, representational Blue Period Picasso.

By comparison with such taste, *Time* was advanced, but then Luce was already friendly with Nelson Rockefeller, Abby's son, by 1936, when Luce first envisaged moving the Time Inc. offices from the Chrysler Building into the not-yet-built Time & Life Building in brand-new Rockefeller Center.[575] Young Nelson was involved in renting out the ambitious city-within-a-city that his multimillionaire father was building in the teeth of the Depression, and Nelson was already nuts about modern art. Needless to say, the Rockefeller family's legendary wealth and social standing must have had their charms for Luce, just as they did for so many other upwardly mobile New Yorkers, but for whatever reason, between 1936 and 1939 *Time* ran four cover stories on MoMA: Abby (January 1936), Dalí (December 1936), Picasso (February 1939), and Nelson, as president of MoMA (May 1939). Soon thereafter, Nelson engineered Luce's election to MoMA's board of trustees.[576] In his own collecting, though, Luce was more conservative. He owned work by John Kane, a self-taught painter, and by David Alfaro Siqueiros, the Mexican muralist.[577] Self-taught artists, called "primitives," and Mexican muralists were "modern" but not abstract, therefore popular among fashionable collectors who wished to appear modern but weren't quite ready to go all the way. Mrs. Luce bought paintings by Frida Kahlo, the Mexican artist who in the postmodernist era has become something of a cult figure but whose style in the '30s wasn't as radical as abstraction, combining as it did academic surrealism with the primitive.[578]

Knowing all this, I should have expected some public hostility when *Picasso: Forty Years of His Art* opened at MoMA in late 1939, but the degree

I found surprised me. *The New York Times* published many letters to the editor about the show, some defending but some bitterly attacking it. It was widely reviewed, and, even before every last painting was hung, averaged 2,000 visitors a day (a lot, for the museum was far smaller than it is now).[579] Most critics agreed that the show was well mounted, but with few exceptions, they were ambivalent about the art, though the show had comparatively few paintings from the period of Analytic Cubism, Picasso's most abstract.

One of the few altogether positive reviews was by George L. K. Morris, the American cubist painter, who defended Picasso's cubism in *Partisan Review* on the basis of its "purity" and ability to convey emotion.[580] But even the most open-minded academic reception evinced a strangely conflicted admiration, at least as indicated by Robert Goldwater, a younger art historian whose then-recent *Primitivism in Modern Painting* (1938) would become a classic. Goldwater reviewed the show for *Art in America* (in those days a scholarly quarterly primarily devoted to art history), finding the work "magnificent" but also representative of the "disquieting" modern era. The scholar spoke of Picasso's "disturbing" succession of styles, suggesting that they might be due to his wish to avoid "banality"and "repetition," and to his being "denied a tradition within which to work." The paradox was that this rapid succession of "periods" accounted for a "recurrent purely decorative tendency of his art."[581]

An unsigned column in *The New York Times* divided ordinary museum-goers at the Picasso show into three groups. First were the young, self-confident visitors, happily discussing the paintings in the formal language of the day: cadences and designs. Third were all the people who got more and more furious at the paintings as they went through the show, and were practically apoplectic by the time they left. The largest group was the second, those who hadn't known what to expect, and wound up no more enlightened. These people could get something out of the Blue Period, the *Times* explained, "But once they are face to face with cubism and the African influence, they are lost....The latest experiments leave them completely shattered."[582]

In this context Clem published "Avant-Garde and Kitsch," which would make him at thirty an overnight celebrity in his small highbrow crowd, and has since become his best-known essay. It appeared in the Fall 1939 issue of *Partisan Review*, just as the MoMA show was opening, and, though primarily concerned with kitsch or mass culture as a threat to high culture, did concede that Picasso still drew crowds. What struck me in 2001 was how much more enthusiastic Clem sounded than any of the commentators on the Picasso exhibition. He spoke of abstract artists deriving their "chief inspiration" from the medium they worked in, and how the "excitement of their art" lay "in its pure preoccupation with the invention and arrangement of spaces, surfaces, shapes, colors, etc...."[583] "Excitement" and "inspiration" implied virtues and vitality for abstraction above and beyond purity or even emotion.

*   *   *

Luce wasn't prepared for abstract expressionism when it surfaced after World War II. Years later, Nelson told how he, fellow MoMA trustees, and Barr among them managed to persuade Luce that "modern art" wasn't a danger for American society, but evidence of how strong and free it was.[584] Although Luce remained dubious about abstract expressionism to the end of his days, he let his magazines deal with it much as its individual editors saw fit.[585] *Life* believed in bringing art to its readers, and would right on through the '50s be more sympathetic to abstract expressionism than any other mass-audience magazine, but most of its art stories in the '40s were about older art, from ancient times on through the early twentieth century, art that its many readers with only high-school educations might be able to appreciate.

In 1948, it organized a "round table" discussion on "modern" art, offering spokesmen both for and against it. The year before, the magazine had done a big article on Stuart Davis, whose semiabstract style had been formed before World War II, but most of its articles about contemporary American art in the '40s featured representational painters who were esteemed in the '40s. As these artists have been mostly forgotten, the articles have, too. *Life* is best remembered for its thoroughly atypical article on Pollock of August 1949, proposed by Daniel Longwell, an executive editor who wasn't part of the regular art section, but read little magazines like *Partisan Review*. The article described Pollock's unorthodox painting techniques, and reproduced paintings in color. Its title, "Jackson Pollock: Is he the greatest living painter in the United States?" referred to the fact that "a formidably high-brow New York critic" made that claim.[586] Pollock was suddenly a national figure, but more notorious than celebrated: the story elicited 532 letters, of which only twenty supported him or his work.[587]

Life's response to this negative barrage was to backpedal. Seven months later, in March 1950, the magazine ran a cover story that must have taken months to prepare, on nineteen younger American painters whom it offered as among the most promising of their generation. Only two, Hedda Sterne and Theodoros Stamos, were abstract expressionists (and lesser ones, at that). The other seventeen were, to one degree or another, representational. All except Stamos are mostly forgotten, and only one scholar whom I've come across mentions the article, though *Life* ran ten pages of color photography with it.[588] The article on Pollock had only two pages of color photography, but it's been cited and discussed ad nauseam.

Much the same has happened with the photograph in *Life* by Nina Leen of the "Irascibles," a group portrait of the abstract expressionists that ran in January 1951. Leen posed the artists together because they'd signed an open letter attacking juries chosen by the Metropolitan Museum of Art for a big show of contemporary art.[589] The *Life* story accompanying Leen's photograph was about this exhibition, with four pages of color photography showing the semiabstract and representational art in it. Again, Leen's photograph has become a classic, but practically nobody I've read mentions the article it accompanied, nor does anybody discuss it at length.[590] Nevertheless, the paintings reproduced there were more what "the media" really welcomed, as something most of their readers might like. Leen's photograph must have made a splash within the "nervous trades." It's a great picture, and shows that she (and *Life*) were in the swim, right up to the moment, au courant with the latest wrinkle of the avant-garde – but in that rather shallow sense of being the latest novelty, abstract expressionism's moment in most of the major media would pass almost before it began.

Having studied the response to the Picasso show, I could see how incredibly far out Pollock's paintings must have seemed to the larger audience of *Life*, as I hadn't been able to earlier. Still, this vision in 2001 tallied with my dissertation findings that neither art magazines nor newspaper critics nor even supposedly sophisticated magazines like *The New Yorker* were overly impressed with the young abstract expressionists before late 1949. Then – zowie! In 1949, *Life* had a circulation of 5.4 million, the largest of the large-format magazines in the country (for a fuller list of magazine circulations, see Appendix). *The Nation*, where Clem's claims for Pollock originally appeared, had a circulation of about 40,000, and *Partisan Review*, where he wrote about art in more theoretical terms, had about 10,000. Thus, in effect *Life* was amplifying his voice more than a hundred times, from a whisper to a trumpet blast.

Whatever *Life*'s less sophisticated readers thought of the article, it seems to have impressed more sophisticated ones. Regardless of its primary audience, the magazine was written and edited by college graduates, and read by many of them, too. Its photography was often superb, and though its texts could be elementary, on occasion it was witty, as recently as the spring of 1949, when it had carried the delightful picture version of Russell Lynes's article on highbrows, upper middlebrows, lower middlebrows and lowbrows. Only after the *Life* article on Pollock appeared did Coates in *The New Yorker* and McBride in the *Sun* begin to take the artist more seriously.[591] *Life*'s less sophisticated readers, however, kept on having trouble with him and with abstract expressionism in general throughout the '50s.

While continuing to offer them plenty of traditional art, the magazine in November 1955 also published closeup views of three representational paintings, showing how abstract these details appeared. This, it probably hoped, would enable readers to relate better to abstraction. In April 1957, *Life* featured Hofmann, the abstract expressionist better known as a teacher, with abstract and representational former students of his: another way of trying to integrate "ab-ex" into readers' ideas of contemporary art. *Life* also dealt with the success that American abstract painting was enjoying abroad. In 1957, it featured Helen Frankenthaler, Grace Hartigan, and Joan Mitchell, but rather because they were women than because their work was abstract (the article included representational women artists, too). As late as 1959, *Life* was still titling a two-part series on abstract expressionism per se "Baffling U.S. Art: What It Is About." The lede summed up the problem: though American abstract expressionism was "the most influential style of art in the world today," it was still "a source of bafflement and irritation to the public at large."[592]

Time's Art page in the later '40s was already written by Alex Eliot. To say that Eliot didn't welcome abstract expressionism would be an understatement: his attacks on Pollock in particular were still remembered as proof of *Time*'s philistinism when I took over the Art page in 1967, especially his epithet for Pollock in 1956, "Jack the Dripper." But Eliot wasn't ignorant about art, or even reactionary. He'd dreamed of becoming an artist himself, and studied under the very modern Josef Albers at progressive Black Mountain College.[593] In the '40s, he wrote favorable stories for *Time* about earlier European avant-garde artists like Klee and Braque, and a cover on Diego Rivera, the Mexican muralist (he wanted to quit *Time* and do a book about Rivera, but Rivera wouldn't let him, because he wasn't a communist). The contemporary U.S. artists whom he chronicled were predominantly representational, but this taste corresponded to that of most of his readers. I'm sure his Art page had a high readership (for an Art page), and was particularly appreciated in towns like Rovere.

In the later '50s, he shared writing the Art page with Cranston Jones, a younger man who by the '60s would be senior editor for the section, and teach me so much about art. Jones liked post-war abstract painting, and most likely wrote the more sympathetic stories about it that *Time* ran in the later '50s, but the magazine continued to devote much more space to representational art, and not until the '60s would it deal with American abstract expressionists in significant depth. In the '50s, *Time* still couldn't believe that artistic leadership had passed from Paris to New York, so it focused on School of Paris equivalents to American abstract expressionism, known as *tachisme* and *l'art informel*. In 1957, the magazine did flattering articles on three of these Parisian painters, while still attacking U.S. abstract expressionism as "the new Academy."[594] The *tachistes* have fallen from favor in the United States, but *Time* was far from alone during the '50s in admiring either them or contemporary representational art. The well-known group shows of contemporary Americans organized for MoMA by Dorothy Miller in 1952, 1956, and 1959 were predominantly abstract, but always included at least a few figurative or semiabstract artists. The paintings acquired by the museum between 1950 and 1959 were likewise divided between abstract and representational or semiabstract, as well as between American and foreign artists. (In fact, as MoMA was acquiring paintings by earlier artists as well as contemporary ones, the balance in favor of foreign and representational or semiabstract artists was quite lopsided).[595]

Newsweek's Art section didn't catch fire until the later '50s, though it was competently written from 1942 to 1946 by Hilda Loveman, a Barnard graduate (like *Time*, *Newsweek* let women write during World War II). When she left to start raising a family, *Newsweek* apparently didn't care enough about art to replace her with anybody who knew much about it. In the late '40s and early '50s, the magazine ran little on art and practically nothing on avant-garde American art (unless the avant-garde was being attacked by politicians). Instead, it dealt with Old Masters, cartoons, photography, and insipid contemporary realists, to the extent, in December 1952, of doing a cover story on John Falter, a second-string *Saturday Evening Post* cover artist, and the general subject of magazine illustration. In August 1954, however, the same month that Kermit Lansner's name appeared for the first time on *Newsweek*'s masthead, a marked improvement in the magazine's art coverage began to take place.[596] The section appeared more often, and became more knowledgeable – though its first big story on an abstract expressionist, Hofmann, didn't run until 1957. This was followed by stories on Barnett Newman (1959), Ad Reinhardt (1960), Rothko (1961), de Kooning, Motherwell, and Gorky (all 1962), and Clyfford Still (1963). Pollock didn't get an article all to himself until 1964, but in 1961, the magazine did a story on a book about him. It was by an English writer who'd never met him, and *Newsweek* described all the complaints that British reviewers and the Manhattan art world had about it. This was real insider stuff.[597]

Admittedly, by the time *Newsweek* was running these articles about the abstract expressionists, *Time* was also dealing with them more sympathetically. But *Time* was committed to addressing the good folk out there in Rovere, and many of them would still say, perfectly openly, that they just didn't understand this kind of painting, so the subject had to be handled in a way that took their attitude into account. Both magazines did stories about *The New American Painting*, a big show of U.S. abstract expressionist paintings organized under the auspices of MoMA's International Council that traveled around Europe in 1958–59. *Time*'s story in August 1958 (most likely written by Jones) was accompanied by four pages of color photography. Its lede concluded that the show was getting "cheers from most younger painters" and "nibbles from some collectors," but it also conceded that the show was causing "cries of outrage from many critics," and "a monumental amount of bafflement from the general public."[598]

The following May, *Newsweek*'s lede brusquely summarized the European reception to the show by saying that everybody loved it, except in France, "which likes no encroachment upon its traditional artistic values" (a euphemistic way of saying it was biased in favor of its own artists).[599] The rest of the story was about Hartigan, one of the youngest artists in the show, and its only woman. The message conveyed to the reader was, you're sophisticated enough to know all about abstract expressionism, so we won't go into detail about this show. Still, you might not have heard about the French reaction, or understand why it was so hostile, and look, here's a younger artist who hasn't gotten the same publicity that the older ones have; she's the real news.

*   *   *

The art magazines were more sympathetic to American abstract expressionism than to its French equivalent, but even at the height of "ab-ex," in the '50s, they regularly ran stories on contemporary representational painting, too. Between 1950 and 1959, the Whitney Museum reproduced about 130 paintings in the catalogues of its annual exhibitions of contemporary art (these shows have always been criticized, but to a degree they must have been representative of the work being done). Of these 130 paintings, I'd consider only about fifty pure abstractions; about fifty were predominantly representational (though rarely naturalistic) and the remainder appear to have been semiabstract (as nearly as I can tell from these small, poor-quality, black-and-white reproductions, and although reviewers were apt to classify these as "abstract," too. Certainly, these paintings often incorporated many busy little shapes, rather than the single large image that distinguished the canvases of the leading abstract expressionists). Among the eighteen better-remembered representational painters whose work was reproduced in those Whitney catalogues, seven were senior figures (born before 1900, including Hopper, Charles Sheeler, Max Weber, and Ben Shahn), but eight were contemporaries of the first-generation abstract expressionists (born between 1900 and 1919, including Wyeth, Jacob Lawrence, Philip Evergood, and Jack Levine), and three were still younger (born 1920 or later: Johns, James McGarrell, and George Tooker).

Other traditional representational and semiabstract painters were also making headway in the '50s, among them Milton Avery (b. 1885), Fairfield

Porter (b. 1907), Nell Blaine (b. 1922), Leland Bell (b. 1922), Jane Freilicher (b. 1924), and Wolf Kahn (b. 1927). An untraditional foe of abstract painting was living in New York in the '50s: Marcel Duchamp, who voiced his dislike for "retinal" painting to anybody who would listen, and who was affectionately described by McBride in 1950 as "the acknowledged but unofficial ambassador of good will from France to this country...."[600] Duchamp was far from invisible, even in the early '50s. Volume 8 of *The Art Index* (November 1950–October 1953) listed eight entries for him, and eight more under "dadaism" (after subtracting for duplication). Besides stories in *Art News* and *The Art Digest*, this list included one in *Time* and two in *Life*.

As nearly as I can reconstruct the milieu of the '50s, there seems to have been a general agreement that abstract expressionism was the accepted vanguard. There were many shows of work by first-, second-, and third-generation abstract expressionists in the '50s, yet in retrospect it seems that many people, inside and outside the art world, apparently still found abstraction difficult, even impossible to respond to, let alone understand. Most of these people appear to have been delighted when de Kooning reverted to the semiabstract, with his much-discussed exhibition at the Sidney Janis Gallery in March 1953 of paintings of bizarre, nightmarish women. Some fervent abstractionists seem to have been very angry at this desertion from the fold, but *Art News* gave the show what in showbiz would have been called a big advance promo, and all the reviews that I've read were – though sometimes stunned – on balance, favorable.[601] In fact, those *Woman* paintings may have done more to establish de Kooning as the "leader" of abstract expressionism than anything else he ever made, although (or rather because) they weren't pure abstractions: people could say that with these paintings, they could finally relate to abstract expressionism, though in fact they weren't truly relating to abstraction at all.

One way around the problems posed by pure abstraction had been offered by Harold Rosenberg, three months before de Kooning's *Woman* show: the critic's dada-inspired article about "action" painting appeared in *Art News* in December 1952. The idea (rightly or wrongly) derived from it – that an abstract expressionist canvas depicted only existential nothingness – would remain popular with postmodernist academics: it jibed with and reinforced Rauschenberg's idea of a gap between art and life. In the '50s, however, this idea was apparently only one of several used by people who liked abstraction and wanted to explain why they liked it to people who didn't.

Commoner was to say that it was difficult or even shocking because it was new; and to try to encourage people who still didn't get it to keep on looking at it – in hopes that eventually they'd be able to appreciate such paintings for the sake of their forms and colors alone, even if they couldn't (and/or were told that they shouldn't) see subject matter comparable to what they'd been raised with.

Abstract painting was also said to be a form of landscape or nature study. This analogy prompted an exhibition at the Whitney Museum called *Nature in Abstraction* (1958). In 1975, this argument would lead to the publication of Rosenblum's *Modern Painting and the Northern Romantic Tradition: Friedrich to Rothko*, but Rosenblum was already making analogies between abstract expressionism and landscape as early as February 1961, when *Art News* published his article on "The Abstract Sublime."

Some people liked to compare abstract art to classical music without words (symphonies, chamber music). At least one abstract painter I know has continued to use this analogy right into the twenty-first century.

Still, perhaps the idea of abstract expressionism as conveying "feeling" was as common as the idea that it was difficult because it was new, and commoner than the analogies with landscape or music. What irony that the '50s, so often called an era of repressed sexuality, should have been a time when art was associated with passionate emotion! True, passion may develop more easily when physical gratification must be delayed, but the "feeling" associated with abstract expressionism in the '50s had little to do with sex. Rather, it was fuzzily defined, amorphous. People talked about abstract expressionism as "subjective" instead of "objective," depicting the artist's inner landscape as opposed to what he or she saw in the external world. They tossed around the words "ambiguous" and "ambiguity" without clarifying what they meant (for, as I pointed out earlier, a painting can be ambiguous in a formal sense as well as an iconographic one – when the artist has rendered foreground and background blended so the viewer can't tell where one begins and the other leaves off; Analytic Cubism was already ambiguous in this sense). There were many references to "the unconscious" as a source for abstract expressionism, Freud being more fashionable than he is now, but again these references were vague. They didn't suggest that the unconscious had assimilated images or information from the external, natural world, still less that it was synthesizing such information and conveying it to viewers.

Clem had often written of feeling, emotion, and "being moved" by art in the '40s and early '50s. He used such phrases much less often in the later '50s, perhaps because so many people had mistakenly begun to assume that any free, loose brushwork must be expressive of emotion, and any painting lacking in such brushwork must lack emotion. Particularly irritating to Clem, I should imagine, would have been the assumption that "feeling" resided exclusively in the overwrought brushwork of "gestural" painting as practiced by de Kooning and his many followers, since Clem considered de Kooning inferior to Pollock, and most of de Kooning's followers second- or even third-rate. (Some of

Clem's friends still took "feeling" very seriously, though, most notably Bill Rubin, who in the '50s was already contributing to the art press.)

The importance of feeling, music, and the new in learning to appreciate modern art had already been suggested by two books published in the wake of the 1913 Armory Show, Arthur Jerome Eddy's *Cubists and Post-Impressionism* (1914), and Willard Huntington Wright's *Modern Painting: Its Tendency and Meaning* (1915). None of these ideas were unique or original with Eddy and Wright. The analogy with music may have begun with Kandinsky, but the idea of feeling as central to abstract art could trace its ancestry back to the pre-Romantic period of the late eighteenth century. It was then that the idea of emotion as central to all art arose (in response to the overemphasis in the Enlightenment on reason, and as a revival of what some call "the emotionalist theory of art," which can even be said to have started with Aristotle, and his idea that tragedy inspires pity and fear). In the late eighteenth century, feeling in art was related to "sentiment," though not identical with it. For Barbara Novak's seminar in nineteenth-century American art, I'd written about sentiment in an American context, but as a synonym for feeling, I see it as having descended to become a way of interpreting abstract expressionism by way of England, Russia, and England again.

Laurence Sterne, the English novelist, was one of many who had underlined the importance of feeling or "sentiment" in *A Sentimental Journey Through France and Italy* (1768). His book was among those that deeply impressed Leo Tolstoy, the Russian novelist.[602] In 1896, Tolstoy published *What Is Art?* In this small book, he maintained that the proper duty of a work of art was to infect the spectator or auditor with a feeling that its creator had experienced. He injected morality into the discussion by arguing that the best art was that which conveyed the "best" emotions, such as heroic self-sacrifice or love of one's neighbor.[603] Despite this caveat (which as Tolstoy saw it, eliminated virtually every artist from Michelangelo to the moderns), *What Is Art?* in turn deeply impressed the English Roger Fry (Clem's best-known predecessor as a formalist critic).[604] Both Fry and Clive Bell, Fry's fellow esthete in Bloomsbury, explored feeling in art (only a few years before Eliot, who had friends in Bloomsbury, was creating poems like *The Waste Land* that relied for their effect upon feeling or mood).

Fry didn't share Tolstoy's moralistic considerations, but in his youth, he thought of a work of art as the result of an emotion felt by the artist and communicated to the viewer by the work of art.[605] Later on, he came to respect the view put forward by Bell that the artist wasn't concerned with conveying any such direct emotions, but rather only "the aesthetic emotion."[606] Fry seems to have been the first critic to apply the idea of feeling to abstract art, in a review of some "improvisations" by Kandinsky that he'd seen at the

Albert Hall in London in 1913. "They are pure visual music," he wrote, "but I cannot any longer doubt the possibility of emotional expression by such abstract visual signs."[607]

By the '50s, the idea of feeling as the subject in art seems to have become so widely accepted that it was even being critiqued. One book to do so was Susanne K. Langer's *Feeling and Form: A Theory of Art* (1953). Langer, a philosophy professor, was one of three writers whom Clem had recommended to me, the first time I met him (along with Kant and Benedetto Croce). She agreed that works of art often expressed "the artist's state of mind," but expressions of feeling "may also be found in wastebaskets and in the margins of schoolbooks," because "all drawings, utterances, gestures, or personal records of any sort express feelings...." To rate as art, Langer believed, the work had to create "forms symbolic of human feeling" – forms that could evoke an esthetic emotion in the viewer that she equated to "exhilaration."[608] Alas, history suggests that for most Americans – and art-world denizens – not even the analogies with music, landscape, existential nothingness, or feeling enabled them to get from an abstract expressionist canvas what they felt somehow entitled to have. They still wanted a rational explanation, a subject that could be defined in words, a more concrete idea of what the work of art was "about."

*   *   *

Besides *Life*, *Time*, and *Newsweek*, the only other consumer magazine that wrote about art regularly was *The New Yorker*.[609] Throughout the '50s, Coates remained on its staff, and his understated urbanity – so much a part of the *New Yorker* mystique – kept him from saying much that was extremely positive about abstract expressionism (though it also kept him from condemning it). In his reviews of the Whitney annuals, he preferred instead to emphasize what a lot of abstract painting there was in them, though by "abstract" he often seems to have meant what I'd be more inclined to call "semiabstract," and also to lump in older abstractionists working in styles that had originated in the '30s with the abstract expressionists themselves.[610]

The *Readers' Guide to Periodical Literature* helped me locate stories about abstract or at least modern art in other major magazines: *Look*, *The Saturday Evening Post*, *Esquire*, *Mademoiselle*, *Vogue*, and *Harper's Bazaar*. Throughout the '50s, these articles were sparse and, with rare exceptions, skirted the subject of abstract expressionism or dumped on it. *Look*, which vied with *Life* for readers with only high-school educations, alluded to art, especially modern art, rarely. Four stories it ran in the '50s dealt with modern art, but "modern" didn't necessarily mean contemporary, let alone abstract.

One story (January 1953) was written by Ben Shahn, an arch-realist.[611] A second (November 1953) featured the art collection of Roy Neuberger, a stockbroker whose tastes, as shown in this article, stopped well short of abstract expressionism. The magazine did reproduce a Hofmann from Neuberger's collection, but it was a semiabstract still life, probably from the '30s, not one of the pure abstracts the artist was known for in the '40s and '50s. Other representational or semiabstract paintings pictured were by Shahn, Avery, Marsden Hartley, and my dissertation subject, the figurative expressionist Abraham Rattner.[612] A third article in *Look* (January 1956) concerned Picasso (hardly a trailblazer at that point). The text, by Russell Lynes, was sensitive but brief, and, although the article reproduced six Picassos in color, all were from his more representational periods (not the near-abstracts of Analytic Cubism).[613] A fourth article (February 1958) concerned "The Taste Shaper," René d'Harnoncourt, director of MoMA. To call modern art "taste" was in effect putting it down (though doubtless not consciously intended that way). The art shown as typical of D'Harnoncourt's "taste" did include one small abstract woodcut, but no painting more radical than a representational Matisse from 1911, and no sculpture more daring than a semiabstract "stabile" by Alexander Calder from 1937.[614]

The only one of these four articles that offered an extended discussion of art as art, and tried to render it more sympathetic and comprehensible to typical *Look* readers, was the piece by Shahn. It dealt with realism, not abstraction. Two of Newman's abstractions were used in September 1951 as backdrops by *Look* for a photo spread featuring two dress designers, a socialite, and an opera star, all wearing ball gowns and illustrating a book extract by Anita Colby, the first supermodel, on how to chose clothes that matched your figure and personality. Nothing was said about Newman's paintings beyond a caption indicating that they'd been photographed during his show at Betty Parsons.[615] Since the show had opened in April, and *Vogue* the month before had run its photo spread featuring models in ball gowns posed in front of Pollock's paintings at the same gallery, it looks to me as though *Look* had been playing copycat (just as it would play copycat with "Swinging London" fifteen years later).

The Saturday Evening Post, *Life*'s other principal large-format competitor, ran an editorial in September 1957 chortling over a chimpanzee named Betsy who'd made news by painting "abstract pictures" at the Baltimore Zoo. The notion that even an animal could make modern art dated back to the nineteenth century, but Betsy enabled the *Post* to argue that collecting abstract art was all about social-climbing anyway.[616] Apparently such philistinism was more than even that magazine could live with, for in August 1959, it published an article by Clem, "The Case for Abstract Art."

One scholar has written that Clem chose the *Post* to express his case for abstract art.[617] Actually, the *Post* asked him to write it.[618] With a circulation in the millions, the magazine must have paid far more than the small-circulation magazines to which Clem normally contributed, but the article wasn't easy to write, and seems to have been less than a complete success. Making no compromises, it suggested to the *Post*'s lower-middlebrow readers that if they couldn't appreciate abstract art, it was partly because it was new, and partly because they didn't engage enough in disinterested contemplation of it, or try to enjoy it for its own sake.[619] In other words (I say cruelly), if they didn't get it, they had only themselves to blame.

This in turn seems to have caused enough consternation so that three months later, the magazine ran "The Anguish of Modern Art," by William Snaith, an industrial designer. He split the difference between formal and philistine by tracing the history of modern art with little illustrations from Matisse to Pollock, and concluding that art had lost its power to communicate.[620] The *Post* then reverted to its earlier skepticism, and in October 1961 ran a jocular piece asking "Is Abstract Art a Private Joke?" Norman Rockwell's equally jocular cover depicting a "connoisseur" gazing at a supposed Pollock appeared three months later, in January 1962. By this time, pop art was already beginning to attract attention.

The situation was no more sympathetic to abstract art at *Esquire*, the gentleman's magazine. In January 1957, it featured Jean Hélion, an older French painter who was courageously fighting fashion by abandoning abstraction for representation; *Esquire* thought this a great idea. *Mademoiselle* was also looking forward to a closer rapport with "nature" in February 1956, when it ran an article called "Is Abstract Art Dead?" In July 1961, when more figurative art was gaining attention, *Esquire* celebrated with an article entitled "A. E....and the hell with it!"

Vogue was the only other national consumer magazine (beside *Life*) to take a more positive view of abstract expressionism, at least in the early years of the movement, and I found four pieces that at least referred to it between 1948 and 1951. The magazine included a Pollock among twenty-four works of art reproduced in April 1948 in a quiz on Manhattan art galleries. In April 1950, it used a full-page color reproduction of a Rothko, accompanied by a glowing description, but only in an article on wall decoration. As indicated earlier, Pollock's classic abstractions were used as backdrops in a spread on spring ball gowns in March 1951. The idea of using modern paintings as a backdrop in fashion spreads was neither new nor unique to *Vogue*, though on this occasion they were accompanied by a respectful but somewhat ambivalent unsigned text block ("dazzling and curious....The puzzled call them idiotic, the admiring call him a genius").[621] Many scholars have reproduced and/or discussed this photo layout, but the text block, if quoted at all, is excerpted only very briefly. The fuller citation is important because it shows how well *Vogue* knew its readers, and how it realized that not all of them (if indeed any of them) were going to find Pollock their cup of tea.

In October 1951, *Vogue* ran an article by Aline B. Louchheim (later Saarinen) on Parsons, whose gallery represented not only Pollock and Newman, but other abstract expressionists as well. While favorable to her and to abstract expressionism, Louchheim conceded that "some of the public" was "baffled by the unfamiliar, non-representational art," and added that "there are many people who think, and many more who hope, that the pendulum of taste will swing again away from these artists."[622] This doesn't surprise me. I grew up in a household where *Vogue* was often on the coffee table. My well-dressed, reasonably affluent mother undoubtedly picked up ideas about clothes and accessories from the magazine, but Pollock – and abstract art in general – weren't her thing. Except for a semiabstract plaster sculpture that I'd made at Dalton, all the art in our apartment was representational (including watercolors I'd made while visiting London in 1949; nothing else could be called original).

Many of my mother's women friends would, I guess, have read *Vogue*. All were successful professionals and/or married to successful professionals, what a social art historian might consider "people of higher status," but none were serious art collectors, either. I was sent to fancy schools. Classmates invited me to their homes, especially when I was at Dalton (between 1950 and 1952, the period when Pollock was being reproduced in *Vogue*). In this way, I saw a number of luxurious Manhattan interiors, furnished by women who might equally well have read *Vogue* and could easily be described as "people of higher status." The decor was always traditional, with grand piano and large, academic oil portrait of the child, children, or lady of the house, prominently hung. I'm sure that some Dalton parents had more avant-garde tastes. So did some *Vogue* readers, and its art director, Alexander Liberman, was a very modern artist himself, but the artistic preferences of the magazine's more typical readers, I suspect, were more nearly indicated by four features it ran in the '50s on prominent private collectors.

In June 1959, it dealt with Robert Lehman's collection of Old Masters, reproducing a Botticelli in color and a drawing by Leonardo da Vinci in black and white. In December 1957, it showed the Stavros Niarchos collection: Van Gogh, Gauguin, Monet, Renoir, plus other impressionists and post-impressionists. In October 1952, it had presented the collection of Mr. and Mrs. Leigh Block. The Blocks were only slightly more daring: they had some early twentieth-century masters, Picasso and Matisse along with the impressionists and post-impressionists. The most adventurous collection shown was that of Mr. and Mrs. Joseph Pulitzer, Jr., seen in May 1957. It included one pure abstraction by Bradley Walker Tomlin, a late cubist from the '40s who adapted his style in the '50s to a conservative form of abstract expressionism. But the Pulitzers also owned a representational drawing by Stephen Greene, a contemporary of the abstract expressionists, and the rest of their collection was again grounded in nineteenth- and early twentieth-century art.

From all this, I conclude that many ladies who read *Vogue* loved art, even modern art, but that by and large, they didn't go for abstraction. True, every December the magazine ran a column called "More Art than Money." Here it showed modestly priced items that might do for Christmas presents, and by 1957 it was even showing little abstract expressionist drawings or small oils, but when it came to the big-ticket items, even the Picassos and Braques in the private collections that it enshrined were almost invariably from those artists' later, more representational periods. Under the circumstances, it's understandable that Liberman chose to do a beautifully illustrated book on elderly, primarily representational School of Paris masters (Rouault, Chagall, Vlaminck, and other painters who'd made their reputations in the early twentieth century). *Vogue* ran eight chapters from this book between October 1954 and November 1955, one chapter per artist. Liberman followed it up with an April 1957 article on five latter-day School of Paris equivalents to abstract expressionism, but only in April 1958 did the magazine offer a two-page layout showing predominantly abstract contemporary American paintings, and they had official endorsement, having been chosen to represent the United States at the Brussels World's Fair. Among artists represented were Motherwell, Reinhardt, and Baziotes, as well as younger and lesser lights.

Harper's Bazaar was even less interested in American abstract expressionism. Its bias in favor of representational art could already be seen in "Five American Painters," an article by James Johnson Sweeney that ran in April 1944. Sweeney, a bona fide critic and future museum director, had done the catalogue statement for Pollock's first solo exhibition in 1943, and Pollock was one of the five painters in his *Harper's Bazaar* article, but the painting reproduced, *The She-Wolf,* is an early, semiabstract Pollock, with an identifiable subject, and the article's theme was how all five of these new painters were returning to "nature." In light of later developments, this may sound strange, but three of the four other pictures reproduced and discussed (by Gorky, Morris Graves, and Avery) were semiabstract to representational. The only abstraction was by Roberto Matta, a surrealist, and Sweeney incorporated it into his argument by saying that it depicted subconscious or inner "nature."[623]

In February 1952, *Harper's Bazaar* ran a short piece on Pollock by Clem. By this time, Pollock had passed through his classic abstract period and was reverting to (uni-referential) representation, so the magazine could bring to its readers more of the kind of news they wanted to hear. Otherwise, all stories dealing directly with painting that I could find in *Harper's Bazaar* concerned artists who were foreign, representational, or both. The abstract expressionists weren't entirely ignored. Their names might be mentioned in a story about Manhattan art galleries or on other group occasions, but none got the star treatment accorded in 1955 to "James W. Fosburgh: An American Painter." The tamest sort of academic realist, Fosburgh was creating anemic still lifes, landscapes, and portraits, yet the magazine gave one of his portraits a full-page color reproduction. The accompanying story, which took another page, reported that he'd sold over 85 percent of the paintings out of his last show, and defiantly suggested that his kind of work was only temporarily out of fashion.[624]

*   *   *

Then there were the academics. In grad school, I'd read how Erwin Panofsky and Ernst Gombrich put down abstract art in their books. Now I saw where Gombrich had also contributed a hostile article, "The Tyranny of Abstract Art," to the April 1958 issue of *The Atlantic Monthly*, a journal of opinion. H. W. Janson, who in 1962 would publish the first edition of his widely assigned survey of art history, expressed his views on modern art in 1959 in a scientific magazine, concluding that it had a growing capacity to "disturb" us – hardly an endearing word.[625] *The Burlington Magazine*, an English publication, reviewed Pollock's first retrospective at MoMA in 1957, calling the artist "talented" but concluding that he was "caught in a bag of his own tricks."[626]

The College Art Association published two journals. Its *Art Bulletin*, which carried footnote-laden, scholarly art-historical articles, wouldn't have dreamt of dealing with recent art in those days (nowadays it's more permissive). Contemporary art (and pedagogical practice) were the bailiwick of the *College Art Journal* (renamed *The Art Journal* in 1960). It published more informal articles by art historians from Ivy League schools as well as less eminent institutions; also, articles or excerpts from speeches by artists who taught (and were known as "studio teachers"). Probably most academics who cared about contemporary art read about it in *Art News* and *Arts*, which published more avant-garde art historian-critics like Rubin, Steinberg, and Rosenblum, but these three were based in or near New York, and the cultural gap between New York and the rest of the country yawned wider in the '50s than it does today.

For academics outside the New York area, the *College Art Journal* might have been equally if not more representative. It carried some pieces sympathetic to abstract expressionism (even a few written by abstract expressionists), but it also had critiques of their style.[627] The articles by abstract expressionists would have interested the studio teachers, in whose classes the style became very popular. Art historians were another matter. Professors from schools as prestigious as Bryn Mawr, Yale, and Boston University contributed articles about contemporary representational artists.[628] Abstract expressionism was sweeping all before it no more in academia than in magazines or museums.

*   *   *

Finally, I surveyed the art market to find out how widely abstract expressionism was accepted by collectors. As Adam Smith said, prices are a yardstick of supply and demand. The greater the demand, the higher prices will go (esthetic quality, as evaluated by critics or posterity, has relatively little to do with it, though a good example of an artist's work will naturally sell for more than a poor one). I'd had a section on prices during the '40s in my dissertation, mainly data I'd come across in museum files and articles on artists in crass periodicals like *Time*. What I'd found correlated with reviews of the period, and showed that the prices that the abstract expressionists were selling for in the '40s were below those of more widely-admired contemporary representational artists. How much had this changed when the abstract expressionists became more widely known? How generally accepted was abstract expressionism, really? The postmodernist desire to prove it as popular as pop developed at about the same time that pop itself came into style. Anticipating postmodernist scholarship, more than one mass-media article in the early '60s would highlight how much money the abstract expressionists were making or had made, implying that the pop artists, with their high prices, were merely following their lead.

As Deirdre Robson reported in her comprehensive study of the market for modern art in the '40s and '50s, prices paid to dealers and artists for abstract expressionist paintings began to escalate in the later '50s.[629] But how was such work doing at auction? The resale market told if it was being accepted by the wider society. At the Archives of American Art, I found microfilms of thirty-six annotated auction catalogues from Manhattan's Parke-Bernet Galleries that included "modern" paintings and drawings between January 1956 and June 1962. "Modern," as then defined by Parke-Bernet, included pretty much anything painted in Europe or America from the mid-nineteenth century onward, abstract or representational, and including much insipid latter-day impressionism by totally undistinguished painters. The only criterion for any these paintings was that they should be salable, and, judged by that criterion, little abstract expressionism made the grade. Two-thirds of those catalogues listed none of it. The first exception seems to have occurred on February 6, 1957, when an Adolph Gottlieb oil, a Motherwell oil, and a Pollock watercolor and gouache were sold for respectively $375, $450, and $600. These weren't the lowest prices at that sale, and even the highest seem laughably low today, but representational work often brought higher prices.[630]

Evidently this reception for abstract expressionism was not as warm as had been hoped, for between then and April 1961, only seventeen more abstract expressionist works were sold in ten auctions (averaging around one hundred paintings and drawings per auction, or a thousand pictures in all). Few if any of the abstract expressionist works seem to have been major. All brought lower prices than more widely admired lesser artists, including the lovable self-taught painter Grandma Moses and Bernard Buffet, a chic Parisian representational artist. The last catalogue in this sequence at the Archives, dated June 7, 1962, suggests that the market was finally beginning to pick up, for it included eight works by abstract expressionists (three each by de Kooning and Gottlieb, one each by Gorky and Baziotes). By this time, pop art was already looming on the horizon, and its presence affecting the market in new and surprising ways.

As for the supposed heyday of abstract expressionism, the secondary market for the style, even in the later '50s, still seemed to be so weak that few collectors would chance it. If somebody wanted to unload an abstract expressionist canvas, the best way was by taking it back to the dealer, who might buy it back or let the collector exchange it for another painting. This was true despite the fact that with the rising level of affluence in the nation as a whole, other auction prices were increasing all across the board.

24. THE RECEPTION OF POP IN THE '60S
(SPRING–SUMMER 2001)

THE ART MAGS were already covering neo-dada in the '50s, though as a minority movement in the art world, meeting with a mixed reception. *Art News* put a target painting by Jasper Johns on its cover when he had his first solo show at the Leo Castelli Gallery in 1958, coupled with a respectful review.[631] Tom Hess, editor of *Art News*, had included a Rauschenberg combine painting in a group show he organized at the Stable Gallery in 1955. The Rauschenberg prompted a wry but tolerant remark from Leo Steinberg, who'd challenged Clem's formalism as far back as 1953, in a famous *Partisan Review* article entitled "The Eye Is a Part of the Mind." Steinberg won a prize from the College Art Association in 1957 for the "Month in Review" column he'd published in *Arts* of 1955–56. Besides noting Hess's Rauschenberg in it, and subjecting the yet more figurative Larry Rivers to prolonged if somewhat ambivalent scrutiny, he explored the "content" of Fritz Glarner's abstractions and toyed with the subject of "meaning" in the abstractions of Philip Guston and Franz Kline (anticipating the insistence on "content" and "meaning" that I'd encounter in grad school in the '70s).[632]

During the 1961–62 season, several future leaders of pop had solo gallery shows. Among them were Lichtenstein, Wayne Thiebaud, and James Rosenquist, while Claes Oldenburg exhibited his work in *The Store*, an "environment" in a storefront on the Lower East Side. By the following season, pop itself had been recognized as a full-fledged artistic movement, with two major group exhibitions, *The New Realists* at the Sidney Janis Gallery in the fall, and *Six Painters and the Object*, at the Guggenheim Museum in the spring. The latter was organized by Lawrence Alloway, who'd been associated with the name of "pop" since the term had been developed in the UK in the '50s to apply to British artists like Richard Hamilton. That same spring, Rauschenberg was having his first major retrospective, at the Jewish Museum. By the spring of 1964, Johns would be having his first museum retrospective, also at the Jewish Museum. Both artists were still in their thirties.

Art News and *Arts* weren't, at first, altogether happy with the popularity of pop. In the Summer 1963 issue of *Art News*, Thomas Hess castigated the vulgar nouveau-riche collectors, critics, curators, and entrepreneurs who were talking about and buying pop because they were eager for novelty, cocktail-party chitchat, and a way to crash society. To hear him tell it, in the good old days, the audience for art had been only artists and their opposite numbers in literature and music, connoisseurs who were capable of appreciating abstract expressionism, even the second generation (Hess's high opinion of this second generation not being one that posterity has shared).[633] In April 1963, *Arts* had published the transcript of a symposium held at MoMA the previous December. In it, Hilton Kramer, Dore Ashton, and Stanley Kunitz, the poet, had attacked pop, while Henry Geldzahler and Leo Steinberg defended it, following a doubtless respectful slide presentation of it by Peter Selz, the moderator.[634]

Both *Arts* and *Art News* had to admit that pop offered a return to figuration which didn't resemble traditional representational painting: it was "new" not only in terms of its brash colors and simple, declarative stylistic devices, but in subject matter: not landscape or still life, but subjects and objects culled from advertisements, comic strips, package design, and other mass-audience or so-called popular culture. Since it was "new" in these respects, and also because of the hullabaloo it kicked up initially, it could claim to be a new avant-garde, thereby deposing abstract expressionism from the throne of prestige (if not profit) that it had occupied since 1950. Pop enabled people who'd loathed abstract expressionism all along to claim that it was now "dead." Even those who'd claimed to admire it were now able to argue that really pop was much more "democratic," whereas abstract expressionism had been "elitist." Accepting the inevitable, *Art News* and *Arts* continued to chronicle pop and its allied movements.

Startled people who didn't know art history, and were perhaps encountering contemporary art for the first time, asked, Can a soup can be art? Can a comic strip be art? This question enabled pop's admirers to provide the standard Duchampian answer that anything can be art if the artist says it is, to label the people asking the question as philistine or rear guard, and to argue that their own answer was the classic response of the avant-garde. All this debate and recognition was coming along much faster than it had with abstract expressionism, but Sidney Tillim, now writing "Month in Review" for *Arts*, had already summarized three reasons for pop's acceptance and even esthetic validity in November 1962: humor, social significance, and a fresh approach to reality and subject matter.[635] Tillim had even anticipated the arrival of pop back in February 1962, when in his review of Oldenburg's *Store* he'd argued that what had hitherto been known as neo-dada was really the product of an artistic personality whom he called "the New American Dreamer."[636] "Pop" seems to have been become the accepted name for the American movement in December 1962, when Selz chose it for the title of his MoMA symposium.

Selz explained that he was rejecting "New Realists" because that was too much like the names of some European movements like the German *Neue Sachlichkeit* of the 1920s; he also rejected "neo-dada" because it had been coined as a pejorative – and because anyway, pop only superficially resembled dada.[637] Henceforth, Rauschenberg, Johns, and Rivers were no longer known as neo-dadaists, but as senior pop artists, alongside the newer arrivals (Warhol, Lichtenstein, Rosenquist, et al.).

Two friends of mine involved in art during this period have told me that one season, every gallery on Fifty-seventh Street seemed to be showing abstract expressionism, and the next, nothing but pop, op, kinetic art, and hard-edge abstraction. Judging from the many capsule reviews that *Art News* still ran, the changeover wasn't quite as rapid and drastic as these friends recalled. Nor, for that matter, had abstract expressionism ever been all that you could see in Manhattan galleries, but a whole new ambiance was certainly ushered in. The great first-generation abstract expressionists would survive and prosper. Indeed, now that they looked like blue chips, people who couldn't stomach them as speculative stocks wanted to invest in them, but many, maybe even most second- and third-generation abstract expressionists ran into difficulty selling their work; some gave up exhibiting or changed styles.[638] Al Held abandoned painterly abstraction for a newer-looking "post-painterly" style. Alfred Leslie quit abstraction for literal realism. Philip Guston evolved from a painterly (if overly dainty) abstract expressionism into a sarcastic semi-figurative cartoonlike style.

Along with adopting pop wholesale, the art world adopted its attitude toward feeling: the less, the better. The big word was "cool." It meant detached, laid-back and unemotional (as opposed to the more recent meaning of great or terrific). *Art in America* (much more concerned with the contemporary than it had been in the '30s and '40s) published "The New Cool-Art," by Irving Sandler, in February 1965. Sandler dealt with the "dead-pan" and "mechanistic" approaches of younger artists, figurative and abstract.[639] Years later, David Bourdon, who in the '60s worked on *Life*, would call the artists of that general period a "comparatively cool, impersonal, and ultrarational generation."[640] *Newsweek* characterized Johns as "mint-cool."[641]

The hallmark of "cool" art was its smooth, clean, impersonal forms and surfaces. The more evident brush stroke of the '50s was satirized (by the smeary paint in Rauschenberg's combine-paintings, and the overly bright "painterliness" of Johns's *Flag* and *Map* paintings). Sometimes it was dispensed with (in Warhol's soup cans, Lichtenstein's comic-strip images, and hard-edged abstractions like those by Ellsworth Kelly and Stella; even the abstracts of Noland and Louis were seen as clean and impersonal by critics who ignored their human side). Impersonal surfaces fit Duchamp's distaste for the artist's *patte*, or paw (personal touch left by a paintbrush); they fitted his machine esthetic (the idea that mass-produced objects like bicycle wheels were superior to the work of a human hand). The figurative side of pop reflected his desire to return art to "the service of the mind," i.e., art that could be described in words. The glorification of "cool" persisted through the '60s. It was so pervasive that not until after I'd spent over a year writing on art for *Time* did I hear (from Rubin) that abstract painting was about feeling. ("Cool" fitted nicely into '60s lifestyles, when many were becoming more open about their sexuality, and less likely to associate it with romantic love.)

*   *   *

Newsweek was far ahead of *Time* in its coverage of the '60s art scene. Its biggest coup was putting de Kooning on its cover in January 1965. The story focused more on pop and its related styles, but Louis and Noland were mentioned, and a photograph of Noland with one of his paintings included (as an exemplar of op).[642] The "inside cover" on new art that the magazine ran in July 1968, though again primarily about what Clem would have called "novelty art," also had a color photograph of and quotations from Dan Christensen, a younger color-field painter, plus a passing allusion to Noland and Olitski.[643] *Time* had run one story in January 1965 on Noland and Louis, with a color page reproducing work by both, but *Newsweek* had already done separate stories on Noland and Louis in 1962, an obituary on Louis in 1962, and a mention of him and Noland in two more general stories.[644] The *Time* story about Louis and Noland ran after the separate stories with color pages done on Rauschenberg and Johns, in September and December 1964. *Newsweek* had done its first story on Rauschenberg and Johns way back in 1958.[645]

During the 1961–62 season, *Newsweek* had written about Lichtenstein's exhibition, using a light touch.[646] *Time*, whose regular Art writer was still Bruce Barton, Jr., had done a faintly sour story on "The Slice-of-Cake-School." It dealt with Thiebaud, Lichtenstein, Warhol, and Rosenquist, implying that their work was only "carbon-copy realism."[647] During the 1962–63 season, *Newsweek* had done separate stories on the Janis and Guggenheim shows.[648] *Time* didn't. Neither Barton nor Fuerbringer liked pop, but it was causing such a stir that they felt obligated to run the four-page color takeout on it in May 1963. This is the first Art story in *Time* that I clearly recall reading: I must have typified thousands of innocents enticed into the world of contemporary art by the satiric flamboyance of pop.

Five months later, Barton died, and Borgzinner took over. He had a lot of catching up to do, and Cran Jones, his senior editor, liked pop no more than Fuerbringer did. Borgzinner's big article on Rauschenberg appeared two months after *Newsweek* had told how the artist won the grand prize for painting at the Venice Biennale, in a two-page account. *Time's* story on Johns trailed that of *Newsweek's* big story on him by ten months. Borgzinner did scoop *Newsweek* with his color takeout on op (a word he coined). The story appeared in October 1964, preceding the big show of op that MoMA was planning for early 1965 (Borgzinner told me Fuerbringer was all for the takeout, hoping that if op was In, it meant pop was Out). *Newsweek* waited until the MoMA show to do its story on op, then titled it "Op: Adventure Without Danger." *Time* ran its color takeout on kinetic art in January 1966. *Newsweek* did a story on kinetic art three months later – in addition to the one it had already done back in 1961.[649]

Many of *Time's* younger readers liked pop. Borgzinner's enthusiastic coverage of it again must have made the section well read. Many older and/ or squarer readers were baffled or outraged. They'd had trouble enough with abstract expressionism, but at least that was paint on canvas. How could a stuffed goat with a tire around its middle (even if assembled by Rauschenberg) be art at all? *Time*, under the leadership of Fuerbringer, still felt obligated to explain such art to such people. Hence the magazine's stories about Rauschenberg and Johns were sympathetic but serious. To convey the fun side of the '60s Manhattan art world, Borgzinner had to introduce Robert Scull, the pop-art collector, with his brassy wife, Ethel.[650] As late as January 1967, *Time* still felt the need to publish an almost despairing Essay on "What Is Art Today?"

Newsweek offered apologias for pop in some of its earlier stories about it. As the '60s progressed, the magazine became more inclined to assume that, just as its readers had known all about abstract expressionism, so, too, they'd moved on to pop and got a kick out of it. This meant that *Newsweek* could deal with it as art and part of a fun lifestyle in the same stories. Such stories must have appealed to adult insiders who knew about pop anyway, and been particularly enjoyable for younger readers on those elite college campuses, where a future generation of museum-goers and collectors might be learning about art for the first time.

The magazine began its story on the Biennale by telling how Venice in the Middle Ages had been "the treasure house, the golden-balled pawn shop, the flamboyant bazaar where East and West simmered together in a happy Turkish bath of commerce and pleasure." The Biennale took place amid "a pizzicato of popping corks."[651] The story on Johns began, "In the hip din of New York art parties the tall, smilingly somber young man doing the twist with a '30s decorousness is Jasper Johns. When he turns on the tart, silent hilarity of his grin he sculpts his own nickname – Jap."[652] What party-going student wouldn't have wanted to pop a cork with Prize-Winner Rauschenberg in Venice, or dance the twist with Johns?

The story on Johns was called "The Younger." On the same page was a story about Adolph Gottlieb, called "The Older." The abstract expressionist was said to have "iron-gray crewcut hair and science-teacher mustache," as well as "science-teacher humor."[653] How many students would have felt they wanted to know Gottlieb better on the basis of that? Barney Newman, back in 1959, had been treated as something of a *bon bourgeois*. His story dramatized what a member of The Establishment he was by telling how close his studio was to Wall Street. "It's convenient," Newman was quoted saying. "I'm near my customers."[654]

The sole Art story on Warhol in *Time* during this period appeared in May 1964. Fuerbringer or Jones must have scheduled it, for it had one paragraph on the artist's exhibition of Brillo boxes at the Stable Gallery, and a second about the abstract paintings that another artist, James Harvey, made at night and exhibited at the Graham Gallery. Harvey's day job was as a commercial artist and he'd designed the Brillo box, so the story implied Warhol was copying him.[655] Seven months later, *Newsweek*'s four-and-a-half-column story about Warhol was called "Saint Andrew." Its lede described a wild party celebrating the opening of his latest show, with guests jammed together and frugging in place, "like a mob of bears back-scratching against the trees of a thick forest."[656] This story was paired with one on Edward Hopper, and the magazine's Top of the Week said that Brian O'Doherty, its new Art writer, had written about the "intensity" with which the 82-year-old realist still worked, while Jack Kroll, the senior editor, had looked at Warhol, who at thirty-two was a member of "'the cooled-off generation.'"[657]

*   *   *

Life, too, was right on top of the pop story. Dorothy Seiberling was its Art editor, Bourdon her assistant. He was friendly with Warhol; she married Steinberg. By November 1961, the magazine was picturing Rauschenberg and one of his combine-paintings as part of an article on *assemblages* (French for concatenations) made from junk. The first article on what would become known as pop appeared in June 1962, after the season when so many future leaders of pop had had solo gallery shows, but before the Janis gallery's group exhibition. In January 1964, a major article on Lichtenstein appeared, called "Is He the Worst Artist in the U.S.?" This playful title harked back to the subtitle of *Life*'s much more famous and much-attacked 1949 article on Pollock ("Is he the greatest living painter in the United States?"). Five more major articles on pop and its ramifications appeared between June

1964 and July 1965, often including sympathetic text blocks explaining the whys and wherefores of the art.[658] Though the magazine showed other kinds of contemporary art as well (including that of David Smith), it also found space to present the art-world fad for sentimental and melodramatic Victorian paintings, thereby confirming what I'd suspected since grad school: that the appeal in academia of the '70s for nineteenth-century academic painting had developed in concert with the advent in the '60s of pop.[659]

By August 1961, *Mademoiselle*'s guest editors (college students, for its annual college issue) were interviewing Rivers; in February 1965, the magazine's authority on culture, Leo Lerman, saluted Rauschenberg and Johns as "The New Old Masters." *Harper's Magazine*, the *Atlantic*'s principal rival, had shown little interest in contemporary art in the '50s, but it greeted neo-dada in March 1962 with an article by Steinberg. He took the argument that all modern art was shocking when it was new, and used it to celebrate Johns, meanwhile observing in passing that abstract expressionism was no longer new. In April 1965, *Harper's* ran a big article by Calvin Tomkins on how Rauschenberg had won the prize at the Biennale. Both Steinberg and Tomkins were graduating from publications that regularly dealt with art to ones that rarely did (Tomkins was doing art reportage for *The New Yorker*, with a Profile of Rauschenberg in February 1964, and one of Duchamp in February 1965.)

Harold Rosenberg was a third art-world insider who made the leap from the art world to the major media – indeed two leaps. First (as I'd discovered, way back in 1969), he'd graduated from *Art News* to *The New Yorker* in 1962 just in time to put his art-world seal of approval on pop as the new avant-garde. By January 1965, he had graduated again, this time to *Esquire*. His article "The Art Establishment" was part of an extended treatment of the hip new art scene that also included "The American Painter as a Blue Chip," by Marvin Elkoff. Both Rosenberg and Elkoff talked about the arrival of big money to the art scene. They suggested that the boom had begun with abstract expressionism, but Elkoff also discussed the success stories of pop stars like Rosenquist, Johns, Rivers, and Jim Dine. A two-page diagram of the "Centers of Power" listed artists, galleries, collectors, writers, and museums in or near the hot New York scene. Castelli, with its pop stars, was very close to the center.

Vogue's coverage of avant-garde American art increased dramatically. After having given "ab-ex" only token coverage since 1951, the magazine published a full-length interview with Duchamp by William C. Seitz in February 1963. The preceding issue had carried an article on Barnett Newman by Rosenberg that showed how even abstract expressionism was benefitting from the increased interest in contemporary art sparked by pop. In April 1963 came an article on "Explosion of Pop Art." In it, Aline B. Saarinen reported that collectors were paying twenty to thirty thousand dollars for some pop art. True, the style was controversial, but she – being a "vulgarian" – liked it.[660] *Vogue* also provided a forum for a negative take on pop, with an article by Seitz that appeared in September 1963, on "The Rise and Dissolution of the Avant-Garde." This article suggested that the new rapprochement between the artist and the bourgeoisie, after a century of alienation, might not be an entirely good thing.

Having become *Vogue*'s editorial director, Alexander Liberman was now able to use the magazine's policy of stories on prominent private collections to feature a couple of more up-to-date ones in January 1964. Besides showing off the treasures that grateful artists had given Clem and Jenny (Noland, Louis, Olitski, Hofmann, Pollock, Motherwell, and Newman), the magazine displayed the Frankenthaler–Motherwell collection (David Smith, de Kooning, Rothko, Noland, and the collection's owners).[661] The rest of the year, Clem's rivals got their innings, with articles by Rosenberg on Johns in February and de Kooning in September. The April 1964 issue carried an account by Betty Rollin of one of those cheerily existential ancestor forms of performance art known as a "happening" and popular in the '60s. The story was illustrated with a small diagram by Allan Kaprow of the "environment" that the happening had happened in.

Harper's Bazaar welcomed pop. Warhol was one of their own: he'd done pre-pop illustrations for the magazine in December 1959 and December 1960, back when he was still primarily (though not exclusively) a commercial artist. In August 1962, he was included as one of the male celebrities who appeared with female celebrities who were modeling the latest fashions in a spread on "the well-mixed party"; the text mentioned that he planned to exhibit in the autumn.[662] In November (when his show opened) came "Deus ex Machina": a brief written passage by Emmanuel Mounier on the poetry of the machine was combined with four pages of Warhol Coke-bottle and automobile paintings, commissioned by *Harper's Bazaar*.[663] The magazine had already run four pages of drawings of "Great Divas" by Rivers (October 1961); reproduced *Alphabets*, a graphite wash drawing by Johns, at full-page size (January 1962); and presented a page of "junk art" by Oldenburg, Dine, Rauschenberg, and two others (May 1962). In March 1963, the magazine published a four-page layout equating pop to the Armory Show of 1913, combining Milton Brown's respectful art-historical assessment of the former with Geldzahler's defense of the latter, and quoting from Brian O'Doherty's rave review of Janis's *New Realists* exhibition for *The New York Times*.

Even the *Ladies' Home Journal* got into the act. One of those huge-circulation women's service magazines, it, too, was addressed to readers with only high-school educations, mainly housewives. Normally, it focused on famous women (preferably presidents' wives or widows), cooking, and fashions, but in March 1964, it published "Can This Be Art?" – a long article by Emily Genauer, with a full-page color photo of Ethel Scull standing in front of Warhol's multiple portrait of her. "Pop art has swept America with a speed and thoroughness approached by no other style in history," Genauer reported.[664] She mentioned exhibitions of it at medium-sized museums in Washington, DC; Oakland, California; Columbus, Ohio; and Waltham, Massachusetts. She also told how three lecture committees at smaller museums where she'd been asked to speak had asked her to bring slides of it along: in Fort Wayne, Indiana; Flint, Michigan; and Cedar Rapids, Iowa, people had never seen the real thing and wanted to know what it was about.

Along came op. Volume 25 of the *Readers' Guide to Periodical Literature* (March 1965–February 1966) listed under "Modernism" twenty-one articles in sixteen publications clearly dealing with everything from how op could be used for food, fashions, and home decoration (in *Look*) to its relationship with mathematics (in *Scientific American*). True, op was abstract, but it was a shallow sort of abstraction, playing entertaining tricks on one's eyesight, and providing facile patterns for striking fabric designs in everything from ties to draperies.

*   *   *

Academia took to pop faster than it had to abstract expressionism: the new style's evident subject matter made it more accessible to interpretation by iconography. Academics also admired some of the younger abstract painters, whose hard-edged forms seemed more intellectually disciplined than abstract expressionism. This was suggested in May 1960, when *The Burlington Magazine* ran an enthusiastic article on painting in contemporary America by George Heard Hamilton, professor of art history at Yale; it singled out Rauschenberg and Kelly for particular praise. In the winter of 1962–63, *The Art Journal* gave nine pages to an article on Duchamp by an assistant professor from Lawrence College in Wisconsin. That summer, the *Journal* published "Warhol at Bennington," by a Bennington student who'd seen slides of Warhol's work in Alloway's class. In the spring of 1964, the magazine used a glass case of Oldenburg's enameled plaster desserts as the cover picture for a ten-page article about pop and neo-dada by an art critic and lecturer who'd taught at Marymount College in Tarrytown-on-Hudson, New York, and the Fashion Institute of Technology in New York City.

*   *   *

The auction picture had begun to brighten for abstract expressionism with the auction at Parke-Bernet of June 7, 1962, that I mentioned in my last chapter – but only in terms of the slightly larger number of works offered for sale, not the prices, which ranged from only $250 for a Gottlieb gouache to $1900 for a de Kooning painting.[665] How dramatically the influx of new money was affecting even the abstract expressionist market may be judged from the next Parke-Bernet catalogue I found in the Archives of American Art, for the sale of May 13, 1964. It listed about thirty drawings and paintings by first- and second-generation abstract expressionists, including at least three major paintings. A Gottlieb brought $7,000, a de Kooning sold for $9,000, and a Rothko went for $10,000.[666] Further evidence of the strength of the market was provided by three pictures listed in the catalogue as Pollocks, though they were withdrawn before the sale after Lee Krasner signed a statement saying that they hadn't been painted by her husband. Grace Glueck said in the *Times* that Parke-Bernet estimated that the three withdrawn pictures, if genuine, would together have been worth about $20,000 – high enough to lure not only imitators but outright forgers into the market. [667] While these prices were still well below the roseate statistics bandied about in the media upon the basis of sales by dealers or artists, at least they indicated that the larger community was beginning to accept abstract expressionism more willingly than it had in the '50s – and, I'd argue, largely because of the interest in art generated by pop.

In February 1965, *Arts* reported on the auction at which *Summer Storm* (1959) became the first large Rauschenberg to go on the block. Though its late owner had bought it for $1,800 about five years earlier, the Allan Stone Gallery paid $13,000 for it. (A new record for de Kooning was also established at this auction when his *Merritt Parkway* (1959) went for $40,000, and a new record for Nicolas de Staël, one of those School of Paris equivalents to American abstract expressionism, at $68,000).[668] Pop artists who came to prominence in the '60s had to wait longer. The 1975 volume of E. Mayer's *International Auction Records* (with prices paid in Europe and the UK as well as the United States) showed that twenty-one Oldenburgs (in all media) brought up to $24,000, twenty-eight Lichtensteins, up to $42,500, and thirty-four Warhols, up to $105,000.

*   *   *

In 1966, after the *Primary Structures* show, minimal art became the latest rage in the galleries. The wider public lost interest, since minimal art (however much it shared the sarcasm of pop) was abstract. The only consumer magazines that continued to cover the art scene were those who'd covered it regularly since the '40s: *Time*, *Life*, *Newsweek*, and *The New Yorker*. I did my best to present minimalism, conceptualism, and so forth sympathetically, but in retrospect, I suspect my very sympathy guaranteed low readership. I also suspect that *Time*, as written in the '40s and '50s, was still better remembered than *Newsweek*, or even *Life* (except for the article on Pollock in 1949).

Time was remembered because Eliot had attacked Pollock and abstract expressionism. I'd tried so hard to live down the philistine reputation he'd given the magazine, but I only knew I'd succeeded when my section was attacked in the article in *Artforum* by Barbara Rose that I'd read in 1969. "The minute Pollock ceased to be 'Jack the Dripper' for the Luce publications," she'd written, "the radicality of extremism was doomed." Apparently, *Time* was needed more as adversary than advocate, for the so-called avant-garde of postmodernism just *had* to have a rear guard to shock and offend; otherwise it couldn't claim to be avant-garde at all. Clem served the same purpose. The communal fantasy of postmodernism set him up as "The Establishment," though at the peak of his influence, only a small percentage of critics and curators shared his outlook. If there had been no Clem, it would been necessary to invent one so that postmodernists could play their adolescent game of Oedipal rebellion against the father.

Still, those four years of saturation coverage of pop and op (1962 through 1965) left an indelible mark upon art and American culture. If, in this chapter, I may not have explored its rationale and outlook in the same depth that I used with abstract expressionism in my last chapter, essentially that's because we're still living with that rationale and outlook. Also, I've already chronicled a good deal of it in earlier chapters about my emergence as a writer on *Time*: how the Beatles displaced Mozart at the top of my personal hit parade, how *Newsweek* dealt with the craze for comic books, even how Lady Jane Ormsby Gore went with her boyfriend to an art gallery in "Swinging London" (since the gallery, Robert Fraser's, emphasized American pop art).

Pop was high style as well as low, of interest not only to the small cities that Genauer wrote about, but to the top echelons of the Kennedy administration. The same issue of *Time* in May 1963 that ran the big color spread on pop art in Art also had a funny story in Show Business on how "Washington, earnestly aspiring to be the new cultural capital of the U.S., was deep in something called 'The Pop Art Festival'...." The big event, preceded by little dinners in Georgetown, and watched breathlessly by ranking members of JFK's New Frontier and/or their wives, was a happening organized by Oldenburg. It climaxed with a striptease by "Miss Washington," attired at the end only in "an aw-gee string," plus a "suggestion of red taffeta there-there and there."[669]

The phenomenal success of this art ensured that its postmodernist attitudes would permeate the art world so completely that modernist values were shoved into the shadows. For the larger community, those four years established the idea that art could be machine-made and fun, and that intellectual stimulus mattered more than emotional power. It enhanced the status of the mass-audience culture that formed the basis for the art, starting the process of substituting the values of mass-audience artistic endeavors for the values of fine art in many areas, from music to literature and not excluding the social sciences.

The upper-middlebrow elevation of mass-audience culture to the level of high culture was already being discussed at cover length by *Newsweek* in 1966. It was still being discussed in 2000 by John Seabrook in *Nob°ow*, and who knows how many other times it's been discussed in the years between and since. While Seabrook suggested that the changeover for society as a whole had occurred gradually over decades, and attributed it in part to the improved quality of mass-audience culture, he also said that it had occurred suddenly, and cited as the key moment Warhol's 1962 exhibition of his soup-can and Coke-bottle paintings.[670] By the twenty-first century, so many people had assimilated Warhol's attitudes so completely that they'd forgotten there was any other way to think. They resented attempts to redress the balance, the more so because many Americans had tended to resent and try to debunk classical culture for decades and even centuries before the rise of abstract expressionism.

In 1949, Russell Lynes (who among other things was one of many such antisnob snobs) had suggested that the upper middlebrows were the axis around which culture revolved. As journalists, curators, book publishers, and educators, they took culture from the highbrows and disseminated it among other upper middlebrows and to lower middlebrows who wanted to be thought cultured. In the '60s, I'd say upper middlebrows stopped looking up to highbrows, and started looking down to lower middlebrows and lowbrows for inspiration.[671] Unlike some other scholars who've written about this development, Lynes didn't equate cultural categories to socioeconomic ones. His whole point was that the intellectual snobbery he described was replacing the old social snobbery based on income and occupation. Highbrows were mostly in "the ill-paid professions," middlebrows (upper and lower) were "at least reasonably well off," and lowbrows existed "in about equal percentages at all financial levels."[672] Still, since he defined the middlebrows (upper and lower) as being "at least reasonably well off," I can't help feeling that the bulk of people in the lower income brackets were more likely to be lowbrows than highbrows (as were affluent and even superrich people and politicians clinging ostentatiously to proletarian tastes).

The first passion for mass-audience culture among the upper middlebrows who disseminate culture may have been comic books in the '60s. This has expanded to include the gimcrack collectibles on *Antiques Roadshow* and trivia on *Jeopardy!* Scholars who fixate on TV shows and Hollywood blockbusters at the expense of live theater I see partially as a spinoff of this same outlook. So is the way that *The New York Times* now reviews pop music and club acts as respectfully as opera, ballet, and classical concerts, and the way that *Publishers Weekly* treats "graphic novels" (i.e., glorified comic books) as literature.

Not all mass-audience culture is bad (just as all high culture isn't good). Clem used to say that he wasn't satisfied with "Avant-Garde and Kitsch"; he also loved the Beatles (I watch a lot of junk TV myself). Yet, though admirers of mass-audience culture like to call it "pop culture" or "popular culture," and think of it as more "democratic" than high culture, it isn't made by *das Volk*, merely consumed by them. It's made (and sold) by a talented, highly paid elite of its own. The revolution brought about by the upper-middlebrow appetite for mass-audience culture hasn't eradicated high art. Classical music, art films, books of lasting value, and serious theater still exist. Sometimes they do very well. In the visual arts, however, the substitution of postmodernist values for those of modernism has ushered in a new chapter of the ongoing debate about how to evaluate the quality of a creation of any kind.

As I said in my Introduction, the biggest debate among students of creativity is how to distinguish between the merely new and the truly creative, for everything we do or say is an "invention," in the sense that nobody else has ever said or done exactly the same thing before. Thus, to be truly creative, a product or process must be "useful," according to some creativity consultants (such as an ad campaign to sell more beer). Scholars of creativity, aware that inventions like $E=MC^2$ don't come bearing price tags, still insist on the need for a creation to be "significant," "appropriate," "of value," or "worthwhile," but even that begs the question, for who decides what's valuable or worthwhile? In academia, there is only "peer review," where fellow scholars decide whether a manuscript is worthy of publication. But an MD in *The New York Times* downgraded the "sacrosanct ritual" of peer review by saying that "More than one critic has pointed out that reviewers may react favorably to research that supports their own, and harshly to research that might undermine their own academic reputation."[673]

According to John Gedo, a psychoanalyst who has written on creativity, "a person with creative achievements is least likely to receive positive feedback from those most qualified to judge the value of those accomplishments, his peers within the same discipline."[674] The response of my various proposal readers to multireferential imagery confirms these two observations. Mihaly Csikszentmihalyi, a psychologist dealing with creativity, claimed the "gatekeeper" role in the visual arts for a consensus of art teachers, curators, collectors, critics, administrators of foundations, and government agencies that deal with culture.[675] Again, all these people have a vested interest in the status quo. Charles Brenner, another psychoanalyst, wrote that "creativity, like beauty, lies in the eye of the beholder....Those who are honored by being *called* creative are the special few...whose creations are judged to be successfully innovative by the members of the society to which they belong."[676] But *which* members of society? I thoroughly agree that communication must take place between a creator and his or her audience, but what audience are we talking about? In the visual arts, are we going to count *every* member of society, including the curmudgeons who lavish scorn on "modern art" to long-suffering art critics at parties where everybody's had a bit too much to drink? What about all those worthies who take their children to movies, zoos, theme parks, science museums, and historical sites instead of art museums? If they're going to be included among those who determine "societal norms," Disney might be judged more creative than Pollock or Warhol, maybe even more creative than Phidias.

Do we really feel that majority vote should prevail, in art as in politics? Should whatever sells the most and/or attracts the most attention be considered best (which amounts to the same thing)? By that standard, *The Da Vinci Code* is a greater novel than anything Roth or Mailer ever wrote, and Britney Spears a better actor than Meryl Streep. It seems to me that in the arts one must venture beyond the value-neutral category of creativity per se, into the value-conscious realm of esthetic appreciation. I quite agree that anything can be art if the artist says it is, but I would add that this doesn't necessarily make it good art, and I think we should consider the possibility that some people may be better qualified than others to evaluate esthetic excellence.

In 1948, *Look* listed the top ten painters in America, according to a poll of sixty-eight "leading" museum directors, curators, and art critics. John Marin, aged sixty-seven, was Number One; Pollock, aged thirty-six, wasn't even Number Ten.[677] In 1948, only Clem, who was not yet widely recognized, said Pollock was the greatest painter of his generation (I doubt that he was included in *Look*'s poll). Marin is still admired by scholars and collectors of American art, but when in 1998, MoMA staged a Pollock retrospective, 329,330 people came to see it from many countries. Was Greenberg better qualified to pass judgment than *Look*'s authorities? I say yes.

I think some people *are* more sensitive to esthetic quality in art than others, just as some can better distinguish between how different pianists play the same concerto, and some can better tell the difference between a curve ball and a slider. Everybody should have equal opportunities to life, liberty, and the pursuit of happiness, but I don't believe that all people being created equal in this sense means that all are created the same. All have different aptitudes, or what Howard Gardner, another psychologist who has written on creativity, called different "intelligences." To Gardner, for instance, Einstein had outstanding logical-mathematical intelligence and extraordinary spatial capacities, while Stravinsky's musical and other artistic intelligences were excellent.[678]

Clem said that his "eye" told him what was good and what wasn't. I'd argue that the brilliance of this "eye" derived at least in part from superior "intelligence" about (or sensitivity to) color and line, compositional and spatial effects. He spoke of having learned from "experience." As most people, it seemed, hadn't shared this experience, he was called an elitist. He agreed, adding that over time, a consensus would emerge among educated people who shared his choices. Given his opinion of most academics, I think that by "educated" he meant primarily having looked at more art, but I also think that the right sort of formal education, the right sort of art, and the right critical encouragement can help to develop one's capacity to admire great art. Alas, neither today's higher education nor the galleries in Chelsea nor our most popular critics offer any real assistance in this department. I was among the lucky ones who came in at the right time, and at the right place, so that my experience has developed my capacity to tell better art from worse. Still, I can't prove my choices are right any more than Clem could. He said you couldn't prove an esthetic judgment – that there are criteria that determine quality, but none that can be put into words. This infuriated his antagonists. They liked to say that art was subjective (a matter of taste), or that quality was determined by the culture that produced the art (relative, not absolute). To me, these are ways of justifying the criterion that the art world has in practice adopted from mass-audience culture: popular opinion.

Commercial manufacturers aim to maximize profits by appealing to the widest possible audience through the lowest common denominator. This policy is what the artistic subcommunity has adopted, along with the design of soup cans and comic-strip conventions. No longer has it room for a critic with Clem's standards, or even mine, unless what we admire appeals to a big enough audience – within the art world, not society at large, but art today is big business. Huge museums must break even by offering shows that will entertain millions of art-lovers, far too many for most to be able to respond to the best art. True, some of these art-lovers may have the aptitudes to appreciate the purely visual. They could go beyond the various forms of mostly uni-referential art that dominate the marketplace because even people with little or no visual aptitude feel (rightly or wrongly) that they can relate to them: assemblage, installation, conceptual art, photography, representational painting (both first- and second-rate), sizeable quantities of second-rate abstract painting and sculpture, as well as video. At least such people could go beyond them, other things being equal, but the schooling they most likely received, and the "experience" they've most likely had since completing their formal education, gives them little opportunity to develop whatever visual aptitudes they may have, and conditions them to prefer contemporary art (abstract and representational) that may be intellectually clever, but is at best emotionally bitter and/or hollow.

I quite agree that there should be a place for the fun kind of art. Not all artistic humor, even within the tradition of dada, is tendentious, and when it's innocent I, too, enjoy its humor. A ten-year-old may have trouble with Rothko, but what kills me is all the art-lovers who never outgrow their adolescent tastes, but hang on to them ever more fervently through their middle and elder years, along with the conditioning they received as young people to ignore or resent the best contemporary art. Such people, it seems to me, may not really want art that can move them on a deeper level. Even if they have the sensitivity to be able to see the difference between a Kelly and a Noland, they don't want the deeper emotional experience that the Noland can give. They'd much rather just glance at it, then dismiss it as "decoration."

What such people really want is light entertainment, art they can take or leave, art they can feel superior to, art that might offer mental stimulation, but not command respect or possess the capacity to move that fine art historically has been endowed with. I'm not alone in perceiving the current postmodernist art scene as being more about entertainment than art: I heard a younger art historian from a distinguished university recently express such a point of view at a panel discussion.[679] And I wouldn't complain about the lesser art if it didn't crowd out the good art, making it virtually impossible for a younger modernist to become known. In postmodernism, whatever sells the best, was made by the newsiest minorities, and/or garners the most flattering write-ups by celebrity critics, must be the best. It's art by any criterion except the esthetic. Postmodernist critics may distinguish between better and worse postmodernist art, but rarely do they step outside the postmodernist box and see it for what it is, as I can (though not full-time in the modernist box, as multireferential imagery isn't approved by every formalist).

Not least among the reasons for the original triumph of the pop-art esthetic was its use in the struggle over Vietnam, coupled with Clem's unwillingness to talk politics. During the '60s, he said he was only interested in art for art's sake, and accepted a grant from the State Department to talk about art in Japan. To many in the art world, this was like sending boys to be killed. Vietnam meant that even art with no political viewpoint acquired political significance. Abstract artists marched in protests, signed petitions, and donated work to auctions for antiwar causes, but because pop art and its allied styles could be used more easily to convey political messages, the myths arose that abstract artists weren't concerned, and that Clem was a political reactionary. I won't say that without Vietnam and the social upheavals of the '60s, color-field painting could have enjoyed even the limited acceptance that abstract expressionism got in the '50s. Other artists would still have wanted to react back into figuration, and this reaction would still have been welcomed by the art-lovers who couldn't relate to abstract expressionism, either. Still, Vietnam helped to turn a rebellion into a revolution by aligning postmodernist art with the leadership of the protest provided by youth.

In 1965, *Newsweek* was already highlighting the role of youth in the antiwar protest. *Time* carried on with this emphasis in 1967. As I've already said, the idea that youth was opposed to the war in Vietnam must have helped to win over moderates. Instead of a conflict between right and wrong, the war became a generational thing, enabling moderates to say, well, if the young people don't want it, we should go along with them. From what little I'd heard at *Time* about the impossibility of winning the war, I felt that my colleagues (and other media) may have played up the youthful aspects of the protest because on a very deep level they instinctively felt this was the best way to force withdrawal. From attitudes that persist in the art world of the twenty-first century, I can see how such media treatment reinforced the idea that the pop artists, too, represented a rebellion of youth against age.

When the pop artists became famous in the early '60s, they were younger than the abstract expressionists. They'd become famous at earlier ages than the abstract expressionists had. But it was so much easier on the ego to say that one liked pop because it represented "youth" than it was to admit that one hadn't related to abstract expressionism in the first place and welcomed the reaction back into figuration, so much easier to ignore the fact that most color-field painters were the same age as the top pop artists. The youth cult was still big in art in the early twenty-first century. One elderly critic apologized to me because she hadn't liked a high-tech show at the Whitney. She knew "the young" liked it, so she felt she ought to like it, too.

> The Sixties was a great decade for myth creation [I wrote, in *From the Mayor's Doorstep* for January 1999]. I had a hand in creating some of the best, but how and where is a tale to be told elsewhere. Here I will say only that no myth was more powerful or appealing than the myth that Youth Is Always Right. It was a necessary myth back then. There was a horrible war on, and this myth seemed the only honorable way to get us out of it, so a lot of people who weren't themselves that young put their muscle into promulgating it (I simplify somewhat, but not much).[680]

Neither youth nor age guarantee quality in art, but my added experience has helped me know whether or not the "new" art in Chelsea was or is really new. Younger critics and art-lovers apparently didn't and don't realize how fundamentally familiar was and is almost all of it – yet simply because they go for it, I'm expected to go for it, too.

Newsweek had been right in step in the '60s with pop as the art of the young. This enhanced the magazine's appeal within the art world, but its coverage of Vietnam added impact to its art coverage, just as its art coverage lent an extra dimension to its Vietnam position. The magazine's synthesis of pop art, youth, and protest was more an expression of the times than a shaping force behind them, only a minor reason that postmodernism gained such a stranglehold – yet whatever modest effect it had was the grain of sand around which had formed the baroque fantasies I'd had about the magazine in 1969. In the '60s, I say in retrospect, this synthesis of pop with youth answered a need. Who could have foretold what a grotesque perversion of esthetic values it would have contributed to forty years later?

The professors of *Newsweek*'s younger readers in the '60s may have been earnestly (but alas, in most cases, without real sympathy or understanding) trying to teach them about abstract expressionism. To the youngsters, that would have seemed like school, while pop was play. Ab-ex was "high seriousness." Pop was relaxed and easy to relate to, almost part of daily life. You didn't have to worry about those boring abstract expressionists: they were for old folks anyway. The way *Newsweek* told the story, pop art let you feel like a member of the inside circle of art lovers, frugging away in spirit with Jap and Saint Andrew at those crazy parties in Manhattan.

25. FROM VIETNAM TO 9/11
(SUMMER–FALL 2001)

THE VIRGINIA CENTER for the Creative Arts had accepted me for another residency from August 27 to September 16. During the spring and early summer of 2001, I was piling up what I hoped would be my final mountain of Xeroxed research. Much of it was about Vietnam, which was still haunting me. I'd never written about it for *Time*. I couldn't claim to be an expert on it, but I'd lived through that era, and witnessed its major events more intensely than most Americans – perhaps because I'd been working in an environment where every news event became the subject of informed speculation, perhaps because the printed word, even in a novel, has always seemed more real than to me than I think it does for most people. Whatever the reason, my immersion in that far-off conflict of the '60s would ultimately furnish me with a key to 9/11.

The home-front battle about Vietnam had never really ended. Hawks and doves were still at it, though their battlefields had shifted from the media to books. In April 2001, the conflict again erupted in the media, when an article in *The New York Times Magazine* told how in 1969, former Senator Bob Kerrey of Nebraska, at that time a lieutenant, and six other Navy Seals, had killed as many as twenty unarmed civilians while searching for a Vietcong official in the village of Thanh Phong. Kerrey had suffered guilt, shame, and remorse ever since. His story, said a *Times* editorial, summed up "the madness of a war that then, as now, seemed to lack any rationale except the wreckage of as many lives as possible on both sides."[681] William Safire, the paper's conservative Op-Ed columnist, reminded readers that there had been a rationale. Prior to the '70s, he continued, most people in and out of the government of the United States had no problem with the proposition that aggression by undemocratic, communist nations had to be combated, if necessary by force. It was only because we'd lost the war in Vietnam, he added, that "ex post facto morality kicks in and it becomes wrong to have sent our young into battle....Are there no voices left...to reject the...humiliating accusation of national arrogance – and to recall a noble motive?"[682]

There it was: a war without a rationale v. a war with a noble motive. Earlier, I'd examined books about Vietnam in relation to the media, youth, and/or dissent, but in 2001, I was focusing on three books primarily about the war itself: A. J. Langguth, *Our Vietnam: The War, 1954–1975* (2000); George C. Herring, *America's Longest War: The United States and Vietnam, 1950–1975* (3rd edition, 1996); and Melvin Small (not *Covering Dissent*, but *Johnson, Nixon and the Doves* (1988)). None explained to my satisfaction how Nixon got elected, or why the war should have gone on for another five years. All three were on the usual dovish side (with varying degrees of detachment). As remarked earlier, I'd seen only a few, mostly poor hawkish books, but I felt I needed more if I were to get a balanced picture of the situation. Serendipity came to my aid. In my apartment, I accidentally ran across an article by Gaines M. Foster in the Winter 1990 issue of *The Virginia Quarterly Review* on "Coming to Terms with Defeat" (I'd bought many copies of that issue of the *VQR* because it had my memoir of North Country School). Foster, who taught at Louisiana State University, cited a handful of what sounded like better-than-average hawkish books on the war, and showed how the hawks had survived and were gathering strength. He recalled Ronald Reagan in 1980 calling Vietnam "a noble cause." Maybe hawks weren't great writers but they could be awfully smart politicians.

I looked up the hawkish books cited by Foster. Columbia had them all, some in multiple copies (though in total, not as many copies as the dovish books). The hawkish ones I liked best were by Guenter Lewy and Harry G. Summers, Jr. I agreed with Foster that as a group, these books argued the war had been justified, moral, noble, and could have been won militarily but had been lost because of "timidity and a failure of will at home." Foster called this "a frontal assault on the doves who condemn the American war effort as both hopeless and wrong," and added that many leaders of this hawkish charge "come from the ranks of the right, and it clearly supports conservative political and foreign policy objectives."[683] Many Americans liked this interpretation of the war. "In 1980," he said, "47 percent of Americans strongly agreed and another 26 percent somewhat agreed with the statement: 'The trouble in Vietnam was that our troops were asked to fight a war which our political leaders in Washington would not let them win.'"[684]

Having sent six cartons of research to the VCCA via UPS, I arrived there August 27, and started writing. On previous visits, I'd listened to readings other writers gave in the evenings, and to music written by the composers. I'd attended open studios given by artists, and read from my manuscript myself, but in 2001, I raced back to my studio every evening right after dinner. My only contact with the other VCCA Fellows was at dinner or breakfast, though I used those meals to bounce ideas from my manuscript off other people, and had some good conversations.

My greatest struggles were still with the chapter on Vietnam. Having now read the points of view of hawks and doves, I could see that, while the doves had accused the media of being overly influenced by the Administration and hostile to the protesters, the hawks accused it of being overly influenced by dovish war correspondents and too favorable to the protest. Formerly, I'd felt that the media had been sympathetic to the protest, but with good reason: they'd known how badly the war was going. In 2001, I saw the conflict over the media more as a microcosm of the larger conflict in U.S. society. Responsible publications like the *Times* had been caught in the crossfire between hawks and doves. Trying to be fair to both sides, such publications had satisfied neither. In retrospect, this seems obvious, but a lot of writers apparently hadn't seen it.

Another thing that troubled me was my long-held belief that the end of the war had been set in motion through the electoral process in 1968. The only book I'd read that emphasized this point was by Thomas Powers. He argued that "It was Lyndon Johnson's fate neither to start nor to end the war in Vietnam, but rather to preside during the period when the nation, in its broadest sense, changed its mind about the war."[685] Previously, I'd believed that Nixon's victory was due to voters who'd felt he was more likely to end the war than Humphrey, but after being inaugurated he hadn't started to withdraw troops until June 1969, after that spring of campus unrest whose turbulence I so well remembered. Despite disclaimers in the epilogue, the Powers book really ended in the spring of 1969. In the fall, I'd left *Time*, and begun ignoring the news. Maybe I saw things as Powers had because I'd exited the scene at so nearly the same time that the events chronicled in his book had concluded.

I went over to the Sweet Briar library that I'd consulted on previous visits, and glanced through *The New York Times Index* for the period between the fall of 1969, when I'd quit, and 1972, when I'd become aware of the news again. Nixon had continued with his "Vietnamization" of the war (i.e., withdrawing U.S. troops, for the spring of 1969 had marked their peak number).[686] But he'd also invaded Cambodia in 1970, ordered U.S. forces to support the attempted South Vietnamese invasion of Laos in 1971, and in 1972, besides ordering the mining of Haiphong harbor and other North Vietnamese ports, begun bombing the country again. All this had prompted more massive antiwar demonstrations. Dimly, I thought, Nixon may have been a bastard, but he wasn't stupid. His actions must have been a response to what some people who'd voted for him wanted. During the campaign, he hadn't committed himself to any specific solutions for Vietnam. Some people might have voted for him because they thought he favored withdrawal, others because they thought he'd escalate. His policies in office could be construed as shifting back and forth between these constituencies.

I remembered, from my earlier reading, that NBC poll taken in 1968 among Democrats voting in the New Hampshire primary: more than five out of ten hadn't known that Gene McCarthy was a dove, and six out of ten who'd voted for him thought that Lyndon Johnson should use more force in Vietnam, not less. I also remembered the poll taken in the fall of 1967 that showed only 28 percent of the respondents approving of how Johnson was conducting the war, but the rest divided over whether he should try to end it or escalate it further. Had surveys been taken in 1968 of why people had really voted for Nixon? I wanted to look that up – and began to wonder whether democracy had in fact triumphed through the electoral process.

Gaines Foster had alerted me to the persistent presence of hawks, but I didn't think that they represented a majority of the population. I still believed, with Powers, that the country as a whole had changed its mind about the war, and that the doves had therefore become the majority. If so, democracy had triumphed, but maybe not all through the electoral process. After all, Nixon hadn't started to withdraw troops until after those spring campus upheavals – suggesting that they might have been a factor, perhaps even *the* determining factor – not the mere fact that Nixon had been elected in and of itself. Therefore I qualified my view of Powers by inserting a passage in my manuscript: "My only caveat is that I think Powers overemphasized the role that the political process in itself played as an expression of public opinion, and underrated the extent to which the street protests also expressed public opinion and impacted on the political process." Even that left me dissatisfied.

On Tuesday, September 11, I got up early, breakfasted in the dining room, and went up to my studio at 8:30 or 9 AM. Throughout the morning, I wrote. One of the beauties of the VCCA is that there's nothing to impede concentration – no telephones in the studios, no e-mail to distract one. At noon, I picked up my box lunch from the table near my studio where the kitchen staff had left it. I didn't see anybody else around, and the rule at the VCCA was that people were not to knock on the doors of other people, and interrupt them when they were trying to create. I returned to my studio, scarfed down my lunch, and wrote on. Around 6 PM, I went down to dinner. After I'd assembled my meal from the buffet, I sat down at a table already mostly filled with people. The woman to my right said, "You're from New York, aren't you?" I said yes, and, thinking she was making small talk, asked her cheerfully where she was from. Then somebody told me about the attack on the World Trade Center. I went into shock.

First, the shock meant denial. I went back to my studio after dinner, and kept on writing (my engagement calendar says I put in 14½ hours that day).

Everybody else seemed to be clustered around the Center's one TV, in the main building, but I couldn't look at what I was told were endless reruns of the second terrorist plane smashing into the second tower, and both towers collapsing. I couldn't even start telephoning friends in New York to be sure that they were all right until Wednesday evening. Some art-world friends lived or worked in SoHo, Greenwich Village, and the financial district, all close to Ground Zero, but none had been involved in the catastrophe.

I kept on writing, as I'd have to leave the VCCA on Sunday, September 16, and I still hadn't finished my revisions. The work eased my anguish, but I had to eat dinner with other VCCA fellows, and some of what they said was more frightening than the catastrophe. One evening, I heard a crescendo of angry voices, saying we Americans must stand together and stamp out terrorism, this has to be *war* because we can't let those terrorists get away with it, if it did it would be *appeasement*, like Neville Chamberlain at Munich in 1938. Instinctively, I shoved my chair back away from the table, saying to myself, no, no, no, no, this is all wrong. War is *not* the answer.

This was initially an instinctive reaction, but when I began to think about it, I realized it was also based on the books I'd been reading. All I'd read was reordering itself in my mind, especially the roles that the hawks and doves from Vietnam had been playing ever since. Those dumb doves, I thought. Like all liberals, so damned naive. For the last thirty years, they've been sitting around, writing books, while the hawks have been organizing politically. Those hawks put Reagan in the White House, where he could build up the military. This had contributed to the demise of communism, which in turn had destabilized the Middle East. The United States had backed Israel for decades, but in the past, the Arabs had been able to live with that because they always knew that as a last resort, they could get the Soviets to help them. Now they no longer had that security. No wonder they felt threatened enough to resort to terrorism.

I saw events leading up to and helping to explain the attack on the World Trade Center, but not solely in terms of the terrorists. Also included was how the United States (without meaning to) had contributed to the disaster – a reaction derived at least partly from my experience of psychoanalysis, and its principle of taking responsibility for whatever happens to one. In the wake of 9/11, our country was laying all the blame on the terrorists, explaining it in terms of their fanatical religious beliefs. But not since the Dark Ages had Moslems tried to conquer the world. I felt that we were about to go to war for purely emotional reasons, the need to strike back, blindly, and that if we thought about the situation, we might come up with wiser answers.

The publisher of *NYArts*, to which I'd previously contributed excerpts from my online column, had invited me to do an article about the VCCA, so

I used that as my forum. The article was written after I'd left the VCCA, but before I returned to New York. I couldn't face flying, but a friend who lived in nearby Lynchburg invited me to stay with her until I felt up to going home. I e-mailed the article from her computer. It began with a warm description of the VCCA itself, and people I'd met there. Then I segued into my explanation for 9/11: how the collapse of communism had destabilized the Middle East.

> Now that Communism is no longer around to play the role of Evil Empire [I wrote], we have become the Evil Empire in its stead, not because we are inherently evil but because we have left the Arabs and the rest of the third world with no other choice but us, and people MUST have choice. They MUST have an option. This is the essence of democracy: if you don't like what one party is doing, you can throw it out and see what the other party can do. We Americans all say we believe in democracy, yet we are asking the rest of the world to live in a world-wide one-party state. If the only option that the Arabs have is between that state and terror, then that's the option they will exercise...and in ways I don't like to think about....Everybody has got to have choice....Choice allows us to hope, and humanity can't live without hope.[687]

In Lynchburg, my friend took me out to dinner. Flags hung in shop windows and were posted on restaurant doors, with signs saying "God Bless America." They were meant to make me feel safe and secure, but I'd never been comfortable with ostentatious displays of patriotism. I'd always loved my country, and treasured its democracy, but maybe that's why I didn't need to advertise my feelings about it. My patriotism was so deep within me that I didn't think I should have to go around shouting about it, and people who did made me nervous. I thought of a phrase I'd learned in childhood, to wrap oneself in the American flag. It meant a person who used patriotism as an excuse for immorality. Another phrase passing through my mind was the famous one of Dr. Johnson: "Patriotism is the last refuge of a scoundrel."

I felt that many people in Virginia, a conservative part of the country, were seizing upon the WTC disaster as an excuse to do what they'd wanted to do all along – go to war. Here they had ideal targets, the autocratic Taliban and Al Qaeda, the terrorist organization of Osama bin Laden, both said to be headquartered in Afghanistan. Bin Laden and the Taliban were clearly wickedness personified. They made much better enemies than the communists in Vietnam, who might have been said to have egalitarian ideals. All the same, my Lynchburg friend was no more enthusiastic about a war than I was. She, too, believed that it would only provoke more terrorism.

On Friday, September 21, I took the train back to Manhattan. Looking out of the cab taking me to my Upper East Side apartment, I saw even more flags than I'd seen in Lynchburg. They were in stores and restaurants throughout midtown, but even more numerous on the Upper East Side: on shops, restaurants, town houses, tenements, flying from flagpoles, and hung on the facades and awnings of high-rise apartment buildings. I should have been reassured, but again, I found it disturbing. It was so unlike my New York, the city I loved more than any other. I'd been at Brearley in Manhattan when the United States entered World War II (I didn't go to North Country until the following year). Yet even when Brearley was conducting air-raid drills because of the fear of German bombers, I didn't remember flags all over the place like this. It was my first evidence of how horribly screwed up and turned around the whole city was, how desperately it needed to reassure itself that we were a good country, even if terrorists hated us enough to kill themselves in the act of trying to destroy us.

In my apartment, 172 e-mails had piled up in my computer, spam but also worried inquiries from friends and relatives in England, Germany, Canada, and Los Angeles. This was heartening but again disturbing, to think that our super-efficient media had picked up this ghastly event and broadcast it around the world, evoking floods of sympathy for us and painting our adversaries as the blackest of villains. I somehow kept on feeling this scenario was wrong. I knew that the terrorists were evil, and that incinerating several thousand people in a moment was a crime beyond belief, yet I couldn't escape a sense that our country wasn't entirely blameless, and that the way we were reacting wasn't going to absolve us of guilt. I knew this was a terribly unpopular point of view, but one reason I had it was that my anecdotal evidence differed from that of most New Yorkers.

Few New Yorkers seemed familiar with the Arab point of view as expressed by sane men, not fanatics. Many seemed to have known somebody killed at Ground Zero. I hadn't known anybody who'd been killed there, but I had known a moderate Arab when I was a teenager. This man had studied in American schools, then returned to his native country for a distinguished career as diplomat and teacher. Around 1999 he'd been visiting the United States with his wife, and we'd dined with mutual friends. His wife had been sitting at the table with him, not brutalized the way Oprah Winfrey had been publicizing the treatment of Afghan women. Most of the dinner passed in pleasant conversation, but over dessert we got into politics. This man recalled how much he and everybody he'd known had admired the United States in the late '40s and early '50s, when he'd been in school here. Then he started talking about how nobody liked us anymore. I'd gotten angry. I'd thought it was just his personal hangup and argued with him bitterly, but in the wake of

9/11, I kept remembering what he'd said and thinking that maybe he spoke for many moderate Arabs overseas – and not necessarily just Arabs.

Some e-mails I got right after 9/11 came from artists. Ann Walsh, the artist who lived with her artist-husband Jim in Greenwich Village, had sent out some vivid round-robin e-mails describing the "very surreal" atmosphere of the city around her, an atmosphere augmented by the fact that besides living in the middle of it, she was also watching it on TV. Everybody had watched the destruction of the twin towers on TV, it seemed, when it happened and since. I wasn't watching TV. Why? Because I feared for my sanity. I was under stress, and it was hypersensitizing me. Every impression I received was magnified. I remembered what stress had done to me in 1969, when I'd entered into my two-year flight from reality. I didn't want that again. As soon as I got back to New York, I went to see my psychiatrist, Dr. J (whom I'd moved on to from Dr. I in 1990). Dr. J upped my dose of bupropion, but this time drugs alone weren't going to do it. Nor was I soothed by how Dr. J was talking, especially not by his joking that Afghanistan was like Vietnam without the jungle. That crack made me feel that he was spoiling for battle. I would have to take my own actions to protect myself.

Many factors had contributed to my entering dreamland in 1969, but while writing this book, I'd concluded that a big one had been the stress caused by working in a news-media environment when the political situation was going crazy. After I'd left *Time*, Clem had said I'd be better off if I didn't pay too much attention to the news. His advice had helped so much that in 2001, I decided to follow it again.[688] It was harder on the Upper East Side in 2001 than it had been in an out-of-the-way London neighborhood in 1969. The TV sat in its own little altar in my Manhattan apartment, but I kept the set turned off except for moments to see the temperature (even then, hitting the mute button).

In delis, radios blared the news. Coffee shops all had TVs tuned to the news, and though they cut the sound, I could still see Bush, mouthing whatever words his speechwriters had crafted to rationalize and justify his decision to send the country to war. My health club had so many TV sets that I felt Big Brother was watching me. I couldn't face the *Times*. One friend said it was running columns and columns of obituaries. Max Frankel, the paper's onetime executive editor, had once written that he "wrote and edited with a bias for the home team, the Yanks in the cold war and the Yankees in the World Series."[689] All these obituaries surely reflected this policy, but depressed me still further.

On Wednesday, September 26, I went to my internist for a regular checkup. In his waiting room was that morning's *Times*, with a three-column headline revealing that the Republicans had been trying to capitalize on war fever by proposing to cut the capital gains and corporate income taxes.[690] They'd been claiming that these cuts would "stimulate" the economy, which had gone into a tailspin, but such cuts would give most of the money to the affluent, who already had money to spend and didn't need more. The lower income groups would have spent any money they got as a tax cut much more rapidly, and stimulated the economy far more effectively, but Bush was closer to his wealthy friends and supporters. I got so upset by this abuse of power that I spent the rest of the day writing letters to my representatives in Washington. This took so much time that I made another vow not to read the *Times*.

Even the way it looked on the newsstands dismayed me, with headlines in unnecessarily large type, and unusually upsetting Page One stories. The people who put it together were supposed to be so level-headed. If they couldn't stay calm, who could?[691] The only news I allowed myself was five or ten minutes a day on the radio just to make sure the world hadn't come to a stop, plus glimpses of headlines as I raced past the newsstands. All this seemed to work fairly well (even if Dr. J described it as a "bunker mentality"). By dealing myself out of the media blitz, I was staying saner than I'd otherwise have been. I'd learned over the years to recognize the signals that I was slipping out of touch, but this time, they were minimal (though not altogether absent).

I tried hard to stay sane, but felt almost alone in whatever sanity I retained. Many people were caught up in the angry mood brought on by the disaster. Some friends were so enraged or depressed that I couldn't talk to them on the phone and had to let my answering machine screen my calls for me. A few friends stayed calm (especially four who'd survived World War II in France or England as children, and come out of it with lifelong nerves of steel). This wasn't enough. Just from headlines and fragments of broadcasts, I kept being reminded of how many people were listening respectfully to expressions of grief that would justify retaliation, and admiring the marvelous president so vigorously expressing this angry national mood.

One friend was a fervent Democrat. She'd never said anything kind about Bush, but now she said she thought his last speech very good. If she was any indication, the whole state of New York had gone over to Bush. The radio said that his approval ratings were skyrocketing across the nation. Trying to relax, I'd tuned in to the David Letterman show, only to hear some celebrity talking about the need for "a strong leader." *Der Führer?* I thought (this being German for "leader"), and hastily switched off the TV. It was like people were so frightened by the disaster, and so desperate for revenge, that they wanted to sweep away any obstacles to Bush's assuming single-handed rule. I was reminded of how the original Führer, Hitler, used the burning of the Reichstag in 1933 to try and stampede the German public into accepting his one-party state.

This memory wasn't erased by a letter from Congresswoman Maloney saying that due to the national emergency, there were no longer any Democrats or Republicans, we were all just loyal Americans together. Combined with that, the anthrax scare made me suspect Bush and the Republicans were trying to eliminate their opposition in Congress. Most people thought the anthrax came from Bin Laden, but if so, why should it be sent to the offices of Tom Daschle, Democratic senate majority leader, and Dan Rather, a liberal newscaster? Congress was the only body that could hinder Bush's war plans, so it didn't stand to reason that Bin Laden would want to eliminate it. Similarly, Rather was less likely to push for an invasion than Fox TV. I had to admit that all this sounded paranoid, and that I shouldn't hold the Republican National Committee responsible, but I still felt the criminal was more likely a right-wing Republican crank than a left-wing Democratic one (nor did the suicide in 2008 of a government scientist suspected of sending the anthrax do anything to alter this view).

The more that cries of war mounted, and the media filled with pictures of people in uniform; the more I had to present ID when I went into office buildings, and have my tote bag searched upon entering libraries and museums, the more I felt that the war was a gigantic mistake. I disliked Bush more than ever as he gained more power and appeared to be using it yet more ruthlessly. I didn't like to think what this might mean for my book. No longer could I bask in the sensation of belonging to a great majority, or offer readers the comfort that in politics, at least, we shared a common outlook.

I did subscribe to the weekly *New York Observer*. Its October 22 issue had an article saying that the red states were united in their determination to back Bush in his war against Afghanistan. "The decadent left" (apparently the blue states that had voted for Gore) was riven with dissension. Some members of it, like Susan Sontag, felt the tragedy was ultimately America's fault, but her son disagreed, as did many other radical leftists.[692] I was distressed by the idea that if you didn't support Bush, this made you a member of the radical left (and a splinter member of that). I'd never seen myself as a radical, only a liberal, a Democrat (occasionally a centrist, when I felt my fellow liberals were being naive). Now, the country had apparently swung so far to the right that I was left high and dry, cast up on a beach because the moon was pulling the tides so far in the opposite direction. I was a radical simply because I was a liberal (even a centrist).

In the United States, we had moderates, who'd vote Republican or Democratic. We had the so-called Radical Right, which would always vote Republican, but we no longer had a radical (or even liberal) left to balance the radical right, and keep the ship of state on an even keel. The *Observer* article was reassuring because Sontag and I agreed that we'd brought the war upon ourselves, but my sense of being marooned was reinforced by remembering how nobody in the media or government had paid attention to my concern about faith-based initiatives the previous winter. Liberals like myself could safely be ignored, it seemed: we were an elderly, dying breed.

Then I had a moment of – well, revelation. Some people might call it an epiphany. Today, I'd describe it as the flash of illumination that accompanies a creative insight or discovery on the Eureka model, and again I had serendipity to thank.

26. Second Eureka
(Fall 2001)

TRYING TO CAPITALIZE on the momentum for the book developed at the VCCA, I'd Xeroxed Gallup polls about American attitudes toward communism in the '40s and '50s that I've since incorporated into Chapter Six. Before inserting them, though, I had to get cracking with the October 15 issue of my online art column, though I was still disturbed about the rightward swing of public opinion. Sitting at my computer, I glanced down at the floor. There lay those Xeroxes, and I saw another poll on the same page as a poll about communism I'd wanted. This other poll had been taken in November 1949, when Harry Truman was President, and liberalism was riding high. The question was, "As you feel today, which political party, the Republican or Democratic, do you think serves your interests best?" The answers were tabulated by occupational groups.

Omitting those with no opinion, here is what the poll showed. Among business and professional people, 59 percent preferred the Republicans, 24 percent preferred the Democrats, and 9 percent saw no difference. Among white-collar workers (primarily sales and clerical people), 37 percent preferred the Republicans, 33 percent preferred the Democrats, and 19 percent saw no difference. Only 16 percent of the farmers favored the Republicans, and 65 percent favored the Democrats, while 10 percent saw no difference. The blue-collar workers were divided into two categories. The skilled workers preferred the Democrats to the Republicans, 59 percent to 12 percent, with 11 percent seeing no difference; unskilled workers preferred the Democrats to the Republicans 64 percent to 10 percent, with 10 percent seeing no difference.[693]

This was it, the open sesame that explained everything – why we'd had Truman in the White House in 1949 and were stuck with Bush in 2001 – because I somehow mysteriously also knew that in the decades between, the number of blue-collar workers and farmers had declined in proportion to the rest of the population, while the white-collar, professional, and managerial workers had increased proportionately. Since voters to whom the status quo had been kindest were usually most eager to conserve it, this occupational shift canted the whole body politic in a more conservative direction. Liberal leaders might come from any segment of the population, of course, but a movement must have followers as well as leaders, and without enough followers, any liberal leader in the new millennium was doomed to lose out in a general election.

The Republicans weren't wiser or worthier to lead the country in 2001. Books claiming the emergence of a new conservative "philosophy" were only rationalizations and justifications for right-wingers to do what they'd wanted to do for sixty years: undo the New Deal. This wasn't conservatism. It was reaction, turning back the clock to the 1920s and before. They were getting away with it because more Americans, by virtue of their occupations, were apt to vote for them. It was disheartening, but encouraging, because it made me feel I wasn't alone in my outlook, that I spoke for the millions of blue-collar workers and farmers whose output was consumed by the American public, and who, by virtue of their occupations, would have been more likely to vote against Bush. Most were probably younger than the people who'd voted for Bush, but they lived in other countries around the world, so they couldn't vote in U.S. elections, and thus – as far as our government was concerned – constituted a "disenfranchised left."

I knew this because the Gallup poll hooked up with other information I'd amassed over the years. As with my theory of multireferential imagery, it was an instinctive synthesis of bits of material that had sunk into my unconscious, but guided my conscious mind to its conclusion. Once I'd reached that conclusion, those bits began pushing their way into consciousness, and demanding further research to document and/or update them (the need for "verification" developing almost simultaneously with the discovery itself). As I'd arrived at my insight without thinking about it, you could call it creative thinking (not unlike how an abstract painting synthesizes in an artist's unconscious). Doubtless the stress of the moment helped as catalyst. Without 9/11, and the climate that 9/11 engendered, I might not have arrived at my concept of "the disenfranchised left," but Graham Wallas's four stages of creation hadn't in this case occurred in the sequence he described.

First, the "illumination" came before I knew I was trying to solve a problem, though in retrospect I can now define two related problems I'd been grappling with: most importantly, how to explain the proto-fascist climate after 9/11; next, how to interpret Nixon's victory in 1968 – had he won election as a hawk or as a dove?

Second, the period of "incubation" could have been described as short or long. It all depended on whether you assumed that I could only begin incubating after I'd acquired that final bit of "preparation," the Gallup poll of party preferences, *or* that the incubation had really begun in 1967, when I started focusing so exclusively on art, and pushing everything to do with politics and economics more or less to the back of my mind. As for "preparation," who knew how much longer before 1967 it had gone on? Besides employing the economics I'd learned as a researcher in *Time* Business, I was rediscovering the concept of the egalitarian society I'd learned as a child and adolescent, as well as recalling things I'd seen in the world around me over many years.

From somewhere (perhaps a college course) I knew that in the '30s and '40s, the Democrats had relied on the votes of farm workers and blue-collar workers. This support had put them in office, and let them use the taxes of the more affluent to help the less affluent get a fair shot at the pursuit of happiness; it had also let them regulate the most powerful forces in the economy so the least powerful suffered less. But I also knew that since the '40s, fewer younger Americans had entered the work force as farmers or blue-collar workers, while more had become white-collar workers, managers, or professionals. In terms of the U.S. population, this was something of a generational thing – the widespread phenomenon of the blue-collar worker who labors to put his child through college, so that the child can get a white-collar job – but whatever the reasons, it had caused the proportion of the population in the upper classes to grow and the proportion of the population in the lower ones to shrink. With this change, power had shifted gradually from Democrats to Republicans, and from more to less egalitarian governmental policies, as even the Democrats had be forced to move to the right in order to compete for this increasingly conservative electorate.

I knew that the United States still relied heavily upon blue-collar and farm workers, because, by comparison with years past, its economy in 2001 was consuming far more, not fewer of the products of their labor. But many of these products were now being made abroad, either because U.S. manufacturers had shut down unionized, high-wage plants in this country and transferred operations to nonunion, low-wage plants overseas, or else because foreign manufacturers were also producing low-priced products and exporting them to the United States. It didn't matter who owned these overseas plants. As they were still producing goods for the U.S. market, the people who worked in them were part of the U.S. economy, but because they were outside the borders of the United States, they weren't part of its body politic. Here was a worldwide pool of millions of blue-collar and farm workers whose lives were influenced by decisions made in Washington, yet who had no influence over those decisions because they weren't U.S. citizens and therefore couldn't vote. This was the "disenfranchised left" that had no way to provide a counterweight to the radical right.

Conservative politicians claimed that class warfare was "outmoded"; all they meant was that so many Americans now belonged to the upper levels of society that those in the lower levels could safely be shortchanged. This was the basic reason for the frightening shift I was perceiving in the wake of 9/11 toward the far right, with its ties to the military and religious fundamentalism. The state of emergency brought on by the attack had ripped away political platitudes and shown the increasingly upper-class body politic beneath, but the underlying shift had been going on gradually for a long time.

It might well be responsible for the long-lived angst of Vietnam, and the reason why that war's issues had never been fully resolved. As recently as the spring of 2001, I'd still believed that democracy had triumphed when U.S. forces were forced by U.S. public opinion to withdraw from Vietnam. Looking at that 1949 Gallup Poll about party preferences, though, it seemed possible that Nixon had really been bowing to minority pressure in withdrawing the troops, and that even by the '60s, the hawks had already been in the majority, among professionals and managers, white-collar workers and elderly blue-collar workers who belonged to the more conservative unions or had risen to the upper income levels in their line of work. I didn't welcome this idea. I still felt the hawks had been wrong to want to stay in Vietnam, but at least (I reflected sourly) making allowance for their influence restored my faith in democracy.

This whole situation explained why America had changed so much in the mind of my Arab moderate friend. When he'd been at school in the United States, the Democrats had been in control, put there by working-class votes, and the rest of the world could identify with those working-class voters. Now America was ruled by Republicans and bosses. While this might be what U.S. voters wanted, it was nothing that exported well.

What other information learned over the years led me to this conclusion? The first thing I remembered (dimly) was a story I'd researched back in the Business section of *Time* in the early '60s about how more people were occupied in the service-producing sector of the U.S. economy than in the goods-producing sector, but that didn't quite seem to fit. The next thing I remembered was what Tony Lukas had said during our lunch in 1991 about his new book being about "class," and his apparent conviction that "class" was the biggest problem in America of the '90s. Another place where I'd encountered "class" was in Howard K. Smith's *The State of Europe*, which I'd read in high school and reread in early 2001. Particularly, I remembered this passage (which I've already quoted in Chapter One):

> Another prime social requisite for the functioning of democracy
> is the existence of a large middle class – people who own something,
> like the possessing classes, and at the same time live principally by
> their own efforts, as does labor – to act as a go-between through

which compromises can be negotiated. In a Western democracy neither owning-class nor working-class political parties can hope to win an election without support from this broad stratum, and the need to woo it saves party politics from being narrow, antagonizing class politics.

I'd always thought of this idea in connection with developing countries, and concluded that until they'd acquired a middle class, they'd have trouble maintaining democracy. The idea had colored my feeling about Vietnam in the '60s, but in the wake of 9/11, I realized we also needed a working class in this country, to counteract the owning classes. Without a big enough working class, and leaders representing it to argue the need for social services, the middle class could be persuaded by the owning classes to vote for decreased government spending and lower taxes, even when that middle class might lose more by decreased social services than it gained by tax cuts.

Somewhere I'd read that union membership had declined. Conservatives claimed that people had become disenchanted with unions because of corruption or featherbedding, but I thought I remembered hearing that service-industry workers were harder to organize than workers in manufacturing, if only because it was more difficult to go on strike. With a factory, you could picket without appearing antisocial, but if you were a teacher, you stood accused of neglecting your little charges, and if you were a hospital worker, you were depriving sick people of their care.

White-collar workers, I'd also read, were even harder to organize than service industries. I supposed that since some managers had risen from the ranks, others dreamed of rising, too, especially if they adopted management's point of view. *Time* was a classic example. We'd had a union, a local of the American Newspaper Guild. Our contracts had covered most editorial employees, but the company kept the writers' salaries well above contract minimums, so few writers joined the union, and senior editors were management, so they couldn't join. Researchers were paid the minimum wage in their category, so more researchers joined. I'd joined (after Bob McLaughlin, my mother's friend, pointed out I'd be getting a free ride if I didn't), but I never wanted to strike because it was so evident that we couldn't win. Seven years after I'd quit, the Guild went on strike. The outcome didn't surprise me: the strikers couldn't shut down the magazines, so they had to accept the same contract they'd originally rejected.

I remembered many things about imports. Farm products, for instance. I'd heard warnings on TV against contaminated strawberries from Mexico, or was it raspberries from Guatemala? I'd heard something like that about imported cantaloupes, too. Picking crops took hours of labor, but could be done by unskilled workers available for lower wages in Central and South America.

The U.S. garment industry had been decimated by imports, I knew. Besides having read it, I looked at labels when I bought clothes. Most had come from India, Sri Lanka, the Pacific Rim, and more recently, Eastern Europe. I'd owned a purse made in China. My Reeboks came from the Philippines. I remembered the little wholesale shops of dresses in Manhattan's garment district, where as a teenager I couldn't buy anything because I was only a retail customer. In those days, I'd also seen many racks of dresses being shoved along Seventh Avenue, but walking to Macy's along those same streets in the new millennium, I'd seen few racks of dresses, and noticed how most of the little shops along the side streets were import-export businesses now.

For decades, I'd heard that Japan was a leader in electronics. Reviewing my possessions, I saw my TV set was a Sony, and Sony was a Japanese company. My portable radio was a Sony, though made in Malaysia. My VCR was a Mitsubishi, another Japanese make. My computer printer was an Okidata, a third Japanese company. My tape recorder's brand name was General Electric, but it had been made in Malaysia. My Dell computer was made in Malaysia, too.

Then there were automobiles. Back in the '50s and '60s, we'd done a number of stories on imported cars in Business, and there were still plenty of Honda and Toyota ads on TV, but I hadn't heard as much about imports recently. Why?

Steel? I'd heard for years that much of it was imported. While at Bethany, I'd seen how much the domestic steel industry, and the coal used to process steel, had declined. Much land near the campus (so I heard) was honeycombed with old, uneconomic, disused coal mines. Weirton and Wheeling, the nearest cities, had steel companies that had dwindled to a fraction of their former size. Wheeling, where I'd gone for my doctor and dentist, was trying to develop a tourist industry: it had shops selling antiques, fresh seafood, and art jewelry, as well as a parkland lit up with fancy lights at night so that tourists could drive through it. Pittsburgh, the closest big city and once the center of the U.S. steel industry, now had clean air. Johnstown, east of Pittsburgh, had huge Bethlehem Steel mills. To demonstrate new uses for steel, a group of brightly painted steel sculptures by a modernist sculptor, James Wolfe, had been commissioned in Johnstown in 1989. I'd taken students to see them, and marvel at the town's geography. Standing on the bluff overlooking the city, you could see where those dreadful floods of 1889 and 1936 had swirled, but the mills were closed; so were the coal mines that had fueled them. The man who showed us around said that mostly older people lived there, with the young going elsewhere in search of jobs.

Partly because of my adolescent exposure to Marxism, partly because of my experience in Business, I'd always paid more attention to economic issues than to "social" or "post-materialistic" ones (equality for minorities, gays, and women; abortion rights, gun control, the environment). This orientation branded me a member of the Old Left of the '30s and '40s, and may have made me less conscious of the social issues, but commentators influenced by the New Left of the '60s sometimes let their interest in social issues obscure the economic ones. I wasn't nostalgic for the old days, though. I've always felt that, on balance, the present is better than the past (if only because of scientific advances, and because the present gives us hope of changing the future).

Trying to relocate articles that had prompted my flash of illumination, I found three. One was indeed the story I'd checked for *Time* in October 1960 on "the service economy." It said there were now more people employed in the service-producing segment of the U.S. economy than in the goods-producing one. Some services mentioned were provided by white-collar workers (doctors, teachers), but some were blue-collar kinds of jobs (doormen, diaper services). It didn't say how many service jobs altogether were white- or blue-collar types. *Time* had explained the shift in employment by saying that there had been a change in the buying habits of U.S. consumers: with increased affluence, they had more discretionary income, and were choosing to spend more of it on services like trips to Europe or greens fees than on durable goods. Nothing was said about the possibility that proportionately fewer American workers might be producing goods because U.S. consumers were buying more imports. This was, after all, decades before the media discovered "globalization."

The second article was the one on automation that Bob Christopher had ordered up for the "Year End Review" in 1961; I'd done a big piece of research for it. This story did deal with the shift from blue-collar workers to white-collar ones, explaining that due to the increased use of computers, more clerks and technicians were needed and fewer production-line workers. This was bad news for organized labor, since assembly-line workers had formed the backbone of the union movement since the '30s, and, said *Time*, clerical employees and those in services were the most difficult to organize. Union membership had declined from 18.5 million to 18.1 million in five years.

This story must have contributed most to my epiphany, but it didn't suggest that imports might be partially responsible for the decline in assembly-line jobs (all the talk about foreign trade was of exports, not imports). I would have to revise my thinking in order to take automation and the trend toward service industries into my explanation for the relative decline in numbers of blue-collar workers, along with the impact of imports. Still, the shift away from goods and into services, even the shift away from blue-collar jobs and into white-collar ones, couldn't be explained entirely by the changed buying habits of the U.S. consumer and the rise in automation. Even if imports weren't the whole story, I felt that they must be an important element in it – though equally obviously, all the information in that article needed to be brought up to date.

The third article was the one I'd published in the January 1985 issue of *Arts* on the art audience, in which I'd said that the average museum-goer was apt to be more rather than less educated, and either a student or a white-collar worker. I'd quoted official statistics to show that those segments of the U.S. population had grown faster than the population as a whole.

27. Verification
(Fall 2001–Fall 2008)

THE FOURTH STEP in Graham Wallas's creative process is "verification," and the first piece of it that I did was update my population statistics.

I found that in 1950, four out of every ten workers in the U.S. labor force had been in white-collar occupations: professional, managerial or technical, clerical, and sales. Six out of every ten workers had been in the non-white-collar occupations, including blue-collar jobs (skilled, semiskilled and unskilled – including crafts and factory jobs), service jobs (from janitors to food-service employees), and farmers.

In 2001, the proportions were reversed: six out of every ten workers were in white-collar occupations, and four were in the non-white-collar occupations. Overall, the work force had more than doubled, but the category of professional, managerial, and technical had more than quadrupled, far in excess of the averages. The number of people employed in the clerical and sales group, and the number of those in the service jobs, had both tripled – again, well beyond the averages. The blue-collar group had grown, but far less than the total labor force – up only about a third, and the farm group had declined about 50 percent.[694]

This shift from a 40:60 ratio to a 60:40 ratio correlated to a degree with the shift from goods-producing industries to service-producing industries ("service-producing industries" differing from "service jobs" by also including professionals and technical people providing services on a more elevated level than cashiers or nannies). But the service-producing sector had already begun to employ more people than the goods-producing sector in actual numbers in the '40s.[695] Since then, the ratio had become more and more lopsided, until in 2001, 76.1 percent of the labor force was in the service industries, and only 21.6 percent in the goods-producing sector (the agricultural sector accounted for the remaining 2.3 percent).[696] Goods-producing industries had white-collar workers, of course (clerks and managers, for example), just as service-producing industries had blue-collar type jobs (bus drivers, busboys), but only one-third of those in the goods-producing segment of the economy were white-collar workers, while in the service-producing industries, more than two-thirds were.[697]

Still, this begged the question: why the shift toward services and/or white-collar jobs? Where did the money come from to pay those doctor bills (for elective as well as essential surgery) and legal expenses (for litigation that might in earlier years have been settled out of court)? Less affluent consumers might only want to cruise the malls or get a manicure, but they, too, needed money to do so. I suspected that part of it came from the fact that they didn't have to spend such a large proportion of their income on goods like TV sets or designer jeans as they had. Studying the consumer price indices, I found that the prices for consumer durables had risen much less than the prices for services, and less than prices as a whole. Since more people were buying these goods than ever before, I concluded that businessmen had been able to sell them at cheaper prices partially because with automation they could produce them more cheaply – but also because they were importing more of them than ever before.

Take TV sets. The number of them sold in the United States had nearly tripled since 1970, though the population had increased by less than half. Originally, sets made in the United States had dominated this market, but by 2001 as many as three-quarters of the total number of sets available to U.S. buyers were imports, and imported TVs were on average cheaper than domestically produced ones.[698] The story was similar, though not as extreme, with computers. The first successful general digital computer had been developed in this country during World War II, but by 2001, the market for computers in the United States seemed to have been divided approximately evenly between domestic products and imported ones, and again it was the smaller, cheaper PCs that were flooding the U.S. market from abroad.[699]

The story of the once-proud U.S. garment industry was poignantly told by Gus Tyler in his history of the International Ladies' Garment Workers' Union. Imports were already a problem by the '60s, when Local 142, neckwear makers, complained that they were being "destroyed" by silk scarves from Japan.[700] The next year, the blouse makers' local was "furious" at a one-dollar blouse imported from Japan, and underselling the local product. The manufacturer was an American who'd folded his plant in the United States to take advantage of the low wages in Japan.[701] In 1955, imports claimed only 3 percent of the apparel market. By 1965, they were up to 12 percent, to 31 percent by 1976, to 45 percent by 1986, and to 60 percent by 1991.[702] In 2001, imports accounted for more than half of the apparent consumption in ten out of eleven categories of men's, women's, girls', boys', and infants' apparel, and in most cases, 75 percent or more.[703]

Faced with losses of U.S. jobs for its members, the ILGWU tried to bargain with foreign governments, and lobby in Washington for quotas, if not tariffs. At one time or another, unions and some employers from other light industries shared in these efforts: makers of boots, shoes, plastics, dolls, toys, novelties, and electronics.[704] Nothing helped. Americans would walk barefoot if imports of shoes and boots were stopped, since the imports represented 96.6 percent of total apparent U.S. consumption in 2001.[705] The Toy Industry Association estimated that 80 to 85 percent of all the toy products sold in the United States were made offshore.[706]

The steel industry had been bewailing its woes since the '60s. By becoming more efficient and specializing in certain types of more refined steel products, it had become somewhat better able to compete in the international market. The fact remained that big integrated mills in the areas of Pittsburgh and Johnstown had been closed down, and many operations shifted to smaller, more efficient "mini-mills," often in out-of-the-way corners of the country where the steelworkers' union had trouble penetrating. This meant not only a loss in numbers of manufacturing jobs, and consequent diminution of union power, but also a relative decline in the country's capacity to produce the raw material that went into all the refined products. In 1961, the United States had been the world's largest producer of raw steel; in 2001, it was the third largest (after China and Japan).[707] In 1957, imports of steel products to the United States were still only 1.6 percent of the net shipments of domestic steel products; by 2001, that total was up to 30.4 percent.[708]

In 2001, only a quarter of the passenger cars sold in the United States were imports, but another fifth had been produced domestically by foreign-owned companies.[709] Although these foreign companies were employing American workers, the Japanese in particular had been very effective in keeping costs down by keeping unions out.

Food and drink in the United States had always been plentiful, but the small number of Americans employed in the agricultural sector continued to decline, thanks in large measure to technologically advanced "agribusiness." Nearly 90 percent of the food that Americans consumed in 2001 was still domestically grown, but the import share of U.S. lamb consumption had quadrupled since the early '80s. The import share of fresh and frozen fruits had also quadrupled, and that of fresh and frozen vegetables had tripled.[710] Some of this growth must have been due to the fact that it had become easier to ship produce from countries with different growing seasons than the United States, but an article in *The New York Times* in 2002 indicated that here was another domestic industry that felt itself threatened by the growth of imports.[711]

To be sure, not all kinds of workers had been rendered superfluous by foreign competition. Those with "capital-intensive" jobs (where much money had been invested in state-of-the-art plant and equipment) were less vulnerable to competition from developing nations. The more money an employer had put into new plant and equipment, the smaller the percentage of his expenses that went to labor costs, and the less the need to relocate. The "capital-intensive" businesses were most competitive on the international market, but employed proportionately fewer U.S. workers. The "labor-intensive" jobs could most easily – and profitably – be exported: assembly-line work that involved more direct and individual participation on the part of the worker, hence requiring a larger number of workers. Assembly-line workers in manufacturing had been among the most highly organized members of the labor force in the United States, so the strength of organized labor had been eroded over the decades by the failure of blue-collar manufacturing jobs to match population growth.

In actual numbers, total U.S. union membership hadn't peaked until the early '80s, but as a percentage of the labor force, its high point had come in 1956, at around 25 percent, and by 2000 it amounted to only 13 percent.[712] The AFL-CIO, to which most unions belonged, had tried hard to organize service and white-collar workers, and since the '60s they'd met with some success. By 2001, the union movement was almost 50 percent white-collar workers, especially in government, where 37.2 percent of the employees were organized (including schoolteachers). In transportation, public utilities, and communications, 23.4 percent were union members, but only 14.6 percent of the workers in the now highly automated manufacturing segment belonged to unions; only 5.9 percent in lower-paying service jobs (doormen, dishwashers), and only 2 percent in the predominantly white-collar sector of finance, insurance, and real estate.[713]

Many of the largest and once most militant unions in manufacturing had suffered substantial losses. Membership in the United Steelworkers of America had declined by 46 percent since 1960, and the United Auto Workers (though it had been particularly active in organizing nontraditional industries) had still lost 30 percent. In 1960, there had been three separate unions for ladies' garments, men's clothing, and textiles. By the millennium, these unions (plus others) had merged into one called UNITE, but its combined membership was down at least 65 percent since 1960. The two principal unions representing electrical workers in manufacturing were still separate entities, but their combined membership had declined by 63 percent.[714] The loss of membership in these four industries alone added up to more than two million workers.

The loss of these union workers must have been particularly hard on the Democratic Party, for union members had voted predominantly Democratic for decades. Union leaders also got out the vote (important, when you bear in mind that in 2000, 49.4 percent of those who had only graduated from high school voted, while 72 percent of those with college degrees did). Nonunion workers were more apt to be voiceless, apathetic. But the loss of those blue-collar union members was even harder on those voters in white-collar jobs

407

who considered themselves liberals, for unions had always supported health insurance, higher minimum wages, unemployment insurance, and other economic issues that kept the Democrats more firmly anchored on the left.

*   *   *

What about class? Could one equate blue-collar workers to the working class, and how should the rest of the population be divided among middle and upper classes? This had to be doable, if Howard K. Smith's analysis of how democracy worked applied in the twenty-first century. In the "Author's Note" to *Big Trouble*, Tony Lukas said he'd kept stumbling over the "twin issue of class" when he was working on *Common Ground*, his book about the Boston school-bussing crisis, though he'd expected to be dealing only with race. He'd wanted to deal with class in his next book, but felt it would be hard when writing about current American society, since it was so "professedly egalitarian that as late as 1991 one survey showed that 93 percent of all Americans regarded themselves as members in good standing of the great middle class." Thus, he'd chosen an episode from the early twentieth century, hoping it would still help to "illuminate the class question at a time when the gap between our richest and poorest citizens grows ever wider."[715] This gap had continued to grow since his death – yet more evidence for me that the poorest Americans may have been as poor as they were because they were competing for jobs with yet lower income foreign-born workers, in the United States or abroad. Indeed, one sociologist offered statistics to show that the growing disparity in the United States had less to do with the rich getting richer than it had to do with the incomes of lower- and middle-class families stagnating.[716]

Tony's saying that 93 percent of all Americans thought of themselves as middle class didn't surprise me, but it underlined for me the importance of psychological factors. We didn't have the landed aristocracy that had formed the upper class in eighteenth-century France and nineteenth-century England, so people tended to think we didn't have classes, or to confuse class with income – yet, in my experience, few people knew how their incomes compared with the averages, so their ideas about their own class became highly subjective. I'd often noticed (with private amusement) how professionals whom I had good reason to believe were in the top fifth or even the top tenth income brackets nonetheless saw themselves as "middle class."

The desire to think of oneself as "middle class" also arose from the favorable connotations of the term, as used in literature and politics over the centuries. Americans in upper income brackets might associate "middle class"" with ideas like "hard-working, thrifty, solid citizens," whereas "upper class" might

408

carry less desirable connotations of "decadent" and/or "snobbish." Lower-income Americans similarly might prefer "middle class" to "working class" because "working class" implied menial toil, and because a working-class person expected to be working class forever, whereas we, with our confidence in the American dream, always assumed that someday we'd be better off.

On the whole, Americans were affluent by comparison with most countries, especially in the third world, but that didn't mean we didn't have classes, even if defining them took more than one criterion. Many, maybe most authors on the subject based their hierarchies upon income (plus sometimes education). Some considered the use of occupation as a criterion to be Marxist, but a political economist named Michael Zweig was also concerned with occupations. To him, both blue-collar and white-collar employees were working class if they had little or no control over their workplaces.[717]

Some scholars looked to lifestyles and cultural tastes to define class, but (as Russell Lynes well knew) these could be deceptive. A millionaire Texan with an MBA from Harvard would qualify as upper class, though his cultural activities centered around golf and barbecues, while a high school dropout from the Bronx would still be lower class, though his choice in footwear or music might be setting styles for New York and Hollywood society. Obviously, income, education, even how much control people had over their jobs helped to define class, but a fourth key determinant was how many other people envied a given job – because of how pleasant it was to pursue, its status or prestige, the degree of upward mobility it offered, and whether it was varied and rewarding in ways beyond the purely financial. Since these were all subjective factors, I agreed with Zweig that the boundaries between classes were "fuzzy."[718]

Using these four determinants, I found that the upper classes in American society were still the managerial and professional occupations, including country music stars and CEOs but also members of the clergy, college professors, even artists (who, however struggling, were doing something that many people in routine jobs secretly wished they could do). The working class still had the traditional blue-collar and low-paid service occupations. The middle class was white-collar workers, mostly in sales and clerical occupations, together with some technicians and low-level administrators, some less well-paid professions (schoolteachers, nurses), and some of the highest-paid blue-collar jobs (truck drivers, unionized workers near retirement).

This was the undecided middle class, as defined by Howard K. Smith when I was in high school, the ones who'd cast their ballots with owning or working classes, so keeping democracy in working order. One article by Thomas E. Cavanagh, a political scientist, described them well in 1990. "Meet the swing voters of the 1990's," it said. "They are secretaries and store clerks, salesmen and high school teachers, nurses, and truck drivers. They're not the 'have-nots,' but they don't have much, and they're trying to hold on to what little they've got."[719] The article explained that these voters were fed up with what they looked upon as the "tax and spend" policies of big government, because of the savings and loan fiascoes. But (I'd add) this discontent had been fueled by years of hearing Republicans, led by Reagan and representing the affluent, insisting that big government was bad government, and the only good way for taxes to go was down.

Job classifications for "undecided" voters were similar in 2000, to judge from the anecdotal evidence of interviews conducted by correspondents of *The New York Times* right after the Republican and Democratic conventions.[720] A very large percentage of these would evidently vote in November for Bush, not Gore (though Gore was a "centrist" rather than a "leftist," and the votes cast for Ralph Nader, a relict of old-style liberalism, had been minuscule). The problem hadn't changed since Smith had written his book: without enough input from the working class, the middle class would be inclined to identify with the owning class. If only because they wanted to be like them, they would tend to see things their way, and consider their interests identical with their own.

*   *   *

In 1968, Nixon, a more conservative candidate, had triumphed over Humphrey by a very slim margin. Had he owed his victory to doves who'd crossed party lines, as I'd thought for all these years, and did this therefore mean that the country as a whole had changed its mind about the war? One Gallup Poll taken in April 1968 had been discussed by Michael Wheeler, in his book on pollsters. The major candidates at that moment had been Nixon, Humphrey, George Wallace (the racist governor of Alabama), and Senator Eugene McCarthy. McCarthy's surprising showing in the New Hampshire primary in March had been widely interpreted as an antiwar statement, yet, according to Wheeler, the constituencies of the four candidates "were remarkably similar in how they responded to the hawk/dove question. Forty-six percent of Wallace supporters described themselves as hawks, 33 percent as doves. For Nixon, the division was 44 percent hawks, 43 doves. Humphrey's supporters were also evenly split, 39 percent and 41 percent respectively. Eugene McCarthy...had surprisingly similar support; 37 percent of his followers described themselves as hawks and 41 percent as doves."[721]

I saw this poll as evidence that Nixon was appealing as much to the hawks as he was to the doves, but I didn't want to rely on Gallup any more than I had to. Wheeler's point was that such polarized questions (where the interviewee had to specify either dove or hawk, with no gradations or alternatives) didn't tell as much about the true opinions of voters as more nuanced questions might. I turned to the National Election Studies, sponsored by the University of Michigan, and said to be the leading academically run national survey of U.S. voters. Its statistics went back to 1948. The questions in its surveys (especially the recent ones) were more nuanced, and the answers were online in ASCII characters, but since I panic at the sight of ASCII characters, I commissioned two Columbia sophomores to interpret them for me.

With data derived from the NES, Shanshan Ding (with Brandon Batista) showed me that 42 percent of the people who'd voted for Nixon in 1968 thought he was a little bit to very hawkish, and another 30 percent thought he was neutral on the subject. Only 21 percent of those who'd voted for him thought he was at all – let alone very – dovish (the remainder fell into inconclusive categories like "don't know" or "N/A").[722] This confirmed my suspicion that his aggressive policies in Vietnam, after he took office, reflected the outlook of a sizeable plurality of the voters who'd elected him, and explained why the war had gone on for another five years – but how about that 21 percent that had voted for him and thought he was dovish? Could this have been his margin of victory? If so, it might explain why he'd alternated between hawkish and dovish stances once elected.

Tricky Dick (as he was called in my youth) won a comfortable majority of 301 votes in the electoral college (to Humphrey's 191), but only seventy-nine of those votes came from states where he'd won a majority of the popular vote (mainly on the Great Plains and in the Rockies). In every other state he carried, he had only a plurality, and only a plurality in the nationwide popular vote, 43.4 percent (Humphrey got 42.7 percent, and George Wallace, 13.5 percent). In six of the more liberal states where the dove vote might have helped Nixon, his margin of victory averaged only 3.35 percent. Those six (California, Illinois, New Jersey, Oregon, Wisconsin, and Ohio) had a total of 127 electoral votes. If they'd gone for Humphrey, they would have put him well above the 270 votes needed to elect, so it may be argued that a small slice of the antiwar voting public shifted from the Democratic to the Republican column in those crucial states. (Then again, it may simply have been that white blue-collar Democrats abandoned Humphrey to vote their racist sympathies with Wallace. Probably a combination of the two.)

Most antiwar activists probably didn't vote for Nixon. More likely, they didn't vote at all. But even if it was only moderate doves who went for Nixon in those six states, still there was that 21 percent who voted for him, thinking that he was (or might become) a dove, and one can certainly argue that they were enough to flip the election in his favor. As early as March 1968, in the wake of the traumatic Tet offensive, Gallup pollsters had begun to ask whether interviewees would approve if the U.S. government decided to gradually withdraw its troops from Vietnam, and, when the question was phrased that way, 56 percent said yes, they'd approve.[723] By June of 1969, that majority had even grown to 59 percent, but when in March 1969, the question had been phrased differently, and interviewees were asked what they thought the United States should do next in Vietnam, the largest number (32 percent) were still in favor of more escalation. Twenty-six percent favored pulling out, and leaving the job of defending South Vietnam to the South Vietnamese, 19 percent favored continuing present policies (which at that point included no withdrawals), and 19 percent favored ending the war "as soon as possible."[724] In retrospect, it appears that the campus disorders in the spring of 1969 that I remembered so vividly may to some extent have forced Nixon to announce the specific withdrawal of 25,000 troops on June 8. After all, such disorders were making mincemeat of his campaign promises to restore law and order. But the fact that he would be withdrawing unspecified numbers of troops at some future point was already known, having been discussed by him in a nationally televised speech on May 14.

Ding and Batista also compiled statistics derived from the NES on party preferences by occupation in 1948, 1968, and 2000. In general, they found that the higher on the social ladder an individual might be, the more likely he or she would be to favor the Republicans. Still, the proportion of professionals and semiprofessionals who according to the NES usually voted Democratic in 1948 was far higher than Gallup would have had you think (43 percent v. 27 percent Republican), although the proportion of managers, supervisors, and the self-employed remained substantially in the Republican column (43 percent v. only 29 percent Democratic). Blue-collar workers (skilled, semiskilled and unskilled) gave the most lopsided endorsement to the Democrats (50 percent for them v. 13 percent for the Republicans). The 1948 survey had a third category, "inconsistent." This apparently referred to people who voted a split ticket, and/or hadn't consistently voted for either party, and was highest among the professionals (21 percent). It was still high among managers (15 percent), but lower among blue-collar workers (9 percent).

The many professional people favoring the Democrats in 1948 didn't surprise me, given my progressive upbringing, but the picture changed with the NES surveys for 1968 and 2000. "Inconsistent" was replaced by "independent," and this nomenclature was more popular: between a quarter and a third of all interviewees now called themselves "independents." In 1968 and 2000, slightly more of the remainder in managerial and professional groups favored the Democrats, but the situation evolved with blue-collar workers. In 1960, they still favored the Democrats heavily (51 percent to 19 percent for the Republicans), but by 2000, those favoring the Democrats were down to 35 percent (though still with only 20 percent favoring Republicans).[725] Sales and clerical workers slotted in between blue-collar workers and professionals, favoring Democrats over Republicans by 43 percent to 32 percent in 1948, by 42 percent to 27 percent in 1968, and by 31 percent to 27 percent in 2000.

The declining proportion of voters willing to declare themselves Democrats was accentuated by the dwindling proportion of people engaged in those blue-collar occupations most inclined to support Democrats. The 1970 census would show that the ratio between white-collar and non-white-collar jobs was nearing 50:50.[726] Though it didn't say so, the average age in the blue-collar group must also have been increasing, since younger people were more likely to have college degrees and be moving into white-collar occupations. As most people tend to become more conservative with age, the aging of the blue-collar group contributed to its increasing defection from the Democratic column, though not all children from working-class backgrounds abandoned their parents' allegiances when they moved up in the world.

The tendency to stay Democratic was probably most pronounced among the "creative" occupations I'd grown up with: advertising, public relations, journalism, fashion, design, and the arts. The growth in some of these occupations outpaced the overall growth in the work force by sometimes startling numbers.[727] In terms of voting, however, the increase of professionals and technical workers in other fast-growing fields wasn't necessarily good for the Democrats. Although college professors were inclined to vote Democratic, nurses and physical therapists might be less likely to, and the finance industries (bankers, brokers, insurance salesmen, real estate agents), from what I'd seen, tended to favor Republicans.

What I took to be representatives of the "disenfranchised left" had demonstrated at meetings of the World Trade Organization in Seattle in 1999, and the Group of Eight at Genoa in 2001. Both protests were against how free trade was exploiting poorer nations. People don't demonstrate when they have peaceable options, only when the democratic process has failed. The demonstrators mostly came from comfortable backgrounds, but lacked the following in their own countries to bring pressure to bear. Somewhere in the developing nations were their constituents, but the demonstrators couldn't use this "disenfranchised left" as a voting bloc any more than could liberal politicians in the United States. According to polls taken shortly after 9/11 by a Canadian organization, 85 percent of Americans, and from 58 to 66 percent of people in the other seven wealthier countries, supported war in Afghanistan, but it was opposed by 70 to 75 percent of the population in the world's poorer countries.[728] Here was more evidence of my "disenfranchised left," able to vote only in polls without any legal force.

I introduced the "disenfranchised left" in a "special triple issue" of *From the Mayor's Doorstep* in January 2002. Verifying (and qualifying) the concept, and finishing my manuscript, took another six years. During that time, much changed, the most dramatic change being the rise of China and India to the status of economic superpowers, thus potentially also political superpowers. Although these rises had been at the expense of millions of American jobs, white collar as well as blue collar, on the whole it benefitted America, paradoxically enough because it showed that we weren't the only superpower, the only game in town. Another factor conducive to world stability was the rise of the euro, relative to the U.S. dollar. As I see it, both developments tamped down paranoia among disadvantaged people who might otherwise support terrorism, while the emergence of Russia as a corrupt, rapacious example of nineteenth-century capitalism helped to reclaim America's somewhat tarnished reputation as the land of the free and home of democracy. I even welcomed the emergence of what in the old days would have been called "neutralist" powers like Venezuela and Brazil, countries that again offered alternatives (however unpalatable) to America's one-party world state.

On the home front, developments were less sanguine. After driving the Taliban out of Afghanistan, the Bush administration embarked on an immoral and unnecessary war against Saddam Hussein in Iraq. Even had it been founded (as it was not) upon reliable evidence that Hussein possessed weapons of mass destruction, only fascist nations should undertake unprovoked attack, certainly not peace-loving democracies. Nevertheless, Bush managed to use the war, billed as a war against terrorism, to win a second term in 2004, despite (or more likely because of) the reactionary economic policies he'd pursued, including more tax cuts for the affluent, enhanced provisions for the oil industry, further deregulation of telecommunications, and so on. Although the United States deposed Hussein, Iraq then bogged down in rival factions warring for control. This miserable situation enabled the Democrats to win control of Congress in 2006.

By 2008, the U.S. military was having more success in suppressing the Iraqi insurgencies, but such news took a back seat to national concern over the state of the domestic economy. The downturn had begun in 2006, when it became apparent that more and more homeowners who had taken out subprime mortgages were falling behind in their mortgage payments, and foreclosures by banks were increasing. The stock market, similarly inflated by unregulated, risky speculations, peaked in October 2007, and began to drift downward, propelled by the mess in housing and other increasingly negative economic indicators. In 2008, the Republicans nominated for the presidency John McCain, a Vietnam war hero in his seventies, while the Democrats, after a unusually long primary campaign, nominated Barack Obama, the 47-year-old son of a white American woman and a Kenyan man.

The fact that Obama was the first African American to become a major party candidate for the presidency led many (including myself) to worry that racism would tilt the balance of an already conservative electorate in favor of McCain, but Obama mounted an extraordinarily effective campaign, raising many millions of dollars, largely (though hardly exclusively) from small contributors. He outspent McCain, but an even more decisive factor in his favor was the increasingly dramatic downturn in the economy. The stock market, which by November had lost 40 percent of its value since its peak in October 2007, lost half of that – 20 percent – in six catastrophic weeks between mid-September and Election Day. This appalling performance sent Bush's already low approval ratings into the cellar, and rendered Obama's stirring call for "change" especially appealing. He won by a handsome majority – not a landslide like FDR's 1936 victory, but (accompanied as it was by increased Democratic majorities in Congress) a generous mandate.

How does this seeming turnaround jibe with my thesis that the American electorate had been moving slowly rightward for the past sixty years? It doesn't disprove it. Only the choice of a black man for the presidency was truly radical – a social issue, not an economic one. On other social issues, Obama wasn't that much more radical than McCain, and though the candidates differed on economic issues, the differences weren't that dramatic, either (both candidates calling for tax cuts, for example, though McCain favored more tax cuts for the affluent, while Obama favored tax cuts for the lower and middle classes; both candidates calling for national health insurance, though McCain favored a greater role for the private sector, while Obama wanted a bigger role for the government). It remained to be seen whether the U.S. presidency – and its electorate – would move still further left.

Somebody (I wish I could remember who) has written that the reason America moved to the left in the '30s was that the Crash of 1929 impoverished (and accordingly radicalized) the middle class. Conceivably, the bear market of 2007–2008 could result in another such shift, but in November 2008 this was still not certain. Many middle-class Americans were mourning steep declines in the value of their 401(k)s, but it also remained to be seen how deep and prolonged the recession of 2008 would become. I suspected there was still a good deal of fat in the U.S. economy, and many Americans who might still not be desperate. In July 2006, two reporters on *The New York Times* had reported that millions of American men in the prime of life who had lost relatively high-paying blue-collar jobs were unwilling to accept lower-paying ones, apparently able to subsist in reasonable comfort on savings and/or their wives' incomes.[729]

In one sense, I even feel that the housing crisis, and the stock market decline, reinforce my argument. That is because it seems, upon the basis of my previous observations, that the conservative, affluent temperament (which has had a better deal from society) is more inclined to be optimistic and if anything, overconfident, while the liberal, less affluent temperament (whose treatment by society has been less kind) is more inclined to anxiety and pessimism (aside from occasional bursts of euphoria, such as followed Obama's election). In my chapter on how *Newsweek* and *Time* covered civil rights in the '60s, I showed how conservative *Time* looked on the bright side of race relations, and emphasized how far "the Negro" had come, while liberal *Newsweek* looked on the dark side, and emphasized how far he still had to go. Similarly, in my chapter on Vietnam coverage of the magazines, I showed how *Time*'s emphasis on the victories that the United States was supposedly winning reflected the more optimistic view of the war taken by Otto Fuerbringer, the magazine's managing editor, while the emphasis on flaws in the South Vietnamese government, the questioning of casualty statistics, and the doubts about where the war was going, reflected *Newsweek*'s more pessimistic, liberal point of view.

Since the '70s, at least, a more optimistic view of the U.S. economy had been growing, out of proportion to the economy's actual growth.[730] Credit mushroomed, far beyond the capacity of many Americans to repay their debts – in terms of mortgages, as we'd already seen by 2008, but also in terms of credit cards, as we might well see in 2009. Stocks had been trading far in excess of their growth expectations. All this optimism, I'd argue, reflected the fact that middle-class Americans were listening more to the upper classes, and adopting their overly optimistic point of view, while ignoring ever less numerous working-class complaints and provisos. Capitalism, rampant, had come to dominate everybody's thinking, while more egalitarian economic values as even espoused by socialism, let alone communism, sank into disrepute.

Capitalism is built upon the principle of self-interest. It argues that when everybody is working for themselves, society benefits, but that doesn't mean everybody benefits equally, and for decades, too few were getting rich at the expense of too many. Communism was intended to counteract the injustices of capitalism. It was built (in theory, not practice) upon the principle of cooperation: subordinating one's self-interest to the good of the community. Liberalism tries to combine the best of both systems. In his earlier, more optimistic books, Freud liked to cite Schiller, the German poet, to the effect that "hunger" and "love" are what move the world. This meant humanity had two drives, to survive and to perpetuate the species.[731] The first led people to exercise their aggressive instincts and try to outdo their fellow humans. The second led them to love and cooperate in the begetting and raising of children. To me, liberalism came closest to balancing cooperation (or constraint) off against liberty (or license). Was that why Freud – as the philosophical corollary to liberalism – was so out of style?

*   *   *

Such as it was, the creativity of my insight into the "disenfranchised left" required synthesizing two sets of statistics, one from business and/or economics, one from politics and/or political science. Some journalists did this; most covered politics or business. They tended to stick to recent developments, while I (being outside the box of daily and weekly journalism) could take a somewhat longer view. Most writers (journalistic and academic) assumed that the U.S. political economy was synonymous with its territorial borders, but I seemed to be outside the box which equates political economies to nation-states. I'm not a political scientist, economist, or sociologist. In fact, as an independent scholar, I'm only a borderline academic, but being outside the boxes of all these disciplines may help explain why I came up with an analysis of voting trends (studied by political scientists) based upon class analysis (studied by sociologists) and business conditions (studied by economists). It wouldn't surprise me to learn that pollsters for both parties know about the situation I've outlined, but they don't seem to want to publicize it. I think we should. Otherwise, how are we going to figure out how to cope with it? Psychoanalysis taught me to face up to nasty realities, because the only way they can be abreacted is by having them out in the open.

Conclusions: Putting It All Together
(2008)

ON NOVEMBER 8, 2001, I went to see a big exhibition of Thomas Eakins at the Philadelphia Museum of Art. Two Philadelphia friends, Marion Steinmann and Charles Joiner, had invited me to stay over with them, and we talked about Marion's latest project. She'd written about science for *Life*, and since then had done a number of medical books, but now she was working on a study of the job experience of women in her class of 1950 at Cornell. I asked whether any of the men in her class had been studying under the GI Bill of Rights, that great government program to fund college educations for vets that had begun at the end of World War II. "77 percent!" she replied, and at this, my mental wheels started turning.

I remembered the research and thinking I'd done in 1995 about my own highbrow upbringing at North Country, as compared with the much larger numbers of children my age and slightly older who read comic books, listened to jukeboxes in drugstores, went to the movies on Saturday afternoons, and ate Campbell's soups in their mothers' kitchens a lot more often than I had. In 1995, I'd seen all those other children as typical, and myself as the exception, but now I realized there must have been other children like myself with maybe not highbrow parents, but definitely upper-middlebrow ones. The attitudes toward culture such children had been raised with would have been more like mine. True, Russell Lynes hadn't believed the hierarchy of brows equated to a hierarchy of incomes, but the idea of lowbrows reading comic books and going to grade-B double features suggested to me that there were more of them among the less educated and affluent, if only because there were more of the less educated and affluent. The children of these less affluent parents would have most likely been reading comic books themselves in the '30s and '40s – as well as being the ones whose cultural horizons would have been most dramatically expanded if they'd been drafted as adolescents and then gone to college on the GI Bill.

Many writers had commented on the new, larger audiences that began to enter the art scene in the later '50s and early '60s. These audiences were usually described in terms of their higher levels of affluence and education, but Marion's 77 percent made me think about the colleges they must have attended to fit them for better-paying and usually white-collar jobs. At college, they might very well have taken art-history courses (surveys, if nothing else), but if they'd come originally from lowbrow families (or even lower-middlebrow ones), they wouldn't have been exposed as children to avant-garde art the same way that children from homes like mine had been. As a result, they wouldn't have been nearly as familiar with its whole modernist tradition from the semiabstractions of Analytic Cubism on through Mondrian to the pure abstractions of Pollock, Rothko, etc. They would been more likely to have been baffled by it, while soup-can paintings and comic-strip imagery would have reminded them of their childhoods.

I looked for books about the GI Bill, and found three particularly relevant: one by Norman Frederiksen and W. B. Shrader, one by Keith W. Olson, and one by Michael J. Bennett. They told me that although my initial hypothesis was in line with reality, it needed qualification. While ex-servicemen attending college under the GI Bill did tend to come from families with less education, they didn't necessarily come from families with lower incomes. Most said that without the GI Bill, they'd have gone to college anyway, but with it, they could and did go to better colleges.[732] Ivy League schools and the Big Ten state universities were more likely to offer (even require) courses in art history than teachers' colleges or vocational schools. And the GI Bill was only half the story. Before World War II, the country, with its huge numbers of unemployed, had been poor. During it, full employment in the armed services and defense industries put more money into more pockets, but as factories were manufacturing guns and tanks, consumer products were in short supply.

After the war, savings that had been forced on consumers during the war, combined with the end of wartime shortages, touched off a consumer-products boom that meant the continuance of full employment. Thus, in the post-war world, more blue-collar workers could afford to send sons and daughters to college straight from high school, and college prepared these boys and girls, too, for better jobs in white-collar positions. The number of college-educated men rose from 10.3 percent of the population in 1940 to 15.7 percent in 1952, an increase of 52 percent, and the number of college-educated women rose from 9.7 percent of the population to 13.4 percent, an increase of 38 percent. This could not have been achieved without many more students from less privileged backgrounds among those totals – many more college grads who as children would have had less exposure to Picasso, and more to *Batman* and the drugstore hamburgers Oldenburg would be celebrating in the '60s.

This elevation from working class and/or lowbrow homes happened with artists as well as art-lovers. Calvin Tomkins discussed Rauschenberg's childhood in Port Arthur, Texas, the small Gulf Coast refinery town where he lived until he was eighteen. Art was at a minimum in the future artist's lower-class family home, and the notion of becoming an artist inconceivable. Rauschenberg didn't see his first Old Master paintings until after he'd gone into the Navy, and didn't enroll in art school until after the war – on the GI Bill of Rights.[733]

Warhol was too young to be drafted, but he came from a working-class family in Pittsburgh. It had little interest in high culture, but seems to have been sufficiently comfortable by the post-war period to enable him to attend the Carnegie Institute of Technology.[734] Like Rauschenberg, Warhol early displayed skill in drawing, and must have seen paintings in the Carnegie Museum of Art (he took art classes there when he was in high school), but as a child he was more interested in movie stars and movie magazines, suggesting that the culture in his home environment was to have a deeper and more lasting effect.[735]

Assaulting the avant-garde culture of the '50s with reminiscences of their lowbrow childhoods was highly creative of Rauschenberg, Warhol, and their compeers. It was "thinking outside the box" with a vengeance, but that was the trouble: they were so far outside the box, and so angry at abstract expressionism, the avant-garde culture they couldn't understand, that their art took the form of revenge upon it.

Returning to New York from Philadelphia, I was confronted by a mammoth retrospective for Norman Rockwell at the Guggenheim Museum. I didn't like Rockwell, but to say this response was somewhat atypical was to put it mildly. Michael Kimmelman praised the show in *The New York Times* as particularly relevant to the city's distressed but patriotic state of mind in the wake of 9/11. He maintained that the saccharine emotion in a painting like *Freedom from Fear* could, in the wake of the World Trade Center tragedy, move viewers even if they didn't want to be moved. "What Rockwell painted," the critic argued, "was not what America, in its complexity, ever quite looked like. But at his best he captured what many Americans really felt and desired – and many now feel and desire – which is truth on a level deeper than surface appearance."[736] Kimmelman's employer evidently agreed, for it ran a series of full-page house ads, using altered Rockwell images to point up the analogies between our heroic past and traumatized present.[737] *Newsweek* used reproductions of Rockwell's "Four Freedoms" series for an article on "Living a New Normal."[738]

I became jarringly aware of how Rockwell had become a city-wide sacred cow when I said that I didn't think much of him to a friend of more than thirty years' standing. She landed on my head like a ton of bricks, insisting that the paintings were "sweet." When I attempted to protest, she snapped that she didn't want to talk about it anymore and forcibly changed the subject.

It was depressing to have somebody I'd known for more than half of my life, and considered one of my best friends, treating me like shit because I wasn't being "patriotic"about Rockwell.

In the Columbia library, I compared the *Saturday Evening Post* covers for which he was best known with other *Post* covers. He'd been very good at what he did, far better than other *Post* cover artists in portraying different types of people, and with a sense of humor that they lacked, but his ambitions weren't on a par with his prowess as an illustrator. After all, he'd perfected this formula of his for a specific publication and its audience. He wasn't creating art for a few sophisticated viewers, in hopes that forty or fifty years later, many more people would become able to appreciate it. He wanted to make as much money as possible as fast as possible. His prestige client was the *Post*, but advertising has always paid much better than journalism, and, in a two-volume catalogue of his complete output, I saw that his talents had also been used in dozens of ads, promoting GM as well as Ford, Coke as well as Pepsi, Budweiser as well as Ballantine's beer – but you get the idea.[739]

The *Post* was a lower-middlebrow publication (and as such, with an audience not far removed from that of *Time* in the '50s and '60s, although more sophisticated people read *Time*, too). While lower middlebrows might or might not be prosperous, they were apt to be square, the sort who could admire Michelangelo and Rembrandt, but, when the subject of "modern art" came up, say that they didn't know much about art but they knew what they liked. (Also the *Post* was browsed by bright, upper-middlebrow children like myself, who liked its humorous anecdotes and cartoons.)

During the '60s, when *Life*, *Look*, and the *Post* were fighting their ultimately losing battle to compete for ads with TV, all three became more with-it (apparently trying to appeal to the smaller but more sophisticated college-educated audience whom advertisers still wanted to reach through print). Rockwell's few paintings dealing with race relations (done for *Look*, not the *Post*) dated from this final period, when the cause was so widely backed that even Republicans endorsed it. Glancing back, over earlier, more representative phases of the *Post,* I perceived 1) articles and illustrations focusing on native-born white people in smaller cities and rural surroundings; 2) a bias in favor of management at the expense of labor; and 3) a preference for Republicans over Democrats. In presidential election years, the magazine did articles on both candidates before the election, but the Republican always came last, just before Election Day, when memory of the article would be freshest as people went to vote.

The Guggenheim show was subtitled "Pictures for the American People" – but which American people were we really talking about? In "Avant-Garde and Kitsch," Clem had equated Rockwell's *Saturday Evening Post* covers to the Stalinist kitsch that a Russian peasant would like, but I discovered a little booklet which told a very different story. Published by the *Post* in 1940, and entitled *What Post Advertising Means to You*, this booklet was designed to persuade potential advertisers to buy space in the magazine. The many statistics carefully assembled for this purpose showed that *Post* readers were inclined to be native-born whites, richer and better educated than the average American, more likely to have life insurance, automobiles, and servants.[740] Apparently *Post* readers were less likely to be the humble little people whom Rockwell depicted in his *Post* covers. In fact, although the common idea was that the *Post* was read by practically everybody in the country, its circulation in 1940 had been 3.3 million, and the total population of the United States had been 131.7 million, meaning that only one American in forty was actually buying the *Post*.

More statistics in the booklet showed that the magazine was most likely to be read in affluent towns and suburbs across the country: Larchmont and Scarsdale in New York, Princeton in New Jersey, Winnetka and Lake Forest in the Chicago area, and Beverly Hills in southern California. It was more likely to be read in big, industrialized cities than in rural areas, and least likely to be read in working-class cities and boroughs with high concentrations of the foreign-born and African Americans. Earlier, I suggested that the reason 93 percent of all Americans considered themselves middle class was the fact that many upper-class people preferred to see themselves as middle class. For such people, Rockwell's images of cute children, gossiping housewives and lovable codgers would have furnished ideal surrogates for their own self-images. There must also have been some city-dwellers who felt the need to fantasize themselves as members of conservative, Republican, small-town, lily-white Middle America. To judge from the *Post*'s booklet, they were fewer in 1940, but, to judge from the adulation Rockwell was receiving in the wake of 9/11, even the editors of *Newsweek* and *The New York Times*, normally liberal, big-city publications, thought their readers would want to see themselves in this light – yet more evidence, however subliminal, of the swing in the country's political orientation to the right.

While Clem had been wrong in seeing Rockwell's *Saturday Evening Post* covers as intended for peasants, he was right with his larger insight that Soviet realism and art for art's sake were opposed. In "Avant-Garde and Kitsch," he'd equated "art for art's sake" with the trend toward abstraction, and many later critics and art historians had used this idea to contrast "art for art's sake" with representational art. For me, the larger distinction was between art for the sake of politics, story-telling, or propaganda, and art for its own sake, as originally discussed in France – long before the arrival of abstraction – by Théophile Gautier in the preface to his novel *Mademoiselle de Maupin* (1835). For Gautier, art for art's sake merely meant that art was to be evaluated upon the basis of its own merits, not for any practical or moral purposes it might serve, the enemies as he saw it being clericalism and the Christian socialism of the followers of Henri de Saint-Simon. In that sense, art for art's sake went back to the Renaissance, when secular painting attained a status equal to religious art. The mythological paintings by Titian and Bellini in the sixteenth-century *camerino* of Alfonso d'Este, Duke of Ferrara, were as much art for art's sake as a Noland, since neither the Duke nor any other Renaissance Italian thought of the Greek and Roman gods portrayed as religious icons.

To the extent that Rockwell's *Saturday Evening Post* covers told their own moral little stories, they weren't art for art's sake. The irony was that their programmatic nature rendered them equally desirable to conservative Republicans on the right and esthetic "radicals" on the left, as the catalogue for the Guggenheim show attested. Dave Hickey, who'd contributed one essay to that catalogue, was much admired by postmodernists. He taught at the University of Nevada, Las Vegas, but he'd also delivered lectures in New York and I'd heard that people had lined up around the block to hear him, at ten bucks a pop. Hickey's essay (also published as an article in *Vanity Fair*) maintained that in the last forty years, the commercial illustrators who'd furnished Rockwell's competition, and 99 percent of the modern artists whose work was said to have been far better than his, "have become historical footnotes...as, in fact, has modernism itself."[741] Employing a detailed iconographic discussion plus loving formal analysis of Rockwell's *After the Prom*, Hickey argued that in paintings such as this, showing a pair of teenagers at a soda fountain to epitomize young love, Rockwell had "invented democratic history painting." It was this achievement of "investing the daily activities of ordinary people with a sense of historical consequence" that to Hickey best explained "Rockwell's survival as an artist."[742]

Hickey's presentation was impressive, but for me the sentimentality of *After the Prom* relegated it to the humbler category of genre painting, not the more elevated one of history painting. Sentimentality is a sign of stale thinking, and the sticky-out noses and apple cheeks of Rockwell's faces were cartoon conventions, cliches for unsophisticated people who (without knowing it) were more at home with cliches than with fresh thinking. Rockwell's humor was what saved him. Because of it, I can see why Clem enjoyed him (as he did), but I'm also sure he would have considered Rockwell minor art, not major. This was still business as usual for an upper middlebrow trying to entertain as many lower middlebrows as possible. Rockwell wasn't painting for people on his own cultural level. He was talking down to his audience, condescending to it. He didn't read the *Post* himself, but subscribed to the *Atlantic* and *The*

New Yorker, upper-middlebrow magazines.[743] Wanda Corn, in her essay in the Guggenheim catalogue, maintained that he cared about art history and was familiar with Pollock's painting.[744] Why not? As an upper middlebrow, it was his job to know about highbrow art and purvey it to lower middlebrows (much as upper-middlebrow commercial artists haunted Manhattan galleries in the '60s, while I was on *Time*, looking for ideas to use in ads and packaging).

Russell Lynes had made clear this prime function of the upper middlebrow, and distinguished between the two types of middlebrow in his article. Corn quoted from that article, but didn't distinguish between the two middlebrows. For me, this distinction between upper middlebrow and lower middlebrow is crucial, because it tells me which way Rockwell was looking while he was making his images, whether his head was facing down toward the ground, where his feet were firmly planted in the realistic world of making a steady living, or up toward the stars, in hopes of creating an art that would outlast the conventions and accommodations of the moment.

Which way somebody is looking is the essence of the difference between the idealist and the realist. This distinction had become clear to me when I was reading the memoir of Oz Elliott, top editor at *Newsweek* in the '60s. As he told it, the people on the publishing side at *Newsweek* had been trying to sell ads in it by looking down upon *U.S. News & World Report*, the newsweekly with the third-largest circulation, and arguing that *Newsweek* was the bigger and therefore the better of the two. Elliott and his "editorial types" decided to look upward instead, setting their sights on *Time*, the biggest newsweekly. By so doing, they cast themselves in the role of the crusading underdog during a decade when many underdogs were on the move, and their idealistic, crusading spirit became the basis of their reputation.

Rockwell wasn't looking upward, in the sense that he was making art he hoped would rival or excel the art of the ages. Rather, he was looking downward, using his knowledge of that greater art to create lesser, safer, more conventional work for people with unsophisticated tastes, yet Hickey compared *After the Prom* to paintings by Fragonard, Chardin, and other eighteenth-century masters. Evidently, he couldn't see the difference in quality between them and Rockwell. In this, he reminded me of John Ashcroft, George W. Bush's first attorney general, who apparently disliked the National Endowment for the Arts because it funded opera and not, by and large, "the art of the great masses," like the country-Western music of Willie Nelson and Garth Brooks.[745]

It was under the oppressive pressures of the adulation surrounding Rockwell in the wake of 9/11, and how this adulation correlated with the reactionary, not to say almost fascistic, political climate of that moment, that

425

I became conscious of the esthetic parallels between Hickey and conservatives like Ashcroft. It was also in this context that I recalled how abstract expressionism had been the reigning avant-garde in the '50s, a period when neither the radical right nor the radical left were overwhelming factors on the political scene, and liberalism remained the guiding governmental philosophy. Eisenhower had been a Republican, but he hadn't tried to dismantle the New Deal, and upon leaving office in 1961, had delivered a speech warning against the influence of the military-industrial complex.

In the late '60s, Clem's antagonists called him a political reactionary, and implied that abstract expressionism caught on only because the CIA used it as a weapon in the cold war.[746] True, abstract painting's lack of obvious political message does lay it open to exploitation by right-wingers: Dick Cheney displayed a (borrowed) Frankenthaler in his official residence. But even if abstract expressionism was used to demonstrate Western freedom of expression, this would have seemed reactionary only in a post-Vietnam world. For the '50s, it would have seemed like a normal liberal thing to do, and one recent essayist has written that in the '50s, Clem was a liberal.[747] To me, in the '70s and even later, he called himself a socialist, but as I've said (in relation to Howard K. Smith) these two identities were not as mutually exclusive as they might appear today, given the enthusiasm that many American liberals felt in the '40s and '50s for British socialism and Scandinavia's modified welfare states.

Recent historical experience therefore suggested that art for art's sake stood its best chance of acceptance when the political climate was liberal, not reactionary or radical, and when the country as a whole was peaceful, prosperous, and with an economy closing the gap between its poorest and wealthiest citizens. Under such optimal conditions, prevailing audiences might be able to accept art that rose above the merely political, and was philosophical in nature. Even then, though, the way wasn't easy. The increased number of more well-to-do white-collar workers from less sophisticated family backgrounds in the decades after World War II also contributed to the difficulties encountered by abstract expressionism in the '50s, and the enthusiasm with which pop art was received in the '60s. This economic explanation for the rise in postmodernism complements the artistic and political ones I've already explored.

God knows, I wouldn't want the '50s back again, with their stuffiness and conventionality (to say nothing of how women and minorities were kept in subordinate roles). Still less would I shoehorn anybody back into a blue-collar job in order to reinstate the primacy of fine abstraction or a more liberal political climate. I do see a parallel between the spirit in which such paintings were (and are) made, and the spirit of reform that can animate have-nots in a society. In socioeconomic and political terms, the underclass looks to the future for improvement over the present, and the upper classes cling to the status quo (or would react back to earlier phases of it when they had even more advantages). Similarly, in the art world, the mass of critical opinion clings to the status quo, while our best artists, especially the younger ones, must (as always) look to the future for widespread recognition.

Norman Rockwell had painted realistic (or rather, representational) pictures. He was also a realist in his outlook on life (at any rate, his professional relationships). In painting, the principal alternatives to realistic painting were fantasy and abstraction, while with life, the alternative to realism was idealism. These two sets of alternatives ran along parallel tracks. The realist in social outlook (and the representational painter) made the best of the present. The idealist (in art as in politics) believed that no matter how bad things were now, they could get better if people worked to make them better.

Realists call idealists innocent or naive; idealists often consider realists cynical or skeptical. To me, most people are neither pure realists nor pure idealists. Even the most dedicated realist has a streak of idealism somewhere, while no idealist could survive if she or he were 100 percent idealistic. It may only be a question of emphasis, but I visualize it as a continuum or even a semicircular arrangement, comparable to the political semicircle I'd learned about in eighth grade. In the idealist/realist semicircle, the idealists sit just to the left of the center aisle, and the truly innocent or naive to the far left. The realists sit just to the right of the center aisle, with cynics and skeptics beyond them to the far right.

I see a correlation between the two hemicycles, with idealists corresponding to political liberals, and realists to political conservatives. That makes the reactionaries into cynics, and places the radicals in the same part of the semicircle as the naive. Within the realm of art, I define the reactionary temperament originally in relation to Duchamp. His Readymades were a reaction against the multireferential imagery of Analytic Cubism, a lapse back into the uni-referential imagery of bottle racks and bicycle wheels, just as the soup cans and stuffed goat of Warhol and Rauschenberg were uni-referential reactions back against abstract expressionism. Reaction of any sort (going back instead of forward) reflects an abandonment of confidence in the capacity of humanity to learn from its mistakes, and move ahead. This contributes to bitterness, anger, and frustration, leading to an art that denies traditional canons of beauty, and sets up canons based on traditional ugliness. Duchamp's art wasn't a total loss, but he seems to have lacked faith in science and language as well as art.[748]

Equating political radicals with the naive or innocent might seem a stretch, but I feel that by and large, radical schemes for solving society's ills have proved unworkable unless modified by liberals, conservatives, even reactionaries. The unworkable solutions to me show naivete about what humanity can live with on a long-term basis. Radicals (or at any rate, Marxists) tended to assume that the rational, logical side of human nature had more control than it did; likewise, they tended to underrate the power of the emotions. This for me was another big reason why Freud's prestige had declined since the '60s. Only Freudians, perhaps, could appreciate an art supposedly expressing nothing but emotion, but it also took a Freudian like myself to discover the ambiguous mimesis of abstract painting. We must learn to live with that ambiguity: it represents in concrete form how the modern mind must accept a far greater range of past, present, and multiple societies than did the minds of any previous era.

*   *   *

What can I add to what I've already said that will help readers enhance their own creativity? Throughout this narrative, I've tried to show the many elements that went into my three major insights, but in no case did I deliberately or consciously set out to be creative: the insights simply happened. In all three cases, I must have known, on some level or other, that a problem had to be solved, but in no case was I more than marginally conscious of it when the insight itself occurred. With "Swinging London," the problem was superficially how to write a cover story, but on a deeper level, I'd wanted to deal with youth since I'd written that interoffice memo to Otto Fuerbringer. With multireferential imagery, the problem was how to rehabilitate modernist abstraction by rendering it more accessible. With the "disenfranchised left," the problem was to explain – in hopes of combating – the rightward swing in the political climate after 9/11.

This book – itself a creative effort – began with the need to reach a wider audience for multireferential imagery, but while writing it, I've discovered much else I also wanted to say. Even the theme of creativity didn't emerge until after the first draft of the book was almost all written. Then I attended a workshop on publicizing one's book sponsored by a writer's organization. The workshop leader told us to sum up our books in as few words as possible, and, when the word "creativity" sifted up from somewhere into my consciousness, her enthusiastic reaction to it made me investigate it further and realize how closely related its basis in unconscious synthesis was to multireferential imagery. Therefore, I urge you, my readers, to try and respond to any problem that strikes you as needing a response, however seemingly irrelevant it appears to be, for eventually your response may lead you in a very relevant direction.

Keep yourself open to new experiences. Look upon everything that you do or that happens to you as a way to learn – including rejection, even insanity. Never underestimate serendipity. Seize every opportunity to let it work for you, whether you're casing the other books on a library shelf besides the one you came to get, or trolling for information on the Web (in both cases, bearing in mind that all sources are not created equally reliable, and that many Web sites in particular are rife with misinformation).

Try different ways of seeing, even in the most literal sense. Most people think of the *Readers' Guide to Periodical Literature* and *The New York Times Index* as resources to look *into*, but I also looked *at* them, and saw that their columns of entries could tell me how much attention a given subject was attracting in the press at a given moment. I had two inspirations here. First, I'd quoted Clem, in my 1983 article on multireferential imagery, on the difference between looking *into* pictures (the way many people did, looking for subject matter) and *at* them (standing back from them, as he preferred to do in order to evaluate their formal values).[749] Second, I'd quoted Stanley William Hayter, in my 1984 article on him. To quote him once again, he'd said: "How are you going to explain to the public...that somebody they look on as a naive source of genius – like Pollock – this was a man who *saw*, who *looked* at things. Much harder, and with greater intensity, with greater insight, if you like...and the result of this was that something came out of him, having been completely assimilated...."

Be ambitious: use your creativity to tackle the big problems (if you're looking for big solutions). I see no hard-and-fast rule about whether or not a creative effort needs to wait for widespread recognition. Much depends on the genre. When I was in college, I wondered how both Eliot and Shakespeare could be great, when Shakespeare had already been popular while he was still quite young, and Eliot didn't win the Nobel Prize until he was old. I decided that, while great poetry might have to wait for widespread recognition, plays had to be accepted when they were produced, else they'd never get produced again. Nonfiction books like this one could go either way, but the visual arts as I saw them were more like poetry. The nasty cracks I've read about the younger painters I admire tells me they're the true avant-garde of our time, and will in time receive the recognition they deserve, but at least a small number of people have to pay attention to them now, lest their work be lost or destroyed when they die.

How did I solve my three problems once they'd been defined? By stretching my mind, I suppose, since they forced me to reach out to many experiences I'd had over sizeable periods of time and a range of places. North Country laid the basis for this, because Leo and Walter Clark encouraged us to integrate life with art, and art with life. They tried to turn us into whole little people, good at schoolwork and also social beings in bodies as well developed as our minds.

How can one bring about that mysterious synthesis that leads to illumination? As Wallas knew, it can't be forced into existence, but not all creative endeavors demand it, either. A book like this one required rather an extended period of putting one thing next to the other, and trusting to whatever skill I'd acquired plus the willingness to keep on plugging in hopes of bringing it all into a harmonious end result. To prepare for such an experience, though, I think that you must strive, even during your daily rounds, to take in as many impressions as possible from the natural world, friends, colleagues, books, media, and cyberspace (unless, of course, this leads to emotional overload, as it did with me after 9/11, in which case it becomes necessary to close off some sources of your impressions).

You might try to think about how all the disparate impressions you receive can be related to each other, and above all withhold judgment until all the pieces fit. Convergent thinking is drummed into most children through the all-too-common kinds of education that rely on tests to measure results, but both children – and adults – need to develop their capacities for divergent thinking as well, because it is only through reconciling contrasting, even opposed points of view and widely differing pieces of information that creative synthesis can take place.

It's necessary to continue to withhold judgment even after you've arrived at your insight, for other people and information may help you improve upon it. One test of the value of an insight may even be the extent to which it can be developed, improved upon, and contribute to new insights. I don't know how much or little *Time's* cover on "Swinging London" contributed to its cover on the March on the Pentagon, but the latter took the idea of youth in revolt further than the former could have taken it. Anne Truitt, Helen Harrison, even some of those deplorable academic readers of my early proposals helped or forced me to revise and develop my theory on multireferential imagery, just as the editors and agent who'd rejected my book manuscript taught me how to improve upon it. I can't begin to say how much I got from the friends who read and critiqued the manuscript for me, too, though I didn't take all their advice, nor (I say again) do I hold any of them responsible for anything wrong with the result. Only you can decide whether the changes people recommend will enhance your creation. Sometimes, the best way to fix a problem may be the opposite of the fix your commentator wants. You can learn a lot from criticism if you analyze it properly, but you must also have the courage to stand by your own work.

SELECTED MAGAZINE AND NEWSPAPER CIRCULATIONS

1950		1966	
Reader's Digest	6,045,000	*Reader's Digest*	16,858,661
Life	5,364,567	*McCall's*	8,566,910
Ladies' Home Journal	4,564,101	*Look*	7,671,328
Saturday Evening Post	4,069,220	*Life*	7,449,865
McCall's	3,807,101	*Saturday Evening Post*	6,858,305
Look	3,200,145	*Ladies' Home Journal*	6,804,779
Time	845,359	*Time*	4,270,572
Newsweek	815,359	*Newsweek*	2,357,122
Esquire	784,665	*Glamour*	1,243,983
Glamour	600,078	*Esquire*	994,696
Mademoiselle	478,141	*Mademoiselle*	664,277
Vogue	371,183	*New Yorker*	472,853
Harper's Bazaar	342,012	*Vogue*	441,971
New Yorker	332,324	*Harper's Bazaar*	424,802
Atlantic Monthly	176,068	*Atlantic Monthly*	284,256
Harper's Magazine	159,357	*Harper's Magazine*	279,282
Nation	35,106	*Art News*	35,420
Art News	22,666	*Art in America*	33,354
Art Digest	15,943	*Nation*	29,470
Partisan Review (est.)	10,000	*Arts Magazine*	18,261
		Artforum (est.)	10,000
New York Times:			
Weekday	505,451	*Weekday*	767,239
Saturday	410,679	*Saturday*	603,028
Sunday	1,109,491	*Sunday*	1,473,981

(Source: *N. W. Ayer & Son's Directory:*
Newspapers and Periodicals, 1951 and *1967*)

Endnotes

1. *The Dictionary of Art*, s.v. "Abstract art"; updated in *Grove Art Online*, via http://www.nypl.org (accessed June 18, 2008).

2. Cf. Sidney Geist, *Interpreting Cézanne* (1988). This fascinating book details the secondary and tertiary implications of Cézanne's paintings, but of course Cézanne was a representational painter, not an abstract one, and Geist argued that his complexity was at least unique to the artists of his generation, and at most, unique to him alone.

3. I am indebted to Sandra Shapiro for suggesting to me that the blots in the standard test were chosen because they did suggest images. See also Hermann Rorschach, *Psychodiagnostics: A Diagnostic Test Based on Perception*, trans. and English ed. by Paul Lemkau and Bernard Kronenberg, 4th ed. (Berne: Verlag Hans Huber, 1949), 15.

4. "Heiress to a New Tradition," *Time*, March 28, 1969, 69.

5. Sigmund Freud, *On Dreams* (1901), in *The Standard Edition of the Complete Psychological Works of Sigmund Freud*, trans. James Strachey et al., 24 vols., (London: Hogarth Press, 1953–1974), 5:649.

6. See Sam Wang and Sandra Aamodt, "Your Brain Lies to You," *New York Times*, June 27, 2008; Benedict Carey, "While a Magician Works, the Mind Does the Tricks," *New York Times*, August 12, 2008; and Benedict Carey, "For the Brain, Remembering Is Like Reliving," *New York Times*, September 5, 2008. None of these articles dealt specifically with my problem, but all indicated that recent research may be along relevant lines.

7. Wallas actually posited five stages in his model of the creative process, with "intimation" as a third stage, when the person begins to sense that "illumination" is on the way, but later writers treated the model as only four stages, with "intimation" just a preliminary stage of "illumination."

8. Robert J. Sternberg, *Cognitive Psychology*, 2nd ed. (Fort Worth, TX: Harcourt Brace College Publishers, © 1999, 1996, # ISBN 9780155083547), 351–54. By permission of Wadsworth, a division of Thomson Learning: www.thomsonrights.com Fax 800-730-2215. See also Jonah Lehrer, "The Eureka Hunt," *New Yorker*, July 28, 2008.

9. Leonardo da Vinci, *Treatise on Painting*, trans. A. Philip McMahon, 2 vol. (Princeton, NJ: Princeton University Press, 1956), 1:199.

10. Quoted by Jacques Hadamard, in *The Mathematician's Mind: The Psychology of Invention in the Mathematical Field* (Princeton, NJ: Princeton University Press, 1996), 16.

11. T. S. Eliot, "The Metaphysical Poets" (1921), in T. S. Eliot, *Selected Essays: New Edition* (New York: Harcourt, Brace, 1950), 247. World rights outside the U.S. courtesy Faber and Faber Ltd. and © The Estate.

12. Clyde Haberman, "J. Anthony Lukas, 64, an Author, Is Dead," *New York Times*, June 7, 1997.

13. Piri Halasz, "Growing Up Progressive," *Virginia Quarterly Review*, 66:1 (Winter 1990), 104–27.

14. Piri Halasz, "Manhattan Museums: The 1940s vs. the 1980s; Part One: Overview," *Arts Magazine*, January 1985, 122.

15. In the '90s, I saw some of these paintings at the Bley house in New Hampshire.

16. Most material about Henry Luce, Briton Hadden, and early *Time* is from Robert T. Elson, *Time Inc.: The Intimate History of a Publishing Enterprise, 1923–1941*, ed. Duncan Norton-Taylor (New York: Atheneum, 1968). Also consulted: John Kobler, *Luce: His Time, Life and Fortune* (Garden City, NY: Doubleday, 1968); W. A. Swanberg, *Luce and His Empire* (New York: Scribner's, 1972); James L. Baughman, *Henry R. Luce and the Rise of the American News Media* (Boston: Twayne, 1987), and Robert E. Herzstein, *Henry R. Luce: A Political Portrait of the Man Who Created the American Century* (New York: Scribner's, 1994).

17. Baughman, 50–51.

18. Elson, 373–74.

19. Wolcott Gibbs, "Time...Fortune...Life...Luce," originally published in *The New Yorker*, November 28, 1936.

20. Russell Lynes, "Highbrow, Lowbrow, Middlebrow," *Harper's Magazine*, February 1949; and "High-brow, Low-brow, Middle-brow," *Life*, April 11, 1949.

21. Sylvan Keiser, MD, "A Manifest Oedipus Complex in an Adolescent Girl," *Psychoanalytic Study of the Child*, 8 (1953), 101. Dr. Keiser used no proper names in the article, but all the details in it correspond to my experience.

22. C. P. Trussell, "Reds Are Defeated in Hollywood, Union Leader Tells House Group," *New York Times*, May 18, 1951; "Miss Morley Balks at Red Questions," *New York Times*, November 14, 1952.

23. What I probably saw was *Selections from the Art Lending Service*, held at the MoMA Guest House October 16–28, 1956. Among much else, this show had pictures by four reasonably well-known second-generation abstract expressionists and four quite well-known contemporary Parisian abstractionists. Press release and checklist supplied by Rona Roob and Michelle Elligott.

24. Herbert L. Matthews, in *The New York Times*, and Percy Knauth, in the *Saturday Review of Literature*, both called Smith a "liberal." Quoted in *Book Review Digest*, 45th ed. (March 1949–February 1950), 853.

25. Howard K. Smith, *The State of Europe* (New York: Knopf, 1949), 407.

26. Smith, 275.

27. Michiko Kakutani, "Was Eliot Anti-Semitic? An Author Says He Was," *New York Times,* June 4, 1996; and Wendy Lesser, "The T. S. Eliot Problem," *New York Times Book Review*, July 14, 1996.

28. Egon Mayer, *A Demographic Revolution in American Jewry* (Ann Arbor, MI: Jean and Samuel Frankel Center of Judaic Studies, University of Michigan, 1992), 6; *The National Jewish Population Survey 2000–2001: Strength, Challenge and Diversity in the American Jewish Population* (New York: United Jewish Communities, 2003), 16–17. These statistics are controversial, but correspond to my anecdotal experience.

29. All circulation statistics in this book from relevant issues of N. W. Ayer & Son's annual directories of newspapers and periodicals (issues cited referring to previous year's audited statistics or estimates – 1957 issue for 1956 circulations, etc.). For "pass-along" readership of *Time* in 1967, see "Hot line to 14,500,000 influential people," *Time* advertisement, *New York Times*, February 2, 1967.

30. People, *Time*, November 24, 1952, 48.

31. Elson, 8.

32. Elson, 8–9.

33. I believe, but am not positive, that Tatum told me about the relationship before it reached gossip columns in the fall of 1959. See Swanberg, 402–4.

34. One psychoanalyst described how during the later '50s, he experimented with "behavior modification, a type of treatment in which the therapist avoids interpretations, and offers the patient advice instead." Herbert S. Strean, as told to Lucy Freeman, *Behind the Couch: Revelations of a Psychoanalyst* (New York: John Wiley, 1988), 114. In 1953, Robert Knight, president of the American Psychoanalytic Association, commented in a speech on the growing scarcity of "pure" psychoanalysts, and suggested that "many analysts would privately admit" to employing "modified techniques." Quoted in Reuben Fine, *The History of Psychoanalysis:*

New Expanded Edition (Northvale, NJ: Jason Aronson, 1990), 122. Dr. G may have been most influenced by the "adaptational technique" of Sandor Rado, director of the Psychoanalytic Clinic for Training and Research at Columbia's College of Physicians and Surgeons while Dr. G was undergoing his own training at Columbia. Rado argued that, after bringing under control the "faulty emergency responses" that the patient had developed in childhood, the analyst should generate in the patient "welfare emotions (pleasurable desire, joy, affection, love, self-respect, and pride)," then "guide the patient in learning how to *act* upon the promptings of his now liberated welfare emotions...." Sandor Rado, "Adaptational Development of Psychoanalytic Therapy," in *Changing Concepts of Psychoanalytic Medicine: Proceedings of the Decennial Celebration of the Columbia University Psychoanalytic Clinic, March 19 and 20, 1955,* ed. Sandor Rado and George E. Daniels (New York: Grune & Stratton, 1956), 95. Dr. G often guided me in "learning how to act."

35. "The Explorer," *Time*, April 23, 1956, 76.
36. "Psychoanalysis: In Search of Its Soul," *Time*, March 7, 1969, 68.
37. "The Explorer," 76.
38. Elson, 72.
39. E.g., "Crash Warning," *Time*, May 20, 1957; "The Soil Bank: A $700 Million Failure?" *Time*, June 3, 1957; "Challenge to Cotton," *Time*, June 10, 1957.
40. "The Younger Generation," *Time*, November 5, 1951, 46: "It has been called the 'Silent Generation.'" See also Thornton Wilder, "The Silent Generation," *Harper's Magazine*, April 1953; and Joel Raphaelson, "The labeled generation," *Mademoiselle*, August 1953. Raphaelson tried but failed to discover the source whom *Time* had been quoting.
41. Margo Jefferson, "Haunted by Ghosts of Pinter Past," *New York Times*, August 12, 2001.
42. Donald J. Bogue, *The Population of the United States* (The Free Press of Glencoe, Illinois, 1959), 225, 234. Other population statistics extrapolated from relevant issues of the *Statistical Abstract of the United States*.
43. In Grunwald's autobiography, he denied that he'd successfully edited copy while he was carrying it around, though admitting he'd once done so unsuccessfully. The "psychoanalyst" seems to have been a therapist to whom his mother sent him while he was in college, and whom he soon abandoned. Henry Grunwald, *One Man's America: A Journalist's Search for the Heart of His Country* (New York: Doubleday, 1997), 79, 72–74.

44. Richard Severo, "Henry A. Grunwald, Editor Who Directed Shift in Time Magazine, Is Dead at 82," *New York Times*, February 27, 2005.

45. "Christmas Rush," *Time*, December 21, 1959, 70.

46. "The Service Economy," *Time*, October 31, 1960.

47. See "School in the Adirondacks," *Architectural Record*, December 1942, 28–35. The diagram on page 30 makes the modular point, although the term itself isn't used. Haskell used it with me, however, when I interviewed him in 1968 for a projected series of articles on the school for *The New Yorker*.

48. "Taking Stock," *Time*, April 12, 1963, 91n.

49. Kennedy "thought nothing of talking to reporters in his bedroom or while taking a swim in the nude." Sally Bedell Smith, *Grace and Power: The Private World of the Kennedy White House* (New York: Random House, 2004), 123.

50. For (often repetitive) discussions of Kennedy's dislike of *Time*, see Theodore C. Sorensen, *Kennedy* (New York: Harper & Row, 1965), 316–17; Paul B. Fay, Jr., *The Pleasure of His Company* (New York: Harper & Row, 1966), 195; Joseph P. Berry, Jr., *John F. Kennedy and the Media: The First Television President* (Lanham, MD: University Press of America, 1987), 62–64; Robert Dallek, *An Unfinished Life: John F. Kennedy 1917–1963* (Boston: Little, Brown, 2003), 368, 371–72, 478, 528; and James N. Giglio, *The Presidency of John F. Kennedy,* 2nd ed. (Lawrence, KS: University of Kansas Press, 2006), 276. For JFK's favorable opinion of Sidey, see Kenneth P. O'Donnell and David F. Powers, with Joe McCarthy, *"Johnny, We Hardly Knew Ye"* (Boston: Little, Brown, 1972), 408. For a *Time*-oriented view of JFK's relations with *Time*, see Sally Bedell Smith, 128–30, 362–63 (she once worked for it).

51. According to Frankel's memoir, he never was a copyboy for the *Times,* but started out as its Columbia stringer. Max Frankel, *The Times of My Life, and My Life on The Times* (New York: Random House, 1999), chapter 11.

52. "Business in 1961: Automation Speeds Recovery, Boosts Productivity, Pares Jobs," *Time*, December 29, 1961, 52.

53. Marya Mannes, *New York Herald Tribune*, and Lucy Freeman, *New York Times,* both quoted in *Book Review Digest*, 59th ed. (March 1963–February 1964), 355.

54. Volume 28 (March 1968–February 1969) was typical of most of the '60s, with nineteen entries under "Woman–Equal Rights," and no separate category for "Women's liberation movement." Volume 29 (March 1969–February 1970) had twelve entries in the first category,

and, though it added the category for "Women's liberation movement," there were only three entries in it. Volume 30 (March 1970–February 1971) had thirty entries under "Woman–Equal Rights," and seventy-eight under "Women's liberation movement."

55. "Pop Art – Cult of the Commonplace," *Time*, May 3, 1963, 72.

56. See Chris Welles, "*Newsweek* (a fact) is the new hot book (an opinion)," *Esquire*, November 1969, 152.

57. Alex Kuczynski, "Kermit Lansner, 78, Former Newsweek Editor," *New York Times*, May 22, 2000.

58. Osborn Elliott, *The World of Oz* (New York: Viking, ©1980 by Osborn Elliott), 51, 52–53. Used by permission of Viking Penguin, a division of Penguin Group (USA) Inc.

59. Curtis Prendergast, with Geoffrey Colvin, *The World of Time Inc.: The Intimate History of a Changing Enterprise, Volume Three: 1960–80*, ed. Robert Lubar (New York: Atheneum, 1986), 129–30.

60. See George H. Gallup, *The Gallup Poll: Public Opinion 1935–1971*, 3 vols. (New York: Random House, 1972), 2: 943, 960–61, 993, 1052–53.

61. "Syngman Rhee Dies an Exile From Land He Fought to Free," *New York Times*, July 20, 1965.

62. Walter Sullivan, "Korea's Fate Held Resting on U.S. Aid," *New York Times*, January 31, 1950; Walter Sullivan, "Police Brutality in Korea Assailed," *New York Times*, February 1, 1950; and Walter Sullivan, "U.S. Advisers in Korea Troubled by Trend to Centralized Authority," *New York Times*, February 2, 1950.

63. "Preview in Korea," *New York Times*, July 19, 1950.

64. Prendergast and Colvin, 236–37.

65. Swanberg reported two of these occasions – one in a press conference at Yale, and another in a speech at William Penn College in Oskaloosa, IA. Swanberg, 463–64.

66. "To See Life in Its Full Dimensions," *Fortune*, January 1967.

67. Milestones, *Time*, August 9, 1963, 58.

68. "South Viet Nam: Birth at Geneva," *Time*, September 20, 1963, 34.

69. See David Halberstam, *The Making of a Quagmire* (New York: Random House, 1965), 191–92, 242–43, 266–69; David Halberstam, *The Best and the Brightest* (New York: Random House, 1972), 205–6, 208, 263, 280, 282; and David Halberstam, *The Powers That Be* (1979; repr., with new introduction, Urbana, IL: University of Illinois Press, 2000), 445–46, 450. Halberstam suggested that Kennedy was ultimately angry not because he didn't believe what the media were saying, but because he did, and feared that publicizing the dissension within

his own administration and the failure of his foreign policy would give opponents issues to use against him in his 1964 campaign for reelection.

70. 1) Halberstam, *Quagmire*, 269–74; 2) Kobler, 174–76; 3) Swanberg, 440–41; 4) Halberstam, *Best and Brightest*, 523 (brief reference); 5) Glenn MacDonald, *Report or Distort?* (New York: Exposition, 1973), 25–26; 6) Halberstam, *Powers That Be*, 461–67; 7) Herbert J. Gans, *Deciding What's News: A Study of CBS Evening News, NBC Nightly News, Newsweek, and Time* (1979; repr., with new preface, Evanston IL: Northwestern University Press, 2004), 267 (brief); 8) Russ Braley, *Bad News: The Foreign Policy of the New York Times* (Chicago: Regnery Gateway, 1984), 234–35 (comes closest to siding with Fuerbringer); 9) Prendergast and Colvin, 237–41; 10) Baughman, 187; 11) Kim Willenson, with the correspondents of *Newsweek*, *The Bad War: An Oral History of the Vietnam War* (New York: New American Library, 1987), 175–77; 12) Neil Sheehan, *A Bright Shining Lie: John Paul Vann and America in Vietnam* (New York: Random House, 1988), 537 (brief); 13) Clarence R. Wyatt, *Paper Soldiers: The American Press and the Vietnam War* (New York: Norton, 1993), 121–22; 14) William Prochnau, *Once Upon a Distant War* (New York: Times Books (Random House), 1995); 409–11, 425–29; 15) A. J. Langguth, *Our Vietnam: The War 1954–1975* (New York: Simon & Schuster, 2000), 244 (brief); and 16) James Landers, *The Weekly War: Newsmagazines and Vietnam* (Columbia, MO: University of Missouri Press, 2004), 43–45. On April 28, 2004, Channel 13 in New York broadcast *A Vision of Empire: Henry Luce & Time-Life's America*. In it, Fuerbringer discussed the article on the Saigon press corps. He said that he'd reread it more recently, and now felt that it had been "thoughtless."

71. Gordon Manning to Piri Halasz, August 10, 1963.

72. Robert K. Merton, *Social Theory and Social Structure*, rev. and enlarged ed. (Glencoe, IL: Free Press, 1957), chapter 10, esp. 387–408.

73. See People, *Time*, October 23, 1964.

74. *Newsweek*'s audience was slightly younger than *Time*'s: in 1966, 53 percent of its readers were aged thirty-four or less, as opposed to 50 percent of *Time*'s. *Time*'s readers were slightly more likely to be in professional and managerial occupations, have higher incomes and be college graduates, but the readership of both magazines was well above national averages in education and income. W. R. Simmons Associates Research Inc., *Selective Markets and the Media Reaching Them: 1966 Standard Magazine Report*, Tables I–1, A–1, A–5, and A–15.

75. Elliott, 54.

76. Top of the Week, *Newsweek*, January 11, 1965, 7.

77. Welles, 152.

78. Gans, 74-75.

79. Writers agree that most American students were apolitical, though more participated in antiwar protests during the later '60s and early '70s than did in the earlier phases of the war. According to a report to Lyndon Johnson submitted by Richard Helms, director of the CIA, in September 1968, out of America's 6.3 million students, hardly 35,000 could be considered "hard-core" radicals. Cited by Charles DeBenedetti, with Charles Chatfield, *An American Ordeal: The Antiwar Movement of the Vietnam Era* (Syracuse, NY: Syracuse University Press, 1990), 231. Another book estimated that the activists were most likely never more than 5 percent of student enrollment, though it added that college enrollment was so huge that even 5 percent could mean tens of thousands of demonstrators nationwide – and that additional thousands might join in for rallies and marches. David Chalmers, *And the Crooked Places Made Straight: The Struggle for Social Change in the 1960s*, 2nd ed. (Baltimore: Johns Hopkins University Press, 1996), 75.

80. Gans, 197–98.

81. David W. Levy, *The Debate Over Vietnam*, 2nd ed. (Baltimore: Johns Hopkins University Press, 1995), 106. Levy was the only writer I found who discussed elite schools v. the full range of institutions of higher education in terms of opinion polls about the war, but other authors discussed this same opposition in terms of actual antiwar activity. Most suggested that the elite schools, or at any rate, students from upper-middle-class households (who most likely attended such schools) provided most leadership in the protest, but also that their impact was magnified by national news media reporting to a greater extent upon them, that there were also many less well-known schools where antiwar activities were conducted, and that this was particularly true in the later stages of the conflict, when public opinion in general was turning against the war. According to Gans, initially the protest was conducted nearly completely on the elite campuses, but the media created the impression that such upper-middle-class practices were a characteristic of the whole college population. Gans, 27. Two recent studies that paralleled Levy's findings are Joseph A. Fry, "Unpopular Messengers: Student Opposition to the Vietnam War," in *The War That Never Ends: New Perspectives on the Vietnam War*, eds. David L. Anderson and John Ernst (Lexington, KY: University Press of Kentucky, 2007), 222, 236; and Edward K. Spann, *Democracy's Children: the Young Rebels of the 1960s and the Power of Ideals* (Wilmington, DE: Scholarly Resources,

2003), 81–82, 86. One notable exception is Kenneth J. Heineman, who argued that antiwar activity "germinated" at less prestigious state universities. Kenneth J. Heineman, *Campus Wars: The Peace Movement at American State Universities* (New York: New York University Press, 1993), 2–3.

82. Elliott, 33.

83. Welles, 152, 154.

84. Welles, 154, 244.

85. According to Fuerbringer's obituary, he was responsible for commissioning such well-known artists to paint or sculpt cover portraits. "Otto Fuerbringer, 97, Former Time Editor," *New York Times*, July 30, 2008.

86. "'In Cold Blood'...An American Tragedy," *Newsweek*, January 24, 1966, 60.

87. "The Altered Heart," *Newsweek*, September 21, 1964, 114.

88. "The Good Guy," *Time*, September 25, 1964, 105.

89. "A Case of Forced Faith," *Time*, July 24, 1964.

90. "Name-Dropper," *Newsweek*, July 20, 1964, 83.

91. "The King," *Time*, February 26, 1965; and "Soft Answers," *Newsweek*, March 1, 1965.

92. "Two for a Tommy Gun," *Newsweek*, August 21, 1967, 65; and "Low-Down Hoedown," *Time*, August 25, 1967, 78.

93. "The Shock of Freedom in Films," *Time*, December 8, 1967.

94. Joseph Morgenstern, "The Thin Red Line," *Newsweek*, August 28, 1967, 82.

95. See A Letter from the Publisher, *Time*, July 2, 1965; and "Splendors at Home," *Time*, July 2, 1965.

96. Top of the Week, *Newsweek*, July 19, 1965, 7.

97. "The Desperate Dilemma of Abortion," *Time*, October 13, 1967; "The Springs of Youth," *Time*, April 16, 1965; "Pills to Keep Women Young," *Time*, April 1, 1966; and "Freedom From Fear," *Time*, April 7, 1967.

98. "The Homosexual in America," *Time*, January 21,1966, 41.

99. Thomas Gordon Plate, "Not So Gay," *Newsweek*, October 14, 1968, 108. Quotation from Martin Hoffman, *The Gay World: Male Homosexuality and the Social Creation of Evil* (New York: Basic Books, 1968), 192.

100. "Superfans and Batmaniacs," *Newsweek*, February 15, 1965, 89.

101. "The Modern *Mona Lisa*," *Time*, March 5, 1965, 41.

102. "The Story of Pop: What It Is and How It Came to Be," *Newsweek*, April 25, 1966.

103. During a sample period (April–June 1966), *Newsweek* ran eight stories on popular music, and nine on classical music, while *Time* ran nineteen

stories on classical, and three on popular. Both magazines omitted the Music section in two of thirteen issues.

104. "Message Time," *Time*, September 17, 1965, and "The Folk and the Rock," *Newsweek*, September 20, 1965; "The Nitty-Gritty Sound," *Newsweek*, December 19,1966, and "Open Up, Tune In, Turn On," *Time*, June 23, 1967; "Air Pollution?" *Newsweek*, August 16, 1965, and "Going to Pot," *Time*, July 1, 1966; "No Town Like Motown," *Newsweek*, March 22, 1965, "The Girls from Motown," *Time*, March 4, 1966, and "Heavyweight Featherweight," *Time*, September 8, 1967; "Pop's Bad Boys," *Newsweek,* November 29, 1965, and "The Baddies," *Time*, April 28, 1967.

105. *Time* cover story on rock'n'roll, May 1965, and "Records: The Whole Funky Grown-Up Bit," *Newsweek*, October 11, 1965.

106. "The Messengers," *Time*, September 22, 1967, 60, 61.

107. "'Camp,'" *Time*, December 11, 1964.

108. Carl Rollyson and Lisa Paddock, *Susan Sontag: The Making of an Icon* (New York: Norton, 2000), 86.

109. Top of the Week, *Newsweek*, June 24, 1963.

110. "Where the Stars Fall," *Time*, September 27, 1963, 17.

111. "Death and Transfiguration," *Time*, March 5, 1965, 23.

112. "Death of a Desperado," *Newsweek*, March 8, 1965, 24.

113. "Never Again Where He Was," *Time*, January 3, 1964.

114. "'The Awful Roar,'" *Time*, August 30, 1963, 9.

115. *Newsweek* cover stories with Harris polls on race: July 29, 1963; October 21, 1963; July 13, 1964, and August 21, 1967. Other issues with Harris polls about race: February 15, 1965 and October 25, 1965.

116. "Is White America Listening?" *Newsweek*, December 4, 1967.

117. Romain Gary and James S. Plaut, "Art in New York," *Newsweek*, January 25, 1965; Willard Van Dyke, "The Lower Depths?" *Newsweek*, March 6,1967; and Joshua Logan, "Reviews Reviewed," *Newsweek*, September 11, 1967, 4.

118. Truman Capote, "Party Poop," *Time*, December 16, 1966; Roy Wilkins, "Merit Is the Measure," *Time*, June 9, 1967; Tony Barrow, "Just the Family," *Time*, September 15, 1967; I. M. Pei, "Pei & Partners," *Time*, October 6, 1967; and Jerry Lewis, "More Than He Can Chew," *Time*, October 13, 1967.

119. According to Grunwald's autobiography, Fuerbringer proposed a Man of the Year cover on the Beatles in 1965; he himself thought this was meant as a joke. Grunwald, 337. Halberstam also speaks of the idea as Fuerbringer's. *Powers That Be*, 457. But Grunwald, from what I heard, was given credit by the office grapevine around 1964 for supporting a

Beatles cover. If Fuerbringer did suggest a Man of the Year cover on them, he can't have been very serious, considering how long it would take *Time* to do a regular cover on them.

120. Michael Wheeler, *Lies, Damn Lies, and Statistics: The Manipulation of Public Opinion in America* (New York: Liverwright, 1976), chapter 3; also 80, 97.

121. Louis Harris, "U.S. Handling of Viet-Nam Issue Has Public Confused, Cautious," *Washington Post*, March 30, 1964.

122. See Fredrik Logevall, *Choosing War: The Lost Chance for Peace and the Escalation of War in Vietnam* (Berkeley: University of California Press, 1999), xvii.

123. Gallup, 2:787, 809, 844, 853 , 1225.

124. Gallup, 2:852, 932.

125. Gallup, 3:1944, 1957, 1966, 1979, 2009, 2183.

126. "The Task Ahead," *New York Times*, July 2, 1950.

127. "Color Her Blond," *Newsweek*, June 19, 1967, and "She Does," *Time*, August 11, 1967.

128. *Time* said the play had "been interpreted as everything from an allegory of the cold war to a modern view of Christ, man, and Satan...." "*Caretaker*'s Caretaker," *Time*, November 10, 1961, 76.

129. Even the redone item was somewhat suggestive. See People, *Time*, September 11, 1964.

130. "The Regency Firing," *Time*, March 12,1965, 80.

131. Davis returned to Modern Living while I was in Milestones and/or People, but was no longer there when I got to Modern Living myself, in late 1966. To the best of my recollection, she'd gone on a second maternity leave, and never come back. She was killed in a freak traffic accident at the age of thirty-six in 1974, only a year after she'd published a delightful novel, *Life Signs*.

132. "Murder by Marmalade," and "An End to Tears?" both *Time*, March 19, 1965.

133. "The Road to Jerusalem," *Time*, October 11, 1963, 34, and "Man with a Four-Seat Margin," *Time*, April 30, 1965, 36.

134. While I was still at *Time*, a John Scott from "the publishing side" of Time Inc. told me in 1965 that Lael Tucker had been a writer in Foreign News in the '40s. According to him, she was married to Stephen Laird, the senior editor, and Laird killed himself after she left him for Charles Wertenbaker, a correspondent. From Eleanor Tatum, I heard that Ruth Mehrtens (later Ruth Mehrtens Galvin) had been a writer in Foreign News in the early '50s, and that she herself had done some writing for *Time* during World War II. A woman I met at a party

told me that she'd been the Mexico City bureau chief for Time Inc., then written in the Latin America section of *Time* (again, I believe in the early '50s). Research conducted for this book shows that actually, Tucker was a correspondent in London, not a writer in New York, when she fell in love with Wertenbaker. Laird was the London bureau chief, not a senior editor, and though Tucker left him for Wertenbaker, he remarried, and was asked by the Wertenbakers to aid them in helping Charles end his life when he was suffering from cancer. Lael Tucker Wertenbaker, *Death of a Man* (New York: Random House, 1957), 63, 148, 156, 160, 176, 178. Mehrtens did write in Foreign News and other sections. A Letter from the Publisher, *Time*, July 26, 1954. By 1954, she'd become a correspondent, but her name had been on the masthead as contributing editor (i.e., writer) in 1950. North's cover was on Alexander Fleming, discoverer of penicillin. A Letter from the Publisher, *Time*, June 5, 1944. A story on her in *TLAS*, the Time-Life Alumni Society newsletter, described her further achievements, which included a stint as wartime Army and Navy editor, but the story again created the somewhat misleading impression that North was the only woman writer that *Time* had ever had during that era. "Caked Out at 100," *TLAS*, Summer 2008. Actually, she was preceded on the masthead by Pearl Kroll, a Sport writer. Elson, 388. Wartime issues of *Time* listed other women on the masthead in the text blocks with men writers or editors. Some may have been writers, though female chiefs of research and the copy desk were also in these blocks. Some, like Tatum, seem to have written for *Time* without getting their names on the masthead as contributing editors.

135. See Jeffrey Record, *The Wrong War: Why We Lost in Vietnam* (Annapolis, MD: Naval Institute Press, 1998). Chapter 1 explained that since World War II, the U.S. had stayed out of mainland China because its military leaders "cautioned against ground combat involvement in wars on the Asian mainland, where, it was felt, U. S. naval and air power's effectiveness would be diluted, and where Asian foes could exploit their great superiority in manpower and bog the United States down in protracted conflict." Record, 1. Although his whole argument was more complex, he also said that "the peninsular geography and barren topography of Korea permitted a very effective use of conventional U. S. military forces, especially naval and air power." Record, 3. See also John Prados, *The Blood Road: The Ho Chi Minh Trail and the Vietnam War* (New York: John Wiley, 1999), 377: "The antiwar movement did not lose the Vietnam War. Hanoi's ability to sustain the Viet Cong in the face of all Westmoreland's attrition operations turned the tide.

The Trail made that possible." Lewis Sorley described the many fierce and ultimately futile attempts to "interdict" the movement of men and materiel down the trail, in *A Better War: The Unexamined Victories and Final Tragedy of America's Last Years in Vietnam* (1999).

136. "The Quiet Escalation," *Time*, January 22, 1965, and "Infiltration From the North: The Vital Transfusion," *Time*, February 5, 1965.

137. Halberstam, *Quagmire*, 316.

138. A fourth member of that same *Crimson* staff was Ronald P. Kriss, who in the '60s was writing in the Nation section for *Time*.

139. E.g., "We Will Be Far Better Off Facing the Issue," *Time*, February 26,1965; "A Reply to the Critics," *Time*, April 16, 1965; "Exhaustive, Explicit--& Enough," *Time*, February 25, 1966; "More Light, Less Heat," *Time*, May 20, 1966; and "The Value of Bombing the North," *Time*, December 16, 1966. Cover stories that reflected the Administration position include those on McGeorge Bundy (June 1965), Johnson (August 1965), Richard Helms (February 1967), and William C. Westmoreland (February 1965, January 1966, and May 1967).

140. "'A Look Down That Long Road,'" *Time*, February 19, 1965, 16.

141. "Pleiku and Qui Nhon: Decision Points," *Newsweek*, February 22,1965, 32.

142. E.g., "The Guardians at the Gate," *Time*, January 7, 1966; "Curtain of Fire," *Time*, April 29, 1966; "A Savage Week," *Time*, February 24, 1967; "A Terrible Price, *Time*, March 31, 1967; and "Arrow of Death," *Time*, May 12, 1967.

143. E.g., "The Valleys of Death," *Time*, November 26, 1965; and "Progress," *Time*, November 24, 1967.

144. E.g., "'Certain Losses,'" *Newsweek*, August 2, 1965; "A Matter of Candor," *Newsweek*, August 2, 1965; and "Moderation in All," *Newsweek*, December 6, 1965.

145. See esp. *Time* cover stories on Nguyen Cao Ky (February 1966) and Nguyen Van Thieu (September 1967).

146. E.g., "Vietnam: The New War," *Newsweek*, July 5, 1965; *Newsweek* cover story on Ky (September 1965); "An Election, a Barrier and Talk of Peace," *Newsweek*, September 18, 1967; "Trying No. 2," *Newsweek*, September 25, 1967; and "Thieu and Ky Squeak Through," *Newsweek*, October 16, 1967.

147. "The War Within," *Time*, May 28, 1965, 22.

148. E.g., "No Exit," *Time*, February 25, 1966; "Teaching Amid Terror," *Time*, April 21, 1967; "Singled Out for Terror," *Time*, May 26, 1967; "The Organization Man," *Time*, August 25, 1967; and "The Massacre of Dak Son," *Time*, December 15, 1967.

149. E.g., "Profile of the Viet Cong," *Newsweek*, April 12, 1965; and "Outvoting Terror," *Newsweek*, April 17, 1967.

150. Photo of napalm: "U.S. Advisers: The Knife's Edge," *Newsweek*, May 24, 1965, 44. Photo and text block of woman bewailing child, "Peasant Pieta," *Newsweek*, September 20, 1965, 44-45.

151. "The Valleys of Death," 32; "Fury at Ia Drang: Now the Regulars," *Newsweek*, November 29, 1965, 21; and "Paying the Price," *Newsweek*, November 29, 1965, 23.

152. William M. Hammond, *Public Affairs: The Military and the Media, 1962–1968* (Washington, DC: Center of Military History, United States Army, 1988), 181.

153. Todd Gitlin, *The Whole World Is Watching: Mass Media in the Making and Unmaking of the New Left* (1980; repr. with new preface, Berkeley, CA: University of California Press, 2003), 33.

154. Fred Powledge, "The Student Left: Spurring Reform," *New York Times*, March 15, 1965, 26.

155. "Professors Hold Vietnam Protest," *New York Times*, March 25, 1965; McCandlish Phillips, "Now the Teach-In: U.S. Policy in Vietnam Criticized All Night," *New York Times*, March 27, 1965; see also Mitchel Levitas, "Vietnam Comes to Oregon U.," *New York Times Magazine*, May 9, 1965.

156. Gloria Emerson, "Dr. Spock Leads 3,000 Urging Vietnam Peace," *New York Times*, April 11, 1965.

157. "15,000 White House Pickets Denounce Vietnam War," *New York Times*, April 18, 1965.

158. Robert C. Doty, "Pope's Christmas Plea: 'Sincere Negotiation,'" *New York Times*, December 24, 1965.

159. Top of the Week, *Newsweek*, November 1, 1965, 11.

160. "The ABC's of Draft Dodging," *Newsweek*, November 1, 1965.

161. Max Frankel, "Thousands Walk in Capital to Protest War in Vietnam; Demonstrators Decorous," *New York Times*, November 28, 1965; John Herbers, "Typical Marcher: Middle-Class Adult," *New York Times*, November 28, 1965.

162. "Teachers Appeal for Peace in Vietnam," advertisement, *New York Times*, January 4, 1966.

163. "Search for a Mantle," *Time*, March 12, 1965, 25n.

164. Who was really behind the attempted "September 30" coup, and whether the military knew that it was coming, have never been settled. Many books have been written, all inevitably influenced by the fact that Suharto, the general who would ultimately succeed Sukarno, inaugurated decades of pro-Western peace, prosperity, brutality,

repression, and corruption on a monumental scale before being forced to resign in 1998. In 1965, the U.S., which backed the military, believed that the Indonesian communist party (PKI) was behind the attempted coup, while Sukarno (who had taken an increasingly procommunist line in the months immediately preceding it) maintained that the CIA was plotting against him. Two recent books continued these rivalries, with John Roosa, a sometime anti-Suharto activist, suggesting that the military prodded the communists into staging the coup by leading them to believe that the military were going to stage one themselves, and Helen-Louise Hunter, a sometime CIA political analyst, insisting that the September 30 movement was a complete surprise to the generals, but that Sukarno may have known about it. See John Roosa, *Pretext for Mass Murder: The September 30th Movement and Suharto's Coup d'État in Indonesia* (Madison, WI: University of Wisconsin Press, 2006), esp. chapter 7, and Helen-Louise Hunter, *Sukarno and the Indonesian Coup: The Untold Story* (Westport, CT: Praeger Security International, 2007), esp. 1–45. Neither completely refuted the other, since both suggested that communists and the CIA appear to have been involved. I fall back on M. C. Ricklefs, in his standard textbook on Indonesia. Of the attempted coup, he wrote that "complicated and sometimes partisan arguments continue over who masterminded the events and what manoeuvres lay behind them. The intricacies of the political scene, the contacts, friendships, and hatreds that linked most of the major participants to one another, and the suspect nature of much of the evidence, make it unlikely that the full truth will ever be known. It seems improbable that there was a single mastermind controlling all the events, and interpretations which attempt to explain events solely in terms of a PKI, army, Sukarno, or Soeharto plot must be treated with caution." M. C. Ricklefs, *A History of Modern Indonesia since c. 1200*, 3rd ed. (Stanford, CA: Stanford University Press, 2001), 338. © 2001 M. C. Ricklefs. Worldwide rights by permission of Palgrave Macmillan.

165. "Merry *Bonenkai*," *Time*, December 31, 1965, 18-19.
166. "The Jungle Marxist," *Time*, July 16, 1965, 27.
167. "The Trial Begins," *Time*, February 18, 1966, 32.
168. "Emergency Time," *Time*, March 25, 1966, 25.
169. "All's Swell at Mattel," *Time*, October 26, 1962.
170. E.g., David Boroff, "Protests Added to Campus Scene," *New York Times*, January 13, 1965; Lawrence Stessin, "They're Not Trying to Succeed in Business," *New York Times Magazine*, March 28, 1965; Albert L. Kraus, "3.7 Million to Reach the Job-Hunting Age in 1965," *New*

York Times, January 11, 1965; "Teen-Age Jobless Stir U.S. Concern," *New York Times*, March 5, 1965; Eileen Shanahan, "Economy Absorbs Teen-Ager Influx," *New York Times*, August 6, 1965; and Albert L. Kraus, "Manpower Rise Poses Challenge," *New York Times*, January 17, 1966.

171. E.g., Joan Cook, "It's the Youth Kick – and Age Is No Barrier," *New York Times*, September 11, 1965; "Nation's 24 Million Teen-Agers Make Money Talk," *New York Times*, January 17, 1966; and Peter Bart, "Standing Up To the Teen-Agers," *New York Times*, August 15, 1965.

172. E.g., Murray Schumach, "Teen-Agers (Mostly Female) and Police Greet Beatles," *New York Times*, August 14, 1965; Murray Schumach, "Shrieks of 55,000 Accompany Beatles," *New York Times*, August 16,1965; Marya Mannes, "But, M. Courrèges, What About Mrs. Bottomley?" *New York Times Magazine*, March 28, 1965; and Phyllis Lee Levin, "The Short, Short, Short Skirt Story," *New York Times Magazine*, March 20, 1966.

173. Susan E. Tifft and Alex S. Jones, *The Trust: The Private and Powerful Family Behind the New York Times* (Boston: Little, Brown, 1999), 41–46.

174. "Long and Short of It," *Newsweek*, September 27, 1965.

175. E.g., "Leadership readership: 34% of all college graduates in the U.S. read *TIME*," advertisement, *New York Times*, February 24, 1966; "College market your target? Zero in with *TIME's* College Student Edition," advertisement, *New York Times*, January 19, 1966.

176. "The Short & the Long of It," *Time*, October 1,1965.

177. James A. Michener, "One Near-Square Who Doesn't Knock the Rock," *New York Times Magazine*, October 31, 1965; Russell Baker, "Observer: The Latest in Revolution," *New York Times*, September 14, 1965; and Russell Baker, "Observer: Father With a Middle-Aged Teen-Ager," *New York Times*, October 31, 1965.

178. "You Can Walk Across It On the Grass," *Time*, April 15, 1966, 30.

179. "You Can Walk Across It...," 31.

180. "The Free-Sex Movement," *Time*, March 11, 1966, 66.

181. Jagger quote, "You Can Walk Across It...," 32. Statistics on British youth, Michael Schofield, *The Sexual Behaviour of Young People* (Boston: Little, Brown, 1965), 29–30. My source was a summary of its UK edition in a British newspaper or magazine.

182. "You Can Walk Across It...," 34.

183. English clippings in this scrapbook from *Financial Times, Observer, Daily Express, Daily Telegraph, Evening News, Sun, Guardian,* and *Cambridge News.*

184. *Time Letters Report*, May 5, 1966.

185. Lenore Hershey, "Sight and Sound From London," *McCall's*, September 1966; "London: The Cutting Edge," *Look*, September 20, 1966; "England Gambles for Survival," *Look*, November 29, 1966.

186. "How the Tea Break Could Ruin England," *Time*, September 2, 1966, 20.

187. Henry Brandon, "State of Affairs: Behind Britain's Swingers," *Saturday Review*, July 16, 1966; Frank Getlein, "The British Renaissance," *New Republic*, September 3, 1966; and William Pfaff, "Swing, Britannia," *Commonweal*, 84:248–9 (May 20, 1966).

188. "A Surfeit of Money and Honey," *Business Week*, July 16, 1966.

189. Nancy Randolph, "Society: PB Swings as the Young Hold Sway," New York *Daily News*, March 7, 1966.

190. "Here's a Real Swinger," caption for boxing picture, New York *Daily News*, February 18, 1966; David McLane, "For Swingers Only," story about golf clubs, New York *Sunday News*, March 27, 1966.

191. William Reel, "She Doesn't Want to Be a Sexpot: But until the true muse knocks, swingin' Joey Heatherton rocks," New York *Sunday News*, September 25,1966; Frank Mazza and William Rice, "Day Girl, Night Girl," New York *Daily News*, October 1, 1966; and George Dzienis and Henry Lee, "Police Collar Swinging 7 In Dope-Filled Village Pad," New York *Sunday News*, October 9, 1966.

192. E.g., Nan Ickersgill, "College Girls on College Fashion: It's Cute, but...," *New York Times*, August 9, 1966; and Nan Ickersgill, "Miss Carnaby Takes Up Residence on 42d St.," *New York Times*, August 11, 1966.

193. "Our Girl in London," *Seventeen*, March 1966.

194. "Riotous with June roses...," advertisement for Bonwit Teller, *New York Times*, May 16, 1966.

195. "The 'waif' look in the swinging new corduroys!," advertisement for Gimbel's, *New York Times*, June 5, 1966.

196. Gloria Emerson, "Goma and His Girls Make a Hit at Paris Showings," *New York Times*, July 28, 1966.

197. "Body and sun; Shirt and skirt idea – everything skimped," *Vogue*, January 1, 1966, 70.

198. E.g., Betsy Hunter, "Shop Here Boutique, The IN Gear for College," *Mademoiselle*, August 1966, 216–217; "Class Jazz: Zip, Zoom, but No Kook," same issue, 248; and "Class Jazz: Suits with Snazz," same issue, 257.

199. "Carnaby Street: USA," *Seventeen*, August 1966, 248.

200. Mary Quant, "The Young Will Not Be Dictated To," *Vogue*, August 1, 1966, 86. Condensed from Mary Quant, *Quant by Quant* (New York:

Putnam, 1966), 74–76. *Glamour, Mademoiselle*'s principal competitor, and *Harper's Bazaar*, which competed with *Vogue*, both conceded the existence of the miniskirt, but avoided crediting it to London – *Glamour* opting to focus on Sweden instead, *Harper's Bazaar* on Paris. "Editors' Travel Notes," *Glamour*, August 1966, and Faith Berry, "Scene and Not Herd: Paris Reoccupied." *Harper's Bazaar*, September 1966.

201. E g., "This is the snap of things...," advertisement for B. Altman & Co. college shop, *New York Times*, August 2, 1966, and "Very Saks Fifth Avenue...where Varsity Gear is the Greatest," advertisement for Saks Fifth Avenue college shop, *New York Times*, August 3, 1966.

202. "Up, Up & Away," *Time*, December 1, 1967, 78.

203. George Nobbe, "Campus Sexplosion: The Most Popular Courses Today: Girls, Dope, Booze," New York *Sunday News*, April 17, 1966; George Nobbe, "Campus Sexplosion: Dope and Girl Raids Bring Scandal at Many Colleges," New York *Sunday News*, April 24, 1966. These stories were more lurid than *Time*'s story on the "free-sex movement" that had appeared a month earlier.

204. Tom Wolfe, *In Our Time* (New York: Farrar, Straus, 1980), 4.

205. Daniel Yankelovich, *The New Morality*, quoted in Chalmers, 143.

206. E.g., "Joke Y'Can See Through," New York *Daily News*, April 16, 1966, and "New Angle on Fashion," New York *Daily News*, May 4, 1966.

207. E.g., "The Orlon® Coat Sweater," advertisement for Gimbel's, New York *Sunday News*, August 7, 1966; "Ribbing Goes Girlish," advertisement for "mini-skirt" in Franklin Simon's children's department, New York *Sunday News*, August 7, 1966.

208. Peter Cadres, "While the Gals Thigh for Freedom: The Dresses Get Lesser, Lesser, & Wow!" New York *Daily News*, August 5, 1966.

209. Arthur Marwick, *The Sixties: Cultural Revolution in Britain, France, Italy, and the United States, c. 1958–c. 1974* (Oxford: Oxford University Press, 1998), 467.

210. "Britain at the Brink," *Newsweek*, July 25, 1966, 34.

211. Anthony Lewis, "Frivolity in Britain: Nation's Problems Are Dull Stuff to People Bent on a Swinging Time," *New York Times*, June 8, 1966.

212. Henry Fairlie, "'Britain Seems Willing to Sink Giggling Into the Sea,'" *New York Times Magazine*, June 12, 1966.

213. Maureen Cleave, "Old Beatles: A Study in Paradox," *New York Times Magazine*, July 3, 1966, 10–11: "This was the first time...visiting foreigners pointed out to alarmed Londoners that they had a swinging city on their hands"; Stephen Watts, "London, In and Out of Focus," *New York Times*, July 31, 1966: "The film [*Blow-Up*], made entirely

on location in London, is concerned with that 'swinging city' persona the town has recently acquired, somewhat to the astonishment of the natives."

214. Herbert L. Matthews, "'There'll Always Be an England,'" *New York Times*, August 22, 1966.

215. Art Buchwald, "Capitol Punishment," *Washington Post*, July 21, 1966.

216. A Letter from the Publisher, *Time*, August 5, 1966.

217. Russell Baker, "Observer: Cold Feet in Swinging London," *New York Times*, November 16, 1966.

218. Russell Baker, "Observer: Ominous Calm on the Cultural Front," *New York Times*, February 2, 1967.

219. "Dropouts with a Mission," *Newsweek*, February 6, 1967; and "Love on Haight," *Time*, March 17, 1967. *Time* did a cover on the hippies July 7, 1967. *Newsweek* didn't deal with them at cover length until "Trouble in Hippieland," October 30, 1967.

220. Nigel Buxton, "In Defense of London – It Is Not a Swinging City," *New York Times*, February 19, 1967.

221. See "The Pot Problem," March 12, 1965.

222. Hollis Alpert, "Le Roi du Crazy," *New York Times Magazine*, February 27, 1966; Victor G. Fourman, "England Revisited," *New York Times*, August 29, 1966.

223. M. Pezas, "The British Celebrate," *New York Times Magazine*, June 26, 1966, and Richard Blomfield, "Modern Britain Hailed," *New York Times*, July 4, 1966.

224. Gloria Emerson, "New Job for Shrimpton: Model to Be a Designer," *New York Times*, May 21, 1965; Jean Antel, "Julie Christie: I Am Not 'Darling,'" *New York Times*, November 21, 1965; and Godfrey Smith, "England's Stingingest Gadfly," *New York Times Magazine*, January 9, 1966.

225. "'Go' Fever: Europe's Biggest Season," *Newsweek*, July 19, 1965, 58.

226. Not even the phrase, "Swinging London." Brian Masters said it was coined by Melvin Lasky, editor of *Encounter*, in conversation with Horace Judson, who may have been interviewing him for *Time*'s cover story. Brian Masters, *The Swinging Sixties* (London: Constable, 1985), 13. In 1966, though, I heard that the phrase had been coined earlier by John Crosby, the American former TV critic then living in London; see Getlein, 27. Crosby didn't use the actual phrase, but he certainly conveyed the idea and made liberal use of the term "swinging" in relation to London in his key article, "London, The Most Exciting City in the World," in the *Weekend Telegraph*, a London Sunday supplement,

April 16, 1965. Shawn Levy suggested that *England Swings*, a hit pop song by the American Roger Miller, fed into the mix. Shawn Levy, *Ready, Steady, Go! The Smashing Rise and Giddy Fall of Swinging London* (New York: Doubleday, 2002), 203. I myself believe that "swinging" was one of a number of musical slang terms from the '30s that were popular in both the U.S. and the UK in the early '60s. At any rate, people were already speaking of "Swinging London" by the time I started work on the cover; the phrase was in the air and being used by my colleagues before we went into print.

227. "The Storm Breaks," *Time*, April 15, 1966, 28.

228. "Turmoil in Vietnam: War Within a War?" *Newsweek*, April 18, 1966, 25.

229. "Poets Hold 'Read-In' in Oregon To Protest U.S. Role in Vietnam," *New York Times*, March 6, 1966.

230. Tony Egan to Piri Halasz, April 19, 1966.

231. David Merrick to Sherry W. Arden, June 2, 1967.

232. Among naysayers: Christopher Booker, *The Neophiliacs: A Study of the Revolution in English Life in the Fifties and Sixties* (London: Collins, 1969; Boston: Gambit, 1970; reissue, with new introduction, London: Pimlico, 1992); Bernard Levin, *The Pendulum Years: Britain and the Sixties* (London: Cape, 1970; New York: Atheneum, 1971, as *Run It Down the Flagpole: Britain in the Sixties)*; Roy Porter, *London: A Social History* (Cambridge, MA: Harvard University Press, 1995); Stephen Inwood, *A History of London* (New York: Carroll & Graf, 1998); Peter Ackroyd, *London: The Biography* (New York: Nan A. Talese/Doubleday, 2001). More favorable comment: Masters; Steve Humphries and John Taylor, *The Making of Modern London, 1945–1985* (London: Sidgwick & Jackson, 1986); Robert Hewison, *Too Much: Art and Society in the Sixties 1960–75* (London: Methuen, 1986); and Marwick, *The Sixties....* Marwick had already dealt less favorably with the subject in *British Society Since 1945* (1982), *Britain in Our Century* (1984), and *Culture in Britain since 1945* (1991).

233. Booker, 310 (Gambit edition); Porter, 362; Inwood, 867; Ackroyd, 741, Masters, 13, Humphries and Taylor, 27, Hewison, xv, 55, 77–78, and Marwick, *The Sixties....*, 456.

234. Lesley Jackson, *The Sixties: Decade of Design Revolution* (London: Phaidon, 1998), 21, 37–38, 39.

235. Chris Stephens and Katharine Stout, "This Was Tomorrow," in *Art & the 60s: This Was Tomorrow,* ed. Chris Stephens and Katharine Stout (London: Tate Publishing, 2004), 9; "Groovy Galleries," in *Art & the 60s*, BBC Television, first broadcast July 1, 2004.

236. David Kemp, "London Swings! Again!" *Vanity Fair*, March 1997, 210; Simon Brooke and Rory Knight Bruce, "granny takes a trip," *ES Magazine*, April 12, 1996, 8; Roger Sabin, "Swinging London: If London really is the coolest city on the planet, why can't Roger Sabin get into the groove!" *Speak*, Winter 1999, 63.

237. Shawn Levy, 200–203, 204, 205, 219, 222, 234; Max Décharné, *King's Road: The Rise and Fall of the Hippest Street in the World* (London: Weidenfeld & Nicolson, 2005), xi, xv–xvi, xviii, 172, 207–8.

238. Dominic Sandbrook, *White Heat: A History of Britain in the Swinging Sixties* (London: Little, Brown, 2006), 245–46, 260.

239. "The Story of Pop," 56.

240. See People, *Time*, February 2, 1968.

241. Jones's books included *Architecture Today and Tomorrow* (1961); *Homes of the American Presidents* (1962); and *Marcel Breuer: Buildings and Projects, 1921–1961* (1962).

242. "The Wild Ones," *Time*, February 20, 1956, 75.

243. "Novelist, 56, Dies in a Restaurant," *New York Times*, January 10, 1962.

244. "Hoving of the Metropolitan," *Newsweek*, April 1, 1968, 55.

245. "When Dutchmen Disagree," *Time*, April 12, 1968.

246. "Pollock Revisited," *Time*, April 14, 1967, 85.

247. According to my recollection, though *Time* didn't mention the dice. It did give two contrasting associations to another sculpture, *Marriage*. "Presences in the Park," *Time*, February 10, 1967, 74.

248. Positive reviews: *Publishers Weekly*, *Library Journal*, *Time* (review written by a Books researcher named Martha McDowell, later Martha Duffy and, after I left, a senior editor). Positive brief references: *Los Angeles Times*, *Virginian-Pilot* (Norfolk, VA). Negative reviews: *Esquire*, *National Review*. Noncommittal: *Kirkus Reviews*. My father suggested that since he owned a bookstore, and I was an author, we should appear together at the American Booksellers Association convention. A press conference for me there led to articles in the *Chicago Tribune*, *Washington Post*, *Cleveland Plain Dealer*, and *Saturday Review*. Coward McCann also arranged for me to appear on the TV quiz program *To Tell the Truth* as "the real Piri Halasz."

249. In the first two weeks after the Smith cover, twenty-one letters about it came in; only four quoted were flatly favorable, while two more approved the sculpture but had other objections. *Time Letters Report*, October 19, 1967, and October 26, 1967.

250. "De Kooning's Derring-Do," *Time*, November 17, 1967, 88.

251. "Minimal Cartwheels," *Time*, November 24, 1967.

252. What Rubin said to me was evidently based upon what Miró told him: see similar account in William Rubin, *Miró in the Collection of the Museum of Modern Art* (New York: Museum of Modern Art, 1973), 30–33. In 1976, the first of a number of Miró drawings was published that appeared to be preliminary studies for *The Birth of the World*, with details supposedly added in the final stages of the painting already in the drawings. See Christopher Green, *Cubism and its Enemies: Modern Movements and Reaction in French Art, 1916–1928* (New Haven, CT: Yale University Press, 1987), 267–71, and David Lomas, *The Haunted Self: Surrealism, Psychoanalysis, Subjectivity* (New Haven, CT: Yale University Press, 2000), 12–22. Green and Lomas agreed that although *The Birth of the World* wasn't automatist, Miró did use an automatist method in some drawings, and it was Rubin's explanation of this method that contributed to my theory, rather than the painting itself.

253. Rubin may have been reading the March issues of *Arts Magazine* and *Artforum*, since they featured and/or carried ads for most of these shows.

254. "The Hobbyhorse Rides Again," *Time*, April 5, 1968, 84. The formal name for the Yippies was the Youth International Party.

255. Based on circulation statistics (audited or estimated) in *N. W. Ayer & Son's Directory: Newspapers and Periodicals 1968*.

256. Calvin Tomkins, "The Space Around Real Things," *New Yorker*, September 10, 1984, 85.

257. Halasz, "Overview," 122–23.

258. "Color It Color," *Time*, June 14, 1968, 60.

259. See Clement Greenberg, "Where is the Avant-Garde?" (1967) in Clement Greenberg, *Clement Greenberg: The Collected Essays and Criticism*, ed. John O'Brian, 4 vols. (Chicago: University of Chicago Press, 1986–1993), 4:259–65.

260. Top of the Week, *Newsweek*, July 29, 1968, 3.

261. "The Avant-Garde: Subtle, Cerebral, Elusive," *Time*, November 22, 1968, 70.

262. "Show of Sculpture by Smith Postponed," *New York Times*, February 12, 1969.

263. Thomas Messer, director of the Guggenheim, had stated in a letter that no other show would be on view at the museum while the Smith show was up. Thomas M. Messer to Clement Greenberg, June 15, 1966, Clement Greenberg papers, 1937–1984, Archives of American Art, Smithsonian Institution, box 8 (David Smith Estate).

264. Clement Greenberg, marginal note, in Piri Halasz, "Get Thee Glass Eyes" (manuscript, 1974, private collection), 200. *Life* thanked

Greenberg for reading and correcting the manuscript of its article, but said it would not be used. Kate Ganz to Clement Greenberg, February 14, 1969. Clement Greenberg papers, 1937–1984, Archives of American Art, Smithsonian Institution, box 3.

265. One psychiatrist I knew socially suggested this to me in the mid-'70s, after I'd recovered. A similar example is cited by Alfred Margulies, in *The Empathic Imagination* (New York: Norton, 1989), 120–21.

266. Carolyn M. Mazure and Benjamin G. Druss, "A Historical Perspective on Stress and Psychiatric Illness," in *Does Stress Cause Psychiatric Illness?* ed. Carolyn M. Mazure (Washington, DC: American Psychiatric Press, 1995), 1.

267. For a general introduction to stress and its biological correlates, see James N. Butcher, Susan Mineka, and Jill M. Hooley, *Abnormal Psychology*, 13th ed. (Boston: Pearson Education, 2007), chapter 5, "Stress and Adjustment Disorders." For a sampling of recent findings, see International Society of Psychoneuroendocrinology. Congress (34th: 2003: New York, NY), *Biobehavioral Stress Response: Protective and Damaging Effects*, ed. Rachel Yehuda and Bruce McEwen (New York: New York Academy of Sciences, 2004).

268. E.g., *Evaluating Stress: A Book of Resources*, ed. Carlos P. Zalaquett and Richard J. Wood (1997); *Occupational Stress: A Handbook*, ed. Rick Crandall and Pamela L. Perrewé (1995); and Julian Leff, *The Unbalanced Mind* (2001).

269. Yehuda and McEwen, "Introduction," in *Biobehavioral Stress Response*, xii.

270. The most persuasive case for a link between artistic creativity and bipolar disorder that I've seen was put by Kay Redfield Jamison in *Touched with Fire: Manic-Depressive Illness and the Artistic Temperament* (1993). But even she was far from being able to show that every modern writer, painter, and composer is or was bipolar.

271. "Bold Emblems," *Time*, April 18, 1969, 74.

272. The disruptions at the CUNY campuses weren't directly related to the antiwar protest, but rather to problems with integrating increased numbers of black and Puerto Rican students into their programs. Nevertheless, the fact that unrest was spreading from the elite schools to less prestigious ones reflected the situation with the antiwar protest as well. According to one book on the SDS, nearly three hundred institutions of higher education throughout the country witnessed various kinds of antiwar protests that spring, and nearly a third of the nation's students were involved. Kirkpatrick Sale, *SDS* (New York: Random House, 1973), 511–12.

273. Grace Glueck, "Lowry Out as Director of the Modern Museum," *New York Times*, May 3, 1969.

274. "Departure at the Modern," *Time*, May 16, 1969, [93].

275. MoMA still refused to explain what precipitated Lowry's firing to Russell Lynes, for *Good Old Modern: An Intimate Portrait of the Museum of Modern Art* (New York: Atheneum, 1973), 416. David Rockefeller, who was MoMA's board chairman at the time, wrote in his memoir that William S. Paley, its president, fired Lowry after seeing the bill for the renovation of Lowry's office suite, done without board approval. David Rockefeller, *Memoirs* (New York: Random House, 2002), 452. Lowry's obituary repeated Rockefeller's explanation. Grace Glueck, "Bates Lowry, 80, Head of Building Museum," *New York Times*, March 18, 2004. To me, this doesn't account for the suddenness or secrecy surrounding the firing; both would have been needed if Lowry had begun behaving oddly, as evidenced by how he was rearranging the gallery.

276. "Monument to an Occasion," *Time*, May 23, 1969.

277. See Lee Hall, *Elaine and Bill, Portrait of a Marriage: The Lives of Willem and Elaine de Kooning* (New York: HarperCollins, 1993), esp. chapter 7.

278. Harold Rosenberg, "The American action painters," *Art News*, December 1952, 22. Copyright © 1952 ARTnews, LLC, December.

279. Barbara Rose, "Problems of Criticism VI: The Politics of Art, Part III," *Artforum*, May 1969, 47.

280. Rose, 48.

281. "Prospero's Progress," *Time*, May 23,1969, 90.

282. Though Hughes's name remained on the masthead until mid-September.

283. Robert M. Coates, "The Passage of Time," *New Yorker,* January 18, 1964.

284. Harold Rosenberg, "A Risk for the Intelligence," *New Yorker*, October 27, 1962, 152.

285. Harold Rosenberg, "The Game of Illusion," *New Yorker*, November 24. 1962, 160.

286. Rose, 50.

287. "Soul-Searching on the Left," *Time*, April 2, 1951; "The State of the Nation," *Newsweek*, April 2, 1951.

288. Rose, 47.

289. Though the disruptions at Princeton were not nearly as extensive as those at Columbia and Harvard, they were still more dramatic than any at Yale. See "Students Occupy a Princeton Hall," *New York Times*,

March 12, 1969; Richard J. H. Johnston, "Princeton S.D.S. Backers Slow Marine Recruiting," *New York Times*, April 22, 1969; Richard J. H. Johnston, "S.D.S. Blockades Princeton Institute," *New York Times*, April 24, 1969; and John Darnton, "Yale Has Been Spared Campus Strife, but Some Administrators Are Nervous," *New York Times*, April 20, 1969.

290. Hedrick Smith, "Nixon to Reduce Vietnam Force, Pulling Out 25,000 G.I.'s by Aug. 31; He and Thieu Stress Their Unity: A Midway Accord," *New York Times*, June 9, 1969.

291. "Not All That Square," *Time*, June 20, 1969.

292. "Class of '69: The Violent Years," *Newsweek*, June 23, 1969, 70.

293. Peter Blake, "Yale on Ice," *New York*, August 11, 1969, 54.

294. Charles Schulz, *Peanuts*, *New York Post*, June 24, 1969.

295. "Sex as a Spectator Sport," *Time*, July 11, 1969, 62.

296. Piri Halasz, *Quidnunc* (manuscript, 1969, private collection). As the manuscript is unpaginated, I'm sparing the reader any endnotes to quotations from it.

297. Charles Schulz, *Peanuts*, *New York Post*, August 29, 1969. Peanuts: ©United Feature Syndicate, Inc.

298. Margulies, 10.

299. Jane Pearce and Saul Newton, *The Conditions of Human Growth* (1963; repr., New York: Citadel, 1969), 220–21.

300. Pearce and Newton, 192.

301. First story, published only in the Latin American edition, but quoted in E. W. Kenworthy, "Capital Voices 'Grave Concern' On Anti-U.S. Violence in Bolivia," *New York Times*, March 4, 1959; second story, as published in the domestic edition, "The Fanned Spark," *Time*, March 16, 1959.

302. Clement Greenberg to Piri Halasz (postcard), April 13, 1970, private collection.

303. Clement Greenberg to Piri Halasz, May 22, 1970, private collection.

304. Pearce and Newton, 224.

305. Pearce and Newton, 195.

306. "Oh, To Be In London," *Time*, April 15, 1966, n.p. [facing 30].

307. Shawn Levy associated the "grass" in the two-hed with marijuana. Shawn Levy, 201–2. Consciously or unconsciously, marijuana may have been on Fuerbringer's mind, as he'd just deleted the reference to pot parties. He may even have been thinking, rather cynically, that the whole cover story was really a dope addict's pipe dream, bearing no serious relation to journalistic reality – but it was too late for him to do anything about it (and besides, he liked it).

308. Of a total of fifty-two letters received about this story in the first two weeks after it appeared, forty-nine attacked it. *Time Letters Report*, April 17, 1969.

309. Erwin Panofsky, *Problems in Titian, mostly iconographic* (New York: New York University Press, 1969), esp. 120, 125.

310. H. W. Janson, *History of Art: A Survey of the Major Visual Arts from the Dawn of History to the Present Day*, with Dora Jane Janson, rev. ed.(Englewood Cliffs, NJ and New York: Prentice-Hall and Abrams, 1969), color plate 81, text, 541.

311. Between 1968 and 1974, MoMA had devoted an exhibition to one contemporary artist whom Greenberg admired (Anthony Caro), but at least six to contemporary art and artists whom he didn't, on balance, admire. The museum had acquired about fifteen works by artists born since 1920 that Greenberg would or might have admired: one each by David Annesley, Darby Bannard, Frank Bowling, Ron Davis, Helen Frankenthaler, Philip King, Kenneth Noland, Jules Olitski, William Pettet, Tim Scott, Anne Truitt, William Tucker, and Larry Zox, plus two by Caro. But MoMA had also acquired at least one hundred and twenty works that Greenberg would most likely have considered lesser if not "novelty" art. See accession numbers in *Painting and Sculpture in the Museum of Modern Art with Selected Works on Paper: Catalogue of the Collection January 1, 1977*, ed. Alicia Legg (New York: Museum of Modern Art, 1977).

312. Piri Halasz, "Homage to Meyer Schapiro, 'the compleat art historian,'" *ARTnews*, Summer 1973.

313. "Heiress to a New Tradition," 69.

314. Heinrich Wölfflin, *Renaissance and Baroque*, trans. Kathrin Simon (Ithaca, NY: Cornell Paperbacks (Cornell University Press), 1967), 30–31, 34.

315. Piri Halasz, "19th Century Painting" (notebook [Fall 1974], private collection), entry for September 9.

316. John Rewald, *The History of Impressionism*, 4th rev. ed. (New York: Museum of Modern Art, 1973), 21.

317. Rewald, 331. For a revisionist discussion of the reviews that this exhibition received, see Jane Mayo Roos, *Early Impressionism and the French State (1866–1874)* (Cambridge, UK: Cambridge University Press, 1996), chapter 12. Although Roos cited many more favorable reviews than Rewald, in the end she concluded that the most hostile one was the truest index of the public response to the show.

318. Rewald, 20.

319. "Issues & Commentary," and Rosalind Krauss, "Changing the Work of David Smith," *Art in America*, September–October 1974, 30–34.

320. Hilton Kramer, "Altering of Smith Work Stirs Dispute," *New York Times*, September 13, 1974; Hilton Kramer, "Questions Raised by Art Alterations," *New York Times*, September 14, 1974; R[obert] H[ughes], "Arrogant Intrusion," *Time*, September 30, 1974, 73; and "Alter Ego," *Newsweek,* September 30, 1974, 105.

321. Greenberg said eight to me, but in a letter dated September 28, 1974, to Stanley A. Frederick, Jr., he said seven, and in a letter to Ira Lowe and Robert Motherwell, dated February 19, 1975, he said five. Clement Greenberg papers, 1937–1984, Archives of American Art, Smithsonian Institution, Box 8 (David Smith Estate). Calvin Tomkins said five, in "Measuring Up to Nature," *New Yorker*, July 19, 1999, 88.

322. Kramer said "several sculptures" had been affected. Hughes set the number at ten, but neither gave a figure for the total number of sculptures in the estate. *Newsweek* used a figure of four hundred for total works in the estate, but said only that paint had been stripped from "several" sculptures, while "others" had been left outdoors.

323. I consulted the Smith estate papers at the Archives of American Art in the '90s. Since then, they have been closed to researchers, so I was unable to confirm or correct my notes while fact-checking the manuscript.

324. See Sylvia Hochfield, "Problems in the Reproduction of Sculpture," *ARTnews*, November 1974.

325. Rewald, 25, 89.

326. Piri Halasz, "Proseminar" (notebook [Fall 1974], private collection), entry on first page.

327. Halasz, "Proseminar," entry for September 26.

328. Piri Halasz, "French Painting 1774-1830" (notebook [Summer 1975], private collection), entry for May 20.

329. Piri Halasz, "German Expressionism" (notebook [autumn 1975], private collection), last page.

330. Piri Halasz, "Romantic Landscape Seminar" (notebook, [spring 1975], private collection), entry for February 18.

331. Erwin Panofsky, "The History of Art as a Humanistic Discipline," in *Meaning in the Visual Arts* (Garden City, NY: Doubleday Anchor Books, 1955), 14.

332. Panofsky, "The History of Art," 14.

333. E. H. Gombrich, *Art and Illusion: A Study in the Psychology of Pictorial Representation* (1960; rev. pb ed., Princeton, NJ: Princeton University Press, 1969), 7, 26–27.

334. Gombrich, 5.
335. Piri Halasz to Clement Greenberg, September 2, 1975, Clement Greenberg papers, 1937–1984, Archives of American Art, Smithsonian Institution, box 3.
336. Clement Greenberg to Piri Halasz, January 10, 1975, private collection.
337. Greenberg to Halasz, January 10.
338. Halasz, "German Expressionism," entry for September 11.
339. See Rose-Carol Washton Long, *Kandinsky: The Development of an Abstract Style* (Oxford: Oxford University Press, 1980).
340. Halasz, "German Expressionism," entry for December 11.
341. Halasz, "German Expressionism," entry for September 25.
342. Donald B. Kuspit, *Clement Greenberg: Art Critic* (Madison, WI: University of Wisconsin Press, 1979), 116; Robert Hughes, *The Shock of the New* (New York: Knopf, 1981), 156.
343. Piri Halasz, "American Painting" (notebook, Fall 1975, private collection), entry for September 29.
344. Piri Halasz, "Architecture" (notebook, [Spring 1976], private collection), entry for April 15.
345. Halasz, "Architecture," entry for April 22.
346. Hilton Kramer, "The Sixties In Retrospect," *New York Times*, July 2, 1967, and Brian O'Doherty, "What is post-modernism?" *Art in America*, May–June 1971, 19. According to O'Doherty, "post-modernism" was a term that had been often employed for several years.
347. Leo Steinberg, "Other Criteria," in *Other Criteria: Confrontations with Twentieth-Century Art* (1972; repr. with new preface, Chicago: University of Chicago Press, 2007), 91. The article in which the term appears was based on a lecture given in 1968, but Steinberg's notes for this lecture didn't indicate that he used the word then, and he thought it more likely that the term first appeared in the 1972 article. Leo Steinberg, telephone interview with Piri Halasz, October 26, 1998.
348. Steinberg, 84.
349. Steinberg, 84.
350. William S. Rubin, *Dada, Surrealism and Their Heritage* (New York: Museum of Modern Art, 1968), 16.
351. Halasz, "Modern Sculpture [I]" (notebook [Spring 1976]), entries for April 9 and 20. Among references to "frustration" that Varnedoe might have known: Arturo Schwarz, *The Complete Works of Marcel Duchamp* (New York: Abrams, [1969]), 105, 111, 485, 560; Anne d'Harnoncourt, "Introduction," in *Marcel Duchamp*, ed. Anne d'Harnoncourt and Kynaston McShine (New York: Museum of Modern Art, 1973), 35; and

Joseph Masheck, "Introduction," in *Marcel Duchamp in Perspective*, ed. Joseph Masheck (Englewood Cliffs, NJ: Prentice-Hall, 1975), 23.

352. Pablo Picasso, "Statement by Picasso: 1935," in Alfred H. Barr, Jr., *Picasso: Fifty Years of His Art* (1946; repr. New York: Museum of Modern Art, 1974), 273.

353. Quoted by Gelett Burgess, "The Wild Men of Paris," *Architectural Record* (New York), 27:5 (May 1910), 405.

354. Halasz, "Modern Sculpture [I]," entry for April 9.

355. Halasz, "Modern Sculpture [I]," entries for March 23 and April 6.

356. Halasz, "Modern Sculpture [I]," entries for April 6 and 9.

357. Emily Braun, "Vulgarians at the Gate," in *Boccioni's Materia: A Futurist Masterpiece and the Avant-garde in Milan and Paris*, ed. Laura Mattioli Rossi (New York: Solomon R. Guggenheim Foundation, 2004), 1.

358. Halasz, "Modern Sculpture [I]," entry for April 20.

359. Arthur E. McGuinness, *Henry Home, Lord Kames* (New York: Twayne, 1970), 88.

360. Eliot, 247.

361. Piri Halasz, "Changes in the Concept of Sentiment in the Nineteenth Century" (manuscript, October 1976, private collection), 68–69.

362. Piri Halasz to Clement Greenberg, November 12, 1976, Clement Greenberg papers, 1937–1984, Archives of American Art, Smithsonian Institution, box 3.

363. Piri Halasz to Clement Greenberg, November 14, 1976, Clement Greenberg papers, 1937–1984, Archives of American Art, Smithsonian Institution, box 3.

364. Clement Greenberg to Piri Halasz, November 19, 1976, private collection.

365. Piri Halasz, "American 20th Cent[ury] Art" (notebook, [Autumn 1976], private collection), entry for December 13.

366. Halasz to Greenberg, November 12. Varnedoe was apparently referring to Greenberg's "Sculpture in Our Time" (1958), as quoted in Ruth Butler, *Western Sculpture: Definitions of Man* (Boston: New York Graphic Society, 1975), 1.

367. Halasz to Greenberg, November 12.

368. Paul N. Siegel, "Introduction," in Leon Trotsky, *Art and Revolution: Writings on Literature, Politics and Culture*, 2nd ed., 4th printing (New York: Pathfinder, 1992), 13, 7–8.

369. Clement Greenberg, "Avant-Garde and Kitsch" (1939), in Greenberg, *Collected Essays,* 1:22.

370. Clement Greenberg, marginal note in Halasz, "Get Thee Glass Eyes," 233.

371. Clement Greenberg to Piri Halasz, August 8, 1974, private collection.

372. Clement Greenberg to Piri Halasz, March 24, 1981, private collection. The "Frenchman in charge" was Serge Guilbaut, coeditor of the published version of the conference (1983).

373. T. J. Clark, *Image of the People: Gustave Courbet and the 1848 Revolution* (1973; repr., Princeton, NJ: Princeton University Press, 1982), 86–98. Weasels: 1) page 86: single sentence devoted to overall election returns, fact that the conservatives had huge majority; rest of paragraph and indeed next eight pages devoted almost exclusively to prolonged discussion of *la France rouge* and its vicissitudes; 2) page 98: single sentence conceding that the opposition to Louis Napoleon's coup d'état was minimal and soon put down; rest of paragraph and indeed most of rest of page devoted to description of this opposition, before another five lines are used to concede that only two weeks were required to crush it.

374. Karl Marx, *The Class Struggles in France, 1848–1850* (New York: International Publishers, 1964), 90.

375. Marx, 91, 134.

376. Marx, 71–73.

377. Karl Marx, *The Eighteenth Brumaire of Louis Bonaparte* (New York: International Publishers, 1963), 123–26.

378. Marx, *Brumaire*, 125.

379. Roger Price, *The French Second Republic: A Social History* (Ithaca, NY: Cornell University Press, 1972), 235–42.

380. Piri Halasz, "Modern Painting I" (notebook [Autumn 1976], private collection), entries of November 9 and 23.

381. Piri Halasz, "Modern Painting II" (notebook [Spring 1977], private collection), entry for January 8.

382. Halasz, "Modern Painting II," entry for January 8.

383. Piri Halasz, "Modern Sculpture II" (notebook [Spring 1977], private collection), entry for February 16.

384. Greenberg, "Where is the Avant-Garde?" 4:263.

385. Halasz, "Modern Sculpture II", entry for January 26.

386. Milton W. Brown, *American Painting from the Armory Show to the Depression* (1955; repr. Princeton, NJ: Princeton University Press, 1970), 65.

387. William C. Agee, *Synchromism and Color Principles in American Painting, 1910–1930* (New York: M. Knoedler & Co., 1965), 19–20. Courtesy of Knoedler & Company.

388. Gail Levin, *Synchromism and American Color Abstraction 1910–1925* (New York: George Braziller and the Whitney Museum of American Art, 1978), 22–23, pls. 63, 64, 66–70.

389. Halasz to Greenberg, November 12.

390. Florence Rubenfeld, *Clement Greenberg: A Life* (New York: Scribner, 1997), 220.

391. Dodie Kazanjian, "On Target," *Vogue*, February 1990, 352.

392. See Clement Greenberg, *Homemade Esthetics: Observations on Art and Taste* (New York: Oxford University Press, 1999), esp. 132–34.

393. Greenberg, *Homemade Esthetics*, 131–32, 144, 153.

394. Rubenfeld, 297.

395. Piri Halasz to Clement Greenberg, January 23, 1977, Clement Greenberg papers, 1937–1984, Archives of American Art, Smithsonian Institution, box 3.

396. Kirk Varnedoe, "On Degas' Sculpture," *Arts Magazine*, November 1977.

397. "So Big: The all-time mass market bestsellers," *Publishers Weekly*, May 26, 1989, S31.

398. See *The Harold Letters 1928–1943: The Making of an American Intellectual*, ed. Janice Van Horne (2000).

399. Clement Greenberg to Piri Halasz, August 23, 1974, private collection.

400. See Harry Rand, *Arshile Gorky: The Implications of Symbols* (1980).

401. See esp. Clement Greenberg, "Changer: Anne Truitt" (1968), in Greenberg, *Collected Essays*, 4:288–91.

402. *Daybook: The Journal of an Artist* (1982); *Turn: The Journal of an Artist* (1986); and *Prospect: The Journal of an Artist* (1996).

403. See Judith Kaye Reed, "New Artists Honored, Abstraction Crowned at Whitney Annual," *Art Digest*, January 1, 1950, 78, and Thomas B. Hess, "8 excellent, 20 good, 133 others," *Art News*, January 1950, 34-35+. Reed said straight out that abstract art was the reigning monarch at the show; Hess got across the same idea by starting his article with a discussion of de Kooning, Pollock, and John Marin, a semiabstract master from an earlier generation, then reviewing the rest of the show roughly in order from more abstract to more representational.

404. First solo exhibitions, in descending order of age: Hoffman, 1944; Rothko, 1945; Gottlieb, 1942; Gorky, 1945; de Kooning, 1948; Still, 1946; Pollock, 1943; Baziotes, 1944; Reinhardt, 1944; Motherwell, 1944; Stamos, 1943.

405. Piri Halasz, "Directions, Concerns and Critical Perceptions of Paintings Exhibited in New York, 1940–1949: Abraham Rattner and His Contemporaries" (PhD diss., Columbia University, 1982), 270–89.

406. See Harold Rosenberg, "The Shapes in a Baziotes Canvas," *Possibilities 1* (Winter 1947/8); Harold Rosenberg, "Introduction to Six American

Artists," *Possibilities 1* (Winter 1947/8); and Harold Rosenberg, "Reminder to the growing: To Patia, for a painting by William Baziotes," *The Tiger's Eye 7* (March 1949). The periodical that Rosenberg co-created (with Motherwell) was *Possibilities*. See Ann Eden Gibson, *Issues in Abstract Expressionism: The Artist-Run Periodicals* (Ann Arbor, MI: UMI Research Press, 1989), 33–34, 38–39.

407. Robert M. Coates, "Abroad and At Home," *New Yorker*, March 30, 1946, 83. Before World War II, Kandinsky had similarly been called an "abstract expressionist" to distinguish him from the other, more representational German Expressionists.

408. Gordon's book would be published after his death in 1984 as *Expressionism: Art and Idea* (New Haven, CT: Yale University Press, 1987). For references to Rattner, Greenberg, and my writing, see 195–98; also notes 116–19, 241.

409. See Kenneth E. Silver, *Esprit de Corps: The Art of the Parisian Avant-garde and the First World War, 1914–1925* (1989).

410. [? Howard Devree], "In the Galleries: Shows One by One," *New York Times*, January 11, 1948.

411. Emily Genauer, "Ethel Edwards Proves Mature Artist," *New York World-Telegram*, February 7, 1949.

412. "Into the Void," *Time*, October 3, 1949, 38.

413. Henry McBride, *The Flow of Art: Essays and Criticisms*, ed. Daniel Catton Rich (New Haven, CT: Yale University Press, 1997), 425.

414. Sam Hunter, "Among the New Shows," *New York Times*, January 30, 1949.

415. Clement Greenberg, "Towards a Newer Laocoon" (1940), in Greenberg, *Collected Essays,* 1:28. He reiterated this distinction in "In Our Own Time," *Art of the Western World: From Ancient Greece to Post-Modernism*, VHS, produced, directed and written by Perry Miller Adato (© 1989 Educational Broadcasting Corporation).

416. Piri Halasz, "Art Criticism (and Art History) in New York: The 1940s vs. the 1980s; Part Three: Clement Greenberg," *Arts Magazine*, April 1983, 88.

417. Halasz, "Art Criticism...Part Three," 88.

418. My 1982 engagement calendar has entries for "research on Pollock" on November 15, "Pollock research – The Interpretation of Dreams," on November 26, and "Pollock/psychology research" on November 29.

419. Piri Halasz, "Stanley William Hayter: Pollock's Other Master," *Arts Magazine*, November 1984, 74.

420. Most Pollock scholars prefer to stress his earlier experiments with dripped or spattered paint in the Manhattan workshop of David Alfaro

Siqueiros, the Mexican muralist, but European surrealism enabled Pollock to link up such pouring with the unconscious, and this link must have lent fresh resonance to the technique.

421. Interview with William Wright taped around 1950, transcript in Jackson Pollock papers, ca. 1914–1975, Archives of American Art, Smithsonian Institution, r. 3048.

422. Quoted in Selden Rodman, *Conversations with Artists* (New York: Capricorn, 1961), 82.

423. Halasz, "Hayter," 75.

424. Lawrence Alloway, "Adolph Gottlieb and Abstract Painting," in *Adolph Gottlieb: A Retrospective*, organized by Sanford Hirsch and Mary Davis MacNaughton, text by Lawrence Alloway and Mary Davis MacNaughton (New York: The Arts Publisher, in association with the Adolph and Esther Gottlieb Foundation, 1981), 58.

425. Piri Halasz, "Abstract Painting in General; Friedel Dzubas in Particular," *Arts Magazine*, September 1983, 77.

426. Halasz, "Abstract Painting," 79.

427. Halasz, "Abstract Painting," 81.

428. Ellen Johnson, "Jackson Pollock and Nature," *Studio International*, 185:956 (June 1973): 257–59, and B. H. Friedman, *Jackson Pollock: Energy Made Visible* (1975; rev. ed., New York: Da Capo Press, 1995), 97.

429. Halasz, "Abstract Painting," 82.

430. Halasz, "Abstract Painting," 82; Friedman, 87, 90.

431. Halasz, "Abstract Painting," 82; Friedman, 92–93.

432. Halasz, "Abstract Painting," 82. I am far from alone in associating Pollock's poured paintings with male sexuality. In addition to Sam Hunter's "ravaging, aggressive virility," the artist Ethel K. Schwabacher, student and biographer of Gorky, was also equating Pollock's painting to "the sheer act – the ever flowing act of potency" during his lifetime. See unpublished notes for a projected book, variously dated "1948" and "1953–1960" in the Ethel Schwabacher papers, 1940–1975, Archives of American Art, Smithsonian Institution, r. N69-64. In 1964, *Time* described how friends witnessed Pollock, "a cigarette smoldering on his lip, emerge from his studio limp as a wet dishrag." "Beyond the Pasteboard Mask," *Time*, January 17, 1964, 69. This suggestive passage was probably written by Jon Borgzinner and edited by Cranston Jones, both of whom would have been familiar with what may well have been inside humor within certain circles of the Manhattan art world at that moment. The *Time* example is one of three analogies with ejaculation cited by Anna C. Chave, in "Pollock and Krasner: Script and Postscript"

(1993), in *Jackson Pollock: Interviews, Articles and Reviews*, ed. Pepe Karmel (New York: Museum of Modern Art, 1999), 265. I do seem to be unusual in equating the image on the picture surface with semen, as opposed to equating the act of painting to ejaculation, and may even be unique in taking the analogy beyond the purely biological, by perceiving semen in human terms as symbolic of aggression, pleasure, love, reproduction, and thus immortality (in the context of Renaissance humanism).

433. For a description of the intentional uni-referential images that underlie the surfaces of Pollock poured paintings, see Pepe Karmel, "Pollock at Work: The Films and Photographs of Hans Namuth," in Kirk Varnedoe, with Pepe Karmel, *Jackson Pollock* (New York: Museum of Modern Art, 1998), 86–137. But results count for more than intentions, and Pollock's finished poured paintings are clearly multireferential, however much postmodernist scholars may try nostalgically to shrink them back into the realm of the comfortably conventional uni-referential.

434. Halasz, "Abstract Painting," 83.

435. Piri Halasz, "New York Museum Exhibitions and Acquisitions, The 1940s vs. the 1980s (With Some Discussion of Multireferential Imagery)," (manuscript, 1983, private collection), 48.

436. Irving Sandler, *The Triumph of American Painting: A History of Abstract Expressionism* (New York: Icon Editions (Harper & Row), [1970]), 98; Dore Ashton, *The New York School: A Cultural Reckoning* (New York: Viking, 1973), 177–84.

437. Steinberg included Noland among artists he maintained had adopted the flatbed picture plane, but only because he felt that Noland's stripe paintings appeared mechanically produced. See Steinberg, 80–81.

438. Halasz, "Some Discussion," 26–27.

439. Halasz, "Some Discussion," 48–49.

440. Halasz, "Some Discussion," 49–50.

441. Halasz, "Some Discussion," 64–65.

442. Halasz, "Some Discussion," 64.

443. Halasz, "Some Discussion, 64–66.

444. Halasz, "Some Discussion," 52–53.

445. Halasz, "Some Discussion," 66–67.

446. Halasz, "Some Discussion," 67–68.

447. See Sigmund Freud, "Jokes and their Relation to the Unconscious" (1905), *SE*, 8 (1960), esp. chapter 3.

448. Halasz, "Some Discussion," 69.

449. Halasz, "Some Discussion," 58, 71; see also Piri Halasz, "Manhattan Museums: The 1940s vs. the 1980s; Part Two: The Metropolitan Museum of Art, *Arts Magazine*, March 1985, 94.

450. T. S. Eliot, "Shakespeare and the Stoicism of Seneca" (1927), in Eliot, *Selected Essays,* 112.

451. Halasz, "Some Discussion," 109.

452. Halasz, "Some Discussion," 76.

453. "Heiress to a New Tradition," 69.

454. Halasz, "Some Discussion," 71–72.

455. In 1985, Greenberg's friend Darby Bannard sent me a greeting card with a picture on it by Benno Friedman, depicting a young housewife wearing an apron smeared with spaghetti sauce that looked like a Pollock. She was offering more spaghetti from a pan to a small boy, and the title was "Jackson's Pollock's Mother." In my article, I'd equated spaghetti sauce with maternal nurturing, and I knew that Greenberg had had problems in his relation to his mother. This for me explained why he'd blocked on his memory of the sauce, and the notion that this seventy-four-year-old man should look upon me as a mother figure gave me the best laugh I'd had in months.

456. Clement Greenberg to Piri Halasz (postcard), December 12, 1984, private collection.

457. I've been unable to find any place where she actually used the term, "multireferential imagery" and believe that the resemblances between her writing and mine that she was alluding to were general rather than specific. See Anne Truitt, *Daybook: The Journal of an Artist* (New York: Pantheon, 1982), 151–52, 163–64, 217–18.

458. Anne Truitt to Piri Halasz, October 9–10, 1983, private collection.

459. Halasz, "Overview," 123.

460. Halasz, "Overview," 123.

461. Halasz, "Overview," 125.

462. For other writing in the '70s and '80s on "subject matter" in abstraction, see Ann Gibson, "The Rhetoric of Abstract Expressionism," in *Abstract Expressionism: The Critical Developments*, organized by Michael Auping (New York: Harry N. Abrams with Albright-Knox Art Gallery, 1987), 92n. Gibson's note gives "a representative list" of nineteen writers who'd explored the "subject matter" of abstract expressionism. The note cites no specific writings, so I can't say exactly what Gibson was referring to, but I found eighteen articles and two exhibition catalogues among those writers whose ideas were new to me, and came remotely near mine. Almost all found only ideological sources for paintings in books the artists had read, and/or only stylistic or ideological sources in other art or museum exhibits they'd seen. In other words, none dealt with mimesis – the imitation of life, or depiction of the world beyond art – to any meaningful extent. Still,

references to ambiguity were common, as were references to the unconscious, and three articles stood out for the intriguing way that they came near to implying multireferential imagery (in individual artists or small groups of artists, and without happening upon it as a guiding principle in abstraction as a whole). The first of these was Jeffrey Weiss's "Science and Primitivism: A Fearful Symmetry in the Early New York School," published in *Arts Magazine* in March 1983. The second was Stephen Polcari's "The Intellectual Roots of Abstract Expressionism: Clyfford Still," which appeared in *Art International* in the May–June 1982 issue. Only Robert S. Mattison, however, connected ambiguity with the unconscious, in "*The Emperor of China*: Symbols of Power and Vulnerability in the Art of Robert Motherwell during the 1940's," published in *Art International* in November 1982. Mattison argued that Motherwell's *Emperor of China* (1947) conflated "after-images" derived by way of the artist's "subconscious" from Picasso, Chinese emperor portraits, prehistoric cave painting, Arp, and Dubuffet. Since he perceived no extra-artistic sources for Motherwell's imagery, however, this was still not mimesis. The painting itself is uni-referential, not multireferential, nor did Mattison apply his ideas to other artists. The more recent state of research into ambiguity in abstraction may perhaps be indicated by Dario Gamboni's *Potential Images: Ambiguity and Indeterminacy in Modern Art* (2002). This intriguing study, however, stops well short of discussing the abstract artist's capacity to synthesize different images derived from his or her own visual experience into a single ambiguous image on the picture plane; as with other postmodernist analyses, the emphasis tends to be on the beholder of the work of art, as opposed to its creator.

463. Robert Rauschenberg, "Robert Rauschenberg" [artist's statement], in *Sixteen Americans*, ed. Dorothy C. Miller (New York: Museum of Modern Art, 1959), 58.

464. Larry Poons, interview by Piri Halasz, East Durham, NY, August 2, 1987, quoted in Piri Halasz, "Poons & Steiner: Growing Up," (manuscript, 1987, private collection), 6.

465. Clement Greenberg, "Oshawa Interview," by Allan Walkinshaw, Oshawa, Ontario, March 15, 1978, Joan Murray Artist Files, The Robert McLaughlin Gallery, Oshawa, Ontario; http://www.sharecom. ca/greenberg/interviewoshawa.html (accessed July 21, 2008).

466. Donald B. Kuspit, *Signs of Psyche in Modern and Postmodern Art*, (Cambridge, UK: Cambridge University Press, 1993), 128.

467. Kuspit, *Signs*, 135,

468. Michael Leja, *Reframing Abstract Expressionism: Subjectivity and Painting in the 1940s* (New Haven, CT: Yale University Press, 1993), 127.

469. I'll spare the reader an overlong footnote on kitchens, dining rooms, and breakfast nooks in the '30s and '40s, as well as Warhol biographies indicating that he almost certainly ate in the kitchen as a child, and report only that his brother, Paul Warhola, said that "their mother habitually served Campbell's Soup at home, and Andy grew up on the product." David Bourdon, *Warhol* (New York: Harry N. Abrams, © 1989, all rights reserved), 99.

470. However, he preferred to stress that his mature comic-strip paintings developed out of the comic-strip drawings he was making for his own children. See, for example, Bruce Glaser, "Oldenburg, Lichtenstein, Warhol: A Discussion," in *Roy Lichtenstein*, ed. John Coplans (New York: Praeger, 1972), 56.

471. Roni Feinstein, "The Early Work of Robert Rauschenberg: The White Paintings, the Black Paintings, and the Elemental Sculptures," *Arts Magazine*, September 1986.

472. Arthur C. Danto, *After the End of Art: Contemporary Art and the Pale of History* (1997); Robert C. Morgan, *The End of the Art World* (1998); and Donald B. Kuspit, *The End of Art* (2004).

473. Cf. "Structuralists and Post-Structuralists typically reject the notion of an Essential Copy derived from Plato's mimetic view of art." Laurie Schneider Adams, *The Methodologies of Art: An Introduction* (New York: Icon Editions, 1996), 162–63.

474. Piri Halasz, *From the Mayor's Doorstep*, 23 (January 15, 2000), 16.

475. William Rubin, *Picasso and Braque: Pioneering Cubism* (New York: Museum of Modern Art, 1989), 210.

476. Pepe Karmel, "Addenda: Lists of Paintings in Picasso's and Braque's Correspondence with Kahnweiler," in *Picasso and Braque: A Symposium*, organized by William Rubin, moderated by Kirk Varnedoe, ed. Lynn Zelevansky (New York: Museum of Modern Art, 1992), 341, and John Richardson, with Marilyn McCully, *A Life of Picasso: Volume II: 1907–1917* (New York: Random House, 1996), 220–21. T. J. Clark captioned the painting *Woman with a Zither ("Ma Jolie")*, in *Farewell to an Idea: Episodes from a History of Modernism* (New Haven, CT: Yale University Press, 1999), 176–77. MoMA itself sanctions alternate titles for this painting.

477. Piri Halasz, *From the Mayor's Doorstep*," 26 (June 1, 2000), 12–13. For an argument that Picasso originally intended *"Ma Jolie"* to incorporate shapes relating to a mandolin, tenora, and even a clarinet, see Pepe Karmel, *Picasso and the Invention of Cubism* (New Haven, CT: Yale

University Press, 2003) 145–46, and figs. 130, 189, and 191–93. Once again, results to me count for more than intentions, but Karmel did confirm my supposition that Picasso knew the zither was played by gypsies.

478. A Letter from the Publisher, *Time*, January 6, 1967, [11].

479. "The Inheritor," *Time*, January 6, 1967, 19.

480. "Youth Questions the War," *Time*, January 6, 1967, 22.

481. "The Wrong Place," *Time*, April 8, 1966, 28. For statistics showing how younger Americans were consistently more hawkish than older ones, see William L. Lunch and Peter Sperlich, "American Public Opinion and the War in Vietnam," *Western Political Quarterly*, 32:1 (March 1979): esp. tables 3 and 4. See also Adam J. Berinsky, *Silent Voices: Public Opinion and Political Participation in America* (Princeton, NJ: Princeton University Press, 2004), 110.

482. "The Dilemma of Dissent," *Time*, April 21, 1967, [20].

483. Douglas Robinson, "100,000 Rally at U. N. Against Vietnam War," *New York Times*, April 16, 1967.

484. "The Peace Marchers," *Newsweek*, April 24, 1967, 27.

485. Melvin Small, *Johnson, Nixon and the Doves* (New Brunswick, NJ: Rutgers University Press, 1988), 93.

486. Robert Dallek, *Flawed Giant: Lyndon Johnson and His Times, 1961–1973* (New York: Oxford University Press, 1998), 485–86.

487. Dallek, 486.

488. Dallek, 486.

489. In 1986, the company history said that a more critical attitude toward the war was first expressed in a story questioning the South Vietnamese army's fighting capabilities in the August 4 issue. Prendergast and Colvin., 250. In 1993, Wyatt found the first evidence of a turnaround in a report by Donovan on a trip to Vietnam in a June issue of *Life*. Wyatt, 177. In 2004, Landers found four references to a "stalemate" in *Time* between June 30 and August 25. Landers, 177n. None of these articles appear to have impressed outside writers at or near the time.

490. Re *Time*: Halberstam, *Powers That Be*, 483; re *Life*: Prendergast and Colvin, 251.

491 14. "The Inheritor," 23. Two months after the Man of the Year cover, Kenneth Crawford, a *Newsweek* columnist, complained that the phrase "generation gap" was over-used. Kenneth Crawford, "Washington: Generation Gap," *Newsweek*, March 13, 1967, 48. But *The New York Times Index* and the *Readers' Guide to Periodical Literature* indicate that neither the phrase nor the subject of a generation gap received much attention before 1967. In 1966, the *Times Index* had a subcategory of

"Psychology and Training" under the general category "Children and Youth"; this subcategory was approximately one column long. In 1967, this subcategory was changed to "Behavior and Training," and took up six columns, including an entry on C. D. B. Bryan's story on the "generation gap" (see below) plus dozens of stories on hippies. Volume 27 of the *Readers' Guide* (March 1967–February 1968) instituted the category "Youth-adult relationship" in addition to its regular category of "Youth." The category "Youth-adult relationship" listed twenty stories, of which eight mentioned the "generation gap" or just the "gap" in their titles (in Volume 26, there were no references at all to this term). The only time I came across the phrase "generational gap," prior to the Man of the Year cover, was in "Protecting the Flank," *Time*, November 4, 1966, [25]. It was probably a parallel construction derived from "missile gap" and "credibility gap."

492. C. D. B. Bryan, "Why the Generation Gap Begins at 30," *The New York Times Magazine*, July 2, 1967, 39.

493. Ramsey Clark, quoted by Small, 110.

494. See Thomas Powers, *The War at Home; Vietnam and the American People, 1964–1968* (New York: Grossman, 1973), 232–33, 234–36, 238–42; DeBenedetti, 187–89, 196–98; Tom Wells, *The War Within: America's Battle over Vietnam* (Berkeley, CA: University of California Press, 1994), 174–81,184–91, 195–97, 201–3.

495. A Letter from the Publisher, *Time*, October 27, 1967, [21].

496. "The Banners of Dissent," *Time*, October 27, 1967, [26-27].

497. "The Banners of Dissent," [23].

498. "The Banners of Dissent," 24.

499. Joseph A. Loftus, "Guards Repulse War Protesters at the Pentagon," *New York Times*, October 22, 1967; John Herbers, "Youths Dominate Capital Throng," *New York Times*, October 22, 1967; and "Scene at Pentagon: Beards, Bayonets and Bonfires," *New York Times*, October 22, 1967.

500. Robert S. McNamara, with Brian VanDeMark, *In Retrospect: The Tragedy and Lessons of Vietnam* (New York: Times Books (Random House), © 1995 by Robert S. McNamara), 304.

501. James Reston, "Everyone Is a Loser," *New York Times*, October 23, 1967.

502. "March on the Pentagon," *Newsweek*, October 30, 1967, 20-21.

503. Jules Witcover, *The Year the Dream Died: Revisiting 1968 in America* (New York: Warner Books, 1977), 32.

504. Doris Kearns [Goodwin], *Lyndon Johnson and the American Dream* (New York: Harper & Row, 1976), 312. While Johnson was President,

though, he was angry with the demonstrators, and suspected that they were controlled by communists. The CIA was asked to discover connections between the two. George C. Herring, *America's Longest War: The United States and Vietnam, 1950–1975*, 3rd ed. (New York: McGraw-Hill, 1996), 198.

505. Prendergast and Colvin, 249.

506. For an argument that the protest was effective, see Small, chapter 8; for a more recent assessment (and agreement), see Fry, 238–39.

507. Halberstam, *Powers That Be*, 484; also Hedley Donovan, *Roosevelt to Reagan: A Reporter's Encounters with Nine Presidents* (New York: Harper & Row, 1985), 103.

508. Prendergast and Colvin, 236.

509. Donovan, 103; also Halberstam, *Powers That Be*, 484.

510. Eugene J. McCarthy, *The Year of the People* (Garden City, NY: Doubleday, 1969), 78–83.

511. McCarthy in 1969 said only that his decision to run had been made in "late October." McCarthy, 53. Other authors suggested or implied more exact dates for the decision, but one of McCarthy's most recent biographers, Dominic Sandbrook, offered well-documented evidence that as late as mid-November, McCarthy still hadn't made up his mind. Dominic Sandbrook, *Eugene McCarthy: The Rise and Fall of Postwar American Liberalism* (New York: Knopf, 2004), 167–68 and 338n.

512. George Rising, *Clean for Gene: Eugene McCarthy's 1968 Presidential Campaign* (Westport, CT: Praeger, 1997), 57–59.

513. Peter Braestrup, *Big Story: How the American Press and Television Reported and Interpreted the Crisis of Tet 1968 in Vietnam and Washington* (1977; abridged ed., New Haven, CT: Yale University Press, 1983).

514. Walter Cronkite, "Who, What, When, Why" CBS broadcast, February 27, 1968. © 1968 CBS Inc.

515. Rising, 68.

516. Herring, 219.

517. Hammond, 372.

518. The other "Wise Men" were George Ball, Douglas Dillon, Cyrus Vance, Arthur Dean, John McCloy, Omar Bradley, Matthew Ridgway, Maxwell Taylor, Robert Murphy, Henry Cabot Lodge, Abe Fortas, and Arthur Goldberg. Herring, 226n.

519. Lyndon B. Johnson, *Lyndon B. Johnson's Vietnam Papers: A Documentary Collection*, ed. David M. Barrett (College Station, TX: Texas A & M University Press, 1997), 713.

520. Books which dealt with the antiwar movement, but discussed the media only in passing, included those by Wells, Chalmers, DeBenedetti, and

Small. The book by Wells also began as a doctoral dissertation for which Gitlin was the principal advisor.

521. Small also thought that *Newsweek* went to press three days later than *Time*, evidently unaware that the two magazines simply dated their issues differently. Melvin Small, *Covering Dissent: The Media and the Anti-Vietnam War Movement* (New Brunswick, NJ: Rutgers University Press, 1994), 69, 79, 72, 80.

522. *Deciding What's News* describes the turnaround in media coverage as taking place in the wake of the Tet offensive, attributing to it the media becoming persuaded that the war couldn't or shouldn't be pursued, and claiming that while earlier TV coverage had focused upon agitators with beards, later coverage emphasized the more conventionally dressed. Gans, 54.

523. CLIO (as of March 1999, when I'd partially simmered down) listed six copies of four books that I considered (broadly-speaking) hawkish: one each of William Colby, *Lost Victory: A Firsthand Account of America's Sixteen-Year Involvement in Vietnam* (1989); Edith Efron, *The News Twisters* (1971); and Russ Braley, *Bad News: The Foreign Policy of the New York Times* (1984); plus three of Braestrup. One copy of the Braestrup was on reserve. The six copies of books that I'd called owlish included two by Hammond, three of Wyatt, and one of Prados. I listed six scholarly books on the protest movement as dovish, plus two more theoretical ones with a related attitude toward the media: Gitlin, Hallin, Small (two titles), Chalmers, Wells, Chomsky, and Gans. These eight had a total of sixty-eight copies in CLIO, of which twenty-five were on reserve. CLIO also listed thirteen copies of Neil Sheehan's book, and the three books by Halberstam dealing with Vietnam were represented by twenty-six copies. To these, of course, must be added the hawkish books that I discovered in 2001, and discuss in Chapter 25.

524. Powers, xviii-xix.

525. Landon Y. Jones, *Great Expectations: America and the Baby Boom Generation* (New York: Ballantine Books, 1981), 118–19.

526. Chalmers, chapter 9.

527. Edward P. Morgan, *The 60s Experience: Hard Lessons About Modern America* (Philadelphia: Temple University Press, 1991), 22, 128.

528. Wyatt, 219.

529. "Is the Press Biased?" *Newsweek*, September 16, 1968, 66-67.

530. Dallek, 486–90; and Stephen E. Ambrose, *Nixon. Volume Two: The Triumph of a Politician 1962–1972* (New York: Simon and Schuster, 1989), 261–62, 264–65.

531. Joel Cooper, *Cognitive Dissonance: Fifty Years of a Classic Theory* (Los Angeles: SAGE Publications, 2007), 2–3. For correlation between defense mechanisms and dissonance reduction, see Henry Gleitman, *Psychology*, 2nd ed. (New York: Norton, 1986), 376n.

532. Anna Freud, *The Ego and the Mechanisms of Defense* (1936; rev. ed., based on trans. by Cecil Baines, Madison, CT: International Universities Press, 1966), chapter 9, "Identification with the Aggressor." As Anna Freud's specialty was child psychology, two cases cited were of little boys whose teachers had frightened them; they identified with the teachers in order to feel more secure. In one case, a boy made faces imitating the angry facial expressions of the teacher; in the other, a boy turned up for his session with Freud with a military hat, toy sword, and toy pistol.

533. Subsequent research would show that they were representative in their ages. Part One of *Reporting Vietnam*, an anthology of articles on Vietnam, covering the period between 1959 and 1969, gave birth dates of forty-six journalists included (almost none of them on the newsmagazines). Nineteen were born during the '30s, and eleven more during the '20s. Only eight were born in 1940 or later, and only eight prior to 1920. Biographical Notes, *Reporting Vietnam*, Part One, *American Journalism 1959–1969* (New York: Library of America, compilation, notes and chronology © 1998), 804–16. Part Two of this collection, dealing with later phrases of the war and hence not directly relevant to this book, had a slightly higher proportion of journalists born in the '30s.

534. Louis Menand observed a parallel situation with the leaders of the "youth culture" of the '60s, like Jerry Rubin (b. 1938) and Abbie Hoffman (b. 1936). Menand, "The Seventies Show," *New Yorker*, May 28, 2001, 131.

535. Sheehan, 318.

536. Richard Severo, "John Gregory Dunne, Novelist, Screenwriter and Observer of Hollywood, Is Dead at 71," *New York Times*, January 1, 2004.

537. See U.S. Census Bureau, *Statistical Abstract of the United States*: 2001 (121st edition), Washington, DC, 2001, table no. 46. Descendants of German, Irish and Latino immigrants were more evenly distributed.

538. I say the election was stolen because Gore might have won Florida (and with it, the presidency), if a recount had been made of *all* the ballots cast there, not just the ballots that he asked to have recounted, according to an independent study commissioned by a consortium of

news media. Ford Fessenden and John M. Broder, "Study of Disputed Florida Ballots Finds Justices Did Not Cast the Deciding Vote," *New York Times*, November 12, 2001.

539. *Encyclopedia of the American Presidency*, s.v. "Roosevelt, Franklin D."

540. *The New Encyclopaedia Britannica*, 15th ed. (*Macropaedia*), s.v. "Franklin D. Roosevelt."

541. *Directory of American Scholars*, 7th ed. (1978), 1 (History), s.v. "Braeman, John Albert" and "Freidel, Frank, Jr."

542. David W. Levy, 113–16.

543. Russell L. Riley, *The Presidency and the Politics of Racial Equality: Nation-Keeping from 1831 to 1965* (New York: Columbia University Press, 1999), chapter 5. Riley's further account in this chapter of how and why President Truman took more decisive steps toward ending segregation is also fascinating.

544. James MacGregor Burns, *Roosevelt: The Lion and the Fox* (1956), and Rexford G. Tugwell, *The Democratic Roosevelt: A Biography of Franklin D. Roosevelt* (1957).

545. Robert A. Divine, *American Immigration Policy, 1924–1952* (1957; repr., New York: Da Capo Press, 1972), 104.

546. Leonard Dinnerstein, *America and the Survivors of the Holocaust* (New York: Columbia University Press, 1982), ix.

547. Howard M. Sachar, *A History of the Jews in America* (New York: Knopf, 1992), 553.

548. Jay W. Baird, *The Mythical World of Nazi War Propaganda, 1939–1945* (Minneapolis: University of Minnesota Press, 1974), 170–71; and Michael Balfour, *Propaganda in War, 1939–1945: Organisations, Policies and Publics in Britain and Germany* (London: Routledge, 1979), 303–304.

549. Roberto Finzi, *Anti-Semitism: From its European Roots to the Holocaust*, trans. Maud Jackson (New York: Interlink Books, 1999), 76.

550. "Far better if we cast a cold eye on the legacy of White House deceit – and suspicion of deceit – that FDR left behind him. Equally dubious was his use of the implied powers of the presidency to wage an undeclared war in 1941. Perhaps it was not an accident that the president who considered himself Roosevelt's heir, Lyndon Johnson, fought another undeclared war in Vietnam." Thomas Fleming, *The New Dealers' War: Franklin D. Roosevelt and The War Within World War II* (New York: Basic Books, 2001), 560. Fleming (b. 1927) wasn't a baby boomer, yet still reflected the intellectual climate created in the '60s.

551. Also seeking to reevaluate FDR from a more critical standpoint: Roy Jenkins, with Richard E. Neustadt, *Franklin Delano Roosevelt* (2003),

and Alonzo L. Hamby, *For the Survival of Democracy: Franklin Roosevelt and the World Crisis of the 1930s* (2004).

552. See Nicholas D. Kristof, "The Endorsement From Hell," *New York Times*, October 26, 2008.

553. "Author's Preface," in Patricia Sloane, *T. S. Eliot's Bleistein Poems* (Lanham, MD: University Press of America, 2000), n. p.

554. Ronald Schuchard, "My Reply: Eliot and the Foregone Conclusions," *Modernism/modernity*, 10:1 (January 2003), 67.

555. See, among others: Peter Ackroyd, *T. S. Eliot: A Life* (1984); Denis Donoghue, *Words Alone: The Poet T. S. Eliot* (2000); and esp. Jonathan Freedman, "Lessons Out of School: T. S. Eliot's Jewish Problem and the Making of Modernism," *Modernism/modernity*, 10:3 (September 2003), 419–29.

556. Frederick Crews, "The Unknown Freud," *New York Review of Books*, November 18, 1993, 62. Reprinted with permission from *The New York Review of Books*. Copyright © 1993 NYREV, Inc.

557. See *Stanford Prison Experiment: A Simulation Study of the Psychology of Imprisonment Conducted at Stanford University*, http://www.prisonexp. org (accessed August 9, 2008).

558. Piri Halasz, "Psych BC 1001x" (notebook, Fall 1996, private collection), re unconscious and penis envy: entry for October 18; re recommendation to read Freud: entry for November 11; re worksheet on defense mechanisms: entry for November 18.

559. Stephen A. Mitchell and Margaret J. Black, *Freud and Beyond: A History of Modern Psychoanalytic Thought* (New York: Basic Books, 1995), Preface.

560. Jonathan Redmond and Michael Shulman, "Access to Psychoanalytic Ideas in American Undergraduate Institutions," *Journal of the American Psychoanalytic Association*, 56:2 (June 2008), published online, copy e-mailed to Piri Halasz by Dottie Jeffries, American Psychoanalytic Association, July 16, 2008.

561. Falk Leichsenring, DSc, and Sven Rabung, PhD, "Effectiveness of Long-term Psychodynamic Psychotheapy: A Meta-analysis," *JAMA*, 300:13 (October 1, 2008):1551–65; see also Richard M. Glass, MD, "Psychodynamic Psychotherapy: Bambi Survives Godzilla?" same issue: 1587–89.

562. Crews, 55.

563. "Psychoanalysis: In Search of Its Soul," 68.

564. Re psychoanalysis: Milton Howard, "As We See It: How Can Madmen Truly Define Sanity?" *Worker Magazine*, January 14, 1951; re abstract

art: D[avid] P[latt], "Harry Gottlieb Talks About Realism and Beauty in Art," *Daily Worker*, May 9, 1951.

565. David E. Sanger, "Bush Pushes Ambitious Education Plan," *New York Times*, January 24, 2001.

566. This was still the case. Donald H. McLaughlin and Stephen Broughman, *Private Schools in the United States: A Statistical Profile, 1993–94* (Washington, DC: U.S. Department of Education, Office of Educational Research and Improvement, [1997]), "An Overview of the 9-Category NCES Private School Typology" (chart), 15.

567. *Encyclopedia of the American Constitution*, 2nd ed., s.v. "Separation of Church and State."

568. Re vouchers: Carolyn Maloney to Piri Halasz, March 13, 2001, private collection; re "faith-based initiatives": Carolyn Maloney to Piri Halasz, March 15, 2001, private collection.

569. Elizabeth Becker, "House Backs Aid for Charities Operated by Religious Groups," *New York Times*, July 20, 2001.

570. Laurie Goodstein, "Support for Religion-Based Plan Is Hedged," *New York Times*, April 11, 2001.

571. Becker; also, "How Representatives Voted on Religion-Based Initiative," *New York Times*, July 20, 2001. The bill didn't come up for a vote in the Senate, still controlled by Democrats, either that session or the next. Bush resorted to executive orders to distribute money to churches.

572. A representative (though far from complete) list of publications dealing with the mass-media response to abstract expressionism includes 1) Serge Guilbaut, *How New York Stole the Idea of Modern Art: Abstract Expressionism, Freedom and the Cold War*, trans. Arthur Goldhammer (Chicago: University of Chicago Press, 1983); 2) Bradford R. Collins, "*Life* Magazine and the Abstract Expressionists, 1948–51: A Historiographic Study of a Late Bohemian Enterprise," *Art Bulletin*, 73:2 (June 1991): 293–308; 3) Wanda M. Corn, "Ways of Seeing," in Maureen Hart Hennessey and Anne Knutson, *Norman Rockwell: Pictures for the American People*, (Atlanta: High Museum of Art; Stockbridge, MA: The Norman Rockwell Museum; New York: Harry N. Abrams, 1999); 4) Ann Temkin, "Barnett Newman on Exhibition," in *Barnett Newman*, ed. Ann Temkin (Philadelphia: Philadelphia Museum of Art, 2002); and 5) Maurice Berger, "Abstract Expressionism: A Cultural Timeline, 1940–1976," in *Action/Abstraction: Pollock, de Kooning, and American Art, 1940–1976*, ed. Norman L. Kleeblatt (New York: The Jewish Museum, and New Haven, CT: Yale University Press, 2008). Guilbaut's book concerned primarily the '40s, but his interest in the

media has been shared by and/or influenced writers dealing with the '50s. Collins focused almost exclusively on *Life*.

573. Sandler, 13; Ashton, 59.

574. Complete list of MoMA exhibitions in the '30s: Lynes, *Good Old Modern*, 447–51.

575. According to Daniel Okrent, Luce hired a real-estate firm in 1937 to find new office space for Time Inc., which had outgrown its old space in the Chrysler Building with the launching of *Life* in 1936. Daniel Okrent, *Great Fortune: The Epic of Rockefeller Center* (New York: Viking, 2003), 146. Yet Luce and Nelson were already friendly by this time, according to a statement by Okrent at a meeting of the Time-Life Alumni Society, January 14, 2004. The effusive article about Rockefeller Center in the December 1936 issue of *Fortune* suggests that the friendship had already borne fruit. The article included a photograph of Nelson, with a caption saying that he was the family's representative in the management of Rockefeller Center, Inc., and ending, coyly, "He also does some renting." Sounds like an inside joke to me. The article was accompanied by a drawing of Rockefeller Center seen from the south. In the foreground were the dotted outlines of the as-yet-unbuilt building that would become the new home of Time Inc.

576. Herzstein, 235–36.

577. Re Kane: *Masters of Popular Painting; Modern Primitives of Europe and America*, text by Holger Cahill et al. (New York: Museum of Modern Art, 1938), 121; re Siqueiros: Alfred H. Barr, Jr., *Painting and Sculpture in the Museum of Modern Art, 1929–1967* (New York: Museum of Modern Art, 1977), 589.

578. Sylvia Jukes Morris, *Rage for Fame: The Ascent of Clare Boothe Luce* (New York: Random House, 1997), 328–32; Hayden Herrera, *Frida: A Biography of Frida Kahlo* (New York: Harper & Row, 1983), 288–94.

579. "Picasso Exhibit Now Complete," *New York Times*, December 18, 1939.

580. George L. K. Morris, "Picasso: 4000 Years of His Art," *Partisan Review*, 7:1 (January–February 1940): 52.

581. Robert J. Goldwater, "Picasso: Forty Years of His Art," *Art in America*, 28:1 (January 1940): 43–44.

582. "Topics of the Times, " *New York Times*, November 20, 1939.

583. Greenberg, "Avant-Garde and Kitsch," 1:9.

584. Nelson A. Rockefeller, "The Arts and Quality of Life," *Saturday Evening Post*, Summer 1971, 72.

585. Besides Leah Gordon's recollection of how dubious Luce was about abstract expressionism in 1966, Dorothy Seiberling recalled how she and other *Life* editors had to talk him into letting *Life* do its series on abstract expressionism in 1959. Round-table discussion at Pollock-Krasner House and Study Center, September 27, 1998.

586. "Jackson Pollock: Is he the greatest living painter in the United States?" *Life*, August 8, 1949, 42.

587. Robert T. Elson, *The World of Time Inc.: The Intimate History of a Publishing Enterprise, Volume Two: 1941–1960*, ed. Duncan Norton-Taylor (New York: Atheneum, 1973), 422n.

588. Collins, 285. Although Collins dealt with the *Life* article at some length, he didn't say that all but two of the artists in it were at most semiabstract.

589. "The Metropolitan and Modern Art," *Life*, January 15, 1951, 85.

590. See Collins, 292. A mention, not a discussion.

591. Robert M. Coates, "Persia, 2000 B.C. to the Present," *New Yorker*, December 3, 1949, 95, and McBride, 425. See also Collins, 298–300, who (with the aid of Steven Naifeh and Gregory White Smith, in *Jackson Pollock: An American Saga*) quoted or listed other reviewers, and argued that the *Life* article also boosted Pollock's sales.

592. "Baffling U.S. Art: What It Is About," *Life*, November 9, 1959, 69.

593. This and further biographical data (aside from what *Time* published about him), Alexander Eliot interview by Piri Halasz, July 3, 1987 (transcript, private collection).

594. "Lines of Force," *Time*, April 1, 1957; "In the End, Nothing," *Time*, September 16, 1957; and "Knockout Blow," *Time*, December 2, 1957. "The New Academy," December 2, 1957, was presumably written by Eliot, not Jones.

595. Calculations based upon acquisition numbers and photographs of work in Barr, *Painting and Sculpture*.

596. Although Lansner was listed on the masthead as Books editor, *Newsweek* was still using unsigned articles in those days, and the first two knowledgeable stories in the Art section both dealt with books about art. The magazine also had a section on "The Arts" that combined stories on books, music, art, etc., and could have been written by anybody on the staff.

597. "Stormy Inventor," *Newsweek*, January 9, 1961.

598. "American Abstraction Abroad," *Time*, August 4, 1958, 40.

599. "The 'Rawness,' the Vast," *Newsweek*, May 11, 1959, 113.

600. McBride, 426.

601. Advance promo: Thomas B. Hess, "de Kooning paints a picture," *Art News*, March 1953. Although "so-and-so paints a picture" was a regular feature of the magazine, normally Hess, the managing editor, assigned it to members of his staff. Reviews: Sidney Geist, "Work in Progress," *Art Digest*, April 1, 1953; Henry McBride, "Abstract Report for April," *Art News*, April 1953; James Fitzsimmons, "Art," *Arts & Architecture*, May 1953; Robert M. Coates, "French, Belgian and American," *New Yorker*, April 4, 1953; and "Big City Dames," *Time*, April 6, 1953.

602. See Boris Eikhenbaum, *The Young Tolstoy*, trans. and ed. Gary Kern (Ann Arbor, MI: Ardis, 1972), 52; and Neil Stewart, "From Imperial Court to Peasant's Cot: Sterne in Russia," in *The Reception of Laurence Sterne in Europe*, ed. Peter de Voogt and John Neubauer (London: Thoemmes Continuum, 2004), 142–43.

603. Leo N. Tolstoy, *What Is Art?* (1896), trans. Aylmer Maude (Indianapolis, IN: Hackett Publishing, 1960), 51.

604. Roger Fry, *Vision and Design* (1920), ed. J. B. Bullen (London: Oxford University Press, 1981), 19–20.

605. Roger Fry, 206.

606. Roger Fry, 206–7.

607. Roger Fry, "The Allied Artists," *Nation* (UK), 13:18 (August 2, 1913): 677.

608. Susanne K. Langer, *Feeling and Form: A Theory of Art* (New York: Scribner's, 1953), 25–26, 40, 395. Used by permission of Pearson Education, Inc.

609. *The Nation* and *The New Republic* were journals of opinion, not mass-media or consumer magazines. Both provided ongoing coverage of contemporary art during the '50s and '60s, but their outlooks varied depending on their contributors of the moment.

610. See Robert M. Coates, "Whitney Annual," *New Yorker*, October 31, 1953; and Robert M. Coates, "Another Annual," *New Yorker*, November 24, 1956.

611. Ben Shahn, "What Is Realism In Art?" *Look*, January 13, 1953, 44–45.

612. "Wall Street Art Collection," *Look*, November 3, 1953, 72–74.

613. Russell Lynes, "Every Day A New Picasso," *Look*, January 10, 1956, 54–57.

614. "New York: The Taste Shaper," *Look*, February 18, 1958, 50–51.

615. "Anita Colby's recipe for Well-dressed Beauty," *Look*, September 11, 1951, 71. Ann Temkin construes this rather offhand treatment of Newman as evidence that the major media were welcoming abstract expressionism. Temkin, 45.

616. "Abstract Art Can't be as Mysterious as the Critics Tell Us," *Saturday Evening Post*, September 21, 1957, 10.

617. Caroline A. Jones, *Eyesight Alone: Clement Greenberg's Modernism and the Bureaucratization of the Senses* (Chicago: University of Chicago Press, 2005), 122–23.

618. Janice Van Horne, telephone interview with Piri Halasz, April 25, 2008.

619. Clement Greenberg, "The Case for Abstract Art," *Saturday Evening Post*, August 1, 1959.

620. William Snaith, "The Anguish of Modern Art," *Saturday Evening Post*, November 7, 1959.

621. "Jackson Pollock's Abstractions," *Vogue*, March 1, 1951, 159. For one precedent, see "You'll find yourself sleeveless...," and "You'll find your freedom in a loose blouse top...," *Harper's Bazaar*, April 1944, 68–69, 74–75. These layouts used paintings by Léger, Mondrian, and Picasso as backdrops for their models, though beyond identifying the paintings as by their respective artists, it had no commentary on the art.

622. Aline B. Louchheim, "Betty Parsons: Her Gallery, Her Influence," *Vogue*, October 1, 1951, 141, 197.

623. James Johnson Sweeney, "Five American Painters," *Harper's Bazaar*, April 1944, 76–77+. Guilbaut quite properly pointed out that Sweeney distinguished between the new American art and the illustrative and sociopolitical art of the '30s, but he neglected to mention the equally if not more significant fact that Sweeney also distinguished between the new American art and European modernism. Guilbaut, 225n.

624. "James W. Fosburgh: An American Painter," *Harper's Bazaar*, June 1955, 80–81.

625. H. W. Janson, "After Betsy, What?" *Bulletin of the Atomic Scientists*, 15:2 (February 1959): 93.

626. Edith Hoffmann, "New York," *Burlington Magazine*, 99:646 (January 1957): 68.

627. E.g., Ad Reinhardt, "The Artist in Search of an Academy," *College Art Journal*, 12:3 (Spring 1953); Adolph Gottlieb, "Artist and Society: A Brief Case History," *College Art Journal*, 14:2 (Winter 1955); and Leon Golub, "A Critique of Abstract Expressionism," *College Art Journal*, 14:2 (Winter 1955).

628. E.g., Joseph C. Sloane, "The Lithographs of Benton Spruance," *College Art Journal*, 17:4 (Summer 1958); George Michael Cohen, "The Bird Paintings of Morris Graves," *College Art Journal*, 18:1 (Fall 1958); and Helmut Wohl, "Recent Paintings of Stephen Greene," *College*

Art Journal, 18:2 (Winter 1959). Sloane was at Bryn Mawr, Cohen at Boston University, Wohl at Yale.

629. A. Deidre Robson, *Prestige, Profit and Pleasure: The Market for Modern Art in New York in the 1940s and 1950s* (New York: Garland, 1995), 248–50.

630. A 1950 oil by George Grosz went for $800; a 1943 Milton Avery tempera went for $850, and two oils by Bernard Buffet, dated 1951 and 1952, went for $1300 and $1800. *Modern Paintings and Drawings.... Modern Sculptures....*[annotated], New York: Parke-Bernet Galleries, February 6, 1957, Archives of American Art, Smithsonian Institution, r. NP-B106, frs. 709–38.

631. F[airfield] P[orter], "Jasper Johns," *Art News*, January 1958, 20; editor's note, 5.

632. Leo Steinberg, "Month in Review," *Arts Magazine*, January 1956, 46-47 (Rauschenberg), 48 (Rivers); Leo Steinberg, "Month in Review," *Arts Magazine*, June 1956, 43-44 (Glarner); Leo Steinberg, "Month in Review," *Arts Magazine*, July 1956, 28 (Guston, Kline).

633. See Thomas B. Hess, "The phony crisis in American art," *Art News*, Summer 1963.

634. "Special Supplement: A Symposium on Pop Art," *Arts Magazine*, April 1963.

635. Sidney Tillim, "Month in Review," *Arts Magazine*, November 1962, 36–38.

636. Sidney Tillim, "Month in Review," *Arts Magazine*, February 1962, 34–37.

637. Peter Selz, [introductory statement], "A Symposium on Pop Art," 36.

638. For one all-too-typical example of slumping sales, see correspondence and financial statements sent between 1959 and 1966 by the Samuel M. Kootz Gallery to James Brooks, a well-regarded second-generation abstract expressionist whom the gallery represented. James Brooks papers, 1928–1983, Archives of American Art, Smithsonian Institution, r. N/69-132, frs.1–102. Kootz, who had been among the first dealers to exhibit abstract expressionism in the '40s, opted to close his gallery in April 1966 rather than see it adapted to the new climate.

639. Irving Sandler, "The New Cool-Art," *Art in America*, February 1965, 96–101. Sandler included Louis and Poons (then in his op-art phase) as well as Johns, Warhol, Lichtenstein, and others.

640. Bourdon, 66.

641. "The Younger," *Newsweek*, February 24, 1964, 82.

642. "Vanity Fair: The New York Art Scene," *Newsweek*, January 4, 1965, 58, 55.

643. "The New Art: It's Way, Way Out," *Newsweek*, July 29, 1968, 60, 62, 56.

644. "Peacock Duo," *Time*, January 8, 1965; "Hitting the Bull's-Eye," *Newsweek*, April 16, 1962 (Noland); "Strong Line," *Newsweek*, October 22, 1962 (Louis); also "Died....Morris Louis", *Newsweek*, September 17, 1962; "Americans in Paris," *Newsweek*, January 6, 1964; and "Carnival in Venice," *Newsweek*, July 6, 1964.

645. "Trend to the 'Anti-Art,'" *Newsweek*, March 31, 1958.

646. "Everything Clear Now?" *Newsweek*, February 26, 1962.

647. "The Slice-of-Cake School," *Time*, May 11, 1962, 52.

648. "Products," *Newsweek*, November 12, 1962, and "Pop Goes the Easel," *Newsweek*, April 1, 1963.

649. "For Movement's Sake," *Newsweek*, March 13, 1961.

650. "At Home with Henry," *Time*, February 21, 1964.

651. "Carnival in Venice," 74.

652. "The Younger," 82.

653. "The Older," *Newsweek*, February 24, 1964, 82.

654. "Picture of a Painter," *Newsweek*, March 16, 1959, 58.

655. "Boxing Match," *Time*, May 15, 1964, 86.

656. "Saint Andrew," *Newsweek*, December 7, 1964, 100.

657. Top of the Week, *Newsweek*, December 7, 1964, 15.

658. See "Modern Plaster Master," *Life*, June 19, 1964; "Art Pops In," *Life*, July 10, 1964; "You Think This Is a Supermarket?" *Life*, November 20, 1964; "Far-out Refrigerators," *Life*, February 26, 1965; and "You Bought It Now Live With It," *Life*, July 16, 1965.

659. "Revival of the Throb and Sob," *Life*, February 15, 1963.

660. Aline B. Saarinen, "Explosion of Pop Art: A new kind of fine art imposing poetic order on the mass-produced world," *Vogue*, April 1963, 86, 142.

661. "Private Lives with Art," *Vogue*, January 15, 1964. Beginning the spread was a brief look at the more conservative collection of Mr. and Mrs. William A. M. Burden, featuring Brancusi and Monet.

662. "young Americans and the well-mixed party," *Harper's Bazaar*, August 1962, photo of Warhol, 89; text, 91.

663. Emmanuel Mounier, "Deus ex Machina," *Harper's Bazaar*, November 1962, 156–59.

664. Emily Genauer, "Can This Be Art?" *Ladies' Home Journal*, March 1964, 151.

665. *Modern Paintings and Drawings....Modern Sculptures....*[annotated] (New York: Parke-Bernet Galleries, June 7, 1962), Archives of American Art, Smithsonian Institution, r. NP-B128, frs. 217–49.

666. *Abstract Expressionist and Other Modern Paintings/Drawings. Sculptures....* [annotated], (New York: Parke-Bernet Galleries, May 13, 1964), Archives of American Art, Smithsonian Institution, r. N/69-48, frs. 4–53.

667. Grace Glueck, "5 Works Dropped from Art Auction," *New York Times*, May 14, 1964.

668. Fritz Neugass, "New Records for Abstract Art," *Arts Magazine*, February 1965, 22.

669. "Pop Culture," *Time*, May 3, 1963, 73.

670. John Seabrook, *Nob°ow: The Culture of Marketing, The Marketing of Culture* (New York: Knopf, 2000), 69.

671. Lynes published a version of "Highbrow, Lowbrow, Middlebrow" in *The Tastemakers* (1955). In this book's 1980 edition, he updated the article with an "afterword," but it isn't nearly as successful. Three related books are Herbert J. Gans, *Popular Culture and High Culture: An Analysis and Evaluation of Taste* (1975; rev. ed. 1999); Pierre Bourdieu, *Distinction: A Social Critique of the Judgement of Taste* (1979; English trans. 1984); and Lawrence W. Levine, *Highbrow/Lowbrow: The Emergence of Cultural Hierarchy in America* (1988). For various reasons, none describe the U.S. situation in the twentieth and twenty-first centuries for me as well as Lynes.

672. Lynes, "Highbrow, Lowbrow, Middlebrow," *Harper's Magazine*, 19–20. Copyright © 1949 by Harper's Magazine. All rights reserved. Reproduced from the February issue by special permission.

673. Abigail Zuger, MD, "How Tightly Do Ties Between Doctor and Drug Company Bind?" *New York Times*, July 27, 2004.

674. John E. Gedo, *The Artist & the Emotional World: Creativity and Personality* (New York: Columbia University Press, 1996), 69.

675. Mihaly Csikszentmihalyi, *Creativity: Flow and the Psychology of Discovery and Invention* (New York: HarperCollins, 1996), 28.

676. Charles Brenner, MD, "Creativity and Psychodynamics," *Psychoanalytic Quarterly*, 73:2 (April 2004): 514.

677. "Are These Men The Best Painters in America Today?" *Look*, February 3, 1948, 44.

678. Howard Gardner, *Intelligence Reframed: Multiple Intelligences for the 21st Century* (New York: Basic Books, 1999), 123.

679. David Joselit of Yale University, at "Identity, Engagement, Judgment: Clement Greenberg and Harold Rosenberg Then and Now," panel at the Jewish Museum in New York, NY, May 15, 2008.

680. Piri Halasz, *From the Mayor's Doorstep*, 16 (January 15, 1999), 1.

681. "The War Within Bob Kerrey," *New York Times*, April 26, 2001.

682. William Safire, "Syndrome Returns," *New York Times*, April 30, 2001.

683. Gaines M. Foster, "Coming to Terms with Defeat: Post-Vietnam America and the Post-Civil War South," *Virginia Quarterly Review*, 66:1 (Winter 1990), 31.

684. Foster, 32.

685. Powers, xi.

686. *Encyclopedia of the Vietnam War: A Political, Social and Military History*, ed. Spencer C. Tucker (Santa Barbara, CA: ABC-CLIO, 1998), s.v. "Chronology of Events Touching Vietnam through April 1975."

687. Piri Halasz, "The View from Virginia," *NYArts*, October 2001, 73.

688. For evidence of the high levels of stress suffered by those who watched a lot of television in the wake of 9/11, see Jeffrey Rosen, "Naked Terror," *New York Times Magazine*, January 4, 2004, 10.

689. Max Frankel, "To Whom It May Concern," *New York Times Magazine*, January 18, 1998, 14.

690. Richard W. Stevenson, "Congress Gets Plea to Drop Tax Benefits for Investors and Widen Economic Relief," *New York Times*, September 26, 2001.

691. I later learned that the *Times*'s 9/11 coverage had been orchestrated by a new executive editor, Howell Raines. See Ken Auletta, "The Howell Doctrine," *New Yorker*, June 10, 2002.

692. Rick Perlstein, "Left Falls Apart, the Center Holds," *New York Observer*, October 22, 2001.

693. Gallup, 2: 874–75.

694. Calculations based on U.S. Census Bureau, *Historical Statistics of the United States, colonial times to 1970* (Washington, DC: U.S. Department of Commerce, 1975), table series D 182–232, and U.S. Census Bureau, *Statistical Abstract of the United States: 2002* (122nd Edition), Washington, DC 2002, table 588.

695. "Employment Distribution by Major Industrial Sector, 1900–1997," in Ronald G. Ehrenberg and Robert S. Smith, *Modern Labor Economics: Theory and Public Policy*, 7th ed. (Reading, MA: Addison Wesley, 2000), chart inside front cover.

696. Calculations based on *Statistical Abstract: 2002*, table 591.

697. Calculations based on Bureau of Labor Statistics, unpublished *Current Population Survey*, provided by Steve Hipple of the BLS. Steve Hipple to Piri Halasz, two e-mails, June 11, 2003, private collection.

698. Calculations based on *TVhistoryTV*, http://www.tvhistory.tv/facts-stats.htm (accessed June 28, 2004); and *Current Industrial Reports: Consumer Electronics: 2001*, table 3, http://www.census.gov/industry/1/ma334m01.pdf (accessed June 28, 2004), printouts, private collection.

699. Calculations based on *Current Industrial Reports: Computers and Office and Accounting Machines: 2001*, table 3, http://www.census.gov/industry/1/ma334r01.pdf (accessed June 28, 2004), printouts, private collection.

700. Gus Tyler, *Look for the Union Label: A History of the International Ladies' Garment Workers' Union* (Armonk, NY: M. E. Sharpe, 1995), 265.

701. Tyler, 266.

702. Tyler, 268, 276, 279, 289.

703. *Current Industrial Reports: Apparel: 2001*, table 5, http://www.census.gov/industry/1/mq315a015.pdf (accessed June 28, 2004), printouts, private collection.

704. Tyler, 266–67.

705. *Current Industrial Reports: Footwear Production: 2002*, table 6, http://www.census.gov/industry/1/ma316ra02.pdf (accessed June 28, 2004), printouts, private collection.

706. Toy Industry Association, http://www.toy-tia.org/ (accessed June 25, 2003). Confirmed by Diane Cardinale of the TIA, e-mail to Piri Halasz, July 7, 2003, private collection.

707. "World Production of Steel by Countries," American Iron and Steel Institute, *Annual Statistical Report: 1962* (New York: American Iron and Steel Institute, 1963), 134–35; and American Iron and Steel Institute, *Annual Statistical Report: 2002* (Washington, DC: American Iron and Steel Institute, 2003), table 59.

708. Calculations based on American Iron and Steel Institute, *Annual Statistical Report, 1957* (New York: American Iron and Steel Institute, 1958), 88, 106; and American Iron and Steel Institute, *Annual Statistical Report: 2002* , tables 10 and 19 (although by 2001, what seems to be essentially the same category was now called "steel mill products").

709. Calculations based on *Ward's Motor Vehicle Facts & Figures 2002* (Southfield, MI: Ward's Communications, 2002), 21, 16–20.

710. Calculations based on Andy Jerardo, "U.S. Agricultural Trade Special Report," Economic Research Service, U.S. Department of Agriculture, FAU–79–01, July 2003, at http://usda.mannlib.cornell.edu/reports/erssor/trade/fau-bb/text/2003 (accessed January 5, 2008).

711. Elizabeth Becker, "California Farmers Reconsidering Opposition to Subsidies," *New York Times*, April 8, 2002.

712. *Historical Statistics*, table series D 946–951, and *Statistical Abstract: 2001*, table 637.

713. Data derived from Bureau of Labor Statistics, Current Population Survey. Union membership (annual), 2002, table 3, http://www.bls.gov/webapps/legacy/cpslutab3.htm (accessed January 5, 2008).

714. Calculations based on U.S. Census Bureau, *Statistical Abstract of the United States: 1962* (83rd ed.), Washington, DC, 1962, table 321; and *Profiles of American Labor Unions*, ed. Donna Craft and Terrance W. Peck (Detroit: Gale Research, 1998), 541, 905, 943, 1007, 1090.

715. J. Anthony Lukas, *Big Trouble: A Murder in a Small Western Town Sets Off a Struggle for the Soul of America* (New York: Simon & Schuster, © 1997 by The Estate of J. Anthony Lukas), 13–14. Reprinted by permission of Simon & Schuster Adult Publishing Group.

716. Lane Kenworthy, "Rising Inequality Not a Surge at the Top," *Challenge*, 47:5 (September–October 2004): 51–55.

717. See Michael Zweig, *The Working Class Majority: America's Best Kept Secret* (Ithaca, NY: ILR Press, 2000), esp. Introduction.

718. Michael Zweig, "Introduction: The Challenge of Working Class Studies," in *What's Class Got to Do With It?: American Society in the Twenty-first Century,* ed. Michael Zweig (Ithaca, NY: ILR Press, 2004), 7. In 2005, *The New York Times* ran a major series on "Class in America," published in book form as *Class Matters* (New York: Times Books/ Henry Holt, 2005). Although series and book conceded that Americans encounter class as "indistinct, ambiguous," both focused primarily on objective (not subjective) determinants: education, income, occupation, and assets.

719. Thomas E. Cavanagh, "The New Populism," *New York Times*, November 6, 1990.

720. Interviewees clearly undecided were primarily in low-level managerial or white-collar jobs, though one was a small-businessman and one a construction worker. Tina Kelley, "Watching, Listening, Hoping for a President," *New York Times,* August 5, 2000; James Sterngold, "Some Fence-Sitters Are Staying Put," *New York Times*, August 5, 2000; Rick Bragg, "Finding Some Words to Ponder While Listening for a President," *New York Times*, August 19, 2000; Andrew Jacobs, "In a Swing State, Cheers and Doubts," *New York Times*, August 19, 2000; and Ross E. Milloy, "For Independents, Much Skepticism," *New York Times*, August 19, 2000.

721. Wheeler, 152.

722. Shanshan Ding (with Brandon Batista), *Final Results, Data Based on NES Election Survey,* e-mail to Piri Halasz, August 12, 2005, private collection. The NES asked interviewees to evaluate Nixon's Vietnam position on a seven-point scale, with numbers 1 to 3 favoring to one degree or another a complete withdrawal, 4 as presumably neutral, and 5 to 7 favoring to one degree or another a complete military victory. I

asked Ding to classify answers from 1 to 3 as "dovish," 4 as "neutral," and from 5 to 7 as "hawkish."

723. Gallup, 3:2115–16.

724. Gallup, 3:2199, 2189.

725. Ding's statistics showed that in 1948, blue-collar interviewees were classed as "skilled and semiskilled" or "unskilled." In neither 1968 nor 2000 were any interviewees classed as "unskilled." From the number of interviewees in each category, I conclude that in 1968, "unskilled" were included in the category of "skilled and semiskilled," and that in 2000, many blue-collar workers were in the category of "does not know, refused to answer, retired, unemployed, student, or housewife," so I've given the party allegiances of interviewees classed as "skilled and semiskilled" in 1968 and 2000.

726. U.S. Census Bureau, *Statistical Abstract of the United States: 1976* (97th ed.), Washington, DC, 1976, table 600. The exact percentage of white-collar workers in 1970 was 48.3; it passed the 50 percent mark in 1976.

727. Exact comparisons are difficult because categories change. In 1950, some 16,000 workers were listed as "authors." In 2000, "authors" numbered 138,000, more than eight times as many, but the 2000 category included all those who "originate and prepare written material, such as scripts, stories, advertisements, and other material" (excluding public-relations specialists and technical writers). Many people in this category might have been classified differently in 1950. The number of "artists" had grown by equally huge amounts, but again, with possibly different job descriptions. *Historical Statistics,* table D233–682; *Statistical Abstract: 2001,* table 593; and "Category 27-3043 – Writers and Authors," Bureau of Labor Statistics, http://www.bls.gov/soc (accessed December 1, 2006).

728. Cited by Leo Panitch, "September 11 and Its Aftermath Through the Lens of Class," in *What's Class Got to Do with It?*, 82.

729. Louis Uchitelle and David Leonhardt, "Men Not Working, and Not Wanting Just Any Job," *New York Times,* July 31, 2006.

730. Cf. David Leonhardt, "The Price of Optimism," *New York Times Magazine*, October 26, 2008, 13: "For the better part of the past two decades, Americans have been living in a state of willful optimism about our financial future."

731. Sigmund Freud, "Screen Memories" (1899), *SE*, 3 (1962), 316; and "The Psycho-Analytic View of Psychogenic Disturbance of Vision" (1910), *SE*, 11(1957), 214-15. After World War I, Freud quoted the Schiller again, but only to disavow it in favor of his later, more disillusioned

polarity of "Eros" and "Thanatos." "Civilization and Its Discontents" (1930), *SE*, 21 (1961), 117.

732. Norman Frederiksen and W. B. Schrader, *Adjustment to College: A Study of 10,000 Veteran and Nonveteran Students in Sixteen American Colleges* (Princeton, NJ: Educational Testing Service, 1951), 227–29, 234–35, 310; Keith W. Olson, *The G.I. Bill, the Veterans, and the Colleges* (Lexington, KY: University Press of Kentucky, 1974), 45; and Michael J. Bennett, *When Dreams Came True: The GI Bill and the Making of Modern America* (Washington, DC: Brassey's, 1996), 243.

733. Calvin Tomkins, *The Bride & the Bachelors: Five Masters of the Avant Garde* (New York: Viking, 1968), 195–96.

734. His first year's tuition was paid for by postal bonds his father had bought before dying in 1942. The last three years were covered by scholarships, but living expenses and the upkeep of his mother were apparently financed by his own part-time jobs and the earnings of his two brothers. Bourdon, 17, 21.

735. Bourdon, 17.

736. Michael Kimmelman, "Flags, Mom and Apple Pie Through Altered Eyes," *New York Times*, November 2, 2001.

737. E.g., "Make sense of our times…," advertisements, *New York Times*, November 14, 2001; November 20, 2001, and December 1, 2001.

738. David Gates, "Living a New Normal," *Newsweek*, October 8, 2001.

739. Laurie Norton Moffatt, *Norman Rockwell: A Definitive Catalogue*, 2 vol. (Stockbridge, MA: The Norman Rockwell Museum at Stockbridge, 1986), 1:384–391 (Ford); 1:412 (GM); 1:344–346 (Coca-Cola); 1:503 (Pepsi-Cola); 1:339 (Budweiser); and 1:263 (Ballantine's).

740. For details, see Piri Halasz, "Pictures for Which American People?" *NYArts*, January 2002, 42–43.

741. Dave Hickey, "America's Vermeer," *Vanity Fair*, November 1999, 177.

742. Hickey, 180.

743. Laura Claridge, *Norman Rockwell: A Life* (New York: Random House, 2001), 337.

744. Corn, esp. 81, 93.

745. "Up Close: Ashcroft on the Issues," *New York Times*, December 23, 2000.

746. For a salutary (if somewhat philistine) revision of this line of thinking, see David Caute, *The Dancer Defects: The Struggle for Cultural Supremacy During the Cold War* (New York: Oxford University Press, 2003), chapter 19.

747. Karen Wilkin, "Clement Greenberg: A Critical Eye," in Karen Wilkin and Bruce Guenther, *Clement Greenberg: A Critic's Collection* (Portland, OR: Portland Art Museum; Princeton, NJ: Princeton University Press, 2001), 21.

748. Tomkins, 18–19, 31–33.

749. Quoted in Halasz, "Abstract Painting," 77.

Index of Names

Aamodt, Sandra, 433*n*

Acheson, Dean, 324

Achimore, Stephen, 309

Ackroyd, Peter, 452*n*, 476*n*

Adams, Laurie Schneider, 469*n*

Adato, Perry Miller, 46

Adler, Renata, 106

Agee, James, 51

Agee, William C., 243, 273, 301, 462*n*

"Agent S," 332

Agnew, Spiro, 334

Albers, Josef, 353

Alexander, Roy, 37, 51, 56, 62, 99

Alfonso d'Este, Duke of Ferrara, 424

Allen, Robert M., 269

Alloway, Lawrence, 140, 273-274, 367, 375, 465*n*

Allston, Washington, 224

Alma-Tadema, Laurence, 218, 221

Alpert, Hollis, 451*n*

Alsop, Joseph, 71

Ambrose, Stephen E., 473*n*

Amburn, Ellis, 125-126

Anderson, David L., 440*n*

Anderson, Marian, 338

Annesley, David, 458*n*

Annigoni, Pietro, 80

Antel, Jean, 451*n*

Antonioni, Michelangelo, 132

Archimedes, 13

Aristotle, 358

Arp, Jean, 260, 468*n*

Ashcroft, John, 425-426, 489*n*

Ashton, Dore, 255, 286, 347, 349, 368, 466*n*, 478*n*

Atkins, Robert, 205, 250

Aubrey, James T., 93

Auchincloss, Louis, 82

Auletta, Ken, 485*n*

Austen, Jane, 245

Avery, Milton, 355, 360, 363, 482*n*

Bacall, Lauren, 264

Bach, J. S., 84

Baird, Jay W., 475*n*

Baker, A. T. (Bobby), 63-64, 155, 160, 166-168, 172, 174, 176, 179, 184, 189

Baker, Lucy, 267, 309

Baker, Russell, 118, 132, 448*n*, 451*n*

Bakunin, Mikhail, 29

Baldwin, Hanson W., 101

Balfour, Honor, 98, 120

Balfour, Michael, 475*n*

Bannard, (Walter) Darby, 296, 458*n*, 467*n*

Barr, Alfred H., Jr., 144, 168-169, 273,

491

38-39, 158, 202, 205, 207, 250, 269, 270, 273, 290, 300, 301, 304, 329, 342-345, 357, 416, 417, 428, 433*n*, 466*n*, 476*n*, 488*n*

Friedan, Betty, 62

Friedlaender, Walter, 218

Friedman, B. H., 263, 276, 294, 465*n*

Friedman, Benno, 467*n*

Fry, Joseph A., 440*n*, 472*n*

Fry, Roger, 358, 480*n*

Fuerbringer, Otto, 51-52, 55, 56, 62, 63, 64, 66, 71-76, 80, 81, 88-89, 91, 93, 94, 99, 100, 102, 103, 111, 113, 114-115, 119, 123, 125, 126, 127, 133, 136, 141, 142, 144, 147, 148, 151, 161, 179, 184, 186, 188-189, 200, 201, 202, 318, 370-372, 416, 428, 439*n*, 441*n*, 442-443*n*, 457*n*

Fulbright, William J., 319

Galassi, Peter, 316

Gallup, George, 89-90, 396, 397, 399, 410-412, 438*n*, 443*n*, 485*n*, 488*n*

Galton, Francis, 10

Gans, Herbert J., 76-77, 326, 439*n*, 440*n*, 473*n*, 484*n*

Ganz, Kate, 455*n*

Gardner, Howard, 380-381, 484*n*

Gart, Murray J., 98, 120

Gary, Romain, 87, 442*n*

Gauger, Marcia, 57, 59

Gauguin, Paul, 362

Gautier, Théophile, 423-424

Gedo, John E., 379, 484*n*

Geist, Sidney, 433*n*, 480*n*

Geldzahler, Henry, 368, 374

Genauer, Emily, 262, 276, 375, 377, 464*n*, 483*n*

Gérard, Baron François, 222

Getlein, Frank, 449*n*, 451*n*

Getty, John Paul, 125

Gibbs, Wolcott, 24, 434*n*

Gibson, Ann Eden, 259, 464*n*, 467*n*

Giglio, James N., 437*n*

Girtin, Thomas, 218

Gitlin, Todd, 325-326, 446*n*, 473*n*

Giuliani, Rudolph, 252

Glarner, Fritz, 367, 482*n*

Glaser, Bruce, 469*n*

Gleitman, Henry, 474*n*

Gleizes, Albert, 230

Glueck, Grace, 141, 376, 456*n*, 484*n*

Goldwater, Robert J., 350, 478*n*

Golub, Leon, 481*n*

Gombrich, Ernst H., 217, 219-220, 224, 314, 364, 459*n*, 460*n*

Goodstein, Laurie, 477*n*

Goodwin, Doris Kearns, 322, 471*n*

Gordon, Donald E., 260-261, 264-265, 266, 286

Gordon, Leah Shanks, 141, 143, 144, 479*n*

Gore, Al, 335, 346, 394, 410, 474*n*

Gorky, Arshile, 256, 259, 354, 363, 366, 463*n*, 465*n*

Gottlieb, Adolph, 259, 273, 274, 366, 372, 376, 463*n*, 465*n*, 481*n*

Gottlieb, Harry, 477*n*

Gough, Lloyd, 26, 345

Goya, Francisco, 294

Graham, Katharine, 67-68, 81, 176

Graham, Philip, 67, 68

Graves, Morris, 363, 481*n*

Green, Christopher, 454*n*

501

CPSIA information can be obtained
at www.ICGtesting.com
Printed in the USA
LVHW090502070219
606719LV00006B/136/P

9 781440 123221